ANNALS OF THE NEW YORK ACADEMY OF SCIENCES
Volume 281

INTERACTIONS OF DRUGS OF ABUSE

Edited by Elliot S. Vesell and Monique C. Braude

The New York Academy of Sciences
New York, New York
1976

Library of Congress Cataloging in Publication Data

Main entry under title:

Interactions of drugs of abuse.

(Annals of the New York Academy of Sciences; v. 281)
"This series of papers is the result of a conference . . . held on March 9, 10, and 11, 1976, sponsored by the New York Academy of Sciences and the National Institute on Drug Abuse."
1. Drug interactions—Congresses. 2. Tetrahydrocannabinol—Congresses. 3. Narcotics—Congresses. 4. Drug abuse—Congresses. I. Vesell, Elliot S., 1933– II. Braude, Monique C. III. New York Academy of Sciences. IV. National Institute on Drug Abuse. V. Series: New York Academy of Sciences. Annals; v. 281.
Q11.N5 vol. 281 [RM302] 508'.ls [615'.78] 76-54861
ISBN 0–89072–027–4

BC
Printed in the United States of America
ISBN 0–89072–027–4

ANNALS OF THE NEW YORK ACADEMY OF SCIENCES

VOLUME 281

December 10, 1976

INTERACTIONS OF DRUGS OF ABUSE*

Editors and Conference Chairmen

ELLIOT S. VESELL AND MONIQUE C. BRAUDE

CONTENTS

* This series of papers is the result of a conference entitled Interactions of Drugs of Abuse, held on March 9, 10, and 11, 1976, sponsored by The New York Academy of Sciences and The National Institute on Drug Abuse.

Narcotics and Narcotic Antagonists

Depressants

Stimulants

Hallucinogens and Others

Financial assistance was received from:

- National Institute on Drug Abuse

The New York Academy of Sciences believes it has a responsibility to provide an open forum for discussion of scientific questions. The positions taken by the participants in the reported conference are their own and not those of The Academy. The Academy has no intent to influence legislation by providing such forums.

PREFACE

Monique C. Braude

Division of Research
National Institute on Drug Abuse
Rockville, Maryland 20852

Elliot S. Vesell

Department of Pharmacology
The Pennsylvania State University College of Medicine
Hershey, Pennsylvania 17033

This volume contains the proceedings of the first Conference on Interactions of Drugs of Abuse. The conference was held in New York, March 9–11, 1976, under the joint sponsorship of the National Institute on Drug Abuse and The New York Academy of Sciences. Increasing polydrug use in the United States prompted the National Institute on Drug Abuse (NIDA) to continue to support and further develop a comprehensive research program to define potential interactions of drugs of abuse with other compounds. Initiated in 1972 by the Division of Narcotics and Drug Abuse of the National Institute of Mental Health, the program concerned mostly interactions of cannabinoids and marihuana with other compounds. Later, under NIDA, the program was extended to encompass interactions of drugs of abuse, such as stimulants and depressants, or of new treatment modalities, such as *l*-alpha-acetylmethadol and naltrexone, with other compounds, used either on the street or therapeutically.

Although the literature dealing with drug interactions from the pharmaceutical standpoint is extensive, it usually consists of testimonial reports of adverse interactions but lacks in-depth studies of the mechanism underlying these effects. NIDA's approach has been to investigate interactions not simply from a forensic standpoint but rather at the behavioral, pharmacological, and biochemical levels.

Surprisingly, we did not find standard, well-accepted methodology for these studies. We had to develop methodology as we progressed. By the same token, new techniques of reporting the extensive data collected represented a problem, particularly in maintaining a multidisciplinary, rather than limited, view of interactions; new systems of reporting and analyzing the data had to be developed.

The complexity of these studies and the difficulties encountered by all participants led us to believe it essential that, for this conference, factual reporting of interaction studies be preceded by a general chapter describing in detail potential levels and mechanisms of drug interaction.

Drugs can interact at various sites and through different pathways, as shown in FIGURE 1. They can interact with one another at sites of drug absorption, distribution, biotransformation, excretion, or a combination of these. Such interactions are called pharmacokinetic. In addition, drugs can interact at their receptor sites; such interactions are called pharmacodynamic. Another reason why drug interactions are exceedingly complex is that numerous factors can alter the nature and extent of both pharmacokinetic and pharmacodynamic

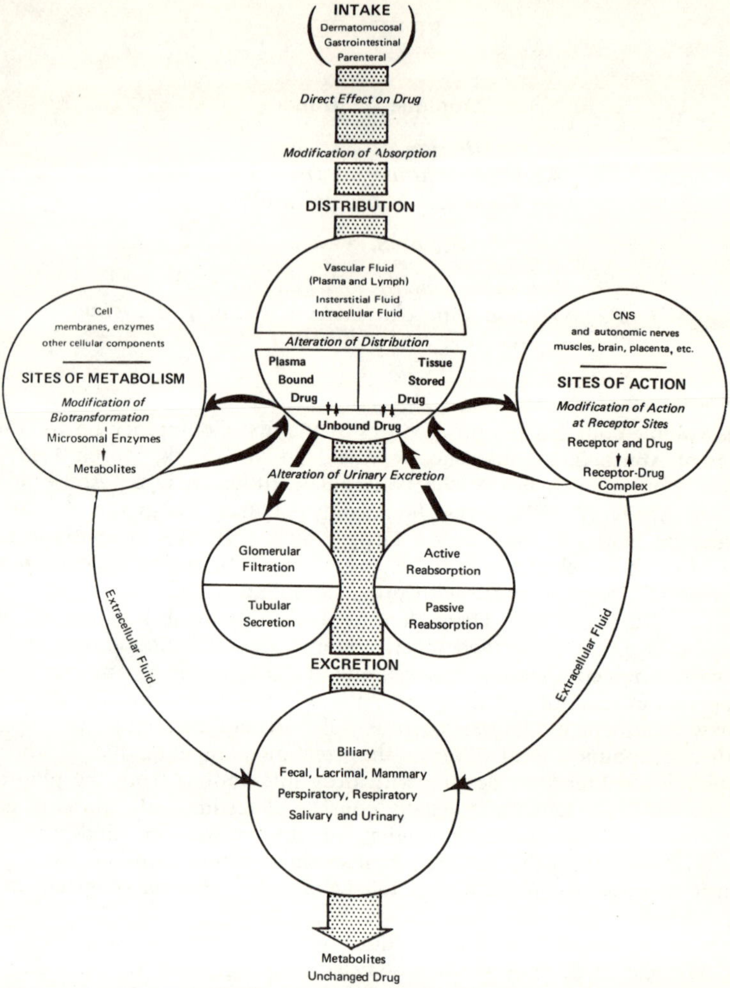

FIGURE 1. Sites and pathways for potential drug interactions. (From E. W. Martin. 1971. *In* Hazards of Medication. J. B. Lippincott. Philadelphia, Pa. By permission of the publisher.)

interactions. A partial list of these is offered in TABLE 1. In designing experiments on drug interactions, it is incumbent on the investigator to make sure that these factors are adequately controlled. Many discrepancies that appear in the literature on drug interactions arise from failure to hold these factors constant during the experiment.

The simplest model for pharmacodynamic interactions is that in which both the drug and interacting compound compete for binding at the same receptor site. We could not resist the temptation to present another model.

FIGURE 2 offers a more complicated model for pharmacodynamic drug interactions. In this conception, an allosteric effect occurs between two separate

TABLE 1

A PARTIAL LIST OF VARIABLES AFFECTING DRUG DISPOSITION IN EXPERIMENTAL ANIMALS

I. Variables in the External Environment	II. Variables in the Internal Environment	III. Pharmacologic Variables
Air exchange and composition	Adjuvant arthritis	Drugs
Barometric pressure	Age	acute vs. chronic administration, bioavailability, dose, withdrawal, presence of other drugs or food, routes of administration, tolerance, vehicle, volume of material injected, etc.
Cage design-materials (crowding, exercise)	Alloxan diabetes	
Cedar and other softwood bedding	Cardiovascular function	
Cleanliness	Castration and hormone replacement	
Coprophagia	Circadian and seasonal variations	
Diet (food and water)	Dehydration	
Gravity	Disease:	
Hepatic microsomal enzyme induction or inhibition by insecticides, piperonyl butoxide, heavy metals, detergents, organic solvents, ammonia, vinyl chloride, aerosols containing eucalyptol, etc.	Hepatic, renal, malignant endocrine (thyroid, adrenal)	
Handling	Estrous cycle	
Humidity	Fever	
Light cycle	Gastrointestinal function, potency and flora	
Noise level	Genetic constitution (strain and species differences)	
Temperature	Hepatic blood flow	
	Infection	
	Malnutrition, starvation	
	Pregnancy	
	Sex	
	Shock (hemorrhagic or endotoxic)	
	Stress	

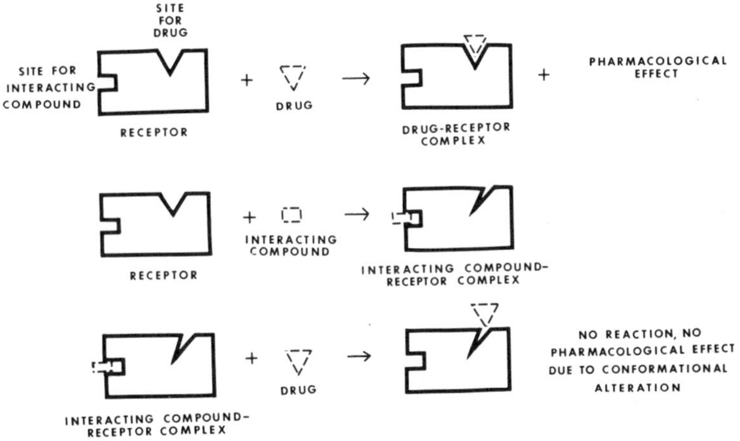

FIGURE 2. Diagrammatic representation of drug-receptor complex formation as affected by an interacting drug.

sites: one site for the interacting compound and another for the drug. When the interacting compound binds to its site, the conformation of the adjacent receptor site for the drug is changed so that the drug no longer fits and thus no pharmacological effect ensues. If the site for binding of the interacting compound is structurally altered, the interacting compound no longer binds to its site and the drug will continue to bind to its normal receptor site, thereby producing its pharmacological effect. This model is currently entirely hypothetical, and many other models for pharmacodynamic drug interactions could be offered. Now that receptor sites for drugs are being isolated and characterized, future models for pharmacodynamic drug interactions should be based firmly on experimental data. Finally, many of the factors listed in TABLE 1 can affect pharmacodynamic drug interactions either by changing the rates of association and dissociation of drug or interactive compound with receptor or by altering the avidity of the binding of the drug by receptor.

We hope to achieve through a study of interaction of drugs of abuse a better understanding of fundamental biological and physiological principles or mechanisms. In this sense, drug interactions were viewed as probes or tools to explore fundamental biological principles or mechanisms. The 38 papers presented at the conference and contained in this volume illustrate how far our expectations have been realized. We recognize that all our expectations have not been fulfilled, but we hope that this conference will stimulate further work and contribute to future progress in this area. We believe that the experiments and approaches described in this volume show that drug interactions are important not only in clinical medicine, where their better understanding will lead to improved patient care, but also in biology where, with well-controlled and defined techniques, their use as a potent tool can illuminate new principles and mechanisms.

In closing, we would like to thank all the participants of the conference, the excellent and very competent staff of The New York Academy of Sciences, and all those who participated, attended, and made this endeavor possible. We enjoyed working on this project, and it is our hope that this volume will be of interest not only to the biomedical scientific community but also to a much broader audience interested in polydrug use.

INTRODUCTORY REMARKS

Chauncey D. Leake

Department of Pharmacology, School of Medicine
University of California, San Francisco
San Francisco, California 94143

A large part of the counterculture of the past couple of decades has involved self-experimentation with drugs. These drugs have been chiefly "uppers" such as amphetamines or cocaine, or "downers" like the barbitals, or alcoholic beverages. In addition, there was, and still is, much experimentation with heroin and the ubiquitous marijuana.

These popular pastimes were usually random, not quantitated or "controlled" in any satisfactory manner. Reports on them came chiefly from clinical studies when things went wrong. Yet, the findings clearly supported well-known pharmacological information on drug antagonisms, synergisms, and incompatibilities.

This symposium gets into the gritty details of what happened. It analyzes the many complexities of the neuronal, extra-neuronal, and genetic factors involved. Many behavioral aspects are explored, and clinical effects examined. Experimental designs for assessment of drug interactions are proposed.

This symposium clearly answered D. G. Walizer's* complaint that there are no reliable quantitating criteria in drug abuse research. The experts gathered here from widely scattered laboratories seemed to be in full agreement on the validity of the quantitative methods they used in studying drug interactions.

The various reports of this symposium are of great importance, clinically. We are a drug-oriented society. Physicians, dentists, pharmacists, veterinarians, nurses, and other health personnel are continually being bombarded by advertisements from our highly competitive pharmaceutical concerns. The public is continually assaulted by such advertising in all media from print to television. The result is that a great number of people regularly take several drugs at once. It is increasingly important for health-guiding personnel to be aware of the dangers of multiple drug use. The ubiquitous consumption of alcoholic beverages may complicate many effects of whatever drugs may be prescribed, purchased over-the-counter, or obtained from a street dealer.

One should remember that undesired side-effects of drugs, either alone or in combination with others, are unpredictable, as was clearly recognized by the great Berlin toxicologist, Louis Lewin (1850–1929).† There are so many unpredictable variations in human beings, such as genetic makeup, allergic tendencies, age, sex, nutritional status, pathological condition, endocrine balance, metabolic stability, nervous sensitivity, and disease, that one may never be sure what may happen when a drug is taken. The chances of untoward effect go way up when more than one drug gets into the body.

This symposium has done a good job of covering what is now known about drug interactions in relation to drug abuse. Those who arranged it are to be congratulated on the quality of the many reports presented. It will be interesting to observe how much of the information offered here passes into clinical awareness and practice.

* 1975. Intern. J. Addict. **10:**927–936.

† 1881. Die Nebenwirkungen der Arzneimittel. Berlin.

Part I. Molecular, Cellular, and Clinical Aspects of Drug Interactions

SOME EXTRANEURONAL INTERACTIONS OF DRUGS OF ABUSE: AN OVERVIEW

Marcus M. Reidenberg

Departments of Pharmacology and Medicine
Cornell University Medical College
New York, New York 10021

In the annotated bibliography, *Drug Interactions,* published by the National Library of Medicine, a drug-drug or drug-chemical interaction is defined as "the interrelationship(s) of the effects of two or more substances (drugs, chemicals, natural products, foods, or devices) in humans, experimental animals, isolated organs, tissues, cells, or subcellular components derived from humans or animals."

Since a drug is broadly defined as "any chemical agent that affects living processes,"[1] a definition concentrating more on the nature of the interrelationship than on the description of what constitutes a drug or a living process might be more helpful.

I propose defining a drug interaction as the modification of the dose-response or time-action characteristics of one drug by another. This definition requires that a drug interaction involve more than the simple algebraic addition of the independent effects of two drugs.

Examples of drug interactions at various extraneuronal sites will be presented to support this concept and to provide an overview of the subject.

Absorption

Most drug absorption takes place in the small intestine. Drugs with anticholinergic activity can slow gastric emptying and thereby delay absorption. An example of this is the delay in absorption of acetaminophen by the concurrent administration of propanetheline.[2] Metoclopramide, a drug that accelerates gastric emptying, accelerates drug absorption as measured with acetaminophen.[2]

Antacids can also modify drug absorption. Both magnesium hydroxide and aluminum hydroxide given to mice prior to oral pentobarbital delayed the onset of sleep. The decrease in response resulting from this drug interaction was due to the fact that the antacids caused retention of most of the pentobarbital dose in the animal's stomach, thereby inhibiting absorption.[3]

Drugs can interact physically or chemically in the gastrointestinal tract to affect the absorption of one or more of the drugs involved. Cholestyramine is an ion-exchange resin used to bind cholesterol and bile acids in the gut in order to prevent their absorption. It binds basic and neutral drugs to a small extent. This binding is easily dissociable. On the other hand, acidic drugs are substantially bound, and this binding persists despite washing of the resin (Table 1).[4] When the drugs in Table 1 were given to animals concurrently with cholestyramine, the absorption of the acidic drugs was impaired. For example, a

TABLE 1

BINDING EFFECT OF CHOLESTYRAMINE ON ACIDIC AND BASIC DRUGS

Drug	Type of Drug	Percent Initially Bound	Percent Bound to Resin after 4 Washes
Warfarin	acidic	97	95
Phenylbutazone	acidic	98	94
Chlorthiazide	acidic	88	70
Digoxin	neutral	33	0
Tetracycline	basic	60	0
Quinidine	basic	28	4

smaller fraction of the dose of warfarin was absorbed when given with cholestyramine than when given alone. This decreased the anticoagulant response to the dose of warfarin. Conversely, neither the absorption of basic drugs nor the response to them was altered by concurrent administration of cholestyramine.[4]

Thyroxine is an acidic or anionic drug. A hypothyroid patient controlled with thyroxine medication began taking cholestyramine in addition and rapidly became hypothyroid. *In vitro* studies showed that both thyroxine and tri-iodothyronine are bound by cholestyramine. Two patients were then given I^{131} labeled thyroxine with and without cholestyramine to evaluate the effect of this binding on thyroxine absorption. The results are given in TABLE 2.[5] Thus,

TABLE 2

PERCENTAGE OF DOSE OF THYROXINE EXCRETED IN STOOL AND URINE

Drug	Route	Patient 1	Patient 2
Thyroxine alone	stool	42	47
	urine	28	40
Thyroxine plus cholestyramine	stool	84	83
	urine	9	11

cholestyramine has been shown to tightly bind acidic drugs *in vitro*. This tight binding has been shown to decrease absorption of the acidic drugs in both laboratory animals and man, and this decreased absorption has been correlated with a decreased intensity of effect. Thus, a drug interaction that causes a decreased dose-response relationship has been identified and evaluated.

DRUG DISTRIBUTION

While many drugs can be shown to displace other drugs from plasma protein binding sites, it must be demonstrated that this displacement actually modifies the dose-response or time-action characteristics of the drug before the significance of this displacement can be evaluated.[6] For instance, many drugs displace phenytoin from plasma protein binding sites, but there is no evidence that this displacement modifies the response of the patient to phenytoin.[6, 7]

An example of a real redistributional drug interaction is the transient increase in the anticoagulant effects of warfarin produced by chloral hydrate. At ordinary therapeutic levels, about 2.5 mg of warfarin is bound to the proteins in 1 liter of plasma. Thus, during therapy, a significant fraction of the body content of warfarin is bound to plasma proteins. Displacing some of this inactive bound warfarin into the unbound pharmacologically active pool would be equivalent to giving an additional dose of anticoagulant. Chloral hydrate is metabolized to trichloracetic acid, which is highly protein bound and can displace warfarin from its binding sites. This has been shown to occur. Patients receiving chloral hydrate need less warfarin to induce therapeutic anticoagulation than patients not receiving chloral hydrate. Once a steady-state of anticoagulation is obtained, then chloral hydrate-treated patients require the same average maintenance dose of warfarin as patients not receiving chloral hydrate. Thus, their rate of warfarin elimination or sensitivity is not altered, and a true redistributional drug interaction is demonstrated.[8]

An example of a drug interaction erroneously considered to be due to plasma protein binding displacement is that of phenylbutazone potentiating the hypoglycemic effects of tolbutamide. The mechanism for this potentiation is not the displacement of tolbutamide from plasma protein binding sites, which does occur but is unimportant, but rather the slowing of the elimination of tolbutamide by phenylbutazone.[9]

Drug Biotransformation

Some drugs can increase the rate of microsomal oxidation of other drugs. This phenomenon, the induction of drug metabolism, will, of course, decrease the response produced by any dose of a drug inactivated by the induced pathway. Conversely, if a drug is activated by the induced pathway, the result of this interaction can be an increased response.

Patients with severe asthma are often treated with adrenocortical steroids. Concurrent phenobarbital administration was found to shorten the dexamethasone half-life in 11 asthmatic patients from a mean $\pm$S.E. of 262 ± 21 minutes before phenobarbital to 144 ± 6 minutes. Dexamethasone volume of distribution was not changed by the barbiturate treatment. Therefore, phenobarbital acted to almost double the metabolic clearance rate of the steroid, a clear example of the effects of enzyme induction. Three prednisone-dependent patients showed clinical worsening, deterioration of spirometric tests, and increased eosinophil counts when given phenobarbital. Phenobarbital withdrawal reversed these changes. Patients not dependent on steroids did not show similar changes after phenobarbital therapy. Thus, enzyme induction can accelerate drug metabolism and lead to a decreased intensity of drug effect.[10]

The extent of induction caused by a given dose of phenobarbital was first shown to be under genetic control in man by Vesell and Page in 1969.[11] They also showed that the slower the initial metabolism of the drug, the greater the change following the phenobarbital. Using the degree of induction as the response, one can demonstrate both dose-response and blood-level response relationships for barbiturates in man.[12]

Cigarette smoking is an unequivocal stimulus for enzyme induction. Smokers have been shown to have a decreased response to standard doses of propoxyphene and benzodiazepins.[13]

Drugs can also slow the metabolism of other drugs. This leads to an increased intensity of effect for any particular dose of the drug if the inhibited metabolic pathway is an inactivating one. While alcohol taken chronically induces drug metabolism, acutely this chemical inhibits drug metabolism. Alcohol has been shown to slow warfarin metabolism and increase the anticoagulant effect observed from a constant dose of warfarin.[14] Chloramphenicol prolongs the half-life of phenytoin.[15] A profound increase in the intensity of effect was observed in a patient on constant phenytoin dose following the administration of chloramphenicol.[16]

There also appears to be a dose-response and blood-level response relationship for enzyme inhibition, at least when phenytoin half-life is measured and phenylbutazone is the inhibitory drug.[17]

Drug Excretion

A major mechanism of importance in drug excretion is reabsorption of drug molecules filtered at the glomerulus by nonionic diffusion across the renal tubule back into the blood. Most drugs are weak acids or weak bases. A weak acid will exist in aqueous solution partly as the undissociated (un-ionized) acid and partly as the anion. The ratio of un-ionized molecule to anion will depend on the pH of the solution and pKa of the weak acid. The more acidic the solution, the greater the percentage of drug in the un-ionized form. The renal tubule cell permits un-ionized molecules to diffuse across it but blocks the passage of ionized compounds. A weakly acidic drug will be filtered at the glomerulus and will enter the glomerular filtrate partly as an anion and partly as the un-ionized weak acid. As the filtrate passes down the tubule, water is reabsorbed, increasing the concentration of drug in the lumen. The un-ionized drug molecules can then diffuse across the wall of the tubule back into the blood. As the urine continues down the tubule, it normally is acidified as well as concentrated. This acidification increases the percentage of drug present in the un-ionized form, further increasing the rate of diffusion of the drug back into the plasma. The effect of this diffusion back into plasma is to slow excretion of the drug. Drugs, such as sodium bicarbonate, that alkalinize urine minimize this back diffusion of weak acids, thereby accelerating their excretion. This phenomenon has been studied by experimenting with phenobarbital[18] and the results used to develop the therapeutic regimen of forced diuresis with alkalinization of urine, used in treating phenobarbital poisoning.[19] It is important to note that urinary excretion of many drugs that are lipid-soluble weak acids is not accelerated by alkalinizing the urine. Thus, while this interaction of urine alkalinizers with anionic drugs is theoretically a general one, in practice, the excretion rate of only a small number of anionic drugs is significantly altered by alkalinizing the urine.

Drugs that are organic bases are also subject to nonionic back diffusion. For these drugs, alkaline urine increases the un-ionized fraction, favoring reabsorption and slowing excretion. Amphetamine is a good example. When the urine of five subjects was acidic during a period of NH_4Cl ingestion, amphetamine half-life ranged from 4.2–6.8 hours, with 59–68% of the dose being excreted unchanged in the urine. When the urine was alkaline during a period of $NaHCO_3$ ingestion, only 1–5% of the dose of amphetamine was recovered unchanged in the urine, and the duration of central nervous stimulation was markedly prolonged compared with the duration of effect of the same dose taken during the urine-acidification experiment.[20, 21]. Thus, alkalinizing the urine slowed excretion and prolonged the effect of amphetamine.

The physical/chemical properties of these organic bases that make their urinary excretion rate so pH dependent are:

1. The pKa favors the un-ionized form at pH values achievable in urine.
2. The un-ionized form is lipid soluble.[22]

It has been street knowledge for a while that taking baking soda with amphetamine prolongs its effects. Athletes may take these two drugs concurrently not only to prolong the effect but also to lower the amount of unchanged amphetamine in their urine to below the limits of analytical detection. Since they normally excrete an acidic urine, excretion of an alkaline urine is grounds for suspecting that suppression of excretion of a weak base has been attempted.[22]

Drug Receptors and Effector Organs

Drug Antagonism

The interactions of drugs at receptor sites are the pharmacological basis for the development of competitive antagonist drugs. Such well-known compounds as naloxone or propranolol markedly reduce the response to narcotics or catecholamines respectively when given concurrently or shortly before the appropriate agonist. When given alone, these drugs cause little pharmacologic response. Thus, their effects are primarily to decrease the dose-response relationships of the agonists.

An interesting example of an interaction of drugs of abuse related to effector organs is that of alcohol antagonizing the antidiuretic effects of cigarette smoking. Cigarette smoking has repeatedly been shown to decrease urine output. This effect is thought to be due to stimulation of vasopressin release by the nicotine absorbed from the smoke. In fact, lack of an antidiuretic response to cigarette smoking has sometimes been accepted as evidence confirming a clinical diagnosis of diabetes insipidus. Alcohol has been known to inhibit vasopressin release during mild stimuli; its effects during the strong stimulus of cigarette smoking have been studied only recently. When people drank 3 ounces of whiskey prior to smoking, there was little or no increase in serum vasopression following smoking.[23] While urine flow rate was not measured simultaneously in this particular study, enough is known about vasopressin levels and antidiuresis for one to be confident that the antidiuretic response to the smoking was suppressed or abolished as well. Thus, alcohol interacts with nicotine at the level of the posterior pituitary to block the normal increase in antidiuretic hormone secretion caused by smoking. In this way alcohol antagonizes the antidiuretic effects of smoking at an organ site distant from the kidney.

Two Agonists

One of the problems in evaluating a potential drug interaction involving two agonists is whether the response observed is really different from the algebraic sum of the responses of the individual drugs given separately. The importance of this can be developed by examples. Suppose we want to study the depressant effects of some drugs. We have a container labeled pentobarbital sodium and a container labeled Nembutal®, which is one of the American brand names for pentobarbital sodium. We find that the dose-response and time-action characteristics of the contents of one container are identical with those of the other. Combining a standard dose from each container produces an effect greater than either of the individual doses but equal to the effect produced by taking both of the standard doses from either container. Have we demonstrated a drug interaction? Since each container contained the same drug even though the labels differed, this cannot be defined as a drug interaction. The same chemical compound under different names is still only one drug, and a drug interaction requires that more than one drug be involved.

Now suppose we repeat the above experiment with pentobarbital in one bottle and secobarbital in the other and observe the identical effects. Has a drug interaction occurred? While chemically the active principles in each bottle are different, pharmacologically this experiment was no different from the previous one. Therefore, I would suggest that pharmacologically this is not a drug interaction either. It is this reasoning that has led to the requirement that a drug interaction involve more than the algebraic sum of the responses to two drugs given independently. Simple additive effects of drugs are not usually considered drug interactions.

Gessner has recently applied a graphic method to analyze potential drug interactions from this point of view. It is called the isobolographic method. It enables one to evaluate the additive effects of two agonist drugs given separately and in combination to learn if the effect produced by the combination is greater than the sum of the independent effects of each of the two drugs in the combination.[24] Using this method, Gessner showed clearly that the combination of ethanol plus chloral hydrate caused more depression than the additive effects of the two drugs alone, while ethanol plus trichlorethanol were simply additive.[24]

Degree of Confidence that a Putative Drug Interaction Really Exists

The examples of drug interactions presented so far have been well described and evaluated interactions. Unfortunately, many of the so-called drug interactions tabulated in various compendia and secondary sources are poorly described and unevaluated. Some probably do not even exist! Richard Kern, M.D., a retired Professor of Medicine at Temple University, used to say, "It isn't what you don't know that gives you trouble. It's what you know that isn't so." To conclude this paper, I would like to present several examples leading from well-evaluated interactions to what I consider to be drug noninteractions.

Several case reports describe very intense effects in patients who were given meperidine while also receiving monoamine oxidase inhibitor drugs.[25] The effects included both respiratory depression and seizures. An experiment was done in mice in which the meperidine LD_{50} was determined with and without monoamine oxidase inhibitor pretreatment. The meperidine acute LD_{50} in control mice was 145 mg/kg. Other mice were treated with phenylzine, an antidepressant drug that inhibits monoamine oxidase. These mice showed some excitement 15 minutes after the phenylzine but appeared completely normal 1 hour later, when meperidine was given. The meperidine LD_{50} in these mice was 28 mg/kg.[26] Thus, a clear-cut interaction between these drugs has been identified but not described in detail.

The following have all been listed in a tabulation of "Some Potentially Lethal Drug Combinations," footnoted "Lethal with high dosage or in susceptible patients":[27]

Alcohol with Nitrates and Nitrites

The basis for this is two papers. One is a study showing that alcohol caused increase in skin temperature, while nitroglycerine increased blood flow to the calf muscles. This was interpreted as showing that these two drugs dilate different parts of the vasculature. The two drugs were not given together in this study.[28] The other paper, a letter to the editor, simply stated:

"A commonly prescribed drug, nitroglycerine, can result in cardiovascular collapse when taken in conjunction with alcohol. Although nitroglycerine only occasionally leads to hypotension when taken alone, when it is combined with alcohol this risk is considerably increased. Since the risks inherent in such a combination are not too well known the subsequent collapse is often attributed to coronary insufficiency or occlusion."[29]

Documentary evidence that alcohol plus nitrates or nitrites produces an effect greater than the independent effects of these drugs given alone has not been included in the reference list of the tabulation. While I suspect that this will happen, it would be nice to have the proof, at least in an animal experiment, before declaring that a drug interaction exists between alcohol and nitrites.

Tricyclic Antidepressants with Methyldopa

The basis for this putative interaction is the following case report:

"Investigation of a 50-year-old man with hypertension showed that the left kidney was smaller than the right and was supplied with two renal arteries, the lower of which was stenosed near its origin. He became moderately depressed after treatment with a reserpine derivative; this was therefore discontinued, and his blood-pressure was thereafter controlled at 120/80–150/90 mm Hg by methyldopa, 250 mg thrice daily, and a thiazide diuretic. He complained of some mental slowing, but continued work. During the following 2 months he again became depressed, and was treated with amitriptyline, 25 mg thrice daily, at home. On attendance at the medical clinic, 10 days after commencing amitriptyline, he was agitated, and there was a fine tremor in his hands. He was no longer depressed, but complained of palpitations. On examination, his pulse, usually 80 per minute, had risen to 148 per minute, and his blood-pressure was 170/110. All treatment was stopped forthwith. A week later he stated that he felt "a different person"; his pulse and blood-pressure had fallen to 100 per minute and 160/90 respectively."[30] Since the agitation, tremor, and palpitations are all well-described side effects of amitriptyline alone, and since genetic slow metabolizers of this drug can have very high levels and side effects while on this dose, there is no evidence in this case report that the methyldopa interacted with the amitriptyline. Certainly, better documentation of an interaction, even in a single case study, should be required before tabulating this as a potentially lethal interaction between tricyclic antidepressants as a class and methyldopa.

Problems have arisen as a result of this tabulation. Conscientious community pharmacists, maintaining proper patient medication profiles, have identified hypertensive depressed patients receiving this drug combination. At least one such pharmacist has warned his customer that he was taking a potentially lethal drug combination and had better check with his doctor right away. What should the doctor then do? The alternative antihypertensive medications are reserpine, a potentially lethal choice for a depressed patient; guanethidine, a drug that is completely antagonized by tricyclic antidepressants and worthless when given concurrently with them; or hydralazine, a drug with very real side effects and toxicity. This is an example of the seriousness with which adverse drug interactions are considered and the importance of publishing only what is really so.

Salicylates with Tricyclic Antidepressants

The potential lethality of this drug combination is documented by a single case report of a 38-year-old woman treated with imipramine 250 mg daily and chlorpromazine 225 mg daily for depression. While on treatment, she was reported to have ingested 11.3 g of aspirin. Six hours later, she developed seizures followed by fever, shock, and death. Autopsy revealed a subdural hematoma, cerebral edema, and "minimum coning into the foramen magnum."[31]

To use this case report to include the combination of aspirin with tricyclic antidepressants on a list of potentially lethal drug combinations, implying that patients taking these antidepressants risk death by also taking aspirin, would be irresponsible. Certainly, it is the responsibility of the writers of reviews, and the compilers of compendia, to be sure that what they say is in fact true.

References

1. Fingl, E. & D. M. Woodbury. 1975. *In* The Pharmacologic Basis of Therapeutics. L. S. Goodman & A. Gilman, Eds. Chap. **1:** 1. Macmillan Co. New York, N.Y.
2. Nimmo, J., R. C. Heading, P. Tothill & L. F. Prescott. 1973. Pharmacological modification of gastric emptying: Effects of propantheline and metoclopramide on paracetamol absorption. Brit. Med. J. **1:** 587–589.
3. Hurwitz, A. 1974. Gastrointestinal drug absorption: effects of antacids. *In* Drug Interactions. P. L. Morselli, S. Garattini, & S. N. Cohen, Eds.: 21–31. Raven Press. New York, N.Y.

4. Gallo, D. G., K. R. Bailey & A. L. Sheffner. 1965. The interaction between cholestyramine and drugs. Proc. Soc. Exp. Biol. Med. **120:** 60–65.
5. Northcutt, R. C., J. N. Steil & J. W. Hollifield. 1969. The influence of cholestyramine on thyroxine absorption. JAMA **208:** 1857–1861.
6. Wardell, W. M. 1974. Redistributional drug interactions: a critical examination of putative clinical examples. *In* Drug Interactions. P. L. Morselli, S. Garattini & S. N. Cohen, Eds.: 123–134. Raven Press. New York, N.Y.
7. Lunde, P. K. M., A. Rane, S. V. Yaffe, L. Lund & F. Sjoqvist. 1970. Plasma protein binding of diphenylhydantoin in man. Clin. Pharmacol. Therap. **11:** 846–855.
8. Koch-Weser, J. & E. M. Sellers. 1971. Drug interactions with coumarin anticoagulants. N. Engl. J. Med. **285:** 487–498, 547–558.
9. Christensen, L. K., J. M. Hansen & M. Kristensen. 1963. Sulfaphenazole-induced hypoglycemic attacks in tolbutamide-treated diabetics. Lancet **2:** 1298–1301.
10. Brooks, S. M., E. E. Werk, S. J. Ackerman, I. Sullivan & K. Thrasher. 1972. Adverse effects of phenobarbital on corticosteroid metabolism in patients with bronchial asthma. New Engl. J. Med. **286:** 1125–1128.
11. Vesell, E. S. & J. G. Page. 1969. Genetic control of the phenobarbital-induced shortening of plasma antipyrine half-lives in man. J. Clin. Invest. **48:** 2202–2208.
12 Breckenridge, A., M. L. 'E. Orme, H. Wesseling, M. Bending & R. L. Lewis. 1974. Increased rates of drug oxidation in man. *In* Drug Interactions. P. L. Morselli, S. Garattini & S. N. Cohen, Eds.: 223–230. Raven Press. New York, N.Y.
13. Jick, H. 1974. Smoking and clinical drug effects. Med. Clin. N. Amer. **58:** 1143–1149.
14. Breckenridge, A. 1971. Pathophysiological factors influencing drug kinetics. Acta Pharmacol. Toxicol. **29**(Suppl. 3)**:** 225–232.
15. Christensen, L. K. & L. Skovsted. 1969. Inhibition of drug metabolism by chloramphenicol. Lancet **2:** 1397–1399.
16. Ballek, R. E., M. M. Reidenberg & L. Orr. 1973. Inhibition of diphenylhydantoin metabolism by chloramphenicol. Lancet **1:** 150.
17. Andreasen, P. B., A. Frøland, L. Skovsted, S. A. Anderson & M. Hauge. 1973. Diphenylhydantoin half-life in man and its inhibition by phenylbutazone: the role of genetic factors. Acta Med. Scand. **193:** 561–564.
18. Waddell, W. J. & T. C. Butler. 1957. The distribution and excretion of phenobarbital. J. Clin. Invest. **36:** 1217–1226.
19. Lassen, N. A. 1960. Treatment of severe acute barbiturate poisoning by forced diuresis and alkalinization of the urine. Lancet **2:** 338–342.
20. Beckett, A. H. & M. Rowland. 1965. Urinary excretion kinetics of amphetamine in man. J. Pharm. Pharmacol. **17:** 628–639.
21. Rowland, M. & A. H. Beckett. 1966. The amphetamines: clinical and pharmacokinetic implications of recent studies of an assay procedure and urinary excretion in man. Arzneimittel-Forsch. **16:** 1369–1373.
22. Vree, R. B., A. T. J. M. Muskens & J. J. van Rossum. 1969. Some physicochemical properties of amphetamine and related drugs. J. Pharm. Pharmacol. **21:** 774–775.
23. Husain, M. K., A. G. Frantz, F. Ciarochi & A. G. Robinson. 1975. Nicotine-stimulated release of neurophysin and vasopressin in humans. J. Clin. Endocrinol. Metab. **41:** 1113–1117.
24. Gessner, P. K. 1974. The isobolographic method applied to drug interactions. *In* Drug Interactions. P. L. Morselli, S. Garattini & S. N. Cohen, Eds.: 349–362. Raven Press, New York, N.Y.
25. Sjoqvist, F. 1965. Psychotropic drugs. II. Interactions between monoamine oxidase (MAO) inhibitors and other substances. Proc. Roy. Soc. Med. **58:** 967–978.

26. BROWNLEE, G. & G. W. WILLIAMS. 1963. Potentiation of amphetamine and pethidine by monoamine oxidase inhibitors. Lancet **1:** 669.
27. MARTIN, E. W., S. F. ALEXANDER, D. J. FARAGE & W. E. HASSAN, JR. 1971. Hazards of Medication.: 415–419. J. P. Lippincott Co., Philadelphia, Penna.
28. ALLISON, R. D., J. C. KRAMER & G. M. ROTH. 1971. Effects of alcohol and nitroglycerine on vascular responses in man. Angiology **22:** 211–222.
29. SHAFER, N. 1965. Hypotension due to nitroglycerine combined with alcohol. N. Engl. J. Med. **273:** 1169.
30. WHITE, A. G. 1965. Methyldopa and amitriptyline. Lancet **2:** 441.
31. HOWARTH, E. 1961. Possible synergistic effects of the new thymoleptics in connection with poisoning. J. Mental Sci. **107:** 100.

POSSIBLE SITES IN THE NEURON FOR INTERACTIONS OF DRUGS OF ABUSE

F. E. Bloom

Arthur V. Davis Center for Behavioral Neurobiology
The Salk Institute
San Diego, California 92112

Introduction

The practical results of this conference will depend to a large degree on our abilities to collate and integrate the individual semantic arguments of each speaker in order to achieve the eventual goal of establishing criteria for drug interactions. We must be able to determine and relate potential points of drug interaction on the molecular, cellular, and behavioral levels in order to envision the complete chain of causal events which begin with the initial drug-receptor interactions on key cells and which culminate in the behavioral manifestations of the whole animal. My suggestions for developing these drug interaction criteria for neurons will be based on the analysis of drug actions resolved through the tip of a microelectrode. With this tool, electrophysiological methods can easily resolve the activity patterns of single neurons, achieve some substantial indications of their functional and cellular identity, and in combination with other micro-methods for drug delivery such as microiontophoresis,[1, 2] or with parenteral drug administrations, evaluate the selectivity of the interactions when drugs are introduced into the test system.

Expressed in the simplest terms, what we want to know from the analysis of how different drugs interact on a single nerve cell's activity is whether these cellular interactions explain the ability of the same drugs to alter the animal's behavior in certain reproducible and predictable ways. The brain poses such ominous structural and functional complexity, in which events occur rapidly, and in which many fundamental details still require solution. Therefore, it seems scarcely possible that any randomly selected nerve cell might be able to reveal the key effects of one drug or clarify the interactive effects between any two drugs sufficiently to explain the actions of these drugs on behavior. As cellular pharmacologists interested in behavior, our task must be viewed humbly in the light of so many experiments that have yielded drug-effect data but little understanding of how drugs actually produce such effects. While I have no solutions to offer that do not require an enormous investment of time and critical data analysis, the suggestions now proposed may help to subdivide the tasks and organize the chores we face.

Organization of Neuron-Drug Interactions

When seeking to uncover the "simpler" case of the specific actions of a single drug in the nervous system, one simplifying approach is to enumerate the possible modes of drug/cell interaction (Figure 1). Some such effects can

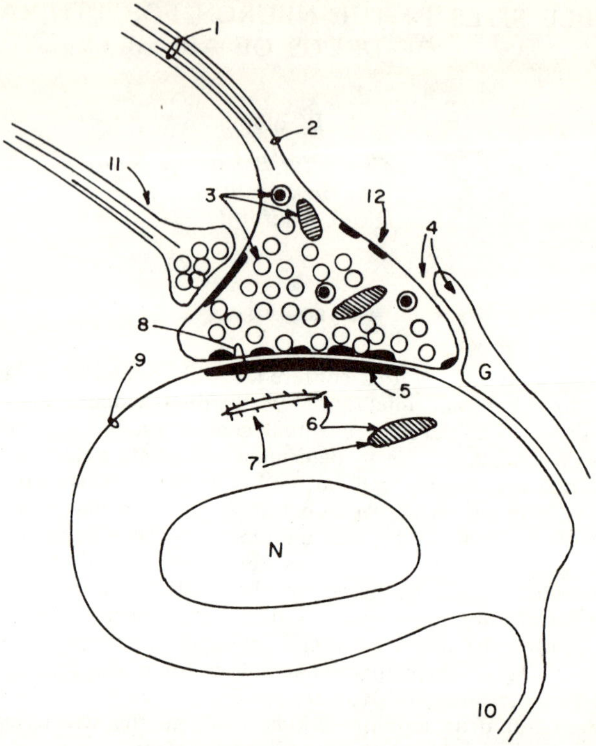

FIGURE 1. Possible steps in the biological cycle of a central neuron at which drugs may interact. Step 1: axoplasmic transport via microtubules. Step 2: electrically excitable components of the axonal and perikaryonal membrane. Step 3: organelles and enzymes present within preterminal axons, synaptic boutons, and some dendritic processes for the synthesis, storage, catabolism, and release of the transmitter, as well as for the active re-uptake and re-storage of the transmitter after release. Step 4: glia-neuronal interaction processes; not yet well characterized, they may assist in policing the extrasynaptic spaces to maintain minimal concentrations of active transmitter molecules. Step 5: postsynaptic receptors which trigger events within the postsynaptic cell initiated by the release of transmitter. Sep 6: intracellular neuronal organelles which may mediate the postsynaptic response in some of the subsequent metabolic aspects, such as ribosomal protein synthesis. Step 7: Cytoplasmic-nuclear interactions which regulate the expression of genetic information possibly sensitive to transmitter-regulated events. Step 8: intrasynaptic events of sensitization, desensitization, habituation, and other physiological modulations of trans-synaptic function. Step 9: the electrical properties of the postsynaptic cell which integrate the simultaneous slow potentials produced by the various excitatory and inhibitory transmitters converging onto the target cell. Step 10: the culmination of the various afferent messages expressed by discharge of the target cell and propagation of a signal down its axon. Step 11: a presynaptic element which is contacting one of the afferent terminals onto the target cell and can regulate its release of transmitter. Step 12: presynaptic autoreceptors by which the release of a transmitter from a synaptic terminal may be modified by the transmitter it has previously released. (Modified from Cooper *et al.*[79])

be attributed to actions which are generalizable to all nerve cells, such as drugs affecting perikaryonal general metabolism, maintenance of membrane integrity and of transmembrane ionic equilibria, and similarly of processes which contribute to the adequacy of the two-way chemical traffic between the perikaryon and the distal neurites of a cell.[3] Thus, drugs such as protein-synthesis inhibitors, mitochondrial poisons, inhibitors of ionic pumps, and disaggregators of microtubules and microfilaments may be expected to have effects on all neurons in some relation to their own structural peculiarities, basal levels of activity, and inherent capacity for resistance to such chemical perturbations. For the most part these actions generally affecting most neurons are not the drug actions this conference seeks to comprehend.

A second large class of drug actions comes closer to the present mark, namely those actions which deal with drugs interacting with specific molecular forms of chemical synaptic transmission. Here the molecular mechanisms for drug specificity are more easily envisioned because of the numerous points within the life cycle of transmitters which have been uncovered through biochemical pharmacology.[4] Such actions as inhibition of precursor amino acid uptake, inhibition or de-regulation of one or more rate-limiting steps in transmitter synthesis (or even in the synthesis of synthesizing or catabolizing enzymes), or in the storage, release, catabolism or re-accumulation and re-storage of the transmitter substance have now been invoked so frequently as potential modes of synaptic transmission regulation that they need no documentary corroboration. Each of these actions is potentially highly specific and restrictable to a single subset of neurons, although in practice achievement of such specific biochemical actions often demands tight selection of treatment times and dose-response curve segments. With these more elemental neuronal processes, one particular transmitter molecule or one particular transmitter-related enzymatic event can be selected out from the mass of brain cells. Then the interactions between drugs and intraneuronal molecular events can be even further simplified with *in vitro* tests of the interactions between the drug and the event (active uptake, enzymatic synthesis, or catabolism, or—under some conditions—transmitter release), and the results can optimally be expressed in kinetic terms to reveal competitive and noncompetitive types of interaction.

A third major category of drug-neuron interactions depends upon the synaptic receptors at which the transmitter released from a synapse can trigger the subsequent actions on the post-synaptic cell and in certain cases on the terminal from which it was released as well.[5, 6] Of these two classes of post-release receptor, the category for which the most experience has accumulated is that of the post-synaptic receptors. The major tool in this analysis has been the method of microiontophoresis,[1, 2] which can administer drugs in minute quantities around neurons while their behavior is monitored with microelectrodes. This procedure not only eliminates many of the diffusional and enzymatic barriers which can restrict and modify the access of drugs to neuronal receptors, but it also restricts the number of possible sites in the environment of the test which could initiate the response. The problems and pitfalls of using this method in an interpretable way to identify transmitter substances and their mechanisms of action have been reviewed countless times with little agreement emerging as to standardized methods of procedure. Nevertheless, for the purposes of trying yet again to devise criteria for establishing the nature of interactions between abusable drugs, some of the features of the use of iontophoresis for pharmacological considerations may bear repetition.[2]

Evaluating Drug Interactions with Iontophoresis

Under proper conditions of testing, iontophoresis can provide descriptive data on the range of responsiveness exhibited by a given set of test cells to a given range of test substances with some assurance that the interactions occurred on the nerve cells examined. The data from iontophoresis experiments can be taken to infer the function of an endogenous chemical substance considered as a potential transmitter. The method can also specify the sites on a test cell at which the transmitter and other drugs interact. In order to derive this degree of information, certain experimental conditions must be explicitly defined.

Identification of Test Neurons

When attempting to evaluate the results of iontophoretic tests in any brain region, the identity of the cells to be tested is of primary concern. Such identifications can be made during the test on the basis of characteristic discharge patterns or from the response of the test cells to stimulation of specific antidromic or orthodromic projections, or by marking recording sites by any of several methods and examining the recording sites cytologically after the experiment.

Such identifications offer several interpretative advantages. Firstly, the cells tested can be categorized into homogeneous functional or cytological groupings for cleaner interpretation of heterogeneous responses. For example, when the differences in responsiveness to norepinephrine were compared between "all-cells-in-a-region" and specific identifiable cell types within a region, for olfactory bulb,[7, 8] hypothalamus,[9–11] cerebral cortex,[12–14] cerebellum,[15] thalamus,[16, 17] limbic system,[18–20] pons,[21–22] and spinal cord,[23–24] the response of identified cells to norepinephrine, for example, was consistently inhibitory. In no case did identified cells exhibit significant instances of mixed responses (i.e., some cells faster, some cells slower) as seen when "all-cells-in-a-region" are artificially lumped together, as was commonly done in the early era of iontophoresis.

Secondly, the identification of test cells is even more important when drug responses are to be compared for their effects on a specific synaptic input to a test cell, or in attempts to determine the molecular basis of the synaptic or drug response. Thus, in order to establish a synaptic inference for iontophoretic responses, the cells tested must be shown to receive this chemical class of synaptic inputs. Thirdly, identification of the test cells can define which of the iontophoretic responses observed may never be utilized by normal synaptic connections (e.g., the excitatory beta adrenergic receptors of neurons in the deep cerebellar neurons of the cat where no evidence for catecholaminergic synapses exists).[25] Finally, identification of test cells is required so that similar drug-test data may be accumulated over multiple experiments on functionally homogenous cell populations for critical evaluation of antagonists or potentiators of the test synapses or test substances.

Presynaptic Receptors

Even though iontophoresis restricts the number of sites onto which a drug can diffuse and start a response, the method does not necessarily limit responses to the single neuron whose activity is being recorded. Indirect effects on the recorded cell could arise from release of another endogenous transmitter or from nearby interconnected neurons whose activity has escaped detection. Elimination of presynaptic responses can be approached by localization of the synaptic terminals which contain the transmitter under test, or by testing specific cells after chronic elimination of specific inputs (as with 6-hydroxydopamine[26]) or during post-natal development before significant numbers of input synapses have formed.[27] This adjunctive approach is applicable to the question of drug interactions as well; for example, desmethylimipramine does not potentiate cerebellar Purkinje cell responses to norepinephrine after 6-hydroxydopamine, indicating the former action to have been presynaptic in nature.[15]

Pharmacologic Considerations

In the founding example of CNS microiontophoresis, carbachol was found to mimic the excitatory actions of acetylcholine on spinal Renshaw cells excited by stimulation of ventral root axon collaterals;[28] cholinesterase inhibitors potentiated these effects. Dihydro-beta-erythroidine, a nicotinic antagonist, diminished both excitatory responses.[28-29] Here, pharmacologic tests extended the level of comparisons between test substance and test synapse beyond simple qualitative effects on discharge rate. Similarly, when the convulsant, strychnine, was found to antagonize glycine,[30-32] or when picrotoxin[32, 34] and bicuculline[35, 36] were shown to antagonize GABA, these antagonisms extended the comparison between the inhibitory actions of the amino acids and inhibitory synaptic transmission in the spinal cord[35, 36] and in several other mesencephalic and cortical areas (see review).[36] However, the actions of an antagonist drug do not necessarily "prove" the identity of a transmitter. Firstly, the specificity of the antagonism should always be questioned because the total list of natural synaptic agonists affecting any neuron is still incompletely defined. If transmitter candidates can elicit actions on neurons which normally do not receive synapses releasing that agent, an antagonist may appear selective only because both the candidate and the antagonist are interacting at some other natural agonist's receptors. Thus, it has been reported that in addition to GABA, bicuculline will block responses to several other natural amino acids (taurine, beta alanine; see[37]) and to monoamines.[38] Secondly, when given parenterally, the dose of picrotoxin or bicuculline required to antagonize the synaptic pathway and the putative transmitter often alters blood pressure and induces convulsant activity; to counteract these side effects, other drugs (sedatives, neuromuscular blocking agents, etc.) are given which further compound the interpretive problems of transmitter identification (see[38]). Similar concerns arise generally over the interpretation of acute parenteral injections of drugs on neuronal unit activity, since a specific direct effect on the test neurons can be established only by extensive sampling of other identified cells.[39]

Nevertheless, many of the potential problems which can confound the analysis of drug interactions can be overcome through application of the principle that specific interactions with a given synaptic transmitter can best be detected and demonstrated when tests are done on a type of identifiable neuron known to receive the type of synapse against which the antagonist drug is thought to act. Recently, Freedman, Hoffer, and Woodward[40] have expanded the quantitative assessments of transmitter-antagonist interactions suggested by Gottesfeld, Kelly, and Renaud[41] through the use of computer-generated drug-response histograms. With this method it is possible to automate iontophoretic test pulses of one or more natural or synthetic agonists, and evaluate the changes in these responses in the presence or absence of an antagonist substance even when the antagonist has some direct depressant action on the test neurons. This study has clarified the need for regularly repeated pulses of norepinephrine in the pursuit of interactions with potential antagonists, and has further demonstrated the pitfalls of interpreting apparent antagonisms of norepinephrine responses by Mn, Co, or verapamil[42, 43] on the basis of an action exclusively as Ca antagonists (also see Phillis[44]).

Neuronal Post-Synaptic Interactions with Drugs of Abuse

Let us now apply some of the experience gained from iontophoretic studies of transmitters and their presumptively related drugs to those recent studies which have attempted to examine the actions of morphine and morphine antagonists. As recently summarized by Satoh *et al.*,[45] although several reports of the iontophoretic interactions of morphine with neurons in the brain stem,[46] spinal cords,[47] thalamus[48] and cerebral cortex[45, 49, 50] have appeared, the results of these studies have thus far failed to incriminate any particular transmitter receptive property as the primary site of the interaction. Firstly, no generalizable response to morphine was observed; some cells showed tachyphylactic (i.e., progressively decrementing responses to identical doses) excitations,[46] while others showed tachyphylactic inhibitions[45] in naive animals. When evaluated against the recurrent excitatory response to ventral root stimulation, spinal cord interneurons showed complex responses including an increased latency of response, with increased excitatory responsiveness to iontophoretic acetylcholine.[47] Most of these actions were reversible by prior or concurrent application of the opiate antagonist naloxone,[46, 47, 49, 50] but no reports of stereospecific opiate agonists simulating any of these reported actions of morphine have yet appeared. In the rat cerebral cortex, two studies have described the effects of chronic morphine administration on the ability of unidentified neurons to respond to acetylcholine[45, 49] and to glutamate;[45, 50] in one case, responses to acetylcholine appeared no different, but the cholinergic responses in the morphine-treated animals could no longer be blocked by iontophoresis of atropine[49] as can control responses.[13, 14] In the second and more recent study, however, after chronic exposure to morphine, unidentified spontaneously active cerebral cortical cells showed enhanced excitatory responses (i.e., lower thresholds) to both glutamate and acetylcholine, and in contrast to the naive animals, morphine did not depress these responses, but instead now showed direct excitatory effects of its own.[45] With great ingenuity, the potential technical artefacts of variable release of drugs from the iontophoretic pipette were controlled by employing the same sets of electrodes "in tandem" on naive and on morphine-treated animals to demonstrate more strongly the morphine-related lowering of the threshold for glutamate and acetylcholine excitations.[45]

From these studies, and from related preliminary intracellular recordings of the effects of morphine on spinal motorneurons (cited by Satoh *et al.*[45]), two major mechanisms of the naloxone-reversible actions of morphine have been proposed: on the one hand, morphine may reduce the natural release of acetylcholine and other excitatory transmitters and thereby induce a type of "transmitter-deficiency" supersensitivity in the absence of structural denervation.[51] Alternatively, these data could suggest that morphine may act specifically to impair the inwardly directed sodium current whose conductance is activated by the combination of excitatory inhibitors with their synaptic receptors.[45]

Although admittedly in their infancy, these studies must nevertheless be analyzed with respect to the question of what the data may signify for the analgesic or euphoric actions of opiates.[52] The general conclusion based on analogy with the nearly two decades of iontophoresis already past is not very heartening. The data available thus far do not tell us whether the effects of morphine in these studies are on presynaptic or postsynaptic sites, nor even whether the actions are on any synaptic sites at all. A very recent paper by Sasa *et al.*[53] has suggested that intravenous morphine can block the ability of the locus coeruleus noradrenergic pathway to inhibit neurons of the spinal trigeminal nucleus, an effect which is compatible with the ability of morphine to impair release of norepinephrine from nerve terminals in both peripheral[51] and central nervous[54] tissues. However, execept for this observation on the spinal trigeminal nucleus and those of Bradley *et al.* on the unidentified neurons of the brainstem,[46] all the data so far reported on the interactions of morphine with neurons have dealt with excitations by acetylcholine and one or another of the excitatory amino acids. As a result, it is not possible to generalize the results. Morphine could either affect responses to all transmitters on a neuron through a generalized presynaptic or postsynaptic mechanisms, or through some specific related synaptic action on an as-yet-undiscovered transmitter.

Much of the foregoing interpretation of the effects of morphine may well be changing even now owing to the demonstration that the transmitter substance with which morphine and other opiates may interact most closely is none of the current crop of recognized agents but rather one or more of the recently discovered endogenous morphine-like substances.[55–62] Thanks to the imaginative work of Hughes and collaborators,[55, 56] the first endogenous morphine-like peptides have been isolated from bovine and ovine material, and the amino-acid sequences of two related pentapeptides have been determined, now termed by Hughes *et al.*[56] as LEU-enkaphalein and MET-enkephalein. MET-enkephalein is wholly contained within a more recently discovered hexadecapeptide isolated from ovine hypothalami by Guillemin *et al.* and termed alpha-endorphine.[62] The previous physiologic data must now be reexamined in the light of these discoveries to determine whether the interactions already observed with morphine may not have been totally unrelated to the actons of acetylcholine, glutamate, or norepinephrine but rather more pertinent to the underlying functional actions of endogenous enkephaleins or endorphines.

The questions on which we now move into the future offer those working in this field the opportunity to apply the historical lessons of the past in attempts to determine when and how the natural morphine-like substances may act on neurons and how this interaction may be disrupted by opiates. At this point of development, we assume that natural opiate alkaloids, synthetic opiates, and the endogenous opioid peptides can all compete for the same stereospecific, naloxone-reversible binding sites in brain homogenates.[60, 61] This must then mean that the reactive components of morphine seen by the receptor bear close resemblance in tertiary structure to the reactive agonist groups on the peptides.

Surely, the race is on to determine ways of revealing those active sites on the pentapeptides and to enhance them through synthetic substitutions. But the important question for such chemical advances will remain: Where and on what should the molecules be tested?

If one were to pursue seriously the possibility that the enkephalein pentapeptides and the endorphine, hexadecapeptide, were likely to have specific effects on synaptic transmission through a receptor which would then, through structural similarity, also be selectively available to the exogenous opiates, the first logical step might be to examine the actions of these materials on the neurons most likely to receive such chemical input. Until antibodies to the peptides become available for immunocytochemical identification[63, 64] of their structural location, it is fortunate that at least three other experimental approaches seem capable of pinpointing logical sites for the preliminary analyses. Unfortunately, the fact that the three independent methods to be mentioned incriminate very few brain sites in common suggests that all must be regarded as equally "helpful." Based on the relative regional distributions of enkephalein[55, 56] and of the relative regional density of stereospecific opiate receptors, the caudate nucleus, which ranks highest on both indices, would be a most reasonable first target,[65] followed by the locus coeruleus and substantia nigra, with their high density of opiate-binding receptors.[66] On the other hand, based upon the points at which morphine can cause analgesia upon microinjections into the brain[67, 68] or at which withdrawal can be precipitated in morphine-dependent animals,[69, 70] the most likely points of analysis would seem to be the central peri-aqueductal grey and mid-line thalamic structures,[48] which also contain significant enicephaleins[55, 61] and opiate receptors.[65, 66] A third possibility for sites of acton would be the nuclei in the ventrobasal thalamus at which pain perception can be shown to be sensitive to parenteral morphine.[71] As judged from the previous literature review, only one of the aforementioned sites has yet been explored for the effects of opiates. That sole study consists of a brief report by Frederickson and colleagues[48] on the relative effects of naloxone and acetylcholine on spontaneous firing rates of unidentified cells within the medial and lateral portions of the rat medial thalamic nucleus. No significant changes were observed in the ability of acetylcholine to change spontaneous activity in either naive or morphine-treated rats. However, the morphine-treated rats exhibited excitatory responses to naloxone (when given either by iontophoresis or by subcutaneous injection), and this excitatory response was not seen in any control animal. The fact that this preliminary study might serve to eliminate further pursuit of altered responses to acetylcholine as the basis for synaptic actions underlying naloxone-precipitated withdrawal offers little solace, considering the larger questions which remain. Were these medial thalamic nucleus neurons the appropriate ones to test? Do they receive any cholinergic inputs, and if so from where? Do these cells receive synapses containing an endogenous morphine-like peptide transmitter? What is its function there? Does it relay sensory information within the thalamus from the nuclei receiving primary spino-thalamic inputs, such as the posterior ventro-basal groups,[71] and thus offer the opportunity to process that potentially painful message before sending it on to the cortex? Does excitation by naloxone in morphine-tolerant animals indicate disinhibition from a tonically induced morphine depression,[45] or greater release of excitatory transmitter from a morphine-suppressed afferent pathway?[51, 53, 54] Clearly, much exciting work awaits those taking up this line of research. Before leaving the interactions of transmitters at the cellular level as possible models for explaining the events of drug dependence and withdrawal, let us consider the recent information gleaned from a study of cultured neurons derived from neuroblastomas.[72, 73, 74] Through the use of hybrid cultures between neuroblastoma and glioma cell lines, the stereospecific, naloxone-reversible binding of morphine and other opiates to these cells was shown to inhibit basal adenylate cyclase activity and to decrease concentrations of intracellular cyclic AMP.[72, 73] This effect reverses spontaneously, accompanied by an increase in the content of adenylate cyclase, which is then found to be activated by the withdrawal of the opiate or presentation of naloxone to the culture.[73] These coupled inhibitory and stimulatory regulations of the cell line's adenylate cyclase have been associated with the previously reported ability of prostaglandin E_1[75] to activate brain-slice adenylate cyclase, an effect which is also acutely antagonized by morphine,[75] to suggest that the adenylate cyclase system of neurons may be the basis of neuronal tolerance and withdrawal phenomena. Compatible with this suggestion is the observation that some phosphodiesterase inhibitors can evoke behavioral symptoms which resemble opiate withdrawal and these drug-induced symptoms are further enhanced by naloxone.[76]

While abundant data now exist to suggest that cyclic nucleotides play important regulatory roles within specific events of interneuronal communication and intraneuronal chemistry (see[77] for review) none of those data are presently capable of establishing cause-and-effect relationships between changes in cyclic nucleotide levels in any neuron and behavioral events on the order of magnitude of withdrawal symptoms. The data which are available, in fact, suggest that the precise mechanism by which a phosphodiesterase inhibitor or a prostaglandin derivative is able to control levels of cyclic AMP or cyclic GMP in a particular cell type may be difficult to generalize to other cell types. In some cases, prostaglandins can activate the synthesis of cyclic GMP, when can then—through de-regulation of a cyclic AMP phosphodiesterase—lead to changes in cyclic AMP.[74] Until studies have been reported on the ability of the endogenous morphine peptides to regulate cyclic nucleotide synthesis and catabolism on specific neurons *in vitro* or *in vivo,* it will be difficult to evaluate how well the effects of opiates on cyclic nucleotide levels in cultured neurons reflect the events of the intact nervous system during tolerance and withdrawal.

Interactions of Other Drugs of Abuse

In the evolving base of work from which specific interactions of opiates may soon become clarified, we have several factors which have contributed to the progress of the analysis: a wide armamentarium of potential agonists and antagonists, often with close stereospecific structure activity properties which eliminate nonspecific effects (in the sense of effects unrelated to specific analgesic or euphoric actions of morphine). With the addition of the detection of natural factors capable of emulating some actions of morphine, a structural thread begins to emerge that may eventually link together all the effects which have so far refused to be organized along the known tracts of existing transmitter systems. This appears now to be a likely point from which to begin. But what about the other drugs of abuse, such as ethanol, or cannabis? For each of these substances, studies now exist which—through biochemical selection of what is measured—show effects on transmitter concentrations, or turnover, or which suggest that one or another transmitter system or cyclic nucleotide is required for an effect (e.g., withdrawal from ethanol[78]). Such studies, in other words, resemble closely the general information available on the chemical epiphenomena of opiate actions or withdrawals. For these two drugs of abuse there are no stereospecific receptor agonists or specific reversible antagonists, and even the molecular nature of the agonistic form of the drug remains to some minds uncertain. Without these pharmacological tools to assist us there seems to be no immediate answer except the difficult challenge of attempting to define the sites and nature of their actions on the nervous system. One approach might be to employ dose-response parametric studies to show that doses and treatment times affecting one or another neuronal process of response are those dose levels and treatment times which are capable of producing behavioral effects in the same species.

Conclusions and Suggested Criteria

Through microiontophoresis aimed at appropriately suspicious target neurons, methods exist for determining whether drugs of abuse produce direct or indirect actions through synaptic or non-synaptic sites of response. In order to establish these various possible sites of action, data are needed as to what cells and pathways are most likely to be affected by the parenteral administration of the drug or by assessment of its general behavioral effects. Against this structural context, augmented by available biochemical measurements of the effects of the compound, tests can be done to determine the interaction of the drug with one or more of the transmitter substances which can be shown to produce natural synaptic actions on the target cell of choice. These natural synaptic transmitters can then be used as a tool to characterize the specificity or generality of the effects of the drug. Since all the chemical transmitters afferent to any target cell have not been defined for any brain cell, it remains possible that none of the testable interactions will establish a specific synaptic interaction for the drug in question. At such a point even innovative iontophoretic applications lose their usefulness, and other methods of neuropharmacological analysis must be developed.

In conclusion, here are some specifically stated criteria for characterizing the interactions of drugs of abuse with neurons which might establish a fundamental basis for the effects produced by these drugs on human and animal behavior:

1. *The interaction of the drug with the neuron must be shown to be directly analogous to the molecular pharmacological characteristics of the substance on clinical and model-preparation indices.* For example, with opiates, is the neuronal effect elicited through a receptor which exhibits the same stereospecific, antagonist-reversible properties as the opiate receptor? In the case of the other, less-characterizable receptors for other drugs of abuse, this criterion cannot yet be applied, but parametric studies of drug response, and time response, should be applied to establish maximally sensitive neurons relative to the response of the whole animal.

2. *The interaction of the drug with the neuron must be defined for specificity or nonspecificity, and for presynaptic, postsynaptic, or nonsynaptic actions by reference to one or more of the systems of neurons contributing*

afferent messages to the test cell. Does the drug interfere with the release or response to a chemical system known to project to whatever test cells are selected for analysis? Here one requires test cells which lie at the intersection of two planes of knowledge: cells which would give the greatest insight would be those surmised to be involved in the behavioral effects of the drug (e.g., analgesia), or cells which reflect the endogenous distribution of the drug-binding receptors, and—at the same time—cells onto which several known systems of chemical transmitter can be demonstrated to act to establish specificity and intraneuronal site of action. In this light, the caudate nucleus, mid-line thalamic nuclei, and amygdaloid complex might all be potentially rich areas to explore for analysis of opiates with only moderate additional characterization of the synaptic systems.

3. *After establishing the interaction as neuronally specific, and chemically specific, the action must be tested for its ability to explain changes in responsivity during the development of drug dependence, tolerance, or withdrawal.* To satisfy this criterion, the same studies of selectivity and specificity must then be repeated under the long-term drug administration condition to establish again that the same key neuronal circuits and actions are the most likely targets of the chronically elicited drug effect.

The nervous system is unlikely to stand still while active drug molecules are presented chronically, and therefore pursuit of the basis for long-term drug interactions and the changes in sensitivity and interneuronal communication which occur under these conditions seems even more difficult. Although modification of naive animal responses with chronic drug treatment seems initially more reasonable than the emergence of new drug-sensitive events, the latter possibility should not immediately be discounted. From the standpoint of cellular biology, the major factors by which cellular level information can be applied to a multi-cellular problem will depend on adequate demonstration of the primary cellular sites of action and the primary molecular mechanisms of this selective effect.

References

1. Salmoiraghi, G. C. & F. F. Weight. 1967. Anesthesiology **28:** 54–68.
2. Bloom, F. E. 1974. Life Sci. **14:** 1819–1834.
3. Kreutzberg, G. W., P. Schubert & H. D. Lux. 1975. *In* Golgi Centennial Symposium. M. Santini, Ed.: 161–166. Raven Press. New York, N.Y.
4. Iversen, L. L. 1974. *In* The Neurosciences, Third Study Program. F. O. Schmitt & F. G. Worden, Eds.: 905–916. MIT Press, Cambridge, England.
5. Bloom, F. E. 1975. Handbook Psychopharmacol. **6:** 1–22.
6. Aghajanian, G. K., H. J. Haigler & J. L. Bennett. 1975. Handbook Psychopharmacol. **6:** 63–96.
7. von Baumgarten, R., F. E. Bloom, A. P. Oliver & G. C. Salmoiraghi. 1963. Pfluegers Arch. Ges. Physiol. **277:** 125–140.
8. Bloom, F. E., E. Costa & G. C. Salmoiraghi. 1964. J. Pharmacol. Exp. Therap. **146:** 16–23.
9. Bloom, F. E., A. P. Oliver & G. C. Salmoiraghi. 1963. Int. J. Neuropharmacol. **2:** 181–193.
10. Barker, J. L., J. Crayton & R. Nicoll. 1971. Science **171:** 208–210.
11. Hori, T. & T. Nakayama. 1973. J. Physiol. **232:** 71–85.
12. Krnjevic, K. & J. W. Phillis. 1963. J. Physiol. **165:** 274–304.

13. STONE, T. W. 1973. Naunyn-Schmiedebergs Arch. Pharmakolog. **278:** 333–342.
14. STONE, T. W., D. A. TAYLOR & F. E. BLOOM. 1975. Science **187:** 845–847.
15. HOFFER, B. J., G. R. SIGGINS & F. E. BLOOM. 1971. Brain Res. **25:** 523–534.
16. CURTIS, D. R. & R. DAVIS. 1962. Brit. J. Pharmacol. **18:** 217–246.
17. SATINSKY, D. 1965. Int. J. Neuropharmacol. **6:** 387–395.
18. SALMOIRAGHI, G. C. & S. STEFANIS. 1965. Int. Rev. Neurobiol. **10:** 1–30.
19. OLIVER, A. P. 1971. EEG Clin. Neurophysiol. **31:** 284–287.
20. SEGAL, M. & F. E. BLOOM. 1974. Brain Res. **72:** 79–97.
21. AVANZINO, G. L., P. B. BRADLEY & J. H. WOLSTENCROFT. 1966. Experientia **22:** 410–412.
22. COUCH, J. 1970. Brain Res. **19:** 137–150.
23. SALMOIRAGHI, G. C. & S. STEFANIS. 1965. Arch. Ital. Biol. **103:** 705–740.
24. CURTIS, D. R., J. W. PHILLIS & J. C. WATKINS. 1961. J. Physiol. **158:** 296–323.
25. YAMAMOTO, C. 1967. J. Pharmacol. Exp. Therap. **156:** 39–47.
26. HOFFER, B. J., G. R. SIGGINS & F. E. BLOOM. 1971. Brain Res. **30:** 425–430.
27. WOODWARD, D. J., B. J. HOFFER, G. R. SIGGINS & F. E. BLOOM. 1971. Brain Res. **34:** 73–79.
28. CURTIS, D. R. & R. M. ECCLES. 1958. J. Physiol. **141:** 435–445.
29. CURTIS, D. R., R. W. RYALL & J. C. WATKINS. 1966. Exp. Brain Res. **2:** 97–106.
30. WERMAN, R. 1972. Annu. Rev. Physiol. **34:** 337–361.
31. CURTIS, D. R. & G. A. R. JOHNSTON. 1970. Nature **225:** 1258–1260.
32. WERMAN, R., K. A. DAVIDOFF & M. H. APRISON. 1958. J. Neurophysiol. **31:** 81–97.
33. OBATA, K. & M. HIGHSTEIN. 1970. Brain Res. **18:** 538–547.
34. TEN BRUGGENCATE, G. & I. ENGBERG. 1971. Brain Res. **25:** 431–448.
35. CURTIS, D. R., A. W. DUGGAN, D. FELIX & G. A. R. JOHNSTON. 1971. Brain Res. **32:** 69–82.
36. CURTIS, D. R. & G. A. R. JOHNSTON. 1974. Ergeb. Physiol. **69:** 97–188.
37. BLOOM, F. E. 1972. Neurosci. Res. Progr. Bull. **10:** 127–246.
38. STRAUGHAN, D. W., M. J. NEAL, M. A. SIMMONDS & G. G. S. COLLINS. 1971. Nature **233:** 352–353.
39. AGHAJANIAN, G. K., H. J. HAIGLER & F. E. BLOOM. 1972. Life Sci. **11:** 615–623.
40. FREEDMAN, R., B. J. HOFFER & D. J. WOODWARD. 1975. Brit. J. Pharmacol. **54:** 529–539.
41. GOTTESFELD, Z., J. S. KELLY & L. P. RENAUD. 1972. Brain Res. **42:** 319–335.
42. PHILLIS, J. W. & J. J. LIMACHER. 1974. Can. J. Physiol. Pharmacol. **52:** 566–574.
43. YARBROUGH, G. G., N. LAKE & J. W. PHILLIS. 1974. Brain Res. **67:** 77–88.
44. PHILLIS, J. W. 1974. Life Sci. **14:** 1189–1201.
45. SATOH, M., W. ZIEGLGANSBER & A. HERZ. 1975. Life Sci. **17:** 75–80.
46. BRADLEY, P. B. & A. DRAY. 1974. Brit. J. Pharmacol. **50:** 47–55.
47. DUGGAN, A. W. & D. R. CURTIS. 1972. Neuropharmacol. **11:** 189–196.
48. FREDERICKSON, R. C. A., F. H. NORRIS & C. R. HEWES. 1975. Life Sci. **17:** 81–82.
49. YARBROUGH, G. G. 1974. Life Sci. **15:** 1523–1529.
50. SATOH, M., W. ZIEGLGANSBERGER, W. FRIES & A. HERZ. 1974. Brain Res. **82:** 378–382.
51. NORTH, A. R. & G. HENDERSON. 1975. Life Sci. **17:** 63–66.
52. JAFFE, J. 1965. *In* The Pharmacological Basis of Therapeutics. L. S. Goodman & A. Gilman, Eds. 3rd edit.: 285–311. Macmillan Co., New York, N.Y.
53. SASA, M., K. MUNEKIYO & S. TAKAORI. 1975. Life Sci. **17:** 1373–1380.
54. MONTEL, H., K. STARKE & H. D. TAUBE. 1975. Naunyn-Schmiedebergs Arch. Pharmacolog. **288:** 427–433.

55. HUGHES, J. 1975. Brain Res. **88:** 295–308.
56. HUGHES, J., T. W. SMITH, H. W. KOSTERLITZ, L. A. FOTHERGILL, B. A. MORGAN & H. R. MORRIS. 1975. Nature **258:** 577–579.
57. TESCHEMACHER, H., K. E. OPHEIM, B. M. COX & A. GOLDSTEIN. 1975. Life Sci. **16:** 1771–1776.
58. COX, B. M., K. E. OPHEIM, H. TESCHEMACHER & A. GOLDSTEIN. 1975. Life Sci. **16:** 1777–1782.
59. TERENIUS, L. & A. WAHLSTROM. 1975. Life Sci. **16:** 1759–1764.
60. PASTERNAK, G. W., R. GOODMAN & S. H. SNYDER. 1975. Life Sci. **16:** 1765–1769.
61. SIMANTOU, R., M. J. KUHAR, G. W. PASTERNAK & S. H. SNYDER. 1976. Brain Res. **106:** 189–197.
62. GUILLEMIN, R., N. LING & R. BURGUS. 1976. C. R. Acad. Sci., Ser. D. (Paris) **282** (In press).
63. HOKFELT, T., S. EFENDIC, O. JOHANSSON, R. LUFT & A. ARIMURA. 1974. Brain Res. **80:** 165–169.
64. HOKFELT, T., K. FUXE, O. JOHANSSON, S. JEFFCOATE & N. WHITE. 1975. Neurosci. Letters **1:** 133–139.
65. KUHAR, M. J., C. B. PERT & S. H. SNYDER. 1973. Nature **245:** 447–450.
66. PERT, C. B., M. J. KUHAR & S. H. SNYDER. 1975. Life Sci. **16:** 1851–1857.
67. SHARPE, L. G., J. E. GARNETT & T. J. CICERO. 1974. Behav. Biol. **11:** 303–313.
68. PERT, A. & T. YAKSH. 1975. Pharmacol. Biochem. Behav. **3:** 133–138.
69. WEI, E., S. SIGEL & E. L. WAY. 1975. J. Pharmacol. Exp. Therap. **193:** 56–63.
70. TESCHEMACHER, H., P. SCHUBERT & A. HERZ. 1973. Neuropharmacol. **12:** 123–132.
71. SHIGENAGA, Y. & R. INOKI. 1976. Brain Res. **103:** 152–156.
72. SHARMA, S. K., M. NIRENBERG & W. A. KLEE. 1975. Proc. Nat. Acad. Sci. **72:** 590–594.
73. SHARMA, S. K., W. A. KLEE & M. NIRENBERG. 1975. Proc. Nat. Acad. Sci. **72:** 3092–3096.
74. TRABER, J., R. GULLIS & HAMPRECHT. 1975. Life Sci. **16:** 1863–1869.
75. ROY, A. C. & H. O. J. COLLIER. 1975. Life Sci. **16:** 1858–1862.
76. COLLIER, H. O. J., D. L. FRANCIS, W. J. MCDONALD-GIBSON, A. C. ROY & S. A. SAEED. 1975. Life Sci. **17:** 85–90.
77. BLOOM, F. E. 1975. Rev. Physiol. Biochem. Pharmacol. **74:** 2–103.
78. KIIANMAA, K., K. FUXE, G. JONSSON & AHTEE. 1975. Neurosci. Letters **1:** 41–45.
79. COOPER, J. R., F. E. BLOOM & R. H. ROTH. 1974. Biochemical Basis of Neuropharmacology. 2nd edit.: 40. Oxford Press. New York, N.Y.

PHARMACOKINETIC APPROACHES TO THE STUDY OF DRUG INTERACTIONS*

Gerhard Levy

Department of Pharmaceutics, School of Pharmacy
State University of New York at Buffalo
Buffalo, New York 14214

Pharmacokinetic investigations of suspected or potential drug interactions are designed to determine the effect of one drug on the absorption, distribution, metabolism, or excretion of another drug and to establish whether any change in the intensity and duration of pharmacologic activity of the affected drug can be explained quantitatively by the altered time course of drug concentrations in plasma or tissues. To determine the clinical significance of a drug interaction, it is usually essential to carry out studies in man under clinically realistic conditions. The purpose of this review will be to consider some pharmacokinetic techniques which are useful in the study of drug interactions, to describe some unusual or interesting types of interactions studied in the author's laboratory, and to emphasize the complexity and multifactorial nature of some drug interactions.

Absorption

The rate and/or extent of drug absorption from the gastrointestinal tract can be altered by a number of different mechanisms. These include changes in gastric emptying rate, in the rate of release of the drug from its pharmaceutical dosage form, in the solubility or thermodynamic activity of the drug in gastrointestinal fluids, and in the permeability characteristics of gastrointestinal membranes.

An interesting example of an effect on gastrointestinal absorption of drugs is the one produced by cola-type beverages. It is described here because it illustrates certain principles and because soft drinks are not generally considered to contribute to drug interactions. Cola beverages contain phosphoric acid and (except for dietary products) sugar. Both substances have been shown to slow gastric emptying in man.[1, 2] Gastric emptying can be a major determinant of drug absorption rate and can also affect the extent of absorption. The water-soluble vitamin riboflavin is absorbed by a specialized saturable process which is located in the proximal region of the small intestine. Because of the limited capacity of the absorption process, the extent of absorption of large doses of riboflavin is a function of the length of time during which ingested vitamin is in contact with intestinal absorption sites. The decrease in gastric emptying rate caused by Coca-Cola® can result in a large increase in the extent of riboflavin absorption[3] (FIGURE 1). This effect is due to both phosphoric acid and sugar since a sugar-free cola beverage (Tab®) also increases riboflavin absorption, but not as much (FIGURE 1).

* Supported in part by grants GM 19568 and GM 20852 from the National Institute of General Medical Sciences, National Institutes of Health, Bethesda, Md.

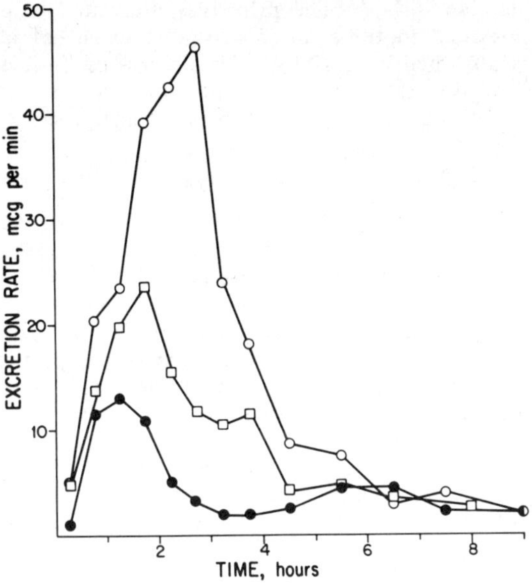

FIGURE 1. Effect of soft drinks on the bioavailability of riboflavin in a healthy adult human subject. Plotted are the excretion rates of riboflavin as a function of time after oral administration of 41 mg riboflavin-5′-phosphate in 450 ml water (●), sugar-free cola (□), and regular cola (○).

A change in gastric emptying rate and a consequent change in the rate of absorption can also modify the biologic fate of a drug. Thus, oral administration of salicylamide with a cola beverage increases the fraction of the dose conjugated with sulfate and decreases the fraction converted to salicylamide glucuronide (TABLE 1). This occurs because the sulfate conjugation process in man is of low capacity and therefore easily saturated. A decrease in the rate of salicylamide absorption results in decreased concentrations of the drug at sites of sulfate conjugation and thereby permits more extensive conversion of

TABLE 1

EFFECT OF A COLA BEVERAGE ON THE METABOLIC FATE OF SALICYLAMIDE IN MAN*

	Urinary Recovery, % of Dose†		
	Control	Cola	
Total metabolites	96.7 ± 3.1	97.0 ± 3.1	N.S.
Salicylamide glucuronide	63.5 ± 6.5	55.2 ± 2.3	$p < 0.05$
Salicylamide sulfate	24.4 ± 4.4	34.1 ± 3.4	$p < 0.001$
Gentisamide	8.8 ± 2.7	7.7 ± 1.9	N.S.

* Salicylamide, 1 g in gelatin capsules, was administered with 450 ml water (control) or Coca-Cola.®

† Mean ± standard deviation, n = 5.

the drug to salicylamide sulfate.[4] The principles illustrated here are that a) a change in gastrointestinal motility can modify the extent of absorption of a substance which is absorbed by a site-specific process of limited capacity, and b) a change in absorption rate can modify quantitatively the metabolic fate of a drug which is subject to biotransformation by saturable processes.

Distribution

The distribution of a drug can be affected by changes in its binding to plasma proteins, its partitioning in and binding to components of various tissues, and by changes in blood circulation. The most frequently recognized change in drug distribution caused by a drug interaction is the partial displacement from plasma protein binding sites of one drug by another. There are, however, more insidious effects which are not as readily recognizable. For example, antipyrine is a drug which is less than 10 percent bound in plasma, and it is therefore not expected to affect the binding of other drugs to plasma proteins. We observed recently that the plasma concentration of dicumarol required to produce a given anticoagulant effect in rats was decreased appreciably by concomitant administration of antipyrine[5] (Table 2). This happens if the protein binding of this very extensively bound drug is decreased. As expected, we found that *in vitro* addition of antipyrine had no effect on the protein binding of dicumarol in plasma. However, we also found that dicumarol is less bound in plasma of antipyrine-treated rats than in control animals (Table 2). The mechanism of this effect is still being investigated; it may be due to a metabolite of antipyrine or to a change in the formation or elimination kinetics of an endogenous substance. If the effective concentration of total (i.e., free and protein-bound) dicumarol in plasma (item A in Table 2) is multiplied by the free-fraction value (item C in Table 2) to obtain the equi-effective concentrations of free dicumarol in plasma, one finds that these are identical in control rats and antipyrine-treated animals. This is consistent with other evidence that the pharmacologic activity of drugs is usually a function of their free rather than total concentration in plasma. The principles illustrated here are a) that it is necessary to determine the potential effect of one drug on the plasma protein binding of another by *in vivo* studies and not only by *in vitro* investigations and b) that the intensity of the pharmacologic activity of drugs should be referenced to their free rather than total concentrations in plasma.

Metabolism

The biotransformation kinetics of one drug can be modified directly or indirectly by another drug in a number of ways, including competitive inhibition, other types of inhibition, and induction of drug-metabolizing enzyme systems. A number of acute drug interactions affect both interacting drugs; a quantitative pharmacokinetic analysis of such interactions therefore requires that the time course of concentrations of both interacting drugs be monitored.[5]

Most formal studies of drug interactions are initiated for one of two reasons: There have been clinical observations which suggest the possibility

TABLE 2

INTERACTION OF ANTIPYRINE WITH DICUMAROL IN RATS

	Control		With Antipyrine	Conditions
A. Dicumarol conc. in plasma which produces 50% of maximum anticoagulant effect, mcg/ml*	17.6		12.6	Antipyrine, 35 mg/kg, injected every 2 hours
		$p < 0.005$		
B. Free fraction of dicumarol in plasma with antipyrine added *in vitro*, ×10,000	1.28		a) 1.30, b) 1.31	Antipyrine concentration in plasma: a) 5 mcg/ml, b) 15 mcg/ml
		N.S.		
C. Free fraction of dicumarol in plasma of antipyrine-treated rats, ×10,000	1.77		2.50	Antipyrine, 35 mg/kg, injected every 2 hours. Antipyrine conc. in plasma ~ 15 mcg/ml.
		$p < 0.001$		

* Calculation of free (not protein bound) equi-effective concentrations by multiplying A and C yields 3.12×10^{-5} mcg/ml for the control and antipyrine experiments, respectively.

of an interaction, or there are theoretical reasons (based on previous experience with drugs of similar structure, activity, or metabolic fate) which make an interaction probable. An example of the latter is the interaction of ascorbic acid with drugs which are subject to conjugation with sulfate. Since man's ability to form sulfate conjugates is limited and since ascorbic acid is biotransformed in part to ascorbic acid sulfate,[6] we suspected that the vitamin may competitively inhibit the formation of drug sulfate. An initial study of the effect of ascorbic acid on salicylamide metabolism in man indicated that our hypothesis may be correct: There was a significant decrease in the fraction of the dose converted to salicylamide sulfate.[7] Salicylamide, in the usual dose range, is largely metabolized in the first-pass and possibly mainly in the intestinal wall. We therefore designed an experiment to determine if ascorbic acid can interact systemically with a drug.

Acetaminophen in rapidly absorbed form (solution) was administered orally to healthy human subjects, and ascorbic acid was given 1½ hours later, i.e. after the acetaminophen had been absorbed.[8] There was a significant decrease in the urinary excretion of acetaminophen sulfate and a corresponding increase in the output of acetaminophen and acetaminophen glucuronide (TABLE 3). This inhibitory effect of ascorbic acid could be prevented by concomitant administration of sodium sulfate (TABLE 4), showing that the availability of sulfate, rather than the capacity of an enzyme, is rate-limiting in the conjugation of acetaminophen. A change in the composition of urinary metabolites of a drug can obviously be caused by a decrease in formation of one metabolite or by an increase in formation of another. The former causes an increase in the biological half-life of the drug, whereas the latter has the opposite effect. In the case of the ascorbic acid-acetaminophen interaction, a decrease in the acetaminophen sulfate fraction was associated with a cor-

TABLE 3

EFFECT OF ASCORBIC ACID ON METABOLIC FATE OF ACETAMINOPHEN IN MAN*

	Urinary Recovery, % of Dose†		
	Control	With Ascorbic Acid	
Acetaminophen	4.5 ± 0.6	5.9 ± 0.7	$p < 0.005$
Acetaminophen glucuronide	46.2 ± 8.7	54.9 ± 8.2	$p < 0.001$
Acetaminophen sulfate	33.3 ± 5.9	23.0 ± 2.7	$p < 0.05$
Total Acetaminophen	84.0 ± 8.4	83.8 ± 8.4	N.S.

* Acetaminophen, 1 g in solution, followed by water or 3 g ascorbic acid in water 1½ hours later.

† Mean ± standard deviation, n = 5.

TABLE 4

EFFECT OF SODIUM SULFATE ON THE BIOTRANSFORMATION INTERACTION BETWEEN ACETAMINOPHEN AND ASCORBIC ACID

	Urinary Recovery, % of Dose*		
	Control	With Ascorbic Acid†	With Ascorbic Acid† and Sodium Sulfate‡
Acetaminophen	4.1, 3.9	5.2, 5.0	4.5, 4.5
Acetaminophen glucuronide	47.7, 53.5	57.8, 62.0	53.8, 52.1
Acetaminophen sulfate	29.4, 32.3	19.6, 23.6	32.7, 31.8
Total acetaminophen	81.2, 89.7	82.6, 90.6	91.0, 88.4

* 1 g acetaminophen orally; data from two healthy men.

† 3 g 1½ hours after acetaminophen.

‡ 1 g at ½, 1½, and 2½ hours after acetaminophen.

responding increase in the biologic half-life of acetaminophen (FIGURE 2), which changed from 2.3 ± 0.2 to 3.1 ± 0.5 hours (mean ± S.D., n = 5).

One interesting and important aspect of competitive drug interactions is the effect of route of administration. This is illustrated by the results of our study of the interaction between ascorbic acid and salicylamide in rats.[9] Intravenous injection of ascorbic acid had no apparent effect on orally administered salicylamide and little effect on intravenously injected salicylamide, but orally administered ascorbic acid had a pronounced inhibitory effect on the formation of salicylamide sulfate from orally as well as intravenously administered salicylamide (TABLE 5). A quantitative assessment of the effect of route of administration on this interaction, particularly as it affects the systemic availability of salicylamide and its body clearance, is obtained from the AUC, i.e. the area under the plasma concentration-time curves (TABLE 6). These show that i.v. as well as oral ascorbic acid inhibited the elimination of i.v. salicylamide, the oral vitamin being somewhat more effective. The effects of these interactions on the concentrations of salicylamide sulfate and glucuronide in plasma are shown in FIGURE 3. The AUC values for orally administered

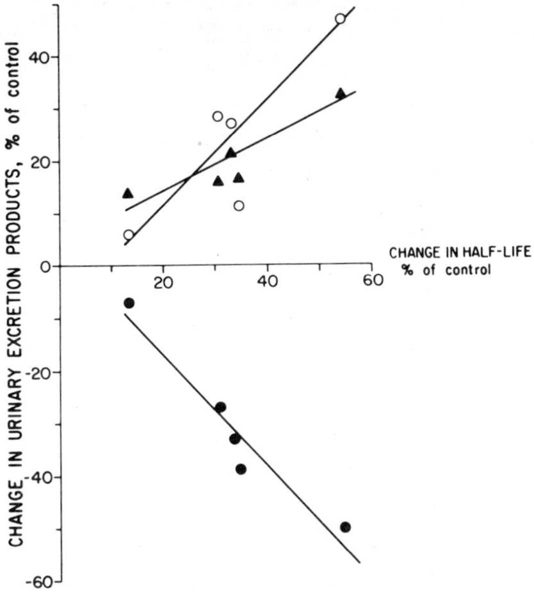

FIGURE 2. Relationship between the change in the apparent half-life of acetaminophen produced by ascorbic acid and the change in the amount of excreted acetaminophen (○), acetaminophen glucuronide (▲), and acetaminophen sulfate (●) in five healthy men.

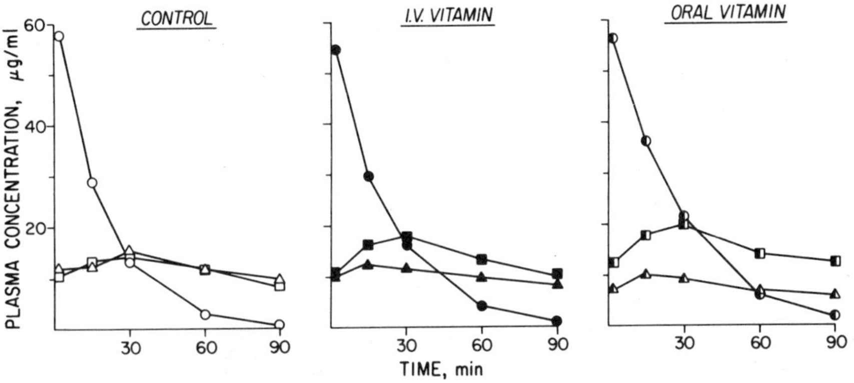

FIGURE 3. Average concentrations of salicylamide (circles), salicylamide glucuronide (squares), and salicylamide sulfate (triangles) in plasma of the same 5 rats after i.v. injection of salicylamide, 100 mg/kg alone (open symbols), with ascorbic acid 500 mg/kg i.v. (closed symbols), and with ascorbic acid 500 mg/kg orally (half-open symbols).

TABLE 5

EFFECT OF ROUTE OF ADMINISTRATION ON THE INTERACTION BETWEEN SALICYLAMIDE AND ASCORBIC ACID IN RATS

	Percent of Dose Excreted in Urine								
	Control			I.V. Ascorbic Acid			Oral Ascorbic Acid		
	SAMG	SAMS	Total	SAMG	SAMS	Total	SAMG	SAMS	Total
I.V. salicylamide*	33.5 ± 1.5	52.8 ± 3	86.3 ± 2.5	41.0 ± 1.6†	44.0 ± 3.0†	85.0 ± 3.2	49.7 ± 2.8†	34.9 ± 1.5†	84.5 ± 2.0
Oral salicylamide*	48.9 ± 3.7	33.4 ± 5.3	82.2 ± 5.3	47.6 ± 4.9	33.4 ± 7.4	80.9 ± 3.8	59.4 ± 1.8†	22.1 ± 4.1†	81.4 ± 3.6

* Mean ± standard deviation for 5 animals.

† Statistically significantly different ($p < 0.01$) from corresponding control value.

TABLE 6

EFFECT OF ASCORBIC ACID ON AREA UNDER PLASMA CONCENTRATION-TIME CURVE FOR SALICYLAMIDE IN RATS

Route of Administration		
Salicylamide	Ascorbic Acid†	Area under Curve (μg/ml) min‡
i.v.*	none	1320 ± 125
i.v.*	i.v.	1453 ± 106§
i.v.*	oral	1708 ± 194§
oral†	none	1028 ± 117
oral†	i.v.	1095 ± 64
oral†	oral	2006 ± 30§

* 100 mg/kg.
† 500 mg/kg.
‡ Mean ± S.D. of area under curve from 0 to 90 minutes.
§ Statistically significantly different from corresponding control value.

salicylamide listed in TABLE 6 are underestimated to some degree because plasma-salicylamide concentrations had not declined to near-zero at 90 minutes (FIGURE 4). An oral dose of 500 mg/kg produced about the same AUC as an i.v. dose of 100 mg/kg, indicating that about 80 percent of the oral dose of salicylamide is metabolized presystemically. Consistent with the metabolite data (TABLE 5), i.v. ascorbic acid had no effect but the oral vitamin had a pronounced effect on the AUC of oral salicylamide (TABLE 6). Thus, the most pronounced interaction occurred when both interactants were administered orally. This is consistent with the concentration dependence of competitive drug interactions and with the fact that the highest concentrations of inter-

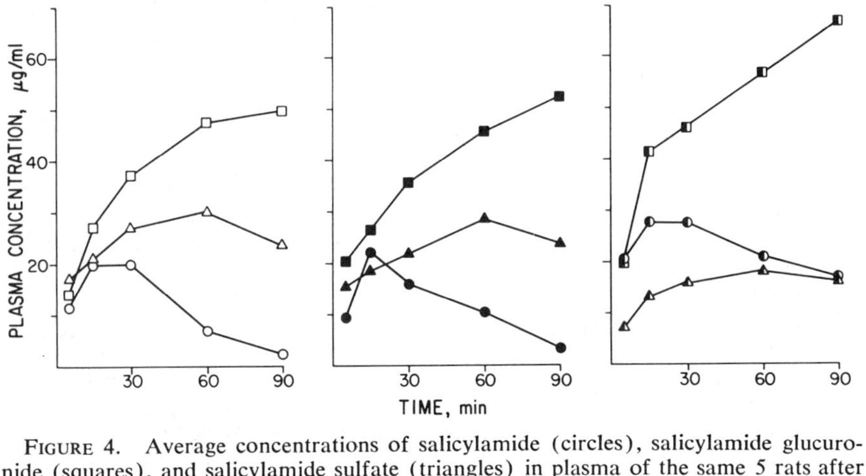

FIGURE 4. Average concentrations of salicylamide (circles), salicylamide glucuronide (squares), and salicylamide sulfate (triangles) in plasma of the same 5 rats after oral administration of salicylamide, 500 mg/kg alone (open symbols), with ascorbic acid 500 mg/kg i.v. (closed symbols), and with ascorbic acid 500 mg/kg orally (half-open symbols).

actants at biotransformation sites (intestinal and hepatic tissues) are obtained upon oral administration.

Some drug interactions are indirect and may not be readily recognizable. We found that the elimination kinetics of phenytoin in rats are unusually nonlinear and not simply of the Michaelis-Menten type[10]: The rate of decline of

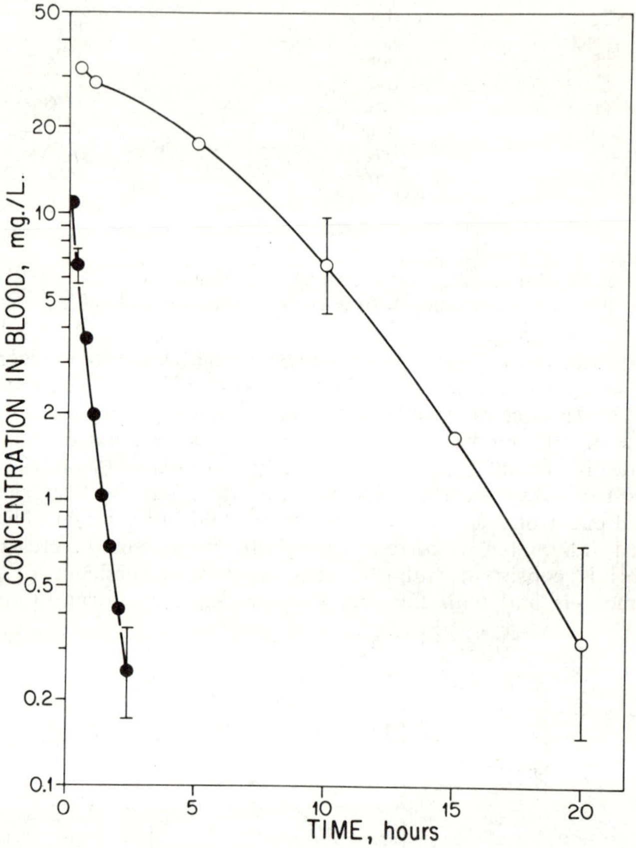

FIGURE 5. Concentration of phenytoin in the blood of rats after i.v. injection of 10 mg/kg (●) and 40 mg/kg (○). Average of five and four rats, respectively. Vertical bars: ± standard error.

phenytoin concentrations in plasma *in a given concentration range* decreases with increasing dose (FIGURE 5). Suspecting the possibility of product inhibition, we administered 5-(*p*-hydroxyphenyl)-5-phenylhydantoin (HPPH), the major metabolite of phenytoin, to rats and found that it does indeed inhibit the elimination of phenytoin (FIGURE 6). HPPH in the body is eliminated by formation of HPPH glucuronide. If this process is inhibited or blocked, HPPH will accumulate at the site of biotransformation and product inhibition should occur. Salicylamide is an effective competitive inhibitor, not only of sulfate but also of glucuronide conjugation.[12] We were not surprised therefore to find

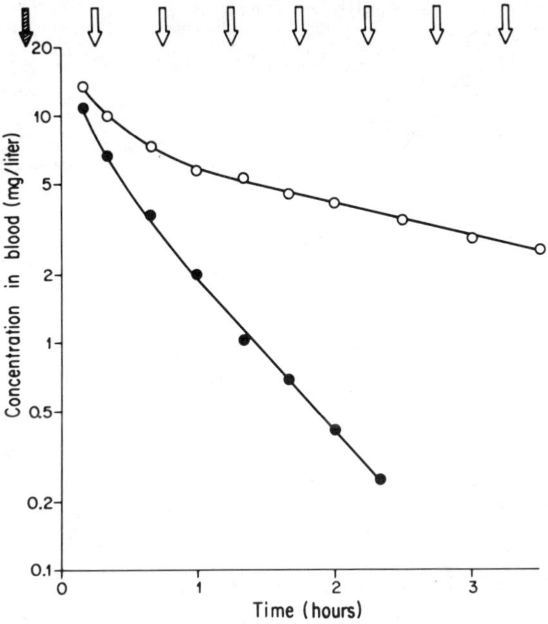

FIGURE 6. Effect of 5-(*p*-hydroxyphenyl)-5-phenylhydantoin (HPPH) on the elimination of phenytoin, 10 mg/kg i.v., by rats. ●, phenytoin alone; ○, phenytoin and HPPH at the times shown by the arrows (striped arrow, 50 mg/kg; open arrows, 25 mg/kg). Mean of 5 rats each.

that administration of salicylamide to rats receiving only phenytoin (no HPPH) had a pronounced inhibitory effect on phenytoin elimination[13] (FIGURE 7). This is an excellent example of an indirect drug interaction: One drug inhibits the elimination of the metabolite of another, which accumulates and thereby inhibits the elimination of its precursor.

RENAL EXCRETION

Renal excretion of a drug occurs by glomerular filtration and often also involves renal tubular secretion and passive or specialized renal tubular reabsorption. All these processes may be affected by other drugs. The most commonly encountered interactions are due to inhibition of renal tubular secretion or to a change in the extent of passive reabsorption. The latter process is pH dependent for drugs which are weak acids or weak bases since such drugs are reabsorbed by passive diffusion of their nonionized molecules from the renal tubular lumen to the general circulation. Ammonium chloride and sodium bicarbonate can modify the pH of urine and are frequently used for this purpose. Not as widely known is that some "non-systemic" antacids, such as aluminum and magnesium hydroxide, can cause a pronounced increase in urine pH.[4] This antacid is often taken by arthritic patients concomitantly with

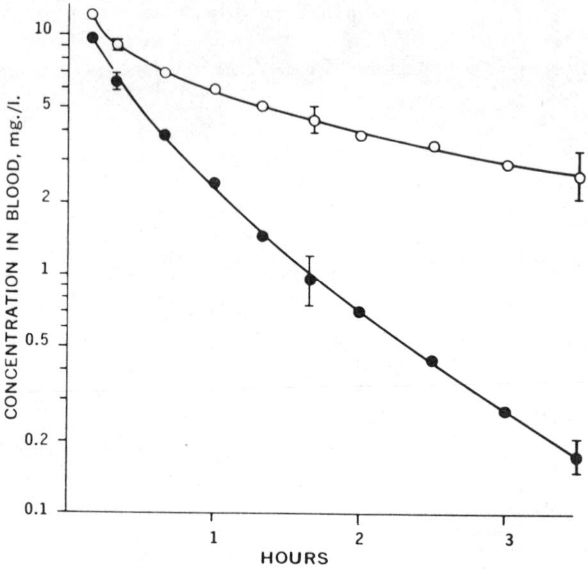

FIGURE 7. Effect of salicylamide on the elimination of phenytoin, 10 mg/kg i.v., by rats. ●, phenytoin alone; ○, phenytoin with salicylamide, 200 mg/kg at −30 minutes and 100 mg/kg every hour thereafter. Means of 5 control and 6 salicylamide-treated animals.

aspirin to reduce adverse gastrointestinal effects. We have found that co-administration of aluminum and magnesium hydroxide with aspirin can increase urine pH and thereby significantly lower the concentration of salicylate in plasma. Conversely, discontinuation of the antacid can cause a decrease in urine pH and consequently a rise of plasma salicylate concentrations to potentially dangerous levels under certain conditions.[15] The antacids have no apparent effect on the bioavailability of aspirin. Since antacids are non-prescription drugs which are often used by patients without the knowledge of their physicians, the occurrence of an antacid-drug interaction may not be readily apparent in many instances.

PHARMACOLOGIC EFFECT

It is always important to determine if a change in the intensity or time course of a pharmacologic effect resulting from a drug interaction is due entirely to the change in the time course of drug concentrations in plasma and tissues produced by that interaction. This has been routine practice in animal studies with barbiturates and zoxazolamine; investigators have measured the concentration of these drugs in the plasma and/or brain of animals upon awakening or recovery from paralysis. It is usually more difficult to do in clinical investigations, but we have been able to make this determination in a pharmacokinetic study of the interaction between heptabarbital and warfarin in man.[16] The barbiturate caused a decrease in the biological half-life of warfarin but had no apparent effect on the relationship between anticoagulant effect and warfarin concentration in plasma (FIGURE 8). Thus, the shorter duration of anticoagulant activity produced by warfarin after treatment of patients with the enzyme inducer could be attributed entirely to the more rapid elimination of warfarin. However, we also found in as yet unpublished studies that pretreatment of rats with phenobarbital, 75 mg/kg/day, caused an increase in prothrombin complex activity, probably due to increased formation rate of

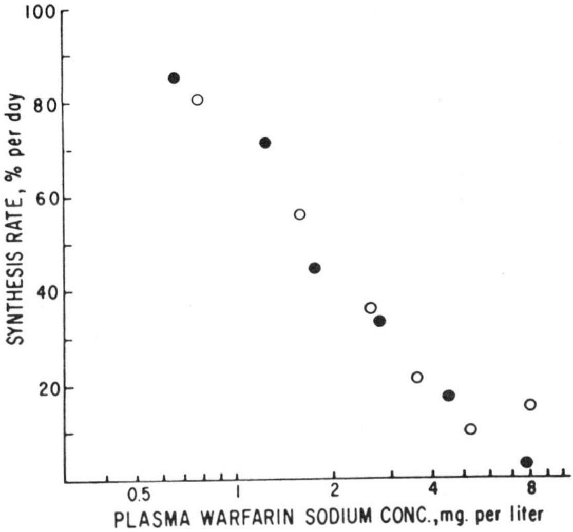

FIGURE 8. Effect of treatment with an enzyme inducer (heptabarbital) on the relationship between synthesis rate of prothrombin complex activity and warfarin concentration in plasma of a healthy human adult. ○, control (warfarin half-life 46 hours); ●, with heptabarbital (warfarin half-life 36 hours).

one or several clotting factors. Whether this is a drug or species difference or due to the higher doses used in rats remains to be established.

THE POTENTIAL COMPLEXITY OF DRUG INTERACTIONS

The most important lesson that I have learned in our investigations of drug interactions is that they can be very complex and multi-factorial. It is often tempting, but dangerous, to conclude from an observation of *one* pronounced alteration in the absorption, distribution, metabolism, or excretion of a drug that this one change accounts for all of the interaction. The multiplicity of mechanisms which may be involved is best illustrated by reviewing the results of our recent investigation in rats of the widely observed interaction between warfarin and phenylbutazone.[17] It is best to begin by pointing out that rats differ widely with respect to the biologic half-life of warfarin (FIGURE 9) and also in the extent to which this drug is bound to protein in their plasma.[18] Based on theoretical pharmacokinetic considerations we developed a mathematical

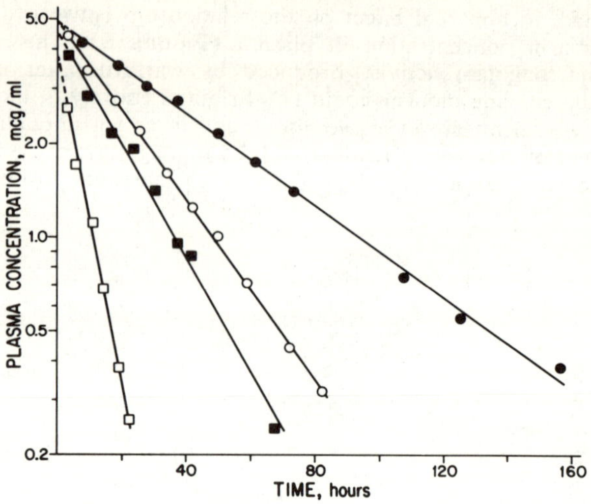

FIGURE 9. Concentration of warfarin in the plasma of rats as a function of time after a 0.6 mg/kg i.v. dose.

model which predicts that the total body clearance (TC) of warfarin is directly proportional to the free fraction of warfarin in plasma (f_p):

$$TC = k''f_p$$

where k'' is an intrinsic clearance constant which reflects the activity of the warfarin metabolizing enzyme system(s).[19] An excellent linear relationship between TC and f was demonstrated experimentally (FIGURE 10), showing that differences in plasma protein binding rather than in enzyme activity account for

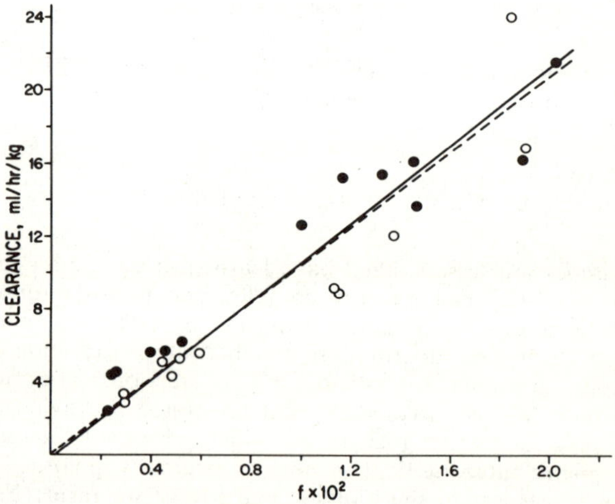

FIGURE 10. Relationship between total plasma clearance of warfarin and free fraction of the drug in the serum of individual animals. Results of two studies.

TABLE 7

EFFECT OF PHENYLBUTAZONE ON THE PHARMACOKINETICS AND SERUM PROTEIN BINDING OF WARFARIN IN RATS*

	Control	With Phenylbutazone
Half-life, hours	16.3	8.66†
Apparent volume of distribution, ml/kg	152	175†
Total body clearance,§ ml/hr/kg	8.88	17.8†
Free fraction in serum ×100	0.908	2.92†

* Average data from 11 rats.
† Statistically significantly different from control value ($p < 0.01$).
§ Calculated from data for individual animals.

the pronounced interindividual variation of warfarin elimination kinetics in rats. We have made similar observations recently in patients with cardiovascular disease who are on warfarin therapy.[20]

Concomitant administration of phenylbutazone with warfarin to rats caused a pronounced decrease in the biologic half-life of warfarin and an increase in apparent volume of distribution, total body clearance, and plasma-free fraction of the drug (TABLE 7). However, body clearance increased only two-fold while the free fraction increased three-fold. A plot of TC versus f_p of warfarin was linear for results obtained in both control and phenylbutazone experiments, but the slope of the regression line was substantially decreased in the experiment with phenylbutazone (FIGURE 11). Thus, phenylbutazone inhibited the activity of the warfarin-metabolizing enzyme system(s) but had an even greater effect in displacing the anticoagulant from plasma protein (and thereby in-

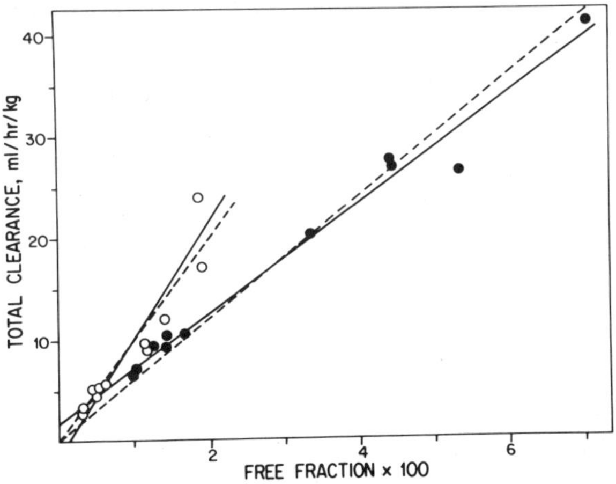

FIGURE 11. Relationship between total clearance and the free fraction of warfarin in plasma of rats in a control experiment (○) and when the same animals were also receiving phenylbutazone, 40 mg/kg at −2 hours and then 20 mg/kg every 4 hours (●). The slopes of the regression lines are significantly different ($p < 0.001$). ——, least-squares regression line;- - -, least squares regression line forced through the origin.

creasing warfarin clearance). The net effect was one of increased warfarin clearance and decreased biological half-life. The situation is actually even more complicated because warfarin is racemic and its two enantiomers interact differently with phenylbutazone.[21] To add further to the complexity, concomitant administration of phenylbutazone causes a lateral shift in the anticoagulant effect-plasma concentration curve of warfarin to a lower concentration range (which is to be expected since phenylbutazone displaces warfarin from plasma protein binding sites, and only *free* warfarin is pharmacologically active[22]), and it even alters the relationship between intensity of effect and concentration of free warfarin (FIGURE 12). It appears that phenylbutazone also interacts directly or indirectly with warfarin at the latter's site of action.

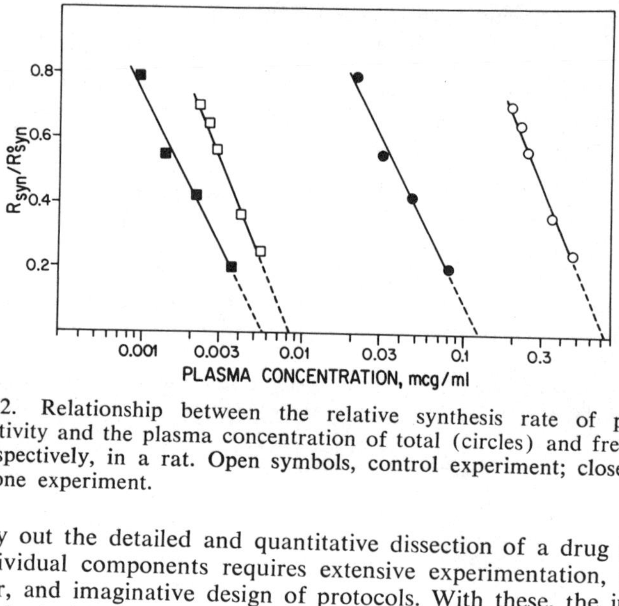

FIGURE 12. Relationship between the relative synthesis rate of prothrombin complex activity and the plasma concentration of total (circles) and free (squares) warfarin, respectively, in a rat. Open symbols, control experiment; closed symbols, phenylbutazone experiment.

To carry out the detailed and quantitative dissection of a drug interaction into its individual components requires extensive experimentation, pharmacokinetic rigor, and imaginative design of protocols. With these, the investigator can often obtain information which not only has a bearing on a particular drug interaction *per se* but will also provide greater insight into the effect of the body on drugs in general and the effect of such drugs on the body.

REFERENCES

1. ELIAS, E., G. J. GIBSON, L. F. GREENWOOD, J. A. HUNT & J. H. TRIPP. 1968. J. Physiol. **194:** 317–326.
2. HUNT, J. N. & M. T. KNOX. 1969. J. Physiol. **201:** 161–179.
3. HOUSTON, J. B. & G. LEVY. 1975. J. Pharm. Sci. **64:** 1504–1507.
4. LEVY, G. & T. MATSUZAWA. 1967. J. Pharmacol. Exp. Ther. **156:** 285–293.
5. LAI, C.-M. & G. LEVY. 1976. To be published.
6. BAKER, E. M., D. C. HAMMER, S. C. MARCH. B. M. TOLBERT & J. E. CANHAM. 1971. Science **173:** 826–827.
7. HOUSTON, J. B. & G. LEVY. 1975. Nature **255:** 78–79.

8. Houston, J. B. & G. Levy. 1976. J. Pharm. Sci. **65:** 1218–1221.
9. Houston, J. B. & G. Levy. 1976. J. Pharmacol. Exp. Ther. In press.
10. Ashley, J. J. & G. Levy. 1973. J. Pharmacokin. Biopharm. **1:** 99–102.
11. Ashley, J. J. & G. Levy. 1972. Res. Commun. Chem. Pathol. Pharmacol. **4:** 297–306.
12. Levy, G. & J. A. Procknal. 1968. J. Pharm. Sci. **57:** 1330–1335.
13. Levy, G. & J. J. Ashley. 1973. J. Pharm. Sci. **62:** 161–162.
14. Gibaldi, M., B. Grundhofer & G. Levy. 1974. Clin. Pharmacol. Ther. **16:** 520–525.
15. Levy, G., T. Lampman, B. L. Kamath & L. K. Garrettson. 1975. N. Engl. J. Med. **293:** 323–325.
16. Levy, G., R. A. O'Reilly, P. M. Aggeler & G. M. Keech. 1970. Clin. Pharmacol. Ther. **11:** 372–377.
17. Yacobi, A., C.-M. Lai & G. Levy. 1976. To be published.
18. Yacobi, A. & G. Levy. 1975. J. Pharm. Sci. **64:** 1660–1664.
19. Levy, G. & A. Yacobi. 1974. J. Pharm. Sci. **63:** 805–806.
20. Yacobi, A., J. A. Udall & G. Levy. 1976. Clin. Pharmacol. Ther. **19:** 552–558.
21. Lewis, R. J., W. F. Trager, K. K. Chan, J. Breckenridge, M. Orme, M. Rowland & W. Schary. 1974. J. Clin. Invest. **53:** 1607–1617.
22. Yacobi, A. & G. Levy. 1975. Res. Commun. Chem. Pathol. Pharmacol. **12:** 405–408.

INVESTIGATIVE APPROACHES FOR THE ANALYSIS OF DRUG INTERACTIONS AT THE GENETIC LEVEL*

Samuel A. Latt and James W. Allen

Division of Medical Genetics
Children's Hospital Medical Center
Boston, Massachusetts 02115

INTRODUCTION

Individuals in modern industrial societies are exposed to a multitude of agents capable of inducing genetic damage. Advances in molecular biology have led to increasingly sensitive tests for mutagenicity and have provided a conceptual framework within which alterations in genetic function can be evaluated. Results thus far have engendered the concern that a number of chemicals, including drugs of abuse, may exert genetically important side effects, even though their primary site of action lies elsewhere.[1] Recent methodological developments should afford improved means of examining the potential of such drugs for causing genetic damage. Of equal importance, new techniques may make it possible to exclude with greater certainty the suspicion that an agent constitutes a genetic hazard. The present review will focus on studies involving psychoactive drugs such as marijuana or lysergic acid diethylamide (LSD), although many of the approaches considered should have wide applicability.

Genetic investigations can be carried out with experimental systems of varying degrees of complexity. Physical/chemical analyses at the macromolecular level provide a well-defined but indirect means of evaluating genetic toxicity. Functional studies offer greater investigative breadth, though they are often limited by incomplete understanding of the processes examined. Mutagenicity tests provide empirical means for screening even those agents for which mechanistic information is scant. However, the high sensitivity of many biologically relevant systems may be associated with a complexity that confounds the interpretation of experimental results.

MOLECULAR INTERACTIONS

Studies of the interaction of drugs with DNA, chromatin, or mitotic spindle components constitute a useful means of assessing the potential for genetic damage. In many instances, it is possible to determine not only the affinity with which a drug binds but also the geometry of binding. Conversely, the

* This work was supported by research grants from the National Institutes of Health (GM 21121), National Foundation March of Dimes (1–353), and American Cancer Society (VC–144A). S.A.L. is the recipient of a Research Career Development Award (GM 00122), and J.W.A. is supported by funds from a postdoctoral training grant (GM 00156).

failure of a drug to bind can be accurately determined. While measurements with purified systems cannot exclude indirect effects of drugs on chromosomes, such as actions dependent on prior host-mediated drug metabolism, they place constraints on the possible mechanisms by which genetic effects might occur.

Optical measurements can be used to characterize binding interactions of psychoactive drugs. While not quantitatively as sensitive as isotopic techniques, spectroscopic approaches can provide qualitative information about the nature of binding interactions. Essential for such studies is the presence of appropriate chromophoric groups. For example, LSD possesses an extended indole group[2] which is suitable for absorption, fluorescence, and optical activity analyses. Delta-9-tetrahydrocannabinol (Δ^9THC) possesses a substituted phenolic group with somewhat less desirable but nonetheless potentially usable spectral properties which, however, have apparently not been extensively exploited.

The interaction of LSD with DNA is associated with a decrease in dye absorption (at 310 nm) and fluorescence (at 450 nm).[3] On the basis of such measurements, it was concluded that LSD bound to double-helical DNA but not to heat-denatured DNA or to RNA. The interaction between LSD and DNA was relatively weak ($K_d \sim 5 \times 10^{-4}$M) however, and both active and inactive optical isomers of LSD were able to bind to DNA. The mode of LSD binding was examined by optical activity[4] and viscosity[5, 6] measurements. Results with these techniques did not support the hypothesis that LSD intercalated between DNA base pairs. However, viscometric analyses have provided evidence suggesting that another hallucinogen, harmine, does intercalate with DNA.[7]

While intercalation does not appear to correlate directly with psychoactive activity, it may increase the likelihood that a chemical exerts a genetic effect. A number of intercalating compounds have been shown to induce frame-shift mutations in bacteria.[8] Presumptive evidence that a number of carcinogenic polycyclic hydrocarbons intercalate is based on their mutagenic activity in the Ames microsomal-mediated *S. typhimurium* histidine auxotroph assay system.[9, 10] Moreover, drugs which interact with DNA may enhance DNA damage by other agents[11] or perturb DNA repair.[12–14] While it is probably incorrect to assume that all drugs containing indole or phenol groups can intercalate with DNA, it is interesting that these groups constitute the sidechains of tryptophan and tyrosine, aromatic amino acids that are capable of modulating protein-DNA interactions by intercalation.[15, 16]

Interactions between drugs and proteins provide another mechanism for genetic effects. Chromosomal proteins may act as receptors for hormones,[17] and the drug-binding properties of protein-DNA complexes may differ significantly from those of DNA alone. Psychoactive drugs may also exert genetic effects via interaction with components of the mitotic spindle, an organelle with a subunit composition similar to that of neurotubules.[18]

Functional Studies

Drug effects may be manifest as alterations in DNA replication, repair, or transcription. A number of new methods for examining these functions have recently been developed, but the details of these processes in mammalian cells are still incompletely understood.

Leuchtenberger and coworkers[19] reported that the smoke from marijuana cigarettes could alter the mitotic index, DNA synthesis rate, and DNA content of fibroblasts from human lung explants. The induction of mitotic abnormalities was also noted. Subsequent feulgen microfluorometric analyses[20] corroborated these findings, which were also extended to include an alteration in chromosome number. However, similar changes related to DNA were induced by smoke from ordinary cigarettes. Trosko[21] was unable to detect effects of LSD on either DNA synthesis or the excision repair of pyrimidine dimers in human amnion cells, although he did not rule out the possibility that more sensitive techniques might detect such effects.

Fluorescence flow techniques now permit determination of the effects of drugs on cell-cycle parameters of very large numbers of cells.[22, 23] Measurements of the distribution of cell DNA content (and indirectly, cycle stage) have been performed on populations of cells treated with various drugs to illustrate the point at which a metabolic block occurred.[24] Similar measurements might provide a highly accurate indication of any effect on cellular proliferation due to drugs such as marijuana or LSD. Importantly, if cells with an irregular amount of DNA were detected, they could then be isolated using the sorting capabilities of flow instrumentation[25, 26] and further characterized.

Experiments examining the effect of marijuana on the ability of lymphocytes to proliferate in response to lectins have yielded conflicting results. Nahas and coworkers[27] reported that the blastogenic response of lymphocytes to *in vitro* stimulation by phytohemagglutinin was depressed in marijuana smokers. However, White *et al.*[28] performed similar experiments and obtained negative results. The influence of interindividual variations in lymphocyte response on these observations remains to be determined. Perhaps a more precise determination of lymphocyte response would follow from differentiation between the number of cells responding to lectins (at all) and the number of divisions undergone by a given responding cell. Growth of cells in medium containing BrdU permits this distinction according to the distribution of lightly and darkly staining chromatids observed following 33258 Hoechst,[29, 30] acridine orange,[31] or Giemsa staining.[32, 33]

Analysis of the time course of DNA replication in different chromosomal regions constitutes an alternative approach for examining drug effects on DNA synthesis. Studies of DNA replication in metaphase chromosomes, previously restricted to autoradiography, can now be accomplished by a variety of fluorescent[34, 35] and Giemsa[36] techniques for detecting BrdU incorporation. These techniques have been used to determine the normal time course of DNA replication in human chromosomes, and they could, in principle, be used to study the impact of exogenous agents on DNA replication kinetics. Subtle effects on the relative timing of the DNA replication in different chromosome regions might constitute early evidence of genetic effects of a drug. Since the functional activity and replication kinetics of chromatin often correlate,[37, 38] such deviations in timing of DNA synthesis might indicate potential alterations in gene expression.

Cytogenetic effects of drugs might conceivably be manifest as an influence on DNA repair. A number of DNA repair systems have been detected and characterized in lower organisms.[39, 40] Perhaps the most familiar system involves the incisional repair of pyrimidine dimers produced by ultraviolet (UV) light. Bacteria lacking the capability for this repair can often survive UV irradiation because of a second system utilizing a recombination-like process for repair.[41, 42]

Evidence for similar processes in mammalian systems is accumulating, although biochemical details are sparse.

Incisional repair can be detected either as unscheduled DNA synthesis[43] or as non-semiconservative incorporation of BrdU.[44, 45] Fibroblasts from patients with xeroderma pigmentosum are defective in the repair of DNA damage by ultraviolet light.[46, 47] In addition to their intrinsic sensitivity to DNA damage, these fibroblasts have been used as a host for detecting low levels of alkylation of adenovirus DNA by psoralen plus light treatment.[48] DNA measurements might also be used to test for indirect drug effects, such as a reduction in the rate with which a cell repairs previously induced damage. Measurements of incisional repair of DNA could be accompanied by analyses of sister chromatid exchanges, events which may reflect recombinational repair (*vide infra*). New methods for detecting these exchanges have been developed and will be discussed in a subsequent section.

Various other functional studies of the effects of drugs of abuse are possible. Two groups of investigations reported that cannabis or Δ^9THC inhibited RNA synthesis in tissue slices or chromatin from rat brain,[49, 50] although a third found that Δ^9THC had no effect on RNA synthesis.[51] Independent estimates of the amount of drug actually reaching target cells in these experiments, and the measurement of the synthesis of specific (e.g., messenger or ribosomal) RNA species, might help to reconcile these observations.

Mutagenesis Testing

Perhaps the greatest concern about the possible genetic effects of psychoactive drugs centers around reports of drug-induced mutagenesis. Mutations may take the form of single DNA base changes, small sequence additions or deletions, or morphologically evident chromosome changes (e.g., breaks or rearrangements).[52, 53] Single-locus mutagenesis can be examined with intact animals[54, 55] or cultured mammalian cells.[56] However, the most heavily utilized single-locus mutagen system involves a test for reversion of *S. typhimurium* histidine auxotrophs.[9, 10] Cytogenetic studies have largely utilized *in vitro* cultures of somatic cells. Most of these analyses have focused on chromosome structural aberrations,[57] although more sensitive means of assaying chromosome damage have recently been developed.

Mutagenesis testing has been greatly improved by host-mediated assays. This approach is capable of detecting mutations due to metabolites of chemicals even if the chemicals themselves are not directly mutagenic. As originally developed,[58] a test chemical and an indicator (e.g., a *S. typhimurium* histidine auxotroph) were injected into an animal, after which the indicator was removed and tested for mutations. Ames simplified this procedure by adding the drug, together with a liver microsomal fraction, directly to the bacteria on a petri dish. Exogenous histidine was not provided, and mutagenesis to a histidine-independent state resulted in bacterial growth.[9, 10, 12, 59, 60] A battery of missense and frameshift Salmonella mutants were employed, allowing assignment of the nature of the mutagenic event.[57] An important aspect of the Salmonella system is the apparently strong correlation between the ability of a drug to induce mutations in bacteria and its carcinogenic activity in different animals.[10, 60]

Cannabis, Δ^9THC, and LSD are not included in the most recent tabulation of results from the Ames test system.[16] However, cigarette-smoke condensate itself is mutagenic in this system, as are benzo[α]pyrene and related compounds. A recent chromatographic study[61] has provided evidence that smoke from marijuana cigarettes contains more potentially carcinogenic polycyclic hydrocarbons, as well as benzo[α]pyrene, than does smoke from regular tobacco cigarettes. It will be important to determine whether the absolute amounts of the hydrocarbons detected are sufficient to constitute a genetic hazard.

Witschi and coworkers have reported that cannabis and its derivatives are capable of inducing aryl hydrocarbon hydroxylase,[62-65] an enzyme which has been implicated in the production of carcinogenic epoxide derivatives of polycyclic hydrocarbons.[66] Oral administration of cannabis or Δ^9THC to rats resulted in enhanced hepatic and pulmonary benzopyrene hydroxylase activities.[62, 63] Aryl hydroxylase activity was also increased in the lungs of rats that had inhaled smoke from burning cigarettes containing cannabis. However, since similar enzyme induction was observed with smoke from cigarettes from material presumably depleted of cannabinoids by extraction,[64, 65] the observed effect may not have been specific.

Early studies with LSD focused attention on the possible cytogenetic impact of drugs of abuse. Cohen and coworkers[67, 68] reported that *in vitro* administration of 0.01–0.10 μg/ml LSD significantly increased the number of chromatid plus isochromatid breaks in peripheral lymphocytes cultured from healthy individuals. Elevated frequencies of chromosome aberrations were also observed in lymphocytes obtained from individuals previously exposed to LSD either directly or *in utero*.[68] Soon afterwards, it was reported[69, 70] that injection of mice with high doses of LSD increased the number of morphological abnormalities in spermatogonial cells as well as in cells at diakinesis or metaphase I of meiosis. However, numerous subsequent studies failed to support the contention that LSD induces significant cytogenetic damage. Negative results were obtained with all but very high doses of LSD added directly to human lymphocyte cultures,[71] and no significant increases in chromosome aberrations were observed in lymphocytes obtained from individuals who had taken LSD.[72-74]

One study[75] concluded that LSD did not induce chromosomal abnormalities in either the bone marrow or spermatogonial cells of mice, although it did appear to increase the frequency of chromosome abnormalities in the lymphocytes of rhesus monkeys. A noteworthy aspect of this latter study is its unusually high control chromosome aberration frequency (11.8%). Jagiello and Polani[76] were unable to show an increase in chromosome aberrations in marrow, spermatogonial, or meiotic cells of mice injected with LSD. Goetz and coworkers[77] found that parenteral administration of 10 or 1000 μg/kg LSD to rats of mice failed to increase significantly the frequency of chromosome breaks or rearrangements in spermatocytes, although the frequency of meiotic univalents was increased, as was the frequency of dominant lethal mutations.[78] In a related study, no cytogenetic abnormalities were observed in lymphocytes of mothers who had received LSD prior to pregnancy or in the offspring of these mothers.[79]

The conflicting results described above may reflect a number of factors: (1) The effects, even if real, may be very small. (2) Considerable variations in the chromosome aberration frequencies in normal individuals exist in consecutive cultures from the same person, as well as between different individuals.[80] (3) Investigators may have different ways of scoring aberrations. (4)

Most of the studies of LSD effects used small numbers of individuals, and (5) the effective concentrations of pharmacologically active LSD reaching cells may have differed widely in the different studies. In addition, gross chromosomal aberrations may reflect only a fraction of the damage incident on chromosomes (see below). Subsequent cytogenetic studies with marijuana and its derivatives also traced a conflicting path,[81-85] although the bulk of the evidence indicates that these agents do not cause chromosome aberrations.

Even if marijuana were found to have no significant effect on chromosome abnormalities in adult human peripheral lymphocytes, its potential for genetic damage in fetal cells might be worth considering. Work with tritiated Δ^9THC indicated that Δ^9THC can cross the placenta in Syrian hamsters.[86] A number of investigators have reported that cannabis extract[87, 88] or Δ^9THC[89] can be teratogenic. One study implicated Δ^9THC in the induction of dominant lethal mutations,[89] although another observed no mutagenic effects due to Δ^9THC.[90] In view of these findings, cytogenetic studies of Δ^9THC effects on amniotic cells might be indicated. However, without a more sensitive assay for chromosome damage than the production of morphological aberrations, a conflicting array of negative and positive reports might result.

Sister chromatid-exchange analysis constitutes a useful new approach for screening for chromosome damage. Sister chromatid exchanges involve breakage and interchange between DNA replication products. As such, they represent a form of chromosome repair in response to damage. Early detection of sister chromatid exchanges relied on autoradiography.[91] Detection of exchanges has been greatly facilitated by fluorescent[29-31, 92] and modified Giemsa techniques,[32, 33, 93] which differentiate sister chromatids according to their substitution with BrdU. Exchanges are at least 200 times as frequent as chromosome breaks,[30] and low doses of clastogens causing only small increases in chromosome breakage can induce marked increases in the sister chromatid-exchange frequency.[94-97] Moreover, there is a high correlation between the exchange-inducing capacity and mutagenicity and/or carcinogenicity of various agents.[97] In two separate hereditary diseases involving chromosome fragility and a predisposition for the development of neoplasia, abnormalities have been noted in either the baseline levels (Bloom's syndrome)[98] or the inducibility by mitomycin C (Fanconi's anemia)[99] of sister chromatid exchanges. Fanconi's anemia cells appear to be highly sensitive to DNA crosslinking agents[100, 101] and might thus be used for sensitive detection of this type of damage. While there is no reason, a priori, to predict that psychoactive drugs of abuse will alter the sister chromatid-exchange frequency in cultured cells, an examination of the exchange-inducing capacity of these drugs might be informative.

Until very recently, sister chromatid-exchange analysis has been limited to *in vitro* studies with cultured cells. Such experiments are subject to reservations about the relevance of the results to mutagenicity in germ cells, as well as the artificial features of culture conditions. It is now possible to detect sister chromatid exchange formation *in vivo* in mouse spermatogonia. This new technique[102, 103] has been used to demonstrate an *in vivo* effect of mitomycin C in inducing sister chromatid exchanges in both the spermatogonia and bone marrow cells of mice. In principle, with suitable technical modifications, this approach could provide the basis for a mutagen assay system combining the metabolic flexibility of host-mediated assays and the sensitivity of sister chromatid-exchange analysis.

It should be stressed that the genetic studies enumerated here were chosen merely to indicate the range of approaches available to investigators interested in possible genetic effects of drugs of abuse. The evidence thus far that the drugs discussed produce severe genetic effects is marginal at best. Application of some of the newer approaches for detecting mutagenesis should provide further information. The usefulness of these new techniques, such as sister chromatid-exchange analysis, for determining the genetic impact of drugs will increase as their molecular bases become understood. Moreover, negative results on all available tests do not guarantee against the possibility that a new and more sensitive assay will ultimately afford detection of a genetic side-effect. Thus in spite of the need for empirical tests of psychoactive drugs for possible genetic effects, attention should be paid to the molecular bases of drug interactions as well as to basic investigations of chromosome structure, replication, and repair.

References

1. J. R. Tinklenberg, Ed. 1975. Marijuana and Health Hazards. Academic Press, Inc. New York, N.Y.
2. T. L. Sourkes. 1972. Psychopharmacology. *In* Basic Neurochemistry. R. W. Albers, G. J. Siegel, R. Katzman & B. W. Agranoff, Eds. Chap. 29: 581–606. Little, Brown & Co. Boston, Mass.
3. Yielding, K. L. & H. Sterglanz. 1968. Proc. Soc. Exp. Biol. Med. **128:** 1096.
4. Brady, A. H., E. M. Brady & F. C. Boucek. 1971. Nature **232:** 189–191.
5. Waring, M. J. 1970. J. Mol. Biol. **54:** 247–279.
6. Smit, E. M. & P. Borst. 1971. Nature **232:** 191–192.
7. Duportail, G. & H. Lami. 1975. Biochim. Biophys. Acta **402:** 20–30.
8. Ames, B. N. & H. J. Whitfield. 1966. Cold Spring Harbor Symp. Quant. Biol. **31:** 221–226.
9. Ames, B. N., W. E. Durston, E. Yamasaki & F. D. Lee. 1973. Proc. Nat. Acad. Sci. USA **70:** 782–786.
10. McCann, S., E. Choi, E. Yamasaki & B. N. Ames. 1975. Proc. Nat. Acad. Sci. USA **72:** 5135–5139.
11. Bearden, J., Jr. & C. W. Haidle. 1975. Biochem. Biophys. Res. Commun. **65:** 317–377.
12. Cleaver, J. E. 1969. Radiat. Res. **37:** 334–338.
13. Schroy, C. B. & P. Todd. 1975. Mutat. Res. **33:** 347–356.
14. Maher, V. M., L. M. Ouellette, M. Mittlestat & J. J. McCormick. 1975. Nature **258:** 760–763.
15. Toulme, J. J., M. Charlier & C. Helene. 1974. Proc. Nat. Acad. Sci. USA **71:** 3185–3188.
16. Anderson, R. A., Y. Nakashima & J. E. Coleman. 1975. Biochemistry **14:** 907–917.
17. Stein, G. S., T. C. Spelsberg & L. D. Kleinsmith. 1974. Science **183:** 817–824.
18. Olmstead, J. B. & G. G. Borisy. 1973. Annu. Rev. Biochem. **42:** 507–540.
19. Leuchtenberger, C., R. Leuchtenberger & A. Schneider. 1973. Nature **241:** 137–139.
20. Leuchtenberger, C., R. Leuchtenberger, U. Ritter & W. Inui. 1973. Nature **242:** 403–404.
21. Trosko, J. 1971. Biochem. Pharmacol. **20:** 3213–3218.
22. Crissman, H. A., P. F. Mullaney & J. A. Steinkamp. 1975. **9:** 179–246.

23. TOBEY, R. A. & H. A. CRISSMAN. 1975. Exp. Cell Res. **93:** 235–239.
24. TOBEY, R. A. & H. A. CRISSMAN. 1972. Cancer Res. **32:** 2726–2732.
25. HULETT, H. R., W. A. BONNER, J. BARRETT & L. A. HERZENBERG. 1969. Science **166:** 747–749.
26. ARNDT-JOVIN, D. & T. JOVIN. 1974. J. Histochem. Cytochem. **22:** 622–625.
27. NAHAS, G. G., N. SUCIO-FOCA, J. P. ARMAND & A. MORISHIMA. 1973. Science **183:** 419–420.
28. WHITE, S. C., S. C. BRIN & B. W. JANICKI. 1975. Science **188:** 71–72.
29. LATT, S. A. 1973. Proc. Nat. Acad. Sci. USA **70:** 3395–3399.
30. LATT, S. A. 1974. Science **185:** 74–76.
31. FRANCESCHINI, P. 1974. Exp. Cell Res. **89:** 420–421.
32. PERRY, P. & S. WOLFF. 1974. Nature **251:** 156–158.
33. KIM, M. A. 1974. Humangenetik **25:** 179–188.
34. DUTRILLAUX, B., C. LAURENT, J. COUTURIER & J. LEJEUNE. 1973. C. R. Acad. Sci. Ser. D **276:** 3179–3181.
35. LATT, S. A. 1975. Somat. Cell Genet. **1:** 293–321.
36. GRZESCHIK, H. H., M. A. KIM & R. JOHANNSMANN. 1975. Humangenetik **29:** 41–59.
37. LYON, M. J. 1972. Biol. Rev. **47:** 1–35.
38. LIMA-DE-FARIA, A. & H. JAWORSKA. 1967. Nature **217:** 138–142.
39. SETLOW, R. B. & J. K. SETLOW. 1972. Annu. Rev. Biophys. Bioeng. **1:** 293–346.
40. GROSSMAN, L., A. BRAUN, R. FELDBERG & I. MAHLER. 1975. Annu. Rev. Biochem. **44:** 19–43.
41. RUPP, W. D. & P. HOWARD-FLANDERS. 1968. J. Mol. Biol. **31:** 291–304.
42. RUPP, W. D., C. E. WILDE, D. L. RENO & P. HOWARD-FLANDERS. 1971. J. Mol. Biol. **61:** 25–44.
43. CLARKSSON, J. M. & H. J. EVANS. 1972. Mutat. Res. **14:** 415–430.
44. HANAWALT, P. C. & P. K. COOPER. 1971. Methods Enzymol. **21:** 221–223.
45. REGAN, J. D., R. B. SETLOW & R. D. LEY. 1971. Proc. Nat. Acad. Sci. USA **68:** 708–712.
46. SETLOW, R. B., J. D. REGAN, J. GERMAN & W. L. CARRIER. 1969. Proc. Nat. Acad. Sci. USA **64:** 1035–1041.
47. KRAEMER, K. H., E. A. DE WEERD-KASTELEIN, J. H. ROBBINS, W. KEIJZER, S. F. BARRETT, R. A. PETINGA & D. BOOTSMA. 1975. Mutat. Res. **33:** 327–340.
48. DAY, R. S. III, A. A. GIUFFRIDA & C. W. DINGMAN. 1975. Mutat. Res. **33:** 311–320.
49. JAKOBOVIC, A. & P. L. MCGEER. 1972. Can. J. Biochem. **50:** 654–662.
50. HODGSON, J. R., G. J. WOODHOUSE & T. R. CASTLES. 1973. Can. J. Physiol. Pharmacol. **51:** 401–403.
51. ROBERGE, M. & H. WITSCHI. 1972. Toxicol. Appl. Pharmacol. **23:** 455–458.
52. FREESE, E. 1971. Molecular mechanisms of mutations. *In* Chemical Mutagens. A. Hollaender, Ed. Vol. 1, Chap. 1: 1–56. Plenum Publishing Corp. New York, N.Y.
53. VOGEL, W. & R. RATHENBERG, 1975. Adv. Hum. Genet. **5:** 223–318.
54. RUSSELL, L. B., 1971. Mutat. Res. **11:** 107–123.
55. CATTANACH, B. M. 1971. Specific locus mutation in mice. *In* Chemical Mutagens. A. Hollaender, Ed. Vol. 2, Chap. 20: 535–539. Plenum Publishing Corp. New York, N.Y.
56. THOMPSON, L. & R. BAKER. 1973. Methods Cell Biol. **6:** 209–281.
57. BUCKTON, K. E. & H. J. EVANS, 1973. Methods for the analysis of human chromosome aberrations: 1–66. World Health Organization, Switzerland.
58. LEGATOR, M. S. & H. V. MALLING. 1971. The host mediated assay, a practical procedure for evaluating potential mutagenic agents in mammals. *In* Chemical Mutagens. A. Hollaender, Ed. Vol. 2, Chap. 22: 569–590. Plenum Publishing Corp. New York, N.Y.

59. AMES, B. N., 1971. The detection of chemical mutagens with enteric bacteria. *In* Chemical Mutagens. A. Hollaender, Ed. Vol. 1, Chap. 9: 267–282. Plenum Publishing Corp. New York, N.Y.
60. AMES, B. N., J. MCCANN & E. YAMASAKI. 1975. Mutat. Res. **31:** 347–364.
61. LEE. M. L., M. NOVOTNY & K. D. BARTL. 1976. Anal. Chem. **48:** 405–416.
62. WITSCHI, H. P. & B. SAINT-FRANCOIS. 1972. Toxicol. Appl. Pharmacol. **23:** 165–168.
63. SKELTON, F. C. & H. P. WITSCHI. 1974. Toxicol. Appl. Pharmacol. **27:** 551–557.
64. MARCOTTE, J. & H. P. WITSCHI. 1972. Res. Commun. Chem. Pathol. Pharmacol. **4:** 561–568.
65. MARCOTTE, J., F. S. SKELTON, M. G. COTE & H. WITSCHI. 1975. Toxicol. Appl. Pharmacol. **33:** 231–245.
66. SICILIANO, M. J., D. A. WRIGHT & C. R. SHAW. 1974. Prog. Med. Genet. **10:** 17–53.
67. COHEN, M. M., M. J. MARINELLO & N. BACK. 1969. Science **155:** 1417–1419.
68. COHEN, M. M., K. HIRSCHHORN & W. A. FROSCH. 1967. N. Engl. J. Med. **277:** 1043–1049.
69. SKAKKEBREK, N. E., J. PHILIP & O. J. RAFAELSON. 1968. Science **160:** 1246–1248.
70. COHEN, M. M., & A. B. MUKHERJEE. 1968. Nature **219:** 1072–1074.
71. DORRANCE, D. L., D. J. BEIGHLIE, V. YOSHIR, O. JANIGER, A. M. BRODETSKY & R. L. TEPLITZ. 1974. J. Lab. Clin. Med. **84:** 36–41.
72. SPARKES, R. S., J. MELNYK & L. P. BOZZETTI. 1968. Science **160:** 1343–1345.
73. TJIO, J. H., W. N. PAHNKE & A. A. KURLAND. 1969. JAMA **210:** 849–856.
74. FERNANDEZ, J., I. W. BROWNE, J. CULLEN, T. BRENNAN, H. MATHEU, I. FISCHER, J. MASTERSON & G. LAW. 1973. Ann. Hum. Genet. **37:** 81–91.
75. EGUZCUE, J. & S. IRWIN. 1969. Humangenetik **8:** 86–93.
76. JAGIELLO, G. & P. E. POLANI. 1969. Cytogenetics **8:** 136–147.
77. GOETZ, P., R. J. SRAM & Z. ZUDOVA. 1974. Mutat. Res. **26:** 513–516.
78. GOETZ, P., R. J. SRAM & Z. ZUDOVA. 1973. Mutat. Res. **21:** 189–190.
79. FERNANDEZ, J., T. BRENNAN, J. MASTERSON & M. POWER. 1974. Brit. J. Psychiatry **124:** 296–298.
80. LITTLEFIELD, L. G. & K. O. KOH, 1973. Cytogenet. Cell Genet. **12:** 17–34.
81. NEU, R. L., H. O. POWES, S. KING & L. F. GARDNER. 1965. Lancet **1:** 675.
82. NICHOLS, W. W., R. C. MILLER, W. HENEEN, C. BRADT, L. HOLLISTER & S. KANTER. 1974. Mutat. Res. **26:** 413–417.
83. STENCHEVER, M. A. & M. ALLEN, 1972. Amer. J. Obstet. Gynecol. **114:** 819–821.
84. GILMOUR, D. G., A. D. BLOOM, K. P. LELE, G. S. ROBBINS & C. MAXIMILIAN. 1971. Arch. Gen. Psychiat. **24:** 268–272.
85. STENCHEVER, M. A., T. J. KUNYSZ & M. A. ALLEN. 1974. Amer. J. Obstet. Gynecol. **118:** 106–120.
86. ISAPAAN-HEIKKILA, J., G. E. FRITSCHIE, L. G. ENGLERT, B. T. HO & N. M. MCISAAC. 1969. N. Engl. Med. **281:** 330.
87. PERSAVO, T. V. N. & A. C. ELLINGTON. 1968. Lancet **2:** 406–407.
88. GEBER, N. F. & L. C. SCHRAMM. 1969. Toxicol. Appl. Pharmacol. **14:** 276–282.
89. MANTILLA-PLATA, B., G. L. CLEWE & R. D. HARBISON. 1973. Fed. Proc. **32:** 746.
90. STOECKEL, M., E. WEBER, T. CONNOR & M. S. LEGATOR. 1975. Mutat. Res. **31:** 313–314.
91. TAYLOR, J. H., P. S. WOODS & W. L. HUGHES. 1957. Proc. Nat. Acad. Sci. USA **43:** 127–138.
92. DUTRILLAUX, B., A. M. FOSSE, M. PRIEUR & LEJEUNE. 1974. Chromosoma **48:** 327–340.
93. KORENBERG, J. & E. FREEDLENDER. 1974. Chromosoma **48:** 355–360.

94. Latt, S. A. 1974. Proc. Nat. Acad. Sci. USA **71:** 3162–3166.
95. Kato, H. 1974. Exp. Cell Res. **89:** 416–420.
96. Latt, S. A., L. A. Juergens, G. Stetten, H. F. Willard & C. D. Scher. 1975. J. Histochem. Cytochem. **23:** 493–505.
97. Perry, P. & H. J. Evans. 1975. Nature **258:** 121–125.
98. Chaganti, R. S. K., S. Schonberg & J. German. 1974. Proc. Nat. Acad. Sci. USA **71:** 4508–4512.
99. Latt, S. A., G. Stetten, L. A. Juergens, G. R. Buchanan & P. S. Gerald. 1975. Proc. Nat. Acad. Sci. USA **72:** 4066–4070.
100. Sasaki, M. S. & A. Tonomura. 1973. Cancer Res. **33:** 1829–1836.
101. Sasaki, M. S. 1975. Nature **257:** 501–503.
102. Allen, J. W. & S. A. Latt. 1976. Mutat. Res. (Abstract, in press.)
103. Allen, J. W. & S. A. Latt. 1976. Nature **260:** 449–451.

INTERACTIONS OF BEHAVIORAL EFFECTS OF DRUGS

P. B. Dews

Laboratory of Psychobiology
Harvard Medical School
Boston, Massachusetts 02115

Interest in the joint effects of two drugs administered simultaneously is as old as scientific pharmacology. Frazer[1] systematically explored the joint effects of physostigmine and atropine, and Bernard[2] studied the effects of curare and (without knowing it) acetylcholine. The general pharmacological principles for assessment of joint effects are also of some antiquity and are widely accepted among pharmacologists, although there has been bickering, of course, about nomenclature. As good a scheme as any was provided by Gaddum[3] over 35 years ago (FIGURE 1). It is presented here as a reminder of a principle not infrequently overlooked by nonpharmacologists: Both dose *and* effect must be taken into account in determining the nature of the joint action of two drugs—whether they are antagonistic or synergistic. If drug A in dose a causes effect of intensity x and drug B in dose b causes the same effect of intensity y, the joint effect of drugs A and B taken simultaneously in doses a and b would not be expected, in general, to be of intensity $x + y$. The reason that effects are not simply algebraically additive, even for drug pairs whose effects are strictly additive in Gaddum's sense, has been emphasized repeatedly: Dose-effect curves are generally not straight lines through the origin. When either a threshold

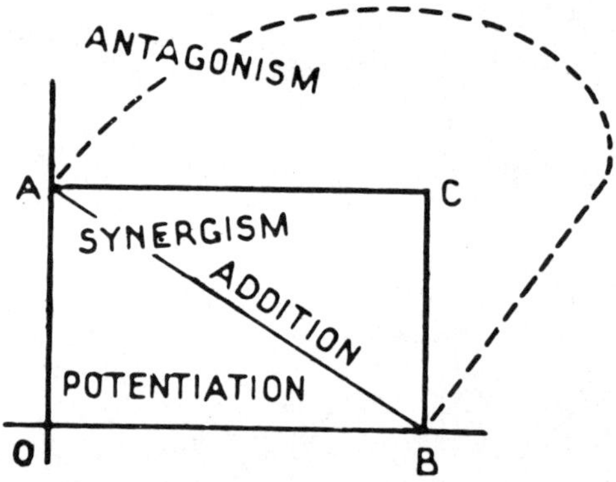

FIGURE 1. Gaddum captioned his figure thus: "Diagram showing the terms to describe the combined effects of two drugs. The dose of one drug is plotted on the horizontal axis and OB represents the dose which is just enough to have some definite effect, such as anesthesia or oestrus or death. OA represents the corresponding dose of the other drug." It is interesting that Gaddum called the doses OB and OA, rather than B and A. Was he thinking of vectors? It is also noteworthy that the examples of effects—anesthesia, oestrus, death—are unidimensional and unambiguously quantified, usually as 0 and 1. (From Gaddum.[3] By permission of Oxford University Press.)

dose is necessary to cause an effect or the dose-effect curve is sigmoid or other shape, then effects are not simply additive. The dose-effect curve of FIGURE 2, from the work of Kelleher *et al.*,[4] is taken out of context for illustrative purposes. A dose of 0.5 mg/kg amphetamine causes effect of intensity 3. If effects were simply additive, a dose of 1.0 mg/kg, which is 0.5 mg/kg + 0.5 mg/kg, would be expected to cause effect of intensity 3 + 3 = 6. The observed effect was 35. Yet the "two" drugs, amphetamine and amphetamine, are strictly addi-

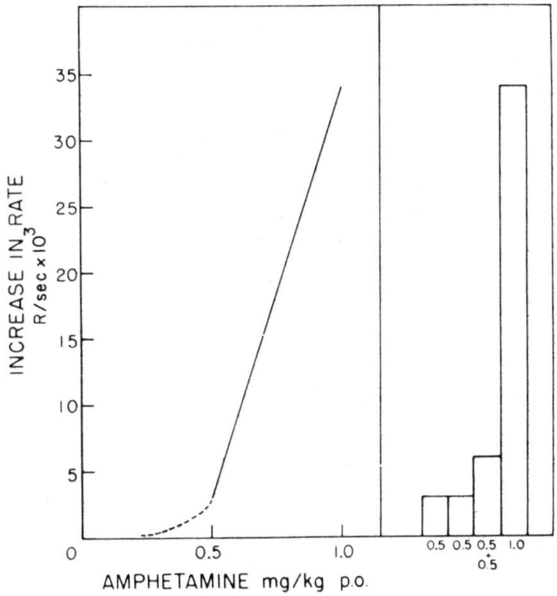

FIGURE 2. Why effects may not generally be simply added. Ordinate is increase in rate of responding. Doses of 0.5 and 1.0 mg/kg (and higher doses) were studied and are plotted on abscissa. The dotted part of the curve is extrapolated; it must reach zero by zero dose. The same effects are represented by bar graphs in the right hand part of the figure: twice the effect of 0.5 mg/kg is far less than the effect of 1.0 mg/kg. (After Kelleher *et al.*[4])

tive in Gaddum's sense, one molecule of amphetamine being equivalent to every other in causing an effect.

The simplicity and clarity of the general principles has often been lost, unfortunately, in dealing with actual experiments. Too often, the results of the joint effects of two drugs resemble more the types of relations illustrated by Loewe[5] (FIGURE 3). Working out such relationships as these may be empirically useful, but for theoretical purposes the results are impossibly complicated. The problem is that the dependent variables in these experiments were subjected to a variety of pharmacological effects from each of the drugs; the isobols peter out as one effect occludes another. The present concern is with joint effects of drugs on the behavioral activities of an intact, unanesthetized subject, a matter regarded by most people as the most complicated situation of all. Do the results of Loewe mean that it is futile to try to make any sense of joint effects of drugs on behavior? We should take encouragement from history. While a whole subject in a behavioral experiment may seem to be an impossibly complicated unit, so, as Clark[6] pointed out long ago, does even a single cell, but that does not daunt us from studying cellular physiology and pharmacology. Much of the progress in studying the joint effects of drugs has come from studies on isolated tissues such as guinea pig ileum and frog heart, but note

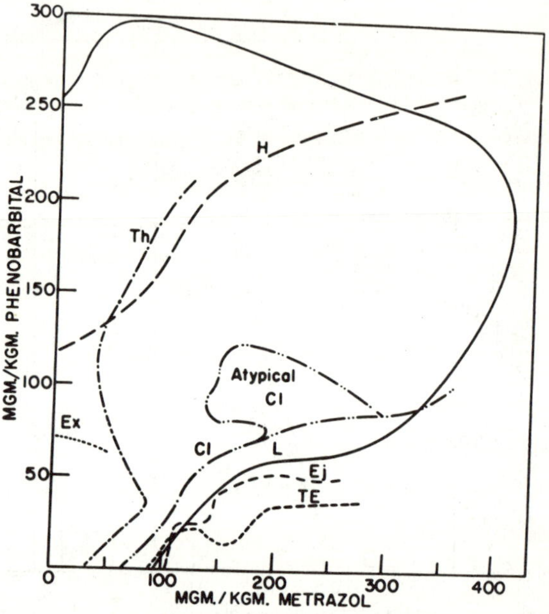

FIGURE 3. "Survey of isobologram of combined phenobarbital—Metrazol effects. Isobols are those of median effective doses for threshold seizure (Th), generalized clonic seizure (C1), tonic extensor seizure (TE), ejaculation (Ej), prehypnotic excitation (Ex), Hypnotic (H) and lethal effect (L)." Notice the clear relationship for lethality, showing antagonism at all doses and the indeterminate curves for much of the dose ranges for the other effects as one effect, for example, lethality occludes another and prevents it from being manifest. (From Loewe.[5] By permission of Williams and Wilkins.)

that even in FIGURE 1 the isobol for lethality is clear, complete, and interpretable, showing that the drugs antagonize one another at all lethal doses. What seems to matter is not the complexity of the preparation, but rather that the dependent variable be unidimensional, clearly quantifiable, and not confounded with other effects of the drugs. It is surely worthwhile to attempt to make sense of joint effects of drugs on behavior, but we should start with a unidimensional, simply quantified dependent variable. The behavioral variable that immediately comes to mind as eminently qualified in these respects is rate of responding. A subject is trained to operate a device that automatically records each operation and has physical characteristics that permit rapid repetitions. The dependent variable is simply the rate of responding from time to time. Many arguments have been advanced for rate of responding being a generally useful dependent variable in behavioral studies: for present purposes it suffices to point to its unidimensional and simply quantified properties. There is, in fact, far more good quantitative information on drug effects on rate of responding than on any other behavioral phenomena, and so the rest of this presentation will be confined to consideration of joint effects of drugs on rates of responding.

The first general finding to be faced in studying the effects of drugs, even the effects of single drugs, on rate of responding, is that the drug effect, however expressed, changes when the rate of responding on which the drug effect is superimposed is changed. Whether the drug effect is expressed as the difference between control rate and rate after drug, or as the ratio of rate after drug to control rate, or according to any other convention, the effect characteristically changes as the control rate of responding changes. There are a great many illustrations of the phenomenon in the literature. In a recent review of the literature on rate-dependent effects of amphetamine,[7] results in rats were grouped according to the rate of responding on which the effects of amphetamine were superimposed. Composite dose-effect curves were then drawn for each of the broad ranges of control rates of responding: more than 1 response/sec; from 0.1 to 1.0 responses/sec; from 0.01 to 0.1 responses/sec, and less than 0.01 responses/sec. The dose-effect curves were dramatically different for the different ranges of control rates. For rates above 1 response/sec, no dose of amphetamine caused a consistent increase in rate of responding, and already in the dose range 1.8 to 5.6 μM/kg (roughly 0.3 to 1.0 mg/kg) the rate of responding is reduced by amphetamine. On control rates of 0.1 to 1.0 responses/sec there is also little increase with amphetamine, but on rates from 0.01 to 0.1 responses/sec doses around 3.0 μM/kg cause on the average a twofold increase in rate of responding. On rates of less than 0.01 responses/sec, doses even as high as 18 μM/kg cause a three- or fourfold increase in responding.

Such profound effects of control rate of responding on the effect of a single drug may seem at first to complicate matters so much as to make the possibility of interpretation of the joint effect of two drugs very remote. Fortunately it has been found that the relation between the effect of a drug and the control rate of responding is generally rather simple. The relation may be examined by graphing the effect of the drug as ordinate against the control rate of responding as abscissa. Because the control rates of responding may vary over a very wide range, of more than three orders of magnitude, it is convenient to graph the control rates logarithmically. If the effect of the drug is expressed as the ratio of responding after the drug to the control rate (or its logarithm), the relationship shown in Figure 4 emerges. Each section of the figure shows a single experiment on a single subject: the effect of a dose of amobarbital on the rate of responding of a pigeon as a function of the control rate of responding. The particular schedule engendering responding (a modified fixed-interval) need not concern us here except to note that it engendered a wide range of rates of responding, over a thousandfold range, consistently from time to time during the session. Over this wide range, the effect of the drug was related to the log of the control rate of responding in a sensibly linear fashion, the slope being negative.[8]

This unexpected result has since been shown to be a finding of considerable generality. A few illustrations will be given.

The experiments just described were on the effects of amobarbital on a

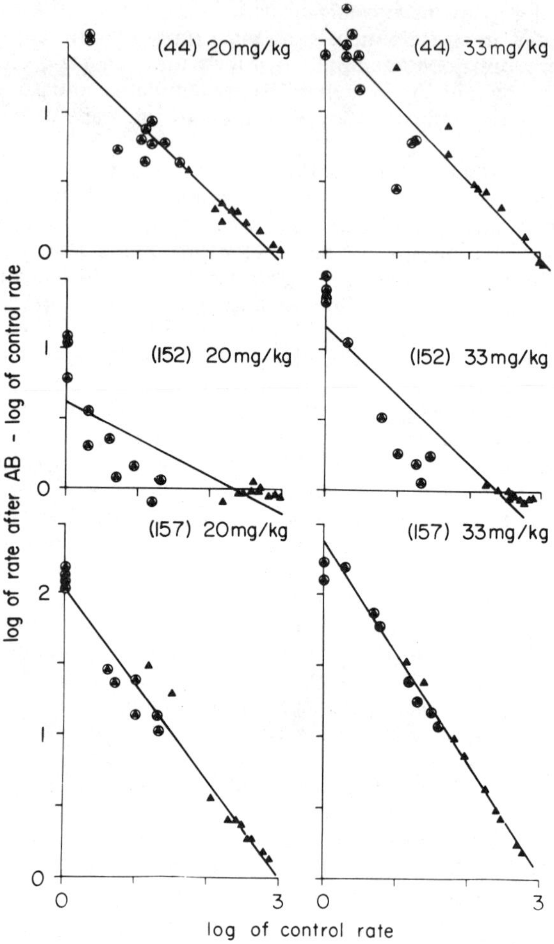

FIGURE 4. Rate-dependent effects of amobarbital on responding of pigeons under FI. Each panel shows results of a single experiment on a single subject (designated in parentheses). Abscissa: log of rate in responses/500 sec. Ordinate: log effect. The 20 points on each graph are for 20 consecutive segments of each FI cumulated over the session. A clear dependence of effect on control rate is shown, with good linearity on log-log plot for subjects 44 and 157. (From Dews.[8] By permission of Springer-Verlag.)

pigeon pecking a key. The effects of amphetamine on the rate of responding of rats operating a key, in the form of a lever, have been studied by several groups of investigators. Will and Checchinato[9] reported an approximately linear relationship, as did Heffner *et al.*[10] In the experiments of Heffner *et al.*, the different rates of responding were engendered by different schedules of reinforcement, variable-interval, fixed-interval, and fixed-ratio, indicating (as, indeed, had been much earlier reported in the squirrel monkey by Kelleher and

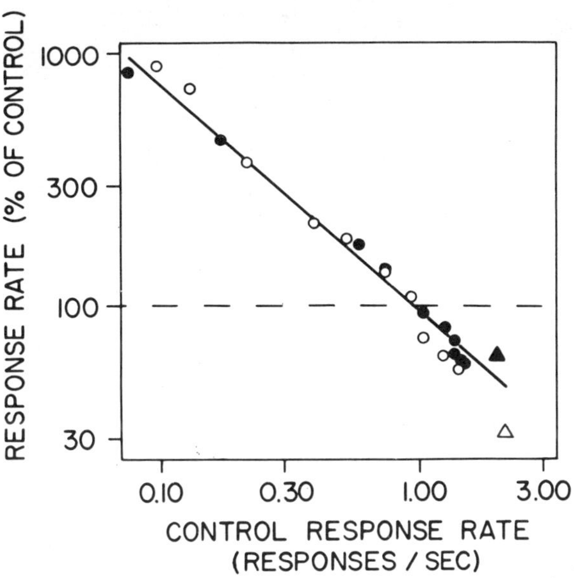

FIGURE 5. Rate-dependency of effects of amphetamine on responding of squirrel monkeys under FI (circles) and FR (triangles). Open points and filled points each represent one session. The FI was divided into 10 segments after the manner of FIGURE 4. Abscissa: responses/sec on logarithmic scale. Ordinate: effect on logarithmic scale. Note that points for FR responding conform with general trend of points from FI segments. (From Kelleher and Morse.[11] By permission of Springer-Verlag.)

Morse,[11] FIGURE 5) that the linearity of the regression of effect on log control rate generalizes for amphetamine across the different patterns of responding maintained by different schedules. For pentobarbital, however, at some dose levels the rate-dependency function, though still linear for a particular schedule performance, was different in pigeons for different schedule performances[12] (FIGURE 6). The slope of the regression lines decreases (becomes increasingly negative) with increase in dose, as indeed it must over some range since at zero dose the slope must be zero. Rate-dependency of the effects of chlordiazepoxide, diazepam, chlorpromazine, *d*-amphetamine, and pentobarbital in the pigeon[13] and of diazepam, nitrazepam, and imipramine in the squirrel monkey[14] have been reported.

The preceding list of findings, although by no means exhaustive, serves to illustrate that the phenomenon of rate-dependency occurs with a variety of different schedules, species, and drugs. The maximum negativity of the slopes of most of the lines is between —0.5 and —1.0. A slope of negativity greater than —1.0 has an interesting consequence. If D_1 is the rate of responding after a particular dose of a drug has been given to a subject at a control rate of C_1, and D_2 the rate after the same dose at a control rate of C_2 then, by the dependency relation:

$$\log (D_1/C_1) = a + b \log C_1 \quad \text{or} \quad \log D_1 = a + (b + 1) \log C_1$$

and $$\log (D_2/C_2) = a + b \log C_2 \quad \text{or} \quad \log D_2 = a + (b + 1) \log C_2$$

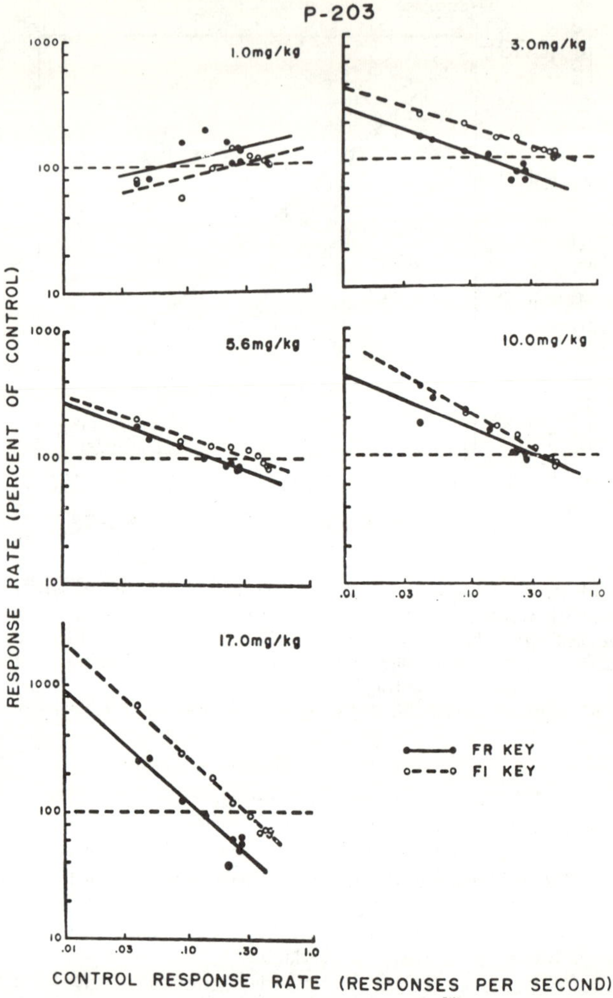

FIGURE 6. Rate-dependency of effects of pentobarbital on responding of pigeons under FI and FR. The FI was divided into 10 segments after the manner of FIGURE 4. Abscissa: responses/sec on logarithmic scale. Ordinate: effect on logarithmic scale. Note that slope of the lines becomes more negative with increasing dose and that points for FI and FR tend to follow separate, though here sensibly parallel, functions. (From Barrett.[12] By permission of *The Society for the Experimental Analysis of Behavior.*)

where a and b are constants of the linear dependency function. Then, by subtraction, $\log (D_1/D_2) = (b + 1) \log (C_1/C_2)$. When b is more negative than -1, then $b + 1$ is negative and $\log (D_1/D_2)$ and $\log (C_1/C_2)$ must be of opposite sign, so if $C_1 > C_2$ then $D_2 > D_1$; that is, the actual rate of responding after the drug is greater when the control rate is less. Such a relationship has been reported.[15, 16]

The relevance of rate-dependency to the joint effects of two drugs is as follows: In the examples of rate-dependency given above the control rate of responding has been changed by manipulation of the schedule or the parameters of the schedule. The rate of responding can, however, be changed by a drug. If a second drug is given simultaneously, it may be considered to be operating on a different control rate from what would have obtained if the first drug had not been given, and therefore its effect will be changed, not because of a physiological interaction between the drugs, but because any factor changing the control rate would change the effect of the second drug. Of course, the relationship is reciprocal; we can consider the effects of drug B to be changed because drug A has changed the rate of responding on which drug B operates; but equally, we could consider that the effects of drug A are changed because drug B has changed the rate on which drug A operates. Inasmuch as the parameters of the rate-dependency functions of drugs A and B will generally not be the same, the two different ways of predicting the effects of the combination will give different answers. There may be a pharmacological interaction between the effects of the drugs in that the effects of each drug are affected by the action of the other, but at the same time each drug may be acting as it would have if the rates had been produced by nonpharmacological means. It may be useful in considering drug interactions to use terminology analogous to that used in studies of pharmacological dependence on a drug where the distinction is made between physiological and behavioral varieties of pharmacological dependence. We may distinguish between physiological (including chemical) and behavioral varieties of pharmacological interactions. In terms of Gaddum's diagram, then, for behavior-affecting drugs, in order to say that two drugs are potentiating or antagonizing one another rather than algebraically adding, we must show that the combined effects, which may be much larger or much smaller than expected from casual inspection of the effects of each alone, cannot be accounted for by the rate-dependency functions of the two drugs. To make the calculations we must know the effects of the particular dose of each of the drugs alone, and be able to estimate the rate-dependency function for each of the drugs. For the latter, the effect of the particular doses on more than one control rate of responding is needed. As a first approximation, we are willing to assume that the rate-dependency is a linear function of log effect on log control rate. The calculated joint effect can then be compared with the observed joint effect. There are few studies in the literature that provide enough information for the calculations; indeed, the number of systematic studies of the joint effects of two drugs on behavior of any kind is relatively small. In the examples to be presented, it must be remembered that the experiments were not designed, conducted, or presented with a view to the type of analysis being attempted. Inferences and assumptions are necessary to fill gaps in the information for present purposes, so the analyses should be regarded as examples of analytical methods, rather than as establishing reliable pharmacological relations between the drugs. I am indebted to J. Goldfarb (personal communication) for pointing out the following additional difficulty, arising from the non-linearity of dose-effect curves. A dose d of amphetamine on control rate C_1 leads to rate of D_1 (effect $E_1 = D_1/C_1$). The effect of a second dose d of amphetamine would be estimated from the dose-dependency function treating D as though it were the control rate subject to an effect of magnitude E_1. But because of the non-linearity of the dose-effect curve, the effect of dose d is not the same when another dose d is also present; therefore, rate-dependency analysis will not give exact predictions of combined effects, even when the combination consists of two doses of the same drug. The solution to the dilemma turns on the nature of the scales of the coordinates of Gaddum's diagram (FIGURE 1). If the log dose-effect curves are symetrical sigmoid curves following the logistic function then the curves could be linearized, over at least most of the range, by transformation of the *dosage* variable by the inverse logit function and normalized by making the slope function the scale unit. The modified diagram would then permit addition of effects of simply additive drugs even if the dose-effect curves were not identical in position. Rarely or never, however, for the type of situation under consideration are the data adequate in precision and over a wide enough range of the dose-effect curve to permit so sophisticated an analysis, and simple rate-dependency analysis should reveal significant physiological interactions.

The effects of pentobarbital and methamphetamine combinations on rate of responding of pigeons were studied by Rutledge and Kelleher.[17] Responding was maintained by a multiple schedule, multiple fixed-interval, fixed-ratio (mult FIFR), and as the rate of responding in the FI and FR components differed by a factor of 4, rate-dependency functions for each of the drugs could be estimated. FIGURE 7 shows the results of the analysis of the effects of 1 mg/kg methamphetamine and 10 mg/kg pentobarbital. The first column in the left-hand part of the figure shows the control rate of responding under FI, and the next three columns the rates after 10 mg/kg pentobarbital alone, after 1 mg/kg methamphetamine alone, and after 10 mg/kg pentobarbital and 1 mg/kg methamphetamine given together. Both 10 mg/kg pentobarbital and 1 mg/kg methamphetamine cause an increase in FI responding, but the effect of the combination seems larger than might have been expected. The next column, marked +, shows a simple algebraic summation of the effects of the two drugs alone. If D_P is the rate after pentobarbital and D_M the rate after methamphetamine, then $D_P - C$ is the increase due to pentobarbital and $D_M - C$ is the increase due to methamphetamine. The additive effect would then be $(D_P - C) + (D_M - C)$, the expression giving the effect as the increase above control caused by the combination. The actual rate after the combination is therefore predicted as $(D_P - C) + (D_M - C) + C$. The column is considerably below the observed value following the combination. The next column is the estimated effect of the combination on the assumption that methamphetamine is operating, not on the control rate, but on the rate resulting from the effects of pentobarbital. The rate-dependency regression for amphetamine was calculated from the effects of the dose of amphetamine on the different control rates engendered by the FI and FR schedules. The regression line permits estimation of the expected effect of amphetamine on the rate resulting from the effects of pentobarbital. The estimate also falls short of the observed value. The final column shows the estimate of the effect of the combination if pentobarbital is assumed to be operating on a rate resulting from the effects of methamphetamine. This last estimate comes closest to the observed.

The right half of FIGURE 7 shows a similar analysis of responding under FR. Again, algebraic addition of the effects gives a result widely divergent from the observed effect of the combination, but rate-dependency analysis provides excellent agreement with the effects of the combination, particularly the calculation of the effects of methamphetamine on a rate resulting from pentobarbital. The excellent agreement of a prediction of the combination on FR responding and the lack of a gross discrepancy of prediction on FI responding

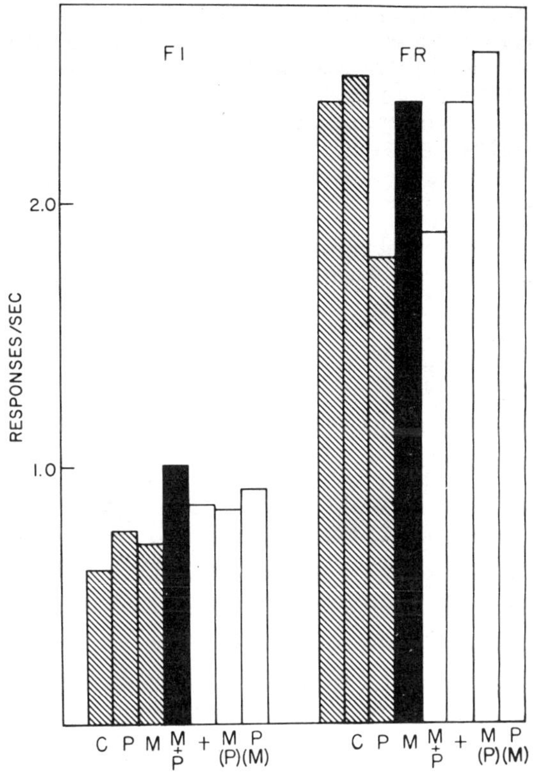

FIGURE 7. Bar diagrams of effects of 10 mg/kg pentobarbital and 1.0 mg/kg methamphetamine and of both on responding of pigeons under FI and FR. Ordinate: rate of responding in responses/sec. Abscissa: conditions: C—control; P—10 mg/kg pentobarbital; M—1.0 mg/kg methamphetamine; M + P—10 mg/kg pentobarbital and 1.0 mg/kg methamphetamine; +—algebraic summation of effects (see text); M(P)—calculated effects of combination on assumption that methamphetamine is operating on the rate produced by pentobarbital alone; P(M)—calculated effect of combination on assumption that pentobarbital is operating on the rate produced by methamphetamine alone. Note that the observed effect of the combination (black bar) can be reasonably matched by a calculated value (open bars). (After Rutledge and Kelleher.[17])

suggest that there is no significant physiological interaction between the effects of the two drugs; in other words, each drug is affecting the rate of responding as though the other drug were not present except for its direct effects on rate of responding.

The combined effects of amphetamine and imipramine on responding in rats have been studied by Ray and Bivens[18] (FIGURE 8). The effects were not very large, and only at the 0.5 mg/kg dose on FI responding was there a convincing discrepancy between even the algebraic addition estimate and the observed effect of the combination. Under these circumstances, again, there is no justification for invoking a physiological interaction.

The combined effects of amobarbital and trifluperazine on suppressed and unsuppressed responding in rats also provided no evidence of a physiological interaction[19] (FIGURE 9). Only at the highest dose levels was there a serious discrepancy between the algebraic summation estimate and the observed effect of the combination, and even here the discrepancy can be resolved by rate-dependency analysis.

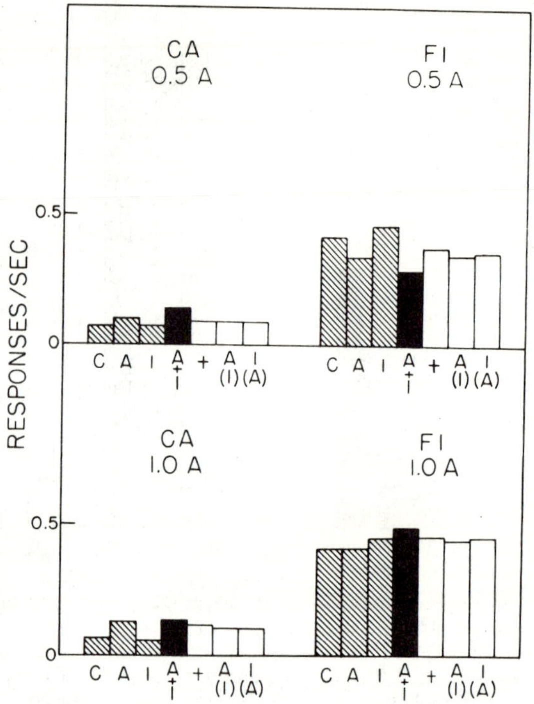

FIGURE 8. Bar diagrams of effects of 0.5 mg/kg amphetamine (above) or 1.0 mg/kg amphetamine (below), imipramine and of both amphetamine and imipramine on responding of rats under a continuous postponement schedule and under FI. Arrangement as in FIGURE 7 except that A represents amphetamine and I imipramine. The effect of the combination does not depart systematically from the calculated values. (After Ray and Bivens.[18])

The final example is a study of the effects of amphetamine and diazepam on FI responding in the cat.[20] The rates in different segments of the FI were segregated, permitting a more detailed rate-dependency analysis than in the preceding examples. The FI were divided into eight segments, but the control rate of responding in the first three segments was too low to permit analysis, so calculations were based on the final five segments (FIGURE 10). Except for the eighth segment, the algebraic summation estimate was a very poor predictor of the effects of the combination, yielding estimates lower by a factor of four or five than thc observed values in the early segments. The rate-dependency analysis yielded estimates of the effects of the combination that were lower than the observed effects in the earlier segments but higher in the later segments. On total responding the combination caused effects as though diazepam were operating on a rate changed by amphetamine (FIGURE 10, upper left), but the substantial and systematic discrepancies in the more detailed analysis suggest that diazepam does indeed interact with the effects of amphetamine through more than behavioral rate-dependencies, for example, by exaggerating the rate-dependency function of amphetamine. As indicated earlier, as the experiments

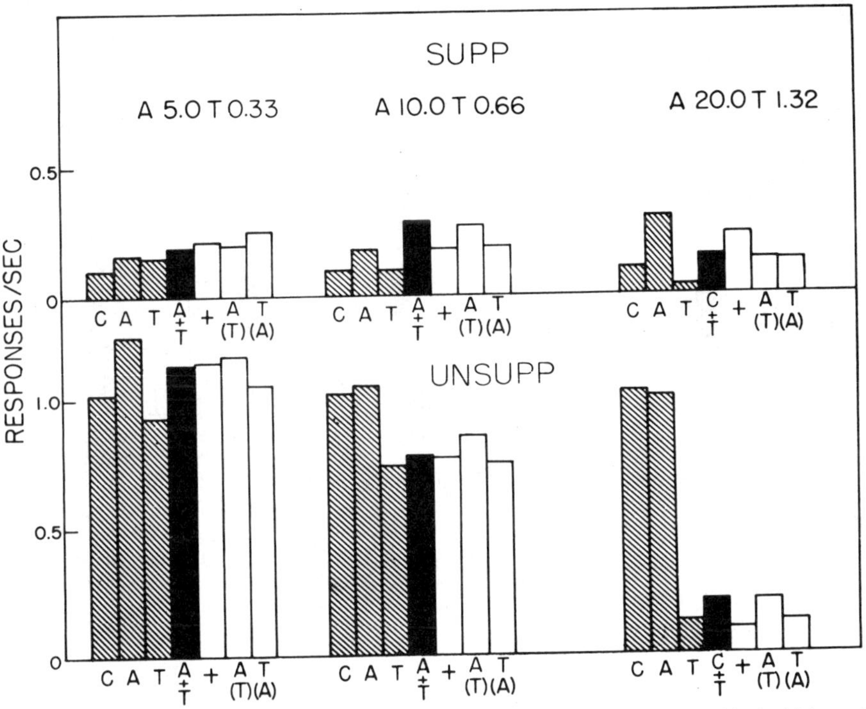

FIGURE 9. Bar diagrams of effects of various doses of amobarbital (A) and trifluperazine (T) alone and in combination on suppressed (above) and unsuppressed (below) responding in squirrel monkey. Arrangement as in FIGURE 7. The concordance between observed and a calculated effect of combination is generally reasonably good. (After Davidson and Cook.[19])

were not intended to yield information for this type of analysis, assumptions had to be made to make the calculations possible, and a physiological interaction cannot be regarded as established. Further work is necessary and should be designed to make rigorous rate-dependency analysis possible.

In conclusion, establishment of a physiological interaction between drugs in their effects on behavior requires the demonstration that the combined effects cannot be accounted for by the drugs acting independently. Since drugs affect the rate of responding and since rate of responding affects the effect of a second drug, physiological potentiation and antagonism cannot be established or refuted without taking account of rate-dependency relations. Judging by the four

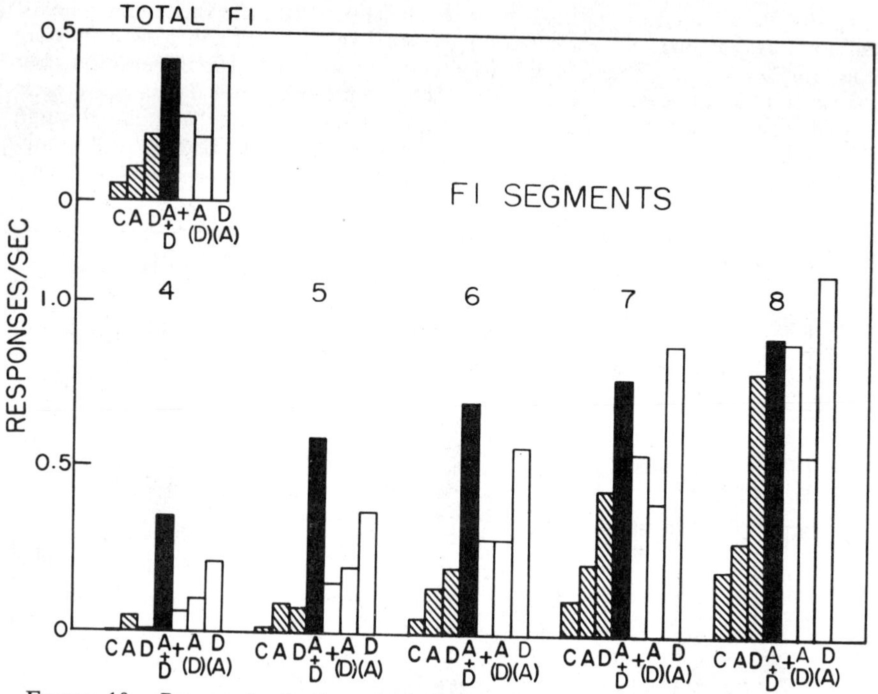

FIGURE 10. Bar graph of effects of 0.5 mg/kg amphetamine (A) and 0.5 mg/kg diazepam (D) on FI responding in a cat. The FI was divided into 10 segments, after the manner of FIGURE 4. In upper left is shown graph for total responding. Arrangement as in FIGURE 7. Although the observed effects of the combination on total responding can be matched by a calculated value, there are systematic discrepancies from under-to-over estimation as the control rate increases. (After Richelle.[20])

examples presented, it appears likely that rate-dependencies can account for many seeming discrepancies of effects of combinations and that significant physiological interactions between the effects of behavior-modifying drugs may be less common than many have supposed.

REFERENCES

1. FRAZER, T. R. 1872. The antagonism between the actions of active substances. Brit. Med. J.: ii 457–459, 485–487.
2. BERNARD, C. 1856. Analyse physiologique des propietes des systemes musculaire et nerveux au moyen du curare. C. R. Acad. Sci. **43:** 825–829.
3. GADDUM, J. H. 1944. Pharmacology. 2nd edit. Oxford University Press. London.
4. KELLEHER, R. T., W. FRY, J. DEEGAN & L. COOK. 1961. Effects of meprobamate on operant behavior in rats. J. Pharmacol. Exp. Ther. **133:** 271–280.

5. LOEWE, S. 1955. Isobols of dose effect relations in the combination of pentylenetetrazole and phenobarbital. J. Pharmacol. Exp. Ther. **114:** 185–191.
6. CLARK, A. J. 1937. General pharmacology. Heffter's Handbuch der Exp. Pharmakol. **4:** 3.
7. DEWS, P. B. & G. R. WENGER. 1977. Rate-dependent effects of amphetamine. *In* Advances in Behavioral Pharmacology. Academic Press, Inc. New York, N.Y. In press.
8. DEWS, P. B. 1964. A behavioral effect of amobarbital. Arch. Exp. Path. Pharmak. **248:** 296–307.
9. WILL, B. & D. CHECCHINATO. 1973. Effects of d-amphetamine on operant behavior in the rat. Psychopharmacologia **29:** 141–149.
10. HEFFNER, T. G., R. B. DRAWBAUGH & M. J. ZIGMOND. 1974. Amphetamine and operant behavior in rats: Relationship between drug effect and control response rate. J. Comp. Physiol. Psychol. **86:** 1031–1043.
11. KELLEHER, R. T. & W. H. MORSE. 1968. Determinants of the specificity of behavioral effects of drugs. Ergeb. Physiol. **60:** 1–56.
12. BARRETT, J. E. 1974. Conjunctive schedules of reinforcement. I. Rate-dependent effects of pentobarbital and d-amphetamine. J. Exp. Anal. Behav. **22:** 561–573.
13. MCMILLAN, D. E. 1973. Drugs and punished responding. I. Rate-dependent effects under multiple schedules. J. Exp. Anal. Behav. **19:** 133–145.
14. WUTTKE, W. & R. T. KELLEHER. 1970. Effects of some benzodiazepines on punished and unpunished behavior in the pigeon. J. Pharmacol. Exp. Ther. **172:** 307–405.
15. DEWS, P. B. 1960. Free operant behavior under conditions of delayed reinforcement. I. CRF-type schedules. J. Exp. Anal. Behav. **3:** 221–234.
16. MORSE, W. H. 1962. Use of operant-conditioning techniques for evaluating the effects of barbiturates on behavior. *In* Psychosomatic Medicine: The First Hahnemann Symposium. J. H. & J. H. Moyer, Eds.: 275–281. Lea & Febiger. Philadelphia, Pa.
17. RUTLEDGE, C. O. & R. T. KELLEHER. 1965. Interactions between the effects of methamphetamine and pentobarbital on operant behavior in the pigeon. Psychopharmacologia **7:** 400–408.
18. RAY, O. S. & L. W. BIVENS. 1968. Anticholinergic potentiation of amphetamine: reinforcement schedule effects. Arch. Int. Pharmacodyn. **172:** 414–420.
19. DAVIDSON, A. B. & L. COOK. 1969. Effects of combined treatment with trifluoperazine-HCl and amobarbital on punished behavior in rats. Psychopharmacologia **15:** 159–168.
20. RICHELLE, M. 1969. Combined action of diazepam and d-amphetamine on fixed-interval performance in cats. J. Exp. Anal. Behav. **12:** 989–998.

BEHAVIORAL METHODS FOR THE STUDY OF DRUG INTERACTIONS

Charles R. Schuster

Departments of Psychiatry and Pharmacological and Physiological Sciences
The University of Chicago
Pritzker School of Medicine
Chicago, Illinois 60637

A variety of behavioral methods have been used to investigate the interaction of drugs of abuse. Rather than covering all of them, however, this review will discuss only 1) behavioral studies using the methods of operant conditioning and 2) opiate agonist and antagonist interactions.

The methods of operant conditioning are particularly appropriate for the study of drug interactions since they allow precise quantification of behavior and, as well, generate behavioral baselines which are stable over many sessions. Such quantification and stability are essential if full dose-response relationships of interacting drugs are to be studied in the same organism. Long-term stability is particularly important if investigations of changes in drug sensitivity as a function of drug history are to be carried out. Although this review will be restricted to the illustration of drug interactions with opiate agonists and antagonists, the studies have been chosen because the behavioral methods could be used to study the interactions of drugs from other pharmacological classes. For this reason, measures of analgesia will not be reviewed since this involves methodology of limited usefulness in the study of other classes of drugs.

Three general areas of behavioral methodology will be used to illustrate the study of drug interactions: 1) schedule-controlled operant behavior sensitive to the actions of opiate agonists, 2) opiate agonists as discriminative stimuli for operant behavior, and 3) opiate agonists as reinforcing stimuli for operant behavior.

Investigation of Drug Interactions Using Schedule-Controlled Operant Behavior

Opiate agonists have been shown to produce a broad spectrum of behavioral actions. Food- and shock-maintained operant behavior of a variety of species is modified by opiate agonists. Such agonistic behavioral effects can be used to investigate the ability of other drugs to act as antagonists.

McMillan *et al.*[1] have utilized the food-maintained key-pecking response of the pigeon to study the interaction of several opiate agonists and antagonists. The data presented in this section come from that study, unless otherwise noted. In this investigation, key-pecking behavior was maintained on a multiple fixed-ratio 30 fixed-interval 5 min (MULT FR 30 FI 5′) schedule of food reinforcement. The components of this multiple schedule alternated, and the session ended after the first component change after 60 minutes. Injections of drugs were given 10 minutes before the session in the pectoral muscle of the pigeon.

Morphine and methadone at low doses (0.3 and 1.0 mg/kg) produced an increase in rate of responding in some pigeons, while higher doses of both these drugs produced a dose-related decrease in the rate of responding in the fixed-interval component of the multiple schedule in all pigeons. Rate of responding in the fixed-ratio component showed only a dose-related decrease with both morphine and methadone. In a prior study[2] it had been shown that the mixed opiate agonist-antagonists nalorphine, cyclazocine, and pentazocine all produced similar changes in response rate of pigeons on the multiple FR 30 FI 5′ schedule of food reinforcement. Naloxone has been reported to be an opiate antagonist almost completely devoid of agonistic activity in a variety of pharmacological measures.[3, 4] In the study by McMillan *et al.*,[1] however, it produced behavioral effects on the performance of pigeons on the multiple FR 30 FI 5′ schedule comparable to those observed with morphine, methadone, and the mixed agonist-antagonists. The potency of naloxone's agonistic activity was greater than that previously reported for nalorphine.[2] It is possible that the agonistic actions of naloxone are more pronounced in pigeons, since the previous experiments which showed its lack of agonist properties had been carried out in rodents. In combination, however, both the rate-increasing and decreasing effects of morphine and methadone were blocked by naloxone, cyclazocine, and nalorphine, but not pentazocine. The agonistic actions of these drugs occurred at doses far below those which produced agonistic actions. That the antagonism is specific is shown by the fact that naloxone did not antagonize the rate-decreasing effects of chlorpromazine or of cyclazocine. Further, although *d*-amphetamine was able to antagonize the rate-decreasing effects of morphine, it did so only to the extent that it produced rate increases when given alone. This is in contrast to the opiate antagonists, which produced blocking effects at doses below those which produced changes in the rates of key pecking when given alone.

The order of potency of the opiate antagonists found in this study (naloxone = cyclazocine > nalorphine > pentazocine, inactive at the doses employed) using the schedule-controlled key-pecking response of pigeons is the same as that found in man.[5] It would thus appear that the schedule-controlled operant performance of pigeons is a useful procedure for predicting the opiate antagonistic actions of a drug in man.

In a more recent study, Holtzman[6] has investigated the effects of morphine, nalorphine, and cyclazocine alone and in combination with naloxone on shock-avoidance behavior of squirrel monkeys. In this study, squirrel monkeys were conditioned to press a lever to avoid the delivery of electric shock to the tail. After animals showed stable performance over 4-hr avoidance sessions, dose-response relationships were established for morphine, nalorphine, and cyclazocine. Morphine and cyclazocine showed a biphasic effect on rate of lever-pressing, with low doses causing an increase and high doses a decrease in responding. Nalorphine produced only an increased rate of lever-pressing at all doses investigated. Naloxone, at a dose of 1.0 mg/kg, blocked the effects of all three of these drugs. These findings replicate previous investigations of these drugs given alone and in combination under similar shock-avoidance schedules using rats as the experimental animals.[7, 8] The antagonism between naloxone and cyclazocine demonstrated in this experiment is in contrast to the work of McMillan *et al.*,[1] in which naloxone failed to block the rate modifying effects of cyclazocine. Whether this difference is due to the species employed or to differences in the behavioral situations cannot be ascertained from existing data.

In another phase of the same study, Holtzman compared the ability of naltrexone, naloxone, and nalorphine to block the rate-decreasing effects of morphine in squirrel monkeys lever-pressing to avoid electric shock. The potency relationships found (naltrexone > naloxone > nalorphine) and the relative durations of actions were similar to those found in man,[5, 9] rhesus monkeys,[10] and rodents.[11] Further, the greater potency and duration of action of naltrexone as compared to naloxone corroborates previous findings of Dykstra *et al.*,[12] who investigated the ability of these compounds to reverse the rate-decreasing effects of morphine on food-reinforced responding in the pigeon.

In all the experiments reviewed in this section, the interactions investigated were of drugs given concurrently. Drug interactions of great importance, however, may involve changes in sensitivity to a drug induced by the previous exposure of the organism to another drug. An experiment by Goldberg and Schuster[13] illustrates this type of interaction. In this study, two groups of rhesus monkeys were conditioned to lever press for food reinforcement, and the effects of nalorphine were investigated. One group of rhesus monkeys had previously been maintained for 2 months on 12 mg/kg/day of morphine sulfate, given as a subcutaneous injection of 3 mg/kg every 6 hours. These animals were withdrawn from morphine for 3 months prior to the experimental manipulations. The control group of monkeys had never received any opiate agonists or antagonists prior to this experiment. All animals were conditioned to level press for food reinforcement delivered after every 10th response (FR 10) during a daily 1-hr experimental session. When responding had stabilized, saline was infused through chronic jugular catheters during the food-reinforced session. In subsequent sessions, the same procedure was followed, except that increasing doses of nalorphine were dissolved in the intravenous saline infusions. Doses of nalorphine from 0.2 mg/kg to 1.6 mg/kg produced no change in the response rate of the control monkeys. Rate decreases were seen only at doses of 3.2 and 6.4 mg/kg. In contrast, animals previously dependent upon morphine showed significant rate decreases at doses as low as 0.8 mg/kg. At a dose of 1.6 mg/kg these animals showed a 60% decrease in response rate, whereas control animals showed no effect. In addition to the increased sensitivity to nalorphine shown in the food-reinforced lever-pressing behavior, the previously dependent animals showed marked salivation and emesis at the higher doses. Control animals failed to show these signs at any dose. That this change in sensitivity is not limited to opiate agonists or antagonists is demonstrated by the increased sensitivity to amphetamines shown in rhesus monkeys with a history of chronic methadone administration (see Carlson, present volume).

In summary, the methods of operant conditioning for generating a behavioral baseline for characterizing the actions of opiate agonists and antagonists alone and in combination have proven highly productive. The illustrations given demonstrate that such procedures generate stable behavior which allows very precise quantification of drug interactions.

Drugs as Discriminative Stimuli

In most operant-conditioning procedures, an exteroceptive stimulus (e.g., a light or tone) is presented as a signal to the organism that responding will be reinforced. Such stimuli which set the occasion for appropriate responses to be reinforced are called discriminative stimuli (S^D). In experimental procedures where more than one response may be reinforced at different times, such discriminative stimuli are used to indicate which response contingency is operative. Thus, for example, a light might be illuminated over one of two levers to indicate which response will produce a reinforcer.

There now exists a burgeoning experimental literature demonstrating that many drugs, including drugs of abuse, can serve as discriminative stimuli in animals.[14, 15] Opiate agonists, for instance, have been shown to have the capacity to serve as discriminative stimuli for maze performances[14, 16] as well as lever-pressing tasks.[17-20] In this review selected studies will be described to illustrate the use of drug-interaction studies as a means of investigating the nature of the discriminative properties of opiate agonists.

The general procedure in the studies to be reviewed is to train animals to press one lever for food or water reinforcement when in a drug state, and a second lever when in a non-drug condition. Training sessions are run under both conditions until animals attain some criterion of discrimination. There are several problems associated with this type of experiment: 1) Drug states cannot be terminated by the experimenter (and are usually long lasting), thus allowing the organism to be run under only one condition per day, 2) once the animal has been reinforced, this event itself indicates which lever is correct for that session. This makes any subsequent behavior meaningless as an indicator of the drug's ability to serve as a discriminative stimulus. To obviate this latter problem, experimenters have periodically tested for stimulus control in extinction sessions[21] or used schedules in which the delivery of the reinforcer is delayed for the first few minutes of every session.[19, 22] In this latter procedure, estimates of the degree of stimulus control are obtained from the animal's differential responding prior to the delivery of the first reinforcer.

Hirschhorn and Rosecrans[19] trained rats to press one of two levers in order to obtain milk reinforcement delivered on a variable-interval (VI) schedule. Responding on one of the two levers produced reinforcement when the animal had received a pre-session drug injection, and responses on the other lever were reinforced when the animal had received a presession injection of saline. No responses were reinforced for the first 2.5 minutes of every session. Sessions where drug interactions were studied were terminated after the 2.5-minute unreinforced period so that subsequent discriminative responding was not influenced by learning under these altered drug states. Two different groups of animals were trained: one to discriminate morphine (10 mg/kg) from saline and a second to discriminate LSD 25 (0.15 μmol/kg) from saline. Following behavioral stabilization, various doses of morphine (5, 10, and 20 mg/kg) were tested in the group trained with LSD. Animals responded under these circumstances almost exclusively on the lever reinforced after saline administration. Similarly, animals trained to discriminate morphine responded primarily on the saline lever when various doses of LSD (0.075, 0.15, 0.3, and 0.6 μmol/kg) were given. Thus, animals trained to discriminate morphine from saline and LSD from saline showed no generalization of the stimulus control exerted by one drug to the other. Subsequently, the effects of naloxone on the stimulus control exerted by LSD and morphine were assessed. At doses of 0.1, 0.2, and 0.4 mg/kg, naloxone caused little change in the stimulus control exerted by LSD. In contrast, the stimulus control exerted by morphine showed a dose-related disruption by these same doses. At the dose of 0.4 mg/kg naloxone, more than 80% of the animals' total responses were made on the saline-correct lever. These data demonstrate, therefore, that naloxone is capable of blocking the stimulus properties of morphine. The fact that the stimulus control exerted by LSD was not changed by naloxone indicates that the effects on morphine stimulus control were specific.

In a more recent study, Kuhn *et al.*[20] investigated the interaction of pentazocine and naloxone. In this study, rats were trained to press on one of two levers when 10 mg/kg of pentazocine was given 30 minutes prior to the session. On days when saline was administered prior to the session, responding on the second lever was reinforced. The schedule of reinforcement used (Tandem VI 1′ FR 10) was chosen in order to maximize response rates during an initial 5-minute period of no reinforcement at the beginning of each session. Estimates of stimulus control were obtained by determining the relative proportion of total responses occurring on the drug-correct and saline-correct levers during this initial 5-minute period. Further, on sessions where pharmacological manipulations were made, sessions were terminated after the 5-minute non-reinforced period so that further learning under these altered conditions would not confound the results of subsequent testing.

Following the establishment of stimulus control by the injections of 10 mg/kg pentazocine and saline, test sessions were run in which various doses of pentazocine and morphine were tested. It was established that the ED_{50} dose of pentazocine was 4.2 mg/kg in this procedure. Further, when animals were given morphine, they showed a dose-related increase in responding on the pentazocine-correct lever. At the highest dose of morphine tested (7.5 mg/kg) over 80% of the animals' total responses occurred on the lever associated with pentazocine. The ED_{50} dose of morphine was calculated to be 1.7 mg/kg. When the ED_{50} doses of pentazocine and morphine were given concurrently, animals responded almost exclusively on the pentazocine-correct lever. Taken together these manipulations strongly suggest the similarity of the stimulus properties of pentazocine and morphine. It must be considered, however, that tests of stimulus similarities of this sort do not mean that the two drug states may not be discriminable. All that this study demonstrates is that the stimulus properties of morphine are more like those of pentazocine than those of saline. It is quite conceivable that with appropriate training animals might learn to discriminate morphine from pentazocine. (For a fuller discussion of this issue, see Overton.[23])

In a final manipulation in this experiment, the interaction of naloxone with morphine and pentazocine was studied. At a dose of 0.4 mg/kg of naloxone the stimulus control exerted by 7.5 mg/kg of morphine was completely blocked, as indicated by the fact that animals responded almost exclusively on the saline-correct lever. In addition, 0.4 mg/kg of naloxone produced a lesser but significant disruption of the stimulus control exerted by pentazocine. The authors of this experiment interpret their data as indicating a great similarity between the stimulus properties of pentazocine and morphine. The fact that naloxone blocks the stimulus properties of both drugs suggests that their stimulus actions are mediated at least in part by a common mechanism of action. There is clinical evidence that pentazocine and morphine produce similar subjective effects in man.[24-26] This suggests that the comparison of drugs as discriminative stimuli in animals may be an effective manner of predicting their comparability in the production of subjective effects in man.

If it is assumed that the subjective effects of drugs are at least in part the basis of their abuse, then investigations of the modification of the stimulus properties of drugs in animals may suggest possible therapeutic interventions for man. The finding that naloxone blocks the stimulus control of opiates and the subjective euphoric effects of these drugs in man lends credence to the application of the animal procedures for this purpose. A more straightforward approach to this problem, however, can be obtained by investigating drug interactions using a second stimulus property of drugs—their ability to serve as reinforcing stimuli.

Drugs as Reinforcing Stimuli

It is now well established that a wide variety of psychotropic drugs can serve as reinforcers in laboratory animals.[27, 28] Those drugs capable of serving as reinforcing stimuli in laboratory animals are, in the main, those which are commonly abused by man. Furthermore, drugs which possess subjectively dysphoric properties in man can be shown to act as negative reinforcers in laboratory animals.[29–31]

Given this correspondence between drugs of abuse in man and those serving as reinforcers in animals, it has been suggested that such procedures can be used as an animal model of drug abuse.[28] Such a model could be useful in a variety of ways, including the development of possible pharmacotherapeutic agents for the treatment of humans who abuse drugs.

Previous studies have established that in physically dependent rhesus monkeys, administration of a low dose of nalorphine can increase responding previously maintained by morphine reinforcement.[13, 30, 32] Higher doses of nalorphine resulted in a suppression of morphine-reinforced behavior.[30] These effects of nalorphine could have been caused by the drug's ability to elicit withdrawal, or by its ability to block the reinforcing actions of morphine, or a combination of both. In a recent study[33] the interaction of naloxone in animals self-administering heroin was investigated. To clarify whether naloxone-induced changes in responding were due to changes in motivation (i.e., withdrawal) or reinforcement, animals were only allowed to self-inject heroin intermittently to avoid physical dependence. In this experiment, animals were conditioned to lever press for cocaine (200 μg/kg/inj) or heroin (6 μg/kg/inj) delivered after every 10th response (FR 10) in a 2-hr daily session. Sessions in which cocaine or heroin was used as the reinforcing stimulus were associated with specific discriminative stimuli, and the sessions were randomly presented. Following stabilization of the animals' responding for both drugs, animals were pretreated 5 minutes before each session with an intramuscular injection of saline or naloxone. Each dose of naloxone was continued until it had been given prior to 7–10 heroin sessions. Between each dose of naloxone tested, a minimum of 10 saline pretreatment sessions were given. Figure 1 shows the average number of heroin and cocaine injections earned for the last three sessions at each dose level of naloxone for one of the subjects. Under baseline conditions, this monkey received approximately the same number of cocaine and heroin injections. At doses of naloxone up to 100 μg/kg, the number of heroin injections received increased. At higher doses (500 and 1,000 μg/kg), naloxone caused a suppression in responding. In contrast, the animal's cocaine-reinforced behavior was unaffected by any dose of naloxone. Figure 2 shows the same animal's performance when saline was substituted for heroin for 10

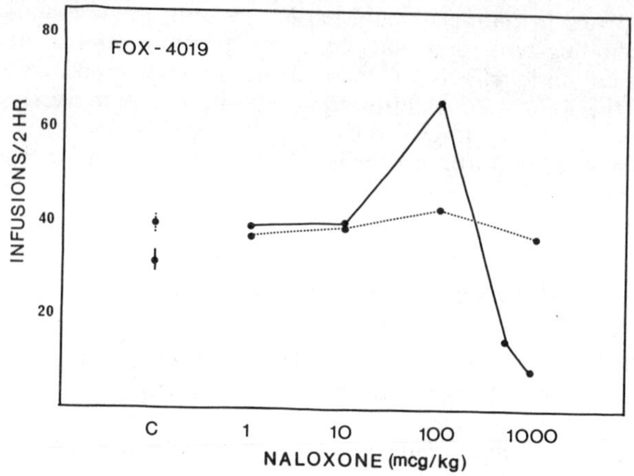

FIGURE 1. Mean number of infusions earned of heroin (solid line) and cocaine (dashed line) for the last three sessions at each dose level of naloxone.

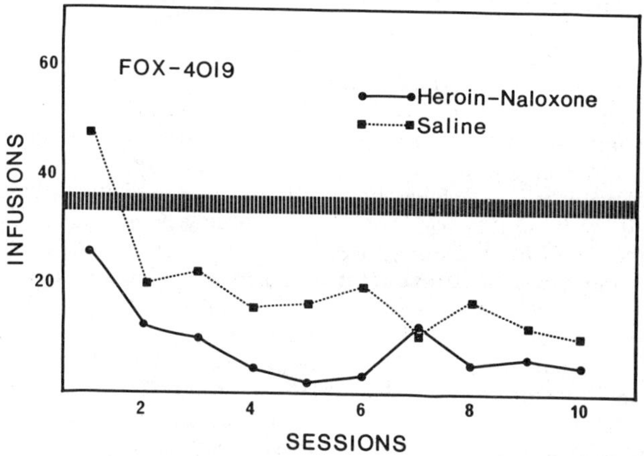

FIGURE 2. Number of infusions earned over 10 consecutive sessions in which: 1) saline was substituted for heroin (solid squares), 2) subject was pretreated with 500 μg/kg of naloxone. The shaded area represents mean and range of the number of heroin infusions earned under baseline conditions.

days (saline extinction) and the animal's performance when 500 μg/kg of naloxone was given prior to 10 heroin-reinforced sessions. Under both conditions the number of injections received showed a progressive decline over the 10-day period. The similarity of these curves suggests that naloxone at this dose was blocking the reinforcing effects of heroin and thus producing extinction of the drug-reinforced behavior.

This experiment demonstrates that naloxone can block not only the discriminative effects of opiates but their reinforcing actions as well. This is, of course, the basis for the use of opiate antagonists in the treatment of former heroin-dependent patients. The similarity of effects produced by naloxone in our animal model of drug abuse and in man further validates the animal model as a means of developing possible pharmacotherapeutic agents for treatment.

Summary and Conclusions

Three different types of behavioral methods have been shown to be useful in the study of the interaction of opiate agonists and antagonists. These procedures can also be applied to the study of interactions of drugs from other pharmacologic classes.

The study of the ability of drugs to modify the discriminative and reinforcing actions of drugs of abuse has both theoretical and practical implications. Theoretically, such interactions may help to unravel the neurochemical mechanisms underlying discriminative and reinforcing effects of drugs. From a practical viewpoint, these drug interactions may suggest new agents for the treatment of drug dependence.

References

1. McMillan, D. E., P. S. Wolf & R. A. Carchinian. 1970. Antagonism of the behavioral effects of morphine and methadone by narcotic antagonists in the pigeon. J. Pharmacol. Exp. Ther. **175:** 443.
2. McMillan, D. E. & W. H. Morse. 1967. Some effects of morphine and morphine antagonists on schedule-controlled behavior. J. Pharmacol. Exp. Ther. **157:** 175–184.
3. Blumberg, H., P. S. Wolf & H. B. Dayton. 1965. Use of the writhing test for evaluating analgesic activity of narcotic antagonists. Proc. Soc. Exp. Biol. Med. **118:** 763–766.
4. Pearl, J. & L. S. Harris. 1963. Inhibition of writhing by narcotic antagonists. J. Pharmacol. Exp. Ther. **154:** 310–323.
5. Jasinski, D. R., W. R. Martin & C. A. Haertzen. 1967. The human pharmacology and abuse potential of N-allynoroxymorphone (naloxone). J. Pharmacol. Exp. Ther. **157:** 420–426.
6. Holtzman, S. G. 1976. Effects of morphine and narcotic antagonists on avoidance behavior of the squirrel monkey. J. Pharmacol. Exp. Ther. **196**(1): 145–155.
7. Holtzman, S. G. & R. E. Jewett. 1973. Stimulation of behavior in the rat by cyclazocine: Effects of naloxone. J. Pharmacol. Exp. Ther. **184:** 528–541.
8. Holtzman, S. G. 1974. Tolerance to the stimulant effects of morphine and pentazocine on avoidance responding in the rat. Psychopharmacologia. **39:** 23–37.
9. Martin, W. R., D. R. Jasinski & P. A. Mansky. 1973. Naltrexone, an antagonist for the treatment of heroin dependence. Arch. Gen. Psychiatry **28:** 784–791.
10. Villarreal, J. E. & M. G. Karbowski. 1974. The actions of narcotic antagonists in morphine-dependent rhesus monkeys. *In* Narcotic antagonists. M. C. Braude, L. S. Harris, E. L. May, J. P. Smith & J. E. Villarreal, eds.: 273–289. Raven Press. New York, N.Y.

11. Blumberg, H. & H. B. Dayton. 1974. Naloxone, naltrexone, and related noroxymorphones. *In* Narcotic Antagonists. M. C. Braude, L. S. Harris, E. L. May, J. P. Smith & J. E. Villarreal, Eds.: 33–43. Raven Press. New York, N.Y.
12. Dykstra, L. A., D. E. McMillan & L. S. Harris. 1974. Antagonism of morphine by long acting narcotic antagonists. Psychopharmacologia **39:** 151–162.
13. Goldberg, S. R. & C. R. Schuster. 1969. Nalorphine: Increased sensitivity of monkeys formerly dependent on morphine. Science **166:** 1548–1549.
14. Overton, D. A. 1973. State dependent learning produced by addicting drugs. *In* Opiate Addiction: Origins and Treatment. S. Fisher & A. M. Freedman, Eds.: 61–75. Winston & Sons. Washington, D.C.
15. Schuster, C. R. & R. L. Balster. 1976. The discriminative stimulus properties of drugs. *In* Advances in Behavioral Pharmacology. T. Thompson & P. B. Dews, Eds. Vol. I. Academic Press, Inc. New York, N.Y.
16. Hill, H. E., B. E. Jones & E. C. Bell. 1971. State-dependent control of discrimination of morphine and pentobarbital. Psychopharmacologia **22:** 305–313.
17. Belleville, R. E. 1964. Control of behavior by drug-produced internal stimuli. Psychopharmacologia **5:** 95–105.
18. Rosecrans, J. A., M. H. Goodloe, G. J. Bennet & I. D. Hirschhorn. 1973. Morphine as a discriminative cue: Effects of amine depletors and naloxone. Eur. J. Pharmacol. **21:** 252–256.
19. Hirschhorn, I. D. & J. A. Rosecrans. 1974. Morphine and *d*-9-tetrahydrocannabinol: Tolerance to the stimulus effects. Psychopharmacologia **36:** 243–253.
20. Kuhn, D. M., I. Greenberg & J. B. Appel. 1976. Stimulus properties of the narcotic antagonist pentazocine: Similarity to morphine and antagonism by naloxone. J. Pharmacol. Exp. Ther. **196**(1)**:** 121–127.
21. Harris, R. T. & R. L. Balster. 1971. The discriminative control of a food reinforced operant by interoceptive stimulation. *In* Stimulus Properties of Drugs. T. Thompson & R. Pickens, Eds. Appleton-Century-Crofts, Inc. New York, N.Y.
22. Kuhn, D. M., I. Greenberg & J. B. Appel. 1974. An analysis of some discriminative properties of *d*-amphetamine. Psychopharmacologia **39:** 57–66.
23. Overton, D. A. 1974. Experimental methods for the study of state-dependent learning. Fed. Proc. **33:** 1800–1813.
24. Keats, A. S. & J. Telford. 1964. Narcotic antagonists as analgesics: Clinical aspects. Advan. Chem. Ser. **49:** 170–176.
25. Keats, A. S. & J. Telford. 1964. Studies of analgesic drugs. VIII. A narcotic antagonist and analgesic without psychotomimetic effects. J. Pharmacol. Exp. Ther. **143:** 157–164.
26. Jasinsky, D. R., W. Martin & R. Hoeldtke. 1970. Effects of short and long-term administration of pentazocine in man. Clin. Pharmacol. Ther. **11:** 385–403.
27. Schuster, C. R. & T. Thompson. 1969. Self-administration of and behavioral dependence on drugs. Annu. Rev. Pharmacol. **9:** 483–502.
28. Schuster, C. R. & C. E. Johanson. 1974. The use of animal models for the study of drug abuse. *In* Research Advances in Alcohol and Drug Problems. R. J. Gibbins, Ed.-in-Chief. Vol. I: 1–31. John Wiley & Sons, Inc. New York, N.Y.
29. Goldberg, S. R., J. H. Woods & C. R. Schuster. 1971. Nalorphine-induced changes in morphine self-administration in rhesus monkeys. J. Pharmacol. Exp. Ther. **176**(2)**:** 464–471.

30. Goldberg, S. R., F. Hoffmeister, U. Schlichting & W. Wuttke. 1971. Aversive properties of nalorphine and naloxone in morphine-dependent rhesus monkeys. J. Pharmacol. Exp. Ther. **179**(2): 268–276.
31. Hoffmeister, F. & W. Wuttke. 1974. Self-administration: positive and negative reinforcing properties of morphine antagonists in rhesus monkeys. *In* Narcotic Antagonists. M. C. Braude, L. S. Harris, E. L. May, J. P. Smith & J. E. Villarreal, Eds. Raven Press. New York, N.Y.
32. Thompson, T. & C. R. Schuster. 1964. Morphine self-administration, food-reinforced and avoidance behaviors in rhesus monkeys. Psychopharmacologia **5**: 87–94.
33. Killian, A. K., K. F. Bonese & C. R. Schuster. 1976. Personal communication.

CLINICAL EFFECTS OF PHARMACOLOGIC AGENTS ON PREGNANCY, THE FETUS, AND THE NEONATE

Loretta Finnegan

Philadelphia General Hospital and
University of Pennsylvania School of Medicine
Philadelphia, Pennsylvania 19104

Pharmacologic agents administered during pregnancy may have an adverse effect on the developing fetus and neonate. Although data concerning the effects of pharmacologic agents have been available for a long time, the seriousness of their significance in the obstetrical patient is not totally appreciated. Despite recent advances in the area of fetal and neonatal pharmacology, many physicians continue to prescribe drugs to the pregnant woman without considering the untoward effects upon the fetus. Moreover, during the past decade, narcotic addiction in the United States has reached epidemic proportions, and the ratio of addiction in women of child-bearing age has been steadily increasing, with the resultant birth of a large number of infants who have been exposed to the prenatal stress of illicit drug usage.

In addition to physician-prescribed drugs and those utilized by the drug-dependent individual, the vast majority of pharmacologic agents used in pregnancy are those that are self-prescribed by the obstetrical patient. The United States has become a chemically oriented country, and recent observations have revealed that an enormous number of drugs are used by pregnant women. The thalidomide tragedy drew attention to the induction of congenital malformations even with a drug generally accepted as innocuous for man. The result was a marked decrease in the use of drugs during pregnancy in those countries in Western Europe where thalidomide had been used. Unfortunately, there has not been an apparent change in maternal drug consumption in this country, where thalidomide was never approved for marketing. One recent study of 67 private patients in the last trimester of pregnancy revealed that each mother took an average of 4.5 drug preparations (including combinations) for a total of 8.7 different drug entities during the period of study. Eighty percent of the drugs were taken without a doctor's supervision or knowledge; the remaining 20% were prescribed by a physician. The drugs included vitamin preparations (86% of the patients), aspirin (69%), antacids (60%), diuretics (30%), cathartics (26%), antibiotics (16%), antihistamines (14%), and barbiturates (12%).[1]

Peckham and King[2] reported that the average pregnant woman receives 3.6 or more drugs during pregnancy, and 4% receive 10 or more drugs. Another series[3] increased this figure to 6.3 per patient. Hill[4] reported that gravid women from a middle socio-economic population received 10.3 drugs, with a range of from 3 to 29 drugs. The mean or range did not include vitamins, iron, intravenous fluids, anesthetic agents, and tobacco or exposure to pesticides, paints, chemicals, radiation, or alcohol. The greatest incidence of fetal drug exposure occurred between 24 and 36 weeks' gestation and again during labor and delivery. Multiple drugs frequently were ingested concomitantly.

The new drug regulations of 1962, which directly followed the thalidomide disaster, dictate that safety and efficacy of new drugs must be demonstrated in the subject in which the drug is to be employed. Unfortunately, these regulations have been bypassed, and much of the needed information upon which to prescribe drugs to the perinatal host is unavailable. It is extremely difficult for the practicing physician to keep up with the numerous animal and human studies in the area of drug effects and drug interactions. He is generally left with the most available source found on his bookshelf, that is, the "Physicians Desk Reference." Unfortunately, the following statement is included in the description of most drugs: ". . . safe use in pregnancy, lactation, or in women of child-bearing age has not been established. The use of the drug in pregnant women requires that its potential benefits be weighed against possible hazards to the patient as well as to the fetus." Although this may serve as a warning to the physician, it conveys very little information.[5] Thus, since the physician knows the beneficial effects of a specific drug in the non-gravid female and is unaware of its effects on the gravid female and the fetus, he will indiscriminately prescribe one or more drugs. This paper will review the special medical problems faced by the pregnant woman as well as the fetus when various pharmacologic agents are taken during pregnancy.

General Concepts in Maternal and Fetal Distribution of Drugs in Pregnancy

Disposition of drugs during pregnancy takes on a unique pattern in view of the fact that we are not dealing with one specific organism. When considering the distribution of drugs in the gravid female, one must be aware of the maternal feto-placental unit. The disposition of drugs in this unit is influenced by several inter-reacting processes.

Many factors operate to modulate the transplacental passage of pharmacologic agents, while many of the rate-limiting processes are poorly understood and some have probably not been identified as yet. The following characteristics of the placenta and the drugs passing through it are important:[6]

1. *Lipid solubility*. The placenta is generally assumed to be lipoprotein in nature and similar to other biological membranes in the mammalian organism. Compounds possessing a high degree of lipid solubility or those with large partition coefficients are generally considered to permeate the placenta readily.

2. *Degree of drug ionization*. Drugs penetrate biological membranes more rapidly when in their un-ionized state; much less rapidly when highly ionized.

3. *Molecular weight*. Compounds whose molecular weights are less than 600 readily traverse the placenta, whereas those exceeding 1000 do not. Most therapeutically effective agents have molecular weights ranging from 250 to 400 and thus would appear to meet this criterion.

4. *Placental blood flow*. The transfer of highly lipid soluble drugs is proportional to placental blood flow in a manner analogous to the relationship between alveolar ventilation and the uptake of volatile anesthetic agents. The effect of fetal circulation on drug transfer must also be considered and if impaired, secondary to heart failure, erythroblastosis fetalis, or drug intoxication (local anesthetics), will significantly decrease drug-transfer rates from the maternal to fetal compartments.

5. *Placental metabolism of drugs.* Many therapeutic agents can be metabolized by placental homogenates under *in vitro* conditions. The overall significance of these reactions in the intact maternal-feto-placental unit still remains to be defined.

6. *Protein binding of drugs.* Those agents that are tenaciously bound to plasma proteins will probably be transferred less rapidly across the placenta than assiduously bound compounds because the proportion of free to total drug present at any time will be significantly lower. Other types of binding may affect the transfer of drugs across biological membranes, particularly if the agent in question has a relatively high affinity for components present within a specific tissue. This may lead to unusual and unanticipated drug-distribution patterns.

7. *Aging of the placenta.* As the placenta matures, the thickness of its trophoblastic epithelium decreases; this should lead to an increase in the rate of diffusion of drug molecules. Unfortunately, there is scanty information in this area; however, several studies suggest that drugs cross the rodent placenta more rapidly in the first trimester than in the last.

Additional factors that influence the distribution of drugs in the fetus after they traverse the placenta include the following: selective uptake of drugs by specific tissues due to non-specific lipid solubility; specific binding of cellular constituents (binding proteins, enzyme-drug interactions); active secretion of drugs by the yolk sac; permeability of specialized membranes; and distribution of the fetal circulation. It is obvious from the preceding comments that drug disposition in the maternal-feto-placental unit represents a complex integrated series of pharmacodynamic processes. These processes operate in an integrated manner, so that multiple kinetic events occur concurrently in both the maternal and fetal environment.

It is important to discuss what is known about the metabolism of drugs in tissues of the fetus and placenta. Recent observations have shown that human fetal liver microsomes contain necessary electron-transport components (NADPH-specific cytochrome c reductase and cytochrome P-450) for drug hydroxylation reactions. Oxidation of several drugs and endogenous substrates such as testosterone and laurate was demonstrated in human fetal liver preparations *in vitro.* These results stand in marked contrast to the inability of many investigators to detect significant evidence of ctyochrome x P-450 or P-450 dependent drug hydroxylation reactions in liver microsomes from fetuses of a wide variety of animal species, even at comparatively late stages of gestation. Evidence of hydroxylation reactions has been found in other tissues of the human fetus, including the adrenal gland and the placenta.[7]

Drug conjugation reactions (acetylation, glycine conjugation, sulphate transfer) have also been demonstrated in human fetal tissues. Several highly active sulfatase enzymes are present in placenta, and these together with sulfurylation capability in the fetal liver and adrenal gland may represent an extremely important mechanism for regulating fetal drug distribution as well as placental drug movement.[7]

In reference to drug interactions, the maternal-placento-fetal unit also reacts in a unique fashion. In the gravid female we are not only concerned about interactions between two drugs but, moreover, the interaction between a drug or drugs and the specific host, which involves the unique peculiarities of the placenta.

Basic Principles of Teratology

Teratology refers to the study of congenital malformations grossly visible at birth that are induced by exogenous agents during the organogenic period. A broadened definition includes any birth defect—morphological, biochemical, or behavioral—induced at any stage of gestation and detected at birth or later. Multifactorial causes have been found for congenital malformations and generally result from an interaction between genetic and environmental factors. It has been estimated that 25% of human malformations can be attributed to genetic factors, 3% to chromosomal aberrations, and another 3% to environmental factors such as maternal infection, radiation, and drug administration. The etiology of the remaining 69% is still unknown.[7]

The possible occurrence of congenital malformations is dependent on the interaction of the following four teratogenic principles: the nature of the responsible agent and its accessibility to the fetus, the time of its action, the level and duration of its dosage, and genetic constitution. During the pre-implantation period (in man the first 2 weeks following conception) the developing embryo is generally considered to be relatively resistant to environmental influences. If damage occurs during this period it most probably will be severe and cause death of the embryo, with subsequent abortion. Furthermore, there is an increased incidence of abnormalities in the aborted fetuses.[8]

In the organ-forming period (in man approximately 13–56 days of gestation) the type of malformation observed will be closely related to the state of development at the time of exposure. In humans for example, the period of sensitivity for the nervous system is 15–25 days, for the heart 20–40 days, and for the limbs 24–46 days.[8]

Following the first trimester, most organs are already formed, with certain important exceptions such as the genital apparatus, the teeth, and central nervous system, which continue to mature. This is the fetal period when most adverse effects from drugs are similar to those observed in adults. Drug effects may show up much later, during postnatal life or adulthood, even though induced prenatally. Behavioral changes of various types have been noticed following treatment with tranquilizing drugs and sex hormones. The recent observation of vaginal adenocarcinoma among adolescent girls whose mothers were treated with high doses of diethylstilbestrol during pregnancy is a tragic example of a late teratogenic effect.[8]

Genetic makeup is an important factor to consider when different results are obtained under identical environmental influences. The final response varies between species, strains, and individuals. A significant percentage of the mothers who took thalidomide during the susceptible period did not give birth to children with malformations.[8]

A teratogenic dose lies between two extremes: a low one which may cause temporary impairment, and a high one producing fetal death. In most cases the teratogenic zone is narrow, and the dose-effect curve has a steep slope. An exception to the rule is thalidomide: a great increase in dose produces only a small increase in fetal morbidity. In animals, the teratogenic dose is rather close to the maternal LD-50 for that particular substance, although this relationship may vary considerably depending on the drug. Besides single dosage, the total amount of drug (that is, the duration of exposure) must be considered as well.

Repeated dosage can result in enzyme induction or inhibition with consequent alteration of the plasma concentration and, therefore, changes in effect.[8]

Specific Responses to Pharmacologic Agents by the Gravid Female

Metabolic and functional parameters undergo considerable change in the gravid state and, therefore, must modify drug handling by the adult female. Unfortunately, minimal information exists in this regard, despite the high intake of drugs throughout gestation. Tetracycline in high doses has been reported to cause hepatic dysfunction, azotemia, and even death when used for the treatment of pyelonephritis in pregnant and early postpartum patients.[8]

The absorption of certain nutrients seems to be enhanced during pregnancy, but nothing is known about absorption of drugs. Total serum protein concentrations, especially albumin, decrease in pregnancy. The binding capacity for sulfisoxazole and Congo Red is also lower in pregnant women at term. Both hypoalbuminemia and increased loading with endogenous material are considered causative factors. Total water content and body volume increase gradually during pregnancy and probably influence the volume of distribution of any potential drug. Kidney function also changes during pregnancy in that there is hypertrophy which tends to shift the normal values for clearance of substances downwards, modifying renal excretion of drugs as well. Tetracycline, which is excreted unaltered, is handled similary by the pregnant and nonpregnant woman.[8]

Studies of drug-metabolizing capacity *in vitro* in pregnant rats have shown that a decreased metabolism exists for oxidative and reductive pathways, whereas sulfation is increased. The mechanism behind these changes during pregnancy is not fully understood, though it may be related to the known hormonal changes. Increases in the amount of reduced progesterone derivatives formed during pregnancy may exert an inhibitory action on the activities of certain drug hydroxylases in the maternal liver. The picture is not clear, however, as both estrogens and progesterones when administered exogenously gave results that varied depending on the structure of the compound under consideration and the duration of treatment.[8]

Specific Pharmacologic Agents Affecting the Fetus

The magnitude of drugs used in general therapeutics does not permit a description of all of the effects seen during pregnancy. Only the more commonly used pharmacologic agents will be discussed, with special emphasis on drugs of abuse. The effects of antidiabetic agents, antithyroid drugs, antibiotics, hormones, diuretics, common analgesics vitamins, sedatives, hypotensive agents, anticonvulsant agents, cancer chemotherapeutic agents, cigarette smoking, and drugs of abuse will be discussed.

Infants of diabetic mothers have a higher rate of anomalies than those of non-diabetic mothers. Insulin and diet provide the best therapeutic routine in diabetes mellitus. Chlorpropamide-treated diabetic mothers have three times the incidence of fetal death *in utero* as compared with diabetic gravidas on insulin and diet alone. Tolbutamide has been shown to potentiate hypoglycemia in the newborn and to cause thrombocytopenia. In regard to antithyroid drugs, all uracils and imizadoles and perchlorates cross the placenta promptly and are goitrogenic for the fetus. Iodine compounds in excessive amounts (for control of asthma, expectorants) cause fetal non-toxic goiter. I-131 administered to the pregnant woman even in the first trimester of pregnancy may be disastrous for the fetus, causing athyrotic cretinism.[9]

Antibiotics are frequently used to protect the gravid female against the many infections that she may acquire. Tetracyclines traverse the placenta readily and are especially hazardous in the last trimester of pregnancy because they may inhibit skeletal growth, cause anomalous bone development, or initiate enamel dysplasia and discoloration of fetal deciduous teeth.[9] Ampicillin has been shown to decrease maternal urinary and plasma estriol levels, and cephaloridine has caused a false positive direct Coombs test. Streptomycin has been found to cause deafness in the neonate. Sulfonamides, both long and short acting, have caused icterus, hemolytic anemia, kernicterus, and thrombocytopenia.

When androgens, progestrogens, and estrogens are administered to the pregnant woman, even in relatively small doses over a prolonged period of time, they may cause nonadrenal pseudohermaphroditism in the female and, rarely, feminization in the male infant. Androgens and progesterogens given prior to the 20th week of pregnancy may cause labial fusion. If given after the 20th week, they may cause clitoral hypertrophy. Paradoxically, stilbestrol administered during pregnancy may cause virilization for unexplained reasons. Corticosteroids have been implicated in causing adrenal insufficiency, cleft palate, and intrauterine growth retardation. Thiazide diuretics administered to pregnant patients may cause neonatal thrombocytopenia by suppression of the bone marrow. Theories of causative factors include antigen-antibody reaction, isoimmunization, and idiopathically incompetent bone marrow. Common analgesics, including acetylsalycylic acid, used persistently during pregnancy have been held responsible for fetal death *in utero* and bleeding in the newborn. Vitamins, such as vitamin D_2, administered in large quantities indiscriminately to pregnant patients have been implicated in the causation of congenital cardiac malformations.[9]

Hypotensive agents such as hexamethonium have been found to cause paralytic ileus, perforation, and death in the neonate. Reserpine affects neonates by causing nasal stuffiness, bradycardia, respiratory distress, hypothermia, and abnormal muscle tone.

Anticonvulsive agents such as diphenylhydantoin and barbiturates have been implicated in the causation of congenital malformations including cleft lip and palate, congenital heart disease, central nervous system and skeletal anomalies, failure to thrive, and hemorrhage. Barbiturates alone have been shown to cause withdrawal syndromes, including tremulousness, for as long as 4 to 5 months after delivery. Paradione and tridione may be causative in the development of congenital heart disease, micropthalmia, and mental retardation.

Cancer chemotherapeutic agents have caused abortions early in gestation, and, in the first trimester, certain congenital anomalies, such as skeletal and cranial malformations and hydrocephalus.[9] The tragic effects of thalidomide, which causes phocomelia, are well known.

Investigations utilizing C-14-diazepam in the pregnant monkey have demonstrated a rapid transfer across the placenta, with significant uptake and prolonged retention of this compound and its metabolites in the fetal cerebellum, spinal cord, and peripheral nerves. Recent studies in man have shown that C-14-diazepam and its metabolites are rapidly transferred across the human placenta, with much greater concentrations present in cord blood than maternal blood 1 hour after administration. Fetal-tissue concentrations of diazepam and metabolites peak at this time. The highest levels were observed in the fetal liver, brain, and gastrointestinal tract. The metabolism of diazepam by fetal liver microsomes was minimal, constituting about 3% of the added substrate; no metabolism was noted in homogenates prepared from human placenta, fetal brain, or fetal small intestine.[10]

The diazepam plasma apparent half-life was found to be significantly reduced (in comparison with that previously observed in premature infants and full-term newborns) in three newborns whose mothers had received phenobarbital for various lengths of time during gestation and diazepam in the last 24 hours prior to delivery.[11] Many factors could play a role in the observed reduction, and these data alone cannot be taken as clear evidence of an increased drug metabolism; however, other data support the suggestion that the rate at which diazepam is degraded in the newborn increases after phenobarbital is administered.

Recent literature[12] has shown an association between cleft lip with or without cleft palate and prenatal exposure to diazepam. The investigators interviewed 278 women who had infants with selected major malformations. In these women diazepam ingestion in the first trimester of pregnancy was found to be four times more frequent among mothers of children with cleft lip with or without cleft palate than among mothers of children with other defects. This association was one of many that was examined in the analysis and quite possibly may simply be due to chance. The investigators state that the possibility that diazepam is a cleft-lip and cleft-palate teratogen in humans requires further investigation. As it stands now, the possible risk of teratogenesis should be carefully weighed against the expected therapeutic benefit when prescribing the drug in women of child-bearing age. Pregnant women should be advised that no causal relationship has yet been proven in regard to diazepam and cleft lip with or without cleft palate. These authors suggest that if a causal relationship does exist, the risk of having a child with cleft lip with or without a cleft palate is about 0.4% if diazepam is used in the first trimester.

The effects of smoking during pregnancy have recently been delineated. Although nicotine, carbon monoxide, and tars have been held responsible, smoking, like excessive eating or drinking, can be considered a reflection of stress, although how it affects the outcome of pregnancy remains obscure. Certain associations concerning smoking in pregnancy have been shown. Fetal growth is reduced at least 200 grams on the average, with a significant increase in the incidence of low-birth-weight infants. These infants are generally those who are described as intrauterine growth retarded. The effects are the result of chronic fetal asphyxia. The outcome will be an infant poorly grown for his gestational age, who may suffer from aspiration pneumonia, asphyxia neonatorum, polycythemia, hypoglycemia, and long-term mental deficiency and growth retardation. In addition to the decrease in fetal growth, mortality rates are much higher in smoking mothers, particularly during fetal life.[9]

The adverse effects on the fetus of chronic maternal alcoholism have been known for many years, but only recently has a full description become available.[13, 14] The abnormalities include prenatal and postnatal growth deficiency, developmental delay, and craniofacial disorders, including microcephaly, short palpebral fissures, asymetric ptosis, strabismus, epicanthal folds, maxillary hypoplasia, and micrognathia. Skeletal abnormalities include hip dislocation, elbow limitation, phalangeal anomalies, and altered palmar creases. Other associated anomalies which have been described include cardiac anomalies, abnormal external genitalia, capillary hemangiomata, and excess nipples.

It should be emphasized that infants who develop the fetal alcohol syndrome are born to mothers to whom the criteria for alcoholism apply (as published in 1972 by the Criteria Committee of the National Council on Alcoholism). The majority of infants whose mothers moderately abuse alcohol during pregnancy do not demonstrate the fetal alcohol syndrome. These infants do show intrauterine growth retardation and may develop mild symptoms of withdrawal, including tremulousness, hypertonicity, and irritability.

Unfortunately, many women who abuse alcohol are also taking physician-prescribed or self-prescribed pharmacologic agents. This permits specific drug interactions with alcohol. For example, alcohol potentiates the gastrointestinal bleeding which can be seen with salicylates and the CNS-depressant effects of narcotic analgesics. Diphenylhydantoin appears to be metabolized at a faster rate by individuals who utilize alcohol. Ethanol potentiates the sedative effects of antihistamines, and when administered concurrently with reserpine, methyldopa, guanethidine, hydralazine, or diuretics, it has been shown to produce an additive hypotensive effect. This is presumably because ethanol produces renal and peripheral vasodilation. In combination with ethanol, the hypotensive effects commonly produced by phenothiazines may be exacerbated, and both produce CNS depressant effects which are additive, with the combination often resulting in severely impaired psychomotor function. The combination of the sedative hypnotics with ethanol results in potentiation of the CNS-depressant effects and thereby in decreased alertness in judgement as well as impairment of motor coordination and manual skills. It has been reported that diazepam and probably the other benzodiazepines produce a supra-additive hypotensive effect when combined with alcohol and perhaps even a decreased tolerance. Deaths have occurred and are attributed to depressed cardiac functioning, vasomotor collapse and respiratory failure. The presence of alcohol appears to inhibit the hepatic smooth endoplasmic reticulum enzymes, which are responsible for the metabolism and detoxification of barbiturates. This may result in a synergistic CNS depression, which may be fatal.[15]

Effects of Maternal Drug Dependency on the Fetus and the Newborn

The life style of the drug-dependent woman predisposes her to a host of maternal complications, which include toxemia, abruptio placenta, retained placenta, postpartum hemorrhage, and, in the infant, low birth weight, breech presentation, and an increase in neonatal morbidity and mortality. About 10 to 15 percent of drug-dependent women have toxemia at pregnancy, and nearly 50% of women who are heroin dependent and have no prenatal care deliver prematurely. The infant born to the drug-dependent mother is not only born early but also weighs less than other infants.

Maternal narcotic withdrawal has been associated with the occurrence of stillbirth. Severe withdrawal is associated with increased muscular activity, thereby increasing the metabolic rate and oxygen consumption in the pregnant woman. During maternal withdrawal fetal activity also increases; consequently, the oxygen needs of the fetus can be assumed to be increased. The oxygen reserve in the intervillous space of the placenta may not be able to supply the extra oxygen need by the fetus. If the bloodflow through the intervillous space is totally arrested, this oxygen reserve will be completely exhausted in 2 to 2½ minutes. During labor, contractions compromise the bloodflow through the uterus, which consequently has an effect on the oxygen reserve of the intervillous space. The longer and stronger the contractions, the more compromised the circulation through the uterus. If labor should coincide with withdrawal symptoms in the mother, the increased oxygen needs of the withdrawing fetus would coincide with a period of variable uterine bloodflow. If the fetus were exposed to an environment of insufficient oxygen for any length of time, it might suffer hypoxia and possibly death. The older the fetus, the greater the metabolic rate and oxygen consumption. Therefore, a pregnant woman undergoing severe withdrawal symptoms during the latter part of pregnancy would be less likely to supply the withdrawing fetus with the oxygen it needs than would an addict in the first trimester of pregnancy.[16]

Naeye,[17] studying other fetal complications of maternal heroin addiction, found that nearly 60% of the mothers or their newborn infants showed evidence of acute infection. Most of the infected mothers delivered prematurely, whereas those not infected delivered at term. The placentas of the heroin-exposed infants commonly revealed meconium histiocytosis, suggesting that they had experienced episodes of distress during fetal life. The infants born to these heroin addicts were, as a group, small for gestational age, and all their organs were affected. Maternal undernutrition could not always be documented as an explanation for the retardation of fetal growth. Naeye suggested the possibility that periodic episodes of heroin withdrawal during pregnancy might restrict fetal growth by reducing uterine or placental bloodflow. However, it is unlikely that a uterine or placental disorder was responsible for their growth retardation since the organ and cellular growth pattern associated with fetal growth retardation in uteroplacental disorders is quite different from that observed in the offspring of heroin addicts. The high incidence of meconium histocytosis in the placentas of heroin-exposed infants suggests that they experienced episodes of hypoxia or some other form of distress during fetal life perhaps related to episodes of heroin withdrawal. In non-addicted women, undernutrition restricts both size and the number of cells in many organs during the last trimester. The adrenal glands, liver, and adipose tissue are affected more than other organs. By contrast, the smallness of many of these organs in infants exposed to heroin in the third trimester was due mainly to a sub-normal number of cells. Growth retardation of the addicted fetuses was still apparent after cases had been placed in appropriate maternal nutritional categories, suggesting that maternal undernutrition was not the only factor responsible for growth restriction. It seems likely that heroin has a direct effect on antenatal growth.[17, 18]

In addition to the numerous obstetrical complications seen in the pregnant drug-dependent woman, other serious illnesses may exist. These occur not only because of almost total lack of self-care and failure to seek medical care but also because many women support drug habits by prostitution. Syphilis, gonorrhea, urinary-tract infection, and many other infectious problems plague the drug-dependent pregnant woman. In addition, a woman who uses needles is subject to complications such as serum hepatitis, venous thrombosis, thrombophlebitis cellulitis, and abscesses. Medical complications seen in drug-dependent pregnant women who were grouped according to the amount of prenatal care received have ranged from 34% to 48%.[19]

Malnutrition presents another complication troublesome to the maternal fetal unit. The lack of proper food intake that leads to nutritional deficiencies in alcoholics and drug addicts is due largely to inhibition of the central mechanism that controls appetite and hunger. Furthermore, adaptive or toxic responses to alcohol, barbiturates, or narcotics may contribute to malnutrition by interfering with the absorption or utilization of ingested nutrients. Lack of adequate nutrition or possibly malabsorption may lead to iron and folic acid deficiency and thereby result in anemia.[20]

TABLE 1

NEONATAL DEATH STATISTICS FOR 303 INFANTS OF DRUG-DEPENDENT WOMEN AND 1586 CONTROL INFANTS

	PGH	Groups A,B,C	Group A	Group B	Group C
Total live births	1586	303	63	88	152
LBW* infants (<2500 g)	241	88	30	32	26
Incidence of LBW	15.2%	30.9%	47.6%	36.4%	17.1%
Total deaths	26	16	3	9	4
Incidence of death in total births	1.6%	5.3%	4.8%	10.2%	2.6%
Incidence of death in LBW infants	10.0%	13.6%	10.0%	28.1%	3.8%

* LBW = Low birth weight.
A, Heroin-dependent, no prenatal care.
B, Methadone-dependent, inadequate prenatal care.
C, Methadone-dependent, adequate prenatal care.

Neonatal death statistics of 303 infants born to drug-dependent women and 1,586 control infants from the general population of Philadelphia General Hospital were compared for the period 1970–75 (TABLE 1). The drug-dependent mothers were of three types: Group A, heroin-dependent women with no prenatal care; Group B, methadone-dependent women who had an average of 1.8 prenatal visits (women who either registered late for care or who lost interest in rehabilitation despite early enrollment in the program); Group C, methadone-dependent women who averaged 8.2 prenatal visits and received comprehensive care through prenatal, psychosocial, and addictive services at Philadelphia General Hospital. Comparisons of the incidence of low-birth-weight infants (weight less than 2500 grams) show that in the 1,586 controls, 15.2% were low birth weight. The overall mortality was 1.6%; in the low-birth-weight infants it was 10%. The overall incidence of low birth weight in the addictive groups was 30.9% (twice as much as in the controls). The incidence of low-birth-weight infants in Groups A, B, and C was 47.6%, 36.4% and 17.1%, respectively. In the 303 infants born to drug-dependent mothers, the overall mortality was 5.3%, more than three times that of the controls, and in low-birth-weight infants it was 13.6%. The overall mortality rate in each group was 4.8%, 10.2%, and 2.6%, and in the low-birth-weight infants it was 10%, 28.1%, and 3.8%. The most striking mortality rates are those in Group B, where total deaths and incidence of low birth weight are affected. This suggests that uncontrolled methadone use in pregnant women may be more harmful than illicit heroin. In contrast, among methadone-maintained mothers with adequate prenatal and addictive care, overall mortality was somewhat higher but mortality in low-birth-weight infants was lower than in the control population. Comparison of average birth weight in the heroin-dependent group with the methadone-dependent group who received comprehensive care, showed a difference of 367 grams.

In addition to this markedly increased mortality rate in infants of drug-dependent women, one must be concerned about the impact of the large number of low-birth-weight infants born to this population. It is well known that these low-birth-weight infants will contribute heavily to those children who will eventually be mentally retarded (with an I.Q. of 70 or below), as well as to those who will have great difficulty in school because they are poor learners. These handicapped individuals will be unable to compete fully in our increasingly complex society. In addition, there is a high incidence of undersized term infants born to drug-dependent women. The majority of deaths among newborn infants are associated with low birth weight. The death rate of low-birth-weight neonates is 40 times that of the full-size infant born at term. Moreover, the incidence of cerebral palsy associated with prematurity may be as high as 10 times; mental deficiency, 5 times, and lethal malformations in the undersized infants, 7 times that of the full-size infant. Emotional disturbances, social maladjustments, and visual and hearing deficits are also multiplied. With the increasing occurrence of drug dependence in our country, we can expect an increasing need for custodial facilities for those infants who may have motor or mental deficiencies. The medical and custodial costs for these individuals are incalculable.[9]

In addition to the increased incidence of low birth weight, and the resultant rise in neonatal mortality, the infant born to the drug-dependent mother also has a greater chance of having neonatal problems other than the neonatal abstinence syndrome. In our studies at Philadelphia General Hospital, neonatal morbidity was seen in nearly 75% of infants born to drug-dependent mothers, necessitating average hospital stays of between 17 to 26 days. Drug-dependent patients (Groups A, B, C) were compared with control groups of non-drug-dependent patients of the same ethnic and socio-economic class with and without prenatal care (Groups D and E) who delivered at Philadelphia General Hospital during 1970–75 (TABLE 2). Neonatal morbidity ranged from 43% in the non-drug-dependent, no-prenatal-care group to a high of 81.1% in the methadone-maintained patients with insignificant prenatal care. The major causes of morbidity in the infants of drug-dependent mothers included asphyxia neonatorum, aspiration pneumonia, intracranial hemorrhage, hyaline membrane disease, metabolic disorders such as hypoglycemia and hypocalcemia, infection, and jaundice. The neonatal narcotic abstinence syndrome was noted in 94.9% of Group A, which were heroin-dependent, 96.2% of Group B, and 91.9% of group C. In groups B and C are infants born to methadone-dependent mothers with average daily methadone doses of 32 and 37 mg/day, respectively. Severe abstinence, defined as that which necessitated therapy for more than

TABLE 2

INCIDENCE OF MORBIDITY FOR 317 INFANTS OF DRUG-DEPENDENT WOMEN IN COMPARISON WITH 185 CONTROLS

	A (N = 63)	B (N = 90)	C (N = 154)	D (N = 85)	E (N = 100)
Prenatal visits (average)	0	1.9	8.3	0	8.9
Days in hospital (infant)	25.9	18.1	16.6	7.1	6.7
Neonatal morbidity*	74.6%	81.1%	66.2%	43.0%	45.0%
Total withdrawal	94.9%	96.2%	91.9%	0%	0%

* Most frequently occurring infant diagnoses (see text).
A, Heroin-dependent (average-6.1 bags/day), no prenatal care.
B, Methadone-dependent, inadequate prenatal care.
C, Methadone-dependent, adequate prenatal care.
D, Non-drug-dependent, no prenatal care.
E, Non-drug-dependent, prenatal care.

2 weeks, was seen in a larger percentage of infants born to heroin-dependent mothers.

Neonatal abstinence can be described as a generalized disorder characterized by signs and symptoms of central nervous system hyperirritability, gastrointestinal dysfunction, respiratory distress, and vague autonomic symptoms, which include yawning, sneezing, mottling and fever. Afflicted infants generally develop tremors which are initially mild and occur only when they are disturbed, but which progress to the point where they occur spontaneously without the infant being stimulated. High-pitched cry, increased muscle tone, and irritability develop. The infants tend to have an increased rooting reflex and therefore frequently suck their fists or thumbs. They have difficulty with feedings and regurgitate frequently. They feed poorly because their sucking reflex is uncoordinated and ineffectual. They may develop loose stools and are therefore susceptible to dehydration and electrolyte imbalance.[21]

The origin of the neonatal abstinence syndrome seems to lie in the abnormal intrauterine environment. A series of steps appear to be necessary for its genesis and for the infant's recovery. Growth and survival of the fetus in an intrauterine environment are endangered by the continuing or episodic transfer of drugs of addictive potential from the maternal to fetal circulations. The fetus undergoes a biochemical adaptation to the presence of the abnormal agent in its tissues. Abrupt removal of this source of the drug at delivery precipitates the onset of the syndrome. The newborn infant continues to metabolize and excrete the drug, and withdrawal or abstinence signs occur when critically low tissue levels have been reached. Recovery from the abstinence syndrome is gradual and occurs as the infant's metabolism is reprogrammed to adjust to the absence of the dependence-producing agent.[22]

At birth most passively dependent infants, whether born to heroin- or methadone-addicted mothers, appear physically and behaviorally normal. The time of onset of withdrawal ranges from shortly after birth to 2 weeks of age, but for the majority it appears within 72 hours. The type of drug utilized by the mother, her dosage, timing of the dose before delivery, the character of labor, the type and amount of anesthesia and analgesia given during labor, the maturity, nutrition, and presence of intrinsic disease in the infant may all play a role in determining the time of onset in the individual infant. Because of the variation in the time of onset and variation in degrees of severity, a range of types of clinical courses may be delineated. Withdrawal may be mild and transient, delayed in onset, have a stepwise increase in severity, be intermittently present, or have a biphasic course, which includes acute neonatal withdrawal followed by improvement and then the onset of acute withdrawal.[22]

At Philadelphia General Hospital, it has been clinically documented by the nursing staff that passively drug dependent infants have difficulty with the sucking reflex. In addition, by means of a precise instrument developed by Kron *et al.*[23-25] the sucking rate, pressure, and the organization of sucking as well as the amount of nutrients consumed have been studied. These findings have been compared to normal controls and to infants born to toxemic mothers who have received such drugs as magnesium sulfate. Fifty subjects born to known addicts were studied on an as-you-come basis in the high-risk nursery. Infants were tested on the sucking instrument twice daily just prior to the 10 AM and 2 PM routine nursery feedings according to our standard procedures. Thirty-two of the subjects were born to mothers receiving low-dosage methadone maintenance therapy with a mean dose of 42 mg/day. These mothers attended our prenatal care program with the opportunity for frequent examinations by an obstetrician experienced in the care of pregnant addicts. Eighteen babies were born to street addicts taking heroin. Most of them did not come for hospitalization until the onset of labor, thus these women rarely had any prenatal care. All of the 50 infants studied underwent some degree of withdrawal reaction during the first 24 hours after delivery. However, not all were deemed to require specific treatment. Those who did were treated with a variety of agents. Twenty-eight received sedation with phenobarbital. Of the remaining infants, five were treated with paregoric, six with valium, and three with thorazine. Withdrawal symptoms in the remaining eight babies were not considered severe enough to require drug treatment, and this group had received no sedation or narcotic drugs whatsoever during the testing period. One control group consisted of 10 infants born to mothers who received magnesium sulfate and various amounts of barbiturates for treatment of toxemia of pregnancy. These infants were chosen because, like the addicted infants, they received special care in the high-risk nursery and, therefore, experienced a neonatal environment similar to that of the newborn addicts. In addition, a second control group of 10 normal full-term infants were studied, randomly drawn from the apparently healthy populations in the normal nursery, and whose mothers had received no general analgesic or sedative drugs during labor. The results for sucking rates in the addictive and control groups are shown in TABLE 3. Of the several sucking parameters, rates appear to be most sensitive in distinguishing among all four subjects, although the pressure parameters also indicated significant differences between the control and the addict population. It had been previously found that pressure-dependent sucking parameters were consistent attributes of the individual infant and were relatively insensitive to environmental influences. For example, if the infant sucked at all, it tended to generate a characteristic range of sucking pressures. However, the present data showed that one effect of drug addiction is to depress pressures as well as sucking rates. Average values for the toxemic babies

TABLE 3

SUCKING MEASURES FOR ADDICTED AND CONTROL GROUPS

	Addicts		Controls	
	Methadone (N = 32)	Heroin (N = 18)	Toxemia (N = 10)	Normal (N = 10)
Sucking rate, sucks/min.	18.3 = 2.1*	26.2 ± 3.2	32.2 ± 3.9	39.6 ± 4.6

* Mean over 6 trial feedings ± SE, two 10 minute trials per day for 3 days performed just prior to the 10 AM and 2 PM routine nursery feedings beginning at 24–36 hours of age.

appear to fall between the normal and heroin groups, but this is due to the fact that the measures in TABLE 3 are means over six trials. On the first two trials the toxemic babies had scores for sucking rates similar to those of the addicts, but on subsequent trials they rapidly recovered and their scores approached that of the normals. Drug-addicted babies remained depressed throughout. Since these trials were done over the first three to four days of life, one cannot be sure of how rapidly the methadone-dependent infants would recover. It is postulated that, because of the longer action of methadone, the effects may have been more prolonged.[26]

The dependence of sucking behavior upon the type of detoxicant treatment is analyzed in TABLE 4. Paregoric-treated infants tend to suck more vigorously than infants treated with sedatives such as phenobarbital and were even superior to those who received no therapy at all. The paregoric group approached control levels on most of the parameters. The averages for the no-treatment group were consistently lower than those for the paregoric babies, despite the fact that their withdrawal symptoms were judged to be quite mild and did not indicate the need for drug therapy. Valium-treated infants were greatly depressed in feeding behavior. Of the six valium subjects, five hardly sucked at all (however, the high sucking scores of the sixth brought up the group mean).[26]

These results raise questions about a number of *a priori* assumptions regarding the safety and efficacy of current treatment methods for maternal drug dependence and neonatal abstinence. Continuing studies in our nursery are involved in further delineating the behavioral effects of the drugs of abuse on the neonate as well as the efficacy of currently recommended detoxicant drugs used for neonatal abstinence.

In conclusion, the clinician who is involved in the care of the obstetrical patient has a difficult task in trying to satisfy the complex nature of the gravid

TABLE 4

EFFECT OF DIFFERENT DETOXICANTS ON SUCKING BEHAVIOR

	Paregoric (N = 5)	Phenobarbital (N = 28)	Valium (N = 6)	Nothing (N = 8)
Sucking rate, sucks/min.	30.5 ± 3.0*	19.4 ± 2.3	13.4 ± 7.2	23.2 ± 4.3

* Mean over 6 trial feedings ± SD.

state. He must not only be concerned about treating specific illnesses in the pregnant woman but also be aware of the effects and interactions of the drugs acting upon the host, which involves the maternal-feto-placental unit.

The benefits of the drug which is to be given to the pregnant female must be carefully weighed before the fetus is subjected to the many risks encountered with pharmacologic agents used for the usual disorders of pregnancy. With the knowledge already available in regard to the clinical effects on the fetus and neonate of pharmacologic agents used during pregnancy, it appears that, unless otherwise absolutely essential, the clinician should practice therapeutic nihilism.

In the case of the pregnant woman who uses illicit drugs, her situation as well as that of the unborn fetus can pose an overwhelming problem for the clinician. If one is aware of the numerous medical and obstetrical complications seen in these women, as well as the untoward effects expected in the newborn, the problem can be dealt with in order to reverse some of the effects of the prenatal stresses encountered when illicit drugs are used. The enormous problems seen in the drug-dependent woman are presently being defined and dealt with in many centers. There is still much to be delineated in regard to the appropriate treatment for such populations of women, as well as the task of adequate planning for their offspring. Only by more extensive and careful studies can we further define for the clinician the effects of pharmacologic agents on pregnancy, the fetus, and the newborn.

References

1. Bleyer, W. A. & R. J. Breckenridge. 1970. Adverse drug reactions in the newborn. II. Prenatal aspirin and newborn homeostasis. JAMA **213:** 2049–2053.
2. Peckham, C. H. & R. W. King. 1963. A study of intervurrent conditions observed during pregnancy. Amer. J. Obstet. Gynecol. **87:** 609–624.
3. Nora, J. J., A. H. Nora, R. J. Sommerville *et al.* 1967. Maternal exposure to potential teratogens. JAMA **202:** 1065–1069.
4. Hill, R. M. 1973. Drugs ingested by pregnant women. Clin. Pharmacol. Ther. **14:** 654–659.
5. Hill, R. M. 1974. Will this drug harm the unborn infant? South. Med. J. **67:** 1476–1480.
6. Mirkin, B. L. 1973. Maternal and fetal distribution of drugs in pregnancy. Clin. Pharmacol. Ther. **14:** 643–653.
7. Yaffe, S. J. 1974. Fetal and neonatal pharmacology. Clin. Perinatol. **1:** 39–45.
8. Eriksson, M., C. S. Catz & S. J. Yaffe. 1973. Drugs and pregnancy. Clin. Obst. Gynecol. **16:** 199–224.
9. Babson, S. G. & R. C. Benson. 1971. Management of high-risk pregnancy and intensive care of the neonate. C. V. Mosby Co. St. Louis, Mo.
10. Mirkin, B. L. 1973. Drug distribution in pregnancy. *In* Fetal Pharmacology. L. Boreus, Ed. Raven Press. New York, N.Y.
11. Morselli, P. L., M. Mandelli, G. Tognoni, N. Principi, G. Pardi & F. Serent. 1974. Drug interactions in the human fetus and in the newborn infant. *In* Drug Interactions. P. L. Morselli, S. Garattini & S. N. Cohen, Eds. Raven Press. New York, N.Y.
12. Safra, M. J. & G. P. Oakley, Jr. 1975. Association between cleft lip with or without cleft palate and prenatal exposure to diazepam. Lancet **2:** 478–480.

13. TENBRINCK, M. S. & S. Y. BUCHIN. 1975. Fetal alcohol syndrome. JAMA **232:** 1144–1147.
14. JONES, K., D. W. SMITH, C. N. ULLELAND & A. P. STREISSGUTH. 1973. Pattern of malformation in offspring of chronic alcoholic mothers. Lancet **1:** 1267–1269.
15. COLEMAN, J. H. & W. E. EVANS. 1976. Drug interactions with alcohol. Resident and Staff Physician **22:** 34–41.
16. REMENTERIA, J. L. & N. N. NUNAG. 1973. Narcotic withdrawal in pregnancy: stillbirth incidence with a case report. Amer. J. Obstet. Gynecol. **116:** 1152–1156.
17. NAEYE, R. L. 1965. Malnutrition, a probable cause of fetal growth retardation. Arch. Pathol. **79:** 284.
18. GRUENWALD, P. 1963. Chronic fetal distress and placental deficiency. Biol. Neonate **5:** 215.
19. CONNAUGHTON, J. F., L. P. FINNEGAN, J. SCHUT & J. P. EMICH. 1975. Current concepts in the management of the pregnant opiate addict. *In* Proceedings of the 37th Annual Scientific Meeting of the Committee on Problems of Drug Dependence of the National Research Council.
20. JONES, J. 1974. Nutrition, drugs and their interrelations. Penn. Health **35:** 3.
21. FINNEGAN, L. P., J. F. CONNAUGHTON & J. SCHUT. 1975. Infants of drug dependent women: Practical approaches for management. *In* Proceedings of the 37th Annual Scientific Meeting of the Committee on Problems of Drug Dependence of the National Research Council: 489.
22. DESMOND, M. M. & G. S. WILSON. 1975. Neonatal abstinence syndrome, recognition and diagnosis. Int. J. Addictive Dis. **2:** 113–121.
23. KRON, R. E. 1967. Instrumental conditioning of nutritive sucking behavior in the newborn. Recent Adv. Biol. Psychiatry **9:** 295–300.
24. KRON, R. E. 1968. The effect of arousal and learning upon sucking behavior in the newborn. Recent Adv. Biol. Psychiatry **10:** 302–313.
25. KRON, R. E. & M. LITT. 1971. Fluid mechanics of nutritive sucking: The sucking infant's oral apparatus analyzed as a hydraulic pump. Med. Biol. Eng. **9:** 45.
26. KRON, R. E., M. LITT & L. P. FINNEGAN. 1975. Narcotic addiction in the newborn: Differences in behavior generated by methadone and heroin. Int. J. Clin. Pharmacol. Biopharmacy **12:** 63–69.

DEVELOPMENTAL FACTORS INFLUENCING INTERACTIONS OF DRUGS*

Sumner J. Yaffe

Division of Clinical Pharmacology
Department of Pediatrics
University of Pennsylvania
School of Medicine and
Children's Hospital of Philadelphia
Philadelphia, Pennsylvania 19104

In order to delineate the clinical principles of drug interactions in the pediatric patient it is essential to define drug disposition and action in the sick infant and child. During recent years it has become quite clear that age is a major determinant of drug action. Although receptor sensitivity occasionally may account for this phenomenon, it is most often the result of differences in pharmacokinetic processes. While there are a large number of animal studies which have demonstrated that the developmental status of the host is an important mediator of drug action, our knowledge of drug disposition in the sick newborn, older infant, child, and adolescent is scanty indeed. Comprehensive and systematic studies of drug disposition in these different age groups are very limited. In fact, this information gap, coupled with well intended amendments to the Food and Drug Laws in 1962, has led to the concept of the "therapeutic orphan." This term refers to the omission of studies in infants and children by the manufacturer who then substituted on the package insert a statement specifically proscribing use in all or in major segments of the pediatric population, thereby "orphaning" them from possible therapeutic benefit. The manufacturer in doing so was in fact complying with the Food and Drug Regulations which required substantial evidence of safety and efficacy in the age group or population in whom the drug was to be used. The reasons for this lack of information regarding drug disposition in the pediatric population are manifold but include lack of adequate support for the requisite studies, lack of adequately trained personnel, and ethical considerations which have made it difficult to evaluate drugs in the pediatric population.

In the following paragraphs I have attempted to summarize our current state of knowledge regarding dispositional processes in infants and children of various ages. It is this area of research which has attracted my attention for the past several years. I have selected the format of describing the traditional processes of absorption, distribution, metabolism, and excretion not only in newborn infants but also in infants and children of other age groups. It is my belief that the general impression has arisen that the newborn infant is more susceptible to the action of drugs and chemicals than is the adult organism. This concept has been derived from clinical observations in which administration of drugs to the newborn infant has been associated with unexpected adverse and, at times, fatal reactions. The widespread publicity generated has led to changes in the Food and Drug Laws in both 1938 and 1962. It has also served to per-

* Supported in part by U.S. Public Health Service Grant HD10053-01.

petuate the belief concerning the unusual sensitivity of the newborn infant to xenobiotics. My concern is that attached to this belief is the accepted truism that beyond the neonatal period, size alone is the determinant of drug action, and dosage per unit of body weight is similar throughout the remainder of our lifetime. This is not so and should not even be anticipated, if one simply reflects upon the profound changes in bodily function which occur as we undergo the normal sequence of developmental changes which are characteristic of the aging process. Knowledge of the effects of age and the effects of diseases, which are often unique to each stage of postnatal development, upon drug action and disposition is a vital and necessary prerequisite to a discussion of interactions of drugs of abuse in the pediatric population.

During intrauterine existence, the fetus has at its disposal the metabolic and excretory capabilities of the maternal organism (as discussed by Dr. Finnegan in the immediately preceding paper). Once the umbilical cord is severed, the neonate must utilize his own mechanisms to handle drug and chemical substances. Let us now discuss these, but in our discussion of each mechanism I should like to consider other ages as well as the neonatal.

The gastrointestinal tract of the neonate undergoes marked changes in function shortly after birth (e.g., prolongation of transit time, decrease in gastric pH, increase in permeability). In addition, it represents a relatively larger portion of the body at birth than in later life. Therefore, it is not surprising that extent and rate of absorption of drug substances are not the same as in the adult organism. No systematic studies have been conducted of the absorption of pharmacologic agents in the newborn infant or at any other age in the developing organism. Because of the lack of bioavailability data in the pediatric population we have steadfastely refused to approve of substituting one drug for another on a generic basis.

The data that are available deal mainly with the absorption of antibiotics since these are used so frequently in the newborn infant. Certainly for these substances absorption appears to be quite good in contrast to compounds which have an active transport process. Studies of drug absorption following parenteral administration to sick newborn infants are not available but are sorely needed because, under hypoxia, acidotic, or hypothermic conditions, blood flow to muscle and/or skin may drastically decrease in the neonate, decreasing absorption of drugs given by these two routes.

We recently investigated the absorption of riboflavin in the newborn infant.[1] We selected this vitamin for study not only because of its safety but also because a non-invasive approach could be utilized to determine the rate and extent of absorption. Riboflavin is absorbed by a saturable, specialized transport process in the proximal small intestine, and excretion of the vitamin into the urine can be used to measure its absorption from the gastrointestinal tract. The time course of the urinary excretion of riboflavin in the newborn was found to be strikingly different from that observed in older infants, children, and adults. While the maximum urinary excretion rate in the older subject was five to six fold higher than in the neonate, the duration of the maximum rate was much longer in the newborn. Consequently, the total amount of riboflavin excreted into the urine, when expressed as a percentage of the administered dose (6–8%), was quite similar at all ages. The maximum rate of excretion in the newborn was 8.65 $\mu g/min/m^2$. When corrected for differences in body size, this rate is relatively constant over the age range 0.25 to 40 years (40.7 ± 11.7 $\mu g/min/m^2$). The low rate in the newborn may be explained by a much lower activity of the specialized intestinal transport process for riboflavin in the newborn. In addition, one must also consider that capacity of this process in the neonate might actually be negligible and that the slow absorption may be due almost entirely to passive diffusion occurring over a much longer segment of the gastrointestinal tract. Since riboflavin was administered as the phosphate salt, the possibility also exists that the phosphatase mediated conversion to riboflavin in the intestinal mucosa is rate limiting in the neonate and delays the absorption. Regardless of the mechanism for the slow absorption, the total amount absorbed is similar to that absorbed at other ages when dosage variations in the older subject are taken into consideration by expressing results as percentage of adminstered dose. This is true because absorption in the neonate proceeds for more than 16 hours, whereas it only lasts 3 to 4 hours in the older child and adult. These results obtained with riboflavin serve to exemplify and emphasize the differences which may occur in drug absorption as a result of the age of the host.

The next parameter which I should like to examine (all but briefly because of the small amount of time allotted) is that of distribution. Through this process the drug which has entered the circulatory system is delivered to the tissues and produces an effect when the necessary concentration is reached at the receptor site. Distribution is regulated by multiple factors, including rate of transport across biological membranes and extent of binding to protein. The neonate has a much higher extracellular volume and total body water content than the older infant and adult. Fat content is lower in the premature infant (1%) than in the full-term infant (16%).

With these changes in body composition, changes in drug distribution are to be expected. Several studies have also shown a differential permeability from blood to brain as a function of the age of the host. This is of particular importance for drugs of abuse, whose action in the newborn following administration to the mother may also be modified by differences in brain receptors and in brain permeability at this age. It is of interest to note that preliminary experiments in our laboratories have shown that the malnourished pre-weanling rodent is more susceptible to the action of barbiturates, presumably because of variations in distribution within the brain and binding to brain receptors.

Data from our laboratories regarding drug-protein interaction clearly demonstrate that plasma protein binding in the newborn infant differs from that in the adult.[2] Should these observations be operative *in vivo* they would explain in part why drugs administered to the newborn infant are often associated with side effects, even though the dose employed takes into consideration the smaller size of the newborn infant. The changes in binding may be due to lower concentrations of plasma-protein (particularly albumin) seen in the newborn infant; however, the methods employed in the formulation of the Scatchard plot are normalized for the amount of protein present. It is more likely, therefore, that the binding characteristics are due to variations in the nature of the neonatal plasma-protein itself. In addition, endogenous substances, especially hormones transferred across the placenta or fatty acids, may occupy binding sites during the first few days of life and thus reduce binding capacity.

We investigated the plasma-protein binding of diphenylhydantoin (DPH) in heparinized plasma from normal and hyperbilirubinemic infants by means of an ultrafiltration technique utilizing carbon-14-labeled DPH. Fresh cord blood (mixed arterial and venous) was obtained from the maternal end of the cord immediately after birth before the placenta was delivered. Serum was separated by centrifugation and binding to DPH determined. Plasma or serum samples were incubated for 30 minutes with labeled and unlabeled DPH in an approximate ratio of 1:4. Prolongation of the incubation time up to one hour did not affect the results.[3] The final concentration of DPH was 16 μg/ml, which is within the therapeutic range desired for the management of convulsive disorders. The unbound fraction of DPH measured in cord plasma from 13 normal infants was 10.6 ± 1.4%. The corresponding value in adult plasma is 7.4 ± 0.7%.

The range of values in individual samples was much greater in newborn plasma than in the adult. Binding of DPH was also investigated in 20 hyperbilirubinemic infants, in which the concentration of total bilirubin (mainly as the unconjugated form) ranged from 4.5 to 24.5 mg/100 ml of plasma. There is a definite correlation between the size of the unbound fraction of DPH and the total concentration of bilirubin. At concentrations of bilirubin greater than 20 mg/100 ml, the unbound fraction of DPH was twice as high as in plasma from non-hyperbilirubinemic infants. The correlation becomes even greater when bilirubin to albumin ratio is plotted against the percentage of unbound DPH. This strengthens the hypothesis that DPH and bilirubin may compete for the same binding sites on the albumin molecule. While the lower degree of binding of DPH in cord plasma and in plasma from newborn infants may not appear striking when one considers percentage of the drug bound, it is of great significance when expressed as percentage unbound, since this is a fraction which reaches the receptor. In other words, there is up to twice as much free unbound drug in cord plasma as in adult plasma.

When hyperbilirubinemia is present, the unbound fraction of DPH is up to three times greater than in adult plasma. It is reasonable to expect that similar differences in plasma-protein binding between adults and newborn infants may be found with other drugs. Furthermore, when one considers that multiple drugs are administered to sick infants, the interaction may increase still further the amount of free unbound drug present in the newborn infant serum or plasma. Other factors such as acidosis, hypoxia, and hypercarbia, often present in the sick newborn infant, may additionally decrease the degree of drug protein binding in the newborn infant and increase the possibility of drug effect.

Studies of drug protein binding in older infants are very few indeed. Winsberg and co-workers investigated imipramine binding in children age 7–10 years.[4] They found that plasma protein binding was much less variable among the children than had been reported in adults and that there was less actual binding in the children (81%) than in adults (86%). It is interesting to note that in their publication, they mentioned that preliminary studies appeared to indicate that adult binding values were obtained at about the time of puberty. We have also found that protein binding of diphenylhydantoin in older children and adolescents appears to differ from that observed in adults.[5] While we did not assess protein binding directly, we employed the salivary concentration of the anticonvulsant, which has been shown to be similar to the free concentration of the drug in the serum. These two suggestions of alteration in drug protein binding in older children and adolescents warrant additional studies of this phenomenon as a function of the age and disease status of the pediatric host.

Drug metabolism is of considerable clinical importance because this is the mechanism by which the action of most drugs is terminated within the intact organism. Studies of this process in the newborn infant have in general shown that the drug metabolic capability of the neonate is low and that it increases quite rapidly during the post-natal and suckling period and reaches maximum activity at different ages, depending on the pathway being studied. This generality does not apply to all drugs, however, as several recent studies have shown. Rane and co-workers in Sweden have studied disposition of an anticonvulsant, carbamazepine, in four newborn infants who received the drug transplacentally.[6] The mothers had received the drug in a dosage of 400–1,000 mg/day throughout gestation. The half-lives ranged from 8 to 28 hours, much lower than the recorded half-lives of the drug in adults (24–46 hours) following a single oral dose. Carbamazepine is capable of stimulating its own metabolism, so that after multiple dosing in adults elimination half-lives decrease significantly. The half-lives during elimination of carbamazepine in the newborn are in the range observed at the multiple dosing in adults. The data are therefore consistent with the possible intrauterine induction of the metabolism of the drug and do not necessarily relate to the intrinsic capability of the neonate to metabolize the drug.

Similar results were found with diphenylhydantoin in newborn infants born to mothers who received the drug for therapeutic purposes during pregnancy. In seven newborns who were studied, the half-lives of transplacentally transferred DPH ranged from 6.6 to 34 hours when measured both in plasma and also by determination of the urinary excretion. Rane was able to correlate the decline in plasma concentration of the drug with the rate of urinary excretion of the metabolite, further evidence that metabolism of the drug in the newborn was proceeding as efficiently as in the adult. Here again, as with carbamazepine, the chronic exposure of these newborns *in utero* to DPH administered to the mother may have been responsible for the high rate of metabolism found after birth. Thus these data cannot be extrapolated to the neonate who will be treated with DPH without prior intrauterine exposure, although the same authors did find that administration of DPH to the newborn who had not received intrauterine drug yielded plasma concentrations in the subtherapeutic range suggestive of an increased rate of metabolism.

We have recently had occasion to study the metabolism of theophylline in low-birth-weight infants with apnea. The serum half-life of the parent compound was in the range of 26–36 hours, in marked contrast to half-lives of about 5 hours found in adults and half-lives of 3 hours noted in adolescent children with asthma. Since theophylline is metabolized by demethylation and mixed-function oxidation, pathways similar to those required for the metabolism of carbamazepine and diphenylhydantoin, it is difficult to reconcile these marked discrepancies in data. Other pathways of metabolism such as glucuronidation and sulfation vary considerably in the neonate.

We investigated glucuronide formation in 14 newborn infants following administration of salicylamide in a single oral dose of 20 mg/kg of body weight.[7] Glucuronide conjugation was measured by determining the amount of salicylamide glucuronide found in the urine. This varied widely, ranging from as high as 45% of the dose to as little as 8%. In addition, there was an inverse relationship between the serum indirect bilirubin found on the fifth day of life, when the test was performed, and the urinary percentage of the dose of salicylamide appearing as the glucuronide. It should be emphasized that in a normal adult approximately 40–50% of a single oral dose of salicylamide appears as a glucuronide. Thus several of the newborn infants were glucuronidating at rates comparable to that found in an adult. This widespread variation in the ability to form the glucuronide form of salicylamide is important to consider when drug dosage regimens are established in the newborn infant. The five to six fold difference in ability to glucuronidate would suggest great difficulty in arriving at a uniform dosage schedule other than on the basis of assessment of individual metabolic capability.

Another metabolic process which should be discussed is sulfation. Although it has not been examined directly in the human neonate, a number of animal studies suggest that it is operative at birth to an extent equivalent to that found in the adult organism. Furthermore, the fact that many sulfated derivatives are found in body fluids in the human organism during fetal and early neonatal life suggests that sulfation is active in the human organism as well.

There are several examples of drug metabolism at other ages beyond the newborn period wihch are worthy of mention. The metabolism of theophylline has been studied in a number of asthmatic children and has been found to be much more rapid than in the adult asthma patient.[8] While there was a widespread variation among patients, the mean half-life of theophylline was found to be 200 minutes in children in contrast to 325 minutes in adult patients. Alvares[9] studied antipyrine and phenylbutazone metabolism in 10 children aged 1 to 8 years. The mean antipyrine half-life in the children was 6.6 hours, significantly lower than the mean half-life in adult patients: 13.6 hours. The mean phenylbutazone half-lives in the children and adults, 1.7 and 3.2 days respectively, also differed significantly. Thus children in the age range studied appeared to metabolize the two drugs at almost twice the rate of adults. We have noticed similar results in studying the metabolism of acetamenophen in adolescent patients. Half-lives were significantly lower than in adults. Mean half-life in 11 adolescents was 1.6 hours; in adult patients, 2.4 hours. Thus, as far as drug metabolism is concerned, children do a much better job with a variety of drug substrates than adults. This increased metabolic capability of the child and adolescent must be considered when drugs are prescribed for them.

The final common pathway for the removal from the organism of xenobiotic substances, whether unchanged or metabolized, is via the kidney. It has long been known that renal function in the newborn infant is much less than in the adult. Thus drugs which are not significantly metabolized and depend upon renal excretion for termination of action will have a noticeably longer effect in the newborn infant. Antibiotics are the major prototype of this class of pharmacologic agent, and because of their frequent use during the neonatal period they have been studied extensively. As anticipated, almost all agents follow a pattern of post-natal maturation where adult values were approached at 3 weeks of age irrespective of gestational age. We have recently found several additional exceptions to the rule that adult values are achieved at 3 weeks of post-natal age. These concern the excretion of digoxin and dicloxacillin in older infants and in adolescents with cystic fibrosis.

In an attempt to understand the large dosage requirement of digoxin in infants beyond the newborn period we measured the renal clearances of digoxin and creatinine in 11 infants, age 1–5 months, with congenital heart disease and heart failure. The renal clearances of digoxin were low at 1 month of age (50 ml/min/1.73 m^2) but increased progressively until the adult range was attained at about 5 months of age (130–150 ml/min/1.73 m^2). At any given age, however, the renal clearance of digoxin was twice as great as the simultaneously determined creatinine clearance. This stands in marked contrast to older subjects, in whom creatinine and digoxin clearances are similar. These data explain (in part) the larger digoxin dosage requirement of young infants and also serve to exemplify the fact that renal clearance of drugs may differ at different ages beyond the neonatal period.

Another example of this phenomenon concerns the enhanced renal excretion of dicloxacillin in children with cystic fibrosis.[10] Single oral doses of 6.25 mg/kg of dicloxacillin suspension were given to 10 cystic fibrosis (CF) patients and 8 normal subjects. Peak serum concentrations and areas under the concentration-versus-time curves for dicloxacillin varied, averaging 2½ times lower in the CF patients. The time of occurrence of the peak serum concentration was similar in both groups, and the total urinary recovery of dicloxacillin was normal or increased in the CF patients, suggesting that intestinal absorption of the drug was unaffected by the disease. The low serum concentrations in the CF patients were caused by unusually high renal clearances of dicloxacillin: an average of 282 ± 135 compared to 95 ± 28 ml/min/1.73 m^2 in the normal subjects. Creatinine clearances were also elevated in the CF patients by 55% on average, while urea clearances were normal. The serum protein binding of dicloxacillin was similar in both groups of subjects. Because rapid excretion results in low and variable serum concentrtions of the antibiotic, treatment of CF patients with dicloxacillin may warrant use of increased or more frequent doses and monitoring of serum antibiotic levels.

In this overview, I have attempted to summarize, albeit very briefly, what is known concerning drug disposition in the pediatric patient. It is essential that the developmental status of the host be taken into consideration when examining interactions of drugs in infants and children. The mechanisms of interactions are similar to those seen in the adult patient.[11, 12] The developmental status of the pediatric patient also plays a significant role in the manifestations of disease seen in sick infants and children. These are often profound and consequently may play a major role in modifying drug action and interaction.

References

1. Jusko, W. J., N. Khanna, G. Levy, L. Stern & S. J. Yaffe. 1970. Riboflavin absorption and excretion in the neonate. Pediatrics **45:** 945–949.
2. Krasner, J., G. P. Giacoia & S. J. Yaffe. 1973. Drug-protein binding in the newborn infant. Ann. N.Y. Acad. Sci. **226:** 101–114.
3. Rane, A., P. K. N. Lunde, B. Jalling, S. J. Yaffe & F. Sjöqvist. 1971. Plasma protein binding of diphenylhydantoin in normal and hyperbilirubinemic infants. J. Pediatr. **78:** 877–882.
4. Winsberg, B. G., J. M. Perel, M. J. Hurwic & A. Klutch. 1974. Imipramine protein binding and pharmacokinetics in children. *In* The Phenothiazines and Structurally Related Drugs. I. S. Forrest, C. J. Carr & E. Usdin, Eds. Raven Press. New York, N.Y.
5. Ciancio, S. G., S. J. Yaffe & C. Catz. 1972. Gingival hyperplasia and diphenylhydantoin. J. Periodontol. **43:** 411–415.
6. Hoppel, C., A. Rane & F. Sjöqvist. 1975. Kinetics of phenytoin and carbamazepine in the newborn. *In* Basic and Therapeutic Aspects of Perinatal Pharmacology. P. L. Morselli, S. Garattini & F. Sereni, Eds. Raven Press. New York, N.Y.
7. Stern, L., N. Khanna, G. Levy & S. J. Yaffe. 1970. Effect of phenobarbital

on hyperbilirubinemia and glucuronide formation in newborns. Amer. J. Dis. Child. **120:** 26–31.
8. Ellis, Elliot F. 1975. Personal communication.
9. Alvares, A. P., S. Kapelner, S. Sassa & A. Kappas. 1975. Drug metabolism in normal children, lead poisoned children and normal adults. Clin. Pharmacol. Ther. **17:** 179–183.
10. Jusko, W. J., L. L. Mosovich, L. M. Gerbracht, M. E. Mattar & S. J. Yaffe. 1975. Enhanced renal excretion of dicloxacillin in patients with cystic fibrosis. Pediatrics **56:** 1038–1044.
11. Reidenberg, M. M. This volume.
12. Hurwitz, A. & D. L. Azarnoff. This volume.

CLINICAL PRINCIPLES OF DRUG INTERACTIONS IN THE ADULT PATIENT*

Aryeh Hurwitz† and Daniel L. Azarnoff

Clinical Pharmacology–Toxicology Center
Departments of Medicine and Pharmacology
University of Kansas Medical Center
College of Health Sciences and Hospital
Kansas City, Kansas 66103

New drug interactions are reported almost daily, and encyclopedic compendia listing these interactions are published frequently. The practicing physician faced with this frightening deluge of information is tempted to stop prescribing drugs. An understanding of the mechanism of the prototype drug interactions will allow the physician to select the drug and dosage to minimize any adverse effects that may result.

Cardiovascular

Digitalis

Cardiac glycosides have a narrow range of effective plasma and tissue levels below which desired effect is lost and above which toxicity ensues. These levels vary significantly among patients receiving the same dose. In patients with renal impairment digoxin levels rise while digitoxin, whose elimination is primarily extrarenal, is not affected similarly.[1] Since hypokalemia potentiates digitalis toxicity, drugs which cause potassium loss like diuretics, cathartics,[2] some steroids,[3] or amphotericin B[4] may cause glycoside toxicity in patients with plasma levels in the usual therapeutic range. Digoxin levels are one-third lower than anticipated when the drug is given orally to patients with malabsorption.[5] The anticholinergic drug, propantheline, which slows intestinal motility and prolongs digoxin contact with the absorptive surface of the gut, results in a 33% elevation of mean digoxin levels.[6] Conversely, metoclopramide accelerates gastrointestinal motility and lowers digoxin levels to the same extent. Phenobarbital stimulates hepatic metabolism of digitoxin, lowering plasma levels of unchanged drug, although the clinical significance is not known since several of its metabolites are active.[7]

Antiarrhythmics

Some antiarrhythmic drugs, including quinidine and procainamide, have anticholinergic and cardiac-depressant (negative inotropic) effects. These effects may add to those of other drugs with similar properties and may be significant in patients with congestive heart failure. Cardiac failure reduces hepatic vas-

* Supported by Grant GM 15956 from the U.S. Public Health Service.
† Recipient of U.S. Public Health Service Career Development Award, GM 70250.

cular perfusion and decreases the rate of elimination of lidocaine.[8] Other drugs with an extensive first-pass effect should be altered in the same way. A similar decrease in hepatic blood flow results from the administration of l-propranolol, which can thereby alter its own disposition as well as that of lidocaine.[9] Although the studies on hepatic perfusion have been done in animals, they suggest that similar findings may occur and be important in man. Even the effect of phenobarbital on the disposition of other drugs may be in part due to its effects on hepatic perfusion,[10] as well as its stimulation of biliary drug excretion.[11]

Modifiers of Blood Pressure

Pressor amines and antihypertensive agents act mainly at the adrenergic nerve ending, where they modify the action and/or turnover of norepinephrine. The main mechanism for terminating norepinephrine action depends on the amine "pump" which enhances catecholamine re-entry into the nerve cell where storage in granules takes place. The amine uptake mechanism, which is inhibited by tricyclic antidepressants[12] and phenothiazines,[13] must function for guanethidine to be effective and for some indirectly acting pressor amines, like tyramine, to function. However, the amino acid, methyldopa, can exert its antihypertensive effects even when the amine pump is blocked and can therefore be used in patients taking phenothiazines or tricyclic antidepressants. It is thus evident that psychotropic drugs (MAO inhibitors, tricyclic antidepressants, phenothiazines, which also block alpha adrenergic receptors), nasal decongestants (phenylephrine, pseudoephedrine), antihypertensives (guanethidine, reserpin), and foods containing tyramine (cheeses, wines) when used together may result in a bewildering array of interactions and cause life-threatening swings in blood pressure.

ANTICOAGULANTS

The activity of the coumarin anticoagulants is controlled by their rate of metabolism in the hepatic endoplastic reticulum. The activity of this drug-oxidizing system, involved in the biotransformation of numerous endogenous compounds and drugs, is stimulated by many chemicals, including barbiturates, pesticides, and some carcinogens and is inhibited by others, including disulfiram, chloramphenicol, and isoniazid.[14] Induction of the microsomal drug-metabolizing system accelerates coumarin inactivation and reverses anticoagulant effect,[15] while inhibition enhances anticoagulant effect and may precipitate serious hemorrhage. Warfarin is dispensed as a mixture of two stereoisomers with a five-fold difference in anticoagulant activity. Phenylbutazone stimulates metabolism of the less active isomer while inhibiting inactivation of the more potent one.[16] Thus, this anti-inflammatory drug may cause bleeding by changing the ratio of isomers of warfarin while total levels remain unchanged. Since coumarins exert their anticoagulant effect indirectly by inhibiting synthesis of the vitamin K dependent clotting factors, and their stereoisomers differ in potency, the correlation between plasma levels and effect is very complex.[17] Coumarin anticoagulants are extensively bound to plasma proteins so that displacement from these binding sites may increase the level of unbound, active drug significantly. Bleeding seen in some anticoagulated patients given chloral hydrate has been ascribed to warfarin displacement by the trichloroacetic acid metabolite of the hypnotic.[18] Aspirin may potentiate bleeding by anticoagulated patients because of its ability to disrupt platelet function[19] and decrease prothrombin levels.[20] Barbiturates inhibit the gastrointestinal absorption of drugs with poor dissolution, such as dicumarol[21] or griseofulvin. The former can be prevented by prescribing warfarin sodium, which is highly water soluble, in place of dicumarol.

Gastrointestinal Drugs

Anticholinergics

Thus far we have discussed drugs having narrow margins of safety, in which small modifications in plasma levels of active compound may cause serious consequences by disrupting finely regulated hemostatic or cardiovascular control mechanisms. By comparison, gastrointestinal function can be modified with relative impunity. However, since most drugs enter the body from the gut, drugs or diseases which modify gastrointestinal activity can have profound effects on the rate and/or extent of absorption and thereby on the pharmacological activity of these drugs. The effects of anticholinergic agents and metoclopramide on digoxin absorption have already been noted. Desipramine, a psychotropic drug with anticholinergic effects, delays the absorption and lowers peak levels of phenylbutazone.[22] Parasympatholytic drugs which slow gastrointestinal motility enhance the absorption of a slowly absorbed drug (digoxin) but have the opposite effect on peak levels of a rapidly absorbed drug (phenylbutazone) whose rate of absorption is limited by the rate of gastric emptying.

Antacids

Antacids are known to modify absorption, plasma levels, and pharmacological effects of concomitantly administered drugs. Chelation of aluminum in antacids[23] and of iron[24] or milk calcium by tetracyclines interferes with the absorption and efficacy of the antibiotic. A drug must be in solution to be absorbed, and since most drug absorption occurs in the small bowel, modification of dissolution or gastric emptying can affect the rate and extent of drug absorption. Antacids enhance the dissolution of sulfadiazine,[25] thereby accelerating its absorption, or inhibit the dissolution of quinine,[26] quinidine, and tetracyclines,[27] resulting in decreased plasma levels. Aluminum hydroxide gel delays gastric emptying[28] and thus retards the absorption of rapidly absorbed drugs, like isoniazid,[29] in a manner similar to agents with anticholinergic properties. Since the ingested aluminum must be in solution to inhibit the smooth muscle contractions normally required for gastric evacuation, antacids with ingredients in addition to aluminum hydroxide gel have a much lower aluminum ion concentration and do not usually delay gastric emptying or drug absorption.[30]

L-dopa is metabolized by gastric mucosa in an acidic medium. Antacids, by raising gastric pH, accelerating stomach emptying, and moving unmetabolized active drug to its site of optimal absorption in the small intestine, can result in twofold higher peak DOPA serum levels.[31] Even "non-systemic" antacids are absorbed sufficiently to increase urinary pH by 0.9 units on the average. This rise in urinary pH due to ingestion of Maalox® is enough to increase urinary salicylate excretion and decrease serum levels by 30 to 70%.[32]

Cholestyramine and colestipol are bile acid sequestering resins used to treat elevated serum cholesterol or the itching of incomplete biliary obstruction. These agents bind a variety of drugs, including digitoxin,[33] warfarin,[34] thyroxine,[35] and chlorothiazide,[36] reducing the amount absorbed and decreasing the pharmacological effects of these drugs.

Endocrine and Metabolic Drugs

Hypoglycemic Drugs

Agents that control blood sugar must be present in a narrow range lest hyperglycemia or life-threatening low blood sugar result. Some of the drugs already discussed can affect sulfonylurea absorption, metabolism, or protein binding, while others like ethanol, steroids,[37] diphenylhydantoin,[38] catecholamines, beta adrenergic blockers, and thiazide diuretics[39] have direct effects on insulin release or intermediary metabolism.

Corticosteroids

As noted, enhanced gluconeogenesis secondary to these drugs can cause blood-sugar elevation. Steroids may also cause sodium and fluid retention, potassium loss, gastrointestinal hemorrhage, and psychiatric disturbance, among other numerous effects,[40] thereby modifying the clinical effects of diuretics, cardiac glycosides, anticoagulants, and psychotropic drugs.

Thyroid

Thyroid status, as affected by endogenous hormone release or exogenously administered drugs, may alter responses to other drugs. Hyperthyroidism lessens the response to digitalis,[41] potentiates the effects of catecholamines,[42] warfarin,[43] and tricyclic antidepressants[44] and interferes with the gastrointestinal absorption of some drugs by accelerating intestinal transit.[45]

Musculoskeletal Drugs

Non-steroidal anti-inflammatory drugs and corticosteroids have already been noted to increase the likelihood of serious hemorrhage in patients receiving coumarins.[46] Salicylates interfere with the uricosuric effects of probenecid and sulfinpyrazone.[47] Aspirin has been shown to block the diuretic effect of spironolactone[48] and indomethacin the natriuretic and antihypertensive effect of furosemide in man,[49] perhaps by inhibiting prostaglandin synthesis. Phenylbutazone potentiates the hypoglycemic effect of acetohexamide by impairing the renal excretion of an active metabolite.[50] Allopurinol, another drug used in the treatment of gout, is also not devoid of possible interactions. This inhibitor of xanthine oxidase interferes with the degradation of 6-mercaptopurine[51] and azathioprine, causing bone-marrow depression[52] and agranulocytosis.

Neuropsychiatric Drugs

Neuropsychiatric drugs have been noted to induce the metabolism of other drugs (barbiturates), to inhibit uptake into nerve endings (e.g., tricyclic antidepressants block guanethidine), or to cause precipitous drops in blood pressure (alpha adrenergic blockade by phenothiazines when used in treatment of methamphetamine toxicity). Isoniazid has been shown to inhibit the metabolism of phenytoin leading to toxicity, especially in slow acetylators who have elevated isoniazid levels.[53] The anticholinergic drugs used in the treatment of Parkinsonism (e.g., trihexyphenidyl) can modify the absorption of other drugs, as can anticholinergics used for other indications. In patients taking L-dopa, not only can the absorption of active drug be enhanced in some patients by antacids, but once absorbed its efficacy can be reversed by small doses of pyridoxine[54] which, in turn, may be needed to prevent isoniazid-induced neurotoxicity.[55]

Epidemiological studies have demonstrated that the sedating effect of benzodiazepines is reduced in cigarette smokers.[56] Induction of hepatic metabolism of this drug by smoke components, as shown for phenacetin metabolism in man,[57] probably accounts for the reduced efficacy. Aside from the numerous harmful effects attributed to tars, carbon monoxide, and nicotine from cigarettes, drug interactions may be an indirect danger to the smoker. In fact, even the theophylline which long-term smokers may need to relieve their obstructive lung disease is more rapidly metabolized in smokers[58] and larger doses are required for a satisfactory response.

Alcohol

Often overlooked is that ubiquitous drug ethanol, found not only in the diet but also in elixirs. Inhibition of the oxidation of its metabolite, acetaldehyde, by disulfiram, chlorpropamide,[59] and metronidazole[60] can cause severe discomfort and even death. Alcohol, when ingested chronically, induces microsomal drug-oxidizing enzymes,[61] necessitating higher doses of drugs metabolized by this system. However, when ingested acutely in large amounts, ethanol inhibits these enzymes and may cause intoxication with these same drugs.[62] Alcohol is a central nervous system depressant, and its concomitant ingestion with other sedatives has proved fatal. The problems of chronic alcohol ingestion, especially when exacerbated by acute over-indulgence, may become magnified by administration of other drugs. Examples are the use of anticoagulants in the presence of alcohol-induced gastritis, with other vasodilators in the treatment of hypertension, or of hypoglycemic drugs in the absence of adequate hepatic glycogen stores.

DISCUSSION

In the foregoing sections a few of the numerous known drug-drug and drug-disease interactions have been mentioned to exemplify those which the clinician may commonly encounter. However, other considerations must be borne in mind. These have been illustrated and include: 1) Most drugs have reasonable therapeutic ratios, so that minor alterations in plasma drug levels or pharmacokinetic parameters, such as half-life or volume of distribution, even when statistically significant, may be clinically unimportant. Interactions between single doses of drugs may not occur on repeated or continuous administration. Plasma level data which look at total drug may not reflect levels of unbound drug, active stereoisomer, active metabolite, or storage and distribution factors which make an interaction very important or inconsequential. Animal or *in vitro* data frequently point to interactions in man[63] but unless confirmed may be totally meaningless for patients. Furthermore, psychiatric or subjective clinical responses are nearly impossible to define accurately in animals. 2) Drug, food, and chemical interactions frequently overlooked by physicians are due to exposure to a number of common agents which in themselves are innocuous and available over the drugstore counter or in the environment. These include specific food constituents like milk, carbonated soft drinks,[64] or tyramine,[65] time relationship between drug ingestion and meals, alcohol, vitamins, sedatives, cold remedies, aspirin, antacids, cathartics, tobacco (containing nicotine and various carcinogens), and insecticides. Often these drugs are not only overlooked but may also be concealed by product label. Patients will avoid aspirin but readily take Anacin® or Alka-Seltzer®. Another related problem is the common practice of ingestion of drugs given to a single patient by several physicians or taking of medication prescribed to another family member. Clinically significant interactions can be missed under these circumstances unless specifically sought. 3) Interactions can result from pharmacological effects of drugs other than those desired by the prescribing physician. These "side effects" are often unimportant in themselves but become significant when added to the effects or side effects of other drugs. Additive pharmacodynamic properties of drugs are often overlooked when hunting for sophisticated pharmacokinetic alterations to explain interactions. 4) Not all interactions are undesirable. Probenecid is used to slow the excretion of penicillin, and protamine sulfate to inhibit the action of heparin. When they are predictable and reproducible, we may choose to utilize or to avoid the interactions. Unfortunately, many interactions between drugs and with disease states remain to be elucidated, making the work of the physician more difficult, more challenging, and more interesting.

REFERENCES

1. DOHERTY, J. E. 1973. Ann. Intern. Med. **79:** 229.
2. FLEISCHER, N., H. BROWN, D. Y. GRAHAM & S. A. DELENA. 1969. Ann. Intern. Med. **70:** 791.
3. BAGSHAWE, K. D., J. R. CURTIS & E. S. GARNETT. 1965. Lancet **I:** 18.
4. MILLER, R. P. & J. H. BATES. 1969. Ann. Intern. Med. **71:** 1089.

5. Heizer, W. D., T. W. Smith & S. E. Goldfinger. 1971. N. Engl. J. Med. **285:** 257.
6. Manninen, V., A. Apajalahti, J. Melin & M. Karesoja. 1973. Lancet **I:** 398.
7. Solomon, H. M. & W. B. Abrams. 1972. Amer. Heart J. **83:** 277.
8. Branch, R. A., D. G. Shand & A. S. Nies. 1973. J. Pharmacol. Exp. Ther. **187:** 133.
9. Nies, A. S., G. H. Evans & D. G. Shand. 1973. Amer. Heart J. **85:** 97.
10. Branch, R. A., D. G. Shand, G. R. Wilkinson & A. S. Nies. 1974. J. Clin. Invest. **53:** 1101.
11. Klaassen, C. D. 1970. J. Pharmacol. Exp. Ther. **175:** 289.
12. Mitchell, J. R., J. H. Cavanaugh, L. Arias & J. A. Oates. 1970. J. Clin. Invest. **49:** 1596.
13. Fann, W. E., D. S. Janowsky, J. M. Davis & J. A. Oates. 1971. Lancet **II:** 436.
14. Conney, A. H. 1967. Pharmacol. Rev. **19:** 317.
15. Koch-Weser, J. & E. M. Sellers. 1971. N. Engl. J. Med. **285:** 487, 547.
16. Lewis, R. J., W. F. Trager, K. K. Chan, A. Breckenridge, M. Orme, M. Rowland & W. Schary. 1974. J. Clin. Invest. **53:** 1607.
17. Levy, G., R. A. O'Reilly, P. M. Aggeler & G. M. Keech. 1970. Clin. Pharmacol. Ther. **11:** 372.
18. Sellers, E. M. & J. Koch-Weser. 1970. N. Engl. J. Med. **283:** 827.
19. Stuart, M. J., S. Murphy, F. A. Oski, A. E. Evans, M. H. Donaldson & F. H. Gardner. 1972. N. Engl. J. Med. **287:** 1105.
20. Quick, A. J. 1960. J. Pharmacol. Exp. Ther. **128:** 95.
21. Aggeler, P. M. & R. A. O'Reilly. 1969. J. Lab. Clin. Med. **74:** 229.
22. Consolo, S., P. L. Morselli, M. Zaccala & S. Garattini. 1970. Eur. J. Pharmacol. **10:** 239.
23. Waisbren, B. A. & J. S. Hueckel. 1950. Proc. Soc. Exp. Biol. Med. **73:** 73.
24. Neuvonen, P. J., G. Gothoni, R. Hackinan & K. af Björk. 1970. Brit. Med. J. **4:** 532.
25. Peterson, O. L. & M. Finland. 1942. Amer. J. Med. Sci. **204:** 581.
26. Hurwitz, A. 1971. J. Pharmacol. Exp. Ther. **179:** 485.
27. Barr, W. H., J. Adir & L. Garretson. 1971. Clin. Pharmacol. Ther. **12:** 779.
28. Hurwitz, A., R. G. Robinson, T. S. Vats, F. C. Whittier & W. F. Herrin. 1976. Gastroenterology. In press.
29. Hurwitz, A. & D. L. Schlozman. 1974. Amer. Rev. Resp. Dis. **109:** 41.
30. Hava, M. & A. Hurwitz. 1973. Eur. J. Pharmacol. **22:** 156.
31. Bianchine, J. R., L. R. Calimlim, J. P. Morgan, C. A. Dujovne & L. Lasagna. 1971. Ann. N.Y. Acad. Sci. **179:** 126.
32. Levy, G., T. Lampman, B. L. Kamath & L. K. Garrettson. 1975. N. Engl. J. Med. **293:** 323.
33. Caldwell, J. H. & N. J. Greenberger. 1971. J. Clin. Invest. **50:** 2638.
34. Benjamin, D., D. S. Robinson & J. McCormack. 1970. Clin. Res. **18:** 336.
35. Northcutt, R. C., J. N. Stiel, J. W. Hollifield & E. G. Stant. 1969. JAMA **208:** 1857.
36. Kauffman, R. E. & D. L. Azarnoff. 1973. Clin. Pharmacol. Ther. **14:** 886.
37. Miller, S. E. & J. M. Neilson. 1964. Postgrad. Med. J. **40:** 660.
38. Farris, B. L. & C. L. Lutcher. 1971. Diabetes **20:** 177.
39. Weller, J. M. 1965. Ann. Intern. Med. **62:** 1076.
40. Azarnoff, D. L., Ed. 1975. Steroid Therapy. W. B. Saunders Co. Philadelphia, Pa.
41. Doherty, J. E. & W. H. Perkins. 1966. Ann. Intern. Med. **64:** 489.
42. Levey, G. S. 1971. Amer. J. Med. **50:** 413.
43. Walters, M. B. 1963. Amer. J. Cardiol. **11:** 112.

44. BREESE, G. R., T. D. TRAYLOR & A. J. PRANGE, JR. 1972. Psychopharmacologia **25:** 101.
45. LEVY, G., M. H. MACGILLIVARY & J. A. PROCKNAL. 1972. Pediatrics **50:** 896.
46. LEVY, M. 1974. N. Engl. J. Med. **290:** 1158.
47. YÜ, T.-F., P. G. DAYTON & A. B. GUTMAN. 1963. J. Clin. Invest. **42:** 1330.
48. TWEEDDALE, M. G. & R. I. OGILVIE. 1973. N. Engl. J. Med. **289:** 198.
49. PATAK, R. V., B. K. MOOKERJEE, C. J. BENTZEL, P. E. HYSERT, M. BABEJ & J. R. LEE. 1975. Prostaglandins **10:** 649.
50. FIELD, J. B., M. OHTA, C. BOYLE & A. REMERS. 1967. N. Engl. J. Med. **277:** 889.
51. RUNDLES, R. W., J. B. WYNGAARDEN, G. H. HITCHINGS, G. B. ELION & H. R. SILBERMAN. 1963. Trans. Assoc. Amer. Physicians **76:** 126.
52. Boston Collaborative Drug Surveillance Program. 1974. JAMA **227:** 1036.
53. KUTT, H., W. WINTERS & F. H. MCDOWELL. 1966. Neurology **16:** 594.
54. LEON, A. S., H. E. SPIEGEL, G. THOMAS & W. B. ABRAMS. 1971. JAMA **218:** 1924.
55. ROSS, R. R. 1958. JAMA **168:** 273.
56. Boston Collaborative Drug Surveillance Program. 1973. N. Engl. J. Med. **288:** 277.
57. PANTUCK, E. J., K.-C. HSIAO, A. MAGGIO, K. NAKAMURA, R. KUNTZMAN & A. H. CONNEY. 1974. Clin. Pharmacol. Ther. **15:** 9.
58. JENNE, J. H., NAGASAWA, R. MCHUGH, F. MACDONALD & W. WYSE. 1975. Life Sci. **17:** 195.
59. FITZGERALD, M. G., R. GADDIE & J. M. MALINS. 1962. Diabetes **11:** 40.
60. PENICK, S. B., R. N. CARRIER & J. B. SHELDON. 1969. Amer. J. Psychiatry **125:** 1063.
61. KATER, R. M. H., G. ROGGIN, F. TOBON, P. ZIEVE & F. L. IBER. 1969. Amer. J. Med. Sci. **258:** 35.
62. RUBIN, E., H. GANG, P. S. MISRA & C. S. LIEBER. 1970. Amer. J. Med. **49:** 801.
63. BURNS, J. J. 1968. Ann. N.Y. Acad. Sci. **151:** 959.
64. HOUSTON, J. B. & G. LEVY. 1975. J. Pharmacol. Sci. **64:** 1504.
65. BLACKWELL, B., E. MARLEY, J. PRICE & D. TAYLOR. 1967. Brit. J. Psychiatry **113:** 349.

METHODOLOGICAL PROBLEMS IN DRUG INTERACTIONS

Salvatore J. Mulé

New York State Office of Drug Abuse Services
Testing and Research Laboratory
Brooklyn, New York 11217

The abuse of several drugs during the chemotherapeutic treatment associated with drug dependence can cause additional difficulties for the analyst concerned with dispositional, pharmacokinetic, metabolic or drug screening of drugs subject to abuse. Of prime concern is the separation, identification and/or characterization of a single drug or its metabolites in the presence of one or more other drugs or metabolites. Normally the analyst must accept the presence of nicotine (metabolites) and caffeine, as well as endogenous hormones, steroids, chemicals from various sundry food stuffs, vitamins, and chemical transmitters in biological tissues and fluids. The addition of two or more drugs simply places a greater stress upon the specificity of the techniques utilized in the identification process. It is, therefore, the purpose of this communication to describe the methods currently in use for the extraction and subsequent identification of a given drug of dependence through the use of ultraviolet and infrared spectroscopy, gas-liquid chromatography, thin-layer chromatography, spectrophotofluorometry, liquid scintillation spectroscopy, immunoassays, and gas chromatography coupled with mass spectroscopy.

Extraction of Drugs from Biological Materials

The choice or approach to an extraction procedure not only involves the nature of the chemical compound (organic acid or base) but also the required degree of specificity and the required purity of the extract, which is related to the analytical method to be used following extraction. There are essentially two basic approaches: 1) solvent-solvent extractions, 2) resin extraction using either paper or column. Essentially, narcotic drugs (organic bases) may be extracted from biological material (urine, plasma, tissue homogenate) by adjusting the pH to 8–10, buffering, saturating the sample with NaCl, and extracting with a pure organic solvent or a mixture of the solvent and alcohol. The drug and/or metabolite may be subsequently re-extracted in 0.1N HCl and then following adjustment of the pH, back-extracted into an organic solvent. In the second approach, primarily designed for analysis of urine, the sample is applied to a column containing Amberlite XAD-2 resin (styrene-divinylbenzene copolymer). The resin may be eluted with a single organic solvent or a mixture of solvents. The solvents are usually shaken with sodium bicarbonate solution and the separated organic phase subsequently analyzed.[2, 3]

Detection Methods

Ultraviolet and Infrared Spectroscopy

Quantitatively, these techniques have somewhat limited value when applied to drugs of abuse obtained from biological material because of the necessity of purifying the extracted drugs prior to analysis and the relatively high concentrations required for analysis. In the case of UV spectrums, information is readily obtained on the absorption maximum and minimum in acids, alkalis, or various solvents.[4] Also, data may be obtained on the shift in spectra in alkaline solution with those drugs that form the phenolate ion.[4] Unfortunately, many drugs of similar structure absorb in the same wavelength region.

IR spectroscopy allows identification of the drug based upon absorption or transmittance showing characteristic peaks within the spectrum at certain wave-numbers (cm^{-1}). IR spectroscopy, however, primarily allows the determination of characteristic features in the structural analysis of complex molecules, such as the appearance or absence of a band of appropriate frequency or intensity, e.g. (C≡N), (S—H), (C═O), (O—H), (N—H). Identification of the substance after exhaustive analysis in various media may be made by comparison with known available spectra.[5]

Thin-Layer Chromatography (TLC)

Thin-layer chromatography is the most widely used analytical tool for the separation and identification of narcotic drugs following the extraction of these drugs from biological materials.[6] This technique when used properly is rapid and relatively sensitive and allows the separation of several drugs and/or metabolites on a single plate in a given solvent system (TABLE 1). The drugs may be detected by ultraviolet light or fluorescence or sprayed with a single or sequential chromophoric reagents.[1, 7, 8] Many modifications of this technique have been introduced over the years, including two-dimensional chromatography, preparation of derivatives, and mini-thin layer plates; almost any and all conceivable substances (gels, powders, emulsions, anion and cation exchangers, resins, salts, bases, etc.) have been used as the solid support on glass plates, plastic sheets, or heavy paper.[7-9]

Gas-Liquid Chromatography (GLC)

Gas-liquid chromatography is an exquisitely sensitive, selective, and specific method for the analysis of drugs subject to abuse and their metabolites following extraction from biological materials. This analytical tool has been in use in our laboratory for several years, and many methods have been developed for the isolation and identification of narcotic drugs and/or their metabolites from biological fluids. TABLE 2 lists the basic GLC data for several narcotic agonists and antagonists—the derivative, retention time (min), column, temperature, carrier gas, detector, sensitivity, and biofluid of determination. It is readily apparent that all these drugs may be effectively separated and identified following the proper choice of GLC conditions. One can readily eliminate drug-drug interference or drug/metabolite interference.

Spectrophotofluorometry (SPF)

The fluorometric technique for the analysis of drugs of abuse following extraction, formation of a fluorophore, excitation, and emission at specific wavelengths provides both sensitivity and specificity for identification. Several

TABLE 1

THIN-LAYER CHROMATOGRAPHIC VALUES FOR VARIOUS NARCOTIC ANALGESICS

Drug (Free Base)	R_f Values (×100)						
	ETOH, PYD	ETOH, HAC	ETOH, NH_3	MeOH, BENZ	t-AMYL, n-BE	n-BUT, HAC	n-BUT, HCl
Iminoethanophenanthrofurans							
Morphine	29	27	11	21 86	7 85	54	34
Normorphine	8	48	4	7 48	STR 25	66	62
Codeine	30	29	39	25 86	8 91	53	30
Norcodeine	12	50	13	9 59	6 56	63	49
Heroin	37	35	76	35 90	15 95	61	32
Ethylmorphine	33	25	46	27 84	8 96	53	33
Dihydromorphine	15	21	10	10 67	STR 73	43	29
Dihydrocodeinone	17	25	41	19 76	STR 94	42	23
Dihydrohydroxycodeinone	46	24	87	29	16	32	34
Iminoethanophenanthrenes							
1-3-Hydroxy-*N*-methylmorphinan	11	47	80	10	7	51	60
1-3-Methoxy-*N*-methylmorphinan	13	43	91	8	7	55	59
1-3-Hydroxy-*N*-allylmorphinan	65	70	98	41	44	64	73
Diarylalkoneamines							
d1-Methadone	34	59	99	17	17	55	62
1-Acetylmethadol	64	60	99	40	38	52	62
d-Propoxyphene	73	68	97	54	56	53	61
Arylpiperidines							
Pethidine	42	41	97	36	20	46	44
Norpethidine	12	65	51	10	11	58	63
Ketobemidone	31	39	47	24	12	42	40
Benzomorphans							
2′-Hydroxy-5,9-dimethyl-2-(3,3-dimethylallyl)-6,7-benzomorphan	73	81	96	25	34	65	77
2′-Hydroxy-5,9-dimethyl-2-cyclopropylmethyl-6,7-benzomorphan	45	71	92	15	16	55	67

From Mulé.[14] By permission of *Analytical Chemistry*.

TABLE 2

GAS-LIQUID CHROMATOGRAPHIC DATA

Drug and Metabolite (M)	Derivative	Retention Time (min)	Internal Standard and Retention Time (min)	Column Packing	Oven Temperature (°C)	Carrier Gas and Flow (ml/min)	Detector Type	Lower Sensitivity	Determination in	
									Plasma	Urine
Morphine	PFPA	5.3	Nalorphine, 7.4	OV-22, 3%	215	Argon-methane, 40	Electron capture, ^{63}Ni	2 PG	+	+
Codeine	PFPA	9.1	Nalorphine, 7.4	OV-22, 3%	215	Argon-methane, 40	Electron capture, ^{63}Ni	20 PG	+	+
Heroin	BSTFA	3.6	Etorphine, 6.6	OV-17, 3%	275	Helium, 60	FID, H_2	10 NG	+	+
Methadone	—	4.7	SKF-525A, 8.8	SE-30, 3%	180	Helium, 32	FID, H_2	15 NG	+	+
(M) Pyrroline	—	3.2	SKF-525A, 8.8	SE-30, 3%	180	Helium, 32	FID, H_2	50 NG		+
(M) Pyrrolidene	—	2.3	SKF-525A, 8.8	SE-30, 3%	180	Helium, 32	FID, H_2	100 NG		+
Etorphine	BSTFA	6.6	B-Naltrexol, 3.6	OV-17, 3%	275	N^2, 60	FID, H_2	10 NG	+	+
Propoxyphene	—	3.4	SKF-525A, 5.2	SE-30, 3%	210	Helium, 33	FID, H_2	10 NG	+	+
(M) Nor-propoxyphene	—	10.1	SKF-525A, 5.2	SE-30, 3%	210	Helium, 33	FID, H_2	50 NG	+	+
Naltrexone	PFPA	5.2	Naloxone, 3.3	OV-22, 3%	215	Argon-methane, 35	Electron capture, ^{63}Ni	10 PG	+	
(M) B-naltrexol	PFPA	4.4	Naloxone, 3.3	OV-22, 3%	215	Argon-methane, 35	Electron capture, ^{63}Ni	5 PG	+	
Naloxone	PFPA	3.3	B-Naltrexol, 4.4	OV-22, 3%	215	Argon-methane, 35	Electron capture, ^{63}Ni	5 PG	+	
Naltrexol	BSTFA	5.1	Etorphine, 6.6	OV-17, 3%	275	Helium, 60	FID, H_2	20 NG		+
(M) B-naltrexol	BSTFA	3.6	Etorphine, 6.6	OV-17, 3%	275	Helium, 60	FID, H_2	10 NG		+
(M) 2-Hydroxy-3-methoxy naltrexol	BSTFA	4.3	Etorphine, 6.6	OV-17, 3%	275	Helium, 60	FID, H_2	<50 NG		+
Cocaine	—	3.5	—	SE-30, 3%	250	N_2, 60	FID, H_2	100 NG		+
Benzoylecgonine	BSTFA	1.8	—	OV-22, 3%	230	N_2, 60	FID, H_2	10 NG		+

PFPA, Pentafluoroproprionic anhydride.
BSTFA, Bis-trimethylsilyl-2,2,2, trifluoroacetamide.
FID, Flame ionization detector.

techniques have been developed for the detection of drugs of abuse by fluorescence.[10] Morphine reacts with sulfuric acid and ammonia to form a highly fluoresecent compound. Morphine may easily be determined in biological material through the use of the automated turret spectrofluorometer (ATS).[11] The assay is sensitive to 220 ng/ml of morphine, and 150 samples can be scanned per hour. However, nalorphine and normorphine yield a fluorescent product identical with morphine. A fully automated technique was developed and applied through use of the Technicon autoanalyzer, whereby morphine was converted to a fluorophore by potassium ferricyanide.[12] Cross reactivity for nalorphine and dihydromorphine was obtained with this assay. Similar oxido-reductions for morphine have been reported.[13, 14] Fluorometric techniques have also been reported for methadone[15] and meperidine.[16] These latter methods are apparently not specific, since quinine and amphetamine may interfere with the assay.

Liquid Scintillation Spectroscopy (LSS)

For the past several years we have utilized radioactive drugs extensively in our studies concerning the pharmacokinetics and metabolism of drugs of dependence as well as narcotic antagonists.[17] The usual approach to such studies is to attempt to develop an extraction technique that is highly specific for the primary drug under investigation. The organic extracts of the biological materials containing the radioactive drug are subjected to liquid scintillation spectroscopy for the estimation of radioactivity and subsequent determination of the concentration of the drug. Metabolic studies of the biological material usually require extraction resin fractionation and separation of the drug and/or metabolites by ITLC and subsequent radioscanning of the plates by LSS. FIGURE 1 shows a typical radioscan of ITLC of an organic extract of dog brain 1 hour after a 2 mg/kg s.c. injection of ^{3}H-methadone and 1 week after the same dose. Methadone and metabolites were apparently present in the brain at both times. The difficulty encountered with these techniques is often related to the quantity of radioactive material available for definitive identification. The use of urine as the primary metabolic material oftentimes provides sufficient labeled metabolite so that such identification can be made. However, the use of a given biofluid or tissue is dependent upon the nature of the investigation.

Immunoassays

The introduction of the immunoassay technique for the identification of drug molecules has provided a new dimension to the field of analysis for the detection and identification of drugs of dependence.

The immunoassay is based simply upon the principle of competitive displacement of a labeled drug from antibody drug complex by a non-labeled drug. The proportion of labeled drug displaced is related quantitatively to the concentration of non-labeled drug present. Three different immunoassays are available today: a) Radioimmunoassay (RIA); b) Enzyme Multiplied Immunoassay Technique (EMIT); c) Hemagglutination Inhibition (HI).

Radioimmunoassay (RIA)

The morphine RIA may be used as a prototype of this method; however, RIA methods for barbiturate, amphetamine, methadone, and benzoylecgonine

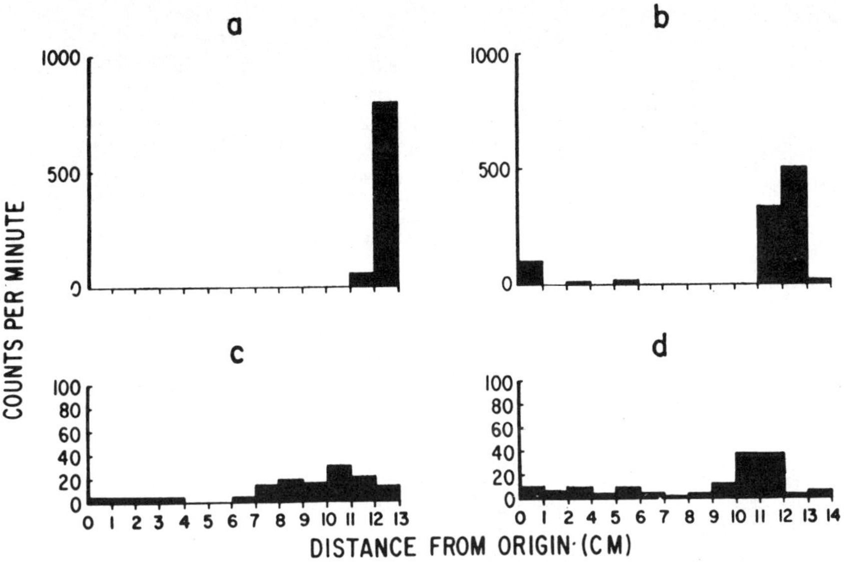

FIGURE 1. Radioscans of: a, Thin-layer chromatogram of chloroform-isopropanol (3:1, v/v) extract of dog brain 1 hour after a single s.c. injection of a 2 mg/kg dose in solvent system ethyl acetate-methanol-concentrated ammonia (17:2:1, v/v); b, ITLC in benzene-ethyl acetate-methanol-concentrated ammonia (80:20:1.2:0.1, v/v); c, Dog brain, 1 week after s.c. injection (2 mg/kg, free base) processed on Amberlite XAD-2 and chromatographed in solvent system ethyl acetate-methanol-concentrated ammonia (17:2:1, v/v); d, Scan of c in benzene-ethyl acetate-methanol-concentrated ammonia (80:20:1.2:0.1, v/v). (From Misra *et al.*[20] By permission of *Journal of Pharmacological and Experimental Therapeutics.*)

are also available. Essentially, the assay consists of competitive binding between non-labeled morphine and radiolabeled (^{3}H or ^{125}I) morphine (antigen) for antibody sites. The displaced labeled morphine (free) must now be separated from the antibody labeled morphine (bound); e.g., by $(NH_4)_2SO_4$ precipitation. The free labeled drug may be estimated in a scintillation counter. This assay is sensitive to 5 ng/ml and quantitative over a concentration range of 40–50 ng/ml. Unfortunately, cross-reactivity with drugs of similar structure occurs. (See TABLES 3–5.) The lack of specificity associated with this assay requires subsequent analysis of the biological material by additional methods (i.e., GC-mass spectrometry) for positive identification of the drug or metabolite.

Enzyme-Multiplied Immunoassay Technique (EMIT)

In the EMIT assay, morphine is coupled to an enzyme lysozyme. The binding of enzyme-labeled morphine to antibodies to morphine renders the enzyme inactive. Free morphine in the biofluid competes with the lysozyme-conjugated morphine for available sites on the antibody. Thus, morphine lysozyme conjugate is displaced from the antibody and the enzyme is activated and catalyzes the hydrolysis of bacterial cell wall (substrate), which is measured spectrophotometrically as a change in optical density (ΔOD). The sensitivity of the assay for morphine is 0.5 μg/ml. EMIT assays are available

TABLE 3

CROSS-REACTIVITY OF DRUGS IN URINE

Drug	Immunoassays						Fluorimetry	
	RIA	RR	HI	RR	EMIT	RR	TAFT	RR
Normorphine	41.6	(0.02)	200.0	(0.00)	44.4	(0.02)	31.0	(0.03)
Codeine	0.76	(1.32)	1.0	(1.00)	0.78	(1.28)	N.R.	—
Diacetylmorphine (heroin)	1.0	(1.00)	2.4	(0.42)	2.4	(0.42)	20.4	(0.05)
N-Allylnormorphine (nalorphine)	10.0	(0.10)	400.0	(0.00)	15.8	(0.06)	2.4	(0.42)
N-Allyl-7,8-dihydro-14-hydroxy normorphinone (naloxone)	290.0	(0.00)	—	—	N.R.	—	N.R.	—
Dihydromorphinone (dilaudid)	1.2	(0.83)	2.0	(0.33)	2.6	(0.38)	N.R.	—
Apomorphine	350.0	(0.00)	—	—	N.R.	—	—	—
Dihydromorphine	1.5	(0.68)	1.5	(0.67)	1.8	(0.55)	0.80	(1.25)
Morphine glucuronide	—	—	—	—	2.6	(0.38)	N.R.	—
1,3-Hydroxy-N-methylmorphinan (levorphanol)	2.0	(0.50)	50.0	(0.02)	6.2	(0.16)	N.R.	—
d-3-Methoxy-N-methylmorphinan (dextromethorphan)	878.0	(0.00)	N.R.	—	268.0	(0.00)	—	—
2-Ethylidene-1,5-dimethyl-3,3-diphenylpyrrolidine (methadone metabolite)	—	—	—	—	N.R.	—	—	—
2-Ethyl-5-methyl-3,3-diphenyl-1-pyrroline (methadone metabolite)	—	—	—	—	1000	(0.00)	—	—
Methadone	1780.0	(0.00)	N.R.	—	N.R.	—	—	—
d-Propoxyphene (Darvon®)	680.0	(0.00)	100.0	(0.01)	N.R.	—	—	—
Cyclazocine	380.0	(0.00)	—	—	N.R.	—	N.R.	—

All values (μg/ml) for each compound are equivalent to 1 μg/ml of morphine.
NR, no reaction at 0.5 mg/ml.
From Mulé *et al.*[18] By permission of *Clinical Chemistry*.

TABLE 4

CROSS-REACTIVITY OF DRUGS IN URINE IN THE RIA FOR BARBITURATES*

Drug	Concentration (μg/ml)	Relative Reactivity (RR)
Secobarbital	0.05	1.00
Pentobarbital	0.15	0.33
Amobarbital	0.25	0.20
Phenobarbital	0.50	0.10
Thiopental	1.00	0.05
Glutethimide (Doriden®)	200.0	0.00025
Others†	N.R.	—

* All values in μg/ml were equivalent to 0.05 μg of secobarbital per milliliter.

† Morphine, dihydromorphine, codeine, methadone, heroin, d-amphetamine, and methamphetamine were nonreactive (NR) at the final concentration of 10 μg/ml.

From Mulé *et al.*[19] By permission of *Clinical Chemistry*.

TABLE 5

CROSS-REACTIVITY OF DRUGS IN URINE IN THE RIA FOR AMPHETAMINE*

Drug	Concentration (μg/ml)	Relative Reactivity (RR)
d-Amphetamine	0.50	1.00
Methamphetamine	22.0	0.022
Phenylpropanolamine	10.0	0.050
Ephedrine	N.R.	—
Methylphenidate	N.R.	—
Secobarbital	N.R.	—
Morphine	N.R.	—
Methadone	N.R.	—

* All values in μg/ml were equivalent to 0.5 μg/ml of d-amphetamine.

N.R., No reaction at 100–1,000 μg/ml.

From Mulé *et al.*[19] By permission of *Clinical Chemistry*.

for methadone, barbiturates, amphetamine, benzoylecgonine, and benzodiazepenes. The major drawbacks associated with the EMIT assays are: 1) sensitivity (μg range); 2) presence of native lysozyme in the biofluids (i.e., urine); and 3) cross-reactivity. (See TABLES 3 and 6.)

Hemagglutination-Inhibition (HI)

In the HI assay for morphine, antibodies to morphine agglutinate red blood cells coated with morphine antigenic material. Free morphine present in the biofluids will bind the antibodies, thus inhibiting the agglutination of the antigenic-coated red blood cells, which then settle as a pellet. In the absence of free morphine, agglutination will, of course, occur. The range of sensitivity is quite adjustable, depending upon the antibody dilution. Normally, this assay for morphine or methadone is sensitive to 30 ng/ml. Cross-reactivity also occurs

TABLE 6

CROSS-REACTIVITY OF COMPOUNDS IN URINE WITH THE VARIOUS EMIT ASSAYS (EQUIVALENT TO 1 μG/ML OF THE ASSAY DRUG)

Methadone			d-Amphetamine			Barbiturate			Cocaine		
Compound	μg/ml	RR	Compound	μg/ml	RR	Compound	μg/ml	RR	Compound	μg/ml	RR
Methadone	1.0	1.00	d-Amphetamine	1.0	1.00	Secobarbital	1.0	1.00	Benzoylecgonine	1.0	1.000
Morphine	N.R.	—	Phenethylamine	3.1	0.32	Phenobarbital	2.0	0.50	Ecgonine	9.5	0.105
Meperidine	1.000	0.001	Phenylpropanolamine	5.0	0.20	Pentobarbital	1.1	0.90	Ecgonine methylester	380	0.003
2-Ethylidene-1,5-dimethyl-3,3-diphenylpyrrolidine	N.R.	—	Methamphetamine (Methedrine®)	0.9	1.08	Amobarbital	1.8	0.55	Cocaine	460	0.002
2-Ethyl-5-methyl-3,3-diphenyl-1-pyrroline	N.R.	—	Methylphenidate (Ritalin®)	50.0	0.02	Thiopental	0.7	1.42	Homatropine	N.R.	—
d-Propoxyphene (Darvon®)	N.R.	—	Phenmetrazine (Preludin®)	0.95	1.05	Glutethimide (Doriden®)	50	0.02	Scopolamine	N.R.	—
			Ephedrine	4.5	0.22				Morphine	N.R.	—
			Mephentermine (Wyamine®)	1.6	0.62				Methadone	N.R.	—
									Secobarbital	N.R.	—

N.R., No reaction at 500–1,000 μg/ml.
From Mulé *et al.*[18] By permission of *Clinical Chemistry*.

(TABLE 3) with this assay. One of the major advantages of HI is the simplicity of the assay, which does not require expensive instrumentation.

Gas Chromatography-Mass Spectroscopy

The analytical laboratory that must identify a single chemical compound within a mixture of several chemical entities will find the mass spectrometer an indispensable tool. Interfacing the mass spectrometer with a gas-chromatograph allows an extremely important prior separation of a complex mixture of molecules. The complexity of the spectra generated usually requires interfacing the mass spectrometer with a computer. This combination of instruments provides the analyst with the optimum capability for detecting and identifying drugs.

TABLE 7

ISOBUTANE CHEMICAL IONIZATION MASS SPECTRA OF DRUGS

Compound	Mol. Wt.	Mass Spectral Peaks in Descending Order of Intensity 1	2	3	Neutral Fragment Lost
Cocaine	303	304	182 (33%)		C_6H_5COOH
Codeine	299	282	300 (22%)		H_2O
Demerol	247	248			
Ethylmorphine	313	296	314 (11%)		H_2O
Levallorphan	283	284	282 (50%)	283 (25%)	
Methadone	309	310			
Morphine	285	268	286 (20%)		H_2O
Oxycodone	315	316			
Oxymorphone	301	302			
Propoxyphene	339	340	266 (63%)		C_2H_5COOH

From Saferstein and Chao.[17] By permission of *Journal of the Association of Official Analytical Chemists*.

TABLE 7 summarizes data obtained on several drugs using chemical ionization mass spectral analysis. Morphine as a typical example of this analysis shows that the dominant ion is 268, which is formed by the protonation of OH group on C-6 and the subsequent loss of H_2O. The peak at 286 was about 20% in abundance.[17]

COMMENT

TABLE 8 summarizes all the essential data on the various analytical techniques described here. It is only necessary to emphasize that normally more than one analytical method is required for the definitive identification of a drug molecule. The presence of several drugs in biological material is the situation usually encountered by the analyst and, in effect, only emphasizes the necessity of applying or developing specificity to the analysis.

TABLE 8

COMPARISON OF ANALYTICAL METHODS*

	Chromatography		Gas Chromatography Mass Spectrometry (GC-MS)	Automated Spectrofluorometry (ATS and Technicon ASA)	Immunoassays			
	Thin-Layer	Gas-Liquid			Free Radical (FRAT)	Enzyme Activation (EMIT)	Radioisotope (RIA)	Hemagglutination Inhibition (HI)
Tests/8 hr/technician	60–100	30–50	30–50	200–500	150–350	200–300	200–400	200–350
Costs†								
Materials/test	0.30–0.50	0.02–0.16	0.50	0.10–1.0	0.30–0.75	0.30–0.75	0.45–1.00	0.15–0.35
Labor/test	0.58–0.60	1.00–1.05	1.00	0.05–0.08	0.10–0.23	0.17–0.20	0.07–0.58	0.10–0.18
Total/test	0.88–1.10	1.02–1.21	1.50	0.15–1.08	0.40–0.80	0.47–0.95	0.52–1.58	0.25–0.53
Start-up	500	5,000–10,000	50,000–100,000	6,000–25,000	27,000	6,000–8,000	8,000–15,000	500
Turn-around time (TAT)	1–2 hr	1–2 hr	1–3 hr	0.5–1 hr	2–4 min	2–4 min	1–2 hr	1.5–2 hr
Equipment maintenance	Negligible (no major equipment)	The GC and GC/MS are the tests most likely to have "down" time. Service contracts are available.		Service contracts available.	Tests depend on one major piece of equipment which could have virtually no "down" time or as much as 25 inoperable days per year. Service contracts are available.			Negligible (no major equipment)
Test result	Intensity of spot on chromatogram (R_f)	Peak height (RT)	Peak height fragmentogram	Peak height (Ex, Em)	Peak height (ESR spectra)	Difference in extinction (Δ OD)	Counts per minute (cpm)	Visual recognition of a pattern of agglutination or non-agglutination
Sensitivity‡ (μg/ml)								
Morphine	0.5–1.5	0.1–2.0	0.0001–0.1	0.20	0.50	0.50	0.03–0.06	0.03–0.06
Barbiturate	1.5–2.0	0.5–3.0	0.0001–0.1	—	1.0–2.0	1.5–2.0	0.05–0.10	—
Amphetamine	1.0–3.0	1.0–2.0	0.0001–0.1	—	1.0–2.0	2.0–2.5	0.10–0.15	—
Cocaine§	1.0–2.0	1.0–2.0	0.0001–0.1	—	0.5–1.0	1.0–1.5	—	0.03–0.06
Methadone	1.0–2.0	0.1–1.0	0.0001–0.1	—	0.5–1.0	0.50	—	0.03–0.06
Specificity (morphine)	Very good	Excellent	Definitive	Fairly specific	No absolute specificity for the immunoassays			

* Portions of these data were obtained from D. Catlin, courtesy Special Action Office for Drug Abuse Prevention, monograph series B, No. 2.

† Cost estimates for immunoassay materials are based on purchase and use of presently available commercial adaptions of each assay. The labor cost is based on a technician earning $40 per day.

‡ Defined as the minimal concentration of a drug or metabolites that can be detected in biological fluid.

§ The principal metabolite of cocaine, benzoylecgonine, is detected.

From Mulé.[7] By permission of *Journal of Chromatographic Science*.

References

1. Mulé, S. J. 1972. Detection and identification of drugs of dependence. *In* Chemical and Biological Aspects of Drug Dependence. S. J. Mulé & H. Brill, Eds.: 277–303. CRC Press. Cleveland, Ohio.
2. Mulé, S. J., M. L. Bastos, D. Jukofsky & E. Saffer. 1971. Routine identification of drugs of abuse in human urine. II. Development and application of the XAD-2 resin column method. J. Chromatogr. **63:** 289–301.
3. Bastos, M. L., D. Jukofsky & S. J. Mulé. 1973. Routine identification of drugs of abuse in human urine. III. Differential elution of the XAD-2 resin. J. Chromatogr. **81:** 93–98.
4. Mulé, S. J. 1964. Determination of narcotic analgesics in human biological materials. Application of UV spectrophotometry, thin-layer and gas-liquid chromatography. Anal. Chem. **36:** 1907–1914.
5. Hubley, C. E. & L. Levi. 1955. Bull. on Narcotics. UN Dept. Social Affairs.
6. Stahl, E., Ed. 1969. Thin-layer chromatography. Springer-Verlag, Inc. New York, N.Y.
7. Mulé, S. J. 1974. Methods for the analysis of morphine and related surrogates: current status. J. Chromatogr. Sci. **12:** 245–253.
8. Mulé, S. J. 1972. Methods for the analysis of narcotic analgesics and amphetamines. J. Chromatogr. Sci. **10:** 275–282.
9. Bastos, M. L. & D. B. Hoffman. 1974. Comparison of methods for detection of amphetamines, cocaine and metabolites. J. Chromatogr. Sci. **12:** 269–280.
10. Bastos, M. L. & S. J. Mulé. 1974. Fluorescence in toxicology. *In* Progress in Chemical Toxicology. A. Stolman, Ed. Vol. **5:** 187–272. Academic Press. New York, N.Y.
11. Mulé, S. J. & P. L. Hushin. 1971. Semiautomated fluorometric assay for submicrogram quantities of morphine and quinine in human biological material. Anal. Chem. **43:** 708–711.
12. Sansur, M., A. Buccafuri & S. Morgenstern. 1972. Automated fluorometric method for the determination of morphine in urine. J. Assoc. Offic. Anal. Chem. **55:** 880–887.
13. Kupferberg, H., A. Burkhalter & E. L. Way. 1964. A sensitive fluorometric assay for morphine in plasma and brain. J. Pharmacol. Exp. Ther. **145:** 247–251.
14. Takemori, A. E. 1968. An ultrasensitive method for the determination of morphine and its application in experiments in vitro and in vivo. Biochem. Pharmacol. **17:** 1627–1635.
15. McGonigle, E. J. 1971. Determination of microgram quantities of methadone by fluorescence. Anal. Chem. **43:** 966–967.
16. Dal Cortivo, L. A., M. M. De Mayo & S. B. Weinberg. 1970. Fluorometric determination of microgram amounts of meperidine. Anal. Chem. **42:** 941–942.
17. Saferstein, R. & J. M. Chao. 1973. Identification of drugs by chemical ionization mass spectroscopy. J. Assoc. Offic. Anal. Chem. **56:** 1234–1238.
18. Mulé, S. J., M. L. Bastos & D. Jukofsky. 1974. Evaluation of immunoassay methods for detection, in urine, of drugs subject to abuse. Clin. Chem. **20:** 243–248.
19. Mulé, S. J., E. Whitlock & D. Jukofsky. 1975. Radioimmunoassay of drugs subject to abuse: Critical evaluation of urinary morphine-barbiturate, morphine, barbiturate, and amphetamine assays. Clin. Chem. **21:** 81–86.
20. Misra, A. L., R. Bloch, N. L. Vadlamani & S. J. Mulé. 1974. Physiological disposition and bitransformation of levo-methadone-1-^{3}H in the dog. J. Pharmacol. Exp. Ther. **188:** 34–44.

THE DESIGN AND ANALYSIS OF EXPERIMENTS FOR THE ASSESSMENT OF DRUG INTERACTIONS

C. L. Mitchell

Riker Laboratories, Inc.
Subsidiary of 3M Co.
St. Paul, Minnesota 55101

The statistician cannot excuse himself from the duty of getting his head clear on the principles of scientific inference, but equally no other thinking man can avoid a like obligation.[1]

INTRODUCTION

In recent years, much has been written concerning the nature of drug interactions. Comparatively little has been said, however, about the design and analysis of such experiments. This is really not surprising since the experimental designs and statistical techniques used in these experiments are the same as those used for other types of experiments. It would, therefore, be trite to discuss the subject if it were not for the fact that most of us, at some time or another, neglect to consider one or more of the principles of sound experimental practice.

This paper summarizes what I believe to be the most important concepts concerning experimental design and its statistical basis and, in addition, discusses some of the statistical procedures that can be used in assessing drug interactions.

EXPERIMENTAL DESIGN AND ITS STATISTICAL BASIS

All fields of biological research have at least one feature in common: inherent variability. The amount present varies among fields, but that it exists in all fields is something of which we are all aware.

When there is considerable variation in the experimental material and when it is not feasible to examine the entire population, the experimenter is forced to give a probability statement concerning any treatment differences observed. In order to do this, it is necessary for the experiment to be designed in such a way that a statistical analysis of the data will yield a valid answer to the question, "What is the probability that the differences observed could have occurred by chance?" In order to do this, there are two requirements which must be met in any design: randomization and replication. Without them, no valid estimate of experimental error can be obtained; a valid estimate of experimental error is necessary in order to make probability statements.

Randomization is necessary in order to introduce the laws of chance into the experiment. A random sample is one in which all individuals in the population have an equal probability of being selected. This principle of randomization is frequently (unconsciously) violated in the selection of subjects. When control data are all collected before the treatment data are obtained, randomization has not occurred. Neither has it occurred when the last group of mice in the cage are left as controls. I could cite numerous other examples, but that is not my point. Rather, it is to remind you that when you select your samples special care should be taken to ensure that all possible sources of bias have been eliminated.

As already stated, replications are necessary in order to provide an estimate of experimental error. In an experiment in which each treatment appears only once, no estimate of experimental error is available since it is possible to explain any difference seen on the basis of either a difference between treatments or a difference between experimental units (subjects). It is not possible to say which is correct. This is straightforward and gives no one any problem. Where the problem arises, however, is in determining how large the sample size should be. There is no easy answer.

The problem of sample size can best be understood by introducing the concepts of the null hypothesis and Type I versus Type II errors. In statistical terms, the null hypothesis is a statement that there is no difference between the parameters or the distributions being estimated by the samples. Taking the simplest case (e.g., the Student's t-test) the null hypothesis is that there is no difference between the means for two populations (e.g., control versus treated). When we accept the null hypothesis, we may be either right or wrong. A Type I error is made when the null hypothesis is rejected and it is, in fact, true. A Type II error is made when the null hypothesis is accepted and it is, in fact, false.

The probability of making a Type I error is called α and is fixed in advance of the experiment. When we state that something is statistically significant at $p = 0.05$, what we really mean is that the probability these results could have occurred by chance is 0.05. We infer that there is a "real" difference but realize we can be wrong, and indeed there is a one in 20 chance that we are.

The probability of making a Type II error is called β. We seldom, if ever, know the value of β. We can say something about its relative magnitude, however. Its value depends upon: 1. The distance between the population parameters being estimated by the samples (population means in the case of Student's t). 2. The value selected for α. 3. The sample size. The larger the distance between the population parameters, the smaller will be β. β varies inversely with α. β decreases as sample size increases.

From the statistical standpoint, then, one is on firmer ground when one rejects the null hypothesis than when one does not, since we know the probability of making a Type I error but not a Type II error. Returning to the problem of sample size, if the data cause us to reject the null hypothesis, then our sample size is large enough. If, on the other hand, we "accept" the null hypothesis, our sample size may be too small. To obtain a "feel" for this possibility one must examine the sample size itself, the degree of variability in the data, and the presence or absence of any trends in the results. If the sample size is small ($n = 3$–5 per group, for example), and a trend exists in the presence of large variability, one should be aware that the probability of a Type II error is high. Whether or not one wishes to repeat the experiment with a larger sample size will depend on the seriousness in the investigator's mind of making the Type II error.

I have dwelled on this subject at some length because it has been my impression that many scientists either are not aware of the Type II error concept or do not understand it. Rather, they tacitly accept the null hypothesis with the same degree of faith as when they reject it.

Besides the requirement of randomization and replication there are certain principles which should be followed. Some of these are non-statistical in nature. A little reflection, however, will show they are logical principles. In other words, the use of common sense is an important factor in the design of experiments.

A scientific experiment should be set up to answer a specific question or questions. The question (or questions) should be precisely formulated before the experiment is designed. Hazily formulated ideas are difficult to discuss and practically impossible to test for correctness. Once the questions are clear, they must then be reformulated into hypotheses which can be tested. I have already mentioned the null hypothesis. If one rejects the null hypothesis, one should have an alternative hypothesis to accept. It should be just as free from vagueness as the null hypothesis.

Only after these things have been done is one able to design the experiment properly. The design includes such things as: 1. The selection of the treatments. 2. The selection of the experimental material. 3. The selection of the characteristics or responses to be measured. 4. The selection of the unit of observation. 5. The number of replications or observations. 6. A decision concerning the things which must be controlled. 7. Determination of the statistical techniques to be utilized.

One should then critically and logically evaluate both the questions one is asking and the experimental design. Included in this step is an examination of the possible outcomes of the experiment and the possible interpretations which can be placed on these outcomes. This is a step which is frequently ignored. Much time, effort, and money could be saved if this step were remembered, because often one sees that the manner in which one intended to approach the problem will not properly answer the questions.

If the investigator has any doubts about the design of the experiment or the manner in which the data will be analyzed, a statistician should be consulted *before* the experiment is conducted, not after it has been completed. Statistics are only tools to help you interpret your data. They are not magic tools. No statistician can extract meaningful results from meaningless data. If the design is faulty, no amount of statistical manipulation can render a decisive interpretation of the results. A final step in the experiment is to re-examine the raw data in light of the results from the statistical analysis. If this inspection of the data does not verify the results of the statistical analysis, then either a mistake has been made in the calculations or the wrong statistical test has been used!

Statistical Analysis of Drug Interactions

From the statistical point of view the study of drug interactions has two main aspects. First, it raises the question as to the probability that the effects observed could have been due to chance rather than representing an interaction. Secondly, if an interaction occurs, the problem is posed as to whether to characterize it as one of addition, potentiation, or antagonism.

It is important to obtain both dose-effect and time-effect information about the substances individually on the responses to be measured before designing any drug interaction experiment. This is necessary for two reasons. First, this information provides a rationale for the doses used in the interaction studies and the time after dosing at which the effect is to be measured. Second, it aids in determining the statistical procedures to be used. The procedures used depend on whether only one or both of the substances affect the response when given alone and whether the measurements are quantitative or quantal in nature.

Procedures Which May Be Used When Both Substances Given Alone Affect the Measured Response

Quantitative Data

The first step is to determine the potency of one substance relative to the other in affecting the response. The purpose of this is to provide a rational basis for the doses used in subsequent studies. The most simple method (and the only one I will mention) assumes that the two compounds yield dose-effect responses which are linear and parallel. The most commonly used parallel line bioassays are 4 point (two dose levels of each substance) and 6 point (three dose levels of each substance) assays.[2] The advantage of the latter is that it provides a test for non-linearity. Both, however, encompass a test for deviation from parallelism.

If the onset and duration of action of the compounds are different (a likely case) then obviously different relative potencies will be obtained depending upon when the measurements are taken. The two most common procedures utilize either the time of peak effect or the area under the time-effect curve. For drug interaction studies I prefer the former since it avoids some of the complications that can arise if the compounds have grossly different time-effect curves. Better yet might be to determine relative potencies at more than one time interval. Most important, though, is to have a reason for the time(s) examined, based either on previous experiments or published information.

Once the relative potency has been determined, subsequent studies involve combining fractional doses of the substances and comparing the responses observed against those obtained using standard doses of the substance individually. The hypothesis to be tested is that, as far as the response being measured is concerned, the two compounds behave as though they were different forms of the same substance. Thus, doses of the combination and single substance(s) are picked such that equivalent responses should be obtained if the effect of the two together is additive. For example, given two compounds (A & B) in which A is 4 times as potent as B, a mixture of 1 part A and 4 parts B should yield a response equivalent to 2 parts A or 8 parts B when each is administered alone if the effect of the two together is additive. If the effect of the mixture is significantly greater than this, potentiation is indicated; if it is significantly less, one infers antagonism. The statistical procedures one uses depend upon the design of the experiment. The Student's t-test can be used if one is only comparing two means. If more than two means are being compared, an analysis of variance followed by designated comparisons of means (i.e., multiple comparison procedures) is more proper. If one has reason to believe that certain requirements of parametric tests are not met (e.g., equality of population variances) non-parametric equivalents may be used (e.g., Mann-Whitney U test instead of Student's t; Kruskal-Wallis one-way analysis of variance instead of analysis of variance).

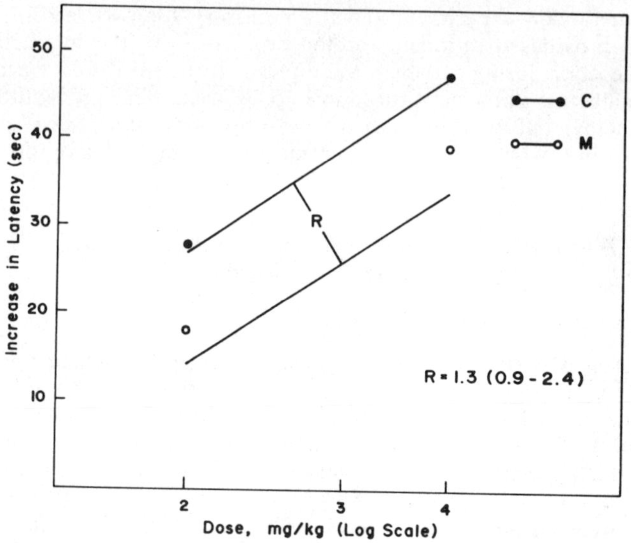

FIGURE 1. Dose-response curves for chlorpromazine hydrochloride and morphine sulfate as determined in the 4 point bioassay. C, chlorpromazine, M, morphine, and R, relative potency. (From Mitchell.[3] By permission of *Archives Internationales de Pharmacodynamie et de Therapie*.)

An example of this technique is presented in FIGURES 1 and 2. The experiment involved determining the effect of morphine and chlorpromazine alone and in combination on the escape response elicited by tooth-pulp stimulation in cats.[3] FIGURE 1 shows the potency of morphine sulfate relative to chlorpromazine hydrochloride when the measurements were taken at the time of peak effect for both compounds. Since the two drugs were virtually equipotent in this test, the combination of 1 part morphine and 1 part chlorpromazine was compared against 2 parts morphine and 2 parts chlorpromazine, each separately, as shown in FIGURE 2. An analysis of variance was performed on these data, following which the means were compared using one of the multiple comparison procedures, Duncan's new multiple range test.[4] No significant difference was obtained between the effect of morphine, 4 mg/kg, chlorpromazine, 4 mg/kg, and the mixture of 2 mg/kg of each. Moreover, morphine, 2 mg/kg, chlorpromazine, 2 mg/kg, and the mixture of 1 mg/kg of each were not significantly different. Thus, it is inferred the effects of morphine and chlorpromazine are additive in this model under the conditions of the experiment.

Quantal Data

These data are first analyzed by probit analysis, with the relative potency determined by the ratio of one ED_{50} versus the other.[2] This second step is sometimes neglected in practice, but it should not be since it encompasses a test for deviation from parallelism. The methods outlined below, like that for quantitative data, assume parallel dose-effect curves. Again different ED_{50}'s may be

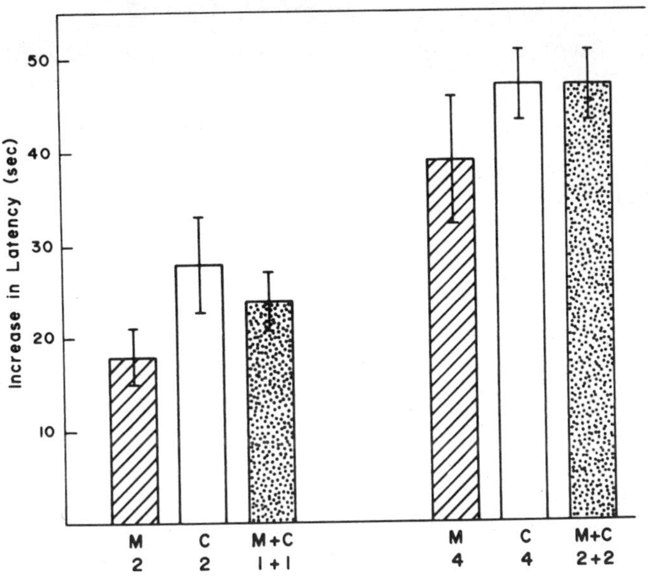

FIGURE 2. Effect of morphine sulfate, chlorpromazine hydrochloride, and their combination on the latency for an escape response to tooth-pulp stimulation in the cat. Bars represent mean change (± standard error) in the average latency for 10 trials after drug and the average latency for 10 control determinations. The observations were made 45 minutes following the administration of morphine and 60 minutes following the administration of chlorpromazine. In all instances the number of animals was 8. The doses were 2 and 4 mg/kg of morphine (M) and chlorpromazine (C) and 1 and 2 mg/kg of each for the combination (M + C). (From Mitchell.[3])

obtained, depending on when the effect is measured. Thus, the comments made above are also relevant here.

Once the ED_{50}'s (and hopefully the potency ratio) have been determined, subsequent studies are conducted in a manner similar to that described for quantitative data except that the statistical procedures are different owing to the nature of the data. Specifically, one might use either the chi-square or Fisher's exact probability tests, depending on the sample size and the expected frequencies. If in doubt which test is appropriate, consult a statistician or examine a statistics book that discusses both methods.

TABLES 1 and 2 show an example of this technique. In this experiment the effects of ethanol alone and in combination with chlorpromazine or chlordiazepoxide on the ability of mice to remain on an inclined screen were examined.[5] TABLE 1 shows the ED_{50}'s and the potency ratios. TABLE 2 shows that when one-half of the ED_{50}'s for ethanol and chlorpromazine were combined, additive effects were obtained. Potentiation was observed when one-half the ED_{50}'s for ethanol and chlordiazepoxide were combined. This was determined by comparing the frequency of mice falling from the inclined screen for the ethanol-drug combination versus the ED_{50} of ethanol alone. For the combination, each drug was administered such that their time of peak effect coincided. It should be emphasized that the finding of addition with the combination of ethanol and

TABLE 1

EFFECT OF DRUGS ON THE ABILITY OF MICE TO REMAIN ON AN INCLINED SCREEN*

Drug	50% Effective Dose† (mg/kg)	Potency Ratio‡
Ethanol	1820 (1436–2043)§	—
Chlorpromazine	11 (9–14)	164 (121–205)
Chlordiazepoxide	65 (57–78)	28 (21–34)

* After Gebhart *et al.*[5] Mice were placed on a 60° inclined screen at the following times after drug administration: ethanol (50% v/v), immediately; chlordiazepoxide, 30 min; and chlorpromazine, 60 min. All drug injections were given intraperitoneally.

† The dose causing 50% of the mice to fall from the inclined screen as determined by the probit method.

‡ The potency ratios were calculated relative to ethanol.

§ 95% confidence interval.

TABLE 2

EFFECT OF DRUGS IN COMBINATION WITH ETHANOL ON THE ABILITY OF MICE TO REMAIN ON AN INCLINED SCREEN*

Drug-Ethanol Combination	Number of Mice: Tested	Number of Mice: Responding†	p‡
50% effective dose of ethanol	20	13	
½ 50% effective doses, ethanol + chlorpromazine	20	10	>0.30
½ 50% effective doses, ethanol + chlordiazepoxide	20	19	<0.05

* After Gebhart *et al.*[5] Chlorpromazine was given 60 min before ethanol; chlordiazepoxide 30 min before ethanol. Mice were placed on the 60° inclined screen immediately after ethanol administration.

† The number of mice falling from the 60° inclined screen.

‡ Probability of χ^2 (ethanol-drug combinations versus ethanol alone); $p \leq 0.05$ is considered significant.

chlorpromazine does not mean that under other conditions potentiation might occur. Indeed, in the same article Gebhart *et al.*[5] did demonstrate potentiation using another endpoint (see below). Also, the study would have been more complete if other fractional doses had been combined and compared with their predicted equivalent doses of the substances alone.

Procedures Which May Be Used When Only One of the Substances Given Alone Affects the Measured Response

The condition in which one of the substances is inactive when given alone results on the one hand in a simpler situation and on the other a more complex situation than when both are active. It is simpler because the potency of one substance relative to the other need not (indeed cannot) be determined. It is more complex because the investigator must now search for another rationale for the doses and times of measurement to be used in the experiment. Once these parameters have been chosen, the procedure is simply to compare the effects of the combinations with those for the active agent alone. The hypothesis to be tested is that, as far as the response being measured is concerned, the "inactive" substance exerts no influence on the other when the two are given in combination. The statistical procedures used depend upon the experimental design and whether the data are quantitative or quantal in nature. In general, any of those mentioned above may be used. It must be remembered, however, that it is mandatory to demonstrate that the one substance is inactive in the doses used unless it is known *a priori* that it is.

An example using quantitative data is illustrated in TABLE 3, which shows the effect on the sleeping time of mice of pretreatment with iproniazid or

TABLE 3

SLEEPING TIME OF MICE TREATED WITH SALINE OR IPRONIAZID 1 HOUR BEFORE INJECTION OF HEXOBARBITAL*

Drug	N	Sleeping Time (in min)†
Saline + hexobarbital	18	24 ± 0.65
Iproniazid + hexobarbital	15	65 ± 4.78‡

* The iproniazid dose was 100 mg/kg, the hexobarbital dose 80 mg/kg; all injections were administered intraperitoneally.

† Defined as length of time between losing and regaining righting reflex. Figures represent mean ± standard error.

‡ Significant difference at $p < 0.05$, t' test.

saline 1 hour prior to the injection of hexobarbital. Since the data are quantitative in nature and only two groups are involved, the first impression might be to analyze the data using the Student's t-test. One of the assumptions of the Student's t-test is that the samples are drawn from populations having equal variances. There is a simple test for this assumption which, unfortunately, is too often ignored by biologists. For the data shown in TABLE 3 the assumption of equality of variance is rejected at $p < 0.005$. In such a case either the t' test or a non-parametric method (in this instance, the Mann-Whitney U test) should be used. The purpose of this illustration was twofold: first, to show how a simple statistical method can be used to study drug interactions; and second, to caution you about inequality of variance. Inequality of variance occurs more often than recognized in biological data. Situations in which one compound inhibits the metabolism of the other frequently present such a case.

The results of an experiment using quantal data and the Fisher's exact probability test are shown in TABLE 4. An ED_{50} for ethanol producing a loss of righting reflex (LRR_{50}) in mice was determined and found to be 4.3 g/kg (95% confidence interval of 3.9–5.2 g/kg).[5] LRR_{50}'s for chlorpromazine and chlordiazepoxide could not be determined that did not also produce varying degrees of lethality. The ED_{50}'s for the three agents in causing mice to fall from

TABLE 4
ABILITY OF DRUGS IN COMBINATION WITH ETHANOL TO PRODUCE A LOSS OF RIGHTING REFLEX (LRR)*

	Number of Mice		
	Tested	Responding†	p‡
½ LRR_{50} of ethanol plus:			
½ PD_{50}§ of ethanol	20	0	
½ PD_{50} of chlorpromazine	20	7	<0.004
½ PD_{50} of chlordiazepoxide	20	13	<0.001

* After Gebhart *et al.*[5] Chlorpromazine was given 60 min before ethanol; chlordiazepoxide 30 min before ethanol. The mice were tested immediately after ethanol administration.

† The number of mice losing the righting reflex.

‡ Fisher's exact probability (½ LRR_{50} ethanol + ½ PD_{50} of ethanol versus ½ LRR_{50} of ethanol + ½ PD_{50} of drug); $p \leq 0.05$ is considered significant.

§ One-half the dose causing 50% of the mice to fall from a 60° inclined screen.

an inclined screen could be determined and were called PD_{50}'s (see above). One-half of the LRR_{50} of ethanol was then given in combination with one-half the PD_{50} for ethanol, chlorpromazine, or chlordiazepoxide. Statistical comparisons were made using Fisher's exact probability test because the expected frequency in the cell "number of mice losing the righting reflex" was less than 5. Otherwise a chi-square test could have been used. Potentiation of the effect of ethanol by both chlorpromazine and chlordiazepoxide was concluded. It should be emphasized that doses of both chlorpromazine and chlordiazepoxide much larger than those used here are required to produce loss of righting reflex in mice.

Probit analysis may also be used for studying drug interactions where one of the compounds is inactive. One approach using this method is shown in FIGURE 3. These data, from a report by Tulunay and Takemori,[6] illustrate the enhanced efficacy of naloxone induced by pretreatment with morphine. The tail flick analgesic assay in mice was used. The animal responses were made quantal by establishing an endpoint at the mean peak effect which represented an increase in the reaction time of an individual animal of greater than 3 standard deviations of the control mean reaction time for all animals used in the group. In control animals, the ED_{50}'s $\pm$ 95% confidence intervals of morphine sulfate, subcutaneously, 30 minutes after administration, were 4.1 (3.2–5.3) mg/kg without naloxone and 35.3 (28.2–41.0) mg/kg with concomitant administration of naloxone, 0.16 mg/kg. In animals pretreated 3 hours earlier with 30 mg/kg of morphine sulfate the ED_{50}'s were 4.8 (3.7–6.2) mg/kg and 82.8 (65.1–108.4) mg/kg, respectively. Thus, pretreatment with a single dose of morphine did not change the ED_{50} of morphine alone but significantly altered the ED_{50} for the morphine plus naloxone combination, demonstrating an increase in the antagonistic potency of naloxone. Had the authors desired, they could have quantified the degree of this enhancement by obtaining the ratio of the ED_{50}'s for the two naloxone groups.

FIGURE 4 illustrates the type of approach just mentioned. Although the data concern the efficacy of morphine in adrenalectomized versus non-adrenalectomized animals, the analogy to the study of drug interactions is apparent. Anal-

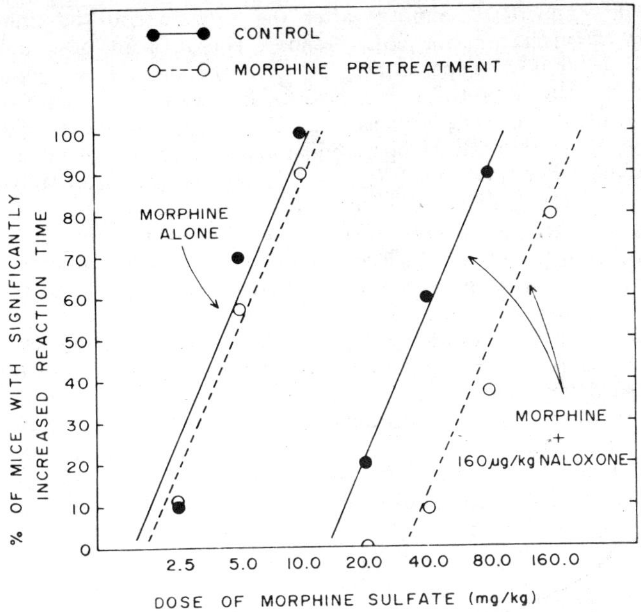

FIGURE 3. The enhanced efficacy of naloxone induced by pretreatment with morphine. See text for details. (From Tulunay and Takemori.[6] By permission of *Journal of Pharmacological and Experimental Therapeutics*.)

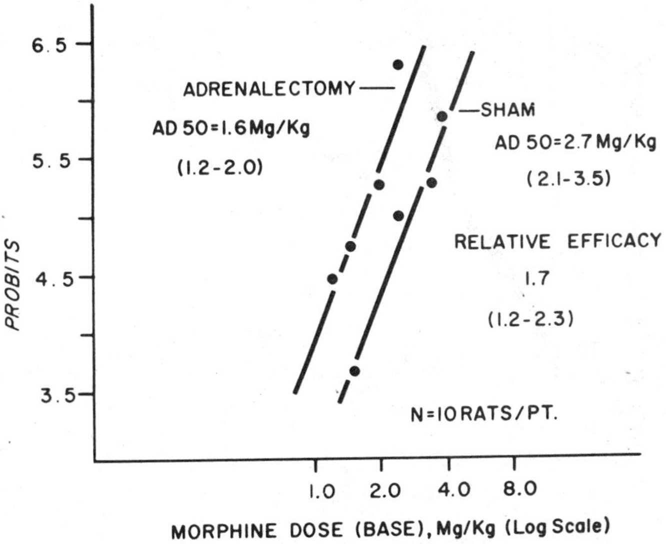

FIGURE 4. Dose-response curves generated while determining equi-analgesic morphine doses on the hot plate. AD_{50}, morphine analgesic dose in 50% of the animals. See text for further details. (From Gebhart and Mitchell.[7] By permission of *European Journal of Pharmacology*.)

gesia was determined 30 minutes after the subcutaneous administration of morphine in rats using the hot plate method.[7] The 50% analgesic dose (AD_{50}) was defined as that dose permitting 50% of the animals to remain on the heated plate for 30 seconds. As can be seen in FIGURE 4, under the condition of the experiment, adrenalectomized rats are more sensitive to the analgesic effect of morphine than sham operated animals. This is demonstrated by the fact that in sham operated rats 1.7 (1.2–2.3) mg/kg of morphine is equivalent to 1 mg/kg in adrenalectomized animals.

The bioassay technique may also be used for quantitative data as shown in FIGURE 5, from the same article as cited above.[7] The experimental procedure was the same as already described except that no cutoff time was used. Before proceeding with the analysis it was verified that adrenalectomy alone did not alter the control reaction times. Thus the data analyzed were the actual increase in reaction times from the control determinations. Results similar to those seen using quantal data were obtained. The utility of this technique for drug interaction studies where one of the compounds is inactive in the test procedure is, I trust, obvious. One advantage of this method lies in the fact it is possible to quantify the potency of one agent relative to another in enhancing or antagonizing the effects of the compound of central interest (i.e., the one which is active in the model when given alone).

Isobolometric Method

Loewe and Muischnek introduced the isobolometric method in 1926,[8] long before the study of drug interactions became as voguish as it is today. The

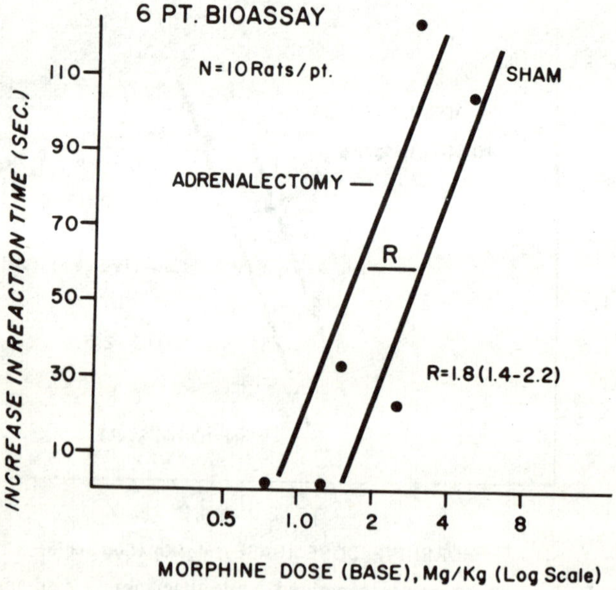

FIGURE 5. Dose-response curves as determined in the 6 point bioassay. R; relative efficacy. See text for further details. (From Gebhart and Mitchell.[7])

method has never been widely accepted for a variety of reasons. Among these are the complex and exotic terminology associated with it, the tedious nature of the method, and the fact that, as introduced by Loewe, it was never a truly quantitative one. Rather than discuss it thoroughly, I simply wish to acknowledge its existence and point out the similarities and differences between this approach and those presented above. The reader interested in examining the method in more detail should consult the articles by DeJongh[9] and Gessner[10] for more complete discussions of the method and for references to Loewe's work.

To determine an isobole one first must choose an effect to be measured. This can be any measurable effect, as for example, a decrease in blood pressure of 20 mm mercury or the incidence of death in 50 percent of the animals. The amount of different mixtures of the two substances necessary to produce the specified effect is then determined. A graph is prepared using doses of one component as the abscissa and doses of the other as the ordinate. Points representing the various combinations tested and found to produce the specified effect are placed on the graph. The line which can be drawn to connect these points is called an isobole; its points represent combinations which cause identical effects. A series of such lines is called an isobologram.[11] There are several types of isoboles. I will present only two.

The first type (Type I) is represented by those situations in which the desired effect can be produced by both substances alone. FIGURE 6 shows a theoretical isobologram illustrating addition, potentiation, and antagonism. If

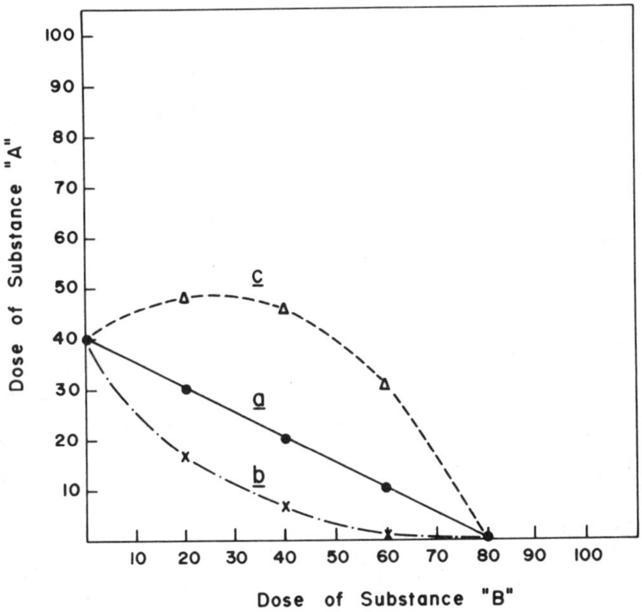

FIGURE 6. Type I isoboles illustrating addition (a), potentiation (b), and antagonism (c). The numbers for the doses are in arbitrary units. See text for further details.

the effect of substances A and B together is additive, the isobole is a straight line connecting the two points obtained for each agent alone (FIGURE 6a). In such a case the specified effect is reached with three-quarters the effective dose of A in combination with one-quarter the effective dose of B, or one-half of each or one-quarter of A and three-quarters of B, and so on. In other words, so far as the effect measured is concerned, one compound is acting as an analytical concentration (or dilution) of the other one. (N.B., This does not imply the same mechanism of action for both substances, however.) If the substances enhance each other's effect, one needs less of both substances in combination

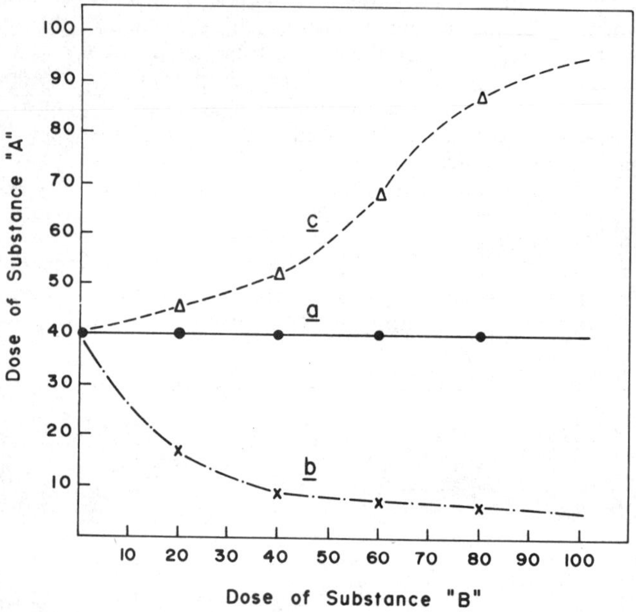

FIGURE 7. Type II isoboles illustrating no effect of substance B (a), potentiation (b), and antagonism (c). The numbers for the doses are in arbitrary units. See text for further details.

to produce the specified effect; hence, this isobole is a curved line situated *below* the line for addition (FIGURE 6b). If the substances have antagonistic effects, one needs more of both in combination to produce the specified effect; thus this isobole is a curved line situated *above* the line for addition. One might also obtain isoboles which indicate mixed effects. One example might be potentiation for a certain range of combinations and addition over the remainder (see below).

A second type (Type II) of isobole occurs when only one of two substances given alone produces the desired effect. A theoretical isobologram illustrating potentiation, antagonism, and no effect for one substance on the other is shown in FIGURE 7. When substance B has no influence on A, the isobole will run parallel to the abscissa (FIGURE 7a). If substance B potentiates A, then less of substance A is needed, and this isobole will lie below the neutral isobole

(FIGURE 7b). Antagonism (FIGURE 7c) is indicated by an upward shift in the line.

Gessner[10] has modified Loewe's method in order to apply a quasi-statistical treatment to the data. He determines the ED_{50} and its 95% confidence interval for each substance alone (if both are active), constructs the expected isobole assuming additivity, and places a confidence interval on it by connecting the lower and upper confidence limits for the two compounds with dotted lines (see FIGURE 9). ED_{50}'s and their confidence intervals for different doses of the combination are then determined using either (1) different doses of both combined

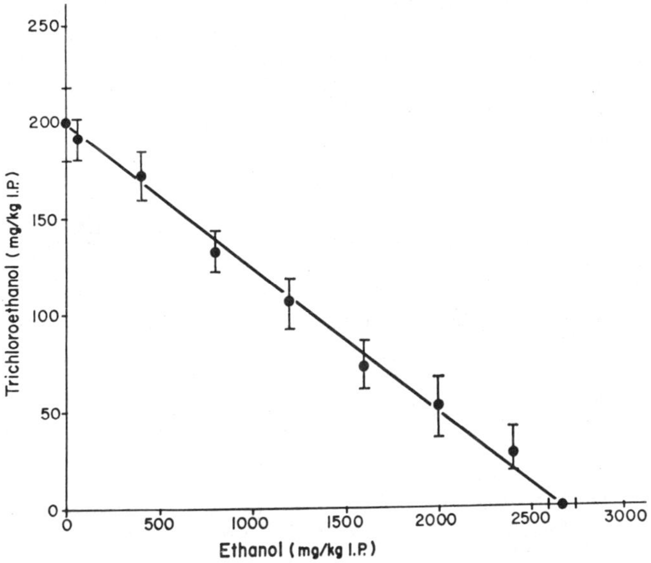

FIGURE 8. Isobole for the interaction of the hypnotic effect of trichloroethanol and ethanol in mice. The ED_{50} points are plotted with their 95% confidence limits. The expected location of the ED_{50} points, given the occurrence of a simple additive synergism, is given by the solid diagonal. See text for further details. (From Gessner and Cabana.[12] By permission of *Journal of Pharmacological and Experimental Therapeutics.*)

in various fixed ratios, or (2) different doses of one compound in the presence of a fixed dose of the other. Additivity or non-additivity is determined by comparing the observed versus expected ED_{50}'s and the 95% confidence intervals.

Actual examples of Gessner's approach with Type I isoboles illustrating addition only and both potentiation and addition are shown in FIGURES 8 and 9, respectively. These data are from Gessner and Cabana.[12] FIGURE 8 shows the isobole for the interaction of the hypnotic effect of trichloroethanol and ethanol in mice. Each of the points represents the ED_{50} ($\pm$95% confidence interval) for trichloroethanol in producing loss of righting reflex in the presence of a fixed dose of ethanol. It is apparent from this graph that the experimental points do not depart from simple additivity. The isobole for the interaction

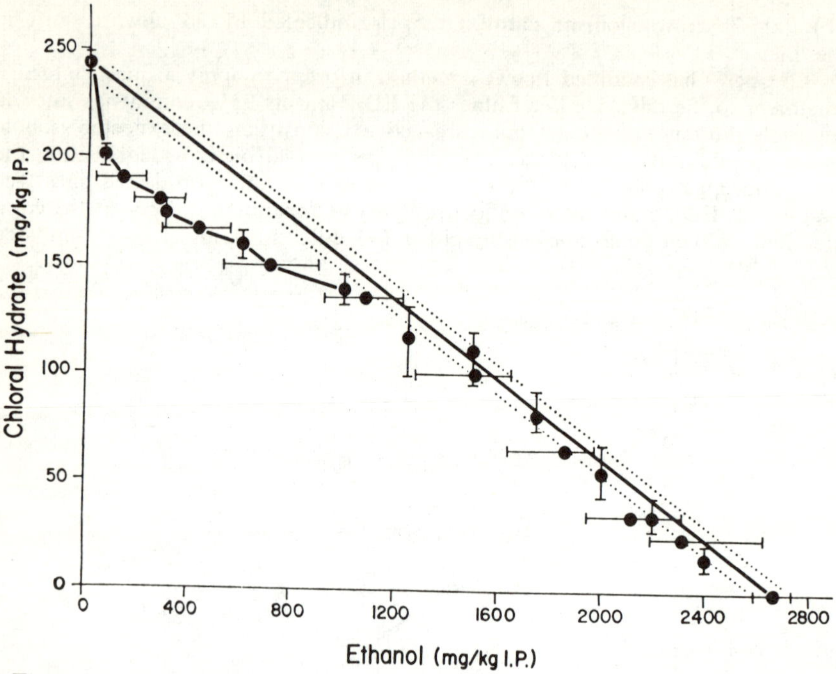

FIGURE 9. Isobole for the interaction of the hypnotic effects of chloral hydrate and ethanol in mice. ED_{50} points are plotted with their 95% confidence limits. The expected location of the ED_{50} points, given the occurrence of a simple additive synergism, is given together with the 95% confidence limits by the solid and dotted straight line diagonals, respectively. In the area of significant potentiation, the ED_{50} isobol has been generated by connecting adjacent points. See text for further details. (From Gessner and Cabana.[12])

of the hypnotic effects of chloral hydrate and ethanol in mice is shown in FIGURE 9. The points represent the ED_{50} ($\pm$95% confidence interval) for either chloral hydrate (vertical confidence interval lines) or ethanol (horizontal confidence interval lines) in the presence of a fixed dose of the other agent. Potentiation was concluded for all mixtures having a chloral hydrate/ethanol ratio greater than 1:7. Addition was concluded for ratios less than this value. The conclusions were based upon a comparison of the observed versus expected ED_{50}'s and their 95% confidence intervals.[12]

The primary disadvantage of the isobolometric approach as modified by Gessner is its tediousness. This arises due to the requirement of determining the exact amounts of a series of mixtures needed to produce a specified effect. It is much easier to measure the effects of given quantities of a mixture. This latter approach is the one utilized in the methods described earlier. It has an advantage, I suppose, in that it *forces* one to examine numerous different concentrations of the mixtures. This is not excluded in the other methods, however. Indeed, the prudent investigator would do this anyway.

Conceptually, both approaches are similar. When the experimental substances, each alone, are active in the test preparation, the working hypothesis is that the two compounds behave as though they were different forms of the same substance, one of which is possibly (depending on the potency ratio) diluted with an inert substance. This is tested in one case by comparing the *responses* of different portions of the mixtures to the *responses* obtained with certain doses of the compounds alone. In the other (isobolometric) case, it is tested by determining the *dose* of the mixture necessary to produce a response equivalent to that for certain doses of the compounds alone. In either case, the doses of both the mixtures and the compounds separately which should give equal effects if the null hypothesis is true, are specified by the potency of one compound relative to the other in the test procedure. One infers additivity if the null hypothesis is accepted. One infers either potentiation or antagonism if the null hypothesis is rejected, depending upon the direction of the deviation from additivity. When one substance is inactive when given alone in the test situation, the null hypothesis for both approaches is that it has no effect when given with the other.

From the statistical point of view there is, however, a major difference between Gessner's modification of Loewe's isobolometric technique and the more conventional methods. With conventional techniques, both the *expected* response (assuming additivity) and the "real" response can be determined experimentally. This is done by comparing the response of a given dose of the mixture with the responses obtained for the appropriate doses of the substances alone; the latter constitute the *expected* response. (Of course, the experiment should be designed such that possible differences due to the time of day in which the three responses are measured are minimized.) With the isobolometric technique, the *expected* dose cannot be determined experimentally. It can only be inferred from the line drawn connecting the ED_{50}'s for the two compounds. Moreover, because of the time-consuming nature of the method, this line is generally based on *historical* data rather than data obtained on the same day as that for the experimental points. From a practical point of view, this may not matter in most cases, since the evidence for potentiation or antagonism may be striking enough that this is of no consequence.

Whatever approach one uses, it is important to be aware of the underlying assumptions. It is likewise important that all possible precautions be taken before, during, and after the experiment to ensure that the reported results are meaningful. This responsibility rests squarely upon the shoulders of the investigator.

Summary

It was pointed out that all fields of biological research have one feature in common: inherent variability. Since this is the case and since it is not feasible to examine the entire population one is interested in, the experimenter is forced to give probability statements concerning any treatment differences observed. In order to do this, it is necessary for the experiment to be designed in such a way that a statistical analysis of the data will yield a *valid* answer to the question, "What is the probability that the differences observed could have occurred by chance?"

The importance of randomization in the selection of the samples was emphasized. The problem of determining the sample size was discussed in relation to Type I (rejecting the null hypothesis when it is true) and Type II (accepting the null hypothesis when it is false) errors. It was suggested that too little attention is given to the possibility of Type II errors in biological research. It was emphasized that the specific question, or questions, one is asking should be precisely formulated prior to the design of the experiment, since hazily formulated ideas are difficult to discuss and virtually impossible to test for correctness. Once the experiment has been designed, both the questions and the design should be critically and logically evaluated for any fallacies. If the investigator has any doubts about the design or the manner in which the data will be analyzed, a statistician should be consulted before the experiment is conducted. A statistician cannot extract meaningful results from data collected with a faulty design.

It was emphasized that it is important to know both the dose effect and time effect of each substance on the responses to be measured, in order to provide a rationale for the doses used in the interaction studies and the time after dosing at which the effect is to be measured.

The design of drug interaction experiments is based, in part, on whether or not both substances when given alone affect the response. If both substances are active, one determines the potency of one substance relative to the other in affecting the response. This can be done for either quantitative or quantal data. Once the relative potency has been determined, subsequent studies involve combining fractional doses of the substances and comparing the results against those obtained using standard doses of the substances individually. Doses of the combination and the single substances are picked such that equivalent responses should be obtained if the effect of the two together is additive. The null hypothesis is that the two compounds behave as though they were different forms of the same substance, one of which is possibly (depending on the potency ratio) diluted with an inert substance. Equivalence of response can be tested using such parametric tests as Student's t or analysis of variance (or their nonparametric equivalents) for quantitative data. The chi-square or Fisher's exact probability test may be used for quantal data. Additivity is inferred if the null hypothesis is accepted. One infers either potentiation or antagonism if the null hypothesis is rejected, depending upon the direction of the deviation from additivity. When one substance is inactive when given alone the null hypothesis is that it has no effect when given with the other. This is tested using the same techniques as mentioned above, except that there is no need, obviously, to determine relative potency.

The isobolometric method for studying drug interactions was compared with conventional techniques. It was emphasized that both approaches have the same conceptual basis. The isobolometric method is more tedious, however, since it requires determination of doses required to cause a specific response, whereas the other methods determine the responses caused by specific doses.

Finally, it was cautioned that, whatever the approach, it is the investigator's responsibility to know what assumptions are being made and to take all possible precautions before, during, and after the experiment to ensure that the reported results are meaningful.

Acknowledgment

I wish to thank Dr. Bernard McDonagh, Manager of Biostatistics, Riker Laboratories, Inc., for reviewing this manuscript and offering his expert advice.

REFERENCES

1. FISHER, R. A. 1960. The Design of Experiments. 7th edit. Hafner Publishing Co., Inc. New York, N.Y.
2. FINNEY, D. J. 1952. Statistical Method in Biological Assay. Hafner Publishing Co., Inc. New York, N.Y.
3. MITCHELL, C. L. 1966. Effect of morphine and chlorpromazine alone and in combination on the reaction to noxious stimuli. Arch. Int. Pharmacodyn. Ther. **163:** 387–392.
4. STEEL, R. G. D. & J. H. TORRIE. 1960. Principles and Procedures of Statistics: 107–109. McGraw-Hill Book Co., Inc. New York, N.Y.
5. GEBHART, G. F., G. L. PLAA & C. L. MITCHELL. 1969. The effects of ethanol alone and in combination with phenobarbital, chlorpromazine, or chlordiazepoxide. Toxicol. Appl. Pharmacol. **15:** 405–414.
6. TULUNAY, F. C. & A. E. TAKEMORI. 1974. The increased efficiency of narcotic antigonists induced by various narcotic analgesics. J. Pharmacol. Exp. Ther. **190:** 395–400.
7. GEBHART, G. F. & C. L. MITCHELL. 1972. The effect of adrenalectomy on morphine analgesia and tolerance development in rats. Eur. J. Pharmacol. **18:** 37–42.
8. LOEWE, S. & H. MUISCHNEK. 1926. Über Kombinationswirkungen. I. Mittelung: Hilfsmittel der Fragestellung. Naunyn Schmiedebergs Arch. Exp. Pathol. Pharmakol. **114:** 313–326.
9. DEJONGH, S. E. 1960. Isoboles. *In* Quantitative Methods in Pharmacology. H. DeJonge, Ed.: 318. North-Holland Publishing Co. Amsterdam, the Netherlands.
10. GESSNER, P. K. 1974. The isobolographic method applied to drug interactions. *In* Drug Interactions. P. L. Morselli, S. N. Cohen & S. Garattini, Eds.: 349. Raven Press. New York, N.Y.
11. LOEWE, S. 1953. The problem of synergism and antagonism of combined drugs. Arzeim.-Forsch. **3:** 285–290.
12. GESSNER, P. K. & B. E. CABANA. 1970. A study of the interactions of the hypnotic effects and of the toxic effects of chloral hydrate and ethanol. J. Pharmacol. Exp. Ther. **174:** 247–259.

OVERVIEW OF FACTORS AFFECTING DRUG INTERACTIONS

James R. Gillette

Laboratory of Chemical Pharmacology
National Heart and Lung Institute
National Institutes of Health
Bethesda, Maryland 20014

Drug interactions are usually classified as either pharmacokinetic or pharmacodynamic in nature. Interactions in which one drug affects the absorption, distribution metabolism, or elimination of another drug and thereby affects its concentration at action sites are frequently called pharmacokinetic interactions. Alternatively, interactions in which one drug displaces another at its action site or changes the responsiveness of the drug-action site complexes are frequently called pharmacodynamic interactions. Before we can properly assess pharmacodynamic interactions, however, it is frequently necessary to carry out studies of drug disposition in order to exclude the possibility that changes in response are caused solely by pharmacokinetic interactions or in order to estimate the contribution of a specific kind of pharmacokinetic interaction to the overall change in the pharmacological response.

Although there has been an increasing awareness that pharmacokinetic interactions may have a profound effect on pharmacological responses, many of these interactions are still incompletely understood by various investigators. For this reason, the importance of some interactions is sometimes exaggerated, and the relative contributions of various kinds of drug interactions are obscured. I shall attempt in this paper to describe situations in which a given pharmacokinetic interaction will be important and situations in which it won't.

Absorption From the Gastrointestinal Tract

Substances can effect the absorption of drugs in several different ways. If the acid form of a weakly acidic drug is insoluble, even alkaline solutions of it may form crystals in the stomach as they are acidified by the gastric juice; under these conditions, the rate of absorption may be altered by substances that affect the emptying time of the stomach. For example, desipramine slows the absorption of phenylbutazone by decreasing gastric motility and delaying the emptying of the stomach.[1] Alternatively, the surface of a tablet containing a soluble form of a drug may be coated with an insoluble layer of its acid form in the stomach, and distintegration of the tablet will therefore be slowed; for this reason, tablets occasionally contain buffers in order to maintain a significantly high pH in the diffusion layer surrounding the tablet.[2] Other substances may decrease the intestinal motility and impair the mixing of the intestinal contents, thereby slowing the absorption of the drug. Finally, cations such as calcium in food may react with a drug to form ionized complexes that are slowly absorbed.

The importance of these interactions that limit the concentration of drugs in plasma depends on the relative rates at which the drug is absorbed into the body and eliminated from it. If the drug is rapidly eliminated, the concentration of the drug in plasma may be markedly altered by changes in the rate of absorption; indeed if the proportional rate of elimination is faster than the proportional rate of absorption, the apparent half-life of the drug may reflect the rate of absorption rather than the proportional rate of elimination. On the other hand, if a drug is eliminated much more slowly than it is absorbed, then changes in the rate of absorption caused by a drug interaction may have very little effect on the concentration of the drug ultimately achieved in plasma. Moreover, if a drug is administered repetitively under conditions in which it is not completely absorbed during the dosage interval, then alterations in the rate of absorption will not have as great an effect on its concentration in plasma as they would if it were administered as a single dose.

Drug Distribution

After a drug is absorbed it is carried by the blood to the various tissues. Binding of the drug to plasma proteins may slow the rate at which the drug enters the tissue by either passive diffusion or by active transport systems. However, the effect of binding to the plasma proteins on the rate of distribution of the drug is usually not as great as might be thought. Indeed, stimulations show that if a drug were not bound to tissues and the unbound drug were distributed with body water, then 90% binding of the drug to plasma proteins would slow distribution of the drug by only twofold (Table 1).

The displacement of one drug by another from plasma proteins also may not increase the concentration of unbound drug at receptor sites as much as might be supposed, especially after the drug in the plasma has equilibrated with that in tissues. If the drug is not bound to tissues and the unbound drug is distributed with body water, then only about 50% of the drug in the body would be bound when 90% of it in plasma is bound (Figure 1). If all of the bound drug were instantaneously displaced, then the unbound concentration of the drug in plasma would initially be tenfold greater than it was before the displacement. However, the drug would leave the blood almost immediately and enter the other tissues that make up the central kinetic pool of the drug. Thus, if the central pool were essentially the extracellular space, the concentration of the drug would decrease to about a third of its initial concentration. However, the drug would then enter the deep kinetic pool, and the concentration of the drug in plasma would continue to decrease until the concentration of unbound drug was only about twice as great as it was when the drug was bound to plasma proteins. In other words, the effect of the displacing agent on the unbound drug on a receptor site in the deep pool would be about the same as the effect of doubling the dose. It is evident, therefore, that the substances that displace drugs solely from plasma proteins will cause significant pharmacological and toxicological effects only when the drug is very highly bound to plasma proteins and only when the unbound concentration of the drug in plasma initially is nearly at toxic levels. It is also evident that substances that displace the drug from sites in tissues (such as muscle) that contain major pools of the drug are more significant than those that displace drugs from plasma

TABLE 1

EFFECT OF REVERSIBLE BINDING TO PLASMA PROTEINS AND INTRACELLULAR COMPONENTS ON THE RATE OF DRUG DISPOSITION*

% Bound	Volume of Distribution (Equilibrium) (liters)	α-Phase Half-life (min)
No binding	45	33
Binding to plasma proteins (central compartment)		
50	25.25	40
75	15.375	51
90	9.45	68
99	5.895	94
Binding to tissue components (peripheral compartment)		
50	75.00	40
75	135.00	44
90	315.00	47
99	3015.00	49

* The following constants were assumed when there is no binding to plasma proteins or tissue components: $k_{12} = 0.0004\ min^{-1}$, $k_{21} = 0.007\ min^{-1}$, $k_{10} = 0$, $V_1 = 15$ l, and $V_2 = 30$ l. The volume of distribution of the plasma protein that binds the drug was assumed to be 5.5 l. In this two-pool kinetic system, k_{12} is the rate constant for the transfer of the drug from the central pool to the peripheral pool, k_{21} is the constant for the transfer of the drug from the peripheral pool to central pool, and k_{10} is the rate constant for the elimination of the drug from the central pool by metabolism and excretion.

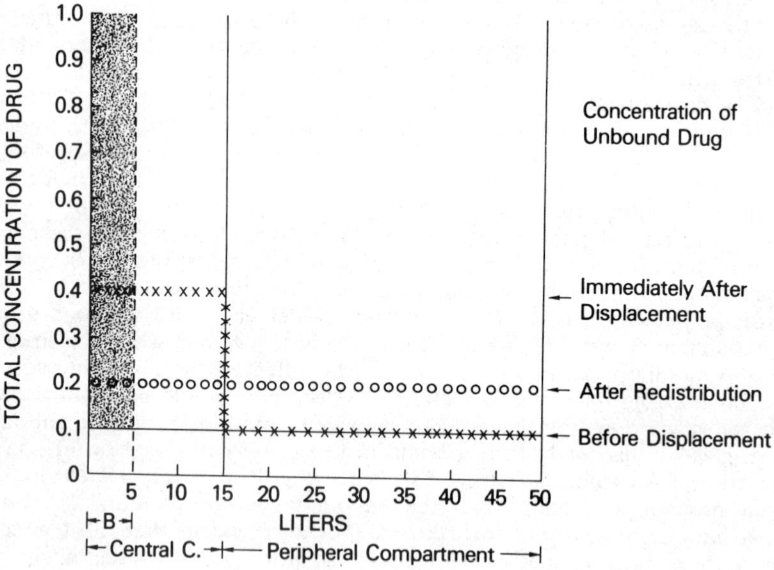

FIGURE 1. Effects of displacement of reversibly bound drugs.

proteins. Unfortunately, the binding of drugs to such tissues is seldom studied or considered.

Effect of Drug Interactions on Drug Elimination

Although polar compounds may be rapidly eliminated from the body by being excreted into urine, most lipid-soluble compounds must be converted to various metabolites of increasing polarity before they can be eliminated by the mammalian kidney. All unbound substances of less than 5,000 molecular weight that are dissolved in blood plasma are filtered by the glomerulus, whereas those as large as plasma albumin are scarcely filtered at all. Compounds having a molecular weight between 5,000 and 69,000 are filtered at intermediate rates.[3] In addition, many ionized substances, including weak acids and weak bases, are actively secreted by active transport systems in the proximal tabules of the kidney.[4] In addition, there are relatively specific transport systems that transfer substances, such as amino acids, glucose, ascorbic acid and uric acid, from the filtrate back into blood, but most drugs are not transported by these highly specific transport systems to any significant extent. Polar substances other than the physiologically important endogenous substances usually are concentrated as the water in the ultrafiltrate is reabsorbed and hence are rapidly excreted. But lipid soluble substances, including the nonionized forms of weak acids and weak bases, diffuse from the lumen of the kidney tubules back into the blood, and hence their concentration in the urine decreases toward the concentration of their unbound, nonionized forms in the plasma. Consequently, even those lipid-soluble compounds that are actively transported into the ultrafiltrate may be slowly eliminated by the kidney.

The rate of excretion of a drug by the kidney may be altered by several different mechanisms, but the importance of any given mechanism will vary with the predominate mechanism by which the drug is eliminated. Since the rate of back diffusion of a weakly acidic or basic drug from the ultrafiltrate to the plasma depends in part on the concentration of its lipid-soluble nonionized form, treatments that alter the pH of the urine will alter its rate of elimination. Moreover, the rates of excretion of this kind of drug will also be affected by the administration of diuretics and other treatments that alter the rate of urinary flow. But treatments that alter either the urinary pH or urinary flow will not affect the excretion of a polar drug that does not back diffuse into blood plasma. On the other hand, substances that inhibit the active transport systems will decrease the excretion of polar drugs that are actively secreted by these systems but will not affect the excretion of drugs that are eliminated solely by glomerular filtration, nor will they necessarily affect the excretion of lipid-soluble drugs, even though the drugs are actively excreted by these systems.

Some polar drugs may be excreted so rapidly by the active transport systems in the kidney that their rate of excretion is limited mainly by the rate of blood flow through the kidney. Under these conditions, their rates of excretion will be altered by substances that change the rate of blood flow through the kidney. For example, isoproterenol decreases the rate of excretion of paraquat, *p*-aminohippurate and *N*-methylnicotinamide by rat kidney in this way, and propranolol prevents this slowing of their excretion.[5] However, alterations in renal blood flow would not be expected to affect the rate of excretion of drugs that are limited mainly by glomerular filtration or by back diffusion.

In addition to being excreted by the kidney, many drugs are excreted directly into the intestine by intestinal mucosa or indirectly by way of the bile. With drugs that are rapidly reabsorbed these processes serve as a buffering mechanism that initially decreases the maximum concentration of drugs in blood plasma but ultimately increases the apparent half-life of the drug. If the rate of reabsorption is slower than the rate of elimination in feces, or if the drug is extensively metabolized by bacterial flora, however, these processes will tend to decrease the bioavailability of the drug. Thus, cathartics, antibiotics, and choleostatic agents may affect the plasma concentration of drugs even when the drugs are administered intravenously.

Relationships Between Drug Metabolism and Urinary Excretion

Most drugs are eliminated from the body not only by being excreted into urine and feces but also by being converted to metabolites that are more readily excreted. Indeed, studies on the pattern of urinary metabolites have become an important area of research in the evaluation of drug action and toxicity. However, such studies of urinary metabolites provide only indirect clues to the amount of drug in the body at any given time and the activities of the various enzymes that catalyze the formation of the various metabolites found in excreta.

In order to illustrate the limitations of studies on urinary metabolites, let us assume that a lipid-soluble compound is infused intravenously into a man. Let us also assume 1) that the drug is so lipid soluble that its clearance is limited by the rate of urinary flow (about 1.0 ml/min), 2) that the rate of excretion of the primary metabolite is limited by the glomerular filtration rate (about 125 ml/min), and 3) that the secondary metabolite is actively secreted so rapidly by the transport mechanisms that its clearance is limited by renal plasma flow (about 1,000 ml/min). Let us further assume that the clearance value for the conversion of the drug to its primary metabolite is similar to the glomerular filtration rate and that the clearance value for the conversion of the primary metabolite to the secondary metabolite is also similar to the glomerular filtration rate (FIGURE 2). After starting the infusion, the concentrations of the drug and its metabolites will increase until they reach steady-state values. Under these conditions, virtually all of the parent drug is eliminated by metabolism, whereas only about 50% of the metabolite is eliminated by metabolism, even though the activities of the enzymes that catalyze these reactions are identical (TABLE 2). For this reason a doubling of the clearance for the metabolism of the parent compound to its primary metabolite will almost halve the plasma concentration of the drug, but it will not markedly alter either the concentration of the metabolites in plasma or the pattern of urinary metabolites. On the other hand, a doubling in the clearance for the conversion of the primary metabolite to the secondary metabolite will affect both the concentrations of the metabolites and the pattern of urinary meabolites (TABLE 3). The effects of alterations of the clearance values of metabolism thus depend on the relative importance of metabolism and excretion in the elimination of drugs and their metabolites and not just on the activity of the enzyme alone.

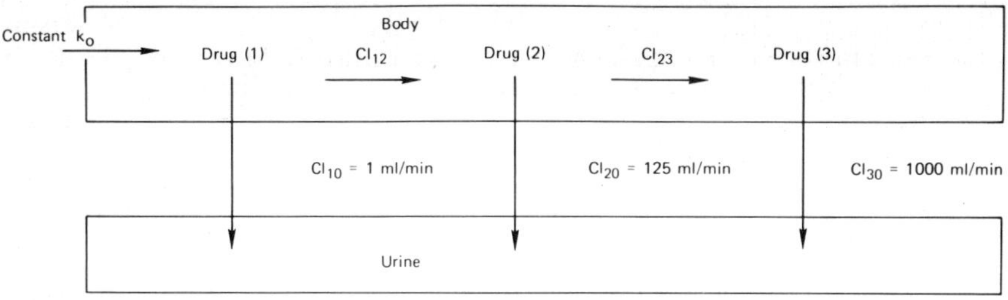

Cl_{12} = 125 ml/min; Cl_{23} = 125 ml/min k_o = 1 mg/min V_d = 50 liters

	Drug 1	Drug 2	Drug 3
Body Conc (μg/ml)	7.94 (.64)	3.97 (.32)	0.496 (.04)
Urine Rate (mg/min)	.008	0.496	0.496

Numbers in parentheses are the fractions of the total concentration of drug in the body.

FIGURE 2. Pattern of urinary metabolites.

TABLE 2
RELATIONSHIP BETWEEN ENZYME ACTIVITIES AND THE STEADY-STATE CONCENTRATION OF DRUGS AND THEIR METABOLITES (FIRST ENZYME)

	First Enzyme (ml/min)	Drug 1	Drug 2	Drug 3
			(μg/ml)	
Plasma (Conc.)	125	7.937 (69)	3.968 (32)	0.496 (4)
	250	3.984 (47)	3.984 (47)	0.498 (6)
	500	1.996 (31)	3.99 (62)	0.499 (7)
			(mg/min)	
Urine (Rate)	125	0.008	0.496	0.496
	250	0.004	0.498	0.498
	500	0.002	0.499	0.499

Numbers within parentheses are percentages of total concentration of drugs in the body. Values of constants, defined in FIGURE 2, are as follows: k_0 = 1 mg/min; Cl_{10} = 1 ml/min; Cl_{20} = 125 ml/min; Cl_{23} = 125 ml/min; Cl_{30} = 1000 ml/min; V_d = 50 l. The activity of the first enzyme (see FIGURE 2) is expressed as a clearance.

RELATIONSHIP BETWEEN TISSUE CLEARANCE AND ENZYME ACTIVITY

The relationship between the activity of an enzyme that catalyzes the metabolism of a drug and the clearance value of metabolism is complex, even when the drug is metabolized and excreted in separate tissues. The tissue clearance (Cl_t) is given by the following equation:

$$Cl_t = \dot{Q}_t ER$$

TABLE 3

RELATIONSHIPS BETWEEN ENZYME ACTIVITIES AND THE STEADY-STATE CONCENTRATION OF DRUGS AND THEIR METABOLITES (SECOND ENZYME)

	Second Enzyme (ml/min)	Drug 1	Drug 2	Drug 3
			(μg/ml)	
Plasma (Conc.)	125	7.94 (64)	3.97 (32)	0.50 (4)
	250	7.94 (71)	2.65 (24)	0.66 (5)
	500	7.94 (77)	1.59 (15)	0.79 (8)
			(mg/min)	
Urine (Rate)	125	0.008	0.496	0.496
	250	0.008	0.331	0.661
	500	0.008	0.198	0.794

The numbers within parentheses are percentages of total concentration of drugs in the body. Values of constants, defined in FIGURE 2, are as follows: $k_0 = 1$ mg/min; $Cl_{10} = 1$ ml/min; $Cl_{12} = 125$ ml/min; $Cl_{20} = 125$ ml/min; $Cl_{30} = 1000$ ml/min; $V_d = 50$ l. The activity of the second enzyme (see FIGURE 2) is expressed as a clearance.

in which $\dot{Q}_t$ is the rate of blood flow through the tissue and ER is the extraction ratio of the drug by the tissue, that is the fraction of the drug entering the tissue that is metabolized by the tissue. In turn, the extraction ratio, ER, is given by the following equation:

$$ER = \frac{pCl_{\text{int}}}{\dot{Q}_t + pCl_{\text{int}}}$$

in which p is the concentration of unbound drug in the tissue divided by the total concentration of drug in the blood, and Cl_{int} is the intrinsic clearance value of the enzyme in the tissue. The intrinsic clearance, in turn, equals $V_m/(K_m + S)$, in which V_m is the calculated maximum activity of the enzyme in the tissue, K_m is the Michaelis constant of the substrate for the enzyme, and S is the concentration of unbound drug in the tissue. When $S \ll K_m$ the equation for the intrinsic clearance degenerates to V_m/K_m. Substitution of the equation for ER into the equation for the tissue clearance gives the following equation:

$$Cl_t = \frac{\dot{Q}_t pCl_{\text{int}}}{\dot{Q}_t + pCl_{\text{int}}}$$

Inverted, this equation becomes:

$$\frac{1}{Cl_t} = \frac{1}{\dot{Q}_t} + \frac{1}{pCl_{\text{int}}}$$

or

$$\frac{1}{Cl_t} = \frac{1}{\dot{Q}_t} + \frac{K_m + S}{pV_{\max}}$$

Inspection of these equations reveals that the tissue clearance equals the intrinsic clearance of the enzyme only when the drug is unbound in blood and when the extraction ratio is very small. At higher extraction ratios, however, the tissue clearance becomes much less than the intrinsic clearance. Thus, the effects of inducers and inhibitors of the enzyme on the tissue clearance of the drug depend on the extraction ratio. At low extraction ratios, the inducer or an inhibitor may profoundly affect the metabolic clearance of the drug, whereas at high extraction ratios, they may have only negligible effects.

When a drug is eliminated solely by the liver, however, alterations in the activity of the liver enzymes will affect the plasma concentration of the drug to a greater extent when it is administered orally or intraperitoneally than when administered intravenously or intramuscularly. After oral administration only a portion of the dose of the drug will escape the liver and enter the peripheral blood as it is absorbed, whereas after intravenous administration, all of the dose enters the peripheral blood. Thus, the area under the plasma concentration curve after oral administration will be:

$$AUC_{(\text{oral})} = \frac{F\,\text{Dose}}{Cl_t}$$

in which F is the fraction of the dose that escapes the liver during the first pass through the liver. By contrast, the area under the plasma concentration curve after intravenous administration will be:

$$AUC_{(\text{iv})} = \frac{\text{Dose}}{Cl_{(t)}}$$

The ratio of the two areas will be:

$$\frac{AUC_{(\text{oral})}}{AUC_{(\text{iv})}} = F = 1 - ER$$

Since,

$$ER = \frac{pCl_{\text{int}}}{\dot{Q}_t + pCl_{\text{int}}}$$

it follows that

$$F = \frac{\dot{Q}_t}{\dot{Q}_t + pCl_{\text{int}}}$$

On inversion, the equation becomes:

$$\frac{1}{\text{Ratio}} = \frac{1}{F} = 1 + pCl_{\text{int}}/\dot{Q}_t = \frac{AUC_{(\text{iv})}}{AUC_{(\text{oral})}}$$

Inspection of this equation reveals that changes in pCl_{int} will have a greater effect on the $AUC_{(\text{iv})}/AUC_{(\text{oral})}$ ratio when $pCl_{\text{int}}/\dot{Q}_t$ approaches infinity than when $pCl/\dot{Q}_t$ is nearly zero.

Relationship Between Binding to Plasma Proteins and Rate Constants of Elimination

Binding of drugs to plasma proteins will alter not only the excretion of drugs by the kidney but also their metabolism. The magnitude of the alteration and its direction depend on the extraction ratios of the drug as it passes through the various organs of elimination.[6, 7] When the extraction ratio is small, binding will tend to decrease the rate of elimination of the drug; when high, binding will tend to increase the rate of elimination.

The rate constant of elimination of a drug for a given tissue depends not only on the clearance of the drug by that tissue but also on the volume of distribution of the drug (V_d). Thus,

$$k = Cl_t/V_d$$

The volume of distribution depends, however, on the amount of drug in the body at any given time and on the concentration of the drug in blood. The total amount of drug (A_t) in turn depends on the total amount of drug that is unbound ($C_f V_f$), the total amount of drug bound to plasma proteins present both vascularly and extravascularly ($C_{bp} V_p$), and the amount of drug bound to tissue components that are not present in the blood ($C_{bt} V_t$). Thus:

$$A_t = C_f V_f + C_{bp} V_p + C_{bt} V_t$$

If we set $C_{bt} = XC_f$ then the equation becomes:

$$A_t = C_f(V_f + XV_t) + C_{bp} V_p$$

Since the total concentration of the drug is $C_f + C_{bp}$, the volume of distribution of the drug becomes:

$$V_d = \frac{A_t}{C_p} = \frac{C_f(V_f + XV_t) + C_{bp} V_p}{C_f + C_{bp}}$$

Let $p = C_f/(C_f + C_{bp})$

$$V_d = p(V_f + XV_t) + (1 - p)V_p$$

Substituting this equation and the equation for Cl_t into the equation for k, the equation becomes:

$$k = \frac{\dot{Q}_t p Cl_{\text{int}}}{(\dot{Q}_t + pCl_{\text{int}})(p(V_f + XV_t) + (1 - p)V_p)}$$

It is evident that the effect of binding of drugs to plasma proteins on the rate constant of elimination can be quite complex.[7] The effects differ, however, when the intrinsic rate constant becomes rate-limiting or when the rate of blood flow becomes rate-limiting. When $\dot{Q}_t \gg pCl_{\text{int}}$ the equation degenerates to:

$$k = \frac{Cl_{\text{int}}}{(V_f + XV_t) + V_p(1 - p)/p}$$

Under these conditions, decreasing values of p invariably decrease k. When $pCl_{\text{int}} \gg \dot{Q}_t$, however, the equation degenerates to:

$$k = \frac{\dot{Q}_t}{p(V_f + XV_t) + (1 - p)V_p}$$

Under these conditions, decreasing values of p will increase k especially when $(V_f + XV_t) \gg V_p$. As p is decreased, however, the assumption that $pCl_{\text{int}} \gg \dot{Q}_t$ no longer becomes valid, and the effect is thus biphasic. It should be evident, however, that the effect of displacing agents on the value of k depends on the intrinsic clearance of the enzyme and on the binding to tissue proteins, as well as on the binding to plasma proteins.[7]

Alteration of Enzyme Activities

Since most drugs are metabolized in the body, it is evident that their biological half-lives may be changed by alterations in the activity of the various enzymes that metabolize the drug. The effect of alterations in enzyme activities on the biological half-life of a drug depends, however, on the extent to which drug metabolism contributes to the total body clearance of the drug. If only a small fraction of the drug is metabolized, then marked changes in the activity of enzymes that catalyze the metabolism of the drug may not significantly alter the biological half-life of the drug. Thus, the greatest change in the biological half-life of the drug for a given change in the activities of the drug-metabolizing enzymes would be expected to occur when virtually all of the drug is metabolized.

Even when most of the drug is metabolized before it is excreted, however, there are many instances in which marked changes in the activity of drug-metabolizing enzymes may not markedly alter the biological half-life of the drug.

Table 4

Activities* of Various Forms of Cytochrome P-450 Isolated From Rabbit-Liver Microsomes

Substrate	Electrophoretic Form 2	4	1,7
Benzphetamine	66	<3.0	7.5
Ethylmorphine	6.1	<3.0	3.0
p-Nitroanisole	6.2	<0.6	0.6
Aniline	1.0	0.8	0.6
Benzpyrene	0.04	Trace	0.5

* nmoles/min · nmol P-450. Modified from Haugen *et al.*[8]

As pointed out above, for example, marked increases in the activity of the enzymes in a given tissue will not markedly affect the clearance of the drug by that tissue when the extraction ratio approaches 1.0. Moreover, a drug may be metabolized to several different primary metabolites. But several of the metabolites may be formed by a single enzyme, or a single metabolite may be formed by several different enzymes. For example, Haugen *et al.*[8] have isolated seven electrophoretic bands of cytochrome P–450 from rabbit-liver microsomes and have obtained three different preparations; one contains predominantly electrophoretic band 2, another predominately electrophoretic band 4, and the third predominately electrophoretic bands 1 and 7. These three preparations had markedly different relative substrate specificities (Table 4). Moreover, the relative rates of hydroxylation in the 6β, 7α, and 16α positions of testosterone differ with the three preparations (Table 5). Furthermore, the body possesses several different esterases,[9] several different acetylases,[10] several different sulfate transferases,[11] and several different glutathione transferases[12] that can catalyze the metabolism of drugs. Hence, alterations in the activity of a given enzyme will alter the biological half-life of a drug only to the extent that the reactions catalyzed by the enzyme contribute to the total body clearance of the drug. If the reactions catalyzed by a given

TABLE 5

HYDROXYLATION* OF TESTOSTERONE BY VARIOUS FORMS OF CYTOCHROME P-450 ISOLATED FROM RABBIT-LIVER MICROSOMES

Position of Hydroxylation	Electrophoretic Form		
	2	4	1,7
6β	<0.02	<0.02	0.32
7α	<0.02	<0.02	<0.02
16α	0.43	<0.02	0.07

* nmoles/min · nmole P-450. Modified from Haugen *et al.*[8]

enzyme constitute a small fraction of the total body clearance, then marked changes in the activity of that enzyme may not markedly alter the biological half-life of the drug.

Although it is well known that species and strain differences in the activities of drug-metabolizing enzymes frequently result in differences in the biological half-life of the drug and thus in its pharmacologic activity, it is becoming increasingly evident that there are species and strain differences in the effects of other foreign compounds and hormones on the activity of the enzymes that metabolize foreign compounds. For example, studies on sex differences in drug metabolism imply that testosterone increases the activity of cytochrome P–450 in rats[13] but apparently decreases them in mice.[14] Moreover, 3-methylcholanthrene induces different cytochrome P–450 enzymes in different animal species. For example, the form of cytochrome P–450 induced by 3-methylcholanthrene in rabbits only slowly hydroxylates 3,4-benzpyrene, whereas that induced in rats and mice rapidly hydroxylates this polycyclic hydrocarbon.[15] There also are genetic differences in the inducibility of cytochrome P–450 enzymes; a given dose of 3-methylcholanthrene may increase the synthesis of cytochrome P–448 in some strains of mice but not in others.[16]

There are also species differences in the mechanism of inhibitors of drug metabolism. For example, SKF 525–A (β-diethylaminoethyl diphenylpropylacetate HCl) inhibits the N-demethylation of aminopyrine by rat-liver microsomes competitively but that by rabbit liver microsomes noncompetitively.[17] Moreover, just as there are species differences in the metabolism of drugs, there are also species differences in the metabolism of inhibitors and thus differences in their duration of action *in vivo*. For example, desipramine inhibits the metabolism of tremorine in rats but not in mice, presumably because desipramine is metabolized considerably more rapidly in mice than in rats.[18]

EXTRAHEPATIC ENZYMES

In recent years, there has been considerable emphasis on the metabolism of drugs by enzymes in extrahepatic tissues and on the effects of other foreign compounds in altering the activities of these enzymes. In most instances, however, the clearances of drugs by these enzymes in extrahepatic tissues are much slower than by those in liver, and hence they contribute very little to the total body clearance of drugs. There are notable exceptions, however: 1) When the enzyme is located at the site of absorption of the drug, the enzyme may decrease the amount of drug entering the body. For example, enzymes in the intestinal mucosa (or in intestinal flora) may extensively metabolize drugs that are slowly absorbed after oral administration. Similarly, enzymes in the skin may extensively metabolize drugs that are applied to the skin. To be effective in decreasing the amount of drug absorbed, however, the clearance of the drug by the enzyme must approach or exceed the clearance of the drug by absorption from the absorption site into the body. 2) Enzymes in the extrahepatic tissues may form a unique metabolite that exerts a pharmacologic or toxicologic response. For example, neuronal tissues contain enzymes that convert sympathomimetic amines to false transmitters that are not formed in the liver. 3) Enzymes in extrahepatic tissues may convert drugs to metabolites that are so chemically reactive that they combine with various substances in the tissue in which they are formed but do not escape the tissue. Thus, a treatment that selectively increases the activity of the enzyme in the extrahepatic tissue may increase the pharmacologic or toxicologic effects of the reactive metabolite in that tissue but may have little effect on the effects of the reactive metabolite in other tissues. On the other hand, a treatment that selectively increases the activity of the enzyme in liver may increase the pharmacologic or toxicologic effects of the reactive metabolite in the liver, but the treatment may not alter the effect of the reactive metabolite in other tissues if the liver enzyme does not play a major role in the elimination of the drug or may decrease the effects of the reactive metabolite in other tissues if the liver enzyme does play a major role in the elimination of the drug.

Perspective on Drug Interaction

The study of drug interactions is complicated by the fact that foreign compounds frequently alter the distribution, metabolism, and elimination of drugs by more than one mechanism. For example, some compounds that displace drugs from binding sites on plasma proteins may also displace them from binding sites of tissue components, or may inhibit active transport systems in kidney or liver, or may inhibit the metabolism of the drug. Unfortunately, most studies on drug interactions are so incomplete that it is impossible to determine the dominant mechanisms. Reporting the unbound fraction of a drug in plasma without reporting the unbound concentration of the drug in plasma does not permit the investigator to decide whether displacement from plasma proteins accounts for all of the changes in the volume of distribution of the drug. Moreover, the failure to correct measurements of the area under the plasma concentration curves for bound drug prevents the investigator from determining whether a treatment alters the clearance of the drug as well as altering its volume of distribution.

In recent years it has become evident that phenobarbital and perhaps certain other inducers increase the elimination of other drugs by increasing not only the activity of cytochrome P–450 enzymes but also the rate of blood flow through the liver. Thus, pretreatment of animals with phenobarbital enhances the elimination of drugs, such as propranolol, that are almost completely extracted by the liver as well as the elimination of poorly extracted drugs, such as antipyrine.[19]

Moreover, the pretreatment of animals with phenobarbital frequently increases the activity not only of the cytochrome P–450 enzymes but also UDP glucuronyl transferase in liver endoplasmic reticulum. Thus, the effects of a given metabolite of the drug depend on the pathway that is preferentially increased in a given animal species. For example, pretreatment of mice with phenobarbital increases the activity of the cytochrome P–450 that catalyzes the conversion of acetaminophen to a reactive metabolite which causes liver necrosis[20] but apparently does not affect the enzymes that catalyze the formation of the sulfate or the glucuronide conjugates of the drug.[21] Since the conjugates are the major pathways of elimination of the drug, pretreatment with phenobarbital increases the toxicity of acetaminophen but does not significantly alter its biological half-life. On the other hand, pretreatment of hamsters with phenobarbital only slightly increases the cytochrome P–450 enzyme in liver endoplasmic reticulum that catalyzes the formation of the reactive metabolite[22] but markedly increases the UDP-glucuronyl transferase.[23] As a result, the pretreatment of hamsters with phenobarbital decreases the biological half-life of acetaminophen and decreases its toxicity.[22] Thus, the effects of phenobarbital on the toxicity of acetaminophen depend on the relative effects of phenobarbital on the activities of cytochrome P–450 and UDP glucuronyl transferase.

Perspectives on Drug Interaction

Although drug interactions have been receiving much attention in recent years, it has become evident that most interactions studied in the laboratory are usually too small to be of medical significance. In the past, the dosage schedules of drugs used in therapy have been developed without the aid of analytical methods, and hence the dose of the drug recommended by physicians may lead to a wide range of plasma concentrations which lie somewhere between the lowest concentration at which the drug evokes its therapeutic effect in most patients and the highest concentration at which the drug evokes a toxic effect in relatively few patients. If a drug were to be therapeutically useful under these conditions, the safety margin would have to be large to encompass the wide individual differences in drug metabolism found by most investigators. Because the safety range is usually large with most drugs, changes of two to tenfold in the concentration of the drug usually do not lead to either toxic or ineffective concentrations of the drug. In order to put drug interactions into perspective, therefore, it should be remembered that a twofold increase in the unbound concentration of a drug caused by a drug interaction would also be expected to occur when the dose of the drug is doubled. It should be evident, therefore, that the drug interactions will be therapeutically important only when the safety margin between the drug concentration required to produce a therapeutic effect and that required to evoke toxic effects is small. Thus, drug interactions will become therapeutically important for only a few drugs.

Nevertheless, studies of drug interactions have been of great use in experimental pharmacology. Indeed, most of our knowledge of the mechanism of drug action is based on the concepts of drug antagonism and the other kinds of drug interactions discussed in this paper. I hope that a clearer understanding of the mechanisms of drug interaction will bring a better understanding of the relative importance of the various mechanisms in given situations.

References

1. Consolo, S. & S. Garattini. 1969. Effect of desipramine on intestinal absorption of phenylbutazone and other drugs. Eur. J. Pharmacol. **6:** 322–326.
2. Levy, G., J. R. Leonards & J. A. Procknal. 1965. Development of *in vitro* dissolution test which correlate quantitatively with dissolution rate limited drug absorption in man. J. Pharm. Sci. **54:** 1719–1722.
3. Weiner, I. M. 1971. Excretion of drugs by the kidney. *In* Handbuch der Experimentellen Pharmakologie, Concepts in Biochemical Pharmacology. B. B. Brodie & J. R. Gillette, Eds. Vol. **28**(1): 328–353. Springer-Verlag. Berlin, Heidelberg & New York.
4. Peters, L. 1960. Renal tubular excretion of organic bases. Pharmacol. Rev. **12:** 1–35.
5. Maling, H. M., W. Saul, M. A. Williams, E. M. Brown & J. R. Gillette. 1976. The relation of the potentiation of paraquat 48-hr mortality in rats and mice by 1-isopropterenol to its effects on renal clearance of paraquat. The Pharmacologist. **18:** 244.
6. Gillette, J. R. 1973. Overview of drug-protein binding. Ann. N.Y. Acad. Sci. **226:** 6–17.
7. Gillette, J. R. 1975. Other aspects of pharmacokinetics. *In* Handbuch der Experimentellen Pharmakologie, Concepts in Biochemical Pharmacology. J. R. Gillette & J. R. Mitchell, Eds. Vol. **28**(3): 35–85. Springer-Verlag. Berlin, Heidelberg & New York.
8. Haugen, D. A., T. A. van der Hooven & M. J. Coon. 1975. Purified liver microsomal cytochrome P-450. Separation and characterization of multiple forms. J. Biol. Chem. **250:** 3567–3570.
9. La Du, B. N. & H. Snady. 1971. Esterases of human tissues. *In* Handbuch der Experimentellen Pharmakologie, Concepts in Biochemical Pharmacology. B. B. Brodie & J. R. Gillette, Eds. Vol. **28**(2): 477–499. Springer-Verlag. Berlin, Heidelberg & New York.
10. Weber, W. W. 1971. Acetylating, deacetylating and amino acid conjugating enzymes. *In* Handbuch der Experimentellen Pharmakologie, Concepts in Biochemical Pharmacology. B. B. Brodie & J. R. Gillette, Eds. Vol. **28**(2): 564–583. Springer-Verlag. Berlin, Heidelberg & New York.
11. Roy, A. B. 1971. Sulphate conjugation enzymes. *In* Handbuch der Experimentellen Pharmakologie, Concepts in Biochemical Pharmacology. B. B. Brodie & J. R. Gillette, Eds. Vol. **28**(2): 536–563. Springer-Verlag. Berlin, Heidelberg & New York.
12. Boyland, E. 1971. Mercapturic acid conjugation. *In* Handbuch der Experimentellen Pharmakologie, Concepts in Biochemical Pharmacology. B. B. Brodie & J. R. Gillette, Eds. Vol. **28**(2): 584–608. Springer-Verlag. Berlin, Heidelberg & New York.
13. Quinn, G. P., J. Axelrod & B. B. Brodie. 1958. Species, strain and sex differences in the metabolism of hexobarbitone, amidopyrine, antipyrine and aniline. Biochem. Pharmacol. **1:** 152–159.
14. Vesell, E. S. 1968. Factors altering the responsiveness of mice to hexobarbital. Pharmacology **1:** 18–97.
15. Kawalek, J. C., W. Levin, D. Ryan, P. E. Thomas & A. Y. H. Lu. 1975. Purification of liver microsomal cytochrome P-448 from 3-methylcholanthrene-treated rabbits. Mol. Pharmacol. **11:** 874–878.

16. NEBERT, D. W. & H. V. GELBOIN. 1969. The *in vivo* and *in vitro* induction of aryl hydroxylase in mammalian cells of different strains, species, tissues and developmental and hormonal states. Arch. Biochem. Biophys. **134:** 76–89.
17. GILLETTE, J. R. 1966. Biochemistry of drug oxidation and reduction by enzymes in hepatic endoplasmic reticulum. Advan. Pharmacol. **4:** 219–261.
18. SJÖQVIST, F., W. HAMMER, H. SCHUMACHER & J. R. GILLETTE. 1968. The effect of desmethylimipramine and other "anti-tremorine" drugs on the metabolism of tremorine and oxotremorine in rats and mice. Biochem. Pharmacol. **17:** 915–934.
19. BRANCH, R. A., D. G. SHAND, G. R. WILKINSON & A. S. NIES. 1974. Increased clearance of antipyrine and d-propranolol after phenobarbital treatment in the monkey. J. Clin. Invest. **53:** 1101–1107.
20. POTTER, W. Z., D. C. DAVID, J. R. MITCHELL, D. J. JOLLOW, J. R. GILLETTE & B. B. BRODIE. 1973. Acetaminophen-induced hepatic necrosis. III. Cytochrome P-450 mediated covalent binding in vitro. J. Pharmacol. Exp. Ther. **187:** 203–210.
21. MITCHELL, J. R., D. J. JOLLOW, W. Z. POTTER, D. C. DAVIS, J. R. GILLETTE & B. B. BRODIE. 1973. Acetaminophen-induced hepatic necrosis. I. Role of metabolism. J. Pharmacol. Exp. Ther. **187:** 185–194.
22. POTTER, W. Z., S. S. THORGEIRSSON, D. J. JOLLOW & J. R. MITCHELL. 1974. Acetaminophen-induced hepatic necrosis. V. Correlation of hepatic necrosis, covalent binding and glutathione depletion in hamsters. Pharmacology **12:** 129–143.
23. JOLLOW, D. J., S. S. THORGEIRSSON, D. J. JOLLOW & J. R. MITCHELL. 1974. Acetaminophen-induced hepatic necrosis. VI. Metabolic disposition of toxic and nontoxic doses of acetaminophen. Pharmacology **12:** 251–271.

THE EFFECTS OF CANNABINOIDS AND OTHER CNS DEPRESSANTS ON CELL MEMBRANE MODELS

E. W. Gill

Department of Pharmacology
Oxford University
Oxford OX1 3QT, England

Interactions between co-administered drugs can occur at a variety of sites and by a variety of mechanisms, and this diversity is clearly demonstrated by the range of presentations at this meeting. The ultimate objective of the molecular pharmacologist is to rationalize drug effects in terms of the interaction, expressed in physico-chemical terms, between the drug molecule and some explicit chemical component of the target cell structure. Such an account of a drug effect is perhaps the most fundamental that can be given, but it presupposes a very high degree of refinement and simplification of the bio-system under consideration. In particular it presupposes that a whole range of pharmacodynamic effects concerning the access of the drug to the site of action, its absorption at extraneous sites, its metabolic conversion, and ultimate excretion are all understood and allowed for in the translation of the initial biophysical changes triggered by the drug molecule into the final gross physiological response we ultimately observe. At our present state of knowledge this might be regarded as an overly ambitious objective, but nevertheless I would like to discuss some experimental observations and hypotheses concerning the possible interactions of Δ9 tetrahydrocannabinol (Δ9 THC)—the major psychoactive component of cannabis—with some other CNS-active compounds at a common site of action on a neuronal cell surface.

Ideas concerning the molecular organization of cellular membranes have been evolving rapidly during the last decade and have been reported on and summarized in several recent publications.[1, 2] Briefly, the most widely accepted view is that the membrane consists for the most part of a bimolecular layer of amphipathic lipids and cholesterol, overlaid and penetrated by protein molecules. The degree of fixation of these protein molecules varies; some are readily detached, whereas others are thought to be firmly embedded in the lipid matrix. The firmly embedded protein molecules are obvious candidates for the many ion-selective pores and drug receptors whose presence has been inferred from many different experiments on membrane permeability. We know that the lipid components of the membrane are closely packed at quite high surface pressures, but that the hydrocarbon chains of the lipids are not completely fixed as in a crystalline lattice. Experiments using electron spin resonance (of a kind referred to below) and ^{1}H and ^{13}C nuclear magnetic resonance techniques have suggested that the hydrocarbon chains of mixed lipid bilayers deviate from close packing and become more disordered and fluid as the central plane of the membrane is approached. The extent of the fluidity depends on the lipid composition of the membrane, and varies between different cells, as their lipid composition varies, and can vary between different parts of the same cell. We also know that the protein components of the cell surface, though firmly embedded in the lipid matrix, are, nevertheless, not rigidly fixed but are capable of lateral diffusion within the membrane surface. Many important differences in detail no doubt exist between different cell membranes, and their elucidation is one of the main objectives of current research on membrane properties, but the broad picture that has been very briefly presented is widely accepted. It is with this complex dynamic structure that most of our drugs interact.

Many classses of drugs are thought to exert their primary chemical effect on the cell surface by combining with a protein receptor molecule. In many cases the arguments for the existence of such a receptor molecule are quite compelling:[3] the drug molecules themselves are complex structures containing ionic, dipolar, and non-polar chemical groupings, and quite small alterations to the chemical structure or spatial arrangement of these groups produce a profound alteration in potency. The opiate alkaloids are a case in point. It is difficult to avoid the conclusion that they are combining with an equally complex complementary structure, and a protein is the most obvious naturally occurring macromolecule affording the necessary diversity and complexity of side-chain groups available for interaction with a combining drug molecule. In the few but steadily increasing number of cases where credible attempts have been made to isolate drug receptors, the material isolated has been a protein.[3] On the other hand an interaction with a membrane-bound protein is not the only possible chemical mechanism of drug action. It has been recognized for many years that the potency of the volatile general anaesthetics correlates very well with their lipid solubility, and one widely accepted mechanism for their mode of action is that they dissolve in and partially disorder the lipid phase of the cell membrane.[4] The evidence that the site of action of Δ9 tetrahydrocannabinol is also the lipid phase of the cell membrane can be summarized as follows:[5, 6]

Experimental Methods

The experimental technique employed was to study the effect of various drugs on the electron spin resonance spectrum obtained from nitroxide-labeled phospholipid vesicles. With the techniques presently available it is not possible by experiments on native cell-membrane preparations to establish whether a drug is exerting its effect on the protein or lipid component. This difficulty can be circumvented by using protein-free lipid preparations that reproduce the structure of the lipid phase of natural membranes. Ultrasonically dispersed suspensions of lecithin and cholesterol mixtures have been shown to consist of spherical bimolecular layers (liposomes), with the lipid molecules stacked together in a manner very similar to that found in natural membranes.[7] Perturbations of these liposome bilayers by drug molecules can be detected by use of the electron spin resonance technique developed by Hubbell and McConnell.[8] Very briefly, the technique is to incorporate in the liposome bilayer a small amount of a reporter molecule, which is either a modified palmitic acid, which has a nitroxide ring structure attached midway along the hydrocarbon chain (1), or a lecithin analog incorporating one molecule of nitroxide-substituted palmitic acid as one of its fatty acids (2). The nitroxide group has an uncoupled electron, and the spin resonance signal of this electron is markedly

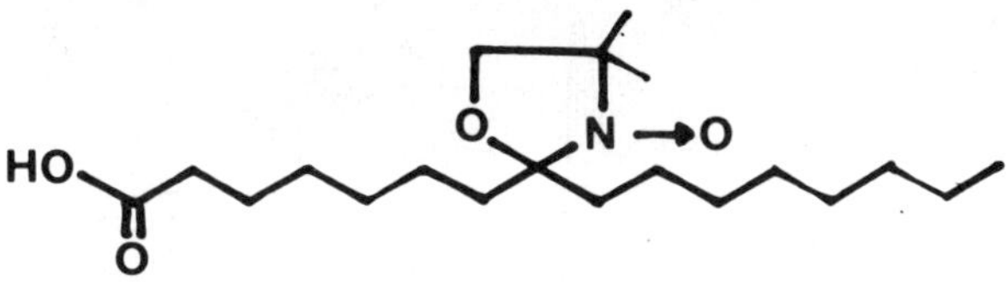

1

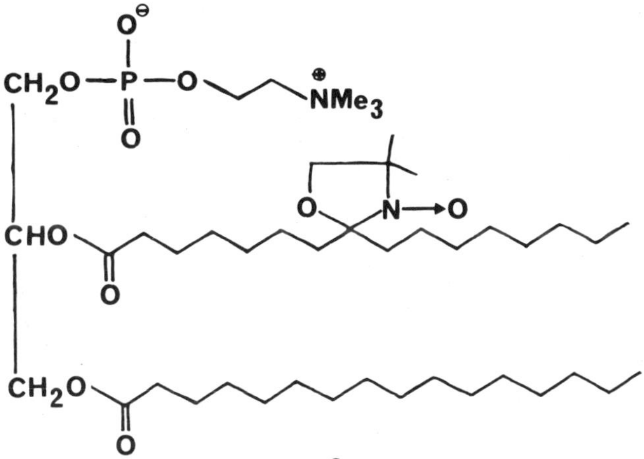

2

affected by the mobility of that part of the molecule to which it is attached, and hence, in a condensed phase such as a closely packed bimolecular layer, by the constraints imposed by adjacent molecules. Hubbell and McConnell[8] showed that measurements of the separation of the inner and outer extrema of the hyperfine interaction components of the spectrum (FIGURE 1) gave a measure of the torsional freedom of the hydrocarbon chain. From these they derived an order parameter, S, which is an index of the degree of local molecular order in the immediate environment of the nitroxide spin label. Trudell *et al.*[9, 10] used spin-labeled liposomes to show that the volatile anaesthetics halothane and methoxyfluorane caused an increase in the mobility of lipid bilayers and that the fluidization, like anaesthesia, could be reversed by the application of external pressure. These simple protein-free structures appeared, therefore, to serve as effective models for the effects of volatile anaesthetics; it remained to be established that they could exhibit the same degree of molecular specificity in their interactions with more complex molecules as does the living cell.

EFFECTS OF STEROID ANESTHETICS

A series of pregnane derivatives (3a, b, c, d) served as an interesting test of the effectiveness of this model system. One of these steroids—3α-hydroxy-5α-pregnane-11,20-one (3a)—is a potent anaesthetic (Alphaxalone) when ad-

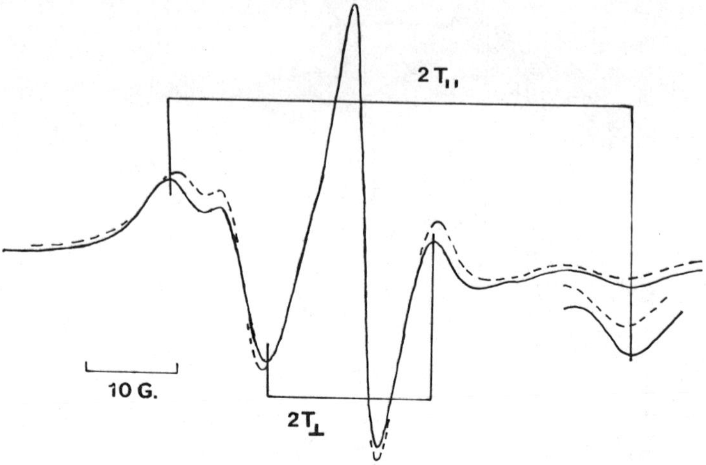

FIGURE 1. Electron spin resonance spectrum of spin-labeled lecithin/cholesterol liposomes (solid line). Toluene (83 mg/g total lipid) reduces the separation of the outer hyperfine extrema and increases the separation of the inner hyperfine extrema (broken line). Calibration line = 10 gauss.

ministered intravenously, whereas its 3-β hydroxy isomer (3b) is devoid of anaesthetic activity.[11] The other two isomeric steroids (3c and 3d) show a similar though less marked difference in anaesthetic potency, and both are less active than Alphaxalone (3a). The effects of this series of steroids and of butobarbitone on the order parameter of spin-labeled liposomes are shown in

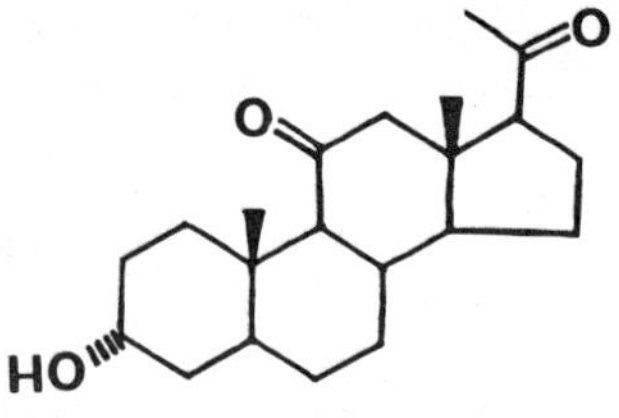

3a

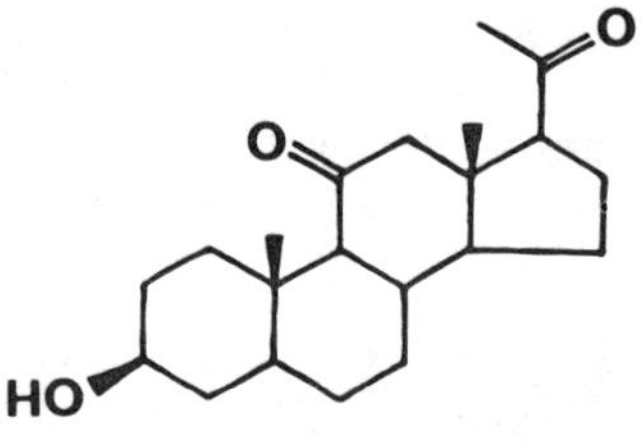

3b

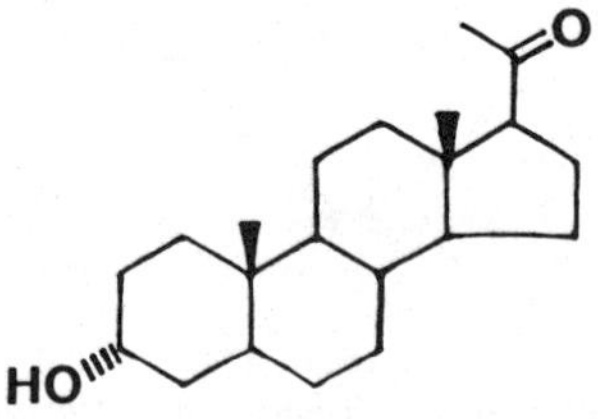

3c

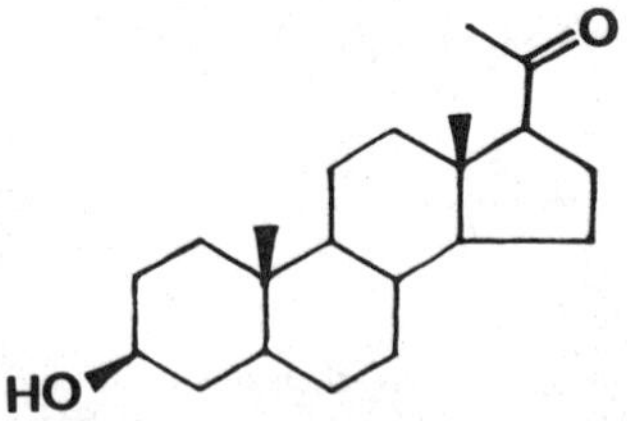

3d

FIGURE 2, together with the effects obtained by Trudell *et al.*[9, 10] for halothane. It can be seen that the potent anaesthetics all produced a marked decrease in the order parameter, i.e., an increased fluidity of the liposome bilayer, the extent of the disordering depending linearly on membrane concentration. When allowance is made for the considerable difference in molecular volume between, say, halothane and the steroid Alphaxalone (the abscissa of FIGURE 2 represents the molal concentration of each drug molecule multiplied by its molal volume, giving a measure of the partial volume occupied by the drug in the liposome bilayer) it can be seen that these two anaesthetics produce, qualitatively and quantitatively, a similar perturbation of the liposome bilayer. Within the series of four related steroid molecules ability to fluidize the liposome bilayer correlates with their effectiveness as anaesthetics. Seeman[4] has estimated

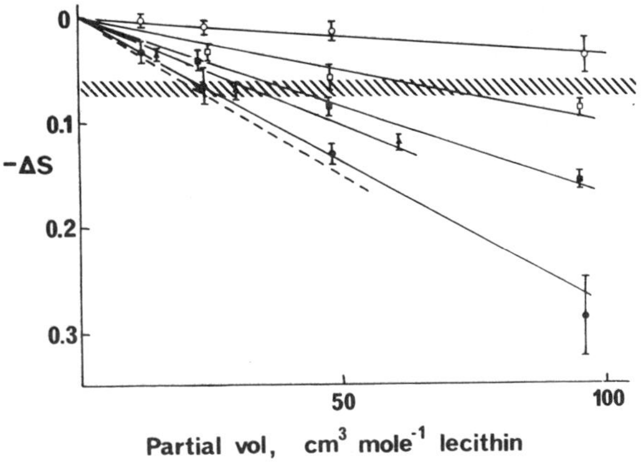

FIGURE 2. Effect of steroids 3a (●), 3b (○), 3c (■), 3d (□), butobarbitone (▲) and halothane (--) on the order parameter (S) of spin-labeled lecithin/cholesterol liposomes. The hatched band indicates the degree of fluidization corresponding to the onset of anaesthesia.

the membrane concentrations of anaesthetics needed to produce anaesthesia, and the correspondent change in the order parameter ($\Delta s = 0.06 - 0.07$) is indicated by the hatched band in FIGURE 2.

From these observations we can construct the following working hypothesis: (1) A wide range of structurally diverse anaesthetics all produce an increase in molecular disorder, or fluidity, of the hydrocarbon phase of phospholipid bilayers; (2) the structure of the liposome lipid bilayer is similar, in composition and organization, to the lipid matrix of nerve cell membranes, and this increase in fluidity is the biophysical change responsible for anaesthesia; and (3) spin-labeled liposomes are realistic model systems for studying this effect.

EFFECTS OF CANNABINOIDS

Tetrahydrocannabinol (Δ9 THC, 4a) and the other psychoactive cannabinoids have many physico-chemical properties in common with the steroid

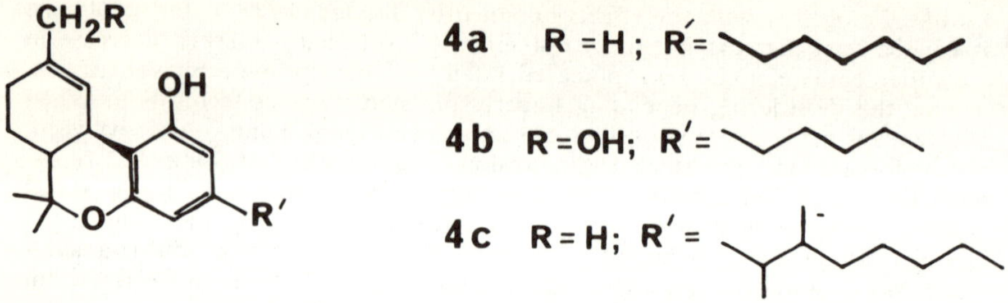

anaesthetics we have been considering. They are very lipophilic, oxygenated hydrocarbons of comparable molecular weight and are devoid of any ionic or strongly dipolar substituent groups. The effect of some cannabinoids on the molecular order of liposomes is shown in FIGURE 3. At low concentrations the

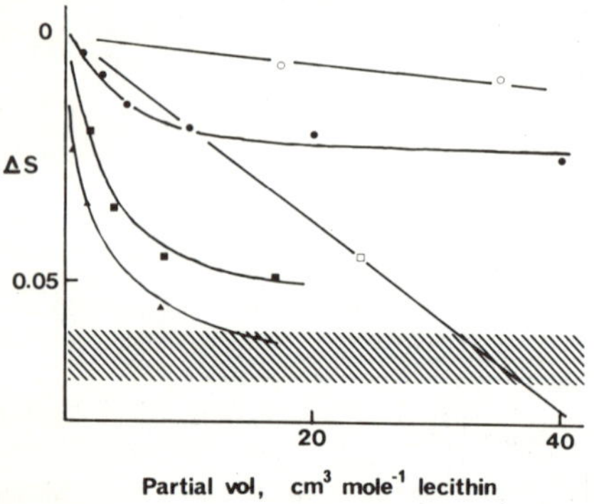

FIGURE 3. Effect of Δ9 THC (4a, ●), 11-hydroxy-Δ9-THC (4b, ■), the dimethylheptyl analog of Δ9 THC (4c, ▲), n-octanol (□), and n-hexadecanol (○) on the order parameter (S) of spin-labeled lecithin/cholesterol liposomes. The hatched band indicates the degree of fluidization corresponding to the onset of anaesthesia.

molecular perturbation produced by the psychoactive cannabinoids is qualitatively the same as that produced by the general anaesthetics, namely, an increase in the molecular disorder of the liposome. At high concentrations the effect levels off, and does not increase as the molecular ratio of Δ9 THC to lecithin is increased. FIGURE 3 also shows the effects of two other psychoactive cannabinoids—11-hydroxy-Δ9-THC (4 b) and the dimethylheptyl analog of Δ9 THC (4 c), both of which have greater CNS activity than Δ9 THC itself. These two derivatives produce similar effects to Δ9 THC on the liposomes but are more potent in that they produce greater fluidization of the liposomes at similar concentrations. This correlation with potency as psychoactive agents encourages us in the belief that this effect is relevant to the *in vivo* actions of the cannabinoids.

The perturbation produced by Δ9 THC does not increase with concentration but levels off to a more or less constant value, substantially below the level of perturbation corresponding to anaesthesia. One possible explanation of the effect is that the solubility of Δ9 THC in phospholipid bilayers is limited and that attempts to increase its membrane concentration result in its being extruded from the hydrocarbon core of the membrane into some alternative configuration having much less effect on the organization of the rest of the membrane system. This limitation on the narcotic effect of Δ9 THC is reminiscent of an effect observed in studies of the narcotic effects of homologous series of organic compounds. It is found that as the chain length of, for example, the series of aliphatic primary alcohols is lengthened, narcotic potency increases in geometric progression until a point is reached when the next highest member is inactive—the so-called cut-off point. Ferguson, in his classic paper on narcosis,[12] explained this effect in terms of a limiting solubility of the narcotic alcohol in the relevant biophase. The inactive members of the series were unable to attain a biophase concentration producing an effect corresponding to the end point of the assay and hence appeared to be inactive. The precise point in the homologous series where the cut-off occurs depends upon the physiological effect that is being recorded. Comparatively gross effects, such as total anaesthesia, would cut off lower down the series than would milder alterations in behavior. This effect can also be reproduced in the liposome model. FIGURE 3 also shows the effects of two aliphatic alcohols—n-octanol and n-hexadecanol. Octanol is an effective anaesthetic when administered intravenously and produces a perturbation of the liposome that at suitable concentrations reaches a level corresponding to anaesthesia. On the other hand, hexadecanol, although it produces "cataleptic"-like conditions in mice similar to those produced by Δ9 THC, is not an anaesthetic, and its ability to fluidize the liposome bilayer is correspondingly limited.

The picture that emerges from these studies is that the psychoactive cannabinoids are members of the class of "cut-off" anaesthetics, exerting their effects predominantly on the lipid phase of nerve cell membranes, producing changes similar to those produced by sub-anaesthetic doses of substances capable of producing full anaesthesia but unable, whatever the dose, to produce anaesthesia by themselves. If we accept this as a working hypothesis for the mode of action of the cannabinoids, we can go on to consider the ways in which they could interact with other agents acting within the central nervous system.

Effects of Other CNS Depressants

The first step is to eliminate those substances that are unlikely to share a common site of action with the cannabinoids. The most obvious example of such a class of substances is the morphine alkaloids. This is not to say, of course, that no interactions between the cannabinoids and morphine derivatives are to be expected. Published reports[13] indicate that such interactions do occur, and others will be given during this meeting. However, all the evidence from structure-action studies, and for the recent isolation of a putative analgesic transmitter substance (enkephalin),[14,15] indicates that the morphine alkaloids interact with a protein-like receptor substance. If the site of action of the cannabinoids is in the lipid phase of the membrane, then these two classes of compound are acting at different sites and any analysis of their interactions would require a much greater knowledge of the molecular nature of the cell response to these compounds than we currently possess.

On the other hand there are some predictions that we can make with some confidence. If we were to seek other compounds that might produce sensory distortions similar to those of cannabis, we might start to look for them amongst the simple aliphatic compounds above the anaesthetic cut-off point, i.e., those of moderately long chain length and low vapor pressure. Unfortunately, such discoveries have already been made by directly empirical means: these compounds are widely used as solvent bases for a wide variety of products and the deliberate inhalation of such vapors—glue sniffing—is a distressing widespread practice, particularly amongst young adolescents. One particular form of the abuse which is currently prevalent in the United Kingdom involves a widely used impact adhesive, the main component of its solvent base being the hydrocarbon toluene. As there is a possibility of these two intoxicants being used simultaneously, we thought it might be of interest to see if there was any summation and, in particular, if there was any synergism between Δ9 THC and toluene. FIGURE 4 shows the effects of toluene on phospholipid vesicles. Rather as expected it shows a typical narcotic-like fluidizing effect. It is not particularly potent in this respect: its molal volume is relatively small, and consequently quite high membrane concentrations must be attained to produce marked effects. When combined with Δ9 THC, the fluidizing effect was augmented,

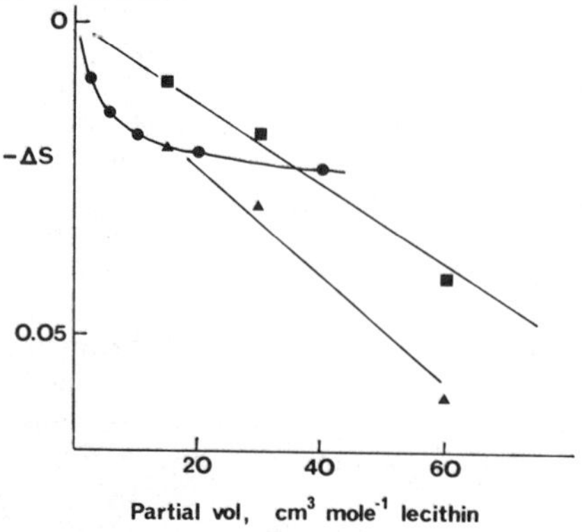

FIGURE 4. Effect of Δ9 THC (●), toluene (■), and a mixture of Δ9 THC (14.2 mg/g total lipid) and toluene (▲) on the order parameter (S) of spin-labeled lecithin/cholesterol liposomes.

the effect of the two substances combined being rather less than the simple sum of the effect produced by either alone.

Barbiturates have been shown to have an effect on liposomes (FIGURE 3), and hence some additivity of their direct narcotic effect with Δ9 THC would be expected. Paton and Pertwee[16] studied the effect of varying doses of Δ9 THC on pentobarbitone-induced sleeping time in mice. They found that low doses of Δ9 THC increased sleeping time but that the effect was limited: further increases in dose of Δ9 THC did not produce any further increase in sleeping time. This observation is concordant with the observations on liposomes: the effect there leveled off with increasing dose, and consequently no further increment of narcotic effect beyond the increase produced by low doses of Δ9 THC would be expected.

The benzodiazepine minor tranquillizers are probably one of the most widely prescribed groups of drugs, certainly amongst those acting on the central nervous system. These drugs evolved, via the quinazolinones, from the barbiturates, and they retain some structural similarities to the latter group (c.f., diazepam (5) and phenobarbitone (6)). The mode of action of these drugs is still a matter of some controversy, and it was thought that these compounds would be worthy of study in their own right, as well as because of the high probability that they might be consumed in conjunction with cannabis.

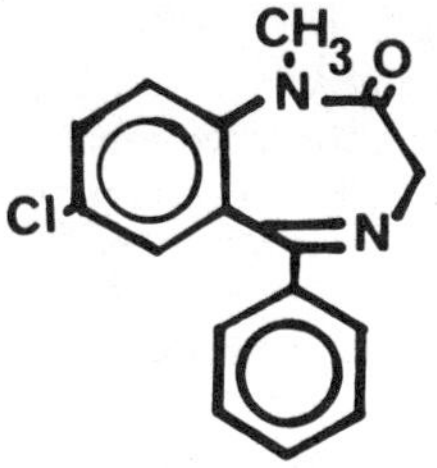

5

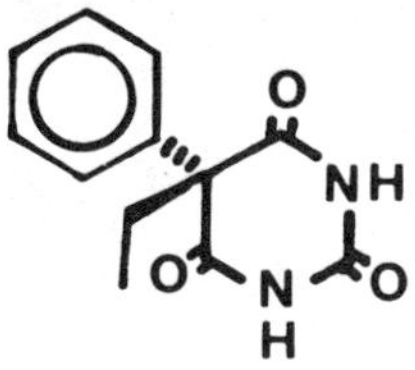

6

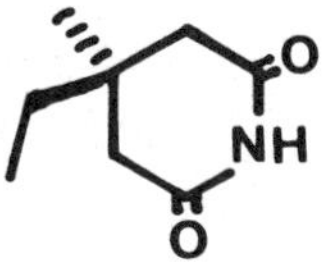

7

The effect, or, rather, the lack of effect of diazepam on spin-labeled liposomes is shown in FIGURE 5. It can be seen that over a wide dose range diazepam had no significant effect on the molecular order of the hydrocarbon chains of the phospholipid components of the membrane. This result is of some interest in that it would imply that although diazepam undoubtedly has

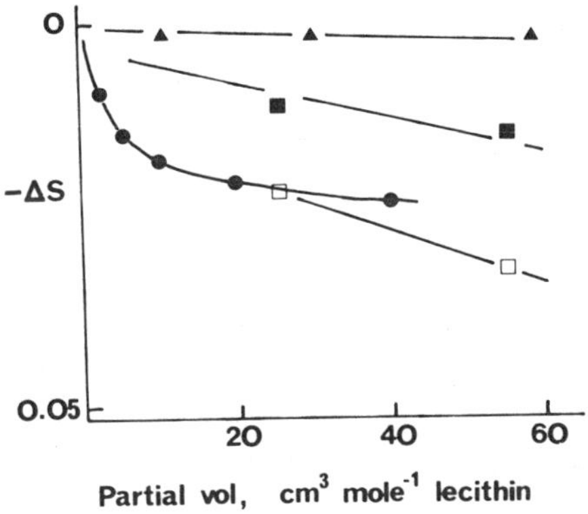

FIGURE 5. Effect of Δ9 THC (●), diazepam (5, ▲), bemegride (7, ■), and a combination of Δ9 THC (14.2 mg/g total lipid) and bemegride (□) on the order parameter (S) of spin-labeled lecithin/cholesterol liposomes.

hypnotic and sedative properties it would appear that it exerts this effect on cell membranes by a molecular mechanism different from that of the barbiturates. These observations need to be extended by studies on other representatives, active and inactive, of the benzodiazepine group, but the conclusion that might be drawn from these experiments is that any summation that might be observed between the effects of diazepam and the cannabinoids is a result of the summation of the physiological responses subsequent to drug combination with the cell, rather than by summation at a common site of action.

One of the most disturbing recent developments in the illicit use of cannabis is the increasing availability of so-called hash-oil—an oily material obtained by solvent extraction from cannabis plants which can contain very high concentrations of the psychoactive cannabinoids. The circulation of this highly concentrated preparation makes it inevitable, one would suppose, that sooner or later cases of massive overdose will begin to appear in the casualty wards.

Several years ago considerable interest was taken in the use of β-methyl β-ethyl glutarimide—bemegride (7)—in the treatment of barbiturate poisoning.

Bemegride is an analeptic, an observation of some theoretical interest in view of its structural similarity to the barbiturates, and particularly as some di α-substituted glutarimides (e.g., glutethimide) are sedative-hypnotics. Bemegride had only a relatively short clinical career as it was found that, although it produced apparently clear-cut reversals of barbiturate-induced hypnosis in experimental animals, its introduction into clinical use as a barbiturate antidote led to a temporary reversal of the steady decline in mortality from barbiturate overdose that the clinicians had achieved over the years. The general opinion nowadays, of course, is that general supportive measures, possibly combined with procedure to accelerate the elimination of the excessive burden of barbiturate, constitute the best therapy for the treatment of overdose.

Nevertheless the idea of a possible hypnotic antagonist is an intriguing one, and consequently the interaction between bemegride and $\Delta 9$ THC on the model system was investigated. FIGURE 5 shows that the effect of bemegride on spin-labeled liposomes is similar to that of the barbiturates in that it increases fluidity and, by that criterion, has a narcotic depressant type of effect, albeit of somewhat limited potency. When combined with $\Delta 9$ THC, the fluidizing effect of bemegride was augmented (FIGURE 5). This result is not too surprising in view of the similarity of its chemical structure to other hypnotic glutarimides. An obvious explanation of the analeptic effect of bemegride is that it has a marginally greater depressant effect on inhibitory synapses within the central nervous system, resulting in some manifestations of central hyperactivity. The failure to act effectively as a barbiturate antagonist would then stem from the fact that an overdose of one depressant of nervous activity was being treated with an additional dose of a second depressant, leading to an improvement in some central mechanisms but to an augmented depression of others. However, notwithstanding the unimpressive clinical record of supposed hypnotic antidotes, the possibility of finding such a substance remains open. The requirement would be to find a compound that reversed the effect of narcotic substances, i.e., increased the molecular order of the lipid phase. Two cannabis constituents—cannabinol and cannabidiol—exert this effect, although they are not very potent.[6] It would be of some interest to endeavor to find a compound that was possessed of considerable potency in this respect.

Two general conclusions may be drawn from these preliminary studies, one pessimistic, one optimistic. The pessimist might point out that a quite detailed description of the molecular mode of action of a drug proves not to be of very much help. Like many other attempts that are being made to correlate drug activities with physical properties, e.g., the linear free energy or QSAR[17] (quantitative structure/action relationship) approaches, such studies seem only to lead to fairly safe predictions of interactions between groups of drugs with similar physico-chemical characteristics at a common site of action, or, more broadly, to new drugs with enhanced potency but with no real novelty of effect. It would seem that the genuinely new drug, or the surprising drug interaction, are more likely to be discovered by the traditional method of animal experimentation. On the other hand, the optimist might conclude that no true understanding of a drug's properties can fall short of an understanding of its action at the molecular level, that such studies prevent the drawing of false analogies between drugs acting in fundamentally different ways, and hence suggest additional directions for investigation, and can also sometimes indicate novel physico-chemical effects that might lead to some new therapeutic agent.

REFERENCES

1. GREEN, D. E., Ed. 1972. Ann. N.Y. Acad. Sci. **195:** 6–519.
2. PARSONS, D. S., Ed. 1975. Biological Membranes. Oxford University Press. Oxford.
3. RANG, H. P., Ed. 1973. Drug Receptors—A symposium. Macmillan Press. London.
4. SEEMAN, P. 1972. Pharmacol. Rev. **25:** 583–655.
5. LAWRENCE, D. K. & E. W. GILL. 1975. Mol. Pharmacol. **11:** 280–286.
6. LAWRENCE, D. K. & E. W. GILL. 1975. Mol. Pharmacol. **11:** 595–602.
7. WILKINS, M. H. F., A. E. BLAUROCK & D. M. ENGELMAN. 1971. Nature New Biol. **230:** 72–76.
8. HUBBELL, W. L. & H. M. MCCONNELL. 1971. J. Amer. Chem. Soc. **93:** 314–326.
9. TRUDELL, J. R., W. L. HUBBELL & E. N. COHEN. 1973. Biochim. Biophys. Acta **291:** 321–327.
10. TRUDELL, J. R., W. L. HUBBELL & E. N. COHEN. 1973. Biochim. Biophys. Acta **291:** 328–334.
11. ATKINSON, R. M., B. DAVIS, M. A. PRATT, H. M. SHARPE & E. G. TOMICH. 1965. J. Med. Chem. **8:** 426–432.
12. FERGUSON, J. 1939. Proc. Roy. Soc., Ser. B **127:** 387–408.
13. JOHNSTONE, R. E., P. L. LIEF, R. A. CULP & T. C. SMITH. 1975. Anesthesiology **42**(6): 674–684.
14. SNYDER, S. H. & S. MATTHYSSE. 1975. Opiate Receptor Mechanisms. Technology Press, M.I.T. Cambridge, Mass.
15. HUGHES, J., T. W. SMITH, H. W. KOSTERLITZ, L. A. FOTHERGILL, B. A. MORGAN & H. R. MORRIS. 1975. Nature **258:** 577–579.
16. PATON, W. D. M. & R. G. PERTWEE. 1972. Brit. J. Pharmacol. **44:** 250–261.
17. HANSCH, C. 1976. J. Med. Chem. **19:** 1–6.

THE COMBINED EFFECT OF MARIHUANA AND DEXTROAMPHETAMINE

R. Forney, R. Martz, L. Lemberger, and B. Rodda

Department of Pharmacology and Toxicology
Indiana University School of Medicine and Lilly Research Labs
Indianapolis, Indiana 46202

M. Evans

Department of Pharmacology
Vanderbilt University
Nashville, Tennessee 37203

Clinical observations and anecdotal accounts of the use of either marihuana (MJ) or dextroamphetamine (d-AMP) have been widely reported. The popularity of each as a recreational agent is generally appreciated. That they were to be so employed conjunctively was inevitable in spite of simple logic, which should have rejected the option to risk damping the exhilaration engendered by an antidepressant or the tranquillity expected from a sedative. Brill *et al.*[1] reported in 1970 that 100% of a sample of college students who used MJ daily also took other drugs on occasion, including amphetamines. Since that observation, Mizner *et al.*,[2] Carlin and Post,[3] Josephson *et al.*,[4] and Fisher and Brickman[5] have confirmed the generalization that MJ smokers are apt also to employ other drugs, including amphetamines, in sensual excursions.

Dagermanjian and Boyd[6] reported in 1962 that dimethyl heptyl pryan and methyl octyl pryan potentiated, in mice, the activity induced by amphetamine or that reduced by barbiturates. In 1967, Garriott *et al.*[7] published data showing that mice in aggregate groups given 95% pure Δ^9-tetrahydrocannabinol (THC) i.p. 1 hr before amphetamine (AMP) treatment experienced stimulation greater than that from AMP alone. Phillips[8] extended this finding to methamphetamine (MAMP) in groups of mice pretreated with incremental amounts of 95% pure THC. The lowest dose, 25 mg/kg, elicited the greatest activity, whereas the highest, 100 mg/kg THC, produced an effect not different from that of AMP alone. The combination of an MJ extract and AMP was studied in single rats and the results described by Perch *et al.*[9] In 1973, they reported that 5, 10, or 20 mg/kg THC in the extract given orally antagonized locomotion stimulated by AMP. Lower doses of 0.625 and 1.25 mg/kg THC were ineffective. Howes[10] reported the effect of THC and a water-soluble derivative on the lethality of d-AMP in aggregated mice. The cannabinoids were administered i.p. 1 hr before i.p. d-AMP. Animals were aggregated four per cage, and number of deaths per 24 hr was recorded. The LD_{50} was calculated. Lethality of d-AMP depended on the dose of THC. A dose of 10 mg/kg THC reduced d-AMP lethality, whereas a dose of 40 mg/kg THC increased toxicity of d-AMP. In isolated mice, the LD_{50} for d-AMP did not change in the presence of 50 mg/kg THC. The mode of action was not determined, but the authors suggested the aggregate mice may have experienced an increased sensitivity to external stimuli from the THC treatment. Craigmill *et al.*[11] have measured motor activity, hyperthermia, toxicity, and brain concentrations of ^{3}H-d-amphetamine induced by d-AMP in aggregated mice pretreated with THC. They reported that 30 min pretreatment with 4.5, 9.0, or 18 mg/kg THC had no effect on toxicity or hyperthermia induced by 5 or 20 mg/kg d-AMP. The high dose of THC did potentiate motor activity. When pretreatment time with 18 mg/kg THC was increased to 1 hr, motor activity and toxicity induced by 5 mg/kg d-AMP were potentiated, hyperthermia was unaffected, and the brain concentration of d-AMP was reduced. This work confirms the observations of Garriott *et al.*[7] and Howes.[10] The authors have concluded that THC potentiates d-AMP toxicity differently than antidepressants, since it did not affect d-AMP-induced hyperthermia and reduced rather than increased brain d-AMP.

Zalcman *et al.*[12] reported the results of giving 15 mg d-AMP or placebo to 10 regular MJ users who immediately smoked either 1 g of MJ containing 1.5% THC or placebo MJ. After 90 min, increased blood pressure and respiratory rate and psychological test scores to be expected when d-AMP with placebo MJ were administered were obtained. Expected MJ effects were also noted in the presence of placebo d-AMP and MJ. Under the test conditions employed, no evidence of drug interaction was noted. Gagnon and Elie[13] have studied the effect of MJ and d-AMP combinations in 63 regular MJ users. d-AMP doses were 0, 7.5, or 15 mg orally and THC by smoking MJ 0, 10 or 20 mg 1.5 hr later. They reported blood pressure increases followed both drug treatments. d-AMP produced a dose-related anorexic effect. With MJ, appetite and food intake were first diminished and then increased. The authors believed an interaction which was not additive occurred when both drugs were given. Kiplinger *et al.*[14] reported in 1971 a dose-related decrement in psychomotor performance in human subjects who had received THC by smoking marihuana. Manno *et al.*[15] showed that this effect is enhanced by ethanol.

An attempt was made to establish a dose relationship of the effect of THC on MAMP-induced locomotor activity in animals. Male Swiss Cox albino mice were used. The studies were conducted in a darkened room at 23° ± 2° C. Treatments consisted of (1) placebo THC + MAMP, (2) THC + placebo MAMP, (3) placebo HC + placebo MAMP, and (4) THC + MAMP. All injections were made i.p. in a volume of 0.5 ml/20 g. THC was suspended in physiological phosphate, and MAMP was dissolved in saline. Placebos were the respective vehicles. Sixteen animals divided into four groups of four mice each were used in each test session. Each group was assigned to one of the treatments and placed in one activity cage. Six sessions were used for each dose level. The doses of THC were 0, 7.5, 15, 30, and 60 mg/kg. The dose of MAMP was 0.5 mg/kg. Under our conditions, 0.5 mg/kg MAMP HCl produced an activity score approximately 25% of maximal activity. THC or placebo THC were gvien 30 min prior to the MAMP. A 5-min acclimatization period for the animals in the activity cage was allowed before the counters were started. Counts were recorded at 30-min intervals for 4 hr.

Placebo treatment produced little or no activity after the first hour of testing and averaged 100 counts/30 min.

TABLE 1 summarizes the activity seen with THC. The values are listed as mean percentage difference from the respective controls for each 30-min interval. With 15 mg/kg, activity increased two to three times over control during the 2 to 2½ hr counting period, with a mean activity for 4 hr of 120% over control value. A summation of the computed ratios for the 4-hr testing period indicated that the low dose of 15 mg/kg doubled locomotor activity, whereas the higher doses of 30 and 60 mg/kg were less effective.

TABLE 1
EFFECTS OF "THC" ON NORMAL LOCOMOTOR ACTIVITY IN MICE

Time	Dose of THC (mg/kg) 15	30	60
0:30	110	−10	20
1:00	80	0	−30
1:30	60	30	80
2:00	280	90	90
2:30	190	100	120
3:00	20	50	0
3:30	110	20	−20
4:00	90	70	−10
Mean total activity for 4 hours	120	40	30

TABLE 2
EFFECTS OF "THC" ON METHAMPHETAMINE-INDUCED LOCOMOTOR ACTIVITY IN MICE

Time	Dose of THC (mg/kg) 7.5	15	30	60
0:30	−30	−60	−60	−70
1:00	−10	10	−30	−40
1:30	30	100	10	30
2:00	150	400	70	120
2:30	310	630	210	170
3:00	110	170	130	100
3:30	150	260	180	160
4:00	70	130	150	125
Mean total activity for 4 hours	100	200	80	70

In TABLE 2, the data obtained with THC effect on MAMP-induced activity are presented as the mean percentage difference from the MAMP control for each time interval. The mean total activity for the 4 hours compared to MAMP control is also given. Animals receiving 0.5 mg/kg MAMP only had increased activity counts during the first 30 min, after which a linear regression of activity was seen. At 3 hr after injection, near-saline control values were observed. Animals pretreated with THC experienced a dose-related decrease in activity during the first 30 to 60 min, compared to MAMP control. As the MAMP effect subsided, the activity of the THC persisted, resulting in counts relatively increased at 2½ hr compared to MAMP controls. The mean relative activity for 4 hr was also maximal when 15 mg/kg THC was given 30 min before MAMP was administered.

FIGURE 1 depicts a dose-response curve at 2½ hr for the effect of THC pretreatment on MAMP-induced locomotor activity. Mean scores from the

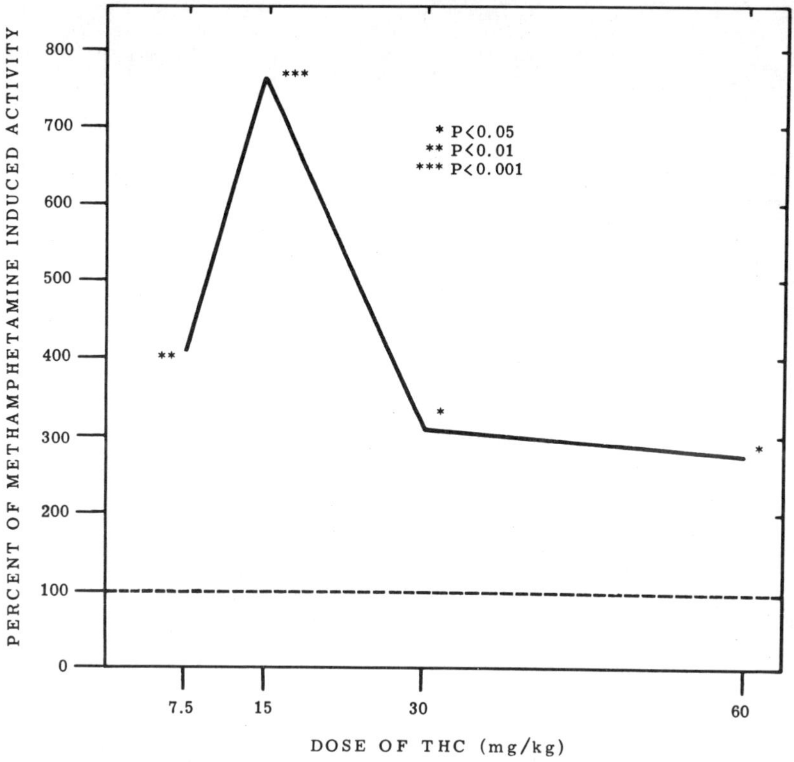

FIGURE 1. Effects of THC on methamphetamine-induced locomotor activity in mice. MAMP dose 0.5 mg/kg.

combination of THC and MAMP were computed as percentage of MAMP only, control. A mean score of 100 thus indicates a mean activity similar to MAMP control. Pretreatment with 15 mg/kg THC enhanced MAMP effect 750%.

The combined effect of MJ and d-AMP on human performance was also examined. Preliminary to this, doses of 0, 5 10, and 15 mg/70 kg d-AMP were administered in capsules to 12 male students in a double-blind random-block design study. Subjects fasted 3.5 hr before the drugs were administered, which was 1.5 hr before testing. Psychomotor performance was measured using a pursuit meter (PM),[16] delayed auditory feedback (DAF),[17] and Wobble Board (WB).[18] Heart rate and arterial blood pressure were monitored, and subjects completed a modified Cornell Medical Index (CMI) questionnaire. Urine was collected for 12 hr in two 6-hr pools and assayed for d-AMP excretion. Heart rate and blood pressure were monitored every 30 min for 1.5 hr before testing. The mean blood pressures and heart rates at time of testing for the doses used are shown in TABLE 3. Systolic pressure rose from a control value of 118 to 141 with 15 mg/70 kg d-AMP. Diastolic pressure with this dose rose from 66 to 73, and the heart rate increase (from 64 to 68) was not significant.

TABLE 3

SUMMARY OF THE EFFECTS OF DEXTROAMPHETAMINE SULFATE ON THE CARDIOVASCULAR SYSTEM

	Dose of Amphetamine (mg/70 kg)				
Cardiovascular Response	0	5	10	15	*p**
Systolic blood pressure					
1½ hr	118	124	134	141	0.0001
Diastolic blood pressure					
1½ hr	66	70	74	73	0.025
Heart rate					
1½ hr	64	70	67	68	N.S.

* Entries indicate the probability that the observed effect occurred by chance alone and, thus, can be considered as "significance levels." A p value which was greater than 0.10 was considered to be not significant and is denoted "N.S."

TABLE 4

SUMMARY OF THE EFFECTS OF DEXTROAMPHETAMINE SULFATE ON PSYCHOMOTOR PERFORMANCE (MEANS AND S. D.)

	Dose of Dextroamphetamine (mg/70 kg)					
Procedure	0	5	10	15	S. D	*p**
Wobble Board						
I	1138	1384	1027	1096	(176)	N.S.
II	1693	1588	1525	1436	(270)	0.01
III	2288	2426	1960	2159	(331)	N.S.
Pursuit Meter						
I	13139	12749	12749	10671	(2600)	0.01
II	10930	10893	10643	10183	(1893)	N.S.
III	11617	11617	11867	11360	(2181)	N.S.
Cornell Medical Index						
Total	5.5	6.3	8.7	10.8	(3.7)	0.01
Pluses	6.0	7.6	10.9	13.6	(5.7)	0.01
No. believed had drug	7/12	6/12	10/12	10/12		

* Entries indicate the probability that the observed effect occurred by chance alone and, thus, can be considered as "significance levels." A p value which was greater than 0.10 was considered to be not significant and is denoted "N.S."

Psychomotor test and symptom scores are shown in TABLE 4. With the WB, a significant ($p < 0.01$ dose-related) improvement in stability of stance occurred in test II (eyes closed). The other two test results were not significant ($p < 0.01$). Test I with the PM was a rapid pattern of 7 cycles/sec. A significant dose-related improvement in performance was seen when it was used. The other two patterns produced no consistent change with dose in either error scores or reaction time. No significant change was observed in any of the tests using DAF.

Both total number of positive responses and symptoms checked on CMI increased significantly ($p < 0.01$) with dose.

Urine analysis indicated that approximately 30% of the dose of d-AMP was excreted during the first 12 hr after it was administered. Urinary pH ranged from 5.3 to 6.6, but the pH of 95% of specimens collected was within 6.0 ± 0.5.

To study the combined effects of THC and d-AMP, oral doses of 0 or 10 mg/kg d-AMP and 0 or 25 μg/kg THC delivered in smoke from a MJ cigarette were chosen. The subjects were 12 male students who had previously used MJ. The study was double blind, with all treatments assigned to each individual according to a randomized complete block design. Each subject was tested at the same time of day, and sessions were each a week apart. Subjects fasted for 3 hr before each session. The d-AMP was given and 1.5 hr allowed to elapse before smoking began. Each MJ cigarette was prepared so as to deliver the calculated dose for each subject, based on previous experience that 50% of its THC content would be absorbed. Each cigarette was smoked in 10 min in a prescribed manner. The experimental treatments consisted of: (1) placebo d-AMP plus placebo THC, (2) d-AMP plus placebo THC, (3) placebo d-AMP plus THC, and (4) d-AMP plus THC. Testing began 1.75 hr after the d-AMP was taken. The testing procedures used were the same as those employed in the d-AMP dose-response experiment.

The mean placebo control value for blood pressure taken 5 min after smoking MJ increased from 86 to 98 after d-AMP. The net change was equal to the sum of those recorded for the agents used singly. Heart rate 5 min after smoking rose 19 beats/min. When the combination was tested, a similar rise occurred. No change was seen with d-AMP or the placebo treatments.

Results obtained with the WB and PM are shown in TABLE 5. The data are presented as mean scores. With d-AMP alone, a slight decrease from placebo suggesting improved standing steadiness was observed. In test III, eyes open and vibrator on, the difference from placebo was significant ($p < 0.05$). MJ treatment alone resulted in decreased steadiness for tests I, II, and III. In test IV (eyes closed, vibrator on), no difference from placebo was detected. The combination treatment scores represent an effect not different from the sum of the two drug treatments used singly.

Digital PM scores in tests I through IV increased significantly ($p < 0.001$) above placebo, with MJ alone indicating a decrease in attentive motor performance. With d-AMP alone, no change from placebo was seen. When the drugs were combined, the loss in attentive performance was similar to that with MJ alone.

Reaction time, for the secondary task of switching off a light signal on cue, demonstrated no consistent change from placebo with d-AMP alone. In test I with MJ, an increase ($p < 0.05$) was recorded. Treatment with both drugs produced no significant difference from placebo. The changes seen were consistent with those associated with MJ alone.

When PM tests I and II were extended from 100 sec duration to 300 sec, a significant decrement in performance was observed with test I ($p < .001$), which was not different from the 100-sec test I result. No change from placebo was recorded with test II.

TABLE 6 presents the subjective impression of the subjects. The CMI indicated a significant increase in the intensity of response symptoms ($p < .001$) over control with MJ. With d-AMP, a slight increase ($p < 0.10$) occurred. The combined treatment result was not different from that with MJ alone. The sub-

TABLE 5

SUMMARY OF THE EFFECTS OF MARIHUANA/DEXTROAMPHETAMINE COMBINATION FOR PURSUIT METER AND WOBBLE BOARD (MEANS AND S.D.)

	Treatment				
Procedure	Placebo Placebo	Amphetamine Placebo	Marihuana Placebo	Marihuana Amphetamine	S.D.
A. Wobble Board					
I	1146	986	1600*	1624	170
II	1448	1287	2167*	1959	320
III	2299	2131†	2947*	2652	305
IV	3825	3659	3769	3720	428
B. Pursuit Meter Test					
I	25605	28036	40993*	37109	8076
II	31090	29940	42456*	43635	8454
III	24605	23985	30345*	31857	5239
IV	27161	28738	43045*	36948	8098
C. Pursuit Meter-RNX time in seconds					
I	1.12	1.22	1.34†	1.29	0.18
II	1.22	1.21	1.32	1.28	0.23
III	1.19	1.14	1.17	1.31	0.26
IV	1.11	1.15	1.28	1.24	0.22
D. Pursuit Meter-Fatigue					
I	78541	72833	111428*	103951	29609
III	74809	64763	80779	80180	10096

Analysis of variance indicated the following:
† $p < 0.05$ * $p < 0.001$ compared with control.

jective impression of the high was improved with MJ alone ($p < .001$) over control. The combined treatment was, again, no different from MJ alone.

The Addiction Research Center Inventory Scale was used for five major drug groups. Mean scores for each group were totaled for treatment effects and then averaged for the 11 subjects completing the Inventory. D-AMP alone produced a negative score in the PCAG (pentobarbital, chlorpromazine, alcohol group), indicating negative sedation or slight stimulation. The MBG (morphine, benzedrine group), B (benzedrine group) A (amphetamine group) scores for d-AMP alone suggest a slight euphoria with some stimulation and a slight psychotomimetic change from the LSD (lysergic acid dietheamide group) score. MJ alone gave a positive sedative score (PCAG) and an increase in euphoria score (MBG) compared to placebo.

The LSD group score was also positive, suggesting dysphoric and psychotomimetic changes. The combination of d-AMP and MJ produced additive scores in all five drug groups.

Eight of the 11 subjects responding felt their driving would be impaired with the MJ-d-AMP combination, and 7 felt this to be true with MJ alone. No real effect on subjective impressions was produced by d-AMP alone.

TABLE 6

SUMMARY OF SUBJECTIVE IMPRESSIONS FOR MARIHUANA DEXTROAMPHETAMINE COMBINATION (MEANS AND S. D.)

Procedure	Treatment: Placebo Placebo	Amphetamine Placebo	Marihuana Placebo	Marihuana Amphetamine	S. D.
A. Cornell Medical Index intensity score	5.7	12.0	18.8*	20.0	9.1
B. Driving impaired	1/11	3/11	7/11	8/11	
C. Drug identification					
Amphetamine	1/11	6/11	1/11	8/11	
Marihuana	1/11	4/11	9/11	11/11	
D. Subjective high	0.4	2.3	5.3*	7.0	2.1
E. Addiction Research Center Inventory					
PCAG	0	−1	3	1	
MBG	1	3	3	6	
BG	0	1	0	1	
A	1	2	3	4	
LSD	0	1	2	2	

* Analysis of variance indicated a p value of less than 0.001 when compared with control.

The subjects' ability to discriminate between drug treatments is also depicted in TABLE 6. When the MJ-d-AMP combination was given, subjects recognized an active treatment. With MJ alone, 9 of 11 identified a drug effect, but d-AMP alone could not be distinguished from placebo treatment.

SUMMARY

The studies in mice indicated that locomotor activity could be stimulated by THC and that this would enhance the effect produced by MAMP.

We have previously shown that when 3, 6, or 9 μg/kg THC were administered to young adult males by MJ smoking, a dose-related impairment in standing steadiness (WB) and attentive motor performance (PM) resulted, although DAF and subjective evaluations were insensitive to these treatments. These same testing procedures after d-AMP 5, 10, and 15 mg/70 kg revealed no important performance effect. Systolic blood pressure was elevated with 15 mg/70 kg d-AMP, and subjective detection was positive and dose related.

A combination of 25 μg/kg THC delivered by smoking an appropriate MJ cigarette and 10 mg/70 kg d-AMP taken orally produced subjective effects and psychomotor performance decrements not different from those with the MJ alone. The doses used were modest, yet most subjects believed their driving performance, a representative motor and metal skill, would be impaired. This judgment is supported by the laboratory measurements made.

It is reasonable that realistically higher doses may not only have adverse psychological and cardiovascular effects but increase an accident potential.

References

1. Brill, N. Q., E. Crumpton, I. M. Frank, J. S. Hackman, P. Lomax, W. H. McGlothlin & L. J. West. 1970. The marijuana problem. Ann. Intern. Med. **73:** 449–465.
2. Mizner, G., J. T. Barter & P. Werme. 1970. Patterns of drug use among college students. Am. J. Psychiatry **127:** 55–64.
3. Carlin, A. S. & R. D. Post. 1971. Patterns of drug use among marihuana smokers. JAMA **218:** 867–868.
4. Josephson, E., P. Haberman, A. Zanes & J. Elinson. 1971. Adolescent marijuana use: Report on a national survey. (Unpublished paper presented, First International Conference on Student Drug Surveys. College of Medicine and Dentistry of New Jersey, Newark, N.J., September 1971.)
5. Fisher, G. & H. R. Brickman. 1973. Multiple drug use of marihuana users. Dis. Nerv. Syst. **34:** 40–43.
6. Dagermanjian, R. & E. S. Boyd. 1962. Some pharmacological effects of two tetrahydrocannabinols. J. Pharmacol. Exp. Ther. **135:** 25–33.
7. Garriott, J. C., L. J. King, R. B. Forney & F. W. Hughes. 1967. Effects of some tetrahydrocannabinols on hexobarbital sleeping time and amphetamine-induced hyperactivity in mice. Life Sci. **6:** 2119–2128.
8. Phillips, R. 1972. Toxicology of delta-9-tetrahydrocannabinol. Ph.D. Thesis. Indiana University School of Medicine, Dept. of Toxicology. Indianapolis, Indiana (136 references).
9. Perch, J. H., R. A. Cohn, K. C. Osterholm & E. S. Barratt. 1973. Antagonism of amphetamine locomotor stimulation in rats by single doses of marihuana extract administered orally. Neuropharmacology **12:** 485–493.
10. Howes, J. F. 1973. The effect of Δ^9tetrahydrocannabinol on amphetamine induced lethality in aggregated mice. Res. Commun. Chem. Pathol. Pharmacol. **6**(3): 895–900.
11. Craigmill, A. L., D. M. Canafax & F. R. Curtiss. 1974. The interaction of Δ^9-tetrahydrocannabinol and *d*-amphetamine in aggregated mice. Res. Commun. Chem. Pathol. Pharmacol. **9**(3): 229–241.
12. Zalcman, S., B. Liskow, R. Cadoret & D. Goodwin. 1973. Marijuana and amphetamine: The question of interaction. Am. J. Psychiatry **130**(6): 707–708.
13. Gagnon, M. A. & R. Elie. 1975. Effect of marijuana and dextroamphetamine on appetite, food intake and some cardiorespiratory variables in man. INRS Sante, Hôp. St. Jean de Dieu, Montreal. Union. Med. Can. **104**(6): 914–921.
14. Kiplinger, G. F., J. E. Manno, B. E. Rodda & R. B. Forney. 1971. Dose-response analysis of the effects of tetrahydrocannabinol in man. Clin. Pharmacol. Ther. **12:** 650–657.
15. Manno, J. E., G. F. Kiplinger, N. Scholz & R. B. Forney. 1971. The influence of alcohol and marihuana on motor and mental performance. Clin. Pharmacol. Ther. **12:** 202–211.
16. Forney, R. B., F. W. Hughes & W. H. Greatbatch. 1964. Measurement of attentive motor performance after alcohol. Percept. Mot. Skills **19:** 151–154.
17. Forney, R. B. & F. W. Hughes. 1961. Delayed auditory feedback and ethanol: Effect of verbal and arithmetical performance. J. Psychol. **52:** 185–192.
18. Shipley, R. E. & R. J. Harley. 1971. A device for estimating stability of stance in human subjects. Psychophysiology **7:** 287–292.

ACUTE AND SUBACUTE INTERACTIONS BETWEEN Δ^9-TETRAHYDROCANNABINOL AND OTHER DRUGS IN THE RAT*

Gordon T. Pryor, Syed Husain, and Chozo Mitoma

Life Sciences Division
Stanford Research Institute
Menlo Park, California 94025

Monique C. Braude

Division of Research
National Institute on Drug Abuse
Rockville, Maryland 20852

In response to the growing interest in the possible implications of increasing polydrug use in our society,[1] we have been studying the interactions between Δ^9-tetrahydrocannabinol (Δ^9-THC), an active ingredient in marihuana,[2] and a number of drugs from various pharmacological classes. The drugs of interest include not only those obtained illicitly and used for recreational purposes, but also socially sanctioned drugs (e.g., alcohol, nicotine, caffeine), drugs prescribed and taken chronically for therapeutic reasons (e.g., the minor tranquilizers, antidepressants, antidiabetics, anorexics), and drugs sold over-the-counter for self-medication (e.g., aspirin, antihistamines).

The drugs and doses we have studied thus far are shown in TABLE 1. Some have been studied much more extensively than others because the results of initial experiments indicated that certain drugs were potentially more interesting in view of the nature and magnitude of their interactions. The purpose of this paper is to present examples of the dose-related interactions observed with several drugs and thereby demonstrate two major points. First, the observed interactions were often complex and depended on a number of factors including (1) the respective doses of the two interacting drugs, (2) the animal's previous history of exposure to either or both drugs, and (3) the methods used to measure the interactions. Although these factors should be self-evident, they are frequently ignored or overlooked. Secondly, in all the interactions between these drugs and Δ^9-THC, the depressant properties of Δ^9-THC generally predominated, regardless of whether the interacting drug was a stimulant or a depressant.

METHODOLOGY

A battery of tests, rather than a single measure, has been used to assess the behavioral and pharmacological effects of drug interactions (TABLE 2). The

* This research was supported by Contract HSM–42–72–182 between the National Institute on Drug Abuse and Stanford Research Institute.

TABLE 1

DRUGS TESTED FOR INTERACTION WITH Δ^9-THC

Drug	Doses Tested*	Units (/kg)
Δ^9-THC	2.5, 5.0, 10.0, 20.0	mg
d-Amphetamine	0.5, 1.0, 2.0, 4.0	mg
Methamphetamine	0.5, 1.0, 2.0	mg
Cocaine	10.0, 20.0, 30.0	mg
Caffeine	25.0, 50.0	mg
Nicotine	0.25, 0.5, 1.0	mg
Chlordiazepoxide	1.0, 2.5, 5.0, 10.0, 15.0	mg
Methaqualone	2.5, 5.0, 10.0, 20.0	mg
Phenobarbital	10.0, 20.0, 40.0	mg
Ethanol	0.5, 1.0, 2.0	g
Phencyclidine	1.25, 2.5, 5.0	mg
LSD-25	0.25, 0.5, 1.0	mg
Lithium chloride	1.0, 2.0, 3.0	mEq
Desmethylimiprimine	5.0, 10.0	mg
Diphenylhydantoin	5.0, 15.0	mg
Tolbutamide	25.0, 50.0, 100.0	mg
Acetylsalacylic acid	120, 240, 320	mg

* Δ^9-THC was given intragastrically in 2 ml/kg of sesame oil; all other drugs were given intraperitoneally in 2 ml/kg of their appropriate aqueous vehicle.

TABLE 2

TEST BATTERY USED IN STUDYING BEHAVIORAL AND PHARMACOLOGICAL INTERACTIONS BETWEEN Δ^9-THC AND OTHER DRUGS*

Test	Measures
Conditioned pole-climb avoidance (two blocks of 30 trials)	Percentage avoidance to tone, nonaversive footshock, or light separately. Percentage total avoidance. Percentage total response (i.e., avoidance or escape). Intertrial responses per minute.
Photocell activity	Cumulative counts: Counts during minutes 0–2. Counts during minutes 2–5. Counts during minutes 5–10.
Heart rate	Beats per minute.
Body temperature	Degrees centigrade.
Rotarod performance	Seconds on rotarod up to 120 seconds.

* The test subjects were male Fischer-strain rats, 55–60 days old, weighing 140–160 g each, housed singly with food and water *ad lib*.

first test consisted of evaluating drug effects on the animals' performance of a conditioned avoidance response (CAR). For this test, one group of animals is first trained to escape and then to avoid an aversive footshock by climbing or pulling a pole; the footshock is signalled by an undulating change in the intensity of a tone or a low-intensity (150 μA), nonaversive current on the grid floor.[3] Use of these three stimuli permits simultaneous assessment of any differential sensory effects of a drug as well as any motor deficits in the same animals. The pretraining takes four days and is done using 12 separate, isolated chambers under computer control.

Another set of animals is used for the other four tests in the battery—photocell activity, heart rate, body temperature, and rotarod performance. The animals are first pretested for photocell activity and trained on the rotarod. They are then assigned to the various drug-treatment groups according to their activity scores so that the mean group scores are equal on this measure. On the following day, subdural electrodes are implanted on both sides of the thorax of each animal for recording the EKG.

TABLE 3

BASIC EXPERIMENTAL DESIGN USED TO STUDY THE ACUTE INTERACTIONS BETWEEN Δ^9-THC AND OTHER DRUGS AND AFTER SUBACUTE PRETREATMENT WITH Δ^9-THC AND/OR OTHER DRUGS*

Group	Subacute Treatment (Days 1–6)	Acute Treatment (Day 7): 2 Hours Before Test	Acute Treatment (Day 7): 30 Minutes Before Test
1	Sesame oil or aqueous vehicle	Sesame oil	Vehicle
2	Sesame oil or aqueous vehicle	Δ^9-THC	Vehicle
3	Sesame oil or aqueous vehicle	Sesame oil	Test drug
4	Sesame oil or aqueous vehicle	Δ^9-THC	Test drug
5	Δ^9-THC	Δ^9-THC	Vehicle
6	Δ^9-THC	Δ^9-THC	Test drug
7	Test drug	Sesame oil	Test drug
8	Test drug	Δ^9-THC	Test drug
9	Δ^9-THC & test drug	Δ^9-THC	Test drug

* The animals were pretrained or pretested before the subacute treatment phase. Δ^9-THC (in sesame oil) and sesame oil were administered intragastrically (2 ml/kg). The test drug (in an appropriate aqueous vehicle) and the vehicle were administered intraperitoneally (2 ml/kg).

Both sets of animals then receive their respective drug treatments daily for the next six days. No further training or testing occurs during this subacute treatment phase. On the seventh day, they are tested following acute drug administration according to the schedule and times described below.

EXPERIMENTAL DESIGN

The basic experimental design used throughout most of these studies is shown in TABLE 3. The objectives were to study both the possible acute interactions between Δ^9-THC and each test drug, as well as how subacute pretreatment with either Δ^9-THC or the test drug or both might affect the interactions.

The first four groups shown in TABLE 3 are used to assess the acute interactions between the drugs. The animals are given sesame oil or an aqueous vehicle during the subacute treatment phase to ensure adequate control comparisons with the last five groups, which are pretreated subacutely with Δ^9-THC and/or the test drug.

On the test day, the animals are administered sesame oil or Δ^9-THC in sesame oil by intragastric intubation 2 hours before testing. Then, 30 minutes before the test, they are injected intraperitoneally with the aqueous vehicle or the test drug in the aqueous vehicle. These times of drug administration were chosen on the basis of results reported in the literature or after preliminary experiments to coincide with times when both drugs would be at effective pharmacological levels at the beginning of testing. The CAR test requires 2 to 2.5 hours, and the other four tests require about 20 minutes to complete.

This experimental design constitutes the necessary minimum basic requirements for testing a drug interaction both acutely and after subacute pretreatment. However, to allow a study of dose effects, the basic design must be expanded considerably. For example, with three doses of Δ^9-THC and three doses of the test drug interacted reciprocally and with one dose of each drug given subacutely, the expanded design requires 25 separate groups. The results reported here were all obtained using such an expanded design.

Behavioral and Pharmacological Effects of Δ^9-THC

Before considering the observed interactions, it may be informative to characterize some of the effects of Δ^9-THC alone in this test system, since this is the primary drug of concern in these studies.

Table 4 summarizes the effects of Δ^9-THC; these results are the combined averages of nine separate experiments. Although the values varied somewhat in the respective experiments, the combined results are fairly typical of each experiment. Photocell activity and rotarod performance were the most variable from experiment to experiment. These measures were also more variable than the other measures within each experiment.

Acute administration of Δ^9-THC caused a dose-related decrease in the values on each of the five measures in the test battery. The magnitude and statistical significance of the effect depended on the particular measure and its variability. Also, the variability increased with increasing doses of Δ^9-THC for all measures except heart rate and rotarod performance. The dose-related decrease in photocell activity shown in Table 4 is actually an oversimplification caused by presenting the combined counts for the entire 10-minute test interval. We have found repeatedly that photocell activity is increased by lower doses of Δ^9-THC during the first 2 to 5 minutes of the test and decreased thereafter. Higher doses of Δ^9-THC typically cause a decrease in photocell activity throughout the test.

Subacute pretreatment with 10 mg/kg of Δ^9-THC for six days caused significant tolerance to develop on all five measures. Again, the magnitude of tolerance depended on the test measure. Thus, almost complete tolerance to the impairment of CAR performance was seen, whereas only partial tolerance to the bradycardia and hypothermia occurred. In some experiments (not shown), this tolerance led to an increase in photocell activity compared with controls.

TABLE 4

ACUTE AND SUBACUTE EFFECTS OF Δ^9-THC
(Combined results from 9 experiments)

Treatment On Days 1–6	Acute Dose of Δ^9-THC On Day 7 (mg/kg)	Test Measure*									
		CAR (%)		Photocell Activity (counts/10 min)		Heart Rate (bpm)		Body Temperature (°C)		Time on Rotarod (sec)	
		Mean	SD	Mean	SD	Mean	SD	Mean	SD	Mean	SD
Sesame oil (2 ml/kg/day)	0.0	88 (136)	8.7	375 (109)	96	489 (107)	25	37.2 (110)	0.37	77 (110)	42
Sesame oil	2.5	86† (136)	12.8	348 (105)	111	439† (104)	35	36.9† (107)	0.49	52† (106)	40
Sesame oil	5.0	78† (137)	16.4	342† (105)	119	412† (106)	39	36.5† (106)	0.67	33† (106)	32
Sesame oil	10.0	63† (137)	23.3	262† (106)	147	382† (107)	35	35.7† (107)	1.05	20† (105)	24
Δ^9-THC (10 mg/kg/day)	10.0	83‡ (135)	13.1	372‡ (104)	136	443‡ (103)	37	36.6‡ (105)	0.71	63‡ (105)	38

* Tests began 2 hours after the last treatment. Combined number of animals is shown in parentheses.
† $p < 0.05$ compared with 0.0 dose by t-test.
‡ $p < 0.01$ compared with acute dose of 10 mg/kg of Δ^9-THC.

PHARMACOKINETICS, DISTRIBUTION, AND METABOLISM OF Δ^9-THC

FIGURE 1 shows the time course of total radioactivity derived from [^{14}C]-Δ^9-THC in plasma as a function of the dose of orally administered Δ^9-THC. The levels are expressed as μg/ml equivalents of the administered Δ^9-THC. They represent the total radioactivity present and, therefore, include both un-

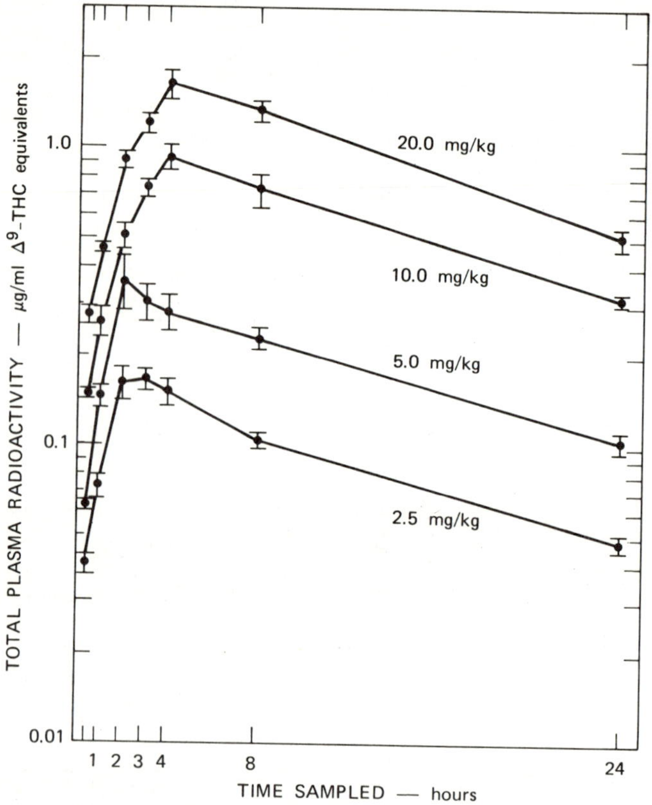

FIGURE 1. Time course of total radioactivity in plasma as a function of the dose of orally administered [^{14}C]-Δ^9-THC (40 μCi/kg).

changed Δ^9-THC and its metabolites. The results were straightforward and do not need extensive discussion. Levels of total radioactivity reached a maximum 2 to 4 hours after administration, depending on dose, and declined thereafter. This time interval—2 to 4 hours—corresponds to the time interval over which the animals were tested for behavioral and pharmacological effects. Therefore, the behavioral and pharmacological effects of Δ^9-THC were directly related to the levels of total plasma radioactivity during testing in these experiments.

The tissue distribution of total radioactivity derived from 10 mg/kg of [^{3}H]-Δ^9-THC (97.9 μCi/kg) after 2 hours is shown in FIGURE 2. By far the highest levels were found in liver at this time, whereas the lowest levels were

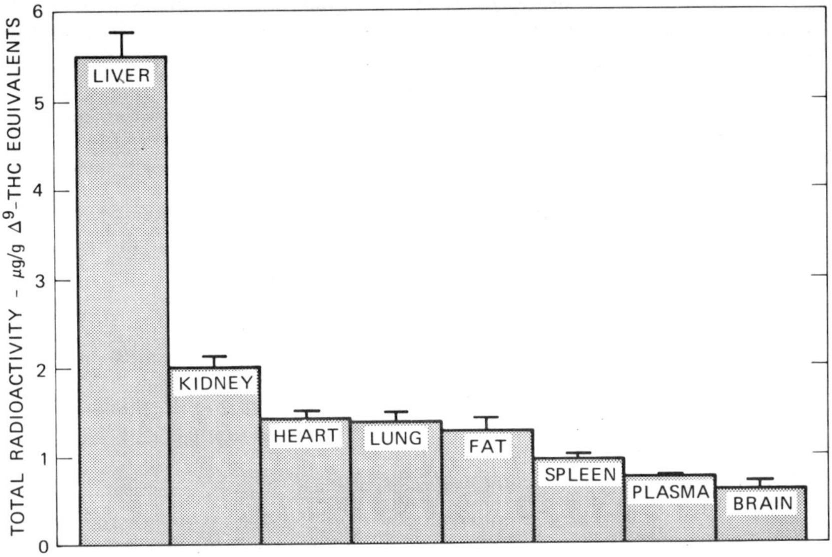

FIGURE 2. Tissue distribution of total radioactivity 2 hours after oral administration of 10 mg/kg of [^{3}H]-Δ^9-THC (98.9 μCi/kg). The results are expressed as the mean (+ SEM) of 5 rats.

found in plasma and brain. Again, these values represent total radioactivity and include both unchanged Δ^9-THC and its metabolites.

The chemical composition of the radiolabeled material in plasma 2 and 4 hours after administration of [^{14}C]-Δ^9-THC (40 μCi/kg) is shown in TABLE 5. The total radioactivity shown on the first line is expressed as μg/ml of Δ^9-THC equivalents and is undifferentiated chemically. Two extractions with 5.0 ml of

TABLE 5

Δ^9-THC AND METABOLITES IN PLASMA 2 AND 4 HOURS AFTER ORAL ADMINISTRATION OF 10 MG/KG [^{14}C]-Δ^9-THC (40 μCI/KG)

	Time after Administration (hours)			
	2		4	
Source of Radioactivity	Mean	SEM	Mean	SEM
Total (μg/ml of Δ^9-THC equivalents)	0.51	0.09	0.33	0.05
Ethyl acetate extract (% total)	73.9	2.8	68.9	2.8
TLC of pooled extract* (% total)				
Δ^9-THC	14.6	—	12.0	—
11-OH-Δ^9-THC	17.5	—	15.3	—
8, 11-diOH-Δ^9-THC	18.8	—	22.2	—
Unidentified	23.0	—	19.2	—

* Tentative identification was made by comparison of Rf's of the samples with authentic standards on the same plate. Five animals were sacrificed at each time point.

ethyl acetate recovered about 70% of the total radioactivity in the samples. The extracted samples were then pooled, evaporated to dryness, and, after being taken up in 0.2 ml of ethyl acetate, spotted on thin-layer plates. After development, sections of the plates were scraped and counted for radioactivity. The migration of authentic standards was used to identify tentatively the unchanged Δ^9-THC and two of its metabolites. Unchanged Δ^9-THC accounted for only 12% and 14% of the total radioactivity in plasma after 2 and 4 hours, respectively. Assuming an approximate plasma/brain ratio of 1.0, the concentrations of Δ^9-THC at the beginning of behavioral and pharmacological testing were probably of the order of less than 100 ng/g in brain after a dose of 10 mg/kg.

Accumulation of Δ^9-THC After Subacute Treatment

As noted earlier, tolerance to the behavioral and pharmacological effects of Δ^9-THC develops rapidly after repeated administration. The mechanism for this tolerance has not been established. However, as shown in Figure 3, plasma and tissue levels of total radioactivity are higher after subacute pretreatment with unlabeled Δ^9-THC than after subacute pretreatment with sesame oil. The results shown in the figure were combined from three separate experiments, each of which showed the same effect. In these experiments, the elevated plasma levels occurred at 2 to 4 hours and then declined to control levels by 8 hours. The magnitude of this effect was larger in brain than in plasma, and the elevated levels persisted for at least 8 hours.

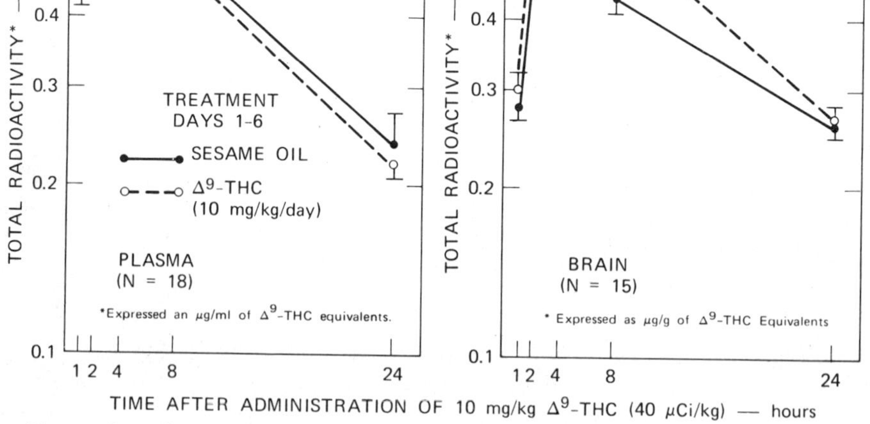

Figure 3. Time course of total radioactivity in plasma and brain after subacute pretreatment with sesame oil or Δ^9-THC.

A separate experiment, summarized in TABLE 6, was conducted to determine how much total radioactivity derived from [^{3}H]-Δ^9-THC accumulated after repeated administration. Two groups of rats were given sesame oil or 10 mg/kg of unlabeled Δ^9-THC daily for six days, and then both were given a labeled dose (80 μCi/kg) of [^{3}H]-Δ^9-THC on the seventh day. The total radioactivity in plasma from the group pretreated with Δ^9-THC was higher than in the group given sesame oil when they were sacrificed 2 hours after administration of the [^{3}H]-Δ^9-THC, although the difference was not statistically significant in this experiment. A third group was given [^{3}H]-Δ^9-THC on the first six days and unlabeled Δ^9-THC on the seventh day to see how much was residual on the seventh day. Residual radioactivity was approximately 3.4 times greater than the radioactivity derived from a single dose of [^{3}H]-Δ^9-THC. Finally, a fourth group was given [^{3}H]-Δ^9-THC on all seven days. The levels in this group were not significantly different from those obtained by adding the levels from the second and third groups, namely 2.7 μg/ml compared with 2.8 μg/ml. This value is almost fivefold higher than the levels obtained after a single administration of [^{3}H]-Δ^9-THC following pretreatment with unlabeled Δ^9-THC for six days. Therefore, a substantial tissue pool of Δ^9-THC-derived substances accumulates after repeated daily administration. The increased radioactivity seen after subacute pretreatment with Δ^9-THC may be caused by an isotope dilution effect as the acute labeled dose interacts with this pool. Whether this pool is in some way responsible for, or related to, the tolerance that develops to Δ^9-THC remains to be established.

TABLE 6

ACCUMULATION OF RADIOACTIVITY IN PLASMA FOLLOWING ACUTE OR SUBACUTE TREATMENT WITH Δ^9-THC OR [^{3}H]-Δ^9-THC

	Treatment		Δ^9-THC Equivalents (μg/ml)	
Group	Days 1–6	Day 7*	Mean	SEM
1	Sesame oil	[^{3}H]-Δ^9-THC	0.59	0.04
2	Δ^9-THC	[^{3}H]-Δ^9-THC	0.69	0.06
3	[^{3}H]-Δ^9-THC	Δ^9-THC	2.01	0.11
4	[^{3}H]-Δ^9-THC	[^{3}H]-Δ^9-THC	2.84	0.09

* Animals (N = 10) were sacrificed 2 hours after the last oral dose of 10 mg/kg of Δ^9-THC or [^{3}H]-Δ^9-THC (80 μCi/kg).

BEHAVIORAL AND PHARMACOLOGICAL INTERACTIONS BETWEEN Δ^9-THC AND OTHER DRUGS

The behavioral and pharmacological interactions discussed below are illustrated by examples from nine experiments in which full reciprocal, dose-response comparisons were made. The examples were chosen to demonstrate specific types of interactions and certain factors that influence these interactions.

Acute Interactions

The depressant properties of Δ⁹-THC generally predominated, regardless of the pharmacological properties of the interacting drug. This common feature of the acute interactions of these drugs with Δ⁹-THC is demonstrated by the results obtained with a single dose of 10 mg/kg of Δ⁹-THC combined with a single dose of each test drug. To make comparison of the results more uniform from experiment to experiment and across measures, the data were normalized with respect to the combined controls on each measure so that the values would have a common scale and could be expressed as a profile of effects in standard units.

The results are summarized in FIGURE 4. Each panel shows the profiles of results for one drug as it interacted acutely with Δ⁹-THC. The profile of each drug alone and of Δ⁹-THC alone are also included for comparison purposes; thus, for each measure there are three overlapping bars beginning at zero. The zero points on the ordinate are the normalized control values for each measure in the test battery.

The acute effects of Δ⁹-THC alone were depressant on all measures in all nine of these experiments. *d*-Amphetamine alone (2 mg/kg) and cocaine alone (20 mg/kg) stimulated photocell activity but had very little effect on the other measures at these doses. Nicotine (0.5 mg/kg) and chlordiazepoxide (5 mg/kg) were essentially inactive alone at these doses on most of the measures, whereas the other six drugs were depressant to varying degrees when administered alone.

The predominant depressant effect of Δ⁹-THC is illustrated by comparisons between the interaction profiles and the profiles for each drug alone. First, the interaction profiles for *d*-amphetamine and cocaine are almost identical with those for Δ⁹-THC alone. That is, at these doses, these stimulants were unable to antagonize any of the depressant effects of Δ⁹-THC. Second, nicotine and chlordiazepoxide, although ineffective alone, strongly potentiated the depressant effects of Δ⁹-THC. Finally, for the other six drugs that showed varying degrees of depression when given alone, the interactions with Δ⁹-THC resulted in mutual enhancement of depression.

FIGURE 5 shows some of the acute interactions in more detail in terms of dose relationships. The results are shown for three drugs as they interacted with Δ⁹-THC in impairing CAR performance. Three somewhat different patterns occurred as a function of the respective doses of the two interacting drugs.

The results for phenobarbital show one pattern. At the doses used, phenobarbital alone did not impair CAR performance appreciably. When given with 2.5 mg/kg of Δ⁹-THC, only the highest dose of phenobarbital (40 mg/kg) caused a slight potentiation of impairment. However, with 5 mg/kg of Δ⁹-THC, the highest dose of phenobarbital severely impaired CAR performance. Finally, with 10 mg/kg of Δ⁹-THC, phenobarbital caused a clear, dose-related potentiation of impairment. These results suggest that a critical level of either Δ⁹-THC or phenobarbital is sufficient to trigger the potentiated impairment of CAR performance.

The results for ethanol show a somewhat different pattern. The interaction between Δ⁹-THC and ethanol, unlike that of Δ⁹-THC and phenobarbital, appears to be more critically dependent on the dose of ethanol than Δ⁹-THC. Thus, up to 1 g/kg of ethanol, there was no significant potentiation of the impairment caused by any dose of Δ⁹-THC, whereas 2 g/kg of ethanol increased

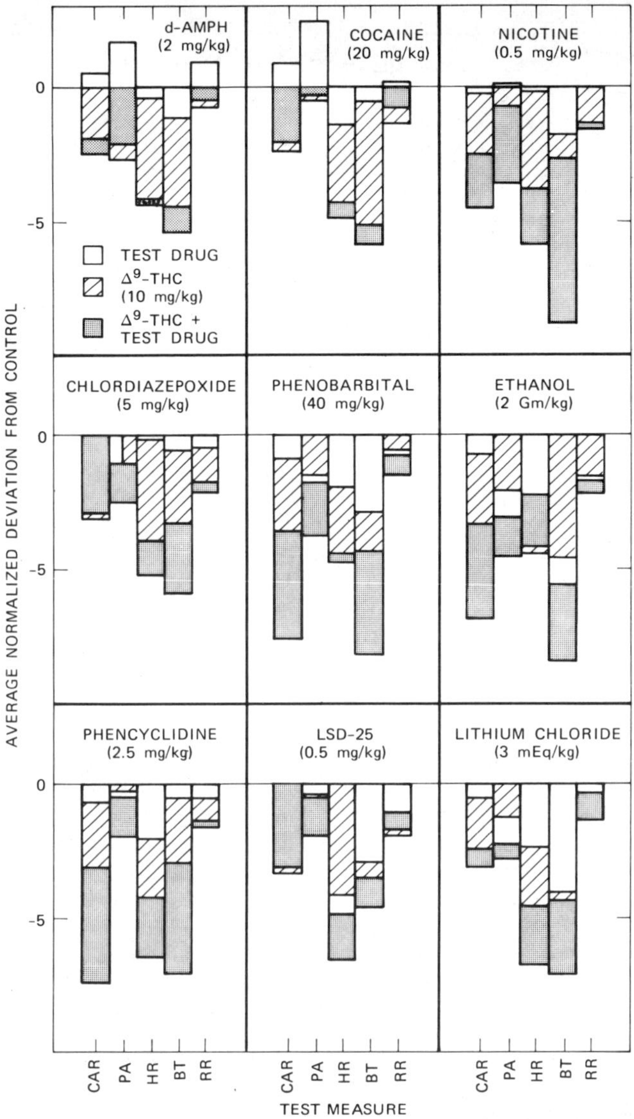

FIGURE 4. Normalized profiles of acute interactions between Δ^9-THC and each of nine other drugs. Open bars represent the effects of the test drug alone (where not shown, the value is zero). Cross-hatched bars represent the effects of 10 mg/kg of Δ^9-THC (where not shown, the value is the same as for the solid bar). The solid bars represent the interaction between 10 mg/kg of Δ^9-THC and the dose of the test drug shown in parentheses. The zero line in each panel corresponds to the normalized control value for each measure; all values are shown as deviations from this zero line in standard deviation units. CAR = conditioned avoidance response to all three stimuli; PA = cumulative photocell activity counts for 10 minutes; HR = heart rate; BT = body temperature; and RR = rotarod performance. There were 10 to 20 animals in each drug-treated group.

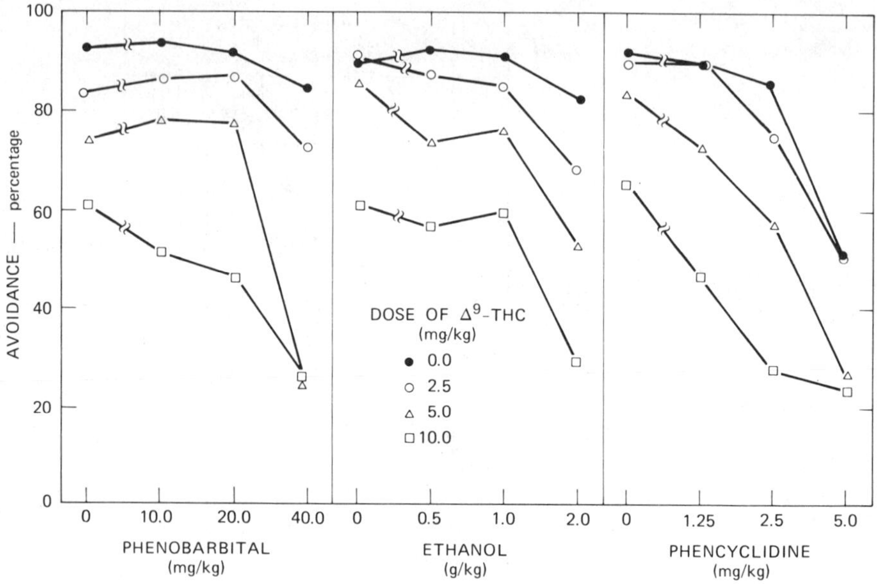

FIGURE 5. Acute reciprocal dose-response interactions between Δ^9-THC and each of three other drugs; effects on CAR performance. The values shown are the means of 14 to 18 rats at each data point.

the effects of all three doses of Δ^9-THC, even though this dose of ethanol was minimally effective alone.

The third pattern is illustrated by the results for phencyclidine. Here, the primary drug appears to be Δ^9-THC. When the dose of Δ^9-THC reached a critical level, in this case 5 mg/kg, phencyclidine caused a graded, dose-related potentiation of impairment. At the lower doses of phencyclidine the potentiation was more than additive, whereas at the highest dose it was less, perhaps because of a floor effect imposed by the lower limit of this test procedure.

Still other dose-related patterns of interaction are shown in FIGURE 6 for photocell activity. Cocaine alone caused a dose-related increase in activity. The interaction with Δ^9-THC on this measure was one of mutual antagonism. The degree of antagonism and which drug predominated depended on the dose of each drug. Thus, at the lower doses of Δ^9-THC, cocaine was still able to stimulate photocell activity. However, at the highest dose of Δ^9-THC, which caused depression alone, the highest dose of cocaine was only able to restore photocell activity to control values (doses much above 30 mg/kg of cocaine caused convulsive activity and, therefore, were not tested).

The results for nicotine are interesting in that doses as high as 1 mg/kg of this drug alone did not alter photocell activity appreciably. However, all doses of nicotine interacted with all doses of Δ^9-THC to cause almost complete suppression of activity.

Phencyclidine alone caused a curious effect depending on dose. Up to 2.5 mg/kg, phencyclidine did not affect photocell activity appreciably. However, at 5 mg/kg, phencyclidine caused a threefold increase in activity that was

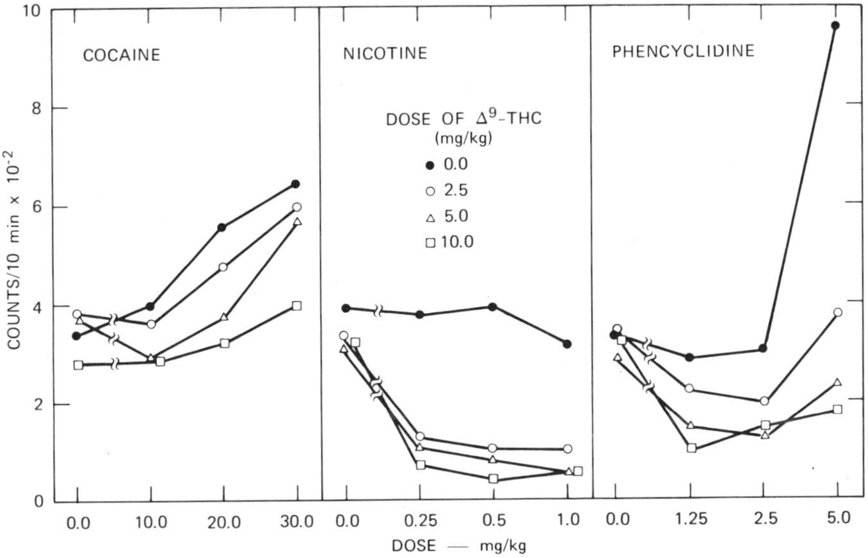

FIGURE 6. Acute reciprocal dose-response interactions between Δ^9-THC and each of three other drugs; effects on photocell activity. The values shown are the means of 10 to 16 rats at each data point.

found by direct observation to be caused by compulsive, although ataxic, forward locomotion. As shown, Δ^9-THC blocked this effect of phencyclidine as a function of dose.

The final illustrations of acute dose-related interactions are shown in FIGURE 7 for heart rate. Acute administration of Δ^9-THC causes a dose-related decrease in heart rate in rats as opposed to the increase seen in humans.[4] Both LSD-25 and lithium chloride have the same effect when administered alone. The difference between these two drugs as they interacted with Δ^9-THC on this measure is seen by comparison of the respective slopes of the dose-response curves. While the interaction of both drugs with Δ^9-THC appeared equally dependent on the doses of Δ^9-THC and the interacting drug, the interaction with LSD-25 was less than additive, whereas the interaction with lithium chloride was almost exactly additive at all doses.

Interactions Following Subacute Pretreatment with Δ^9-THC

The previous section illustrated different acute interaction patterns that occurred depending on the doses of the two interacting drugs. This section compares some of the interactions that occurred after subacute pretreatment with Δ^9-THC with those after acute treatment and demonstrates a second common feature of the interactions we have seen; namely, that tolerance develops to the effects of Δ^9-THC, and, in general, this tolerance extends to the interactions of Δ^9-THC with other drugs, causing an attenuation of the predominant effects of their acute combinations.

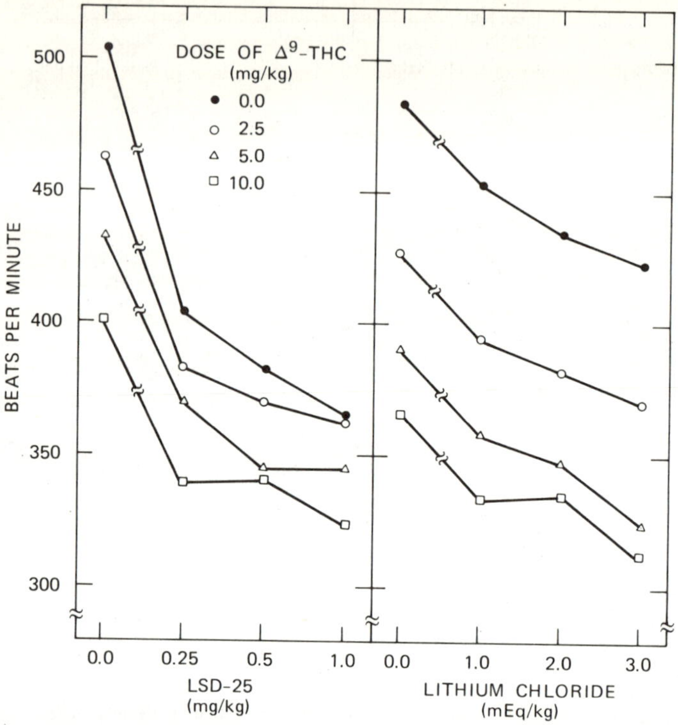

FIGURE 7. Acute reciprocal dose-response interactions between Δ^9-THC and each of two other drugs; effects on heart rate. The values shown are the means of 11 to 15 rats at each data point.

FIGURE 8 shows the effects on CAR performance of the interactions between Δ^9-THC and each of eight drugs after subacute pretreatment with 10 mg/kg of Δ^9-THC for six days; also shown are the acute interactions and the effects of each drug alone. Clearly in all cases except two, the groups pretreated subacutely with Δ^9-THC performed better than the groups treated acutely with both drugs. The two exceptions were the interactions seen with the highest doses of lithium chloride and phenobarbital. (The highest dose of phenobarbital also interacted acutely with a lower dose of Δ^9-THC (5 mg/kg) to cause the same magnitude of impairment, so that this result may not be a true exception.) These results may seem obvious in the sense that if tolerance develops to a drug, then an attenuation of any interactions must follow. However, as will be shown in the next section, this assumption is not always true when the animals are pretreated with the test drugs.

The other data shown in FIGURE 8 (closed squares) are for groups of animals that were pretreated subacutely with both Δ^9-THC and the test drug. For six of the drugs, the results were similar to those seen after subacute pretreatment with Δ^9-THC alone. The exceptions were phenobarbital and phencyclidine. Although pretreatment with Δ^9-THC alone did not appear to attenuate the acute interaction with phenobarbital, pretreatment with both Δ^9-THC and phenobarbital caused significantly better performance than after their acute

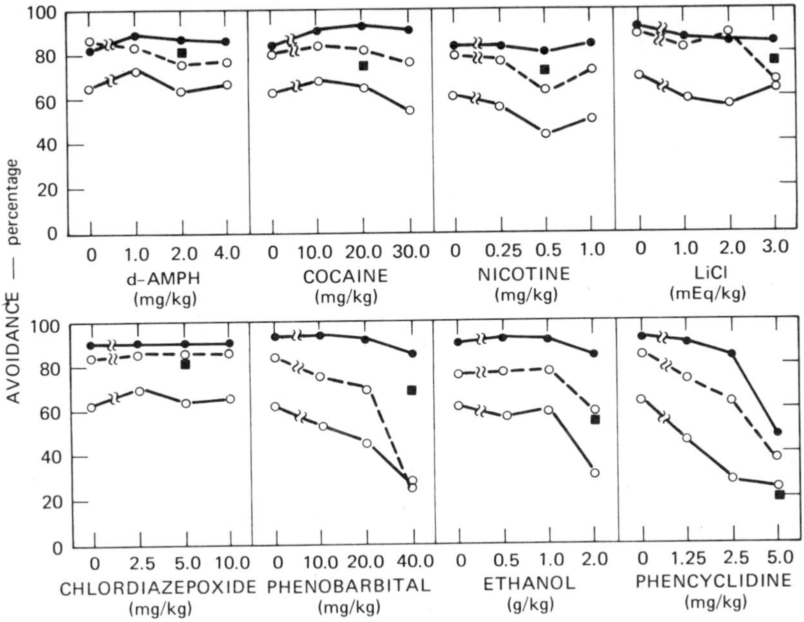

FIGURE 8. Interaction between Δ^9-THC and each of eight other drugs after subacute pretreatment with 10 mg/kg of Δ^9-THC alone or in combination with the other drug; effects on CAR performance. Treatment on Days 1 to 6: —— sesame oil, - - - - - Δ^9-THC. Treatment on Day 7: ● test drug alone, ○ test drug plus 10 mg/kg of Δ^9-THC. The ■ represents groups treated throughout with 10 mg/kg of Δ^9-THC and the indicated dose of the test drug. The values shown are the means of 14 to 18 rats at each data point.

administration. This result suggests that tolerance developed to the effects of both Δ^9-THC and phenobarbital, since the improvement in performance by this group was greater than after subacute pretreatment with phenobarbital alone (see FIGURE 10).

On the other hand, the interaction between Δ^9-THC and phencyclidine was as great after pretreatment with both drugs as after acute administration. Since tolerance to the acute interaction was seen following subacute pretreatment with Δ^9-THC alone, this result suggests cumulative effects of phencyclidine, a conclusion that is supported further below.

The results for photocell activity are shown in FIGURE 9. The same general effects of subacute pretreatment with Δ^9-THC are seen here as were seen for CAR performance. However, the degree of tolerance to the depressant effects of Δ^9-THC alone and its interactions with the other drugs was often less for this measure than for CAR performance, and the doses of the test drugs that were still effective were lower.

The results for phencyclidine deserve special attention. As noted earlier, an acute dose of 5 mg/kg of phencyclidine caused a marked increase in photocell activity counts that was blocked by 10 mg/kg of Δ^9-THC. When the animals were made tolerant to the effects of 10 mg/kg of Δ^9-THC in this experi-

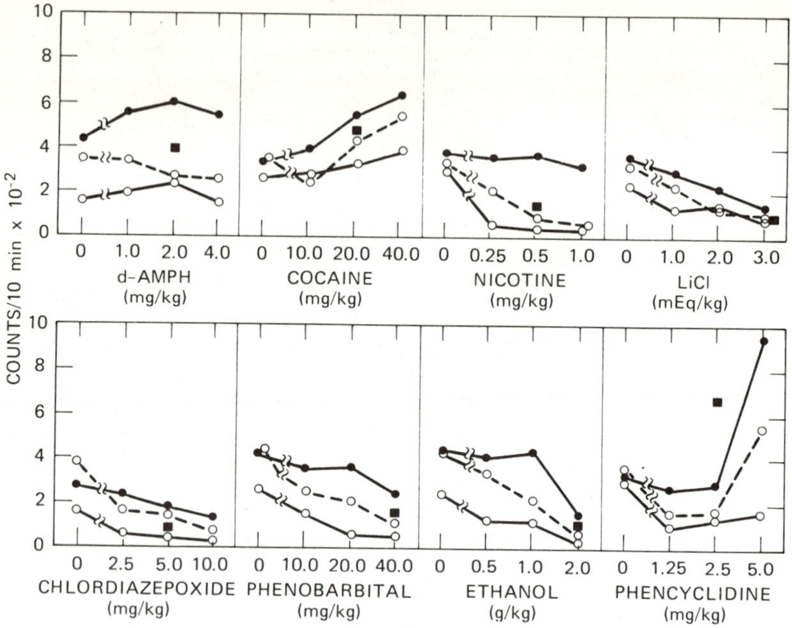

FIGURE 9. Interactions between Δ⁹-THC and each of eight other drugs after subacute pretreatment with 10 mg/kg of Δ⁹-THC alone or in combination with the other drugs; effects on photocell activity. Symbols are the same as in FIGURE 8. The values shown are the means of 10 to 15 rats at each data point.

ment, the increase in photocell activity caused by 5 mg/kg of phencyclidine again appeared. Another point that was raised by the results in FIGURE 8 is supported further by the results in FIGURE 9; namely, that phencyclidine may have cumulative effects. In the group pretreated with both 10 mg/kg of Δ⁹-THC and 2.5 mg/kg of phencyclidine, photocell activity again was increased markedly. Since this dose of phencyclidine was not effective when given acutely, this result also provides evidence for a cumulative or sensitizing effect that was revealed when the animals were made tolerant to Δ⁹-THC.

Interactions After Subacute Pretreatment with the Test Drugs

The interactive effects seen after subacute pretreatment with each of the test drugs, unlike those seen after pretreatment with Δ⁹-THC, are not generally predictable; instead, they depend on the particular drug.

The interactive effects on CAR performance after pretreatment with each of four of the drugs are shown in FIGURE 10 and illustrate three different results. The results after subacute pretreatment with 40 mg/kg of phenobarbital were similar to those seen generally after subacute pretreatment with Δ⁹-THC. Tolerance to the effect of phenobarbital alone and its interaction with Δ⁹-THC was clearly evident. On the other hand, subacute pretreatment with 2 g/kg of ethanol did not alter its interaction with Δ⁹-THC, even though there was evidence of slight tolerance to ethanol itself. Finally, both phencyclidine and

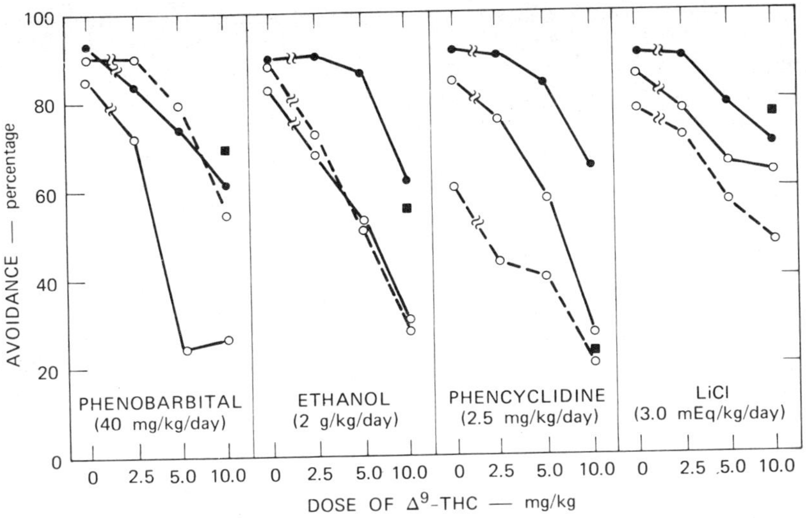

FIGURE 10. Interactions between Δ^9-THC and each of four other drugs after subacute pretreatment with each other drug alone or in combination with 10 mg/kg of Δ^9-THC; effects on CAR performance. Treatment on Days 1 to 6: —— sesame oil, - - - - - test drug. Treatment on Day 7: ● test drug alone, ○ test drug plus 10 mg/kg of Δ^9-THC. The ■ represents groups treated throughout with 10 mg/kg of Δ^9-THC and the dose shown in parentheses of the other drug. The values shown are the means of 13 to 18 rats at each data point.

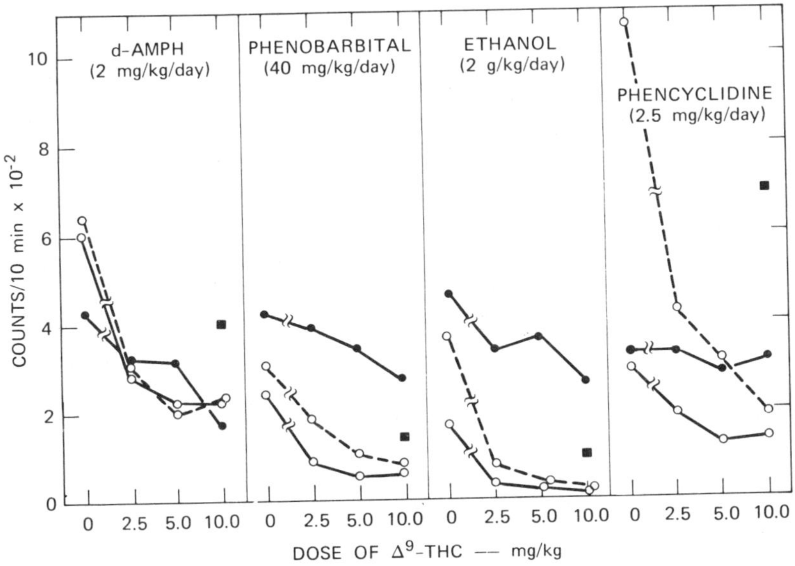

FIGURE 11. Interactions between Δ^9-THC and each of four other drugs after subacute pretreatment with each other drug alone or in combination with 10 mg/kg of Δ^9-THC; effects on photocell activity. Symbols are the same as in FIGURE 10. The values shown are the means of 9 to 15 rats at each data point.

lithium chloride showed evidence of an increase in their effects after subacute pretreatment. This increase in effect was especially pronounced for phencyclidine.

Comparable results for photocell activity are shown in FIGURE 11. The stimulation caused by *d*-amphetamine was effectively antagonized as a function of dose of Δ^9-THC. The magnitude of this antagonistic effect of Δ^9-THC was essentially the same whether *d*-amphetamine was given acutely or after subacute pretreatment. On the other hand, there was significant tolerance to phenobarbital and its interaction with Δ^9-THC, although the tolerance was less for this measure than for CAR performance. Clear tolerance to the depressant effects of ethanol alone followed subacute pretreatment. However, the interaction between ethanol and Δ^9-THC was just as severe as after their acute combination. Finally, the cumulative or sensitizing effects of phencyclidine were more striking than any shown previously. Again, referring back to FIGURE 6, an acute dose of 2.5 mg/kg of phencyclidine was ineffective alone. After six daily injections, the increase in counts caused by this dose was even greater than the increase caused by 5 mg/kg of phencyclidine given acutely. Δ^9-THC effectively antagonized this cumulative effect of 2.5 mg/kg of phencyclidine by about the same amount that it antagonized the acute effects of 5 mg/kg of the drug.

SUMMARY AND CONCLUSIONS

Although more data have been collected than can be reported here, sufficient examples have been presented to demonstrate the points outlined at the beginning of this paper. We have not discussed the results for body temperature, which generally paralleled those for heart rate. Also, results similar to those shown for CAR performance were found for rotarod performance, even though this measure was much less reliable from experiment to experiment than the other measures. Finally, we have not discussed the results of a number of kinetic studies in plasma and brain and how the levels of total radioactivity derived from [^{14}C]-Δ^9-THC or the labeled test drugs are affected by the various interactions. Generally, these latter measures have been less sensitive to the interactive effects of these drugs than the behavioral and pharmacological measures. Therefore, we have been less successful in identifying the possible mechanisms involved than in demonstrating the effects. Although additional work is required, we are hesitant at this time to attribute the observed interactions to grossly altered metabolism in general. Instead, we believe that the sites and mechanisms of these interactions will most likely be found in the ways these drugs interact with the neural substrate.

The behavioral and pharmacological interactions we have observed in rats between Δ^9-THC and a number of other drugs can be summarized as follows:

1. The effects of Δ^9-THC alone are generally depressant and related to dose.

2. When Δ^9-THC is combined acutely with a variety of drugs, its depressant properties generally predominate, regardless of the pharmacological properties of the other drug.

3. The type of interaction seen depends on several factors including:
   (a) The respective doses of the two interacting drugs.

(b) The test subject's previous history of exposure to either or both of the interacting drugs.

(c) The tests used to measure the interaction.

4. Tolerance to the depressant effects of Δ^9-THC develops rapidly, but differentially, depending on the particular test measure. This tolerance generally extends to the interactions between Δ^9-THC and other drugs and results in a reduction of the predominant depressant effects of Δ^9-THC.

5. Finally, the changes in the interactions that follow subacute pretreatment with the other drugs are less general. Some drugs showed selftolerance, but no reduction in their interactive effects with Δ^9-THC, whereas others showed tolerance to both effects. For some drugs there were no differences between the interactions seen after acute and subacute pretreatment, while for still others the effects were greater after subacute pretreatment than after acute treatment.

Acknowledgments

Scheduled drugs, including cannabinoids, were supplied by NIDA. The following persons deserve special credit and thanks for their skilled and conscientious assistance in this project: Ferol Larsen, Janet Carr, Catherine McKenzie, Linda Dixon, Janet Frazier, Tom Steeger, Barbara Lewin, and Dr. Leon Lombrozo.

References

1. Polydrug Use: An Annotated Bibliography. June 1975. National Institute on Drug Abuse. National Clearinghouse for Drug Abuse Information. Rockville, Md.
2. Singer, A. J., Ed. 1971. Marijuana: Chemistry, Pharmacology, and Patterns of Social Use. Ann. N.Y. Acad. Sci. Vol. 191.
3. Pryor, G. T. 1976. Acute and subacute behavioral and pharmacological interactions of Δ^9-THC with other drugs. *In* The Pharmacology of Marijuana. M. Braude & S. Szara, Eds. Raven Press. New York, N.Y.
4. Johnson, S. & E. F. Domino. 1971. Some cardiovascular effects of marijuana smoking in normal volunteers. Clin. Pharmacol. Therap. **12:** 762–768.

INTERACTIONS OF ACTIVE CONSTITUENTS OF MARIHUANA WITH OTHER DRUGS IN THE NEURON*

William L. Dewey, Kenneth M. Johnson, and Alan S. Bloom

Department of Pharmacology
Medical College of Virginia
Virginia Commonwealth University
Richmond, Virginia 23298

A number of papers have appeared in recent years that describe the interaction of other drugs with marihuana or one of its active constituents. These drug interaction studies can be divided into three groups: Some investigators have studied the effects of one other constituent of marihuana on the pharmacological effects of delta-9-tetrahydrocannabinol (Δ^9-THC), which has been shown to be the major active constituent of marihuana.[1–4] In some reports the investigators have studied the interaction of one of the other drugs of abuse with marihuana or its active constituent.[5–10] In the third group of experiments, the interaction of various therapeutic agents with marihuana or one of its active constituents has been investigated.[11–14] The majority of the experiments referred to above have been involved with an *in vivo* interaction of a drug with a cannabinoid. Although the majority of these experiments have been carried out in laboratory animals, some work in human volunteers has been reported. The majority of these papers have been referred to by other speakers in this conference. There are few reports of the interaction of other drugs on the *in vitro* or biochemical effects of the cannabinoids.

In the present communication, it is our intent to discuss two different drug interactions with Δ^9-THC that occur within the neuron. The first of these interactions is concerned with the effect of reserpine and Δ^9-THC on the subcellular distribution of each other in brain tissue. Other investigators have reported on the effects of drugs on the distribution of Δ^9-THC in the whole animal. However, no previous attention has been given to the effect of drugs on the subcellular distribution of Δ^9-THC. In the second portion of this report, we describe the results of our experiments into the effects of the narcotic antagonist, naloxone, on some of the pharmacological effects of an interesting new cannabinoid. Again, we have examined this interaction at a neurochemical level. It is our intent to describe drug interactions of a pharmacodynamic or distributional nature and relate these interactions to alterations in the pharmacological effect of the cannabinoids produced by these other drugs.

Cannabinoids and Reserpine Effects on Subcellular Distribution

We will review what has been reported on the subcellular distribution of Δ^9-THC in the central nervous system prior to describing the effect of

* This work was supported in part by U.S. Public Health Service Grants DA-00326, DA-00490, F32-DA-05012, and T32-DA-07027.

reserpine on this parameter. We have previously reported that the subcellular distribution of Δ^9-THC in the mouse, rat, and dog brain is similar.[15] A summary of the data accumulated on the subcellular distribution of Δ^9-THC in mouse, rat, and dog is presented in TABLE 1. The dogs were given a dose of 0.5 mg/kg tritiated Δ^9-THC by the intravenous route of administration 10 minutes prior to sacrifice. In the mouse and rat experiments, tritiated Δ^9-THC was given at a dose of 50 mg/kg intraperitoneally 1 hour prior to sacrifice. Although different doses of the cannabinoid and different pretreatment times were used in different species, these conditions were chosen on the basis of previous experiments that demonstrated that they produced significant effects on the overt behavior of that species. A more detailed description of the experimental protocol and details about the radiolabeled compound have been reported in previous communications.

TABLE 1

PERCENT OF TOTAL RADIOACTIVITY (Δ^9-THC PLUS METABOLITES FOUND IN TOTAL HOMOGENATES IN EACH FRACTION OR SUBFRACTION OF MOUSE, RAT, AND DOG BRAIN

Fraction	Mouse	Rat	Dog
Crude nuclear (CN)	25	25	22
Crude mitochondrial (CM)	41	49	46
Microsomal (MS)	21	8	12
Supernatant (S)	7	8	15
CM Sucrose density subfractions			
Myelin (A)	8	12	29
Membrane fragments (B)	5	9	3
Cholinergic synaptosomes (C)	13	15	7
Noncholinergic synaptosomes (D)	9	16	6
Free mitochondria (E)	2	2	1
CM osmotic shock subfractions			
Myelin (M_1)	24	35	32
Synaptic vesicles (M_2)	4	12	7
Supernatant (M_3)	5	8	7

As can be seen in TABLE 1, approximately 45% of the radiolabeled Δ^9-THC and its metabolites was found in the crude mitochondrial fraction of each species. Little radioactivity was found in the supernatant, and the crude nuclear contained more than the microsomal fraction in each species. This distribution differs from that of many other psychotomimetic drugs, including morphine, barbiturates, and LSD. The majority of these drugs are found in the supernatant fraction. The distribution of Δ^9-THC in subfractions of the crude mitochondrial fraction of the mouse, rat, and dog is also presented in TABLE 1. As can be seen, a significant quantity of radioactivity was found in the cholinergic nerve endings, the noncholinergic nerve endings, and, when disrupted by osmotic shock, in the synaptic vesicles.

The details of the methodology used and a more complete description of the results obtained in the experiments in which we investigated the effects of Δ^9-THC and reserpine on the subcellular distribution of each other have been submitted for publication elsewhere.[18] Essentially, the distribution of Δ^9-THC was determined *in vitro* following the incubation of the crude nuclear (900 × *g*) supernatant fraction of rat forebrain with reserpine or vehicle for 15 min., followed by the addition of radiolabeled Δ^9-THC and a subsequent 15 min. incubation. The effect of reserpine incubation on distribution of Δ^9-THC in the primary fractions, that is the crude mitochondrial, microsomal, and supernatant as well as in subfractions of the crude mitochondrial fraction, is presented in TABLE 2. There was no difference between the subcellular distribution of Δ^9-THC when it was added to the crude nuclear supernatant and that observed when the radiolabeled Δ^9-THC was administered prior to sacrificing the animals (TABLE 1). TABLE 2 also shows that the incubation of the crude nuclear (900 × *g*) supernatant with reserpine did not alter the

TABLE 2

EFFECT OF 1 μM RESERPINE ON THE DISTRIBUTION OF 100 μM [^{3}H]Δ^9-THC IN SUBSEQUENT SUBCELLULAR FRACTIONS ORAL SUBFRACTIONS OF RAT FOREBRAIN CRUDE NUCLEAR SUPERNATANT

Fraction	Percent of Control in Reserpine-Treated Samples
Crude mitochondrial (CM)*	100
Microsomal (MS)	128
Supernatant (S)	111
CM sucrose density subfractions	
Myelin (A)	92
Membrane fragments (B)	65
Cholinergic synaptosomes (C)	93
Noncholinergic synaptosomes	97
Free mitochondria (E)	127
CM osmotic shock subfractions	
Myelin (M_1)	100
Synaptic vesicles (M_2)	86
Supernatant (M_3)	80

* 357.3 μg [^{3}H]Δ^9-THC plus metabolites in the control crude mitochondrial fraction.

subsequent subcellular distribution of Δ^9-THC in the subfractions of the crude mitochondrial fraction. These results are not surprising in that lower than pharmacologically active doses of reserpine have not been reported to alter the effect of Δ^9-THC in animals or man.

Englert *et al.*[17] have shown, however, that Δ^9-THC caused a shift of 5–HT from the bound to the free intraneuronal pool; in addition, we have shown that Δ^9-THC releases 5–HT from a reserpine-sensitive site.[16] It has also been demonstrated that Δ^9-THC inhibited serotonin depletion and hypothermia induced by reserpine in rats. We therefore proceeded to investigate the effect of Δ^9-THC on the subcellular distribution of reserpine in an attempt to elucidate the mechanism for the reduction of reserpine effects by Δ^9-THC.

It has previously been reported by Ho and Johnson[19] that when the crude nuclear supernatant of unmedicated animals was incubated with Δ^9-THC and then incubated with radiolabeled reserpine, the binding of the radiolabeled reserpine to the particulate matter was greatly increased over control, especially in the mitochondrial fraction.[19] In other words, Δ⁹-THC appeared to increase the binding of reserpine. This observation was repeated and extended to include an investigation into the effects of Δ⁹-THC on the subcellular distribution of reserpine using a different method of fractionation. These experiments were carried out in a fashion similar to those described above when we investigated the effects of reserpine on the subcellular distribution of the cannabinoid. The crude nuclear supernatant from unmedicated rats was incubated with Δ⁹-THC for 15 min. Radiolabeled reserpine was then added for another 15-min. incubation period. This crude nuclear supernatant was then fractionated by the procedures described by DeRobertis *et al.*[20, 21] and Martin *et al.*[22] The percentage changes from controls of the distribution of radiolabeled reserpine following incubation with Δ⁹-THC are presented in TABLE 3.

TABLE 3

EFFECT OF 100 μM Δ⁹-THC ON THE DISTRIBUTION OF 1 μM [^{3}H]RESERPINE ON PRIMARY AND SUBFRACTIONS OF RAT FOREBRAIN CRUDE NUCLEAR SUPERNATANT

Fraction	Percent Change From Control in Δ⁹-THC-Treated Samples
Crude mitochondrial (CM)	+154
Microsomal (MS)	+27
Supernatant (S)	−66
CM sucrose density subfractions	
Myelin (A)	+242
Membrane fragments (B)	+288
Cholinergic synaptosomes (C)	+1020
Noncholinergic synaptosomes (D)	+1169
Free mitochondria (E)	+318
CM osmotic shock subfractions	
Myelin (M_1)	+324
Synaptic vesicles (M_2)	+247
Supernatant (M_3)	+40

As can be seen in this table, there was a significant increase in the amount of reserpine in the crude mitochondrial fraction and significantly less radioactivity found in the supernatant fraction following incubation with the cannabinoid. It appears that the subcellular distribution of reserpine to some extent followed that of Δ⁹-THC. The decrease in radioactivity in the supernatant of the crude mitochondrial fraction suggests that the Δ⁹-THC altered the mitochondrial fractions in such a way that it bound more reserpine molecules, leaving less radioactivity in the supernatant.

The crude mitochondrial fraction was further subfractioned by placement on a discontinous sucrose density gradient, and the results of this experiment also are presented in TABLE 3. As can be seen in this table, there was a highly significant increase in the binding of reserpine in the cholinergic and noncholinergic nerve endings isolated from crude nuclear supernatants that had been incubated with Δ⁹-THC. Again, there is significantly less radiolabeled reserpine in the supernatant fraction obtained from the subfractionation of the crude mitochondrial fraction. It appears that Δ⁹-THC caused the reserpine to go from the final supernatant into the synaptosomal fraction. An aliquot of the crude mitochondrial fraction was also subjected to osmotic shock, which caused a disruption of the nerve endings. In these experiments, the reserpine appeared to be much more highly bound to the synaptic vesicle fraction following incubation with Δ⁹-THC. The supernatant in this preparation, which would be the cytoplasm of the nerve endings, also contained much less radioactivity in the THC incubates than in the controls.

The data presented in TABLE 4 demonstrate that the effect on reserpine binding observed with Δ⁹-THC was also observed with Δ⁸-THC and cannabinol. Other cannabinoids, such as 11–hydroxy–Δ⁹-THC, the primary metabolite of Δ⁹-THC, and 9–nor–9–beta–hydroxyhexahydrocannabinol, which has potent analgesic and cannabinoid-like effects in animals, did not increase the binding of reserpine to this subcellular fraction. This is significant in that Δ⁸-THC, Δ⁹-THC, 11–OH–Δ⁹-THC and 9–nor–9–beta–hydroxyhexahydrocannabinol have cannabinoid-like activity, whereas cannabinol is without activity. It appears, therefore, that there is not a consistent or a predictable correlation between the activity of cannabinoids in altering the distribution of reserpine and their other pharmacological effects in animals. This effect of cannabinoids on reserpine distribution does appear, however, to have specificity in that many other central-nervous-system-active drugs were found not to alter the distribution of reserpine (TABLE 4). The drugs that were found to be inactive in this regard include amphetamine, mescaline, pentobarbital, serotonin, LSD, and others. The narcotic analgesic, morphine, was less active than Δ⁹-THC in this regard. We feel that this interesting interaction between Δ⁹-THC and reserpine

TABLE 4

EFFECT OF Δ⁹-THC AND OTHER DRUGS ON THE *In Vitro* BINDING OF [^{3}H]RESERPINE TO A CRUDE MITOCHONDRIAL FRACTION OF RAT FOREBRAIN

Drug	Inactive Concentrations (μM)	Concentrations That Increased Binding (μM)*
Δ⁹-THC	10	50, 100
Δ⁸-THC	10, 50	100
Cannabinol	10, 50	100
11–OH–Δ⁹-THC	10, 50, 100	none
9–nor–9β–OH–HHC	10, 50, 100	none
Serotonin	1, 10, 100	none
Sodium pentobarbital	1, 10, 100	none
Cocaine	1, 10, 100	none
Amphetamine	1, 10, 100	none
Imipramine	1, 10, 100	none
Chlorpromazine	1, 10, 100	none
Tetrabenazine	1, 10, 100	none
Morphine	1, 10	100
D–LSD	0.1, 1, 10	none

* The maximum concentration of each drug tested was 100 μM (except D–LSD–10 μM). The concentration of [^{3}H]reserpine was 1 μM in each experiment.

merits further investigation. Hopefully, additional experiments will shed some light on the possible meaningfulness of this interaction.

The Inhibitory Action of Naloxone on Cannabinoid Effects

Δ^9-THC and other constituents of marihuana have been reported to produce certain pharmacological effects similar to those produced by morphine, including analgesia,[23-26] increased catecholamine synthesis,[27, 28] and hypo-

Table 5

Effect of Naloxone (2 mg/kg) on the Tail-Flick Activity and Increased Catecholamine Synthesis Produced by 9–nor–9β–OH–HHC*

Dose β-HHC mg/kg	Tail-Flick Activity % MPE		[³H]DA/Spec. Act. Tyrosine μg/g ± SEM		[³H]NE/Spec. Act. Tyrosine μg/g ± SEM	
	Saline†	Naloxone‡	Saline	Naloxone	Saline	Naloxone
0	1	0	0.996 ±0.102	0.936 ±0.095	0.340 ±0.052	0.312 ±0.045
3	21	12	1.334 ±0.140	1.002 ±0.121	0.406 ±0.046	0.342 ±0.038
10	54	34	1.845 ±0.182	1.153 ±0.170	0.549 ±0.065	0.370 ±0.071
20	85	45	2.164 ±0.171	1.244 ±0.186	0.574 ±0.048	0.381 ±0.075
30	97	57	2.308 ±0.192	1.511 ±0.181	0.585 ±0.061	0.414 ±0.050

* Animals were injected subcutaneously with naloxone 10 min. before β-HHC. There were 12 mice in each group in the tail-flick test, and 6 mice in each group in the biochemical studies.

† ED_{50} = 7.4 mg/kg; 95% C.L. 4.8–11.3.

‡ ED_{50} = 21.7 mg/kg; 95% C.L. 9.9–47.7.

thermia.[29, 30] As with morphine, tolerance also develops to these effects of Δ^9-THC.[5, 27, 31-33] Δ^9-THC also has been reported to produce a blockade of naloxone-precipitated abstinence in morphine-dependent rats.[34] In view of the above reports, we decided to examine the effects of the pure narcotic antagonist, naloxone, on some of the pharmacological and neurochemical effects of an interesting new cannabinoid, 9–nor–9β–OH–hexahydrocannabinol (β–HHC). The ED_{50} in the tail-flick test at 30 min. after the subcutaneous administration of β–HHC was 7.4 mg/kg. The ED_{50} of morphine in this procedure is 5.8, and this same dose of Δ^9-THC is not active in this test of antinociceptive potency. It can be seen in Table 5 that β–HHC increases the accumulation of newly synthesized dopamine and norepinephrine formed from an injection of [³H]tyrosine. Pretreatment with naloxone antagonized both the antinociception and increased catecholamine synthesis produced by several doses of β–HHC. The highest dose of β–HHC used appeared to partially overcome the naloxone antagonism. We have previously reported that naloxone also antagonized the tail-flick activity and increased catecholamine synthesis produced by both morphine and methadone.[28] Wilson and May[26] reported that naloxone completely abolished the antinociceptive activity of 11–OH–Δ^8-THC as measured in the mouse hot-plate test. However, others have reported that nalorphine, a narcotic antagonist-analgesia, was not effective in antagonizing the antinociception produced by a cannabis extract in the same test.[25]

We have also found that naloxone is effective in blocking the hypothermia and increased catecholamine synthesis produced by a 30 mg/kg dose of Δ^9-THC. These data suggest the possibility that the cannabinoids and the narcotic analgesics share some common sites of action that can be blocked by naloxone. It is possible, however, that naloxone may be acting at different sites for the cannabinoids than for the narcotics.

However, it is our hypothesis that the inhibitory effects of naloxone on the increased catecholamine synthesis induced by Δ^9-THC and β–HHC take place within the neuron. Although proof is lacking for this conclusion, overwhelming evidence exists to identify the conversion of tyrosine to catecholamines within the neuron. An alternate hypothesis is that the effect of naloxone on the increased synthesis of catecholamines induced by cannabinoids, or for that matter even the effect of cannabinoids, is extraneuronal. They may alter metabolism, protein binding, or another pharmacodynamic parameter, as well as affecting some other component of catecholaminergic function.

We have described the interactions of two drugs, reserpine and naloxone, with the intracellular effects of cannabinoids. In one, Δ^9-THC had profound effects on the intraneuronal distribution of reserpine and has been shown to inhibit the hypothermia induced by this drug. Also, the effect of naloxone on the intraneuronal activity of the cannabinoids (inhibition of the increased synthesis of catecholamines) was reflected in an alteration in their pharmacological effects in the whole animal (antinociception and hypothermia). We feel that additional studies of this type will be useful in identifying possible drug interactions in man, as well as increasing our knowledge of the mechanism of action of the drugs and our understanding of the central nervous system.

References

1. Karniol, I. G. & E. A. Carlini. 1973. Psychopharmacologia **33:** 53–70.
2. Karniol, I. G., R. N. Takahashi & R. E. Musty. 1974. Arch. Int. Pharmacodyn. Ther. **212:** 230–237.
3. Karniol, I. G., I. Shirakawa, N. Kasinski, A. Pfeferman & E. A. Carlini. 1974. Eur. J. Pharmacol. **28:** 172–177.
4. Hollister, L. E. & H. Gillespie. 1975. Clin. Pharmacol. Ther. **18:** 80–83.
5. McMillan, D. E., W. L. Dewey & L. S. Harris. 1971. Ann. N.Y. Acad. Sci. **191:** 83–99.
6. Ng, L. K. Y., F. Lamprecht, R. B. Williams & I. J. Kopin. 1973. Science **180:** 1368–1369.
7. Rafaelsen, O. J., P. Bech, J. Christiansen, H. Christrup, J. Nyboe & L. Rafaelsen. 1973. Science **179:** 920–923.
8. Coldwell, B. B., K. Bailey, C. J. Paul & G. Anderson. 1974. Toxicol. Appl. Pharmacol. **29:** 59–69.
9. Friedman, E. & S. Gershon. 1974. Psychopharmacologia **39:** 193–198.

10. Gough, A. I. & J. E. Olley. 1975. J. Pharm. Pharmacol. **37:** 62–63.
11. Drew, W. G., G. F. Kiplinger & L. L. Miller. 1972. Clin. Pharmacol. Ther. **13:** 526–533.
12. Adams, H. R. & R. D. Sofia. 1973. Experientia **29:** 181–182.
13. Chesher, G. B., D. M. Jackson & G. A. Starmer. 1974. Brit. J. Pharmacol. **50:** 593–599.
14. Chesher, G. B. & D. M. Jackson. 1974. Psychopharmacologia **37:** 255–264.
15. Dewey, W. L., B. R. Martin, J. S. Beckner & L. S. Harris. 1976. A comparison of the subcellular distribution of cannabinoids in the brains of tolerant and nontolerant dogs, rats and mice after injecting radiolabeled Δ^9-tetrahydrocannabinol. *In* Marihuana: Chemistry, Biochemistry and Cellular Effects. G. G. Nahas, Ed.: 349–366. Springer-Verlag. New York, N.Y.
16. Johnson, K. M., B. T. Ho & W. L. Dewey. 1976. Life Sci. **19:** 347–356.
17. Englert, L. F., B. T. Ho & D. Tayler. 1973. Brit. J. Pharmacol. **49:** 243–252.
18. Johnson, K. M., W. L. Dewey & B. T. Ho. 1977. Res. Commun. Chem. Pathol. Pharmacol. Submitted for publication.
19. Ho, B. T. & K. M. Johnson. 1976. Sites of neurochemical action of Δ^9-tetrahydrocannabinol: Interaction with reserpine. *In* Marihuana: Chemistry, Biochemistry and Cellular Effects. G. G. Nahas, Ed.: 367–382. Springer-Verlag. New York, N.Y.
20. DeRobertis, E., A. Pelligrino de Iraldi, G. Rodriguez DeLores Arnaiz & L. Salganicoff. 1962. J. Neurochem. **9:** 23–25.
21. DeRobertis, E., G. Rodriguez DeLores Arnaiz, L. Salganicoff, A. Pelligrino de Iraldi & L. M. Zieher. 1963. J. Neurochem. **10:** 225–235.
22. Martin, B. R., W. L. Dewey, L. S. Harris & J. S. Beckner. 1976. J. Pharmacol. Exp. Ther. **196:** 128–144.
23. Bicher, H. I. & R. Mechoulam. 1968. Arch. Int. Pharmacodyn. Ther. **172:** 24–31.
24. Buxbaum, D. M. 1972. Psychopharmacologia **25:** 275–280.
25. Chesher, G. B., C. J. Dahl, M. Everingham, D. M. Jackson, H. Marchant-Williams, H. & G. A. Starmer. 1973. Brit. J. Pharmacol. **49:** 585–594.
26. Wilson, R. S. & E. L. May. 1975. J. Med. Chem. **18:** 700–703.
27. Maitre, L., P. A. Baumann & A. Delini-Stula. 1972. Neurochemical tolerance to cannabinols. *In* Cannabis and Its Derivatives. W. D. M. Paton & J. Crown, Eds. Oxford University Press. London, England.
28. Bloom, A. S., W. L. Dewey, L. S. Harris & K. K. Brosius. 1976. J. Pharmacol. Exp. Ther. **198:** 33–41.
29. Haavik, C. O. & H. F. Hardman. 1973. J. Pharmacol. Exp. Ther. **187:** 568–574.
30. Bloom, A. S., K. M. Johnson, F. J. Bowman & W. L. Dewey. 1976. Fed. Proc. **35:** 506.
31. Ten Ham, M. & Y. DeJong. 1974. Eur. J. Pharmacol. **28:** 144–148.
32. Liu, R. K. 1974. Res. Commun. Chem. Pathol. Pharmacol. **9:** 215–228.
33. Anderson, P. F., D. M. Jackson, G. B. Chesher & R. Malor. 1975. Psychopharmacologia **43:** 31–36.
34. Hine, B., G. Friedman, M. Torrelio & S. Gurshon. 1975. Science **187:** 443–445.

INTERACTIONS OF Δ^9-TETRAHYDROCANNABINOL WITH OTHER PHARMACOLOGICAL AGENTS*

Paul Consroe, Byron Jones, and Hugh Laird

Department of Pharmacology and Toxicology
University of Arizona College of Pharmacy
Tucson, Arizona 85721

There are convincing demographic data to indicate that marijuana has become one of the most widely used psychoactive substances in this country.[1] Although laboratory animal data[2] and human research[2, 3] have generally established that the margin of physical safety with marijuana and its main psychoactive ingredient Δ^9-tetrahydrocannabinol (THC) is quite high, there is little question that acute marijuana intoxication interferes with immediate intellectual functioning, driving, and other complex psychomotor skills.[2] Additionally, there are many reports of associations of marijuana use and toxic psychological effects, ranging from anxiety states to toxic psychosis,[4] and it is known that, in sufficient doses, THC (like LSD) may induce grossly psychotomimetic reactions.[5] With the emergence in the illicit market of higher potency marijuana preparations like hashish oil, containing in excess of 30% THC,[6] adverse reactions might be expected to increase in both frequency and severity. Because of these considerations indicating a definite potential of THC toxicity, we felt that studies of potential drug antagonists of THC in laboratory animals would be of particular interest. Such studies might provide appropriate correlations for potential human treatment conditions as well as furnish clues to possible mechanisms of action of THC. The present paper provides data on the interactive effects of THC with a number of other drugs in two agonist-antagonist paradigms in the rabbit.

Depressant-Stimulant Effects of THC

As emphasized in a number of reviews of the behavioral pharmacology of marijuana,[7–11] THC elicits a mixture of depressant (e.g., sprawling, decreased locomotion and grooming, etc.) and stimulant (increased ataxic ambulation, etc.) effects on unlearned behavior. Moreover, even when the behavioral sedative effects of THC predominate, as is the case in most species, the THC-treated animals are markedly hypersensitive to external tactile and auditory stimuli.[11] As with behavioral measures, CNS depressant and stimulant correlates of THC action may be inferred from electroencephalographic (EEG) data in laboratory animals. EEG patterns indicative of sedation, i.e., high-voltage slow-wave cortical activity or EEG synchronization[12–16] coupled with a diminution of hippocampal theta rhythm,[14, 16–18] and those patterns indicative

* Supported by Grant #9R01-DA01448 from the National Institute on Drug Abuse (NIDA) of the Alcohol, Drug Abuse and Mental Health Administration (ADAMHA).

of stimulation, i.e., low-voltage high-frequency cortical activity or EEG desynchronization,[17, 19, 20] have been demonstrated after THC administration. Further, many studies (for a review see Consroe and coworkers[21]) have indicated the occurrence of stimulant EEG activity reminiscent of epileptiform or convulsant-like spikes, polyspikes or spike and slow-wave complexes (without behavioral seizures) in THC-treated animals. In the rabbit, Lipparini and coworkers[17] and Fujimori and Himwich[16] have shown a temporally biphasic EEG and behavioral stimulation-sedation property of THC, whereas our initial experiments[15] suggested that the cannabinoid produced mainly sedative effects without any initial stimulation. Since the most obvious basic requirements for drug evaluations are stable and reproducible baselines against which drug-correlated changes are assessed, we first assessed the EEG and behavioral effects of THC with respect to dosage and level of animal habituation (adaptation),[22] two important parameters known to influence the behavioral effects of the cannabinoid.[11]

Five New Zealand White rabbits, previously equipped surgically with permanent cortical and hippocampal recording electrodes and jugular vein injection catheters, were individually test adapted, i.e., given 3 weekly 84-minute exposures to the testing conditions with control THC vehicle (10% polysorbate (Tween) 80-saline solution). Following adaptation, the effects of Δ^9-THC, given intravenously (i.v.) in counterbalanced doses of 0.01, 0.05, 0.1, 0.5, and 1 mg/kg (spaced 1 week apart), were determined on EEG and behavior of freely moving rabbits in a sound-attenuated chamber. THC was administered from outside the chamber via a jugular catheter to minimize experimenter-produced disturbances during testing. Cortical and hippocampal EEG patterns were assessed qualitatively; additionally, the electrical activity occurring between the left motor and right parietal cortices was quantified by means of a Grass (7P10B) cumulative voltage integrator. In order to present relative changes in cortical voltage output, the mean frequency of integrator resets (which is directly proportional to the EEG voltage output) was plotted for each treatment condition. Frequency and duration of the following behaviors were measured by an experimenter-operated digital event recorder (the numbers in parentheses are inter-observer reliability values or Pearson's r): standing ($r = 0.89$), sitting ($r = 0.85$), sprawling ($r = 0.99$), and activity ($r = 0.97$), the latter consisting of a composite of environmental exploration, locomotion, and grooming. Within each treatment session, time sampling of the simultaneous EEG and behavioral effects consisted of five 4-minute periods at 0–4, 20–24, 40–44, 60–64 and 80–84 minutes following drug administration. Testing of a second (nonadapted) group of four rabbits was identical with the above procedure, except that they were treated with a single i.v. dose of THC (1 mg/kg) and tested only once (without prior adaptation) in the chamber. Statistical evaluations of all data presented in this and in following studies were carried out using appropriate analyses of variance tests and subsequent comparison between means using the Dunnett Test and/or the Newman-Keuls Multiple Comparison method.[23]

As illustrated in FIGURE 1, adapted rabbits (open bars), evinced dose-related increases of cortical voltage output, decreases in durations of standing and activity, and marked sprawling behavior following THC administration. Compared to control, EEG was the most sensitive measure of THC action ($p < 0.05$ at 0.05, 0.1, 0.5 and 1 mg/kg), followed by activity ($p < 0.05$ at 0.1, 0.5 and 1 mg/kg), sprawling ($p < 0.05$ at 0.5 and 1 mg/kg), and stand-

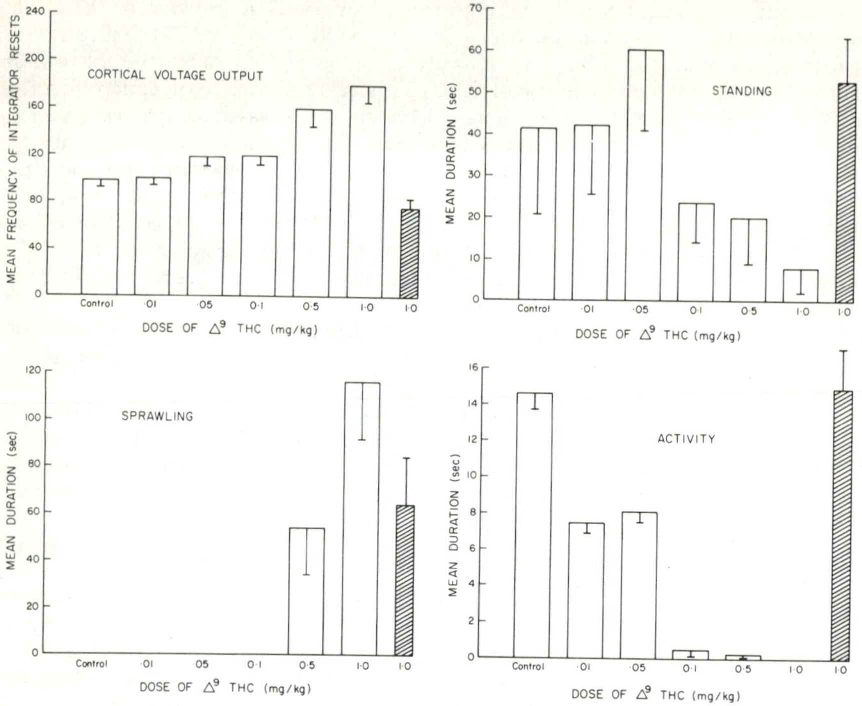

FIGURE 1. Mean frequency of integrator resets (cortical voltage output) and mean duration (in seconds) of standing, sprawling, and behavioral activity in five 4-minute periods (0–4, 20–24, 40–44, 60–64, 80–84) following intravenous injection of control vehicle (10% Tween 80-saline) or graded doses of Δ^9-tetrahydrocannabinol (Δ^9-THC). Open bars represent mean values obtained from rabbits adapted to the testing milieu (n = 5). Shaded bars represent mean values obtained from non-adapted animals (n = 4). Vertical lines are standard errors. (From Consroe *et al.*[22])

ing ($p < 0.05$ at 1 mg/kg). Additionally, there were marked differences between the effects of THC in adapted and nonadapted rabbits. The shaded bars of FIGURE 1 show that the nonadapted rabbits treated with 1 mg/kg THC evinced less cortical EEG voltage output ($p < 0.05$), stood and explored more ($p < 0.05$, $p < 0.01$) and sprawled less ($p < 0.05$) than their identically dosed, but adapted cohorts (open bars). Furthermore, in both groups of rabbits, THC induced bursts of cortical EEG polyspikes (100–150μV, 10–14Hz) and brought about a general disappearance of sinusoidal theta waves from the hippocampus. The present demonstration that the experimental setting is a crucial element in THC studies is in accord with observations of others[24, 25] and taken together these findings suggest that the behavioral and EEG actions of THC are markedly influenced by the animal's existing state of arousal. Moreover, the present findings that quantitative EEG and behavioral measures are highly sensitive to the actions of THC and that the resultant depressant and stimulant effects are largely (although not entirely) separable by carefully controlling environmental factors, prompted us to use the adapted rabbit paradigm to test the effects of some potential drug antagonists.

THC-Drug Interactions in Adapted Rabbits

Since THC causes mainly sedative effects in adapted rabbits and since most of these effects can be reversed by stimuli such as noise,[15, 22] we hypothesized that CNS-stimulant drugs should act as antagonists of THC in our paradigm. Presented in the following text is a compilation of the interactive effects of THC with several cholinergic (physostigmine, arecoline, nicotine), catecholaminergic (methamphetamine, cocaine, apomorphine), and general CNS-stimulant (caffeine) drugs. For each THC-drug interaction study (n = 6), the following counterbalanced crossover treatment design was used: baseline or Tween-saline (10% Tween 80-saline vehicle at time 0, followed 30 minutes later by saline), THC-saline (Δ^9-THC at time 0, followed 30 minutes later by saline), Tween-putative antagonist (10% Tween 80-saline at time 0, followed 30 minutes later by the antagonist), and THC-putative antagonist (Δ^9-THC at time 0, followed 30 minutes later by the antagonist). All drugs and vehicles were given i.v. in an equal volume, and all doses were calculated as the free base. After rabbits had been adapted to the testing milieu, simultaneous EEG and behavioral measures were obtained in each of the above treatment conditions for seven 4-minute time samples, i.e., 0–4, 10–14, 20–24, 30–34, 40–44, 50–54, and 60–64 minutes.

The following composite of three studies[26] represents the interactive effects of THC (0.5 mg/kg) with the cholinomimetics, physostigmine (0.05 mg/kg), arecoline (0.025 mg/kg), and nicotine (0.02 mg/kg). As illustrated in Figure 2, THC (given singly) caused a persistent increase ($p < 0.05$, all time periods) of cortical EEG voltage output and sprawling, and a decrement (n.s.) in activity, whereas both physostigmine and arecoline (but not nicotine) caused a brief decrease ($p < 0.05$) in EEG voltage and increase ($p < 0.05$) in activity, compared to control. In THC-treated rabbits, the effects of physostigmine and arecoline were similar (except for a longer duration of effect for physostigmine) in that both drugs reliably ($p < 0.05$) antagonized the alterations of cortical EEG voltage output, sprawling, and activity induced by the cannabinoid (Figure 2). These two cholinomimetics also elicited prominent hippocampal theta rhythm, thus reversing THC's trend of theta disruption in this species. Additionally, in THC-treated animals, nicotine only briefly reduced ($p < 0.05$) cortical EEG voltage (Figure 2) and caused only a fleeting theta thythm recorded from the hippocampus. Furthermore, nicotine produced behavioral effects which were clearly different from those elicited by physostigmine and arecoline. In all six rabbits given THC, nicotine precipitated brief (2–3 minutes) but dramatic fasciculations and convulsive-like jerking, and subsequently caused a persistent increase ($p < 0.05$) in sprawling behavior (Figure 2). THC's antagonism by physostigmine is consistent with our earlier findings in rabbits[15, 27] and is congruent with physostigmine antagonism of THC-induced hyperthermia in rats[28] and THC-induced tachycardia and conjunctival injection in humans.[29] However, reports of increased lethargy and somnolence in man with the THC-physostigmine combination[29] and augmented frequency of lethality in rodents when THC is combined with physostigmine[30, 31] or arecoline[31] suggest that THC-cholinergic interactions may also be toxic. Certainly, our present results with the THC-nicotine combination are in accord with this supposition.

The following composite of four studies[32] represents the interactive effects of THC (0.5 mg/kg) with methamphetamine (0.1 mg/kg), cocaine (1 mg/kg), apomorphine (1 mg/kg), and caffeine (12.5 mg/kg). Figure 3 shows

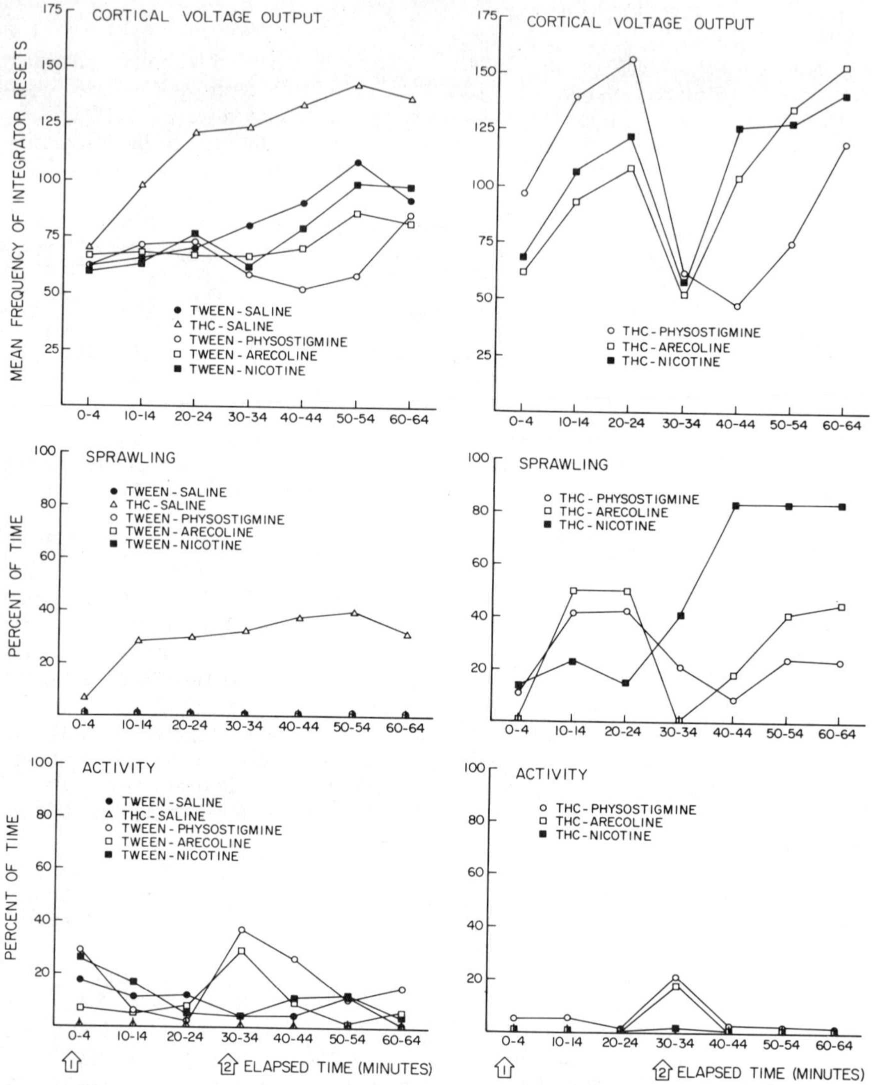

FIGURE 2. Mean frequency of integrator resets (cortical voltage output) and mean percentage of time of sprawling and behavioral activity during each 4-minute time period for drugs given singly (left) and combined (right). Δ^9-tetrahydrocannabinol (THC) or Tween (10% Tween 80-saline) was injected i.v. at 0 time (arrow #1), and saline solution or the stimulant drug was administered i.v. at 30 minutes (arrow #2). For illustration purposes, data points for Tween-saline and THC-saline conditions represent the mean of the three studies (n = 6 rabbits per study).

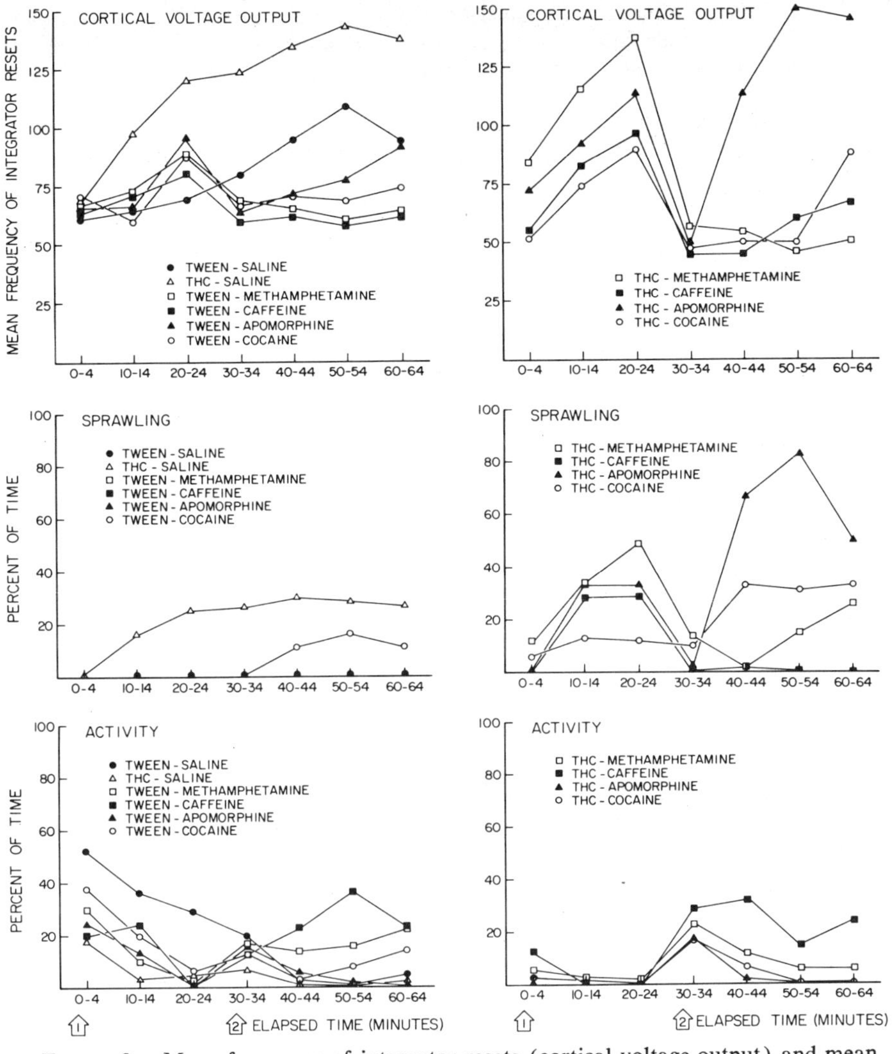

FIGURE 3. Mean frequency of integrator resets (cortical voltage output) and mean percentage of time of sprawling and behavioral activity during each 4-minute time period for drugs given singly (left) and combined (right). Δ⁹-tetrahydrocannabinol (THC) or Tween (10% Tween 80-saline) was injected i.v. at 0 time (arrow #1), and saline solution or the stimulant drug was administered i.v. at 30 minutes (arrow #2). For illustration purposes, data points for Tween-saline and THC-saline conditions represent the mean of the four studies (n = 6 rabbits per study).

that THC given alone once again caused typical EEG and behavioral sedative effects. Each of the potential antagonists given singly initially reduced cortical EEG voltage and increased activity, although persistent and reliable ($p < 0.05$, 40–64 minute time periods) changes in EEG were seen with cocaine, methamphetamine, and caffeine, and in activity behavior only with caffeine and methamphetamine. Cocaine caused a brief period of hyperactivity followed by increased ($p < 0.05$) levels of sprawling. FIGURE 3 also illustrates that caffeine and, to a lesser extent, methamphetamine effectively ($p < 0.05$)

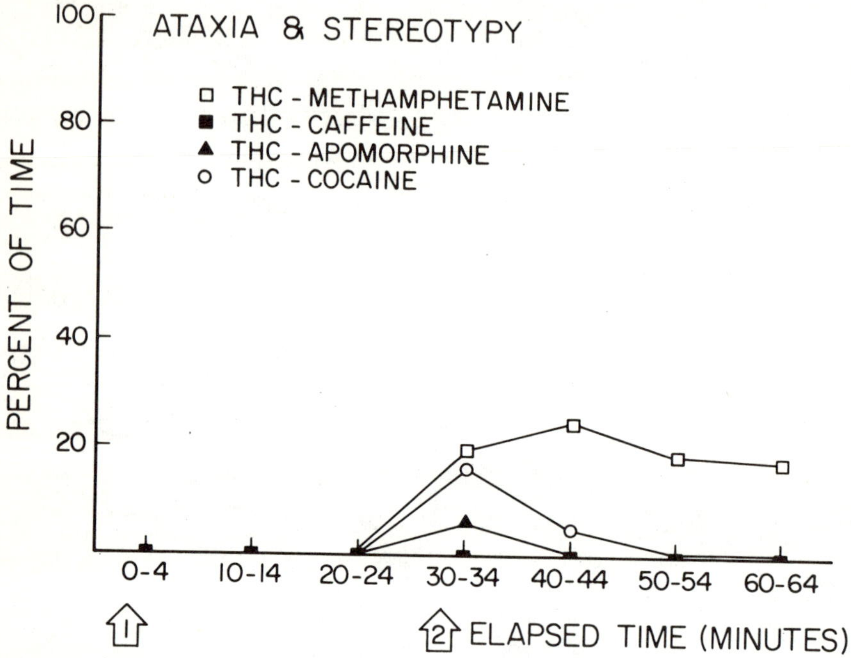

FIGURE 4. Mean percentage of time of ataxia and stereotypy during each 4-minute time period. Δ^9-tetrahydrocannabinol (THC) was injected i.v. at 0 time (arrow #1), and each stimulant drug was administered i.v. at 30 minutes (arrow #2). n = 6 rabbits per study.

and persistently reversed THC's alterations of EEG and behavior. Cocaine and especially apomorphine, although causing an ephemeral EEG and behavioral stimulation, failed to reliably ($p > 0.05$) reverse sprawling and decrements in activity caused by the cannabinoid; indeed, rabbits given apomorphine following treatment with THC evinced sprawling durations greater ($p < 0.05$) than those seen following administration of THC alone (FIGURE 3). The THC-induced disruption of hippocampal theta was generally reversed by caffeine and appeared to be antagonized only briefly by the other drugs. However, in many cases, EEG artifacts caused by abnormal behavior induced by THC-stimulant drug combinations occluded subcortical wave forms. That is, the administration of apomorphine, cocaine, or especially methamphetamine to rabbits previously treated with THC clearly induced behavioral distress (FIGURE 4). This finding is especially noteworthy since none of the drugs, given singly, produced ataxia and stereotypy or any other behavior indicative of extreme behavioral distress. These data extend the findings of other investigators[12, 33–34] and taken together support the concept that, depending upon the parameters being investigated, the interaction of THC with caffeine and catecholaminergic drugs (amphetamine, cocaine, apomorphine) may result in antagonism or potentiation of effect.

Mechanistically, it is interesting that a wide variety of CNS-stimulant drugs are capable of reversing the sedative EEG and behavioral effects of THC. Physostigmine, an anticholinesterase drug that increases levels of acetylcholine available at central muscarinic receptors,[44, 45] arecoline, a direct-acting CNS muscarinic agonist,[45] and caffeine, a phosphodiesterase inhibitor that elevates central levels of cyclic AMP,[46, 47] all acted as THC antagonists without causing behavioral distress. Additionally, nicotine, a drug that directly activates CNS nicotinic receptors[45] and those drugs that augment central catecholaminergic activity, viz., methamphetamine by releasing catecholamines and especially dopamine,[48, 49] cocaine by blocking catecholamine neuronal reuptake,[50, 51] and apomorphine by directly stimulating dopamine receptors,[52, 53] also reversed some of THC's sedative effects. However, in combination with THC, these agents evoked clear signs of behavioral distress (e.g., fasciculations, convulsive-like jerking, or ataxic ambulation and stereotypy) in our rabbits. These bizarre behaviors are indicative of extreme arousal beyond mere reversal of the cannabinoid-induced sedation. Therefore, it appears that antagonism of THC can be mediated by a number of neurochemical events, e.g., cholinergic, adrenergic, cyclic AMP, and that extreme arousal may result from an interaction of the cannabinoid with predominantly nicotinic cholinergic as well as catecholaminergic (dopaminergic?) mechanisms.

Cannabinoids, Seizures, and Antagonists

During our investigations of the EEG and behavioral effects of THC in rabbits, we made a startling discovery. Four rabbit littermates evinced clonic behavioral convulsions after acute administration of an i.v. dose as low as 0.05 mg/kg of Δ^9THC.[22] Although THC-induced behavioral convulsions have occasionally been reported in rats,[54–57] dogs,[54, 55] and monkeys,[54] these drastic effects only occur with extremely high, and often lethal, acute or chronic doses of the cannabinoid. Moreover, literature reports of behavioral seizures in rabbits are noticeably absent despite the administration of Δ^9THC in a wide range of doses given acutely, i.e., 0.01–10 mg/kg, i.v.,[15–18, 22, 58] and chronically, i.e., 3 mg/kg, i.v. for 6 days[17] or up to 153 mg/kg, s.c. for 28 days.[59] We subsequently commissioned our local rabbit breeder/supplier to initiate inbreeding of these rabbits, and FIGURE 5 illustrates the lineage of these four animals (Nos. 20,21,22,24) and of our present population of "Δ^9THC-seizure susceptible" New Zealand White rabbits. In a previous communication[21] we reported some basic pharmacological data on the convulsant effects of Δ^9THC in a group (Nos. 22,24,31,33,34,40,42, FIGURE 5) of our specially bred rabbits. Briefly summarized, nonfatal behavioral convulsions resulted within 3 minutes after giving THC, i.v., in rather low threshold doses (0.1 to 0.4 mg/kg). Seizures typically consisted of front and/or hind limb clonus, mydriasis,

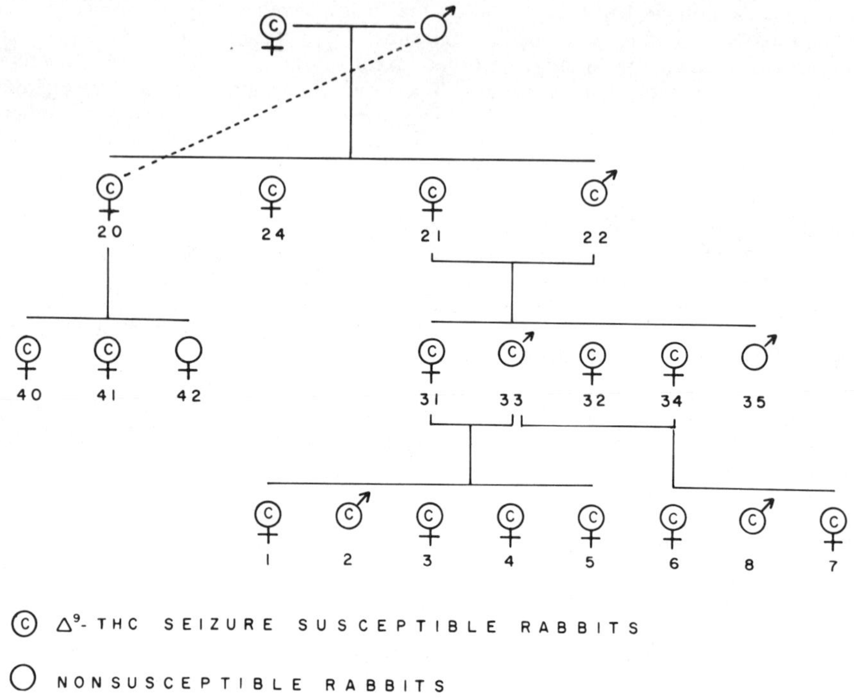

FIGURE 5. Lineage of New Zealand White rabbits sensitive to behavioral convulsant effects of Δ^9-tetrahydrocannabinol (Δ^9THC), given i.v., in doses of 0.5 mg/kg or less. (From Consroe *et al.*[21])

nystagmus, flexure of the head ventrally, body torsion, and front and/or hind limb extension. Convulsive activity persisted for about 5–15 minutes and was followed by postictal depression. Periodic episodes of seizure activity reoccurred during the subsequent 1 to 3 hours, but subjects (*S*s) appeared completely normal within 8–12 hours post injection. Injection of THC vehicle (up to 2 ml of 4% Tween 80-saline solution) did not cause convulsive activity. Although the behavioral stimulant properties of THC may be dependent on many factors, e.g., species, gender, temporal considerations of testing, effects of habituation and dose of cannabinoid administered,[11] the behavioral convulsions we observed appear to represent a unique interaction of Δ^9THC with a genetic animal model in which the stimulant properties of the cannabinoid predominate. In any event, the novel and reproducible occurrence of behavioral seizures in our THC-treated *S*s prompted the following experiments using cannabidiol (CBD) and cannabinol (CBN), two cannabinoids that are essentially inactive in man.[60, 61]

Each of seven rabbits (Nos. 1,2,4,5,6,7,8, FIGURE 5) was injected i.v. with Δ^9THC (0.5 mg/kg), CBN (10 mg/kg), CBD (10 mg/kg), and cannabinoid vehicle (10% Tween 80-saline solution), and behavioral observations were made as previously described.[21] The crossover treatment sequence was counterbalanced with a minimum 5-day rest period between injections for each animal. Characteristically in all *S*s, both THC and CBN produced patterns of nonfatal behavioral convulsant activity that were similar to the rabbit seizure pattern evoked by Δ^9THC in our previous study.[21] In marked contrast, neither the cannabinoid vehicle (1 ml) nor CBD caused seizures; the only observable behavioral effects were some ataxia and a swaying and bobbing of the head in CBD-treated rabbits. Willinsky and coworkers[62] reported ataxia and head swaying with a 10 mg/kg i.v. dose of CBD and a lack of any significant behavioral effect with a 30 mg/kg i.v. dose of CBN in rabbits. Lipparini and coworkers[17] demonstrated that Δ^9THC caused behavioral excitation and depression in rabbits, but the drug failed to produce behavioral convulsions in

TABLE 1

COMPARISON OF THE BEHAVIORAL CONVULSANT ACTIVITY OF INTRAVENOUS Δ^9-TETRAHYDROCANNABINOL (THC) GIVEN ALONE AND 30 MINUTES AFTER INTRAVENOUS CANNABIDIOL (CBD) PRETREATMENT IN CANNABINOID-SEIZURE SUSCEPTIBLE NEW ZEALAND WHITE RABBITS

	THC (0.5 mg/kg)	CBD (10 mg/kg) + THC (0.5 mg/kg)
Latency to convulsion	124.3 ± 9.4	174.3 ± 22.1
Frequency of:		
Clonus	6.8 ± 1.9	5.7 ± 0.9
Front limb extension	3.4 ± 0.9	3.9 ± 1.1
Hind limb extension	4.4 ± 1.0	2.4 ± 0.8
Head tuck	3.4 ± 0.8	2.6 ± 0.9
Body torsion	2.4 ± 0.4	2.4 ± 0.4
Duration of:		
Clonus	64.1 ± 13.9	52.7 ± 6.8
Front limb extension	21.9 ± 6.1	23.3 ± 6.0
Hind limb extension	24.9 ± 8.5	11.3 ± 3.4
Head tuck	52.1 ± 7.6	32.7 ± 9.1
Body torsion	13.0 ± 2.4	20.4 ± 2.9

Numbers are mean values ± standard error obtained in a 5-minute observational period following THC administration to 7 animals. Latency and durations of convulsant activity are in seconds.

i.v. doses up to 10 mg/kg. Thus, it is apparent that our findings of CBN- and Δ^9THC-induced behavioral seizures are indeed unique and perhaps attributable to a novel interaction between specific cannabinoids and our rather specialized population of rabbits.

Recently, CBD has been reported to block various effects of THC in rodents,[63, 64] rabbits,[63, 64] and man,[61] although an additional study in man[65] and in mice[66] failed to confirm a blocking effect of the cannabinoid. In light of the above findings and other data showing an anticonvulsant effect of the cannabinoid in various experimental animal seizure paradigms,[67, 68] we decided to test the effects of CBD on behavioral convulsions produced by THC. After a drug-free interval of 7 days, our seven rabbit *S*s were given CBD (10 mg/kg, i.v.) followed 30 minutes later by Δ^9THC (0.5 mg/kg, i.v.), and quantitative observations of individual rabbit behavior were made as previously described.[21] TABLE 1 illustrates a comparison of the effects of THC given singly and following CBD pretreatment on the various seizure endpoints measured. In all *S*s, CBD failed to block THC-induced seizures; furthermore, there were no significant differences ($p > 0.1$) on any latency, frequency, or duration measures of convulsant activity between the two treatment conditions. While these data suggest that CBD, in a single i.v. dose of 10 mg/kg, lacks anticonvulsant activity in our paradigm, additional studies (currently underway in our laboratory) using higher doses of CBD in combination with THC may provide a more definitive conclusion. Nevertheless, our present and previous findings suggest the occurrence of an animal model that is perhaps uniquely and differentially sensitive to the (extreme) stimulant actions of cannabinoids. In light of this hypothesis, the possible existence of a rather novel biological paradigm to test the effects of marijuana, its congeners, and potential antagonists is an exciting avenue for further research.

Acknowledgments

We thank Dr. Monique Braude of NIDA (ADAMHA) for the generous supply of cannabinoids and for her encouragement of these studies. We also thank Mr. Douglas Eisenstein and Dr. Parthena Martin for their technical assistance.

References

1. Greene, M. H., S. L. Nightingale & R. L. DuPont. 1975. Evolving patterns of drug abuse. Ann. Int. Med. **83:** 402–411.
2. Secretary of Health, Education and Welfare. 1974. Marihuana and Health, fourth report to Congress. U.S. Government Printing Office, Washington, D.C.
3. Rubin, V. & L. Comitas. 1975. Ganja in Jamaica. Mouton & Co. The Hague, Netherlands.
4. Kolansky, H. & W. T. Moore. 1975. Marihuana, can it hurt you? JAMA **232:** 923–924.
5. Isbell, H. & D. R. Jasinski. 1969. A comparison of LSD-25 with (-)-Δ^9-trans-tetrahydrocannabinol (THC) and attempted cross tolerance between LSD and THC. Psychopharmacologia **14:** 115–123.
6. Brown, J. K. & H. Malone. 1975. Status of drug quality in the street-drug market, an update. Pacific Inf. Serv. Street-Drugs **4**(2–4)**:** 11–30.
7. Harris, L. S. 1971. General and behavioral pharmacology. Pharmacol. Rev. **23**(4)**:** 285–294.
8. Carlini, E. A., J. Masur, I. G. Karniol & J. R. Leite. 1972. *Cannabis sativa:* Is it possible to consider behavioral animal data as experimental models for some effects on humans? *In* Cannabis and its Derivatives. W. D. M. Paton & J. Crown, Eds.: 154–175. Oxford Univ. Press. London, England.
9. Pradhan, S. N. & P. T. Bailey. 1972. Behavioral effects of marijuana and its derivatives. *In* Drug Addiction: Experimental Pharmacology. J. M. Singh, L. Miller & H. Lal, Eds.: 17–29. Futura Press. Mount Kisco, N.Y.
10. Paton, W. D. M. & R. G. Pertwee. 1973. The pharmacology of Cannabis in animals. *In* Marijuana, Chemistry, Pharmacology, Metabolism and Clinical Effects. R. Mechoulam, Ed.: 191–285. Academic Press. New York, N.Y.
11. Miller, L. L. & W. G. Drew. 1974. Cannabis: Review of behavioral effects in animals. Psychol. Bull. **81**(7)**:** 401–417.
12. Domino, E. F. 1971. Neuropsychopharmacologic studies of marijuana: Some

synthetic and natural THC derivatives in animals and man. Ann. N.Y. Acad. Sci. **191:** 161–191.

13. Hockman, C. H., R. G. Perrin & H. Kalant. 1971. Electroencephalographic and behavioral alterations produced by Δ^1-tetrahydrocannabinol. Science **172:** 968–970.
14. Martinez, J. L., S. W. Stadnicki & U. H. Schaeppi. 1972. Δ^9-Tetrahydrocannabinol: Effects on EEG and behavior of Rhesus monkeys. Life Sci. **11:** 643–651.
15. Consroe, P. E. 1973. Effect of Δ^9-tetrahydrocannabinol on a cholinergic-induced activation of the electroencephalogram in the rabbit. Res. Commun. Chem. Pathol. Pharmacol. **5:** 705–712.
16. Fujimori, M. & H. E. Himwich. 1973. Δ^9-Tetrahydrocannabinol and the sleep-wakefulness cycle in rabbits. Physiol. Behav. **11:** 291–295.
17. Lipparini, F., A. Scotti de Carolis & V. G. Longo. 1969. A neuropharmacological investigation of some trans-tetrahydrocannabinol derivatives. Physiol. Behav. **4:** 527–532.
18. Fujimori, M., D. M. Trusty & H. E. Himwich. 1973. Δ^9-Tetrahydrocannabinol: Electroencephalographic changes and autonomic responses in the rabbit. Life Sci. **12:** 553–563.
19. Bicher, H. I. & R. Mechoulam. 1968. Pharmacological effects of two active constituents of marihuana. Arch. Int. Pharmacodyn. Ther. **172:** 24–31.
20. Pirch, J. H., R. A. Cohn, P. R. Barnes & E. S. Barratt. 1972. Effects of acute and chronic administration of marijuana extract on the rat electroencephalogram. Neuropharmacology **11:** 231–240.
21. Consroe, P., B. Jones, H. Laird & J. Reinking. 1976. Anticonvulsant-convulsant effects of Δ^9-tetrahydrocannabinol. Conference on the Therapeutic Aspects of Marijuana, November 1975, Asilomar, California. In press.
22. Consroe, P. F., B. C. Jones & L. Chin. 1975. Δ^9-Tetrahydrocannabinol, EEG and behavior: The importance of adaptation to the testing milieu. Pharmacol. Biochem. Behav. **3:** 173–177.
23. Winer, B. J. 1971. Statistical Principles in Experimental Design. 2nd Edit. McGraw-Hill. New York, N.Y.
24. Barry, H. & R. Kubena. 1969. Acclimation to laboratory alters response of rats to Δ^1-tetrahydrocannabinol. Proc. 77th Ann. Amer. Psychol. Assoc. Mfg.: 865–866.
25. Drew, W. G. & L. L. Miller. 1973. Differential effects of Δ^9-THC on locomotor behavior in activity wheel habituated and non-habituated rats. Pharmacology **9:** 41–51.
26. Jones, B. C., P. F. Consroe & H. E. Laird. 1976. The interaction of Δ^9-tetrahydrocannabinol with cholinomimetic drugs in an agonist-antagonist paradigm. Eur. J. Pharmacol. **38:** 253–259.
27. Jones, B. C., P. F. Consroe & F. Akins. 1975. Physostigmine-induced reversal of EEG and behavioral effects of Δ^9-tetrahydrocannabinol. Bull. Psychonom. Soc. **6**(2): 204–206.
28. Johansson, J. O., T. U. C. Jarbe & B. G. Henriksson. 1974. Physostigmine attenuation of Δ^9-tetrahydrocannabinol induced hyperthermia in rats. Experientia **30:** 779–780.
29. Freemon, F. R., J. E. Rosenblatt & M. K. El-Yousef. 1975. Interactions of physostigmine and delta-9-tetrahydrocannabinol in man. Clin. Pharmacol. Ther. **17**(2): 121–126.
30. Rosenblatt, J. E., D. S. Janowsky, J. M. Davis & M. K. El-Yousef. 1972. The augmentation of physostigmine toxicity in the rat. Res. Commun. Chem. Pathol. Pharmacol. **3:** 479–482.
31. Sofia, R. D. & L. C. Knoblock. 1974. Influence of acute pretreatment with Δ^9-tetrahydrocannabinol on the LD50 of various substances that alter neurohumoral transmission. Toxicol. Appl. Pharmacol. **28:** 277–234.
32. Consroe, P., B. Jones & H. Laird. 1976. EEG and behavioral effects of

Δ^9-tetrahydrocannabinol in combination with stimulant drugs in rabbits. Psychopharmacologia. In press.
33. DAGIRMANJIAN, R. & E. S. BOYD. 1962. Some pharmacologic effects of two tetrahydrocannabinols. J. Pharmacol. Exp. Ther. **135:** 25–33.
34. GARRIOTT, J. C., L. J. KING, R. B. FORNEY & F. W. HUGHES. 1967. Effects of some tetrahydrocannabinols on hexobarbital sleeping time and amphetamine induced hyperactivity in mice. Life Sci. **6:** 2119–2128.
35. GRUNFELD, Y. & H. EDERY. 1969. Psychopharmacological activity of the active constituents of hashish and some related cannabinoids. Psychopharmacologia **14:** 200–210.
36. KUBENA, R. K. & H. BARRY. 1970. Interactions of Δ^9-tetrahydrocannabinol with barbiturates and methamphetamine. J. Pharmacol. Exp. Ther. **173:** 94–100.
37. HARDMAN, H. F., E. F. DOMINO & M. H. SEEVERS. 1971. General pharmacological actions of some synthetic tetrahydrocannabinol derivatives. Pharmacol. Rev. **23:** 295–315.
38. COPER, H. & M. FERNANDEZ. 1973. Interaction between cannabis and other drugs. *In* Bayer-Symposium IV, Psychic Dependence. L. Goldberg & F. Hoffmeister, Eds.: 135–141. Springer-Verlag. New York, N.Y.
39. HOWES, J. F. 1973. The effect of Δ^9-tetrahydrocannabinol on amphetamine induced lethality in aggregated mice. Res. Commun. Chem. Pathol. Pharmacol. **6:** 895–900.
40. WATERS, D. H. & S. D. GLICK. 1973. Asymetrical effect of Δ^9-tetrahydrocannabinol (THC) and striatal dopamine and behavior. Res. Commun. Chem. Pathol. Pharmacol. **6:** 57–63.
41. CRAIGMILL, A. L., D. M. CANAFAX & F. R. CURTISS. 1974. The interaction of Δ^9-tetrahydrocannabinol and d-amphetamine in aggregated mice. Res. Commun. Chem. Pathol. Pharmacol. **9:** 229–241.
42. GOUGH, A. L. & J. E. OLLEY. 1975. Cannabis and amphetamine-induced stereotypy in rats. J. Pharm. Pharmacol. **27:** 62–63.
43. CONSROE, P. F., B. C. JONES & F. Akins. 1975. Δ^9-Tetrahydrocannabinol-methamphetamine interaction in the rabbit. Neuropharmacology **14:** 377–383.
44. BARTOLINI, A., R. BARTOLINI & E. F. DOMINO. 1973. Effects of physostigmine on brain acetylcholine content and release. Neuropharmacology **12:** 15–25.
45. YAMAMOTO, K-L. & E. F. DOMINO. 1967. Cholinergic agonist-antagonist interactions on neocortical and limbic EEG activation. Int. J. Neuropharmacol. **6:** 357–373.
46. BUTCHER, R. W. & E. W. SUTHERLAND. 1962. Adenosine 3′, 5′-phosphate in biological materials. J. Biol. Chem. **237:** 1244–1250.
47. FUXE, K. & U. UNGERSTEDT. 1974. Action of caffeine and theophylline on supersensitive dopamine receptors: Considerable enhancement of receptor response to treatment with DOPA and dopamine receptor agonists. Med. Biol. **52:** 48–54.
48. SCHEEL-KRUGER, J. 1972. Some aspects of the mechanism of action of various stimulant amphetamine analogues. Psychiatr. Neurol. Neurochir. **75:** 179–192.
49. VANROSSUM, J. M. 1972. Psychopharmacology of amphetamines. Psychiatr. Neurol. Neurochir. **75:** 165–178.
50. MUSCHOLL, E. 1966. Indirectly acting sympathomimetic amines. Pharmacol. Rev. **18:** 551–559.
51. SNYDER, S. H. 1972. Catecholamines in the brain as mediators of amphetamine psychosis. Arch. Gen. Psychiatry **27:** 169–181.
52. ANDEN, N., A. RUBENSON, K. FUXE & T. HOKFELT. 1967. Evidence for dopamine receptor stimulation by apomorphine. J. Pharm. Pharmacol. **19:** 627–632.

53. Costall, B. & R. J. Naylor. 1973. On the mode of action of apomorphine. Eur. J. Pharmacol. **21:** 350–361.
54. Braude, M. C. 1972. Toxicology of cannabinoids. *In* Cannabis and its Derivatives. W. D. M. Paton & J. Crown, Eds.: 88–100. Oxford Univ. Press. London, England.
55. Thompson, G. R., H. Rosenkrantz, U. Schaeppi & M. C. Braude. 1973. Comparisons of acute oral toxicity of cannabinoids in rats, dogs and monkeys. Toxicol. Appl. Pharmacol. **25:** 363–372.
56. Rosenkrantz, H., R. A. Sprague, R. W. Fleishman & M. C. Braude. 1975. Oral Δ^9-tetrahydrocannabinol toxicity in rats treated for periods up to six months. Toxicol. Appl. Pharmacol. **32:** 399–417.
57. Rosenkrantz, H. & M. C. Braude. 1974. Acute, subacute and 23-day chronic marijuana inhalation toxicities in the rat. Toxicol. Appl. Pharmacol. **28:** 428–441.
58. Segal, M. 1974. Central implantation of cannabinoids: Induction of epileptiform discharges. Eur. J. Pharmacol. **27:** 40–45.
59. Thompson, G. R., H. Rosenkrantz, R. W. Fleischman & M. C. Braude. 1975. Effects of Δ^9-tetrahydrocannabinol administered subcutaneously to rabbits for 28 days. Toxicology **4:** 41–51.
60. Hollister, L. E. 1973. Cannabidiol and cannabinol in man. Experientia **29:** 825–826.
61. Karniol, I. G., I. Shirakawa, N. Kasinski, A. Pfeferman & E. A. Carlini. 1974. Cannabidiol interferes with the effects of Δ^9tetrahydrocannabinol in man. Eur. J. Pharmacol. **28:** 172–177.
62. Willinsky, M. D., A. Scotti de Carolis & V. G. Longo. 1973. EEG and behavioral effects of natural, synthetic and biosynthetic cannabinoids. Psychopharmacologia **31:** 365–374.
63. Karniol, I. G. & E. A. Carlini. 1973. Pharmacological interaction between cannabidiol and Δ^9-tetrahydrocannabinol. Psychopharmacologia **33:** 53–70.
64. Borgen, L. A. & W. M. Davis. 1974. Cannabidiol interaction with delta-9-tetrahydrocannabinol. Res. Commun. Chem. Pathol. Pharmacol. **7:** 663–670.
65. Hollister, L. E. & H. Gillespie. 1975. Interactions in man of delta-9-tetrahydrocannabinol. Clin. Pharmacol. Ther. **18:** 80–83.
66. Ham, M. T. & Y. DeJong. 1975. Absence of interaction between Δ^9-tetrahydrocannabinol (Δ^9-THC) and cannabidiol (CBD) in agression, muscle control and body temperature experiments in mice. Psychopharmacologia **41:** 169–174.
67. Carlini, E. A., J. R. Leite, M. Tannhauser & A. C. Berardi. 1973. Cannabidiol and *Cannabis sativa* extract protects mice and rats against convulsive agents. J. Pharm. Pharmacol. **25:** 664–665.
68. Karler, R., W. Cely & S. A. Turkanis. 1973. The anticonvulsant activity of cannabidiol and cannabinol. Life Sci. **13:** 1527–1531.

INTERACTIONS OF Δ^9-TETRAHYDROCANNABINOL WITH OTHER DRUGS

Leo E. Hollister

Stanford University School of Medicine
and
Veterans Administration Hospital
Palo Alto, California 94304

Interactions of the active component of marihuana, Δ^9-tetrahydrocannabinol (THC), with other drugs are of interest from several points of view. First, hardly any socially used drug is used alone, and marihuana is no exception. Second, interactions may provide a better understanding of the mechanisms of action of THC. Third, interactions with other drugs, or with varying states of the individual, or with the setting in which marihuana is taken may account for some of the great variability in its effects, both between and within individual users.

Many possible interactions of THC might be studied. They may be described in the following general categories: a) pharmacodynamic interactions between THC and another drug with known actions; b) pharmacokinetic interactions with other drugs or substances which might affect absorption, binding, distribution, metabolism, excretion, or access of THC to receptor sites; c) interactions to study the mechanisms of action of THC; and d) interactions dependent on characteristics of the subject taking the drug and/or the setting in which it is taken.

Pharmacodynamic Interactions

The drug most commonly taken with marihuana is ethanol. These drugs are deliberately taken together to enhance the effects of marihuana. Fortified sweet wines are the preferred alcoholic beverage. Not surprisingly, experimental evidence supports the validity of this folk practice. Adding ethanol both to high and low doses of THC increased impairment from the latter drug on several measures, as well as adding to the subjective experiences.[1] Both drugs share somewhat similar properties in being disinhibiting agents and euphoriants when taken in small doses and sedative when taken in larger doses. Thus, the usual clinical sequence of an initial "high" followed by sleepiness is common to both drugs. Comparison between ethanol and THC confirms the similarities, the major distinction being the more distorted time sense and hallucinogenic action of THC.[2]

A situation similar to that of ethanol should prevail with sedatives, but studies in man are few. THC administered in single doses to mice caused potentiation of sleeping time and loss of righting reflex from nine types of sedative hypnotics, including ethanol and barbiturates.[3] Chronic treatment with THC reduced loss of righting reflex in mice by zoxazolamine and hexobarbital, but not potentiation from barbital; as the latter drug, unlike the former, is not metabolized by the liver, possible induction of drug-metabolizing enzymes by the liver could explain this difference.[4] In man, THC given after pentobarbital pretreatment induced hallucinations and anxiety in five of seven volunteers, to the extent that four did not complete the course of five doses of THC because of the severe psychologic effects.[5] The same investigators found that THC potentiated the sedative and respiratory depressant effects of the opioid, oxymorphone, in man. Cardiovascular effects of THC seemed to be unaltered by the presence of either drug.

Stimulants combined with THC have relatively little effect in man, seeming to act in a mildly additive fashion. A dose of 15 mg of dextroamphetamine in man followed by smoking 15 mg of THC equivalent in marihuana cigarettes revealed separate effects from both drugs: marihuana caused tachycardia and conjunctival injection; dextroamphetamine increased blood pressure and respiratory rate. The impairment of performance on cognitive tests produced by marihuana may have been overcome by dextroamphetamine, which improved performance when given alone.[6] Similar additive effects were seen in subjects given 10 mg/70 kg doses of dextroamphetamine and 50 μg/kg doses of THC by smoking. In this case, dextroamphetamine did not counter the adverse effects of marihuana on motor performance.[7] Instances of combined use of amphetamines and marihuana are infrequent in social practice. One would guess that when they occurred, doses of amphetamine would be considerably higher than those given experimentally.

Pharmacokinetic Interactions

Although inadvertent or deliberate overdoses of THC are unusual in social use of marihuana, it might be desirable to have a drug available which would antagonize its effect. Phenitrone, a substance which has little pharmacological activity of its own except in large doses, was thought to be such a substance. Careful experiments in mice and dogs in one case, or dogs and pigeons in another, revealed no evidence of any such antagonistic effects.[8, 9]

Indian folklore recommended the use of tamarind, a tropical fruit, as an antagonist of the effects of bhang. We tried giving the fruit an hour before, simultaneously, or an hour after administration of THC orally to man. In doses up to 180 g, it was totally ineffective. Tamarind juice, as served in subtropical climates, is a generally refreshing drink, and it may be that this nonspecific effect was the basis for assuming it to be an antagonist.

THC is strongly lipid soluble and is bound to lipoproteins in plasma. This property raised the possibility that a high prevailing level of lipids in the plasma, such as might occur following a rich and heavy meal, might alter its distribution characteristics. We studied subjects given orally administered THC either fasting or after a 100 g fat meal based on intake of ice cream, a technique that produces marked alimentary lipemia.[10] Effects of the same dose of THC in the same subject were essentially indistinguishable in either the fasting or lipemic condition.

Giving THC in a lipid vehicle undoubtedly increases the completeness and rapidity of absorption. In our first studies with THC, we administered it orally in a hydroalcoholic solution in doses of from 10 to 70 mg.[11] Other investigators, using 30 mg doses of THC in a sesame oil vehicle, obtained much greater effects than we reported. Mixing marihuana with fatty substances is an old trick for taking it orally for social use. We have used for several years a version of the Alice B. Toklas cookie: a commercial cookie to which THC in alcoholic solution is added, the solvent being evaporated under nitrogen. It is a most satisfactory way to give the drug orally in measured doses which are probably fully absorbed.

The two other major cannabinoids in marihuana, cannabidiol (CBD) and cannabinol (CBN), might interact with THC either by altering the metabolism of THC or by competition for the same receptors.

Studies of interaction between major cannabinoids have suggested a potentiating effect of CBD and a blocking action of CBN. CBN was reported to antagonize the prolongation of hexobarbital sleeping time in mice.[12] Pentobarbital anesthesia in mice, which is prolonged by THC alone, was further enhanced by adding CBD, whereas CBN reduced the effect, the latter result being consistent with the previous study.[13] Hexobarbital sleeping time in rats was prolonged both by THC and CBD, showing an additive effect; CBN blocked the effect of THC. This result also is consistent with the previous study. The enhancement by CBD was thought possibly to be due to inhibition of THC metabolism.[14] This explanation was supported by a study showing that CBD was the most potent cannabinoid for inhibiting hepatic drug-metabolizing enzymes.[15] Intestinal motility in mice from a combination of both THC and CBD was more depressed than by a comparable single dose of THC alone; 10 mg/100 g of THC combined with 40 mg/100 g of CBD induced depression equivalent to that of 40 mg/100 g dose of THC alone.[16] CBD given prior to THC reduced the magnitude and duration of hypothermic effects of THC in rats, as well as its depressant effects on heart rate, respiration, and rectal temperature in rabbits. The action was thought to be due to competitive antagonism.[17] A more complex interaction between THC and CBD was described in rabbits, mice, and rats. CBD was thought to antagonize the excitatory effects of THC while potentiating the depressant effects.[18]

The situation in regard to these interactions in man is somewhat less clear. Oral doses of 30 mg of THC produced strong psychological responses in man, while doses of 15 to 60 mg of CBD alone produced nothing. When the former dose of THC was combined with 15, 30, or 60 mg doses of CBD, most of the effects of THC were blocked.[19] A comparison between smoked THC and marihuana indicated that the subjective, cognitive, and physiologic changes tended to be greater for marihuana.[20] Rather than a blocking effect of other constituents in marihuana, the latter study suggested enhanced effects, even though the amount of other cannabinoids present in the marihuana was miniscule.

Oral doses of 20 mg of THC combined with placebo or 40 mg doses of CBD or CBN showed no apparent interaction with CBN in the quality, intensity, or duration of effects of THC alone. CBD tended to delay onset and prolong effects of THC, while making them somewhat more intense. This interactive effect was slight, providing no reason for abandoning the current practice of basing doses of marihuana for clinical studies solely on THC content.[21] A recent study in mice failed to show any interaction between THC and CBD.[22] Co-administration of THC and CBN in rats accelerated the rate of clearance of THC from the blood, suggesting a possible diminution of effect of THC depending on the amount of CBN.[23]

Interactions Bearing on Mechanisms of Action

Major focus for explaining the mechanism of centrally active drugs is on their effects on neurotransmitters. Reports on interactions of Δ^9-tetrahydrocannabinol with biogenic amines as determined by animal studies have been conflicting. Mice treated with intraperitoneal doses of THC showed a decreased concentration of norepinephrine in brain following low doses but an increase following doses of 200 mg per kg; concentrations of serotonin (5-hydroxyptamine) were increased by both low and high doses.[24] Rats treated with intraperitoneal doses of 80 mg per kg showed slight decreases in endogenous norepinephrine and increases in serotonin; the turnover and metabolism of norepinephrine were increased without any ihibition of its uptake or any decrease of its deamination.[25] Telencephalic levels of serotonin were elevated in mice by doses of 10 mg per kg without any changes in endogenous levels of brain norepinephrine or dopamine.[26] Smaller doses of THC, adequate to produce behavioral effects in rats, had no change in the concentration or turnover of serotonin in brain.[27]

Alphamethylparatyrosine (AMPT), an inhibitor of tyrosine hydroxylase, the rate-limiting step in the biosynthesis of catecholamines, was given prior to treatment with THC in three separate experiments. No major qualitative or quantitative changes in the effect of THC were found. Some accentuation of the total intensity of THC was apparent but impossible to distinguish from some of the reported effects at large doses of AMPT itself. Evidence that recently synthesized catecholamines are of major importance in THC action is lacking.[28] This conclusion is somewhat supported by the fact that the beta-adrenergic receptor blocking agent, propranolol, ameliorated THC-induced tachycardia but had no effect on disturbances of cognitive function.[29]

The role acetylcholine in THC action has been studied using interactions between the acetylcholine esterase inhibitor, physostigmine, and THC. In one study, hyperthermia produced in rats by THC was attenuated by physostigmine, but not by neostigmine, an inhibitor which does not enter the brain. These findings suggested that THC-induced hyperthermia was due to reduced acetylcholine release centrally.[30] A somewhat opposite effect was suggested by the fact that physostigmine toxicity in rats, as measured by lethality, was augmented by THC. The toxicity of the THC-physostigmine combination was reduced both by atropine and methscopolamine, indicating that increased lethality was not solely due to increased central acetylcholine concentrations.[31]

The single study of THC-physostigmine interaction in man revealed amplification of lethargy and somnolence and reduction in tachycardia and conjunctival injection. As physostigmine alone produces a specific syndrome of lethargy, somnolence and bradycardia in man, the observed effects may simply have been additive.[32]

Interactions Between THC and Characteristics of Subject and Setting

Variable responses to the same dose of THC are seen not only between subjects but in the same subject as well. We have been interested in this phenomenon and have begun to study it. One possible explanation for between-subject variability would be different rates of hydroxylation of drugs. If the active metabolite of THC is 11-hydroxy-THC, then subjects with a rapid rate of hydroxylation might be expected to have a more precipitous onset and greater intensity of THC effect than slow hydroxylators. Both metabolism of antipyrine and phenylbutazone were used as indices of hydroxylation rate. It was impossible to correlate either the speed of onset, total intensity, or duration of effects with speed of hydroxylation of drugs.[33] Thus, it seems unlikely that differing rates of drug metabolism account for the widely variable responses between individuals exposed to THC.

It has become axiomatic that the setting in which psychoactive drugs are taken is a strong determinant in the effects they produce. The axiom is seldom tested. A study of marihuana and placebo cigarettes smoked under "favorable" and "unfavorable" conditions found no appreciable contribution of the setting but strong effects for subjects and treatments.[34] Quite possibly the psychological expectations or "set" of subjects are the major determinant of inter-individual differences. This factor has not yet been adequately studied in the case of THC.[35]

Summary and Conclusions

Pharmacodynamic interaction between THC and ethanol is additive and is the only interaction of consequence in the social use of the drug, commonly being sought deliberately. Pharmacokinetic interactions between THC and other cannabinoids, although theoretically possible, do not appear to be of any clinical significance. No antagonist of THC effects has yet been found. Preliminary studies of interactions between THC and drugs affecting activity of neurotransmitters have not provided good tests of the mechanism of action of the drug, showing at best subtle effects of questionable clinical significance. The variable responses of subjects to THC is neither explained by differences in metabolism of drugs nor by differences in the setting in which the drug is taken.

References

1. Manno, J. E., G. F. Kiplinger, N. Scholz, R. B. Forney & S. E. Haine. 1971. The influence of alcohol and marihuana on motor and mental performance. Clin. Pharmacol. Ther. **12:** 202–211.
2. Hollister, L. E. & H. K. Gillespie. 1970. Marihuana, ethanol, and dextroamphetamine; mood and mental function alterations. Arch. Gen. Psychiatry **23:** 199–203.
3. Sofia, R. D. & L. C. Knobloch. 1973. The interaction of delta-9-tetrahydrocannabinol pretreatment with various sedative-hypnotic drugs. Psychopharmacologia **30:** 185–194.
4. Sofia, R. D. & H. Barry. 1973. Interactions of chronic and acute delta-1-tetrahydrocannabinol pretreatment with zoxazolamine and barbiturates. Res. Commun. Chem. Pathol. Pharmacol. **5:** 91–98.
5. Johnstone, R. E., P. L. Lief, R. A. Kulp & T. C. Smith. 1975. Combination of delta-9-tetrahydrocannabinol with oxymorphone or pentobarbital: Effects on ventilatory control and cardiovascular dynamics. Anesthesiology **42:** 674–684.

6. ZALCMAN, S., B. LISKOW, R. CADORET & D. GOODWIN. 1973. Marijuana and amphetamine: The question of interaction. Amer. J. Psychiatry **130:** 707–708.
7. EVANS, M. A., R. MARTZ, L. LEMBERGER, B. E. RODDA & R. B. FORNEY. 1974. Clinical effects of marihuana dextroamphetamine combination. The Pharmacologist **16:** 281.
8. BERGER, H. J. & J. C. KRANTZ. 1972. Phenitrone: ineffective blockade of (- -)-trans-delta-9-tetrahydrocannabinol in mice and dogs. J. Pharm. Pharmacol. **24:** 492.
9. SPAULDING, T. C., R. D. FORD, W. L. DEWEY, D. E. MCMILLAN & L. S. HARRIS. 1972. Some pharmacological effects of phenitrone and its interaction with delta-9-THC. Eur. J. Pharmacol. **19:** 310–317.
10. HOLLISTER, L. E. 1963. Successive trials of induced alimentary lipemia. Amer. J. Clin. Nutr. **13:** 214–218.
11. HOLLISTER, L. E., R. K. RICHARDS & H. K. GILLESPIE. 1968. Comparison of tetrahydrocannabinol and synhexyl in man. Clin. Pharmacol. Ther. **9:** 783–791.
12. 12. KRANTZ, J. C., H. J. BERGER & B. L. WELCH. 1971. Blockade of (- -)-trans-delta-9-tetrahydrocannabinol depressant effect by cannabinol in mice. Amer. J. Pharmacol. **143:** 149–152.
13. CHESHER, G. B., D. M. JACKSON & G. A. STARMER. 1974. Interaction of cannabis and general anaesthetic agents in mice. Brit. J. Pharmacol. **50:** 593–599.
14. FERNANDES, M., A. SCHABAREK, H. COPER & R. HILL. 1974. Modification of delta-9-THC-actions by cannabinol and cannabidiol in the rat. Psychopharmacologia **38:** 329–338.
15. FERNANDES, M., N. WARNING, W. CHRIST & R. HILL. 1973. Interactions of several cannabinoids with the hepatic drug metabolizing system. Biochem. Pharmacol. **22:** 2981–2987.
16. ANDERSON, P. F., D. M. JACKSON & G. B. CHESHER. 1974. Interaction of delta-9-tetrahydrocannabinol and cannabidiol on intestinal motility in mice. J. Pharm. Pharmacol. **26:** 136–137.
17. BORGEN, L. A. & W. M. DAVIS. 1974. Cannabidiol interaction with delta-9-tetrahydrocannabinol. Res. Commun. Chem. Pathol. Pharmacol. **7:** 663–670.
18. KARNIOL, I. G. & E. A. CARLINI. 1973. Pharmacological interaction between cannabidiol and delta-9-tetrahydrocannabinol. Psychopharmacologia **33:** 53–70.
19. KARNIOL, I. G., I. SHIRAKAWA, N. KASINSKI, A. PFEFERMAN & E. A. CARLINI. 1974. Cannabidiol interferes with the effects of delta-9-tetrahydrocannabinol in man. Eur. J. Pharmacol. **28:** 172–177.
20. GALANTER, M., H. WEINGARTNER, T. VAUGHAN, W. T. ROTH & R. J. WYATT. 1973. Delta-9-transtetrahydrocannabinol and natural marihuana. A controlled comparison. Arch. Gen. Psychiatry **28:** 278–281.
21. HOLLISTER, L. E. & H. GILLESPIE. 1975. Interactions in man of delta-9-tetrahydrocannabinol. II. Cannabinol and cannabidiol. Clin. Pharmacol. Ther. **18:** 80–83.
22. TEN HAM, M. & Y. DE JONG. 1975. Absence of interaction between delta-9-tetrahydrocannabinol and cannabidiol in aggression, muscle control and body temperature experiments in mice. Psychopharmacologia **41:** 169–174.
23. MCCALLUM, N. K. 1975. The effect of cannabinol on delta-1-tetrahydrocannabinol clearance from the blood. Experientia **31:** 957–958.
24. HOLTZMAN, D., R. A. LOVELL, J. H. JAFFE & D. X. FREEDMAN. 1969. 1-delta-9-tetrahydrocannabinol: neurochemical and behavioral effects in the mouse. Science **163:** 1464–1467.
25. SCHILDKRAUT, J. J. & D. H. EFRON. 1971. The effects of delta-9-tetrahydrocannabinol on the metabolism of norepinephrine in rat brain. Psychopharmacologia **20:** 191–196.
26. WELCH, B. L., A. S. WELCH, F. S. MESSIHA & H. J. BERGER. 1971. Rapid

depletion of adrenal epinephrine and elevation of telencephalic serotonin by (- -)-trans-delta-9-tetrahydrocannabinol in mice. Res. Commun. Chem. Pathol. Pharmacol. **2:** 382–391.

27. Gallagher, D. W., E. Sanders-Bush & F. Sulser. 1972. Dissociation between behavioral effects and changes in metabolism of cerebral serotonin following delta-9-tetrahydrocannabinol. Psychopharmacologia **26:** 337–345.
28. Hollister, L. E. 1974. Interactions in man of delta-9-tetrahydrocannabinol 1. Alphamethylparatyrosine. Clin. Pharmacol. Ther. **15:** 18–21.
29. Drew, W. G., G. F. Kiplinger, L. L. Miller & M. Marx. 1972. Effects of propranolol on marihuana-induced cognitive dysfunctioning. Clin. Pharmacol. Ther. **13:** 526–533.
30. Johansson, J. O., T. U. C. Jarbe & B. G. Henriksson. 1974. Physostigmine attenuation of delta-9-tetrahydrocannabinol induced hyperthermia in rats. Experientia **30:** 779–780.
31. Rosenblatt, J. E., D. S. Janowsky, J. M. Davis & K. El-Yousef. 1972. The augmentation of physostigmine toxicity in the rat by delta-9-tetrahydrocannabinol. Res. Commun. Chem. Pathol. Pharmacol. **3:** 479–482.
32. Freemon, F. R., J. E. Rosenblatt & M. K. El-Yousef. 1975. Interaction of physostigmine and delta-9-tetrahydrocannabinol in man. Clin. Pharmacol. Ther. **17:** 121–126.
33. Hollister, L. E. & H. K. Gillespie. 1975. Action of delta-9-tetrahydrocannabinol. Clin. Pharmacol. Ther. **18:** 714–719.
34. Hollister, L. E., J. E. Overall & M. L. Gerber. 1975. Marihuana and setting. Arch. Gen. Psychiatry **32:** 798–801.
35. Hollister, L. E. & J. E. Overall. 1975/76. Dimensions of marihuana experience. Drug & Alcohol Dependence **1:** 155–164.

CLINICAL STUDIES ON THE INTERACTION OF PSYCHOPHARMACOLOGIC AGENTS WITH MARIHUANA

L. Lemberger, B. Dalton, R. Martz, B. Rodda, and R. Forney

Departments of Pharmacology and Medicine
Indiana University School of Medicine and Lilly Research Laboratories
Indianapolis, Indiana 46260

We have been interested in the interaction of marihuana and its constituents with other psychopharmacologic agents. The purpose of this paper will be first to describe our recent attempts to study the interactions of the barbiturates with cannabis, and then to discuss the interactions between several of marihuana's constituents.

There is considerable evidence that a segment of the marihuana-smoking population also uses other drugs, either concurrently with marihuana, or on separate occasions. Fisher and Brickman[1] reported that about 17% of occasional users of marihuana may occasionally use barbiturates, whereas 28% and 48% of regular and daily users, respectively, also occasionally use barbiturates. There is much evidence from animal studies in our laboratory, as well as from other laboratories, that marihuana and Δ^9-tetrahydrocannabinol (Δ^9-THC), its major psychoactive component, produce CNS depression, and that an interaction occurs between these drugs and the barbiturates.[2-5] Since no previous clinical studies have been reported on the interaction of cannabis and barbiturates, we embarked on a clinical study to investigate whether these interactions occurred in man, and to determine their clinical significance. Twelve healthy male volunteers were recruited from our student population. All subjects had previous experience with cannabis preparations. Each subject was given a complete history, physical, laboratory evaluation, and electrocardiogram, and the purpose of this study and its associated hazards and risks were explained. Written informed consent was obtained. The basic design of this study was carried out in a double-blind fashion with subjects randomly assigned to one of four groups as shown in TABLE 1. All subjects were tested on each of four weekly sessions, and each subject received all four possible combinations of placebo or drug.

The order of testing and drug administration is shown in TABLE 2. The tests used included a modified Cornell Medical Index, wobble board, pursuit meter,

TABLE 1

EXPERIMENTAL DESIGN FOR STUDYING THE INTERACTION OF MARIHUANA AND SECOBARBITAL

Drug Administration
Placebo capsule + placebo marihuana cigarette
150 mg secobarbital (p.o.) + placebo marihuana cigarette
Placebo capsule + marihuana cigarette (25 μg/kg THC)
150 mg secobarbital (p.o.) + marihuana cigarette (25 μg/kg THC)

TABLE 2

PROTOCOL FOR INVESTIGATION OF MARIHUANA AND SECOBARBITAL INTERACTION

Time (min)	Procedure
0	Secobarbital or placebo administered orally
40	Radial pulse, modified Cornell Medical Index
50	Active or placebo marihuana administered
60	Radial pulse
65	Wobble Board test
70	Pursuit meter tests
80	Delayed auditory feedback tests
95	"Suitcase" tests
105	Modified Cornell Medical Index

delayed auditory feedback, and "Suitcase Test," the details of all of which have been reported previously.[6]

The pursuit meter is an instrument designed to test coordination and tracking ability. Secobarbital alone or Δ^9-THC alone both resulted in a decreased ability to track. The combination of both drugs resulted in a greater decrease in tracking ability, which was additive (FIGURE 1).

The results of the modified Cornell Medical Index questionnaire are shown in FIGURE 2. Minimal symptoms were reported for placebo medication. The administration of secobarbital alone did produce an increase in symptoms, as

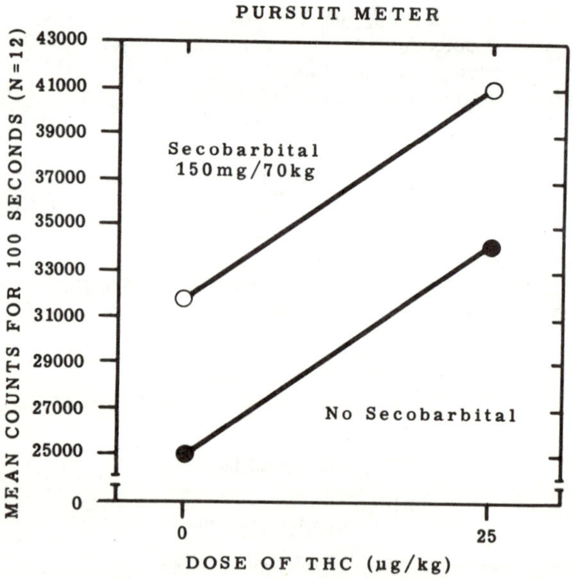

FIGURE 1. The effect of secobarbital and marihuana on tracking ability. Mean error scores of 12 subjects on the pursuit meter. Subjects received cigarettes designed to deliver 0 or 25 μg/kg of THC with and without sodium secobarbital.

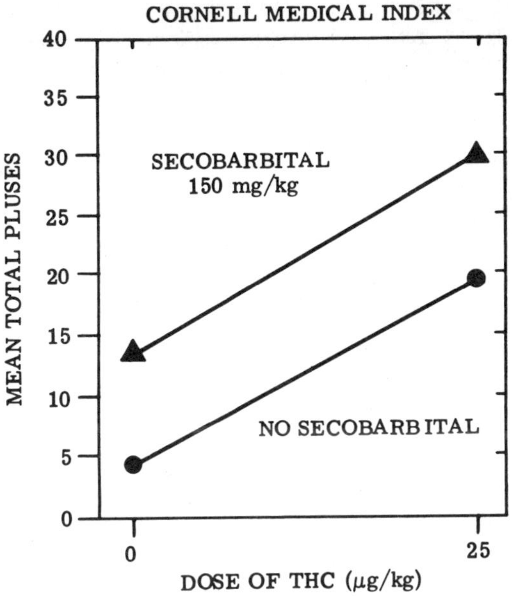

FIGURE 2. The subjective effects of marihuana and secobarbital. Mean total of positive answers in 12 subjects in response to a modified Cornell Medical Index Questionnaire. Subjects received either 0 or 25 μg/kg of Δ^9-THC with and without sodium secobarbital.

did the administration of Δ^9-THC alone. The combination of these drugs resulted in a greater increase in symptoms than either drug alone, and the effects were totally additive.

At the termination of the study, the subjects were asked to give their subjective impressions of what drug they thought they had received and if, in fact, they thought their driving ability would be impaired. The results are shown in TABLE 3. Although only 50% of the subjects thought their driving ability would be impaired with either Δ^9-THC or barbiturate alone, 75% of the subjects felt that their driving ability would definitely be impaired after the combination of both drugs. No significant interaction was found with the "Suitcase Test" and delayed auditory feedback, whereas on the wobble board, secobarbital and Δ^9-THC produced opposite effects.

It is known that certain barbiturates are metabolized by the hepatic microsomal enzymes and that Δ^9-THC is also a substrate for these enzymes.[7-8] Studies in laboratory animals have shown that cannabinoids such as Δ^9-THC and cannabidiol potentiate barbiturate sleep time and also inhibit the metabolism of these drugs by liver microsomal enzymes.[9-14] These studies indicate that Δ^9-THC is a potent inhibitor of the liver microsomal enzymes and that it produces a Type I spectral change when combined with liver microsomes. However, it has been found that cannabidiol is much more potent than Δ^9-THC as an inhibitor of the liver microsomal enzymes *in vitro* and also in its ability to inhibit drug metabolism *in vivo*. Therefore, we decided to study the effects of cannabidiol on secobarbital's pharmacologic actions, as well as on its physiologic disposition.

TABLE 3

IMPRESSIONS OF SUBJECTS REGARDING TREATMENTS

	No Barbiturate		Barbiturate	
Subjective Impressions	0 μg/kg THC	25 μg/kg THC	0 μg/kg THC	25 μg/kg THC
No. believed they had marihuana alone	2/12	6/12	4/12	3/12
No. believed they had barbiturate alone	2/12	0/12	3/12	4/12
No. believed they had both drugs	0/12	3/12	3/12	5/12
No. believed driving would be impaired	1/12	6/12	6/12	9/12

Placebo marihuana or placebo marihuana to which only cannabidiol was added was administered by inhalation to six subjects. The cannabidiol was given at doses of either 150 μg/kg or 500 μg/kg. Each subject was administered secobarbital orally at a dose of 150 mg/70 kg body weight, according to the experimental design in TABLE 4. Cannabidiol, when given alone in much larger quantities, has been shown to be without noticeable pharmacologic activity.[15-16] No significant difference in the response to the modified Cornell Medical Index was observed, whether the subjects received secobarbital with placebo marihuana or secobarbital with either 150 μg/kg or 500 μg/kg of cannabidiol (FIGURE 3). There was also no statistically significant difference in the plasma concentrations of secobarbital and its plasma $t_{1/2}$ (23.3 hr.), whether secobarbital was administered with placebo marihuana or in combination with cannabidiol (FIGURE 4).

Recently, several reports have appeared in the literature suggesting that although Δ⁹-THC is the major active component of marihuana, other constituents of marihuana may modify Δ⁹-THC's effects. Galanter *et al.*[17] reported that subjects evidenced a greater psychologic response from marihuana of known Δ⁹-THC content than from a placebo marihuana cigarette from which all the cannabinoids had been extracted but only the Δ⁹-THC replaced. Animal studies[18-22] have shown that cannabidiol interacts with Δ⁹-THC, enhancing its pharmacologic effects in several test systems. In man, Karniol *et al.*[23] have reported that cannabidiol interferes with the effects of Δ⁹-THC after the oral administration of these drugs. In contrast, Hollister and Gillespie[24] were unable to detect significant behavioral interactions between Δ⁹-THC and cannabidiol

TABLE 4

EXPERIMENTAL DESIGN FOR STUDYING THE INTERACTION OF CANNABIDIOL AND SECOBARBITAL

Drug Administration
Placebo marihuana cigarette + 150 mg secobarbital
Placebo marihuana cigarette (150 μg/kg cannabidiol) + 150 mg secobarbital
Placebo marihuana cigarette (500 μg/kg cannabidiol) + 150 mg secobarbital

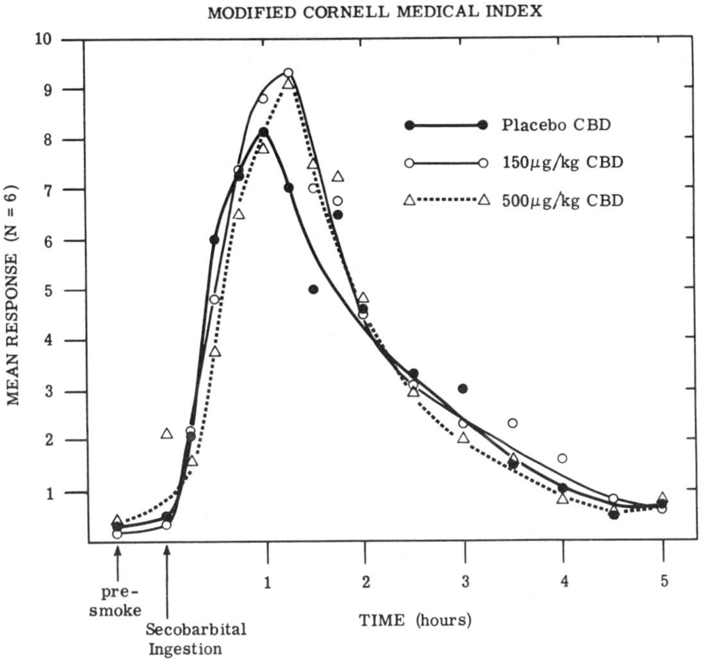

FIGURE 3. The subjective effects of cannabidiol and secobarbital. Mean of 6 subjects and their response to the modified Cornell Medical Index Questionnaire. Subjects received either placebo, 150 μg/kg, or 500 μg/kg of cannabidiol with sodium secobarbital.

after administering them by the oral route. Since, in their usual manner of consumption, Δ^9-THC and cannabidiol are administered by inhalation, we investigated the interaction of these constituents of marihuana after administration to subjects who had inhaled these drugs either alone or in combination. Fifteen subjects were studied in this experiment, which consisted of two separate experimental designs. The design of the study is illustrated in TABLE 5. Subjects received marihuana cigarettes containing either Δ^9-THC or cannabidiol, or both of these drugs in combination. In one instance, cannabidiol was administered 30 minutes prior to Δ^9-THC, and in the other the drugs were administered

TABLE 5

EXPERIMENTAL DESIGN FOR STUDYING THE INTERACTION OF CANNABIDIOL AND Δ^9-TETRAHYDROCANNABINOL

Placebo cigarette (0–CBD) + placebo cigarette (0–THC)
Placebo cigarette (0–CBD) + cigarette with THC (25 μg/kg)
Cannabidiol cigarette (150 μg/kg) + placebo cigarette (0–THC)
Cannabidiol cigarette (150 μg/kg) + cigarette with THC (25 μg/kg)

Study 1. Pretreatment with cannabidiol, 8 subjects.
Study 2. Drugs administered simultaneously, 15 subjects.

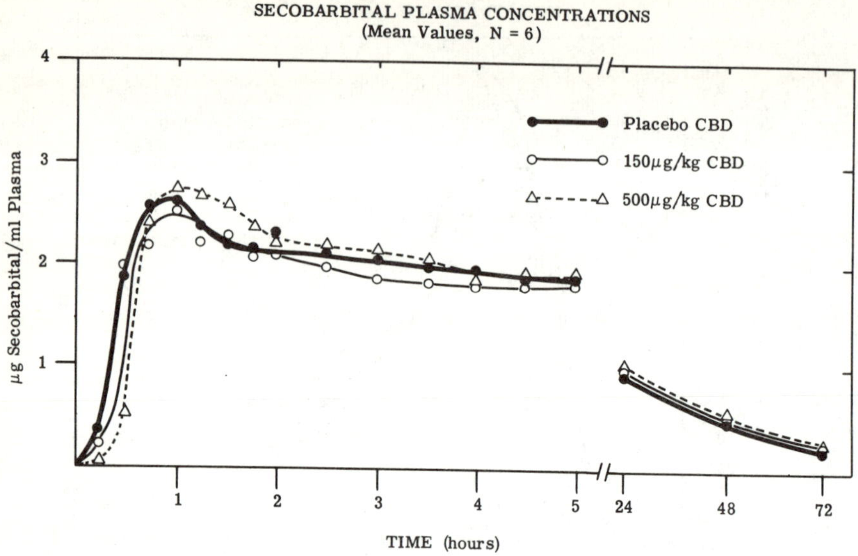

FIGURE 4. Plasma levels of secobarbital following the inhalation of marihuana cigarettes containing cannabidiol. Values represent the mean of 6 subjects who received either 0 CBD, 150 μg/kg CBD, or 500 μg/kg CBD in conjunction with secobarbital.

simultaneously. Subjects were tested at various times over a 1½-hr period to determine the time course for the pharmacologic effects.

Mean pulse rate in the 15 subjects was about 70 beats/minute. Placebo marihuana or cannabidiol alone produced no significant change from basal pulse rate; however, the administration of Δ^9-THC alone or in combination with cannabidiol resulted in a marked tachycardia. There was no apparent difference between the two treatments, i.e., Δ^9-THC alone or Δ^9-THC plus cannabidiol (FIGURE 5). The effects of these drugs on the pursuit meter (i.e., ability to track) and on the wobble board (i.e., stability of stance) revealed that cannabidiol did not differ from placebo treatment in either of these tests. However, Δ^9-THC itself did have a marked effect on these tests, and these effects appeared to be attenuated by the co-administration of cannabidiol. Although these differences were not statistically significant at the 0.05 level, there definitely appeared to be a trend in the direction indicating that cannabidiol attenuated the effects of Δ^9-THC (FIGURES 6 & 7).

During the course of this study, subjects were asked to rate the "high" they may or may not be experiencing. The "high" was rated on a 0–10 scale (0 being no psychologic "high" and 10 representing the "highest" they had ever been on marihuana in the past). Placebo and cannabidiol alone produced only a minimal psychologic effect, whereas Δ^9-THC produced a marked euphoria. This euphorogenic effect of Δ^9-THC was significantly attenuated by the co-administration of cannabidiol (FIGURE 8).

In summary, the studies which we have reported demonstrate that marihuana, when used in combination with the barbiturates, can result in a greater

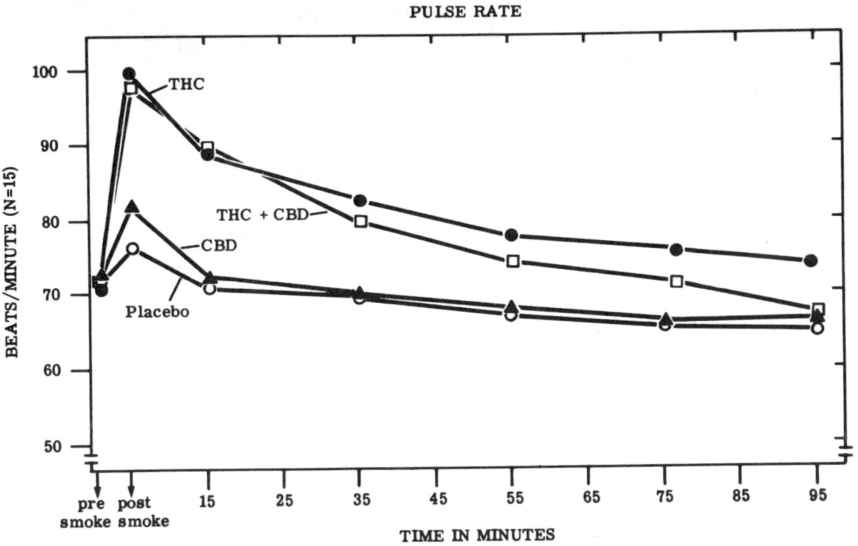

FIGURE 5. The effect of cannabidiol and THC on pulse rate. Values represent the mean of 15 subjects.

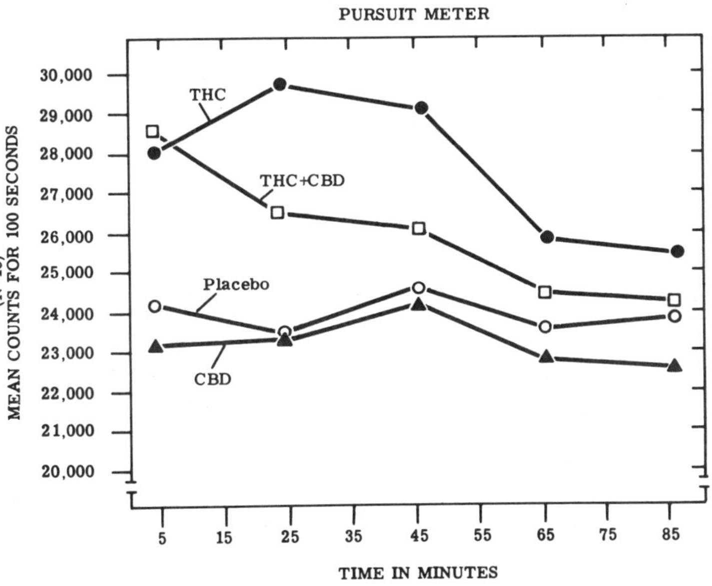

FIGURE 6. The effect of THC and cannabidiol on tracking ability. Time course of the impairment in hand-eye coordination as measured by the pursuit meter. Each point represents the mean of 15 subjects.

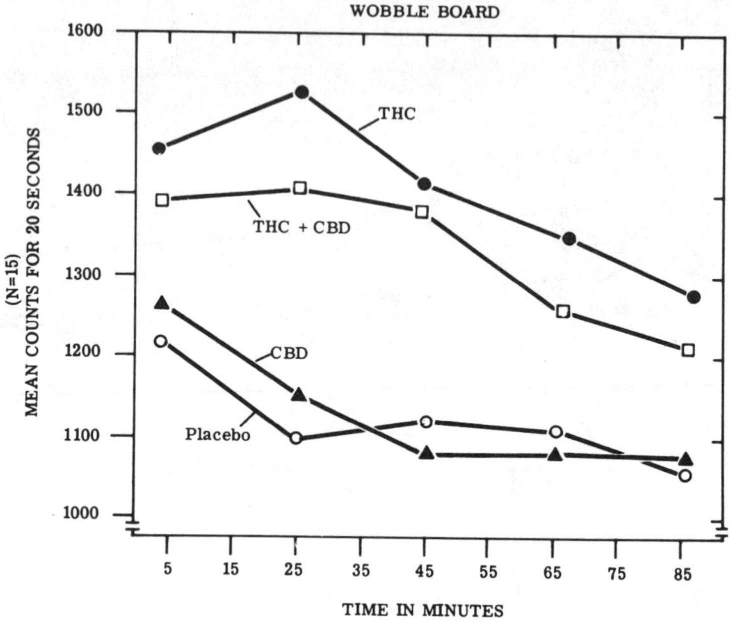

FIGURE 7. The effect of THC and cannabidiol on stability of stance. Time response analysis of the impairment in stability. Each point represents the mean of 15 subjects.

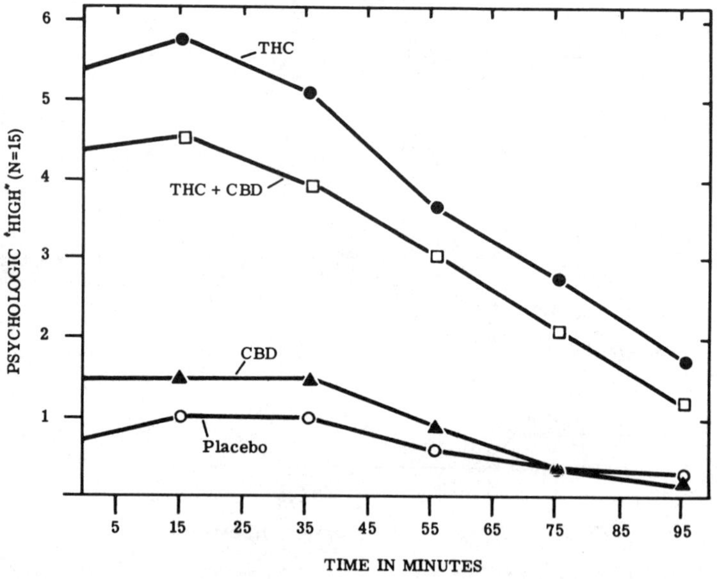

FIGURE 8. The effect of THC and cannabidiol on psychologic "high." Each point represents the mean of 15 subjects.

depression of CNS function than that produced by either drug alone. These agents do not potentiate or synergize with each other, and the interaction appears to be solely an additive effect.

An attempt was made to substantiate in humans the interaction of cannabidiol and barbiturates reported to occur in animals; however, we were unable to demonstrate any interaction between these two drugs with respect to pharmacologic effects such as drowsiness. Moreover, in the dosage used, we were unable to demonstrate any effect of cannabidiol on the physiologic disposition of secobarbital.

Our studies with cannabidiol and Δ^9-THC appear to substantiate the earlier findings of Karniol *et al.*[23] (although in our study the drugs were administered by inhalation, the usual route employed when these drugs are used in actual practice). In most test systems studied, cannabidiol produced a definite trend towards attenuating the effects of Δ^9-THC. Clearly, the effect of cannabidiol on attenuating the psychologic "high" produced by Δ^9-THC was significant.

References

1. Fisher, G. & H. R. Brickman. 1973. Multiple drug use of marihuana users. Dis. Nerv. Syst. **34**(1): 40–43.
2. Bose, B. C., A. Q. Saifi & A. W. Bhagwat. 1963. Effect of *Cannabis indica* on hexobarbital sleeping time and tissue respiration of rat brain. Arch. Int. Pharmacodyn. Ther. **141:** 520–524.
3. Garriott, J. C., L. J. King, R. B. Forney & F. W. Hughes. 1967. Effects of some tetrahydrocannabinols on hexobarbital sleeping time and amphetamine induced hyperactivity in mice. Life Sci. **6:** 2119–2128.
4. Kubena, R. K. & H. Barry. 1970. Interactions of Δ^1-tetrahydrocannabinol with barbiturates and methamphetamine. J. Pharmacol. Exp. Ther. **173**(1): 94–100.
5. Phillips, R. N., D. J. Brown & R. B. Forney. 1971. Enhancement of depressant properties of alcohol or barbiturate in combination with aqueous suspended Δ^9-tetrahydrocannabinol in rats. J. Forensic Sci. **16**(2): 152–160.
6. Dalton, W. S., R. Martz, L. Lemberger, B. E. Rodda & R. B. Forney. 1975. Effects of marihuana combined with secobarbital. Clin. Pharmacol. Ther. **18:** 298–304.
7. Lemberger, L. 1972. The metabolism of the tetrahydrocannabinols. Advan. in Pharmacol. Chemother. **10:** 221–255.
8. Lemberger, L. & A. Rubin. 1976. The Physiologic Disposition of Drugs of Abuse. Spectrum Press. New York, N.Y.
9. Coldwell, B. B., K. Bailey, C. J. Paul & G. Anderson. 1974. Interaction of cannabinoids with pentobarbital in rats. Toxicol. Appl. Pharmacol. **29:** 59–69.
10. Cohen, G. M., D. W. Peterson & G. J. Mannering. 1971. Interactions of Δ^9-tetrahydrocannabinol with the hepatic microsomal drug metabolizing system. Life Sci. **10**(1): 1207–1215.
11. Fernandes, M., N. Warning, W. Christ & R. Hill. 1973. Interactions of several cannabinoids with the hepatic drug metabolizing system. Biochem. Pharmacol. **22:** 2981–2987.
12. Paton, W. D. M. & R. G. Pertwee. 1972. Effects of cannabis and certain of its constituents on pentobarbitone sleeping time and phenazone metabolism. Brit. J. Pharmacol. **44:** 250–261.

13. Dingell, J. V., H. G. Wilcox & H. A. Klausner. 1971. Biochemical interactions of Δ-9-tetrahydrocannabinol. Pharmacologist **13:** 296.
14. Siemens, A. J., H. Kalant, J. M. Khanna, J. Marshman & G. Ho. 1974. Effect of cannabis on pentobarbital-induced sleeping time and pentobarbital metabolism in the rat. Biochem. Pharmacol. **23:** 477–488.
15. Hollister, L. 1973. Cannabidiol and cannabinol in man. Experientia **29:** 825–826.
16. Perez-Reyes, M., M. C. Timmons, K. H. Davis & E. M. Wall. 1973. A comparison of the pharmacological activity in man of intravenously administered Δ-9-tetrahydrocannabinol, cannabinol, and cannabidiol. Experientia **29:** 1368–1369.
17. Galanter, M., H. Weingartner, T. B. Vaughan, W. T. Roth & R. J. Wyatt. 1973. Δ-9-transtetrahydrocannabinol and natural marihuana. Arch. Gen. Psychiatry **28:** 278–281.
18. Jones, G. & R. G. Pertwee. 1972. A metabolic interaction *in vivo* between cannabidiol and Δ^1-tetrahydrocannabinol. Brit. J. Pharmacol. **45:** 375–377.
19. Karniol, I. G. & E. A. Carlini. 1973. Pharmacological interaction between cannabidiol and Δ^9-tetrahydrocannabinol. Psychopharmacologia **33:** 53–70.
20. Anderson, P. F., D. M. Jackson & G. B. Chesher. 1974. Interaction of Δ^9-tetrahydrocannabinol and cannabidiol intestinal motility in mice. J. Pharm. Pharmacol. **26:** 126–127.
21. Fernandes, M., A. Schabarek, H. Coper & R. Hill. 1974. Modification of Δ^9-THC actions by cannabinol and cannabidiol in the rat. Psychopharmacologia **38:** 329–338.
22. Borgen, L. A. & W. M. Davis. 1974. Cannabidiol interaction with Δ^9-tetrahydrocannabinol. Res. Commun. Chem. Pathol. Pharmacol. **7**(4)**:** 663–670.
23. Karniol, I. G., I. Shirakawa, N. Kasinski, A. Pfeferman & E. A. Carlini. 1974. Cannabidiol interferes with the effects of Δ^9-tetrahydrocannabinol in man. Eur. J. Pharmacol. **28:** 172–177.
24. Hollister, L. E. & H. Gillespie. 1975. Interactions in man of delta-9-tetrahydrocannabinol. Clin. Pharmacol. Ther. **18**(1)**:** 80–83.

ENVIRONMENTAL AND DRUG INTERFERENCE WITH EFFECTS OF MARIHUANA*

E. A. Carlini,† C. J. Lindsey,‡ and S. Tufik‡

Departamento de Psicobiologia
Escola Paulista de Medicina
São Paulo 04023 Brasil

It is widely recognized that several factors can have a profound influence on the way that a drug affects living organisms. The previous administration of the drug itself (for example, developing tolerance), interaction with other previously administered drugs, and several forms of environmental stress have been reported as capable of effectively changing some drug effects.[1–6] Obviously, the psychotomimetic drugs are no exception to this rule; on the contrary, several reports emphasize the importance of previous stressful situations in modulating quantitatively or even qualitatively the effects of drugs on mammals. For example, the disrupting effect of mescaline on the behavior of rats trained on DRL schedule of reinforcement is markedly potentiated by a stressful situation.[7] It has been reported also that in the presence of a stressful situation mescaline induces excitatory effects on some aspects of behavior of rats, contrasting with its inhibitory effects in non-stressed controls[8] (however, see[9, 10]). Another psychotomimetic drug, cyclazocine, may induce either behavioral excitation or depression, depending whether the animal is stressed or not.[11] As for marihuana,§ evidence has been accumulating lately suggesting that its effects can be drastically changed by stressful situations.[12, 13]

The present report deals with this subject: interaction between stress and marihuana. I will begin with an incidental observation we made 14 years ago and then proceed to describe the experiments we have done in my laboratory from that occasion up to the present time. In 1963, my colleagues and I began to observe that the effects of cannabis extracts in rats could be changed from one of general depression to one of excitation and aggressiveness,¶ when drug administration was associated with chronic starvation.[14, 15] We further confirmed these results using two different samples of Δ^9-THC, but rather unexpectedly a third sample, although active in several other tests, failed to produce the aggressive behavior in the starved rats.[16] The observation of intraspecific fighting between rats was extended to a form of interspecific aggressiveness, as muricidal behavior appeared in rats after the double treatment marihuana *plus* starvation.[17, 18] Our initial working hypothesis, that starvation could be contributing

* Work financed by grants from FAPESP, FINEP and CNPq.

† Chefe de Pesquisas, CNPq.

‡ With fellowships from FAPESP.

§ The terms "marihuana" and "cannabis" are used here to designate either cannabis extracts, (-) Δ^9-*trans*-tetrahydrocannabinol, or other cannabinoid derivatives with same qualitative effects.

¶ The terms "aggressiveness," "aggressive behavior," and "fighting behavior" are used here as synonymous, meaning the upright position a pair of rats assumes, standing on their hindlegs, including when one animal forces its partner to assume different patterns of submissive postures.

either through hypoproteinemia, hypoglycemia or acidosis, was refuted since it was shown that these factors were not interacting with marihuana to induce aggressiveness.[19] On the other hand, several reports from other laboratories have appeared, confirming that high doses and/or chronic administration of marihuana, associated or not with chronic starvation, induced hyperexcitability and aggressiveness in rats.[20–25]

Our failure to find an "organic" factor connected to starvation which could be responsible for the striking change in the effects of marihuana, led us to hypothesize that the stress of hunger could be playing a role in the phenomenon.[19] This possibility was strenghtened by the demonstrations that several environmental manipulations leading the rats to a state of stress, such as cold,[19] and abstinence from previous morphine or barbiturate administration,[26, 27] also facilitated the appearance of marihuana-induced aggressiveness. It has been also reported that acute administration of Δ^9-THC increases aggression in rats only when they are exposed to unfamiliar environment.[28]

The latest environmental manipulation we have used is to deprive rats of rapid eye movement (REM) sleep.[12, 13] After reading that amphetamine induces aggressiveness in REM-deprived rats,[29] we decided to see whether the same would occur with cannabis. Male rats were deprived of REM sleep for 3 to 4 days through the flower-pot technique (a 6.0-cm platform surrounded by water), and then injected with marihuana extract or Δ^9-THC at doses ranging from 2.5 to 40 mg/kg. As controls we employed either rats which had spent the same period of time on 14-cm platforms (control rats) or animals without any previous manipulation (normal rats). Pairing REM-deprived rats produced a peculiar aggressive behavior, as can be seen in FIGURE 1.

These animals attack nearly everything brought near them, such as a pencil, the experimenter's hand, or a glass rod. It is not possible to identify precisely which stimuli generate the aggressive behavior, as the rats jump spontaneously and are very excited. Sound and other stimuli increase or initiate fighting, although the animals also attack their cagemates spontaneously; sometimes a rat behaves as being attacked by an imaginary foe (FIGURE 1, panel D), as it stands in the corner of the cage with closed eyes, vocalizing and moving the forepaws.[12, 13, 30, 31]

We began to wonder whether the aggressive behavior observed was not, in some way, related to an alteration of brain catecholamine systems brought about by the double treatment, REM deprivation *plus* marihuana. This tentative hypothesis was formulated on the basis of several very indirect indications, such as: a) aggressive behavior has been frequently related to brain catecholamines,[32–34] b) a relationship may exist between brain catecholamines and REM sleep;[35, 36] c) high doses of apomorphine induce aggressive behavior;[37] d) amphetamine induces aggression in REM-deprived rats;[29] e) aggressiveness developed through chronic starvation *plus* marihuana is potentiated by L-dopa pretreatment.[38] In order to test the hypothesis we have carried out a series of experiments demonstrating that: 1) low doses of apomorphine produce aggressive behavior in previously REM-deprived rats;[13] 2) chlorpromazine, haloperidol, and α-methyl-p-tyrosine partially block the aggressiveness induced by marihuana in REM-deprived rats;[13] 3) FLA-63, a dopamine β-hydroxylase inhibitor, which increases three-fold the dopamine (DA) turnover and decreases brain norepinephrine levels, potentiates the cannabis-aggressiveness, and more, it induces *per se* such behavior in REM-deprived rats;[13] 4) L-dopa also potentiates cannabis-aggressive behavior in REM-deprived rats.[13]

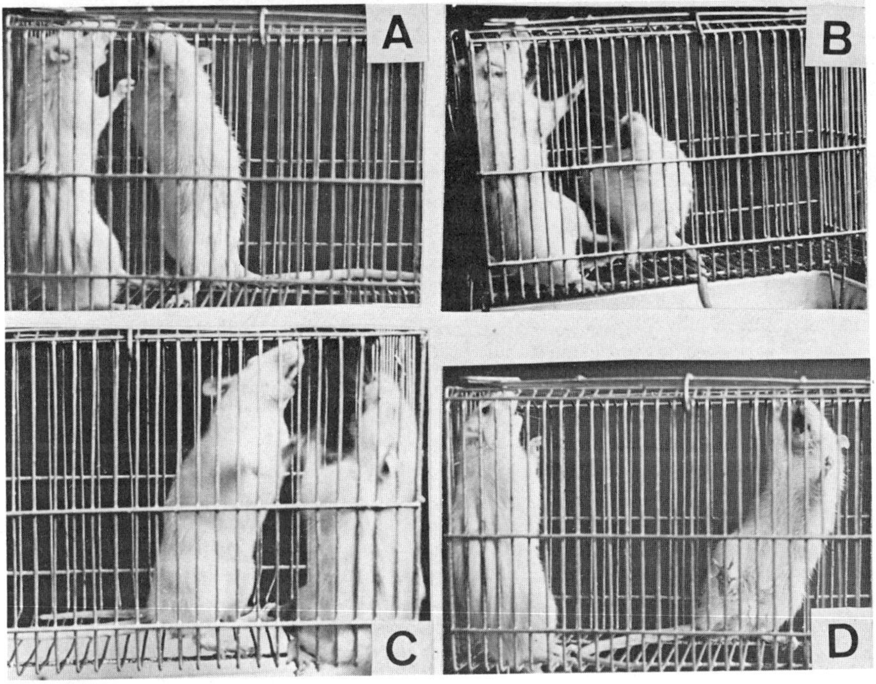

FIGURE 1. Several aspects of the aggressive behavior elicited by 5.0 mg/kg of Δ^9-THC in rats deprived of REM sleep for 4 days. One animal of each pair assumes dominant posture and the partner a submissive one. The submissive posture, however, is not complete as the heads of the animals are not tilted completely upwards, the teeth are exposed, there is vocalization, and the forepaws are not abducted, being constantly moved. In *D* both rats were REM deprived, but only the one on the right was injected with Δ^9-THC. The other rat remains in a complete submissive posture, motionless for long periods of time, whereas its Δ^9-THC-treated partner is very aggressive and "attacks" the ceiling of the cage.

We have further observed[39] that clonidine, a noradrenergic receptor agonist, blocks the aggressive behavior (FIGURE 2), an effect also obtained by intraventricular application of norepinephrine.[30] Finally, nomifensine, an inhibitor of the dopamine uptake by dopaminergic neurons, is able to induce aggressive behavior in the deprived rats,[39] as can be seen in FIGURE 3.

Taken together these data led us to a new working hypothesis: a dual and opposite role played by the noradrenergic and dopaminergic brain systems concerning our model of aggressive behavior,[13, 30] as can be seen in FIGURE 4. A similar mechanism has also been proposed for the shock-induced aggression observed between rats.[40]

Therefore, this scheme theoretically proposes two effects of cannabis on REM-deprived rats: one of blockade of noradrenergic systems, an inhibitor of aggressive behavior, and one of stimulating the dopaminergic system, which would function as an activator of aggression. In addition to our own preliminary data, there are other reports which also suggest a noradrenergic blocking role for Δ^9-THC.[41–43]

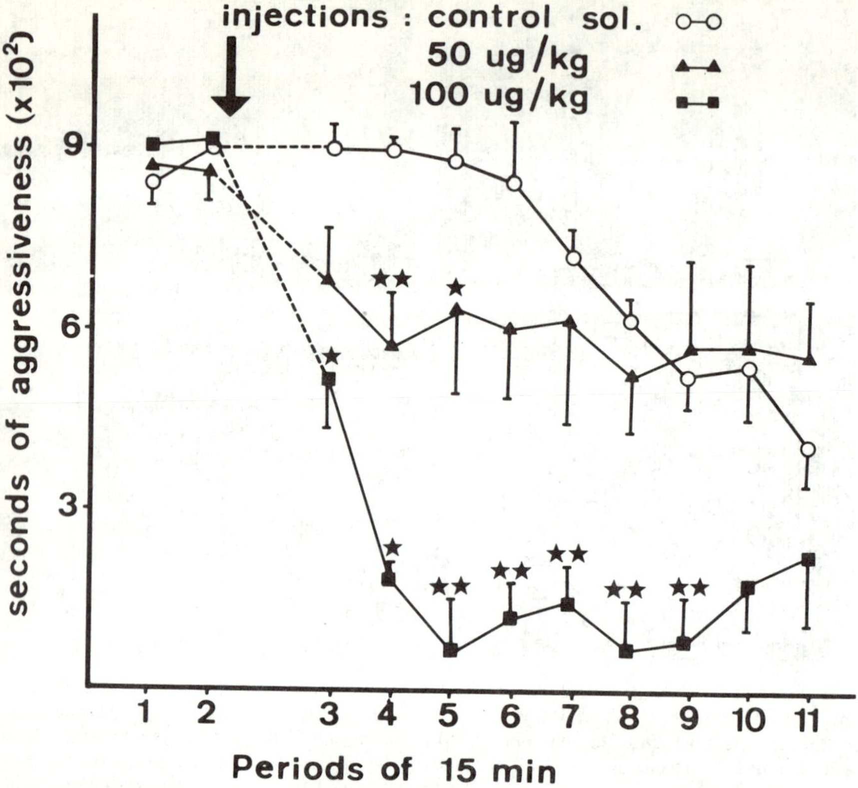

FIGURE 2. Influence of clonidine on the aggressive behavior elicited by 10 mg/kg of cannabis extract in rats deprived of REM sleep for 4 days. Aggressiveness was scored at 15-min intervals, beginning 10 min after marihuana injection. Clonidine, in 50 and 100 μg/kg doses, and control solution were injected immediately after scoring the second 15-min period (40 min after marihuana injection). Each curve averages 6 pairs of rats, and the vertical bars indicate the standard errors. The stars indicate statistically significant differences from the control solution injected group (Student's t-test: $*p \leq 0.05$; $**p \leq 0.01$).

Lately, our attention has been focused on the second point of our working hypothesis, which we could formulate as follows: REM deprivation facilitates an agonistic effect of cannabis on a central dopaminergic system. As cannabis does not produce aggressive behavior in normal (non-REM-deprived) rats, we felt that REM deprivation could be sensitizing such a system, thus facilitating cannabis action, and aggressiveness would appear. In order to test this possibility we carried out a series of experiments comparing the effects of apomorphine, a direct agonist of dopamine receptors,[44] in normal, control, and REM-deprived rats. One typical effect of apomorphine is to elicit stereotyped behavior, characterized by sniffing, licking, and gnawing. TABLE 1 shows that apomorphine provokes stereotypy in REM-deprived rats at smaller doses than it does in normal rats.[45]

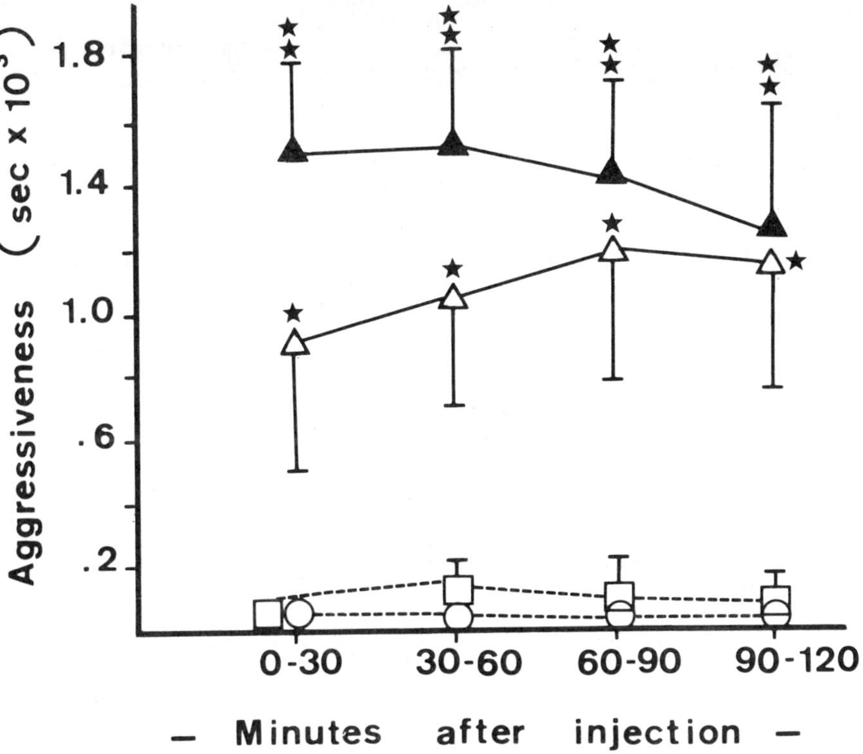

FIGURE 3. Effects of nomifensine on the aggressive behavior of rats, scored at 30-min intervals. Ten mg/kg of the drug did not induce the behavior in normal (○---○) or in control (□---□) rats. However, when 3-day REM-deprived animals were treated either with 5 mg/kg (△——△) or with 10 mg/kg (▲——▲), strong aggressiveness was observed. Each curve averages 6 pairs of rats, and the vertical bars indicate the standard deviations. The stars mean statistically significant differences from the control rats (Student's t-test: $*p \leq 0.05$; $**p \leq 0.01$).

Another effect of apomorphine in rats is to elicit aggressiveness either when injected at doses of 1 mg/kg intravenously or at doses of 10–20 mg/kg subcutaneously.[37, 46] TABLE 2 confirms our previous results[13] and shows that with previous REM deprivation apomorphine i.p. induces aggressiveness at smaller doses.[45]

The third comparison carried out concerns the effect of apomorphine on induced verticalization in animals; when injected with the drug they tend to adopt a vertical position, climbing the bars of the cage.[47, 48] Our initial results,[45] presented in TABLE 3, show that rats previously deprived of REM sleep present a much larger degree of verticalization.

Finally, there are several reports suggesting that the hypothermic effect of apomorphine is mediated through stimulation of dopaminergic receptors in hypothalamus.[49, 52] We have used this knowledge in order to observe whether REM deprivation would potentiate this effect of apomorphine. As seen in

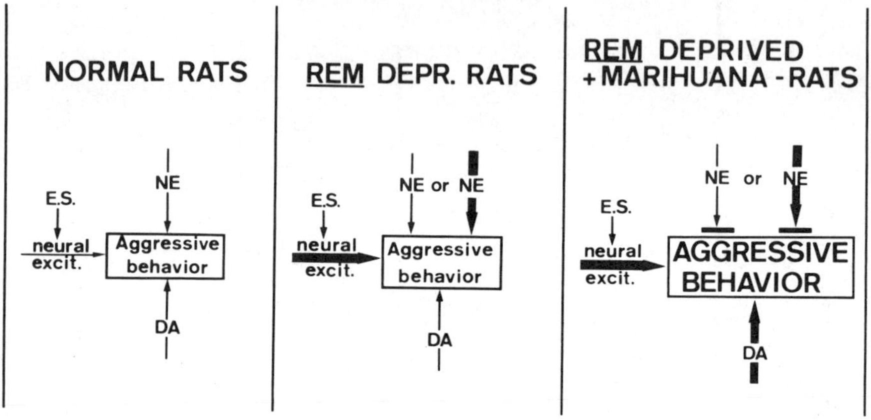

FIGURE 4. Tentative hypothesis to explain the aggressive behavior elicited by marihuana in REM-deprived rats. The size of the arrows and of the rectangles indicates the amount of the function and of the behavior being analyzed. In *Normal Rats,* the normal environmental stimuli (ES) reaches the CNS, which has a normal excitability; the aggressive behavior of these animals is very little, being dependent upon the opposite roles of an inhibitory noradrenergic (NE) and of an excitatory dopaminergic (DA) systems. In *REM Deprived Rats* there is an increase of neural excitability and probably an increase of NE turnover. Consequently, the same ES is not able to considerably increase aggressive behavior. In the *REM Deprived + Marihuana Treated Rats,* in addition to the increased neural excitability, there are simultaneously a blockade of the NE and a stimulation of DA systems, the latter two effects brought about by marihuana. Consequently, even in the presence of normal ES there is much aggressive behavior.

TABLE 4, although no dose-response-curve was obtained, the drug induced larger hypothermic effects in the REM-deprived rats, mainly when measured 5 min after drug injection.

Having obtained data suggesting that REM deprivation sensitizes dopaminergic system(s), at least as measured through the potentiation of several behavioral effects of apomorphine, we turned our attention back to marihuana. The decrease by cannabis of the dopamine turnover in REM-deprived rats, and not in normal rats, as measured after α-methyl-p-tyrosine treatment,[39] and the aggressive behavior induced by cannabis in the REM-deprived rats, which had several similarities with that produced by apomorphine,[13] were obviously in accordance with our hypothesis. Further indication that cannabis is acting in REM-deprived rats through stimulating a sensitized dopaminergic system(s) can be seen in TABLE 5, which shows that REM deprivation potentiates Δ^9-THC-hypothermia. Experiments concerning stereotyped behavior and verticalization are now being carried out in our laboratory.

The critical question raised by these data is: if cannabis acts on a sensitized dopaminergic system, why in larger doses does it not do so in normal receptors (normal rats)? A possible answer is that cannabis may possess a rather weak dopaminergic activity, and in normal rats such effects are masked by the effects on other systems. Cannabis interference on acetylcholine, norepinephrine, and serotonin systems has been claimed by several authors.[53-56] On the other hand, a direct action of cannabis on normal dopaminergic mechanisms in rats is sug-

TABLE 1

STEREOTYPED BEHAVIOR* ELICITED BY APOMORPHINE IN NORMAL AND REM-DEPRIVED RATS

Apomorphine (mg/kg)	No. of Rats per Treatment	Seconds of Stereotyped Behavior (mean ± S.E.) at Several Time Intervals After Apomorphine Injection: 5–10 min		15–20 min		30–35 min	
		Normals	Deprived	Normals	Deprived	Normals	Deprived
0.3	5	62 ± 33	121 ± 25	0	20 ± 12	0	0
0.6	5	31 ± 30	280 ± 19[3]	0	183 ± 53[1]	0	65 ± 39
0.6	9	104 ± 37	192 ± 25[1]	94 ± 36	164 ± 22[1]	29 ± 18	36 ± 10
0.8	9	80 ± 32	197 ± 23[3]	143 ± 29	218 ± 23[1]	108 ± 28	138 ± 31
1.25	5	216 ± 58	262 ± 26	105 ± 48	180 ± 47	69 ± 34	92 ± 35
2.5	5	300 ± 0	300 ± 0	300 ± 0	300 ± 0	264 ± 35	300 ± 0
5.0	5	290 ± 9	300 ± 0	230 ± 59	300 ± 0	240 ± 60	300 ± 0

* Stereotyped behavior was measured in sec, with the help of stopwatches, and corresponds to the time the animals remained sniffing, licking, and/or gnawing.

[1–3] Superscript numbers indicate significant differences from normal rats (one tailed Student's t test; [1] $p \leq 0.05$; [2] $p \leq 0.01$; [3] $p \leq 0.005$).

TABLE 2

AGGRESSIVE BEHAVIOR INDUCED BY APOMORPHINE IN NORMAL, CONTROL AND REM-SLEEP-DEPRIVED RATS. FOR EACH TREATMENT 5 PAIRS OF RATS WERE USED

Rat Condition	Apomorphine i.p. (mg/kg)	Aggressive Behavior (mean ± S.E.) Scored During Consecutive Periods of 30 Min Beginning 5 Min After Injection:		
		0–30	30–60	60–90
Controls	2.5	0 ± 0	0 ± 0	0 ± 0
REM deprived	2.5	127 ± 56[2]	479 ± 139[2]	780 ± 215[1]
REM deprived	—	109 ± 108	78 ± 75	—
Control	5.0	182 ± 181	19 ± 18	—
REM deprived	5.0	1800 ± 0[3]	1780 ± 17[3]	—
Normal	1.25	0 ± 0	—	—
REM deprived	1.25	380 ± 75[3]	—	—
Normal	2.5	0 ± 0	—	—
REM deprived	2.5	1431 ± 357[3]	—	—
Normal	5.0	360 ± 359	—	—
REM deprived	5.0	1739 ± 61[3]	—	—
Normal	10	216 ± 215	—	—
REM deprived	10	1315 ± 93[3]	—	—
Normal	20	345 ± 191	—	—
REM deprived	20	1424 ± 182[2]	—	—

[1–3] Superscript numbers indicate statistically significant difference from control or normal rats ([1] $p \leq 0.05$; [2] $p \leq 0.01$; [3] $p \leq 0.005$. One tailed Student's t test).

TABLE 3

VERTICALIZATION INDUCED BY APOMORPHINE IN NORMAL AND REM-SLEEP-DEPRIVED RATS (6 ANIMALS PER GROUP)

Dose of Apomorphine (mg/kg)	Seconds of Verticalization (mean ± SD) During the 5th to the 20th Min After Injections	
	Normals	REM Deprived
2.5	225 ± 284	897 ± 6[2]
5.0	431 ± 419	886 ± 36[1]
10.0	305 ± 387	883 ± 12[1]

[1,2] Superscript numbers indicate statistically significant differences from normal rats ([1] $p \leq 0.025$; [2] $p \leq 0.01$. One tailed Student's t test).

gested by at least three of its effects: hypothermia,[57–59] rotational or turning behavior,[60, 61] and suppression of prolactin secretion.[62] Other evidence of a marihuana dopaminergic effect are the indications that Δ^9-THC promotes the release from and inhibits the uptake of dopamine by striatal synaptosomal fractions.[63–65] More pertinent is the observation that Δ^8-THC decreases DA turnover only in rats which were previously stressed by cold, starvation, or immobilization.[66] Other authors[61] observing that Δ^9-THC induces a high inci-

TABLE 4

HYPOTHERMIC EFFECT OF APOMORPHINE ON NORMAL, CONTROL, AND 3-DAY REM-DEPRIVED RATS. FOR EACH DOSE AND RAT CONDITION 7–12 RATS WERE EMPLOYED

Rat Condition	Time After Injection	Mean (± SD) Drop in Temperature (in °C) After the i.p. Injections of Three Doses of Apomorphine (mg/kg): 2.5	5.0	10.0
Normal	5	0.56 ± 0.41	0.21 ± 0.21	0.29 ± 0.35
	15	1.01 ± 0.60	0.64 ± 0.32	0.66 ± 0.32
	30	1.19 ± 0.58	1.15 ± 0.52	1.05 ± 0.67
Control	5	0.60 ± 0.29	0.48 ± 0.33[1]	0.24 ± 0.19
	15	0.97 ± 0.35	0.70 ± 0.29	0.36 ± 0.26
	30	1.04 ± 0.48	0.80 ± 0.44	0.68 ± 0.41
REM deprived	5	0.94 ± 0.42[2,3]	1.03 ± 0.65[4]	0.90 ± 0.56[4]
	15	1.06 ± 0.48	1.13 ± 0.74[1]	0.90 ± 0.58[3]
	30	0.93 ± 0.62	1.38 ± 0.92	0.87 ± 0.55

[1,2] Differs statistically from normal rats ([1] $p \leq 0.05$; [2] $p \leq 0.01$; one tailed Student's t test).
[3,4] Differs statistically from control rats ([3] $p \leq 0.05$; [4] $p \leq 0.01$; one Student's t test).

dence of turnings in rats undergoing abstinence from previous morphine administration, contrary to control rats, suggested a dopaminergic role for Δ⁹-THC. This agrees with the observations that during chronic morphine treatment and in abstinence from it there is development of supersensitivity of DA receptors[67–70] (however, see[71, 72]). The same eventual supersensitivity of DA receptors could also explain our previous data showing aggressive behavior produced by Δ⁹-THC in morphine-abstinent rats.[26]

One point deserving further attention is whether the modifications of the effects of cannabis and apomorphine by REM deprivation are due to the deprivation *per se* or are related to the stress that inevitably accompanies the flower pot technique.[73, 74] This question cannot be satisfactorily answered, given the present state of knowledge. Our preliminary comparisons among normal rats, control rats, (exposed to 14-cm platforms), and REM-deprived rats (6.0 cm platforms), favor the view that REM deprivation *per se* is very important. Thus, aggressive behavior does not appear in control rats treated either with a small dose of apomorphine (TABLE 2) or with marihuana,[12, 13] the hypothermic effect of apomorphine and Δ⁹-THC is larger in the REM-deprived than in the control rats (TABLES 4 and 5). However, there are several indications that stressful situations may also be playing a role. Thus, apomorphine and cannabis induce aggressive behavior in rats undergoing morphine abstinence;[26, 29] marihuana aggression also appears in rats stressed by cold, chronic starvation, unfamiliar environment, and abstinence from barbiturates.[15–19, 27, 28] Immobilization stress changes the effects of Δ⁹-THC on serum and medullary dopamine β-hydroxylase from one of a decrease to an increase in the enzyme activity level.[75, 76] It is also pertinent that in the presence of stress levels of corticosterone, Δ⁹-THC stimulates tissue respiration, which contrasts with its depressing effects with low hormone level.[77]

Many reports state that cannabis, stress, and REM sleep are also related

TABLE 5

HYPOTHERMIC EFFECTS OF Δ^9-THC ON NORMAL, CONTROL AND 3-DAY REM-DEPRIVED RATS. SIX RATS PER TREATMENT

Rat Condition	Dose of Δ^9-THC (mg/kg)	Mean Drop (± S.D.) in Temperature at Several Time Intervals (in min) After Injections:					
		15	30	60	120	180	240
Normal	10	0.18 ± 0.66	0.63 ± 0.56	0.88 ± 0.47	0.82 ± 0.44	0.33 ± 0.48	0.40 ± 0.30
	20	0.55 ± 0.34	0.85 ± 0.45	1.13 ± 0.45	1.40 ± 0.39	1.58 ± 0.52	1.75 ± 0.50
Controls	10	0.73 ± 0.50	1.30 ± 0.60[2]	1.85 ± 0.78[2]	1.92 ± 0.58[3]	1.82 ± 0.90[3]	1.25 ± 1.09[1]
	20	0.88 ± 0.08[1]	1.12 ± 0.39	1.40 ± 0.35	1.62 ± 0.34	1.48 ± 0.48	0.68 ± 0.70[2]
REM deprived	10	0.88 ± 0.36[1]	1.22 ± 0.48[1]	1.63 ± 0.70[1]	1.65 ± 0.58[3]	1.22 ± 0.89	0.45 ± 0.63
	20	1.35 ± 0.35[3,5]	1.75 ± 0.52[2,5]	2.11 ± 0.74[2,4]	2.28 ± 0.86[2]	1.28 ± 1.19[2]	1.03 ± 0.62[4]

[1–3] Differs significantly from normal rats (one tailed Student's t test: [1] $p \leq 0.05$; [2] $p \leq 0.025$; [3] $p \leq 0.005$).
[4,5] Differs significantly from control rats (one tailed Student's t test: [4] $p \leq 0.05$; [5] $p \leq 0.005$).

to other neurohumoral systems. For example, it has been suggested that prolonged isolation of mice, a stressful situation leading to aggressiveness, reduces noradrenaline release resulting in a relative supersensitivity of brain norepinephrine receptors;[78, 79] including 4–8 weeks isolation of rats may bring about supersensitivity of peripheral catecholaminergic receptors.[80] It has also been suggested that after chronic morphine treatment, a condition in which cannabis induces aggressiveness, the muscarinic, α-adrenergic and dopaminergic receptors become supersensitive.[67] Until now our efforts have been oriented in quest of data which show a dopaminergic action for cannabis. Our results, we believe, support this supposition.

Nevertheless, we are now prepared to extend our investigations to other transmitter systems which have been implied to play a role in aggressive behavior.

References

1. Kosman, M. E. & K. R. Unna. 1968. Effects of chronic administration of the amphetamines and other stimulants of behavior. Clin. Pharmacol. Ther. **9:** 240–254.
2. Moore, K. E. & E. W. Lariviere. 1964. Effects of stress and d-amphetamine on rat brain catecholamines. Biochem. Pharmacol. **13:** 1098–1100.
3. Huff, J. E., S. M. Shaw & J. E. Christian. 1970. Effect of acute and chronic stress on amobarbital metabolism in the rat. J. Pharm. Sci. **59:** 126–128.
4. Barry, III, H. & J. P. Buckley. 1966. Drug effects on animal performance and the stress syndrome. J. Pharm. Sci. **55:** 1159–1183.
5. Javoy, F., A. M. Thierry, S. S. Kety & J. Glowinski. 1968. The effect of amphetamine on the turnover of brain norepinephrine in normal and stressed rats. Commun. Behav. Biol. **1** (part A): 43–48.
6. Otto, U. & L. Paalzow. 1975. Effect of stress on the pharmacokinetics of sodium salicylate and quinidine sulphate in rats. Acta Pharmacol. Toxicol. **36:** 415–426.
7. Smythies, J. R., R. J. Bradley & V. S. Johnston. 1967. Interaction of "stress" and the response to mescaline. Nature (London) **215:** 1179–1180.
8. Bridger, W. H. & I. J. Mandel. 1971. Excitatory and inhibitory effects of mescaline on shuttle avoidance in the rat. Biol. Psychiatry **3:** 379–385.
9. Gorelick, D. A. & W. H. Bridger. 1974. Interaction of mescaline and stress on shuttle avoidance in rats. J. Pharmacol. (Paris) **5**(sup. 2): 38–39.
10. Gorelick, D. A. & W. H. Bridger. 1975. Does increasing stress change the behavioral action of mescaline from disruption to facilitation? Psychopharmacologia **44:** 307–310.
11. Wray, S. R. 1973. Interaction of stress and psychotomimetic drug-action: possible implication for psychosis. Psychopharmacologia **30:** 263–268.
12. Alves, C. N., A. C. Goyos & E. A. Carlini. 1973. Aggressiveness induced by marihuana and other psychotropic drugs in REM sleep deprived rats. Pharmacol. Biochem. Behav. **1:** 183–189.
13. Carlini, E. A. & C. J. Lindsey. 1974. Pharmacological manipulations of brain catecholamines and the aggressive behavior induced by marihuana in REM sleep-deprived rats. Aggressive Behav. **1:** 81–99.
14. Carlini, E. A. & C. Kramer. 1965. Effects of *Cannabis sativa* (marihuana) on maze performance of the rat. Psychopharmacologia **7:** 175–181.
15. Carlini, E. A. & J. Masur. 1969. Development of aggressive behavior in rats by chronic administration of *Cannabis sativa* (marihuana). Life Sc. 8: 607–620.

16. Carlini, E. A. & J. Masur. 1970. Development of fighting behavior in starved rats by chronic administration of (-) Δ^9-*trans*-tetrahydrocannabinol and cannabis extracts. Lack of action of other psychotropic drugs. Commun. Behav. Biol. **5:** 57–61.
17. Alves, C. N. & E. A. Carlini. 1973. Effects on acute and chronic administration of *Cannabis sativa* extract on the mouse-killing behavior of rats. Life Sci. **13:** 75–85.
18. Ueki, S., M. Fujiwara & N. Ogawa. 1972. Mouse-killing behavior (muricide) induced by Δ^9-tetrahydrocannabinol in the rat. Physiol. Behav. **9:** 585–587.
19. Carlini, E. A., A. Hamaoui & R. M. W. Märtz. 1972. Factors influencing the aggressiveness elicited by marihuana in food-deprived rats. Brit. Pharmacol. **44:** 794–804.
20. Leonard, B. E. 1971. The effect of Δ^{1-6}-tetrahydrocannabinol on biogenic amines and their aminoacids precursors in the rat brain. Pharmacol. Res. Commun. **3:** 139–145.
21. Orsingher, O. A. & S. Fulginiti. 1970. Effects of *Cannabis sativa* on learning in rats. Pharmacology **3:** 337–344.
22. Palermo-Neto, J. & F. V. Carvalho. 1973. The effects of chronic cannabis treatment on the aggressive behavior and brain 5-hydroxytryptamine levels of rats with different "temperaments". Psychopharmacologia **32:** 383–392.
23. Rosenkrantz, H., R. A. Sprague, R. W. Fleischman & M. C. Braude. 1975. Oral Δ^9-tetrahydrocannabinol toxicity in rats treated for periods up to six months. Toxicol. Appl. Pharmacol. **32:** 399–417.
24. Luthra, Y. K., H. Rosenkrantz, I. A. Heyman & M. C. Braude. 1975. Differential neurochemistry and temporal pattern in rats treated orally with Δ^9-tetrahydrocannabinol for periods up to six months. Toxicol. Appl. Pharmacol. **32:** 418–431.
25. Thompson, G. R., M. M. Mason, H. Rosenkrantz & M. C. Braude. 1973. Chronic oral toxicity of cannabinoids in rats. Toxicol. Appl. Pharmacol. **25:** 373–390.
26. Carlini, E. A. & C. Gonzalez. 1972. Aggressive behavior induced by marihuana compounds and amphetamine in rats previously made dependent on morphine. Experientia **28:** 542–544.
27. Carlini, E. A., J. R. Leite, M. Tannhauser & A. C. Berardi. 1973. Cannabidiol and *Cannabis sativa* extract protect mice and rats against convulsive agents. J. Pharm. Pharmacol. **25:** 664–665.
28. Carder, B. & J. Olson. 1972. Marihuana and shock induced aggression in rats. Physiol. Behav. **8:** 599–602.
29. Ferguson, J. & W. Dement. 1969. The behavioral effects of amphetamine on REM deprived rats. J. Psychiat. Res. **7:** 111–118.
30. Musty, R. E., C. J. Lindsey & E. A. Carlini. 1967. 6-Hydroxydopamine and the aggressive behavior induced by marihuana in REM sleep deprived rats. Psychopharmacologia. In press.
31. Carlini, E. A. Further studies on the aggressive behavior induced by Δ^9-tetrahydrocannabinol in REM sleep deprived rats. Submitted for publication.
32. Eichelman, B. S., Jr. & N. B. Thoa. 1973. The aggressive monoamines. Biol. Psychiatry **6:** 143–164.
33. Munkvad, I. 1975. The mechanism of action of psychopharmacological agents. Acta Pharmacol. Toxicol. **36**(sup. II): 20–30.
34. Randrup, A. & I. Munkvad. 1969. Pharmacological studies on the brain mechanisms underlying two forms of behavioral excitation: stereotyped hyperactivity and "rage". Ann. N. York Acad. Sci. **159:** 928–939.
35. Stern, W. G. & P. J. Morgane. 1974. Theoretical view of REM sleep function: maintenance of catecholamine in the Central Nervous System. Behav. Biol. **11:** 1–32.

36. SINHA, A. K., R. D. CIARANELLO, W. C. DEMENT & J. D. BARCHAS. 1973. Tyrosine hydroxylase activity in rat brain following REM sleep deprivation. J. Neurochem. **20:** 1289–1290.
37. MCKENZIE, G. M. 1971. Apomorphine-induced aggression in the rat. Brain Res. **34:** 323–330.
38. PALERMO NETO, J. & E. A. CARLINI. 1972. Aggressive behavior elicited in rats by *Cannabis sativa:* effects of p-chlorophenylalanine and dopa. Eur. J. Pharmacol. **17:** 215–220.
39. LINDSEY, C. J. & E. A. CARLINI. Catecholamine systems in brain—The aggressive behavior elicited by cannabinoids in REM sleep deprived rats. Submitted for publication.
40. GEYER, M. A. & S. SEGAL. 1974. Shock-induced aggression: opposite effects of intraventricularly infused dopamine and norepinephrine. Behav. Biol. **10:** 99–104.
41. GRAHAM, J. D. P., M. J. LEWIS & D. M. F. LI. 1974. The effect of Δ^1-tetrahydrocannabinol on the release of [^{3}H]-(-)-noradrenaline from the isolated vas deferens of the rat. Brit. J. Pharmacol. **52:** 233–236.
42. SOFIA, R. D. & L. C. KNOBLOCH. 1974. Influence of acute pretreatment with Δ^9-tetrahydrocannabinol on the LD_{50} of various substances that alter neurohumoral transmission. Toxicol. Appl. Pharmacol. **28:** 227–234.
43. BENOWITZ, N. L. & R. T. JONES. 1975. Cardiovascular effects of prolonged delta-9-tetrahydrocannabinol ingestion. Clin. Pharmacol. Ther. **18:** 287–297.
44. ANDÉN, N.-E., A. RUBENSON, K. FUXE & T. HÖKFELT. 1967. Evidence for dopamine receptor stimulation by apomorphine. J. Pharm. Pharmacol. **19:** 627–629.
45. TUFIK, S. & E. A. CARLINI. Behavioral effects of apomorphine in control and REM sleep deprived rats. Submitted for publication.
46. SENAULT, B. 1970. Comportement d'agressivité intraspécifique induit par l'apomorphine chez le rat. Psychopharmacologia **18:** 271–287.
47. COSTENTIN, J., P. PROTAIS & J. C. SCHWARTZ. 1975. Rapid and dissociated changes in sensitivities of different dopamine receptors in mouse brain. Nature **257:** 405–407.
48. VON VOIGTLANDER, P. F., E. G. LOSEY & H. J. TRIEZENBERG. 1975. Increased sensitivity to dopaminergic agents after chronic neuroleptic treatment. J. Pharmacol. Exp. Ther. **193:** 88–94.
49. YEHUDA, S. & R. J. WURTMAN. 1972. The effects of d-amphetamine and related drugs on colonic temperatures of rats kept at various ambient temperatures. Life Sci. **11:** 851–859.
50. YEHUDA, S. & R. J. WURTMAN. 1972. Release of brain dopamine as the probable mechanism for the hypothermic effect of d-amphetamine. Nature **240:** 477–478.
51. REID, J. L. 1975. Dopamine supersensitivity in the hypothalamus. *In* Advances in Neurobiology. D. B. Caine, T. N. Chase & A. Barbeau, Eds. Vol. 9: 73–80. Raven Press. New York, N.Y.
52. FUXE, K. & F. SJÖQVIST. 1972. Hypothermic effect of apomorphine in the mouse. J. Pharm. Pharmacol. **24:** 702–705.
53. MAZURKIEWICZ-KWILECKI, I. M. & M. FILEZEWSKI. 1973. The effect of chronic treatment with Δ^9-tetrahydrocannabinol on catecholamine synthesis in the rat. Psychopharmacologia **33:** 71–79.
54. SOFIA, R. D., R. J. ERTEL, B. N. DIXIT & H. BARRY, III. 1971. The effect of Δ^1-tetrahydrocannabinol on the uptake of serotonin by rat brain homogenates. Eur. J. Pharmacol. **16:** 257–259.
55. HO, B. T., D. TAYLOR, G. E. FRITCHIE, L. F. ENGLERT & W. M. MCISAAC. 1972. Neuropharmacological study of Δ^9- and Δ^8-L-tetrahydrocannabinol in monkeys and mice. Brain Res. **38:** 163–170.

56. DREW, W. G. & L. L. MILLER. 1974. Cannabis: neural mechanisms and behavior—a theoretical review. Pharmacology **11:** 12–32.
57. LOMAX, P. 1971. Acute tolerance to the hypothermic effect of marihuana in the rat. Res. Commun. Chem. Pathol. Pharmacol. **2:** 159–167.
58. YAGIELA, J. A., K. D. MCCARTHY & J. W. GIBB. 1974. The effect of hypothermic doses of 1-Δ^1-tetrahydrocannabinol on biogenic amine metabolism in selected parts of the rat brain. Life Sci. **14:** 2367–2378.
59. COX, B., M. ARY & P. LOMAX. 1975. Dopaminergic mechanisms in withdrawal hypothermia in morphine dependent rats. Life Sci. **17:** 41–42.
60. WATERS, D. H. & S. D. GLICK. 1973. Asymetrical effect of delta-9-tetrahydrocannabinol on striatal dopamine and behavior. Res. Commun. Chem. Pathol. Pharmacol. **6:** 57–63.
61. HINE, B., E. FRIEDMAN, M. TORRELIO & S. GERSHON. 1975. Tetrahydrocannabinol-attenuated abstinence and induced rotation in morphine-dependent rats: possible involvement of dopamine. Neuropharmacology **14:** 607–610.
62. KRAMER, J. & M. BEN-DAVID. 1974. Suppression of prolactin secretion by acute administration of Δ^9-tetrahydrocannabinol in rats. Proc. Soc. Exp. Biol. (N.Y.) **147:** 482–484.
63. OSGOOD, P. & J. HOWES. 1974. Cannabinoid induced changes in mouse striatal homovanillic acid and dihydroxyphenylacetic acid: the effects of amphetamine and L-Dopa. Res. Commun. Chem. Pathol. Pharmacol. **9:** 621–631.
64. HOWES, J. & P. OSGOOD. 1974. The effect of Δ^9-tetrahydrocannabinol on the uptake and release of ^{14}C-dopamine from crude striatal synaptosomal preparations. Neuropharmacology **13:** 1109–1114.
65. BANERJEE, S. P., S. H. SNYDER & R. MECHOULAM. 1975. Cannabinoids: influence on neurotransmitter uptake in rat brain synaptosomes. J. Pharmacol. Exp. Ther. **194:** 74–81.
66. LITTLETON, J. M. & K. I. MACLEAN. 1974. The effect of Δ^8-tetrahydrocannabinol on dopamine metabolism in the rat corpus striatum: the influence of environment. Brit. J. Pharmacol. **51:** 117.
67. VASQUEZ, B. J., D. H. OVERSTREET & R. W. RUSSELL. 1974. Psychopharmacological evidence for increase in receptor sensitivity following chronic morphine treatment. Psychopharmacologia **38:** 287–302.
68. PURI, S. K. & H. LAL. 1974. Tolerance to the behavioral and neurochemical effects of haloperidol and morphine in rats chronically treated with morphine or haloperidol. Naunyn-Schmiedebergs Arch. Pharmakol. **282:** 155–170.
69. GIANUTSOS, G., M. D. HYNES, S. K. PURI, R. B. DRAWBAUGH & H. LAL. 1974. Effect of apomorphine and nigrostriatal lesions on aggression and striatal dopamine turnover during morphine withdrawal: evidence for dopaminergic supersensitivity in protracted abstinence. Psychopharmacologia **34:** 37–44.
70. EIDELBERG, E. & R. ERSPAMER. 1975. Dopaminergic mechanisms of opiate actions in brain. J. Pharmacol. Exp. Ther. **192:** 50–57.
71. KUSCHINSKY, K. 1975. Dopamine receptor sensitivity after repeated morphine administrations to rats. Life Sci. **17:** 43–48.
72. KUSCHINSKY, K. 1975. Does chronic morphine treatment induce a supersensitivity of dopamine receptors in rat brain. Psychopharmacologia **42:** 225–229.
73. STERN, W. C., F. P. MILLER, R. H. COX & R. P. MAICKEL. 1971. Brain norepinephrine and serotonin levels following REM sleep deprivation in the rat. Psychopharmacologia **22:** 50–55.
74. VOGEL, G. W. 1975. A review of REM sleep deprivation. Arch. Gen. Psychiatry **32:** 749–761.
75. NG, L. K. Y., F. LAMPRECHT, R. B. WILLIAMS & I. J. KOPIN. 1973. Δ^9-Tetrahydrocannabinol and ethanol: differential effects on sympathetic activity in differing environmental setting. Science **180:** 1368–1369.
76. LAMPRECHT, F., R. KVETNANSKY, L. K. Y. NG, R. B. WILLIAMS & I. J. KOPIN.

1973. Effect of Δ⁹-tetrahydrocannabinol on immobilization-induced changes in rat adrenal medullary enzymes. Europ. J. Pharmacol. **21:** 249–251.
77. List, A. F., S. F. Bartram, B. L. Nazar & J. Harclerode. 1975. Interactions of Δ⁹-tetrahydrocannabinol, adrenal steroids, and ethanol. J. Pharm. Pharmacol. **27:** 606–607.
78. Welch, B. L. & A. S. Welch. 1965. Effect of grouping on the level of brain norepinephrine in white Swiss mice. Life Sci. **4:** 1011–1018.
79. Welch, B. L. & A. S. Welch. 1968. Greater lowering of brain catecholamines in group-housed than in individually-housed mice administered DL-methyltyrosine. J. Pharm. Pharmacol. **20:** 244–246.
80. Speiser, Z. & M. Weinstock. 1974. Supersensitivity to isoprenaline induced in rats by prolonged isolation. Brit. J. Pharmacol. **52:** 605–608.

COMMENT

Dr. David H. Tedeschi (*Lederle Laboratories, Pearl River, N.Y.*): It would seem appropriate for a meeting on drug interactions to call attention to a classic paper on this subject by Weaver *et al.*, who studied combinations of phenobarbital and diphenylhydantoin for their anticonvulsive potencies (1955. J. Pharmacol. Exp. Ther. **113:** 359). One especially important point they made is that the effect of adding two drugs of similar action is not simply the sum total of their independent effects. In other words, if Drug A produces a 25% effect at dose "C" and Drug B a 25% effect at dose "D," the effect of the combination of doses, "C" and "D," is not 50%. The expected effect can be determined as follows: Dose response curves for Drugs A and B are plotted using coordinates such as log dose against probits. (See figure below.) The intersection of the effect point observed for dose "C" of Drug A with the regression line for Drug B is identified, and the dose of Drug B expected to cause this effect is determined (dose "E"). Dose "D" (Drug B) is added to dose "E" (Drug B), and the point noted on the abscissa (point "M"). The point of intersection of a perpendicular line passing through point "M" and the regression line for Drug B represents the effect expected by adding dose "C" (Drug A) to dose "D" (Drug B). Weaver *et al.* also provided a comprehensive discussion of statistical approaches to analysis of data, as well as limitations of applications.

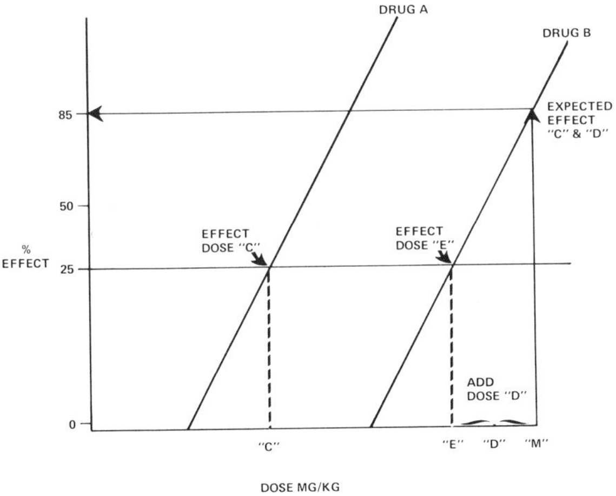

EFFECT OF AGONIST-ANTAGONIST INTERACTION ON THE DEVELOPMENT OF TOLERANCE AND DEPENDENCE*

Joseph Cochin and Barry E. Mushlin

Department of Pharmacology
Boston University School of Medicine
Boston, Massachusetts 02118

The nature of tolerance to and dependence on the narcotic analgesics has been under investigation throughout the world for at least 75 years and has been a continuing interest of the senior author for the past two decades. From the demonstration that the relatively simple explanation of tolerance through changes in the way the body handled the metabolism, distribution, and excretion of morphine was not valid, through the delineation of extremely long-lasting effects of single injections of morphine, we have attempted to describe the mechanisms by which tolerance and dependence are induced, develop, and disappear.

Among the aspects of tolerance and dependence that interested us from the beginning was the fascinating interaction of the agonists and antagonists with respect to the analgesic receptor and with respect to the development of tolerance. In 1952, Woods and Cochin[1] carried out some experiments in which they attempted to measure plasma levels in the dog after prolonged morphine administration followed by an injection of nalorphine. Their assay methods were insensitive (judged by present-day standards), and although it looked as if there was a small increase in plasma morphine levels after the nalorphine injections, the differences were not striking enough to draw any conclusions. Recently, Way[2] has demonstrated decreases in agonist tissue levels after injections of antagonist.

In 1953, Orahovats, Winter, and Lehman[3] reported that rats injected chronically with a mixture of morphine and nalorphine exhibited less tolerance to morphine than animals injected with morphine alone. They used doses of nalorphine that only partially blocked the analgesic effects of morphine, and in addition the mixed agonist and antagonist properties of nalorphine made the outcome less than clear-cut.

In the late fifties and early sixties, a number of investigators studied the effects of concomitant administration of antagonists and agonists. Houde and Wallenstein[4] showed that the analgesic effect of a combination of morphine and nalorphine was biphasic, depending on the ratio of agonist to antagonist, and they interpreted their results as meaning that nalorphine not only progressively interferes with the analgesic effect of morphine but that it begins to exert its own analgesic effect as the amount of nalorphine in the mixture is increased. They did not report on effects on tolerance to and dependence on the various mixtures.

In 1960, Eddy and coworkers[5] reported on a study in man in which

* This work was supported in part by Research Grants #R01–DA–0016 and P01–DA–00257 from the National Institute on Drug Abuse.

morphine and levallorphan were administered together. They found that the coadministration of the two drugs caused a partial blockade of tolerance to morphine. None of the agonist-antagonist mixtures they used, however, completely blocked morphine analgesia. Seevers and Deneau reported in 1963[6] that mixtures of morphine and levallorphan or nalorphine partially or completely prevented the development of physical dependence in the monkey and that the intensity of the abstinence syndrome was dependent on the morphine-antagonist ratio given prior to withdrawal. If nalorphine was administered prior to each morphine dose, no depressant effects of morphine were seen, but the stimulatory effects of morphine were not antagonized by nalorphine, and none of the specific and typical abstinence signs elicited by nalorphine in the tolerant monkey were observed. Seevers and Deneau speculated that because nalorphine was administered before morphine the latter could not occupy the receptors responsible for its depressant actions and could not initiate those mechanisms involved in the iniation of physical dependence.

Because there has been much disagreement and even more controversy surrounding the relationship of the agonists and antagonists and because such questions as do they sit on the same receptor or different receptor sites or do the antagonists just occupy or do they change the agonist receptor are still unanswered, we decided some years ago to explore the problem in depth. More than 20 years ago Axelrod and Cochin[7] looked at the N-demethylation of the narcotic agonists and the effects of the antagonists thereon. They found that the inhibition of this enzymatic reaction was non-competitive. Cochin and Spivak[8] later found, however, that the inhibition was either competitive or non-competitive depending on the nature of the agonist-antagonist pairs and on the ratio of their concentrations.

Since there are so many unanswered questions concerning the interaction of the agonists and antagonists and because much of the contemporary research is concerned with the nature of the receptor (often from the biochemical viewpoint), we decided to attempt to further investigate pharmacologically the question of whether the receptor site activated by the narcotic analgesics is also the site that is occupied by the antagonists and whether complete blockade of agonist action prevents the subsequent development of tolerance and physical dependence. It is our hypothesis that occupation of the receptor site by the agonist will result in tolerance and dependence, even though one cannot detect agonist activity with a particular assay technique. If this occupation is prevented or interrupted, no tolerance or dependence will result.

The first series of experiments we undertook examined the effects of concurrent morphine and naloxone administration on the development of tolerance and physical dependence in the rat. The animals used were adult male Wistar-Lewis rats.[9–11]

In the first experiment, rats were assigned to one of three groups, and received eight daily injections of either 15 mg/kg of morphine, morphine plus 6 mg/kg of naloxone (with naloxone administered 10 minutes before and 110 minutes after morphine), or naloxone alone. On the ninth day, all rats received only morphine. All animals were tested for analgesia, using the hot-plate assay, on days 1, 4, and 9. The results are shown in TABLE 1. As can be seen, no analgesia was evident in the groups receiving morphine plus naloxone or naloxone alone, and the areas obtained are no different than those seen with rats treated with saline. On day 9, when the two naloxone-treated groups received only morphine, the naloxone group was no different from the morphine

TABLE 1

PARTIAL BLOCKADE OF MORPHINE TOLERANCE BY NALOXONE*

Treatment†	Day 1	Day 9
Morphine	2318 ± 224 (21)	831 ± 158‡ (18)
Morphine + naloxone	28 ± 31 (24)	1715 ± 252§ (21)
Naloxone	14 ± 25 (24)	2134 ± 210 (23)

* Areas under the time-response curve, in minute-seconds, are expressed as the mean ± S.E.; the numbers of rats are indicated in parentheses.

† All rats received the indicated drug treatment on days 1–8, and only morphine on day 9.

§ Different from morphine group on Day 1 ($p < 0.05$, single-tailed t-test).

‡ Different from morphine group on Day 1 ($p < 0.001$).

group on day 1. However, the rats that had received morphine plus naloxone did show significant tolerance to morphine. We believe that the explanation for this is that the naloxone blockade was not complete and that some morphine was reaching the receptor site, although we could see no evidence for this with our assay technique.

To determine whether tolerance to morphine was developing in the absence of detectable analgesia, one group of rats was injected daily with 2 mg/kg of morphine for four days; a second group received saline. All animals were tested on the hot plate on days 1 and 4; there was no detectable analgesia. On day 5, both groups were again tested on the hot plate after receiving 15 mg/kg of morphine. The low-dose morphine group exhibited a significant attenuation of morphine effect as compared to the saline group. Thus there was tolerance development in the absence of detectable analgesia in our assay system.

We then decided to give four naloxone injections surrounding each morphine injection in order to assure a complete blockade of morphine effect. Rats received daily injections of morphine or naloxone or morphine plus naloxone for the first eight days, and only morphine on days 9–17. All animals were tested on the hot plate on days 1, 4, 9, 12, and 17. Neither naloxone nor morphine plus naloxone produced any detectable analgesia on days 1 and 4. Unlike the earlier experiment where only two injections of naloxone were given, the administration of four naloxone injections blocked the development of tolerance to morphine; the morphine-naloxone group on day 9, the first day of morphine alone, is no different than the morphine group on day 1. Additionally, the degree of tolerance was not affected by the naloxone pretreatment since the naloxone animals on day 17, their ninth day of morphine only, are as tolerant as is the original morphine group on day 9 (TABLE 2).

In another series of experiments, injections were given at weekly, rather than daily intervals. The results are similar to those obtained in the experiment in which animals received daily injections. Coadministration of naloxone blocked the morphine effect as well as the development of tolerance to morphine.

We then examined the effects of naloxone on the development of physical dependence to morphine, utilizing the same schedule of injections shown previously to be capable of blocking tolerance development. Four groups of rats received daily injections of either morphine, morphine plus naloxone, naloxone

TABLE 2

COMPLETE BLOCKADE OF MORPHINE TOLERANCE BY NALOXONE: DAILY INJECTIONS*

Treatment†	Day 1	Day 9	Day 17
Morphine	1843 ± 238 (15)	410 ± 82 (15)	210 ± 65 (15)
Morphine + naloxone	91 ± 28 (16)	1841 ± 186 (15)	352 ± 48 (14)
Naloxone	84 ± 20 (16)	2241 ± 97 (16)	455 ± 52 (15)

* Areas under the time-response curve, in minute-seconds, are expressed as the mean ± S.E.; the numbers of rats are indicated in parentheses.

† All animals received the indicated drug treatments on days 1–8, and only morphine on days 9–17.

alone or saline for 16 days. Four hours after the last morphine injection on day 16, all rats received an injection of either saline or 10 mg/kg of naloxone and were tested for precipitated abstinence by a modification of the method of Wei *et al.*[12] All animals were observed for escape behavior, wet-dog shakes, diarrhea, and ptosis for 15-minute periods immediately before and after the saline or naloxone injections. No significant abstinence signs were observed in any of the groups prior to the test injections. Following the saline test injection, one rat in the morphine-naloxone group demonstrated wet-dog shakes; no other signs were seen. When the injection of naloxone was given to all groups, significant abstinence signs were observed only in the morphine group. In this group during the 15-minute period after the naloxone injection, 6 of the 17 rats exhibited escape behavior and 15 showed evidence of diarrhea and ptosis. Additionally, one rat exhibited wet-dog shakes.

The final measure of dependence was the acute, 3-hour weight loss following saline or naloxone injections. All rats were weighed at the time of the injections of saline or naloxone, and again 3 hours later. The animals were deprived of food and water during this period. As can be seen in TABLE 3, the

TABLE 3

ACUTE 3-HOUR WEIGHT LOSS FOLLOWING SALINE NALOXONE INJECTIONS IN ANIMALS THAT HAD PREVIOUSLY BEEN GIVEN MORPHINE, NALOXONE, OR BOTH CHRONICALLY*

	Test Injection	
Treatment†	Saline	Naloxone
Morphine	98.2 ± 0.2 (17)	94.3 ± 0.2§ (17)
Morphine + naloxone	98.4 ± 0.2 (15)	98.3 ± 0.1 (15)
Naloxone	98.3 ± 0.1 (15)	98.5 ± 0.1 (15)
Saline	98.6 ± 0.1 (15)	98.8 ± 0.1 (15)

* Percentage of original weight 3 hours after the test injection is expressed in each case as the mean ± S.E.; the number of rats is indicated in parentheses.

† The various treatment groups received 16 daily injections of the indicated drugs; test injections were administered 4 hours after the last morphine injection.

§ Significantly different ($p < 0.001$) from the morphine group tested with saline.

only group exhibiting weight loss beyond control levels is the morphine group that received a naloxone injection; the naloxone-pretreated groups were no different than saline-pretreated controls.

Nine days after the animals were tested for precipitated abstinence, all rats received 15 mg/kg of morphine and were tested on the hot plate for the presence of tolerance. As expected, the morphine-pretreated group showed a very high degree of tolerance as compared to the saline-pretreated group. The groups pretreated with naloxone or with morphine plus naloxone showed no evidence of tolerance or cross tolerance; there were no differences from saline values.

We then turned our attention to the problem of the mixed agonist-antagonists, a class of compounds that has interested and puzzled investigators in this field since the description of N-allylnorcodeine by Pohl.[13] We looked at the effects of concomitant administration of nalorphine and morphine on tolerance and dependence. Nalorphine was given at three dose levels (1.875, 3.75, or 7.5 mg/kg), 30 minutes before and 110 minutes after the administration of 15 mg/kg of morphine. After the first series of experiments when 3.75 mg/kg was seen not to be different from 7.5 mg/kg, we used 15 mg/kg as the third dose level of nalorphine.[11, 14]

Rats received 16 daily injections of morphine, nalorphine, or both. All animals were then tested for evidence of physical dependence. No signs of naloxone-precipitated abstinence were seen in the saline group nor in any of the nalorphine-only groups. However, at all three nalorphine doses, signs of naloxone-precipitated abstinence were seen in the morphine-nalorphine groups, including significant weight loss. These results are somewhat puzzling. The naloxone-precipitated abstinence is not due to the nalorphine treatment directly since the nalorphine-only groups did not show any withdrawal signs. We can only surmise that the nalorphine blockade is incomplete with respect to the initiation of physical dependence or that the nalorphine interacts with morphine to produce an abstinence syndrome. The same doses of nalorphine given without morphine do not result in any detectable abstinence.

Nine days after the test for dependence, all animals were tested on the hot plate for tolerance or cross tolerance to morphine. As expected, the morphine group showed a high degree of tolerance as compared to the saline control group. There was no cross tolerance evident in the nalorphine groups; in all cases the areas obtained with the test injection of morphine were no different from saline control values. In the groups treated with both morphine and nalorphine, there was significant tolerance seen in the group that had received the lowest dose of nalorphine, 1.875 mg/kg, although to a lesser degree than in the morphine control group. We believe that this is due to the inability of this dose of nalorphine to completely block the morphine. This is comparable to that seen with morphine-naloxone mixtures; where there was incomplete blockade, we were able to induce tolerance in the absence of detectable analgesia. When the dose of nalorphine was raised, however, no tolerance was seen, and the two high-dose nalorphine groups are comparable to the saline control group (TABLE 4).

Thus, coadministration of nalorphine in an appropriate dosage schedule will block both the appearance of the morphine effect and the development of tolerance to morphine. With regard to the development of physical dependence to morphine, it appears that the nalorphine blockade was not complete under the conditions of our experiment. Unlike the results with naloxone,

TABLE 4

RESPONSES OF THE VARIOUS DRUG GROUPS TO A HOT-PLATE ASSAY PERFORMED 9 DAYS AFTER A SERIES OF 16 DAILY INJECTIONS

Treatment*	N	Area under Morphine Time-Response Curve†
Morphine	12	572 ± 124‡
Saline	9	2124 ± 297
Nalorphine (1.875)	15	2265 ± 227
Nalorphine (7.5)	13	2257 ± 198
Nalorphine (15)	12	2159 ± 324
Morphine + nalorphine (1.875)	15	1197 ± 190§
Morphine + nalorphine (7.5)	15	2086 ± 248
Morphine + nalorphine (15)	12	2295 ± 269

* Animals received the indicated drug(s) or saline for 16 days, and only morphine 9 days later. The dose of nalorphine, in mg/kg, is indicated in parentheses.

† Areas, in minute-seconds, are expressed as the mean ± S.E. All rats were tested with morphine, 15 mg/kg.

§ Different ($p < 0.05$) from animals that received morphine for the first time on day 9 (saline group).

‡ Different ($p < 0.001$)

some dependence did develop even with the highest doses of nalorphine that we used. There is some evidence that we have separated tolerance blockade from the blocking of physical dependence since at these doses of nalorphine the blockade of tolerance is complete. Whether this phenomenon is dose-related or occurs with other mixed agonist-antagonists as well, only further experiments can determine.

We then turned our attention to the timing of the events initiated by the morphine interaction with the receptor. One of the questions that has been puzzling us is the nature of the combination of morphine with its receptor that leads to tolerance and dependence. Do they occur at the instant that the drug binds to the receptor, or is that link the beginning of a series of events which can be reversed for a time and then become irreversible? Since it is clear from our results and those of other workers that morphine can be prevented from interacting with the receptor site by concomitant administration of an antagonist, thus preventing drug action and its consequences—tolerance and physical dependence—it also follows that by dislodging the analgesic from the receptor, one should be able to prevent the development of tolerance and/or dependence, if the dislodgement occurs early enough in the process.[15]

Four groups of animals were given 15 mg/kg of morphine, and all were tested on the hot plate every 30 minutes for 2½ hours. One group was given naloxone 5 minutes after the 30-minute test, a second, 5 minutes after the 60-minute test, a 3rd, 5 minutes after the 90-minute assay, and the fourth, 5 minutes after the 120-minute test. All groups were given at least one additional injection of naloxone in order to compensate for the differences in half-life of morphine and naloxone. A saline group, a naloxone-only group, and a morphine-only group were also carried through the assay procedure.

Three days later, all seven groups of rats were given a 15 mg/kg injection of morphine and tested on the hot plate (TABLE 5). The saline and naloxone-

TABLE 5

RESPONSES OF THE VARIOUS TEST GROUPS TO AN INJECTION OF MORPHINE (15 MG/KG) 3 DAYS AFTER INITIAL DRUG TREATMENT

Day 1 Treatment*	N	Area under Morphine Time-Response Curve (minute-seconds) on Day 4†
SAL	40	2721 ± 100
MS	42	1975 ± 117¶ (2763 ± 94)‡
NAX	39	2925 ± 101
MS-NAX (35)	39	2739 ± 99
MS-NAX (65)	38	2520 ± 116
MS-NAX (95)	44	2290 ± 117§
MS-NAX (125)	35	1800 ± 129¶

* SAL = Saline, MS = morphine, NAX = naloxone; values in parentheses indicate the time after morphine administration on Day 1 that naloxone administration was begun.
† Mean ± S.E.
‡ MS group area on Day 1.
§ $p < 0.01$ as compared to saline group.
¶ $p < 0.001$ as compared to saline group.

only groups, animals receiving morphine for the first time, gave time-effect areas that are typical for the Wistar-Lewis rat. The group of rats receiving morphine only for the second time with no naloxone following the first injection showed an approximately 30% reduction in area. The 35-minute naloxone group gave responses identical with those in animals that had never received morphine. At 65 minutes, naloxone prevented the initiation of significant tolerance, and the mean area obtained was similar to those seen in animals that received morphine for the first time. Although the 65-minute naloxone group yielded areas somewhat lower than controls, they were not significantly so, and the differences may represent only the variability of the data. The 95-minute naloxone group, however, was significantly lower than the controls, and tolerance was evident. After 125 minutes, administration of naloxone does not seem to alter the course of subsequent tolerance to a second injection of morphine. There is no difference between the morphine-only animals and the 125-minute naloxone animals with respect to sensitivity to a second injection of morphine.

How does one summarize and tie together this mass of experimental data? There is no doubt that complete blockade of agonist by an appropriate schedule of antagonist administration—a schedule that takes into account the differing half-lives of agonist and antagonist—will prevent the subsequent development of tolerance and dependence. We also feel that our experiments lend further support to our belief that agonist interaction with the receptor site is necessary for tolerance and dependence, even though that interaction cannot be measured by a particular assay technique.

Furthermore, we may also have separated the induction of tolerance from the development of physical dependence, since some of our experiments with nalorphine demonstrate that the successful blocking of tolerance does not necessarily completely abort the development of physical dependence.

Finally, we have shown that for the changes that result in tolerance to occur, association of the agonist with its binding site must be maintained for a finite period of time, and this period of time is longer than the time needed for the initiation of the agonist action. Our results indicate that the receptor occupation by itself, although it may be responsible for the events leading to measurable drug effect, cannot be solely responsible for the development of tolerance and that some time-related sequence of events, occurring after the initiation of drug effect, must take place before tolerance can develop.

Acknowledgment

We are grateful to Mrs. Rachelle Grell for her technical assistance.

References

1. Cochin, J. 1954. On the chemical determination of morphine and its biological fate. Dissertation Abst. **15**(4): #11259.
2. Shen, J. W. & E. L. Way. 1975. Antagonist displacement of brain morphine during precipitated abstinence. Life Sci. **16:** 1829–1830.
3. Orahovats, P. D., C. A. Winter & E. G. Lehman. 1953. The effect of N-allynormorphine upon the development of tolerance to morphine in the albino rat. J. Pharmacol. Exp. Ther. **109:** 413–416.
4. Houde, R. W. & S. L. Wallenstein. 1956. Clinical studies of morphine-nalorphine combinations. Fed. Proc. **15:** 440.
5. Eddy, N. B., M. Piller, L. A. Pirk, O. Schrappe & S. Wende. 1960. The effect of the addition of a narcotic antagonist on the rate of development of tolerance. Bull. Narc. **12:** 1–16.
6. Seevers, M. H. & G. A. Deneau. 1963. Physiological aspects of tolerance and physical dependence. *In* Physiological Pharmacology. A Comprehensive Treatise. W. S. Root & F. G. Hoffman, Eds. Vol. 1: 565–640. Academic Press. New York, N.Y.
7. Axelrod, J. & J. Cochin. 1957. The inhibitory action of nalorphine on the enzymatic N-demethylation of narcotic drugs. J. Pharmacol. Exp. Ther. **121:** 107–112.
8. Cochin, J. & C. T. Spivak. 1964. Studies on enzymes N-demethylating narcotic drugs. The Pharmacologist **6:** 88.
9. Mushlin, B., R. Grell & J. Cochin. 1974. Blockade of the development of tolerance to morphine by concurrent naloxone administration. The Pharmacologist **16:** 194.
10. Mushlin, B. E., P. Griffel & J. Cochin. 1975. Blockade of the development of physical dependence to morphine by concurrent naloxone administration. Fed. Proc. **34:** 735.
11. Mushlin, B. E. & J. Cochin. 1976. Some effects of agonists and antagonists on the development of tolerance and dependence. *In* Tissue Responses to Addictive Drugs. L. Roth, Ed. Raven Press. (In press.)
12. Wei, E., H. H. Loh & E. L. Way. 1973. Quantitative aspects of precipitated abstinence in morphine-dependent rats. J. Pharmacol. Exp. Ther. **184:** 398–403.
13. Pohl, J. 1915. Ueber das N-allynorcodeine einen antagonisten des morphins. Z. Exp. Path. Ther. **17:** 370–378.
14. Mushlin, B. E., R. Grell, P. Griffel & J. Cochin. 1975. The effects of nalorphine on concurrent and subsequent morphine administration in the rat. The Pharmacologist **17:** 206.
15. Mushlin, B. E. & J. Cochin. 1976. Tolerance to morphine in the rat: its prevention by naloxone. Life Sci. **18:** 797–802.

RESPONSIVITY TO NALOXONE DURING MORPHINE DEPENDENCE

E. Leong Way and Horace H. Loh

Department of Pharmacology and
Langley Porter Neuropsychiatric Institute
School of Medicine, University of California
San Francisco, California 94143

It is well established that the narcotic antagonists not only can reverse the acute effects of morphine and its surrogates but can also precipitate a severe withdrawal-like syndrome in a subject physically dependent on narcotics. The latter phenomenon was first described by Wikler *et al.* in 1953 using the antagonist nalorphine.[1]

The constellation of signs and symptoms elicited in the narcotic-dependent subject by an antagonist closely resembles that occurring in the addict during abstinence, but the two syndromes differ vastly in onset, intensity, and duration. Whereas the major signs of symptoms of abrupt withdrawal from morphine appear gradually after discontinuance of the drug, peaking usually after 36 to 48 hours and lasting 5 to 7 days, precipitated withdrawal is much more explosive. The syndrome has an onset within 5 minutes after administration of the antagonist, peaks at about 10–20 minutes, and generally subsides within 1 to 2 hours.

Wikler *et al.*[1] found that nalorphine would precipitate withdrawal-like signs in patients physically dependent not only on morphine but on diacetylmorphine and methadone as well, and as consequence suggested that nalorphine could be used as a reliable test for addiction to narcotics. Absence of the withdrawal signs or the presence of nalorphine effects, such as dysphoria, lethargy, sweating, pallor, nausea, vomiting, ptosis, slurring of speech, miosis and respiratory depression, would be indicative that the patient has not received morphine or one of its surrogates, or at least not in sufficient amounts long enough to produce physical dependence. This procedure is usually identified by its place of origin as the Lexington Test.

Terry and Braumoeller[2] noted on applying the Lexington Test that a 5 mg dose of nalorphine produced marked mydriasis in a known woman addict, and this occurred in the absence of other withdrawal signs. Subsequent experimentation and refinement resulted in a standardized pupil test for detecting narcotic usage, and the reliability and limitation of the test have been studied extensively.[3–6] Until the advent of chemical tests on urine, the Nalline test, named after the trade name of the drug, was widely used in the State of California in the 1960's to detect narcotic usage in narcotic probationers and parolees.

Additional experiments by Wikler *et al.*[1] indicated that the intensity of the nalorphine-precipitated withdrawal signs was related to the degree of physical dependence in the addict and the nalorphine dose. A mild abstinence syndrome could be detected after a relatively high dose of nalorphine (15 mg subcutaneously) in subjects who had previously received 60 mg of diacetylmorphine or morphine daily in four divided doses for only 2 or 3 days. As addiction to a constant or increasing daily dose of the narcotic progressed, smaller amounts of nalorphine were required to precipitate abstinence-like changes. Thus, in addicts stabilized on 240 mg of morphine daily for 50 days, 2 or 5 mg of nalorphine initiated effects fully as intense as those elicited by 15 mg of nalorphine in subjects maintained for 2 to 3 weeks on 60 to 120 mg of morphine. In our own experience with addicts heavily dependent on 150 to 200 mg heroin, we observed that 3 mg of nalorphine produced a very severe abstinence-like syndrome.[7] Currently, naloxone has largely replaced nalorphine[34, 35] because it is generally considered to be a pure antagonist. Despite this wealth of information it has been difficult to obtain comprehensive quantitative data on human subjects and to assess the possible mechanisms involved in antagonist-precipitated withdrawal. The results we are about to describe involve studies with naloxone that have been carried out in the experimental laboratory in collaboration with various associates over a period of years.

Rodents as Model for Assessing Physical Dependence

In our laboratory we use the mouse and rat as a model. The classic effects of morphine such as analgesia, tolerance, and physical dependence can easily be demonstrated in both species. By modifying the original morphine pellet reported by Huidobro and Maggiolo[8] with a specially formulated pellet[9] containing 75 mg of morphine base, a high degree of tolerance and physical dependence can be produced within 3 days after subcutaneous implantation.[10, 11]

Tolerance to morphine is measured by noting the increase in the amount of the drug (morphine ED_{50}) required to produce analgesia as measured by the classic tail-flick antinociceptive procedure. Physical dependence on morphine can be assessed after abrupt withdrawal by removing the pellet or by precipitating withdrawal with the narcotic antagonist, naloxone. As in humans, the withdrawal signs after precipitated withdrawal are much more rapid in onset, more intense, and shorter in duration. Precipitated abstinence in mice is characterized by defecation, urination, increased motor activity, tremors, sometimes convulsions, and most characteristically by stereotyped jumping. The degree of dependence on morphine can be quantified by estimating the amount of naloxone required to precipitate the response (ED_{50}).

Relationship Between Degree of Physical Dependence on Morphine and the Naloxone ED_{50}

An inverse relationship was found to exist between the degree of physical dependence and the amount of naloxone necessary to elicit withdrawal jumping. Based on an earlier evaluation of the time relationship of physical dependence development after morphine pellet implantation, it was established by abrupt withdrawal studies (pellet removal) that maximal dependence developed after 3 days.[10] The degree of dependence developing after pellet implantation could be easily followed by determining the naloxone ED_{50} required to elicit jumping

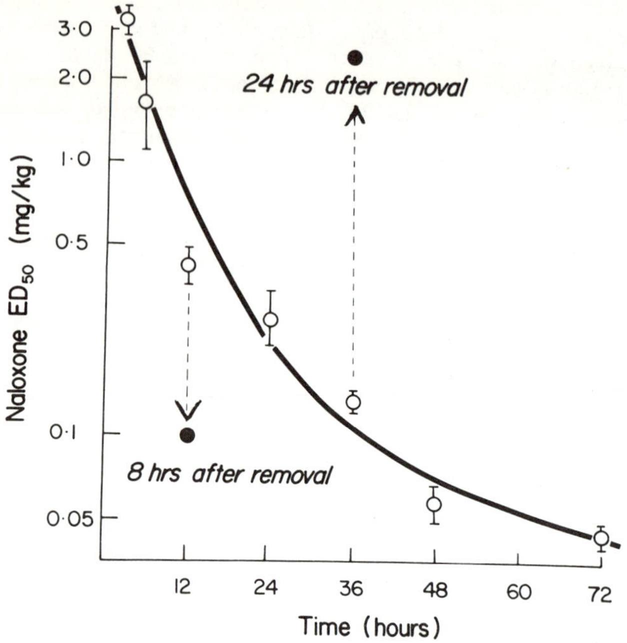

FIGURE 1. Effect of morphine pellet implantation time on the development of physical dependence. The degree of physical dependence at varying periods after pellet implantation was evaluated by determining the dose of naloxone (ED_{50}) required to precipitate withdrawal jumping. Data taken from Way *et al.*[10]

as shown in FIGURE 1. It was possible to precipitate jumping with naloxone after only 3 hours of implantation, and the jumping response was not elicitable by 12 mg/kg of naloxone in animals challenged immediately after implantation.

It was possible to decrease or increase the amount of naloxone for precipitating the abstinence syndrome by removing the morphine pellet and selecting the time for naloxone challenge. Less naloxone was required to elicit withdrawal jumping when the animals were tested at a time when abstinence signs were maximal upon abrupt withdrawal. Conversely, more naloxone was required if the animals were challenged after dependence to morphine had largely subsided. For example, in the 12-hour implanted group which exhibited a naloxone ED_{50} of 0.42 (0.36–0.48) mg/kg, removal of the pellet and retesting 8 hours later resulted in a 4-fold decrease in the ED_{50} to 0.10 (0.079–0.127) mg/kg. It should be pointed out that 12 hours of implantation is not sufficient to elicit jumping by abrupt withdrawal, and the response occurs only after challenge by naloxone. On the other hand, in a group of mice implanted for 36 hours, the naloxone ED_{50} was 0.135 (0.123–0.148) mg/kg. Removal of the pellet and retesting with naloxone after 24 hours yielded a nearly 20-fold increase in the ED_{50} to 2.4 (1.85–3.2) mg/kg. A large percentage of these animals would have exhibited withdrawal jumping without naloxone had they been tested at 8 hours after pellet removal before dependence had subsided.

Displacement of Morphine from the Brain During Antagonist-Precipitated Abstinence

A likely explanation for the precipitated withdrawal syndrome is that it may be due to the sudden displacement of morphine from its receptor site. Studies were initiated, therefore, in an effort to study the effect of naloxone on brain morphine levels during physical dependence.[12]

Mice were rendered physically dependent on morphine by pellet implantation as described previously,[10] and after 72 hours the pellet was removed. The animals were divided randomly into two groups, and 6 hours later one group was injected with physiologic saline and the other with naloxone. Then, after various periods of time, the mice were sacrificed.

Morphine in brain tissues was extracted by the method of Kupferberg *et al.*[13] and analyzed by radioimmunoassay by a slight modification of the method of Catlin *et al.*[14]

The results clearly demonstrated that during the course of antagonist-induced precipitated withdrawal in morphine-dependent mice, a dramatic fall in brain morphine occurred shortly after the administration of naloxone. The time course and duration of the decline in brain morphine levels coincided closely with the onset, peak, and duration of the acute withdrawal signs that were precipitated. A direct dose-dependent relationship was exhibited by the amount of naloxone required to elicit the response and the degree of decrease in brain morphine. Also, the sensitivity in the response to a given dose of naloxone appeared to be related directly to the degree of physical dependence on morphine. Brain morphine levels of mice that received naloxone HCl (10 mg/kg i.p.) 6 hours after removal of the morphine pellet were only 10% of those of the saline-treated mice at 15 minutes after naloxone administration. Full recovery from the effect of this dose of naloxone occurred within 1 hour, as shown by the return to a brain morphine level comparable to that of animals that received saline. However, following a second injection of the same dose of naloxone, the brain morphine levels were again greatly reduced. The results provide strong evidence compatible with the hypothesis that the antagonist displaces morphine from its receptor site. The increase in sensitivity to naloxone with increasing dependence suggests that an alteration in either the amount or the nature of the receptors is involved.

Neurotransmitter Basis for the Expression of Antagonist-Precipitated Withdrawal

Both cholinergic and dopaminergic neurons participate in the manifestation of morphine withdrawal; indeed, the two substances appear to be interrelated. In studies initiated to assess cholinergic mechanisms that might influence naloxone-precipitated withdrawal escape or jumping behavior, naloxone-precipitated withdrawal jumping in morphine-dependent mice was found to be markedly attenuated by elevating brain acetylcholine by choline esterase inhibition. When physostigmine was given immediately prior to naloxone, it greatly decreased the amount of naloxone necessary to induce the withdrawal jumping syndrome, as shown by a striking increase in the naloxone ED_{50} by over 100-fold.[15] Conversely, when hemicholinium-3 was injected intracerebrally in the dependent mouse to inhibit acetylcholine synthesis, naloxone-precipitated withdrawal jumping was enhanced. A dose of hemicholinium-3 that reduced brain acetylcholine by 40 percent was found to reduce the naloxone ED_{50} by 50 percent.[16] Furthermore, cholinergic agonists of both the muscarinic and nicotinic types, including nicotine, tremorine, oxytremorine, arecoline, and physostigmine, significantly reduced naloxone-induced jumping, whereas cholinergic antagonists, such as atropine, benztropine, pempidine and mecamylamine, enhanced naloxone effects.[17] During naloxone-precipitated withdrawal in dependent mice or rats, brain acetylcholine levels were significantly decreased. The decrease occurred only in dependent mice that jumped after administration of naloxone, not in those that failed to jump.[18]

The role of dopamine in naloxone-precipitated withdrawal was studied using the model proposed by Anden *et al.*[19, 20] to differentiate between dopaminergic stimulating and dopaminergic blocking agents. The substantia nigra zona compacta contains dopaminergic bodies of nigro-neostriatal pathways which terminate in the ipsilateral neostriatum. Following a unilateral lesion of the substantia nigra and degeneration of the nerve fibers, there is a dopaminergic imbalance and circling behavior occurs. In lesioned rats, dopamine blockers such as haloperidol or pimozide induced contralateral circling, and dopamine agonists such as apomorphine produced ipsilateral circling. When a lesion was made in the left substantia nigra of the rat and the animal rendered dependent on morphine by pellet implantation, challenge with naloxone not only precipitated the usual withdrawal signs but also contralateral circling similar to that induced by dopamine antagonists. The contralateral circling behavior induced by naloxone was gradually reversed to ipsilateral circling by increasing the dose of the dopamine agonist, apomorphine. Moreover, the severity of the intense withdrawal precipitated by naloxone, as evidenced by the high incidence of escape behavior and wet shakes, was greatly diminished by apomorphine, especially at the highest dose. On the other hand, the dopamine blocker, halperidol, did not modify the naloxone-induced contralateral circling and did not appreciably alter naloxone-precipitated withdrawal.[21, 22] These studies led to the conclusion that activity in the dopaminergic nigro-neostriatal pathway diminishes during naloxone-precipitated withdrawal.

Brain levels of dopamine and norepinephrine and serotonin as well were measured in mice rendered dependent on morphine by pellet implantation after stereotyped withdrawal jumping was provoked by naloxone. Dopamine levels had risen, but norepinephrine and serotonin remained unchanged. The changes in brain dopamine appeared to coincide chronologically with jumping behavior. The increase in dopamine was noted to occur within 2 minutes, reach a maximum between 5 and 10 minutes, when the incidence of jumping was at its peak, and the response was over by 30 minutes. The main increase in dopamine occurred in the striatum, and dopamine levels increased only in dependent mice that jumped after administration of naloxone, not in those that failed to jump.[23] The sudden elevation in brain dopamine substantiates that a temporary diminution of dopaminergic activity occurs in the nigro-neostriatal pathway during naloxone-precipitated abstinence.

A cholinergic-dopaminergic relationship in the jumping response was demonstrated by the fact that elevation of brain acetylcholine by cholinesterase inhibition in the morphine-dependent mouse not only blocked naloxone-precipitated withdrawal jumping but also the accompanying elevation of brain dopamine.[15, 23] Thus, it appears that both substances are associated in the expression of certain signs of morphine withdrawal and that a reciprocal relationship exists between acetylcholine and dopamine. We are looking at relationships between cholinergic pathways and nigrostriatal dopamine release and the possible contributory role of γ-aminobutyric acid as well.

Morphine-Naloxone Interaction in Postaddict Mice

In the experimental laboratory, it has been difficult to demonstrate protracted dependence. Indeed, it has been reported that one cycle of dependence and recovery does not modify the course of a subsequent cycle in mice[24] and that physical dependence on morphine in the rat is not increased by previous dependence.[25] Although protracted abstinence was described in the rat for as long as 4–6 months after withdrawal of morphine, the differences in signs between addicted and control rats were small and not of the magnitude to encourage extensive studies on the syndrome.[26] We noted accidentally in postaddict mice previously unresponsive to naloxone that precipitated withdrawal could be elicited when the animals were primed with a relatively small dose of morphine. The phenomenon was studied in greater detail, and these findings have been published.[27] On the basis of the results, we are proposing that our procedure be evaluated clinically for detecting and quantifying protracted dependence on narcotic drugs.

Mice were rendered dependent on morphine by pellet implantation with morphine for 3 days in the usual manner,[10] after which the pellet was removed. At fixed intervals between 1 and 43 days after initiating abrupt withdrawal, the naloxone ED_{50} required to precipitate jumping in the postaddict mice was determined following a 1-hour pretreatment with morphine sulfate (30 mg/kg, s.c.). Postaddict mice primed with saline served as a control for morphine pretreatment. Placebo pellet-implanted mice pretreated with morphine served as a control for abstinence.

Marked development of physical dependence after a 3-day morphine pellet implantation period was evidenced by the small naloxone ED_{50} required to produce withdrawal jumping with the morphine pellet still retained in the animal. Under such conditions, the naloxone ED_{50} was significantly increased by an injection of morphine. As shown in Table 1, in mice implanted 3 days with a morphine pellet and then given 30 mg/kg of morphine, the naloxone ED_{50} determined 1 hour later was 3-fold larger than the naloxone ED_{50} of the control group receiving saline. This demonstrates that in the fully dependent state, additional morphine antagonizes naloxone rather than sensitizing the animal to naloxone-induced jumping. If, however, the mice were allowed to undergo abrupt withdrawal by removing the morphine pellet, a completely opposite phenomenon was observed. Mice lose much of their jumping response to naloxone within a day after morphine pellet removal,[10] and even convulsant doses of naloxone may not elicit the jumping response.[24] Table 1 also indicates that a large but nonconvulsant dose of naloxone (80 mg/kg) produced minimal jumping effects in mice 3 days or more after morphine pellet removal, and a naloxone ED_{50} could not be obtained in these mice that were pretreated with saline. If, however, abstinent mice were pretreated for 1 hour with morphine (30 mg/kg), the naloxone ED_{50} was easily determinable for quite a long period

TABLE 1

CHANGE IN NALOXONE ED_{50} WITH TIME IN ABSTINENT MICE PRETREATED WITH SALINE OR MORPHINE*

Days after Pellet Removal	Naloxone ED_{50}	
	Morphine Group	Saline Group
0	0.24 (0.15–0.39)	0.070 (0.048–0.103)
1	0.46 (0.26–0.83)	>40[3/10]
3	1.10 (0.52–2.31)	>80[2/10]
7	1.28 (0.61–2.68)	>80[1/10]
17	1.67 (0.73–3.84)	>80[0/10]
43	3.67 (1.96–6.86)	not tested

* Mice were rendered dependent on morphine by a 3-day pellet implantation period. Subsequently, at the indicated times, groups of 10 mice each received saline or morphine (30 mg/kg, s.c.) 1 hour before a s.c. injection of naloxone. The pellet was left intact on day 0. The mice used on the first day after pellet removal were retested on days 3, 7, 17, and 43, thus giving intervals of 2, 4, 10, and 26 days after the previous morphine and naloxone injections. Numbers in parentheses indicate the 95% confidence limits of the naloxone ED_{50}. Numbers in brackets give the jumping incidence at the naloxone dose indicated, which was the highest dose tested. From Brase *et al.*[27]

of time after pellet removal. This effect appeared to decay slowly, and even after 43 days, a naloxone ED_{50} could be determined after the priming dose of morphine. On plotting the reciprocal of the naloxone ED_{50} against time after previous exposure to morphine, this decay process appeared to have two distinct components, one with a fast rate of decay and the other with a relatively slow rate of decay. Approximation of the half-life of the fast component indicates it to be less than 24 hours. The slow component had a half-life of about 2 weeks. This half-life would be extended to approximately 3 weeks if the reciprocal were plotted against time after pellet removal.

Under similar conditions, placebo-implanted animals showed no tendency to increase their jumping response to naloxone when retested after extended periods. When animals previously implanted with a placebo pellet were primed with 30 mg/kg of morphine 43 days after pellet removal, challenge doses of 1.0, 2.0, and 4.0 mg/kg of naloxone failed to elicit jumping significantly in separate groups of 10 mice. Although mice pretreated with a morphine pellet or a single dose of morphine will jump from a platform when injected with naloxone 1 to 4 hours later, huge doses of morphine and naloxone are required for this effect.[10, 26–28] Thus, previous dependence of mice on morphine markedly increases the ability of a single injection of morphine to sensitize the mice to naloxone-precipitated withdrawal jumping behavior. It should be noted that naloxone also produced other withdrawal signs in abstinent mice pretreated with morphine, including rearing, paw tremor, salivation, and body shakes, but these signs were not quantified.

The ability of a narcotic drug to sensitize mice to naloxone depends upon many factors, including prior development of physical dependence, the time interval between the priming dose and the naloxone challenge, the dose of agonist used to prime the mice, and the duration of abstinence. The jumping induced by naloxone in postaddict mice appears to require the presence of an optimal narcotic concentration in the brain and subsides as the narcotic drugs leaves the brain. A minimal effective dose of agonist is required to elicit the response, but large doses of agonist prevent the naloxone antagonist effect from becoming manifest when small doses of naloxone are used. The priming effect could be demonstrated with morphine, levorphanol, and methadone, but not with dextrorphan, the analgesically inactive enantiomorph of levorphanol. Thus, the priming effect is stereo-selective. The rapid reinduction of naloxone-induced jumping after a single narcotic injection in abstinent mice can be attributed to a remanifestation of an existing state of physical dependence, rather than to a redevelopment of physical dependence caused by the single narcotic injection. The initial production of physical dependence may cause a homeostatic adaptation or derangement in the brain which, after primary abrupt withdrawal, persists in a latent state that is relatively insensitive to naloxone. Responsivity of this latent state of homeostatic derangement toward naloxone might then be unmasked by the administration of a single dose of a narcotic agonist.

One possible interpretation of these findings is that the priming dose of narcotic agonist in postaddict mice is inducing the responding receptors to return to a conformational state that becomes sensitive to naloxone challenge again. It has recently been proposed[29-31] that with continuous morphine administration a qualitative change of the opiate receptor occurs that renders it increasingly sensitive to naloxone as tolerance increases. Likewise with increasing dependence, less naloxone is required to precipitate abstinence signs.[10] Following abrupt withdrawal and loss of acute abstinence signs, the receptor may then return to its normal conformational state and the jumping response to naloxone disappears, as does the increased ability of naloxone to antagonize morphine analgesia. However, with an optimal priming dose of morphine, the naloxone-sensitive conformational state that is associated with dependence becomes rapidly manifest again, and upon challenge with naloxone, precipitated withdrawal signs become immediately apparent.

The present studies suggest the feasibility of using the mouse as a model to study protracted physical dependence on narcotic drugs in a quantitative manner. Such a model may facilitate the study of the possible neurochemical mechanisms involved in protracted physical dependence.

References

1. Wikler, A., H. F. Frazer & H. Isbell. 1953. N-allylnormorphine: Effects of single doses and precipitation of acute "abstinence syndromes" during addiction to morphine methadone or heroin in man (postaddicts). J. Pharmacol. Exp. Ther. **109:** 8–20.
2. Terry, J. G. & F. L. Braumoeller. 1956. Nalline: An aid in detecting narcotic users. California Med. **85:** 299–301.
3. Elliott, H. W. & E. Leong Way. 1961. Effect of narcotic antagonists on the pupil diameter of nonaddicts. Clin Pharmacol. Ther. **2:** 713–721.
4. Way, E. Leong, H. W. Elliott & Norman Nomof. 1963. Comparison of chemical tests with the pupillary method for the diagnosis of narcotic use. Bull. Narcot. **15:** 29–23.
5. Chen, I.-Yung & E. Leong Way. 1965. Studies on antagonism of morphine miosis by nalorphine as a diagnostic test for narcotic usage. Brit. J. Pharmacol. **24:** 789–797.

6. WAY, E. LEONG, B. P. N. MO, C. P. QUOCK, P. M. YAP, G. OU, S. C. CHAN & J. CHENG. 1966. Evaluation of the nalorphine pupil diagnostic test for narcotic usage in long-term heroin and opium addicts. Clin. Pharmacol. **7:** 300–311.
7. QUOCK, C. P., J. CHENG, S. C. CHAN & E. LEONG WAY. 1968. The abstinence syndrome in long-term high dosage narcotic addiction. Brit. J. Addict. **63:** 261–270.
8. HUIDOBRO, F. & C. MAGGIOLO. 1961. Some features of the abstinence syndrome to morphine in mice. Acta Physiol. Latinoamer. **11:** 201–209.
9. GIBSON, R. D. & J. E. TINGSTAD. 1970. Formulation of a morphine implantation pellet suitable for tolerance-dependence studies in mice. J. Pharm. Sci. **59:** 426–427.
10. WAY, E. LEONG, H. H. LOH & F. H. SHEN. 1969. Simultaneous quantitative assessment of morphine tolerance and physical dependence. J. Pharmacol. Exp. Ther. **167:** 1–8.
11. WEI, EDDIE & E. LEONG WAY. 1975. Application of the pellet implantation technique for the assessment of tolerance and physical dependence in the rodent. *In* Methods in Narcotics Research. S. Ehrenpreis & A. Neidle, Eds. Vol. **5:** 241–259. Marcel Dekker Inc. New York, N.Y.
12. SHEN, J. & E. LEONG WAY. 1975. Antagonist displacement of brain morphine during precipitated abstinence. Life Sci. **16:** 1829–1830.
13. KUPFERBERG, H., A. BURKHALTER & E. LEONG WAY. 1964. A sensitive fluormetric assay for morphine in plasma and brain. J. Pharmacol. Exp. Ther. **145:** 247–251.
14. CATLIN, D., R. CLEELAND & E. GRUNBERG. 1973. A sensitive rapid radioimmunoassay for morphine and immunologically related substances in urine and serum. Clin. Chem. **19:** 216–220.
15. BHARGAVA, HEMENDRA, N. & E. LEONG WAY. 1972. Acetylcholinesterase inhibition and morphine effects in morphine tolerant and dependent mice. J. Pharmacol. Exp. Ther. **183:** 31–40.
16. BHARGAVA, H. N., S. L. CHAN & E. L. WAY. 1974. Influence of hemicholinium (HC-3) on morphine analgesia, tolerance, physical dependence and on brain acetylcholine. Eur. J. Pharmacol. **29:** 253–261.
17. BRASE, D. A., L. F. TSENG, H. H. LOH & E. L. WAY. 1974. Cholinergic modification of naloxone induced jumping in morphine-dependent mice. Eur. J. Pharmacol. **26:** 1–9.
18. BHARGAVA, H. N. & E. L. WAY. 1975. Brain acetylcholine and choline following acute and chronic morphine treatment during withdrawal. J. Pharmacol. Exp. Ther. **194:** 65–73.
19. ANDEN, N. E., A. DAHLSTROM, K. FUXE, K. LARSSON, L. OLSON & U. UNGERSTEDT. 1966. Ascending monoamine neurons to the telecephalon and diencephalon. Acta. Physiol. Scand. **67:** 313–326.
20. ANDEN, N. E., A. DAHLSTROM, K. FUXE & K. LARSSON. 1966. Functional role of the nigro neostriatal dopamine neurons. Acta Pharmacol. Toxicol. **24:** 263–274.
21. IWAMOTO, E. T., H. H. LOH & E. LEONG WAY. 1976. Circling behavior after narcotic drugs and during naloxone-precipitated abstinence in rats with unilateral nigral lesions. J. Pharmacol. Exp. Ther. In press.
22. IWAMOTO, E. T., H. H. LOH & E. LEONG WAY. 1976. Dopaminergic-cholinergic interactions in naloxone-induced circling in morphine-dependent rats with nigral lesions. Eur. J. Pharmacol. In press.
23. IWAMOTO, E. T., I. K. HO & E. LEONG WAY. 1973. Elevation of brain dopamine during naloxone-precipitated withdrawal in morphine-dependent mice and rats. J. Pharmacol. Exp. Ther. **187:** 558–567.
24. CHENEY, D. L. & A. GOLDSTEIN. 1971. Tolerance to opioid narcotics: time course and reversibility of physical dependence in mice. Nature **232:** 477–478.

25. WEI, E. & H. LOH. 1972. Morphine physical dependence unaltered by previous dependence on morphine. Nature **238:** 396–397.
26. MARTIN, W. R., A. WIKLER, C. G. EADES & F. T. PESCOR. 1963. Tolerance to and physical dependence on morphine in rats. Psychopharmacologia **4:** 247–260.
27. BRASE, D. A., E. T. IWAMOTO, H. H. LOH & E. LEONG WAY. 1976. Reinitiation of sensitivity to naloxone by a single narcotic injection in postaddict mice. J. Pharmacol. Exp. Ther. In press.
28. KOSERSKY, D. A., R. A. HARRIS & L. S. HARRIS. 1974. Naloxone-precipitated jumping activity in mice following the acute administration of morphine. Eur. J. Pharmacol. **26:** 122–124.
29. JACOB, J. J. C., C. D. BARTHELEMY, E. C. TREMBLAY & M. L. COLOMBEL. 1974. Potential usefulness of single-dose acute physical dependence on and tolerance to morphine for the evaluation of narcotic antagonists. Advan. Biochem. Psychopharmacol. **8:** 299–318.
30. SMITS, S. E. 1975. Quantitation of physical dependence in mice by naloxone-precipitated jumping after a single dose of morphine. Res. Commun. Chem. Pathol. Pharmacol. **10:** 651–661.
31. TAKEMORI, A. E., T. OKA & N. NISHIYAMA. 1973. Alteration of analgesic-antagonist interaction induced by morphine. J. Pharmacol. Exp. Ther. **186:** 261–265.
32. TULUNAY, F. C. & A. E. TAKEMORI. 1974. Further studies on the alteration of analgesic receptor-antagonist interaction induced by morphine. J. Pharmacol. Exp. Ther. **190:** 401–407.
33. TULUNAY, F. C. & A. E. TAKEMORI. 1974. The increased efficacy of narcotic antagonists induced by various narcotic analgesics. J. Pharmacol. Exp. Ther. **190:** 395–400.
34. WANG, R. I. W., R. L. WIESEN, S. LAMID & B. L. ROH. 1974. Rating the presence of severity and severity of opiate dependence. Clin. Pharmacol. **16:** 653–658.
35. BLACHLY, PAUL. 1973. Naloxone for diagnosing in methadone programs. JAMA **224:** 334–335.

PHARMACOLOGIC FACTORS WHICH ALTER THE ACTION OF NARCOTIC ANALGESICS AND ANTAGONISTS*

A. E. Takemori

Department of Pharmacology
University of Minnesota Health Sciences Center
Minneapolis, Minnesota 55455

The clinical data regarding the interaction of narcotic analgesics and antagonists with other drugs are sparse, and the reported studies have centered, for the most part, on the increased toxicity of the interaction.[1, 2] Examples of such studies are those involved in the interaction of narcotic analgesics with central nervous system (CNS) depressants, monoamine oxidase (MAO) inhibitors, and β-adrenergic blocking agents. In spite of the lack of clinical data on the effect of other drugs on the analgesic potency or effectiveness of narcotic analgesics, in animal studies, a large number of compounds have been reported to alter the action of narcotic analgesics. The modifying compounds include a wide spectrum of experimentally and therapeutically used drugs. In this article, the listing of many of these drugs which interact with narcotic analgesics and antagonists in laboratory animals should serve to indicate that a number of potential interactions involving narcotic drugs in man is possible.

The various compounds which have been reported to inhibit and potentiate narcotic analgesia are summarized in TABLES 1 and 2. The inhibition of analgesia and other narcotic effects by narcotic antagonists is well established in both animals and man.[3] Among the narcotic antagonists, there are those that are relatively pure antagonists such as naloxone[4] and diprenorphine[5] and those that have both agonistic and antagonistic properties such as nalorphine,[6] levallorphan,[7] pentazocine,[8] cyclazocine,[8] and cyclorphan[9] (TABLE 1). The latter drugs have been termed narcotic-antagonist analgesics, and when they are used in combination with narcotic analgesics one can observe a spectrum of analgesic effects ranging from additive effects to complete antagonism of analgesia depending on the proportional amounts of narcotic and narcotic-antagonist analgesic contained in the combination dose.[10] Study of this unique characteristic of the narcotic-antagonist analgesics has led to the proposal that narcotic and narcotic-antagonist analgesics may interact with analgesic receptors in a different manner.[3, 11] Taking advantage of the fact that the relatively pure antagonists can antagonize the analgesic effects of both the narcotic and narcotic-antagonist type analgesics, it has been shown that when naloxone is used to antagonize narcotic drugs, the apparent affinity of the antagonist for the receptors is significantly higher than when it is used to antagonize narcotic-antagonist analgesics.[12] These observations suggest that narcotic and narcotic-antagonist analgesics interact either with two different populations of analgesic receptors or with the same receptor in a different manner. Aside from the effect of the interactions of these drugs on analgesia, one should note that abstinence syndrome can be acutely precipitated in a narcotic-dependent animal or individual not only by the relatively pure antagonists but by the narcotic-antagonist analgesics as well.

* Supported by U.S. Public Service Health Grant DA 00289 from the National Institute on Drug Abuse.

TABLE 1

COMPOUNDS REPORTED TO INHIBIT NARCOTIC ANALGESIA

Narcotic Antagonists	*Anticholinergic Drugs*	*Amino Acids*
naloxone	atropine	tryptophan
diprenorphine	hemicholinium	α-aminobutyric acid (GABA)
nalorphine		aspartic acid
levallorphan	*MAO Inhibitors*	glutamic acid dimethyl and diethyl ester
pentazocine	pargyline	
cyclazocine	tranylcypromine	*Prostaglandins*
cyclorphan	iproniazid	prostaglandin E
Biogenic Amine Depletors	*Hypnotics*	*Cations*
reserpine	thiopental	calcium
tetrabenazine	pentobarbital	magnesium
α-methyltyrosine (α-MT)	phenobarbital	manganese
6-hydroxydopamine (6-OH-DA)	glutethimide	
disulfiram		*Antibiotics*
diethyldithiocarbamate (DDC)	*Antihistamines*	actinomycin D
p-chlorophenylalanine (pCPA)	promethazine	
p-chloroamphetamine (pCA)		*Antianxiety Drugs*
	Basal Anesthetic	benzodiazepines
Dopaminergic Stimulators	hydroxydione	meprobamate
apomorphine		
L-dopa	*ACTH and Adrenocorticosteroids*	*Antipsychotic Drugs*
dopamine	ACTH	chlorpromazine
amantadine	cortisone	promazine
	dexamethasone	
α-Adrenergic Blockers		*Hallucinogens*
tolazoline	*Adenine Derivatives*	lysergic acid diethylamide (LSD)
phenoxybenzamine	adenine	
	adenosine	
	AMP	
	ATP	
	cyclic AMP	

There is a large controversy in the literature as to the role that the central biogenic amines play in altering narcotic analgesia. For example, reserpine has been reported by numerous laboratories to inhibit morphine analgesia[12–27] as well as to potentiate morphine analgesia.[28–33, 20] Conflicting reports have even come from the same laboratories.[19, 32; 21, 30] Other investigators have observed that reserpine has no influence on morphine analgesia[33, 34] or a marked inhibition of morphine analgesia only in morphine-tolerant animals.[34] Aside from differences in species, dose and pretreatment times, one of the major difficulties of this problem is that the bulk of the studies used only a single dose of morphine and no attempt was made to quantitate the pharmacological effect. In this regard, there are more reports claiming antagonism of morphine analgesia by reserpine in which the effects were quantitated by estimation of ED_{50} values of morphine before and after reserpine pretreatment[15, 17, 18, 24] than reports claiming potentiation of morphine analgesia by reserpine.[29] The evidence for reserpine being an antagonist of narcotic analgesia therefore appears to be stronger. The lack of corroboration with regard to the effect of reserpine has been attributed to the various analgesic assays used; e.g., poentiation of

TABLE 2

COMPOUNDS REPORTED TO POTENTIATE NARCOTIC ANALGESIA

Catecholamines
norepinephrine
dopamine

Biogenic Amine Depletors
reserpine
diethyldithiocarbamate (DDC)
6-OH-DA
pCPA

α-Adrenergic Blockers
phenoxybenzamine
phentolamine

CNS Stimulants
cocaine
amphetamine

Dopamine-β-Hydroxylase Inhibitors
1-phenyl-3-(2-thiazolyl)-2-thiourea (PPT)

MAO Inhibitors
pargyline
tranylcypromine
iproniazid

Dopaminergic Stimulators
L-dopa

Dopaminergic Blockers
haloperidol
primozide
clothiapine
spiroperidol
perphenazine

Serotonin and Precursor
5-hydroxytryptamine (5-HT)
5-hydroxytryptophan (5-HTP)

Anticholinesterases and Parasympathomimetic Drugs
physostigmine
diisopropylfluorophosphate (DFP)
neostigmine
pilocarpine
carbamylcholine
acetylcholine

Adrenocorticosteroids
desoxycorticosterone
dexamethasone
prednisolone
triamcinolone

Cations
lithium

Chelators
EDTA
EGTA
CDTA
sodium citrate
sodium oxalate

Sulfonamides
sulfapyridine

Inactive Analgesic Isomers
dextromethorphan
levopropoxyphene

Antidepressants
imipramine
desipramine

Antibiotics
daunomycin

Antianxiety Drugs
chlordiazepoxide

Antipsychotic Drugs
chlorpromazine

Cardiac Glycosides
ouabain

analgesia by reserpine has been observed using the hot plate assay, but antagonism has been observed using the tail pressure assay.[20] On the other hand, the potentiating effect of reserpine has been observed in one study employing three different analgesic assays: tail flick, tail pressure, and hot plate.[31]

It is generally thought that the effect of reserpine on narcotic analgesia is due to its property of depleting central biogenic amines, although antagonism and potentiation of morphine analgesia have both been attributed to the direct effect of reserpine by a few investigators.[18, 30] It seems likely that the antagonistic property of reserpine is due to the depletion of biogenic amines, since the depletion of catecholamines by different means with different compounds such as tetrabenazine,[17, 35, 36] disulfiram,[23] 6-hydroxydopamine (6-OH-DA),[27, 39–42] alpha-methyltyrosine (α-MT),[21, 32, 37, 38] or diethyldithiocarbamate (DDC)[26] and the depletion of serotonin by para-chlorophenylalanine (pCPA)[24, 26, 32, 37, 43–45] or para-chloroamphetamine (pCA)[45] results in the inhibition of morphine analgesia. It should be hastily added that the results involving 6-OH-DA, α-MT, and pCPA are not uniform. With regard to morphine analgesia, potentiating effects have been reported for 6-OH-DA,[47] α-MT,[26, 33] DDC,[59, 60] and pCPA[48] (TABLE 2), and also pCPA has been reported to have no influence.[33, 38, 46, 49, 50] The conflicting reports concerning the effect of pCPA could be partly due to differences in strain of rats used; e.g., pCPA inhibits morphine analgesia in Sprague-Dawley strain but not in the Fisher strain.[43] The analgesic testing also seems to be an important determinant; e.g., antagonism of morphine analgesic by pCPA can be demonstrated with the writhing assay but not with the hot plate assay.[24]

Studies in which the various biogenic amines or their precursors were replaced after pretreatment of the animals with biogenic amine depletors reveal that all of the amines appear to be involved in the analgesic action of narcotic drugs. One or another of the biogenic amines have been claimed to be more important than the others in the analgesic process. The importance of all biogenic amines,[17] norepinephrine (NE),[15, 38] catecholamines,[21] or NE and 5-HT[14] has been claimed by various investigators. Others have directed attention to the importance of the balance between 5-HT and NE[25] or 5-HT and dopamine (DA)[26, 37] or NE and DA.[51]

There is a vast amount of evidence which indicates that morphine analgesia is enhanced by increased serotonergic activity and reduced by decreased serotonergic activity.[14, 24–26, 32, 37, 43–45, 47, 48, 52–58] Most of the evidence reveals that stimulation of the dopaminergic system inhibits morphine analgesia,[19, 25, 26, 45, 51, 56, 62–64] and dopaminergic blockers potentiate morphine analgesia (TABLE 2).[45, 63, 64] Part of the inhibition of morphine analgesia by dopaminergic stimulators, apomorphine and L-dopa, has been shown to be due to physiologic or functional antagonism[85] since these drugs cause hyperalgesia.[122] Sympathomimetic agents have long been known to produce analgesia in man and laboratory animals.[61] However, the bulk of the data are in agreement that α- and β-adrenergic blockers do not modify morphine analgesia.[22, 24, 37, 45, 54, 64–66] There have been a few reports which claim that α-adrenergic blockers either potentiate,[67, 68] inhibit,[36] or have no effect[69] on analgesia and that β-adrenergic blockers antagonize[67] or do not alter[68] morphine analgesia. In general, it appears that the serotonergic system acts as positive and the dopaminergic system as negative modulators of narcotic analgesia.

There is good agreement in the literature concerning the role of the cholinergic system in narcotic analgesia. Cholinesterase inhibitors and parasympathomimetic agents have not only been shown to potentiate morphine analgesia but have analgesic properties themselves in animals and man (TABLE 2).[45, 54, 56, 62, 70–78] On the other hand, anticholinergic drugs such as atropine[45] and hemicholinium[79] have been reported to inhibit morphine analgesia. Thus, it appears that the cholinergic system, in addition to the serotonergic system, is a positive modulator of narcotic analgesia.

Studies of the effect of inhibitors of enzymes which are involved in the metabolism of biogenic amines have disclosed some unexpected results. MAO inhibitors, paragyline, tranylcypromine, and iproniazid potentiate morphine analgesia,[80] which is what one might expect if the serotonergic system is assumed as a positive modulator of analgesia. However, if animals are pretreated with MAO inhibitors several hours rather than a few hours before analgesic testing, morphine analgesia is unaffected. If they are pretreated 3 or 4 days before analgesic testing, morphine analgesia is inhibited. Further experimentation revealed that these effects are not related to the degree of MAO inhibition, changes in the disposition of MAO inhibitor, or brain levels of morphine. The dopamine-β-hydroxylase inhibitor, 1-phenyl-3-(2-thiazolyl)-2-thiourea, has been reported to potentiate morphine analgesia (TABLE 2),[68, 81] but the effect could not be correlated with changes in brain levels of NE, DA, serotonin, or acetylcholine.

Hypnotics such as thiopental, pentobarbital, phenobarbital, and glutethimide have been shown to antagonize morphine analgesia.[28, 82] In man, barbiturates inhibit not only narcotic analgesia but analgesia induced by nitrous oxide as well.[83, 84] With regard to the barbiturates, they appear to produce increased sensitivity to pain in both mice[82] and man,[83] i.e., hyperalgesia. Thus, the inhibition of analgesia by these agents may be due to physiologic or functional antagonism.[85] It also appears that the inhibition of narcotic analgesia in mice[86] and man[87] by promethazine may be due to the same mechanism.[87]

A number of seemingly unrelated endogenous compounds have been reported to influence the action of narcotic analgesics. Cortisone and ACTH have been shown to antagonize morphine analgesia, whereas desoxycorticosterone potentiates it.[88] Dexamethasone has been reported to antagonize[87] and potentiate[90] morphine analgesia. Potentiation of analgesia has also been observed with other adrenocortocosteroids such as prednisolone and triamcinolone.[90] The basal anesthetic, hydroxydione, which has a steroidal structure, appears to inhibit morphine analgesia.[28] Other compounds which are reported to antagonize narcotic analgesia are adenine derivatives, cyclic AMP,[91, 92] adenine,[92] adenosine,[92] AMP[92] and ATP,[92] several amino acids including tryptophan,[93] α-aminobutyric acid (GABA),[94] aspartic acid,[95] and esters of glutamic acid[96] and prostaglandin E_1[97] (TABLE 1). Curiously, ADP in particular does not influence morphine analgesia.[92] The mechanism of the interaction of these compounds with the narcotic analgesics has not been elucidated.

Cations may play a role in the interaction of narcotic analgesics with their receptors. Ca^{++} has been shown to antagonize and calcium chelators to potentiate morphine analgesia (TABLES 1 & 2).[98] In addition, Mg^{++} and Mn^{++} have also been reported to inhibit morphine analgesia.[99] On the other hand, Li^{+} has been reported to potentiate morphine analgesia.[27] It has been shown that these ions will compete with narcotic analgesics and antagonists for stereospecific binding sites on putative narcotic receptors.[100, 101]

There have been several results of drug interaction attributed to dispositional mechanisms. Sulfapyridine has been shown to potentiate codeine and morphine analgesia,[102, 103] and it has been suggested that the sulfonamide releases the narcotic which is bound to blood and/or tissue components.[103] The potentiation of methadone analgesia by desipramine has been attributed to the inhibition of methadone metabolism by desipramine.[107] Diazepam also inhibits methadone metabolism to enhance narcotic effects.[105] Dextromethorphan and levopropoxyphene have been shown to inhibit the metabolism of their respective analgesically active isomers, levomethorphan and dextropropoxyphene, and to potentiate the analgesic activity of the active isomers.[106] This invites the interesting possibility of using mixtures of enantiomerically related compounds clinically to enhance the pharmacologic activity of the active isomer.

Among the antibiotics, the RNA synthesis inhibitor, actinomycin D, has been reported to inhibit morphine analgesia.[107] However, another RNA synthesis inhibitor, daunomycin, has been shown to potentiate morphine analgesia.[108] The latter effect could not be attributed to alteration of morphine levels in the brain. Although the development of tolerance appears to be inhibited by another protein synthesis inhibitor, cycloheximide, the antibiotic has no influence on morphine analgesia.[109, 110]

There are a number of puzzling interactions involving narcotic analgesics and other psychotropic drugs. Chlorpromazine,[31, 115] imipramine,[36] and chlordiazepoxide[111, 113] have all been shown to potentiate narcotic analgesia. On the other hand, diazepam and a number of other benzodiazepines, including chlordiazepoxide, have been reported to antagonize narcotic analgesia.[111, 114] LSD appears to inhibit morphine analgesia, and this action may be related to its anti-serotonin effect.[116] For the most part, the mechanisms of these interactions are obscure.

The potentiation of morphine analgesia by centrally administered ouabain[117] is a curious observation. The authors suggest that the potentiating action of ouabain is due to the enhancement of dopamine levels in the brain, and the action is mediated by dopamine. However, as stated above, there is overwhelming evidence that stimulation of the dopaminergic system inhibits morphine analgesia.

Table 3

Compounds Reported to Inhibit or Potentiate Narcotic Antagonism

Inhibitors	Potentiators
narcotic analgesics (acute)	narcotic analgesics (pretreatment or chronic)
apomorphine	cortisone
L-dopa	ACTH
atropine	propranolol
physostigmine	pimozide
	5-hydroxytryptophan

The interaction of narcotic antagonists with other drugs has received much less attention than interactions involving analgesics. The drugs which have been reported to alter the action of narcotic antagonists are listed in Table 3. The relatively pure antagonist, naloxone, antagonizes narcotic analgesia; however, the antagonism can be overcome by increasing the analgesic dose.[118] The antagonistic potency of naloxone and other antagonists, including the narcotic-antagonist analgesics, more than doubles when used in animals which have been pretreated with a single dose of a narcotic analgesic.[119, 120] The potency of naloxone increases more than eight-fold when used in morphine-tolerant animals.[110] These results may help to explain why, in clinical trials, the combination of the narcotic-antagonist analgesic, pentazocine, and morphine, although effective in nontolerant patients, becomes less effective than morphine alone in tolerant patients.[121]

ACTH and cortisone have been shown not only to antagonize morphine analgesia but to potentiate the antagonistic effect of nalorphine.[88] The mechanism of this interaction is unknown, but the authors suggested that the potentiation may be related to the direct central stimulating property of cortisone. Corticosterone and ether have also been shown to enhance the antagonistic potency of naloxone, and this effect has been attributed partly to the increase in plasma corticosteroids due to stress (E. L. Way, personal communication).

The role of biogenic amines in modifying the action of narcotic antagonist could be discussed more easily by comparison with their role in narcotic analgesia. TABLE 4 summarizes a study in which such a comparison was made.[45] Whereas compounds which have opposing effects on the central dopaminergic, serotonergic, or cholinergic systems modulate morphine analgesia uniformly in an opposing manner, there is no predictable pattern of the effects of these compounds on naloxone antagonism. Neither α- nor β-adrenergic blockers alter morphine analgesia, yet propranolol but not phenoxybenzamine enhances the naloxone potency. Dopaminergic receptor stimulation inhibits both morphine analgesia and naloxone potency. However, with the use of haloperidol and pimozide, only the latter dopaminergic blocker increases naloxone pontency. Inhibition of serotonin synthesis with pCPA and pCA inhibits morphine analgesia but has no effect on naloxone potency. On the other hand, potentiation of

TABLE 4

COMPARISON OF THE EFFECTS OF VARIOUS DRUGS ON MORPHINE ANALGESIA AND NALOXONE ANTAGONISM

(+ = potentiation; − = antagonism; 0 = no effect)

Drugs	Morphine Analgesia	Naloxone Antagonism
Phenoxybenzamine	0	0
Propranolol	0	+
Apomorphine	−	−
L-dopa	−	−
Haloperidol	+	0
Pimozide	+	+
pCPA	−	0
pCA	−	0
5-HTP	+	+
Atropine	−	−
Physostigmine	+	−

morphine analgesia with 5-hydroxytryptophan also enhances naloxone potency. Atropine and physostigmine, which had opposing effects on morphine analgesia, both lessen naloxone potency. The data reveal that the modulation of naloxone antagonism is much more complicated than that of morphine analgesia, and in addition to the dopaminergic, serotonergic, and cholinergic systems, the β-adrenergic system may be involved in the modulation of antagonism. The findings also indicate that certain drugs which alter the analgesic effect of morphine can have similar effects, no effect, or opposing effects on the antagonistic activity of naloxone. The results support the proposal that although antagonists such as naloxone display an apparent competitive-type antagonism of narcotic analgesia, they may not interact with analgesic receptors in precisely the same manner as narcotic analgesics.

In summary, I would like to stress again that a large number of drugs can alter the activities of narcotic analgesics and antagonists. Chronic intake of narcotic analgesics, of course, leads to a state of tolerance and dependence, and in this state not only are the activities of the analgesics and antagonists altered greatly, but the effects of interacting drugs may also affect the activities differently than in the non-tolerant state. Clinically there are a number of potential interactions, and unusual increases or decreases in the potency of analgesics should not be overlooked.

References

1. Martin, E. W. 1971. Hazards of Medication. J. B. Lippincott Co. Philadelphia, Pa.
2. Hansten, P. D. 1975. Drug Interactions. 3rd edit. Lea & Febiger. Philadelphia, Pa.
3. Martin, W. R. 1967. Pharmacol. Rev. **19:** 463–521.
4. Blumberg, H., H. B. Dayton, M. George & D. N. Rapaport. 1961. Fed. Proc. **20:** 311.
5. Blane, G. F. & D. Dugdall. 1968. J. Pharm. Pharmacol. **19:** 367–373.
6. Unna, K. 1943. J. Pharmacol. Exp. Ther. **79:** 27–31.
7. Benson, W. M., E. O'Gara & S. van Winkle. 1952. J. Pharmacol. Exp. Ther. **106:** 373.
8. Harris, L. S. & A. K. Pierson. 1964. J. Pharmacol. Exp. Ther. **143:** 141–148.
9. Gates, M. & T. A. Montzka. 1964. J. Med. Chem. **7:** 127–131.
10. Blane, G. F. & D. Dugdall. 1968. J. Pharm. Pharmacol. **20:** 547–552.
11. Takemori, A. E. 1974. Ann. Rev. Biochem. **43:** 15–33.
12. Smits, S. E. & A. E. Takemori. 1970. Brit. J. Pharmacol. **39:** 627–638.
13. Schneider, J. A. 1954. Proc. Soc. Exp. Biol. Med. **87:** 614–615.
14. Sigg, E. B., G. Caprio & J. A. Schneider. 1958. Proc. Soc. Exp. Biol. Med. **97:** 97–100.
15. Schaumann, W. 1958. Arch. Exp. Path. Pharmakol. **235:** 1–9.
16. Medaković, M. & B. Banić. 1964. J. Pharm. Pharmacol. **16:** 198–206.
17. Takagi, H., T. Takashima & K. Kimura. 1964. Arch. Int. Pharmacodyn. **149:** 484–492.
18. Rudzik, A. D. & J. H. Mennear. 1965. J. Pharm. Pharmacol. **17:** 326–327.
19. Contreras, E. & L. Tamayo. 1966. Arch. Int. Pharmacodyn. **160:** 312–320.
20. Ross, J. W. & A. Ashford. 1967. J. Pharm. Pharmacol. **19:** 709–713.
21. Verri, R. A., F. G. Graeff & A. P. Corrado. 1968. Int. J. Neuropharmacol. **7:** 283–292.
22. Nott, M. W. 1968. Eur. J. Pharmacol. **5:** 93–99.
23. Vedernikov, Y. P. & I. I. Afrikanov. 1969. J. Pharm. Pharmacol. **21:** 845–847.
24. Fennessy, M. R. & J. R. Lee. 1970. J. Pharm. Pharmacol. **22:** 930–935.
25. Sparkes, C. G. & P. S. J. Spencer. 1971. Brit. J. Pharmacol. **42:** 230–241.
26. Major, C. T. & B. J. Pleuvry. 1971. Brit. J. Pharmacol. **42:** 512–521.
27. Tulunay, F. C., B. K. Kiran & S. Kaymakçalan. 1972. Acta Med. Turcica **8:** 51–60.
28. Tripod, von J. & F. Gross. 1957. Helv. Physiol. Pharmacol. Acta **15:** 105–115.
29. Tardos, L. & Zs. Jobbágyi. 1958. Acta Physiol. Hung. **13:** 171–178.
30. Garcia Leme, J. & M. Rocha e Silva. 1961. J. Pharm. Pharmacol. **13:** 734–742.
31. Dandiya, P. C. & M. K. Menon. 1963. Arch. Int. Pharmacodyn. **141:** 223–232.
32. Contreras, E., L. Quijada & L. Tamayo. 1973. Psychopharmacologia **28:** 319–324.
33. Buxbaum, D. M., G. G. Yarbrough & M. E. Carter. 1973. J. Pharmacol. Exp. Ther. **185:** 317–327.

34. Loh, H. H., F. H. Shen, I. K. Ho & E. L. Way. 1972. Proc. West. Pharmacol. Soc. **15:** 1–3.
35. Takagi, H. & M. Nakama. 1968. Jap. J. Pharmacol. **18:** 54–58.
36. Sethy, V. H., R. J. Pradhan, S. S. Mandrekar & U. K. Sheth. 1970. Indian J. Med. Res. **58:** 1453–1458.
37. Görlitz, B. D. & H. H. Frey. 1972. Eur. J. Pharmacol. **20:** 171–180.
38. Reinhold, K., J. Bläsig & A Herz. 1973. Naunyn-Schmiedebergs Arch. Pharmakol. **278:** 69–80.
39. Friedler, G., H. N. Bhargava, R. Quock & E. L. Way. 1972. J. Pharmacol. Exp. Ther. **183:** 49–55.
40. Bläsig, J., K. Reinhold & A. Herz. 1973. Psychopharmacologia **31:** 111–119.
41. Elchisak, M. A. & J. A. Rosecrans. 1973. Res. Commun. Chem. Path. Pharmacol. **6:** 349–352.
42. Ayhan, I. H. 1972. Psychopharmacologia **25:** 183–188.
43. Tilson, H. A. & R. H. Rech. 1974. Psychopharmacologia **35:** 45–60.
44. Tenen, S. S. 1968. Psychopharmacologia **12:** 278–285.
45. Takemori, A. E., F. C. Tulunay & I. Yano. 1975. Life Sci. **17:** 21–28.
46. Cheney, D. L. & A. Goldstein. 1971. J. Pharmacol. Exp. Ther. **177:** 309–315.
47. Samanin, R. & S. Bernasconi. 1972. Psychopharmacologia **25:** 175–182.
48. Saarnivaara, L. 1969. Ann. Med. Exp. Biol. Fenn. **47:** 113–123.
49. Harvey, J. A., A. J. Schlosberg & L. M. Yunger. 1974. Advan. Biochem. Psychopharmacol. **10:** 233–245.
50. Maruyama, Y., G. Hayashi, S. E. Smits & A. E. Takemori. 1971. J. Pharmacol. Exp. Ther. **178:** 20–29.
51. Nakamura, K., R. Kuntzman, A. C. Maggio, V. Angulis & A. H. Conney. 1973. Psychopharmacologia **31:** 177–189.
52. Mercier, F., P. Etzensperger & J. Mercier. 1959. Anesthesie Analgesie, Reanimation **16:** 70–79.
53. Tamayo, L. & E. Contreras. 1965. Arch. Biol. Med. Expts. **2:** 70–75.
54. Dewey, W. L., L. S. Harris, J. F. Howes & J. A. Nuite. 1970. J. Pharmacol. Exp. Ther. **175:** 435–442.
55. Gardiner, T. H. & G. Eberhart. 1970. Fed. Proc. **29:** 685.
56. Calcutt, C. R. & P. S. J. Spencer. 1971. Brit. J. Pharmacol. **41:** 401 p.
57. Genovese, E., N. Zonta & P. Mantegazza. 1973. Psychopharmacologia **32:** 359–364.
58. Nicák, A. 1965. Med. Pharmacol. Exp. **13:** 43–48.
59. Zebrowska-Lupina, I., Z. Kleinrok. & J. Smolarz. 1971. Dissert. Pharm. Pharmacol. **23:** 33–39.
60. Watanabe, K., Y. Matsui & H. Iwata. 1969. Experientia **25:** 950–951.
61. Ivy, A., F. R. Goetzl, S. C. Harris & D. Y. Burrill. 1944. Quart. Bull. Northwestern Univ. Med. School **18:** 298–306.
62. Pleuvry, B. J. & M. A. Tobias. 1971. Brit. J. Pharmacol. **43:** 706–714.
63. Vanderwende, C. & M. T. Spoerlein. 1972. Res. Commun. Chem. Path. Pharmacol. **3:** 37–45.
64. Vanderwende, C. & M. T. Spoerlein. 1973. Res. Commun. Chem. Path. Pharmacol. **5:** 35–43.
65. Bhargava, H. N., S. L. Chan & E. L. Way. 1972. Proc. West. Pharmacol. Soc. **15:** 4–7.
66. Chipkin, R. E., W. L. Dewey & L. S. Harris. 1974. Pharmacologist **16:** 204.
67. Gupta, S. K. & V. R. Deshpande. 1965. Indian J. Physiol. Pharmacol. **9:** 163–165.
68. Cicero, T. J., E. R. Meyer & B. R. Smithloff. 1974. J. Pharmacol. Exp. Ther. **189:** 72–82.

69. HELLER, B., J. M. SAAVEDRA & E. FISHER. 1968. EXPERIENTIA **24:** 804–805.
70. SLAUGHTER, D. & D. W. MUNSELL. 1940. J. Pharmacol. Exp. Ther. **68:** 104–112.
71. PÓRSZÁSZ, J., J. KNOLL & E. KOMLÓS. 1951. Acta Physiol. Hung. **2:** 469–477.
72. SZERB, J. C. 1957. Arch. Int. Pharmacodyn. **111:** 314–321.
73. BHARGAVA, H. N. & E. L. WAY. 1972. J. Pharmacol. Exp. Ther. **183:** 31–40.
74. PEDIGO, N. W., W. L. DEWEY & L. S. HARRIS. 1975. J. Pharmacol. Exp. Ther. **193:** 845–852.
75. HARRIS, L. S., W. L. DEWEY, J. F. HOWES, J. S. KENNEDY & H. PARS. 1969. J. Pharmacol. Exp. Ther. **169:** 17–22.
76. HOWES, J. F., L. S. HARRIS, W. L. DEWEY & C. L. VOYDA. 1969. J. Pharmacol. Exp. Ther. **169:** 23–28.
77. IRESON, J. D. 1970. Brit. J. Pharmacol. **40:** 92–101.
78. CHRISTENSEN, E. M. & E. G. GROSS. 1948. JAMA **137:** 594–599.
79. BHARGAVA, H. N., S. L. CHAN & E. L. WAY. 1974. Eur. J. Pharmacol. **29:** 253–261.
80. IWAMOTO, E. T. & I. K. HO. 1972. Fed. Proc. **31:** 504.
81. BHARGAVA, H. N. & E. L. WAY. 1974. J. Pharmacol. Exp. Ther. **190:** 165–175.
82. NEAL, M. J. 1965. Brit. J. Pharmacol. **24:** 170–177.
83. DUNDEE, J. W. 1960. Brit. J. Anaesth. **32:** 407–414.
84. CLUTTON-BROCK, J. 1960. Anaesthesia **15:** 71–72.
85. ARIËNS, E. J. 1971. Drug Design. Vol. I: 169. Academic Press. New York, N.Y.
86. LESLIE, G. B. & B. NUNN. 1968. J. Pharm. Pharmacol. **20:** 881–882.
87. MOORE, J. & J. W. DUNDEE. 1961. Brit. J. Anaesth. **33:** 3–8.
88. WINTER, C. A. & L. FLATAKER. 1951. J. Pharmacol. Exp. Ther. **101:** 93–105.
89. GISPEN, W. H., T. B. VANWIMERSMA GREIDANUS, C. WATERS-EZRIN, E. ZIMMERMANN, W. A. KRIVOY & D. DE WEID. 1975. Eur. J. Pharmacol. **33:** 99–105.
90. BROWN, J. H. & R. L. GARRETT. 1972. Arch. Int. Pharmacodyn. **196:** 176–183.
91. HO, I. K., H. H. LOH & E. L. WAY. 1973. J. Pharmacol. Exp. Ther. **185:** 336–346.
92. GOURLEY, D. R. H. & S. K. BECKNER. 1973. Proc. Soc. Exp. Biol. Med. **144:** 774–778.
93. HO, I. K., D. A. BRASE, H. H. LOH & E. L. WAY. 1975. J. Pharmacol. Exp. Ther. **193:** 35–43.
94. HO, I. K., H. H. LOH & E. L. WAY. 1973. Proc. West. Pharmacol. Soc. **16:** 4–7.
95. KOYUNCUOĞLU, H., M. GLÜNGÖR, H. SAĞDUYU & L. EROĞLU. 1974. Eur. J. Pharmacol. **27:** 148–150.
96. WONG, C. & G. G. YARBROUGH. 1975. Can. J. Physiol. Pharmacol. **53:** 509–512.
97. FERRI, S., A. SANTAGOSTINO, P. C. BRAGA & I. GALATULAS. 1974. Psychopharmacologia **39:** 231–235.
98. KAKUNAGA, T., H. KANETO & K. HANO. 1966. J. Pharmacol. Exp. Ther. **153:** 134–141.
99. HARRIS, R. A., H. H. LOH & E. L. WAY. 1975. J. Pharmacol. Exp. Ther. **195:** 488–498.
100. PERT, C. & S. H. SNYDER. 1973. Science **179:** 1011–1014.
101. HITZEMANN, R. J., B. A. HITZEMANN & H. H. LOH. 1974. Life Sci. **14:** 2393–2404.
102. GLAUBACH, S. 1941. Proc. Soc. Exp. Biol. Med. **46:** 53–57.
103. CHRYSSANTHOU, C. P. 1973. Proc. Soc. Exp. Biol. Med. **144:** 770–773.

104. Liu, S. J. & R. I. H. Wang. 1975. J. Pharmacol. Exp. Ther. **195:** 94–104.
105. Spaulding, T. S., L. Minium, A. N. Kotake & A. E. Takemori. 1974. Drug. Metab. Disp. **2:** 458–463.
106. Cooper, M. J. & M. W. Anders. 1974. Life Sci. **15:** 1665–1672.
107. Johanneson, T. & W. J. Steele. 1973. Acta Pharmacol. Toxicol. **32:** 519–524.
108. Ferri, S., I. Galatulas, A. Santagostino & G. Giagnoni. 1975. Eur. J. Pharmacol. **31:** 370–373.
109. Loh, H. H., F. H. Shen & E. L. Way. 1969. Biochem. Pharmacol. **18:** 2711–2721.
110. Tulunay, F. C. & A. E. Takemori. 1974. J. Pharmacol. Exp. Ther. **190:** 401–407.
111. Fennessy, M. R. & J. Sawynok. 1973. Arch. Int. Pharmacodyn. **204:** 77–85.
112. Weis, J. 1969. Experientia **25:** 381.
113. Gupta, S. K. & B. B. Gaitonde. 1964. Indian J. Physiol. Pharmacol. **8:** 27–32.
114. Carabateas, P. M. & L. S. Harris. 1966. J. Med. Chem. **9:** 6–10.
115. Courvoisier, S., J. Fournel, R. Ducrot, M. Kolsky & P. Koetschet. 1953. Arch. Int. Pharmacodyn. **92:** 305–361.
116. Dhawan, B. N. & G. P. Gupta. 1959. Arch. Int. Pharmacodyn. **123:** 132–139.
117. Calcutt, C. R., N. S. Doggett & P. S. J. Spencer. 1971. Psychopharmacologia **21:** 111–117.
118. Takemori, A. E., H. J. Kupferberg & J. W. Miller. 1969. J. Pharmacol. Exp. Ther. **169:** 39–45.
119. Takemori, A. E., T. Oka & N. Nishiyama. 1973. J. Pharmacol. Exp. Ther. **186:** 261–265.
120. Tulunay, F. C. & A. E. Takemori. 1974. J. Pharmacol. Exp. Ther. **190:** 395–400.
121. Houde, R. W., S. L. Wallenstein & A. Rogers. 1972. Report at the meetings of the Committee on Problems of Drug Dependence. Ann Arbor, Michigan.
122. Tulunay, F. C., S. B. Sparber & A. E. Takemori. 1975. Eur. J. Pharmacol. **33:** 65–70.

DISPOSITION OF NARCOTICS AND NARCOTIC ANTAGONISTS*

Charles E. Inturrisi

Department of Pharmacology
Cornell University Medical College
New York, New York 10021

An understanding of the basis of drug interactions requires, among other things, a consideration of the role of pharmacologically active metabolites in the dose-response and time-action characteristics of a drug.

When a drug is intended for use in the maintenance treatment of heroin dependence we can expect it to be administered for some extended period of time. This situation can provide the opportunity for even minor active metabolites to accumulate.

In the past few years, analytical methods for the identification and quantitation of narcotic drugs and their metabolites in biofluids have been developed in a number of laboratories. This paper reviews recent information on the disposition of methadone, alpha-*l*-acetylmethadol,† and naltrexone in relation to the possible contribution of active metabolites to certain of the pharmacological effects of these drugs in man.

METHADONE

The structures of methadone and two biotransformation products are shown in FIGURE 1. Methadone undergoes an *N*-demethylation reaction that is catalyzed by the liver microsomal enzyme system to form an apparently unstable intermediate that rapidly cyclizes and eliminates a molecule of water to yield 2-ethylidene-1,5-dimethyl-3,3-diphenylpyrrolidine (metabolite 1).[1] Metabolite 1 can in turn undergo *N*-demethylation resulting in 2-ethyl-5-methyl-3,3-diphenyl-1-pyrroline (metabolite 2).[2] Metabolites 1 and 2 have both been reported to be devoid of narcotic-like pharmacologic activity in animal test systems.[2] Thus, for methadone, *N*-demethylation can be considered a detoxification pathway.

We have attempted to demonstrate a relationship between the time course of methadone in plasma and the time-action of certain pharmacologic effects. For example, FIGURE 2 shows the plasma levels of methadone following an oral dose of 15 mg to normal volunteers.[3] On the average, the peak plasma level is seen at 4 hours after drug administration. The plasma level of methadone de-

* This work was supported in part by NIDA Grant DA–00297. Dr. Inturrisi is an Andrew W. Mellon Teacher-Scientist, 1975–76.

† This report will be confined to a discussion of the alpha-*l*-isomer of acetylmethadol. Biotransformation of the alpha-*l*-isomer can result only in the corresponding alpha-*l*-metabolites. Hereafter, where a particular isomer of acetylmethadol or its biotransformation products is not designated, the reference is to the alpha-*l*-isomer.

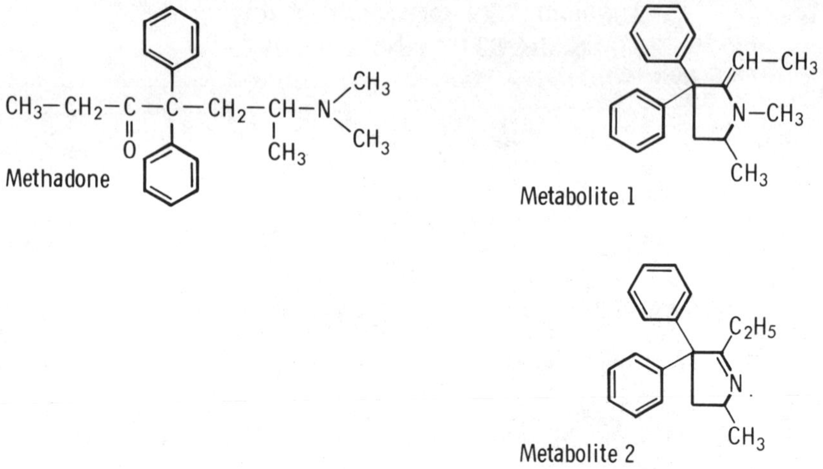

FIGURE 1. Structural formulae of methadone, metabolites 1 and 2.

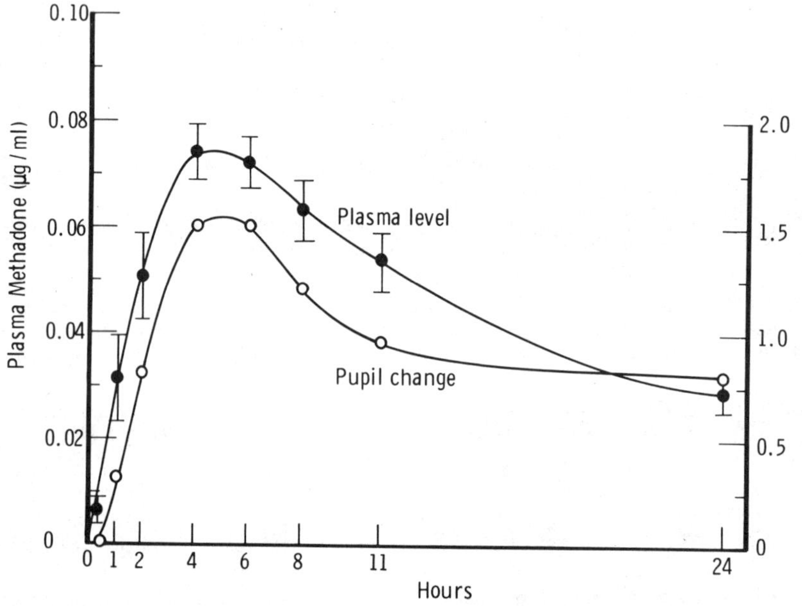

FIGURE 2. Plasma levels of methadone and pupillary constriction following a 15 mg oral dose. The results represent the mean of five normal subjects. Plasma methadone levels are mean ±S.E. (From Inturrisi & Verebely.[3] By permission of *Clinical Pharmacology and Therapeutics.*)

clined during the next 20 hours to a level at the 24th hour that was equal to about 40% of the peak plasma level.

FIGURE 2 includes data on the effect of methadone on the diameter of the pupil. It shows that the onset, peak, and 24-hour duration of methadone-induced pupillary constriction closely coincided with the corresponding time course of methadone in plasma. The miotic effect of narcotics is a centrally mediated effect resulting from an excitatory action on the visceral nuclei of oculomotor nuclear complex.[4] The correlation of the time-course of methadone in plasma with the time-action of methadone-induced pupillary constriction suggests that plasma methadone levels may in some manner reflect the disposition of the drug at those receptors in the central nervous system that mediate pupillary effects. Upon repeated administration tolerance develops only quite slowly, if at all, to the miotic effect of methadone. This is in sharp contrast to many of the characteristic effects of methadone and other narcotics on the central nervous system. Indeed, Verebely *et al.*[5] were able to demonstrate a correlation between the time-course of methadone in plasma and the time-action of the miotic effect during the chronic administration of methadone to maintenance patients. On the basis of a comparison of the duration of the miotic effect of several narcotic analgesics, Fraser and associates[6] suggested that a correlation might exist between the relative miotic potency of a narcotic and its ability to suppress abstinence when substituted in morphine-dependent subjects. As Fraser and associates predicted, acetylmethadol, which produces a miosis that is more sustained than after methadone, will suppress abstinence for a longer time than will methadone.

We have examined the time-course of methadone in the plasma of patients in a methadone-maintenance treatment program. The results of one study are shown in FIGURE 3. The subjects had been stabilized on a single daily oral dose of 100 to 120 mg of methadone for from 6 weeks to 1 year. The characteristics of these subjects are summarized in Reference 7.

The zero time sample was collected just before administration of the daily dose. This sample came approximately 23 hours after the previous dose of methadone. The time at which post-drug samples were taken is indicated on the abscissa of Figure 3. The data reveal large individual differences in plasma methadone levels. For example, the zero-time plasma level ranged from 0.20 to 0.83 μg/ml, whereas the peak plasma level ranged from 0.57 to 1.08 μg/ml. The mean time-course of plasma methadone was obtained by averaging subject plasma levels at each sample time (FIGURE 4). The peak mean plasma level occurred 4 hours after drug administration. The plasma level declined during the next 20 hours to a value approximately equal to the predose level. These data indicate that with the dosage schedule of these subjects, a steady state is achieved between the absorption and elimination of methadone. The mean apparent half-life for the elimination of methadone from the plasma of these subjects was 25 hours, with a range of from 13 to 47 hours.[7] These pharmacokinetic data, confirmed by others,[5, 8] are consistent with the daily dosage schedule developed by Dole and Nyswander on the basis of clinical assessment of patient symptoms.[9]

Although methadone can be demonstrated in patient plasma even after a single dose,[10] we have been unable to identify in plasma either metabolite 1 or 2 by use of a combination of solvent extraction and gas-liquid chromatographic procedures. A number of the products of methadone biotransformation have been identified in human urine after single[1-3, 10] and multiple doses.[5, 7, 8, 11-13]

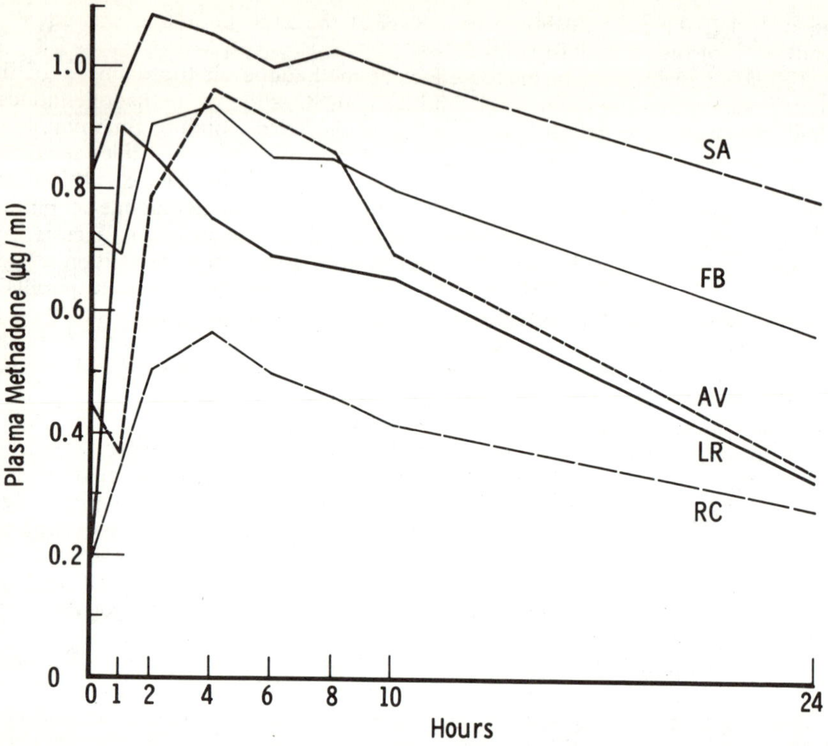

FIGURE 3. The time-course of methadone in the plasma of five methadone maintenance subjects receiving 100 to 120 mg of methadone HCl orally each day. Blood samples were collected as indicated on the abscissa. The zero-time sample was taken 23 hours after the previous dose of methadone.

For example, TABLE 1 shows data on the total urinary excretion of methadone and metabolites for each of five normal subjects for the 96 hours following a single 15-mg oral dose. During this period, an average of 52% of the administered dose appeared in the urine as methadone and metabolites (the recovery ranged from 39 to 64% of the administered dose), 21% as methadone, 30% as metabolite 1, and less than 1% as metabolite 2. These results indicate that metabolite 1 is a quantitatively important biotransformation product of methadone.

The urinary excretion pattern has been compared after acute and chronic administration of methadone to maintenance patients by Anggard and associates[13] and Verebely *et al.*[5] Both groups found an increase in the urinary excretion of metabolite 1 relative to methadone and a decrease in the percentage of the dose excreted as unchanged methadone. This increased urinary excretion of metabolite 1 could result from a methadone-induced stimulation of biotransformation, although other mechanisms may be operative. In the rat, Spaulding *et al.*[14] found that chronic oral ingestion of methadone results in an increase in components of the liver microsomal *N*-demethylating system, including cytochrome P–450 reductase.

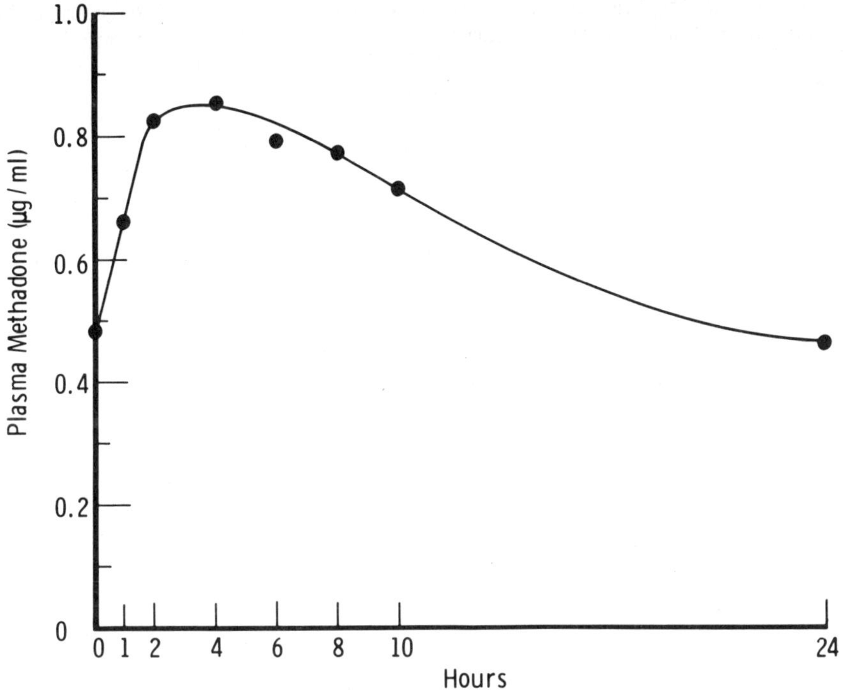

FIGURE 4. The mean plasma time-course of methadone in maintenance subjects. Each value is the mean of each of the five subjects shown in FIGURE 3. (From Inturrisi & Verebely.[7] By permission of *Clinical Pharmacology and Therapeutics.*)

TABLE 1

TOTAL URINARY EXCRETION OF METABOLITES IN THE 96 HOURS FOLLOWING A 15-MG ORAL DOSE OF METHADONE*

	Mg of Base			
Subject	Methadone	Metabolite 1	Metabolite 2	Total Base Recovered
B.R.	2.93	6.50	0.15	9.58
H.R.	4.49	4.80	0.14	9.43
H.L.	3.57	3.47	0.08	7.12
L.R.	2.32	4.65	0.07	7.04
J.S.	2.59	3.16	0.09	5.84
Average	3.16	4.53	0.11	7.80

* From Inturrisi & Verebely.[3] By permission of *Clinical Pharmacology and Therapeutics.*

In addition to biotransformation, renal mechanisms can influence the elimination of methadone. The urinary excretion of unchanged methadone is enhanced by acidification of the urine.[15] In FIGURE 5 the renal clearance values for methadone are plotted as a function of the pH values of the voided urine. The open circles represent the data from methadone maintenance subjects, and the closed circles represent data from normal subjects after a single dose of methadone. A positive correlation was found between increased renal clearance and decreasing urinary pH. This conclusion remains the same when the clearance values are recalculated after correction for the plasma protein binding of methadone. Clearly, methadone is handled by the kidney, as are other organic bases; that is, when the urine pH is lowered, the ionized form of the base is favored in tubular urine, and the passive reabsorption of methadone is decreased by ion trapping.

FIGURE 6 shows the biotransformation pathways for methadone in man, as identified by Anggard and associates.[13] In addition to the major pathway involving mono-*N*-demethylation to metabolite 1 (M_1) and then a minor pathway to metabolite 2 (M_2), ring hydroxylation of parent and mono and di-*N*-demethylated metabolites to yield M_5, M_6, and M_7, respectively, was demonstrated. These ring hydroxylated metabolites appear in urine predominantly as conjugates.

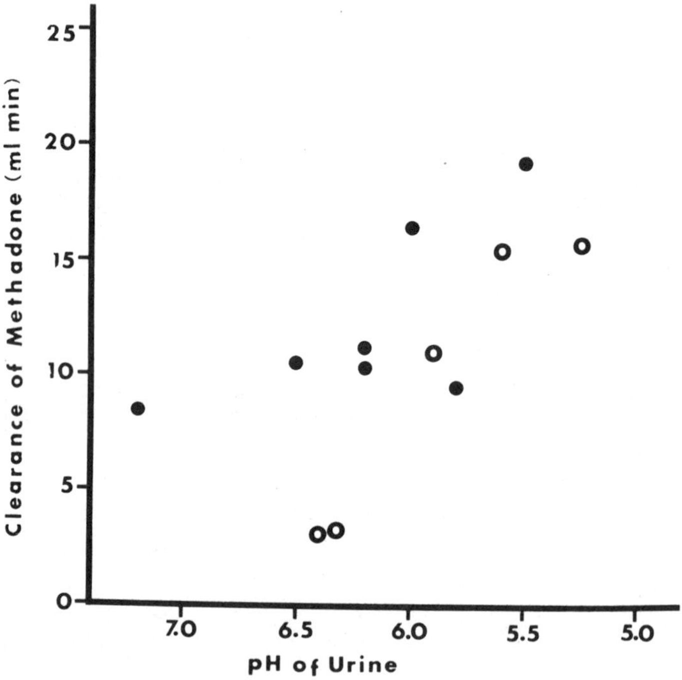

FIGURE 5. Renal clearance of methadone as a function of spontaneous urinary pH. Open circles represent methadone maintenance subjects and closed circles normal subjects. Renal clearance was determined during the 4- to 8-hour period after drug administration, as described in References 3 and 7.

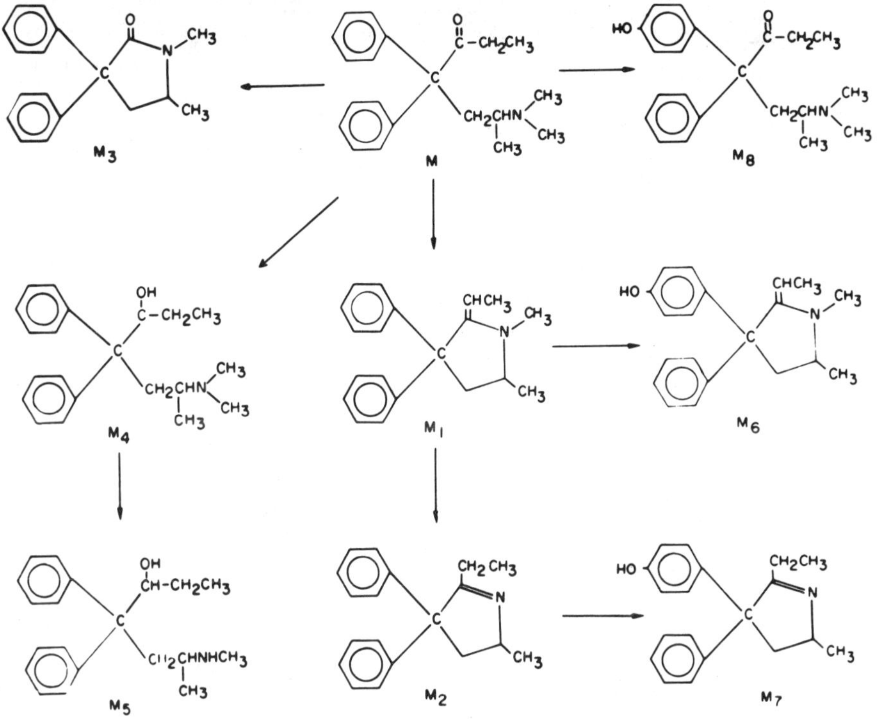

FIGURE 6. Biotransformation pathways of methadone in the human. (From Anggard *et al.*[13] By permission of *Clinical Pharmacology and Therapeutics.*)

There has been speculation as to the role of methadol (M_4) and normethadol (M_5) formed following the reduction of the keto group of methadone. Since this reduction appears to be stereoselective, the pharmacologically inactive *d*-methadone isomer contained in the racemic mixture *d,l*-methadone is biotransformed into the pharmacologically active metabolites *l*-methadol (M_4) and, then, to *l*-normethadol (M_5).[16] However, the data of Anggard *et al.*[13] indicate that reduction of methadone to methadol appears to be a relatively minor pathway. Thus, while a role for active metabolites cannot be ruled out, the evidence to date favors methadone itself as the predominant pharmacologic agent in man.

ACETYLMETHADOL

Alpha-*l*-acetylmethadol (acetylmethadol) is a synthetic narcotic analgesic derived from *d*-methadone. The relatively long duration of certain of the pharmacologic effects of acetylmethadol, in particular, the suppression of abstinence in morphine-dependent subjects, has prompted the clinical evaluation of this drug in the maintenance treatment of heroin dependence.

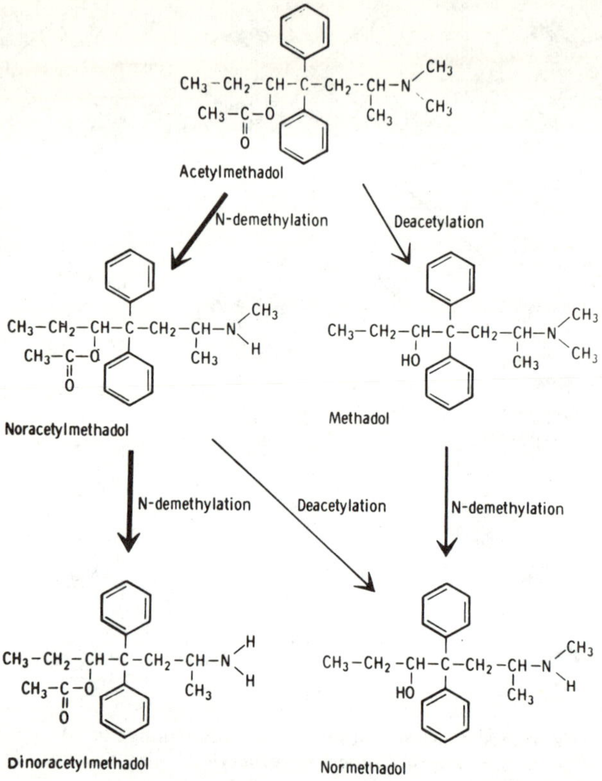

FIGURE 7. Structural formulae of acetylmethadol, noracetylmethadol, dinoracetylmethadol, methadol, and normethadol. (From Kaiko, Chatterjie & Inturrisi.[25] By permission of *Journal of Chromatography*.)

A number of clinical studies indicate that doses of acetylmethadol administered three times per week are as effective as daily doses of methadone in maintenance treatment.[17–20]

In both man and rat, the onset of narcotic effects is more rapid after oral administration than after parenteral. Studies in laboratory animals have suggested that biotransformation of acetylmethadol to active metabolites contributes to its long duration of action.[21, 22] In the rat, acetylmethadol is *N*-demethylated to noracetylmethadol.[23] In addition, ester hydrolysis would produce methadol and normethadol (FIGURE 7), each of which has been found to possess narcotic activity in animal test systems.

We have identified acetylmethadol, noracetylmethadol, methadol, and normethadol (FIGURE 7) in the urine of acetylmethadol maintenance subjects.[24] The presence of these compounds in subject urine was confirmed by use of chemical ionization mass spectrometry[25] (TABLE 2). The presence of a protonated molecular ion (m/e) with a value of 326 had not been anticipated (TABLE 2). This value is 14 mass units lower than the value of 340 for noracetylmethadol. This difference corresponds to the weight of a methylene group

TABLE 2

PARTIAL CHEMICAL IONIZATION MASS SPECTRUM ($i\text{–}C_4H_{10}$) OF AN EXTRACT OF URINE FROM AN ACETYLMETHADOL MAINTENANCE SUBJECT*

m/e†	Associated Compound	Absolute Intensity‡
354	Acetylmethadol	676
340	Noracetylmethadol	2925
326	Dinoracetylmethadol	4600
312	Methadol	384
298	Normethadol	134

* From Kaiko, Chatterjie & Inturrisi.[25] By permission of *Journal of Chromatography*.
† Molecular weight of protonated molecule.
‡ Arbitrary intensity units.

and suggested that noracetylmethadol might be further biotransformed in man to the primary amine dinoracetylmethadol (FIGURE 7). Billings *et al.*[26] were the first to isolate dinoracetylmethadol from rat urine and obtain the compound by chemical synthesis. They found that dinoracetylmethadol possesses narcotic activity in rodent test systems.[26] Thus, consideration must be given to another active metabolite.

Our most recent efforts have been directed toward an understanding of the role of these biotransformation products in the pharmacologic action of acetylmethadol. We have established that acetylmethadol, noracetylmethadol, and dinoracetylmethadol are present in the plasma of maintenance subjects, whereas methadol and normethadol were not detectable in these samples above the limits of sensitivity of the method.[25, 27]

The time-course of acetylmethadol, noracetylmethadol, and dinoracetylmethadol in subject plasma is shown in FIGURE 8. These subjects had been receiving an oral dose of 40 to 60 mg of acetylmethadol three times per week for 6 to 10 weeks. The initial (zero-time) sample was collected 72 hours after the previous dose and just prior to the test dose. As can be seen from FIGURE 8, none of the samples contained acetylmethadol at zero time. The plasma level of acetylmethadol was highest at 4 hours and barely detectable by 24 hours. At zero time the mean plasma level of noracetylmethadol was 0.042 μg/ml. The plasma level of noracetylmethadol reached a peak between 4 and 8 hours and then slowly declined so that at 48 hours it was equal to 60% of the peak level. Mean dinoracetylmethadol levels rose slightly after 4 hours and were not significantly different in subsequent samples.

Individual differences were noted in plasma levels. For example, the peak plasma level of acetylmethadol had a range of nearly 6-fold, whereas the peak for noracetylmethadol had a range of greater than 4-fold. The mean apparent plasma half-life is 7 hours for acetylmethadol and 48 hours for noracetylmethadol. The mean rate of formation of dinoracetylmethadol appears equal to the rate of disappearance from plasma, since the plasma level remains relatively constant during the dosing interval. These observations on the persistence of noracetylmethadol and dinoracetylmethadol in plasma throughout a 72-hour dosing interval are in agreement with the report of Billings *et al.*[28]

The time-action of the miotic effect was assessed in these subjects by measuring pupillary diameter concurrently with the collection of plasma sam-

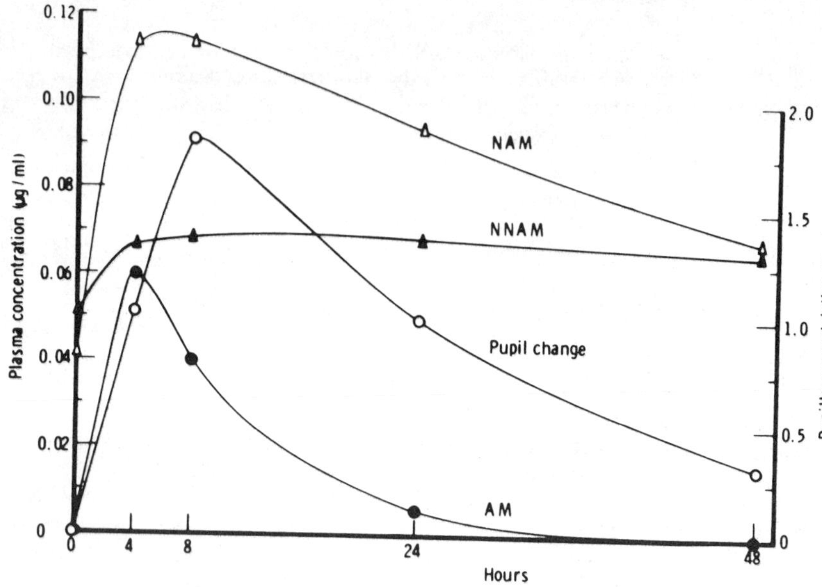

FIGURE 8. Plasma levels of acetylmethadol (AM), noracetylmethadol (NAM), dinoracetylmethadol (NNAM), and pupillary constriction in acetylmethadol maintenance subjects receiving 40 to 60 mg acetylmethadol HCl three times per week. The results represent the mean of eight subjects. (From Kaiko & Inturrisi.[27] By permission of *Clinical Pharmacology and Therapeutics*.)

ples. These data are also shown in FIGURE 8. The mean peak of pupillary constriction occurred at 8 hours. This is after the mean peak plasma level of acetylmethadol and at the time of the highest mean levels of noracetylmethadol and dinoracetylmethadol. Thus, whereas acetylmethadol disappears rapidly from plasma, two biotransformation products persist in plasma, and a pharmacologic effect (miosis) is sustained. We find that the time-action of the miotic effect corresponds most closely to the time-course of plasma noracetylmethadol.[27] Smits,[29] using the mouse-writhing analgesic test, reports that noracetylmethadol is 10 times more potent than either acetylmethadol or dinoracetylmethadol.

Although not conclusive, our results suggest that *N*-demethylation of acetylmethadol to active and persistent metabolites is responsible for the long duration of drug action. It would appear that acetylmethadol is rapidly taken up by tissue reservoirs, followed by a sequence of pharmacokinetic processes involving redistribution and biotransformation to provide active metabolites that result in a smooth and sustained level of pharmacologic activity.

The critical role of biotransformation in the time-action characteristics of acetylmethadol requires a careful evaluation of the influence of concurrent administration of drugs known to affect the enzymes of biotransformation. Although the potential for drug interactions in acetylmethadol maintenance subjects may appear to be great, only careful laboratory and clinical studies will provide the information necessary to predict significant interactions. In addition, much more information is required on the basic pharmacologic properties of each of the recently identified active metabolites. As yet we have no basis for deciding whether the active metabolites completely mimic the pharmacologic profile of a typical narcotic. Do they also possess properties not seen with typical narcotics? A great deal more remains to be learned about this potentially useful and very interesting drug.

NALTREXONE

As a class, the narcotic antagonists may be a useful adjunct in the treatment of heroin abusers. By virtue of their specific antagonist action, as function of dose, they will reverse or prevent most of the effects of narcotics, including euphoria. Upon repeated administration, tolerance does not appear to develop to their antagonist action, undesirable side effects are minimal, and they do not induce physical dependence.[30, 31] Naltrexone, an antagonist with good oral potency and a long duration of action, is currently the focus of clinical and laboratory research aimed at the development of a narcotic antagonist for the treatment of heroin dependence.

Recent efforts have been directed toward an understanding of the disposition of naltrexone in man and laboratory animals. Cone[32] discovered that the major human urinary metabolite of naltrexone is beta (β)-naltrexol (FIGURE 9). This observation drew attention to the stereochemistry of the reduction products of members of the 6-keto morphine series.

In collaboration with Dr. James Fujimoto of the Medical College of Wisconsin, we examined metabolites of naltrexone isolated from human, rabbit, and chicken urine. Proton magnetic resonance spectral studies revealed that the metabolite from human and rabbit was β-naltrexol, whereas that from the chicken was alpha (α)-naltrexol (FIGURE 9).[33] Since the α and β alcohols are chemically distinct compounds and might differ in their pharmacological properties, it appeared important to us to define the routes of biotransformation for naltrexone in the several species involved in the toxicity and other pharmacologic studies.

A major breakthrough came with the discovery of a stereoselective chemical synthesis that provided a quantity of β-naltrexol for use as an analytical standard and for pharmacologic evaluation.[34]

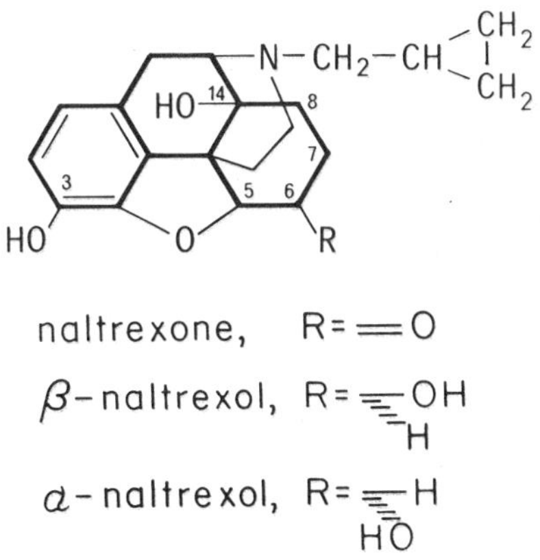

FIGURE 9. Structural formulae of naltrexone, β-naltrexol, and α-naltrexol.

TABLE 3

URINARY EXCRETION OF NALTREXONE AND β-NALTREXOL

Species & Sex	Dose Route*	Dosage Schedule	Collection Period (hours)	Percentage of Administered Dose Recovered					Reference
				Naltrexone		β-Naltrexol		Total Base	
				Free	Conjugated	Free	Conjugated		
Human: male	50 mg po	single dose	144	1.2	9.7	26.2	16.4	53.4	36
male	125 mg po	3×/week for 1 month	48	0.8	7.6	16.8	11.8	37.0	35
Monkey: male	12 mg/kg po	daily for 8 months	24	0.1	8.1	0.3	8.0	16.5	35
female	12 mg/kg po	daily for 8 months	24	1.3	21.0	0.9	15.0	38.2	35
Rabbit: male	30 mg/kg ip	daily for 8 days	24	0.2	14.5	0.1	3.3	18.2	35
Rats: male	100 mg/kg po	daily for 12 months	24	0.1	0.2	0.1	0.1	0.5	35
female	100 mg/kg po	daily for 12 months	24	0.2	0.2	0.3	0.1	0.8	35
Dog	5 mg/kg sc	single dose	48	3.3	51.2	0.0	0.3	54.7	37
Guinea pig	50 mg/kg sc	single dose	48	28.7	16.8	8.5	11.3	65.3	37

* po = oral; ip = intraperitoneal; sc = subcutaneous.

TABLE 3 summarizes the cumulative urinary excretion pattern of naltrexone and β-naltrexol in several species. In all mammalian species studied to date, the predominate 6-keto reduction product of naltrexone is β-naltrexol.[35–37] This metabolite is present in the urine of these species in both the free form and as a conjugate released by acid hydrolysis. Although we were able to identify α-naltrexol in the urine of the chicken,[33] this metabolite was not detected in the urine of several mammalian species.[35] Cone and Gorodetsky,[37] using a more sensitive analytical method, found that less than 1% of a dose of naltrexone was excreted as α-naltrexol.

The contribution, if any, of β-naltrexol to the pharmacologic activity of naltrexone remains a central question. The urinary excretion patterns differ among the several species (TABLE 3). Thus, in man, free and conjugated β-naltrexol are the predominant urinary metabolites, whereas the monkey excretes nearly equal proportions of naltrexone and β-naltrexol as conjugates. In the dog and rabbit, the major urinary metabolite is conjugated naltrexone. In the rat, urinary excretion is a very minor pathway.

In man, the time-course of urinary excretion indicates that naltrexone is rapidly metabolized and excreted, with nearly all of the naltrexone cleared in 16 to 24 hours.[35, 36] Thereafter, β-naltrexol is the predominant and persistent urinary metabolite. The antagonist action of naltrexone is known to exceed 24 hours.[30, 31] Cone *et al.*[36] noted that in the dog, a species that handles naltrexone mainly by conjugation, with little β-naltrexol formed, the duration of antagonist action is quite short, in contrast to man, a species where formation of β-naltrexol predominates (see TABLE 3). This has led to speculation that the presence of β-naltrexol may be responsible for the long duration of action of naltrexone in man.

This hypothesis would be supported by the demonstration of the antagonist activity of β-naltrexol in the usual animal test systems. When compared to naltrexone, β-naltrexol is only 1/50 to 1/80 as potent a narcotic antagonist in mice[34, 38] and approximately 1/12 to 1/15 as potent as naltrexone in precipitating abstinence in the chronic spinal dog.[36] Blumberg and Ikeda[39] found that in the rat, β-naltrexol is approximately 1/50 as potent as naltrexone but has a much longer duration of antagonist action. These data suggest that although β-naltrexol is a much weaker narcotic antagonist, it may contribute to the long duration of action of naltrexone.

A great deal more remains to be learned about the disposition of naltrexone. In man, the pharmacokinetics are currently under study by Verebely and associates.[40] It would be of particular interest to determine whether the reduction of naltrexone to β-naltrexol can occur in the central nervous system. Recently, Misra *et al.*[41] have been able to detect low levels of β-naltrexol in rat brain, but not in plasma, following administration of tritium-labeled naltrexone. In addition to studies of the localization of naltrexone and metabolites in the central nervous system, a comparison should be made of the relative affinities of naltrexone and β-naltrexol for the opiate receptor.

REFERENCES

1. BECKETT, A. H., J. F. TAYLOR, A. F. CASY & M. M. A. HASSAN. 1968. J. Pharm. Pharmacol. **20:** 754–762.

2. POHLAND, A., H. E. BOAZ & H. R. SULLIVAN. 1971. J. Med. Chem. **14:** 194–197.
3. INTURRISI, C. E. & K. VEREBELY. 1972. Clin. Pharmacol. Ther. **13:** 923–930.
4. LEE, H. K. & S. C. WANG. 1975. J. Pharmacol. Exp. Ther. **192:** 415–431.
5. VEREBELY, K., J. VOLAVKA, S. MULÉ & R. RESNICK. 1975. Clin. Pharmacol. Ther. **18:** 180–190.
6. FRASER, H. F., T. L. NASH, G. D. VANHORN & H. ISBELL. 1954. Arch. Int. Pharmacodyn. **98:** 443–451.
7. INTURRISI, C. E. & K. VEREBELY. 1972. Clin. Pharmacol. Ther. **13:** 633–637.
8. KREEK, M. J. 1973. N.Y. State J. Med. **73:** 2773–2777.
9. DOLE, V. P. & M. NYSWANDER. 1965. JAMA **193:** 646–650.
10. INTURRISI, C. E. & K. VEREBELY. 1972. J. Chromatogr. **65:** 361–369.
11. SULLIVAN, H. R. & S. L. DUE. 1973. J. Med. Chem. **16:** 909–913.
12. SULLIVAN, H. R., S. L. DUE & R. E. MCMAHON. 1972. J. Am. Chem. Soc. **94:** 4050–4051.
13. ANGGARD, E., L. M. GUNNE, J. HOLMSTRAND, R. E. MCMAHON, G. G. SANDBERG & H. R. SULLIVAN. 1975. Clin. Pharmacol. Ther. **17:** 258–266.
14. SPAULDING, T. C., A. N. KOTAKE & A. E. TAKEMORI. 1976. Drug Metab. Dispos. **4:** 45–52.
15. BECKETT, A. H. 1969. *In* A Scientific Basis of Drug Dependence. H. Steinberg, Ed.: 129–148. J. & A. Churchill, Ltd. London.
16. SULLIVAN, H. R., S. E. SMITS, S. L. DUE, R. E. BOOHER & R. E. MCMAHON. 1972. Life Sci. **11:** 1093–1104.
17. JAFFE, J. H. & E. C. SENAY. 1971. JAMA **216:** 1303–1305.
18. JAFFE, J. H., E. C. SENAY, C. R. SCHUSTER, P. R. RENAULT, B. SMITH & S. DIMENZA. 1972. JAMA **222:** 427–442.
19. ZAKS, A., M. FINK & A. M. FREEDMAN. 1972. JAMA **220:** 811–813.
20. LEVINE, R., A. ZAKS, M. FINK & A. M. FREEDMAN. 1973. JAMA **226:** 316–318.
21. SUNG, C. & E. L. WAY. 1954. J. Pharmacol. Exp. Ther. **110:** 260–270.
22. VEATCH, R. M., T. K. ADLER & E. L. WAY. 1964. J. Pharmacol. Exp. Ther. **145:** 11–19.
23. MCMAHON, R. E., H. W. CULP & F. J. MARSHALL. 1965. J. Pharmacol. Exp. Ther. **149:** 436–445.
24. KAIKO, R. F. & C. E. INTURRISI. 1973. J. Chromatogr. **82:** 315–321.
25. KAIKO, R. F., N. CHATTERJIE & C. E. INTURRISI. 1975. J. Chromatogr. **109:** 247–258.
26. BILLINGS, R. E., R. BOOHER, S. E. SMITS, A. POHLAND & R. E. MCMAHON. 1973. J. Med. Chem. **16:** 305–306.
27. KAIKO, R. F. & C. E. INTURRISI. 1975. Clin. Pharmacol. Ther. **18:** 96–103.
28. BILLINGS, R. E., R. E. MCMAHON & D. A. BLAKE. 1974. Life Sci. **14:** 1437–1446.
29. SMITS, S. E. 1974. Res. Commun. Chem. Pathol. Pharmacol. **8:** 575–578.
30. MARTIN, W. R., D. R. JASINSKY & P. A. MANSKY. 1973. Arch. Gen. Psychiat. **28:** 784–791.
31. RESNICK, R. B., J. VOLAVKA, A. M. FREEDMAN & M. THOMAS. 1974. Amer. J. Psychiat. **131:** 646–650.
32. CONE, E. J. 1973. Tetrahedron Letters No. **23:** 2607–2610.
33. CHATTERJIE, N., J. FUJIMOTO, C. E. INTURRISI, S. ROERIG, R. I. H. WANG, D. V. BOWEN, F. H. FIELD & D. D. CLARKE. 1974. Drug Metab. Dispos. **26:** 401–405.
34. CHATTERJIE, N., C. E. INTURRISI, H. B. DAYTON & H. BLUMBERG. 1975. J. Med. Chem. **18:** 490–492.
35. DAYTON, H. E. & C. E. INTURRISI. 1976. Drug Metab. Dispos. In press.
36. CONE, E. J., C. W. GORODETZKY & S. Y. YEH. 1974. Drug Metab. Dispos. **2:** 506–512.

37. CONE, E. J. & C. W. GORODETSKY. 1976. Fed. Proc. **35**(1451): 469.
38. FUJIMOTO, J. M., S. ROERIG, R. I. H. WANG, N. CHATTERJIE & C. E. INTURRISI. 1975. Proc. Soc. Exp. Biol. Med. **148:** 443–448.
39. BLUMBERG, H. & C. IKEDA. 1976. Fed. Proc. **35**(1453): 469.
40. VEREBELY, K., J. VOLAVKA, S. J. MULÉ & R. B. RESNICK. 1976. Fed. Proc. **35**(1452): 469.
41. MISRA, A. L., R. BLOCH, J. VARDY, S. J. MULÉ & K. VEREBELY. 1976. Drug Metab. Disp. **4:** 276–280.

DISCUSSION

DR. KARL VEREBELY: (*New York State Drug Abuse Control Commission, Testing and Research Laboratory, Brooklyn, N.Y.*): I'd like to address myself to the last statement of Dr. Inturrisi concerning the pharmacologically active component of naltrexone. We have a great deal of human pharmacokinetic and disposition data on naltrexone, which will be presented at the FASEB meeting in California in April, 1976.

In previous urinary excretion studies, naltrexone was detected only up to 4 to 6 hours after naltrexone administration, yet narcotic antagonism was observed for at least 48 hours. Since β-naltrexol was steadily excreted, it was thought to be responsible for the long time action of naltrexone. For our studies we were able to measure both naltrexone and β-naltrexol in the plasma of subjects up to 72 hours after a single or multiple 100 mg dose(s). β-naltrexol plasma concentrations were 1.5 to 10 times higher than naltrexone. Naltrexone, on the other hand, declined very slowly from 24 to 72 hours, whereas the narcotic antagonism was nearly 100% complete at 24 and 48 hours to a 25-mg heroin challenge. The correlation coefficient (r) between the naltrexone plasma levels and the degree of narcotic antagonism was $r = 0.92$, and the same for β-naltrexol was 0.84. The individual plasma elimination half-life of naltrexone also correlated with the degree of narcotic blockade at the level of $r = 0.99$, whereas β-naltrexol showed no correlative tendency. On the basis of this data, naltrexone appears to be the major pharmacologically active component, and β-naltrexol contributes to the narcotic antagonism to a lesser extent. A conclusive answer cannot be given, however, until the potency of β-naltrexol in man is known.

Regarding the clinical use of naltrexone the following impressions were observed: (1) No evidence of dispositional and pharmacological tolerance during chronic administration; (2) no prolonged induction period is required in chronic treatment because of rapid attainment of naltrexone steady-state equilibrium in plasma; (3) the strong correlation of naltrexone plasma level with the degree of narcotic antagonism ($r = .92$) indicates an opportunity to regulate the doses to achieve therapeutically effective plasma levels of naltrexone; (4) naltrexone and β-naltrexol do not accumulate during chronic administration (100 mg daily doses), which indicates that naltrexone can be used safely in long-term maintenance and; (5) no danger of acute toxicity to naive individuals after accidental ingestion, no danger of overdose deaths, and no abuse potential are evident by naltrexone. Our studies suggest that naltrexone is a safe and reliable therapeutic agent for the maintenance of post-opiate dependence and is a promising drug for preventing relapse to heroin use.

INTERACTIONS OF NARCOTIC ANTAGONISTS

Louis S. Harris

Department of Pharmacology
Medical College of Virginia
Richmond, Virginia 23298

Since the inception of the narcotic antagonists, their interaction with narcotics has produced certain dichotomies and paradoxes that are important in the context of this symposium. This paper will illustrate some of the problems encountered from basic work carried out in our laboratory and others over the past 15 years. Other papers presented at this conference discuss some of the more recent work attempting to explain the paradoxes described herein. For this reason, we will concentrate, in major part, on a review of past work.

The crux of the situation lies in the fact that the basic action of the narcotic antagonists appears to differ markedly, depending on whether the agonist was administered acutely or chronically. Let us look at some data.

One method of evaluating the narcotic antagonists is by the use of a variety of antinociceptive test procedures. Thus, in a test procedure where the narcotic agonists are effective analgesics, it would be expected that the antagonists would prevent or reverse the effects of an agonist. We have extensively used a modification[1] of the D'Amour-Smith[2] tail-flick procedure. In this modification, the stimulus is of a high intensity, giving a short control reaction time (2–4 seconds). We also use a cutoff time (20 seconds in rats, 10 seconds in mice) that is considered as the maximum effect or 100%. Using these conditions, the partial agonists such as nalorphine, pentazocine, and cyclazocine have little or no agonistic activity. This makes the evaluation of antagonistic properties easier.

Using the tail-flick procedure, one can generate good analgesic dose-response curves (FIGURE 1), and there is a good correlation between antinociceptive potency in this test and analgesic potency in man. To test an antagonist, one could give a dose of the drug and repeat the agonist dose-response curve. If the curve is shifted to the right and remains parallel, one has evidence for competitive antagonism. A second method[1] for evaluating antagonists is to give a standard dose of agonist (e.g., ED_{80}) and then graded doses of the antagonist. By doing this, one can generate good antagonist dose-response curves (FIGURE 2). If one plots the data on probit paper, AD_{50} values can be calculated, 95% confidence limits determined, and the parallelism of the curves can be ascertained using the method of Litchfield and Wilcoxon.[3] In this way, relative potencies can be determined. Using this procedure, the commonly used antagonists, nalorphine, levallorphan, and naloxone, as well as a large number of other compounds, look like classical competitive antagonists. For instance, Grumbach and Chernov,[4] in an exhaustive study, compared two antagonists (nalorphine and levallorphan) against a wide variety of agonists varying in potency from meperidine to compounds 1,000 times more potent. What they found was that it took about the same amount of antagonist to reverse equianalgesic doses of agonist despite the fact that the agonist potency varied over a 1,000-fold range. This is illustrated in TABLE 1 for nalorphine. Similar data was obtained for levallorphan. These authors also calculated the Gaddum drug

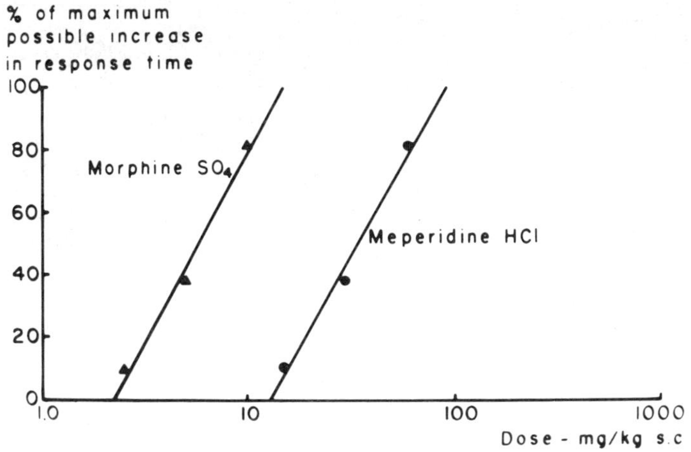

FIGURE 1. Comparison of the antinociceptive activity of morphine and meperidine using the rat tail-flick procedure.

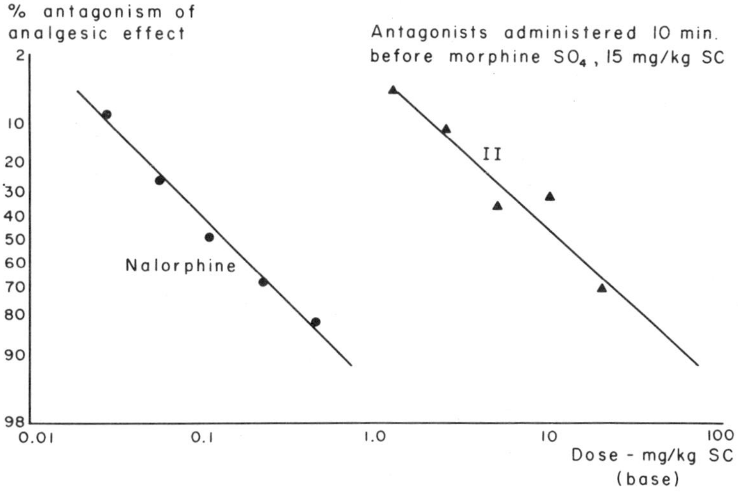

FIGURE 2. Comparison of the activity of nalorphine and pentazocine as antagonists of morphine in the rat tail-flick procedure.

ratios[5] for four opiate-antagonist pairs. These data lent strong support for a demonstration of the competitive nature of the antagonism.

We have examined some 20 antagonists versus the ED_{80}'s of three narcotics (TABLE 2).[6] Spearman rank order correlations[7] were then carried out. As can be seen, there is a nearly perfect correlation between the potency of these antagonists between all three agonists, despite the fact that the antagonistic potency of the compounds varies over a nearly 4,000-fold range—again, evidence for the competitive nature of the agonist-antagonist interaction.

TABLE 1

ANTAGONIST ACTIVITY OF NALORPHINE AGAINST VARIOUS ANALGESICS AS DETERMINED BY THE ORIGINAL D'AMOUR-SMITH PROCEDURE IN THE UNANESTHETIZED RAT*

Analgesic	Analgesic ED_{80} (mg/kg, s.c.)	% Rats of Group of 60 Rats Going to Cutoff Time of 20 Sec: Saline control	Nalorphine HCl (mg/kg, s.c.) 0.063	0.125	0.250	% Antagonism of 80% Analgesic Effect: Nalorphine HCl (mg/kg, s.c.) 0.063	0.125	0.250	Antagonist Dose-50 of Nalorphine HCl (mg/kg, s.c.)	Antagonist Dose-50 Derived from Probit Analysis
Meperidine HCl	120	74 (61–84)†	48 (35–61)	36 (24–49)	22 (12–39)	35	51	70	0.112	0.093
Morphine sulfate	15	78 (66–88)	43 (30–56)	30 (19–43)	10 (4–21)	45	62	87	0.078	0.075
Ketobemidone HCl	3.75	85 (73–93)	48 (35–61)	37 (25–50)	2 (0.5–9)	43	58	98	0.085	0.086
Methadone HCl	3.75	90 (80–96)	63 (50–75)	37 (25–50)	5 (1–14)	30	59	94	0.100	0.103
Phenazocine HBr	0.670	77 (64–87)	40 (28–54)	17 (8–29)	3 (0.5–12)	48	78	96	0.065	0.063
N-Ph(C4)-A	0.663	84 (73–93)	62 (49–74)	30 (18–43)	12 (5–23)	26	64	86	0.100	0.101
N-Ph-O-(C4)-P	0.234	78 (66–88)	37 (25–50)	17 (8–29)	3 (0.5–12)	52	78	96	0.056	0.058
N-Ph(C4)-P	0.166	73 (60–84)	45 (32–58)	15 (7–27)	7 (2–16)	38	80	90	0.078	0.067
N-Cinnamyl-P	0.150	85 (73–93)	60 (47–72)	48 (35–61)	18 (10–30)	30	44	79	0.120	0.126
N-Ph(O)(C4)-P	0.125	88 (77–95)	68 (55–79)	43 (30–56)	20 (11–32)	23	51	77	0.125	0.157
Mean values		81.2	51.4	31.0	10.2	37.0	62.5	87.3	0.0919 ±0.0233‡	0.0928

* From Grumbach & Chernov.[4]
† The values in parentheses are the 95% binomial confidence limits of the percentages.
‡ Standard deviation of the grand mean AD_{50}.

TABLE 2

A RANK ORDER CORRELATION OF VARIOUS ANTAGONISTS AGAINST THE ANALGESIC ACTION OF THREE NARCOTICS

A vs. Meperidine		B vs. Morphine		C. vs. Phenazocine	
Rank	AD_{50} mg/kg s.c.	Rank	AD_{50} mg/kg s.c.	Rank	AD_{50} mg/kg s.c.
1	0.0135	1	0.018	1	0.019
2	0.018	7	0.048	5	0.033
3	0.019	2	0.029	2	0.028
4	0.019	3	0.030	3	0.029
5	0.024	6	0.046	7	0.048
6	0.034	4	0.038	8	0.054
7	0.046	8	0.057	9	0.09
8	0.049	5	0.044	4	0.030
9	0.052	9	0.058	6	0.046
10	0.092	12	0.26	12	0.2
11	0.094	11	0.19	13	0.37
12	0.134	10	0.130	10	0.098
13	0.146	13	0.46	11	0.19
14	0.37	14	0.60	14	0.40
15	0.45	15	0.63	15	1.0
16	0.66	16	2.2	16	1.4
17	3.9	17	9.0	17	6.3
18	10.9	18	11.6	18	11.0
19	14.5	19	18.0	19	29.0
20	48.0	20	50.0	20	70.0

Rank order correlation coefficients:

A vs. B = 0.962
B vs. C = 0.952
B vs. C = 0.970

Of course, other *in vivo* test procedures can be used to evaluate narcotic-narcotic antagonist interactions. One of these involves the reversal of the respiratory depression induced by a narcotic. This is illustrated by FIGURE 3, where the reversal of morphine by an experimental antagonist is shown. Using this technique in a quantitative fashion is difficult since a large number of animals would be required and things are complicated by the fact that the partial agonists, such as nalorphine and pentazocine, produce respiratory depression themselves. This fact did lead us to examine the ability of naloxone, the relatively pure antagonist, to antagonize the respiratory depression produced by the partial agonist pentazocine (TABLE 3). Thus, naloxone has become the drug of choice in treating pentazocine overdosage.

Let us turn now to the chronic situation. We have recently had the relatively unique experience of setting up *de novo* a colony of morphine-dependent monkeys patterned after that of Dr. Seevers and his colleagues at the University of Michigan.[8, 9] These animals from the first day have received 3.0 mg/kg subcutaneously every 6 hours. There is no interruption of medication for weekends, holidays, etc. We have carried out a relatively systematic study of the development of physical dependence over a period of time in these animals,

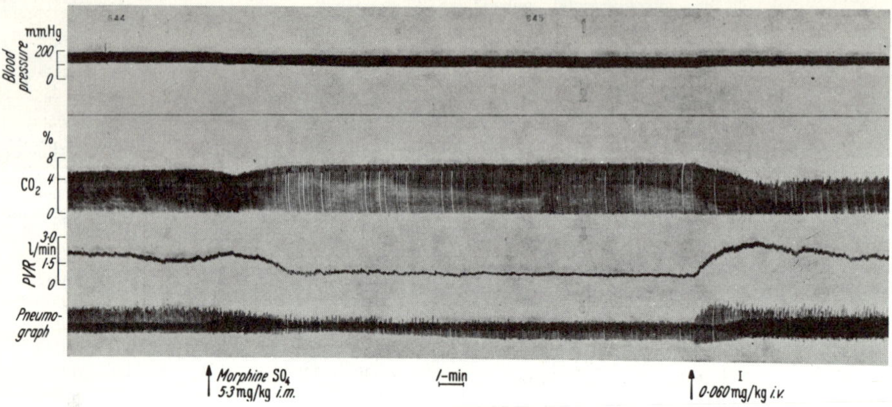

FIGURE 3. Reversal of morphine-induced respiratory depression in the barbitalized dog by 2-allyl-5-ethyl-2′-hydroxy-9-methyl-6,7-benzomorphan(I).

TABLE 3
NALOXONE REVERSAL OF PENTAZOCINE DEPRESSION IN DOGS

Parameter	Percent Change from Preinjection Value			
	Pentazocine (15 mg/kg)		Naloxone (0.5 mg/kg)	
	Direction	Percent	Direction	Percent
Blood pressure (mm Hg)	Decrease	13.6 ± 4.4*	Increase	11.6 ± 4.8
Heart rate (beats/min)	Decrease	9.5 ± 5.7	Increase	4.9 ± 2.5
Pulmonary ventilation rate (1/min)	Decrease	26.8 ± 9.7	Increase	40.6 ± 6.2
pCO_2	Increase	40.6 ± 9.0	Decrease	15.4 ± 5.0
Percent carbon dioxide	Increase	52.4 ± 17.5	Decrease	12.8 ± 2.4
Respiration rate (resp/min)	Decrease	64.9 ± 5.9	Increase	42.4 ± 11.2
pO_2	Decrease	30.6 ± 2.6	Increase	30.9 ± 3.4

* Average ±s.e. for 5 dogs. Naloxone alone at 0.5 or 1.0 mg/kg caused minimal changes.

using precipitated abstinence with nalorphine and naloxone.[10] All experiments were carried out blind, and a wide variety of signs and symptoms were observed and scored. AD_{50} values were calculated, where possible, for all these signs and symptoms. In general, what we observed was that the animals became more sensitive to the antagonists with time. This only reached a peak 9 months after initiation of the morphine dosing. The phenomenon is illustrated for vomiting in TABLE 4.

These findings, of course, fit in with similar data in rodents described by Way and his colleagues,[11] Muruyoma and Takemori,[12] and Cheney *et al.*[13] The work by Cheney and his colleagues is particularly elegant. They used levorphanol-dependent mice and measured the fluctuation of the naloxone ED_{50} between doses of levorphanol and time of injection. They found that naloxone

TABLE 4

CALCULATED ED_{50}S FOR VOMITING INDUCED BY NALOXONE AND NALORPHINE DURING THE DEVELOPMENT OF MORPHINE DEPENDENCE*

Precipitated Withdrawal	Naloxone (mg/kg/s.c.)	Nalorphine (mg/kg/s.c.)
30 days	N.S.†	N.S.
60 days	0.069 (0.045–0.101)	N.S.
90 days	0.057 (0.042–0.072)	N.S. EST—1.08 (0.00–2.30)
9 months	0.021 (0.011–0.035)	—‡

* From Aceto *et al.*[10]
† Not significant at $p = 0.05$ or less.
‡ Not tested.

acts noncompetitively to precipitate withdrawal jumping and that the withdrawal could not readily be overcome by the agonist. Similar findings were noted by Wikler and his colleagues in their early studies with nalorphine in man.[14] They found that a single dose of nalorphine precipitated a severe abstinence syndrome in a morphine-dependent subject which could not be relieved by large doses of morphine.

Recently, we have been looking at another model of dependence in the rodent, first described by Teiger.[15] In this model, rats are prepared with an indwelling intraperitoneal catheter, which is led out through a stab wound in the back. They are then fitted with a harness and allowed to roam freely within their home cage by use of a spring and swivel arrangement (FIGURE 4). The catheter is attached to a Harvard Pump, and morphine or other drugs are infused continuously at a slow rate. Using an appropriate dosage schedule, one can produce a thoroughly dependent animal in a week or less. On abrupt with-

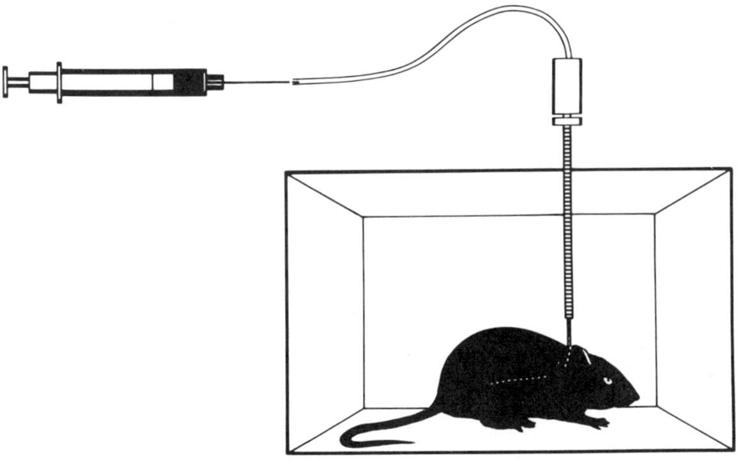

FIGURE 4. The continuous intraperitoneal infusion technique in the rat.

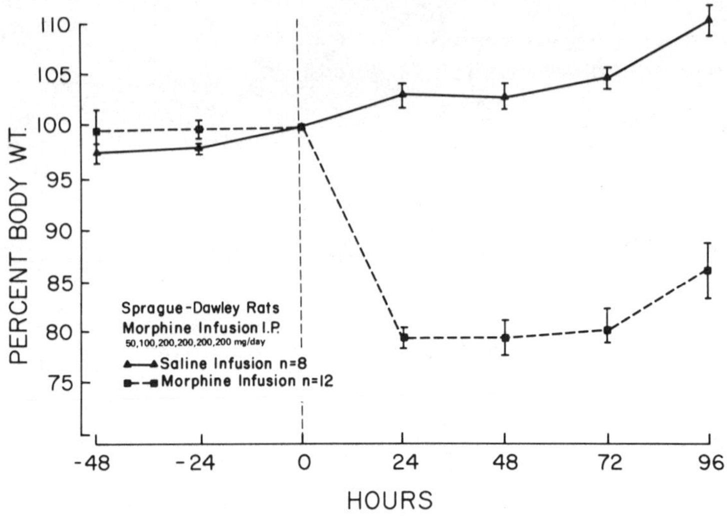

FIGURE 5. Demonstration of physical dependence to morphine in the rat, using the continuous intraperitoneal infusion technique.

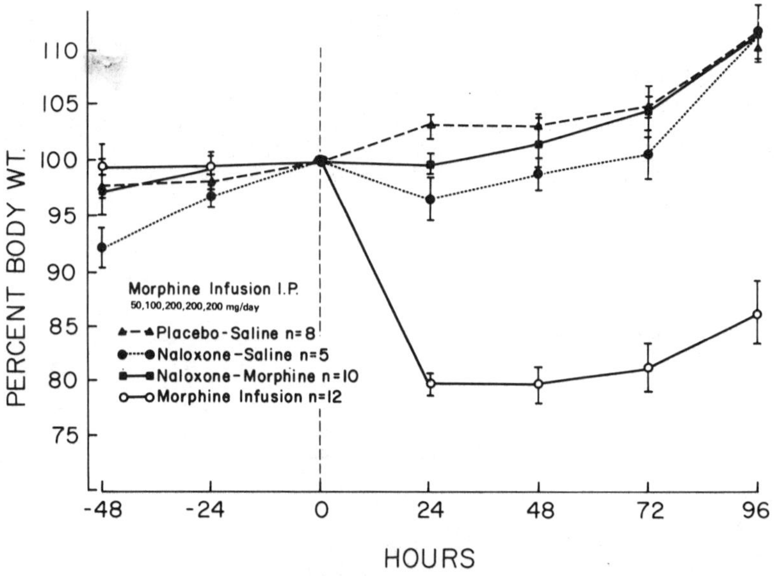

FIGURE 6. Prevention by naloxone of the development of physical dependence to morphine in the rat, using the continuous intraperitoneal infusion technique.

TABLE 5
SUBSTITUTIONS OF NARCOTIC ANTAGONISTS FOR MORPHINE IN THE RAT INFUSION PROCEDURE

Drug	Dose (mg/kg/day)	Substitute
Morphine sulfate	200	Yes
Naltrexone	20	No
	200	No
Buprenorphine	10	No
Pentazocine	20	No
	200	Yes

drawal or administration of an antagonist, the typical signs of abstinence are seen. We have found loss of body weight to be the most reliable sign and, although we record the other symptoms, only weight loss data will be reported here. A typical experiment[16] is shown in FIGURE 5, where the effects of morphine are compared to a saline control. On abrupt withdrawal there is a precipitous fall in body weight, peaking at about 24 hours and only slowly returning to control levels. The beauty of this technique is that it provides a steady-state animal, which is not readily obtained using repeated injections or pellet implantation.

We can now interpose the antagonists into this system. FIGURE 6 compares a morphine group with a morphine-plus-naloxone group. Note the complete lack of weight loss in animals concomitantly treated with morphine and naloxone. This was also true of all the other signs of abstinence. The results of preliminary studies[17] with several antagonists are shown in TABLE 5. We can readily produce a complete block of dependence with all the compounds except pentazocine, which gives only a partial blockade. We have also examined a number of the new long-lasting antagonist preparations, and this method appears to offer promise as an evaluation procedure to assess the potency and duration of action of these agents.

REFERENCES

1. HARRIS, L. S. & A. K. PIERSON. 1964. J. Pharmacol. Exp. Ther. **143:** 141–148.
2. D'AMOUR, F. E. & D. L. SMITH. 1941. J. Pharmacol. Exp. Ther. **72:** 74–79.
3. LITCHFIELD, J. T. & F. WILCOXON. 1949. J. Pharmacol. Exp. Ther. **96:** 99–113.
4. GRUMBACH, L. & H. I. CHERNOV. 1965. J. Pharmacol. Exp. Ther. **149:** 385–396.
5. GADDUM, J. H. 1957. Pharmacol. Rev. **9:** 211–218.
6. ARCHER, S. & L. S. HARRIS. 1965. Prog. Drug Res. **8:** 262–320.
7. SIEGEL, S. 1956. Nonparametric Statistics for the Behavioral Sciences: 202–212. McGraw Hill Book Co., Inc. New York, N.Y.
8. SEEVERS, M. H. 1936. J. Pharmacol. Exp. Ther. **56:** 147–156.
9. SEEVERS, M. H. & G. A. DENEAU. 1963. *In* Physiological Pharmacology. W. S. Rost & F. G. Hofmann, Eds. Vol. I: 565–670. Academic Press. New York, N.Y.
10. ACETO, M. D., R. E. FLORA & L. S. HARRIS. 1976. Pharmacology **15:** 1–10.

11. WAY, E. L., H. H. LOH & F. H. SHEN. 1969. J. Pharmacol. Exp. Ther. **167:** 1–8.
12. MURUYAMA, Y. & A. E. TAKEMORI. 1973. J. Pharmacol. Exp. Ther. **185:** 602–608.
13. CHENEY, D. L., B. A. JUDSON & A. GOLDSTEIN. 1972. J. Pharmacol. Exp. Ther. **182:** 189–194.
14. WIKLER, A., H. F. FRASER & H. ISBELL. 1953. J. Pharmacol. Exp. Ther. **109:** 8–20.
15. TEIGER, D. G. 1974. J. Pharmacol. Exp. Ther. **190:** 408–415.
16. DEWEY, W. L., G. A. PATRICK & L. S. HARRIS. 1975. Personal Commun. Comm. Probs. Drug Depend.: 64–73.
17. DEWEY, W. L. & L. S. HARRIS. Unpublished data.

INTERACTIONS OF NARCOTICS, NARCOTIC ANTAGONISTS, AND ETHANOL DURING ACUTE, CHRONIC, AND WITHDRAWAL STATES*

Andrew K. S. Ho and Raymond C. A. Chen

Division of Pharmacology
Peoria School of Medicine
University of Illinois
Peoria, Illinois 61606

J. Michael Morrison

Division of Research
National Institute on Drug Abuse
Rockville, Maryland 20852

Introduction

Interactions between narcotics and ethanol have been reported in human and in animal studies. Heroin addicts maintained on prolonged methadone treatment who became secondarily addicted to ethanol develop a syndrome with a tenfold increase in mortality rate over those on methadone maintenance alone.[1] Other studies indicated that many opiate addicts have had earlier problems with ethanol[2] and that some of these persons would use ethanol when drugs such as heroin, morphine, or cocaine were not available.[3] In mice, ethanol pretreatment followed by morphine administered after blood alcohol levels had returned to zero resulted in a marked increase in lethality.[4] Similarly, potentiation of the depressant effects of ethanol by morphine and an increase in mortality rate have also been reported.[5, 6] Recently, Sinclair *et al.*[7] reported that the selection of ethanol in Sprague-Dawley rats was suppressed after a single injection of morphine (60 mg/kg). Despite these reports, no detailed studies have been reported on interactions between narcotics and/or narcotic antagonists and ethanol during acute and chronic administration and during withdrawal in animals.

In this paper, we present observations on interactions of various narcotics and antagonists, especially morphine, methadone, and naloxone with ethanol, during acute and chronic administration and during withdrawal in various strains of rats and mice.

Methods and Procedures

The following strains of rats and mice were used:

1. Adult male Sprague-Dawley rats weighing 180–200 g.
2. Adult male Long-Evans Hooded rats weighing 180–200 g.
3. Adult male C57BL/6J mice weighing 20–25 g.
4. Neonatal Sprague-Dawley rats.

* Supported by NIDA contract ADM-45-74-220. Presented in preliminary form at the Fall Pharmacology Society Meeting, Davis, Calif., August 1975.

Effects of Drugs on Volitional Consumption of Ethanol

Animals were housed individually in standard stainless steel wire mesh cages. After at least 4 days of acclimatization to the laboratory conditions (temperature, 68–70° F, light-dark cycle, 14–10 hr), the animals were used for experimentation. Except when otherwise specified, animals had free access to food (Purina lab chow), water, and/or ethanol (prepared fresh daily from 95% ethanol in distilled water). All fluids (water, ethanol, morphine, etc.) were placed either in 100 ml (in the case of rats) or 25 ml (in the case of mice) graduated Richter-type drinking tubes fitted onto the outside of each cage. Daily consumption of each of these fluids was recorded between 11 AM and 2 PM. The tubes were randomly rotated each day so as to prevent the development of a position habit. In most experiments, food consumption and body weight were also monitored daily. Under a free-choice situation, stable baseline consumptions of water, ethanol, and/or drug were established for at least 4 days (usually the last 4 of 7 days) prior to drug treatment. The means of the 4 stable days was taken as base-line values for these factors. Results after drug treatment are expressed as a percentage of this base-line consumption (TABLES 1, 2). In some experiments, the preference-aversion cutoff concentration for ethanol was determined in individual rats. The concentration of ethanol was increased by 1% daily until the animal consumed no measurable amount of ethanol on 2 consecutive days. This concentration of ethanol is the preference-aversion cutoff concentration.

The following drugs were used:

- Morphine sulfate (Merck Chemical Co.)
- Methadone hydrochloride and *l*-α-acetylmethadol (LAAM) (Eli Lilly & Co.)
- Levorphenol hydrochloride, dextrorphan hydrochloride (Hoffman La Roche Co.)
- Naloxone hydrochloride and naltrexone hydrochloride (Endo Lab.)
- Ethanol, 95% (Scientific Products Co.).

Acute Studies

The effects of single doses of morphine, methadone, levorphanol, and dextrorphan on the volitional consumption of ethanol were studied in rats and mice. The following doses were used for each drug studied:

Morphine	10, 30, and 60 mg/kg s.c.
Methadone	2, 5, 10, and 30 mg/kg s.c.
Levorphanol	2, 10, 30, and 60 mg/kg s.c.
Dextrorphan	2, 10, 30, and 60 mg/kg s.c.

Chronic Experiments

Physical dependence on morphine in adult rats and mice was produced by one of two procedures:

(1) Daily subcutaneous injections for 14 days based on an incremental dose regimen as follows:

10 mg/kg to 50 mg/kg twice daily from days 1–5

50 mg/kg to 150 mg/kg twice daily from days 6–11
160 mg/kg to 200 mg/kg twice daily from days 13–14
(2) Pellet implantation using a 75 mg/kg morphine pellet subcutaneously for 72 hours.

In neonatal rats, morphine was given at 5 mg/kg from day 3 to day 8, and the daily s.c. dose was subsequently increased to 10, 20, 30, and 40 mg/kg on the 9th, 15th, 21st, and 27th days, respectively. Methadone dependence was produced by subcutaneous injections twice daily using 5 mg/kg for 2 days and increasing the dose by 2.5 mg/kg every 2 days up to a dose of 40 mg/kg at 30 days.

Morphine Withdrawal

The following abstinence signs due to morphine withdrawal precipitated by naloxone or naltrexone were observed and recorded:

a. Body weight loss at 24 and 48 hours after morphine.
b. Rectal temperature 90–180 minutes after the antagonist.
c. Number of spontaneous withdrawal jumpings in each of the animals over a period of 30 minutes following antagonist and the percentage of animals that showed jumping behavior.
d. The frequency and severity of naloxone- or naltrexone-induced diarrhea was estimated by counting the number of watery or soft stools produced by each animal over 30 minutes.
e. Teeth chattering was estimated by counting the number of audible teeth chattering sounds made by each animal in 30 minutes after the antagonist.
f. The number of animals that showed ptosis was noted.
g. The number of both head and body shakes (wet dog shakes) was counted for 30 minutes after naloxone or naltrexone.
h. Irritability to handling and touch was noted in each animal after naloxone or naltrexone.

Ethanol Withdrawal

The abstinence signs due to ethanol withdrawal were observed in rats with a scoring system as follows:

Loss of 20% or more of control body weight	1
Mild tremor, hyperreflexia, compulsive drinking	2
Continuous tremor, provoked convulsions (by ringing a bunch of keys around the animal for 1 minute)	3
Jumping, clonic-tonic convulsions (at least 2 or more/hr)	4
Severe clonic-tonic convulsions (at least 2 or more/hr)	5
Coma and/or death	6

Ethanol withdrawal signs were examined in rats that had been exposed to ethanol alone administered chronically for 1 to 5 months on a forced-drinking schedule. On this schedule the only fluid available to the animals was an ethanol solution. The initial concentration of ethanol in this drinking solution was 5% (v/v), which was increased with daily increments of 1% until it reached 40% (v/v). The animals were then maintained at this concentration of ethanol.

Blood Ethanol Levels

The effects of acute narcotics on blood ethanol levels after a loading dose of ethanol were determined in Sprague-Dawley rats. Ethanol was prepared by diluting 95% ethanol with distilled water to a final concentration of 30% (v/v) and was injected intraperitoneally at a dose of 2 g/kg, 45 minutes after a single subcutaneous injection of either morphine (2 mg/kg, 10 mg/kg, and 20 mg/kg) or methadone (1 mg/kg, 5 mg/kg, and 10 mg/kg). Blood was sampled from the tail vein over a period from 10 to 280 minutes after ethanol administration. Blood ethanol was measured by the enzymatic assay using NAD-ADH.[13] Control rats were treated similarly with normal saline.

Results

Modification of Volitional Consumption of Ethanol by Narcotics

Acute Studies

The effects of an acute dose of morphine on the daily consumption of water, ethanol, and food and on body weight were studied in the C57BL/6J mice and Long Evans Hooded rats. Our observations showed that morphine (10–60 mg/kg) induced a dose-related suppression of voluntary ethanol consumption in the mice given free choice between water and 10% ethanol but caused no statistically significant inhibition of food and water intake and had no effect on body weight. A reduction of approximately 40% in mean ethanol consumption was noted with 60 mg/kg of morphine, compared with a smaller but significant reduction of about 20% with a 10 mg/kg dose (Table 1). The suppressive effect of morphine on ethanol consumption was transient, and recovery to base-line levels of consumption was seen within 2 days after morphine administration (Figure 1). In mice, 30 mg/kg of methadone and 5 and 10 mg/kg LAAM also produced significant suppression of ethanol consumption. These drugs also caused a significant decrease in food consumption. In the Long-Evans Hooded rats, ethanol consumption was significantly reduced by morphine (10 mg/kg and 30 mg/kg) and by methadone (15 mg/kg) (Table 2). In both species, there was a very large individual variation in water consumption, particularly among drug-treated animals, which may be due, at least in part, to increased spillage by these animals. Thus, no meaningful conclusions can be drawn with regard to this parameter.

In order to test the relative specificity of these narcotic effects, levorphanol and its inactive stereoisomer, dextrorphan, were studied. In mice, treatment with levorphanol caused a significant and dose-related suppression of ethanol and food consumption at 30 and 60 mg/kg, whereas treatment with dextrorphan at similar doses failed to cause any significant change in these parameters (Table 1). Similar effects were seen in rats, although only a single dose (30 mg/kg) of each drug was used (Table 2). Rats treated with either naloxone (up to 5 mg/kg) or naltrexone (up to 5 mg/kg) showed no significant reduction in ethanol consumption (Table 2).

TABLE 1

EFFECTS OF SINGLE INJECTION OF DIFFERENT DOSES OF OPIATES ON CONSUMPTIONS OF ETHANOL, WATER, AND FOOD, AND BODY-WEIGHT CHANGES IN C57BL/6J MICE

	Mean Percent of Base-Line Values†			
Treatment (s.c.)	Ethanol (10%) Consumption	Water Consumption	Food Consumption	Body Weight
Saline controls (N = 30)	102.6	115	99	100.4
Morphine				
10 mg/kg (N = 7)	81.0* ($p < 0.005$)	130	117	98.1
30 mg/kg (N = 7)	70.3* ($p < 0.005$)	186	103	97.8
60 mg/kg (N = 15)	62.2* ($p < 0.0005$)	162	97	99.4
Methadone				
2 mg/kg (N = 8)	99.2	86	93	99.4
5 mg/kg (N = 10)	103	75	91	99.8
10 mg/kg (N = 8)	99	90.7	88.6* ($p < 0.05$)	98.1
30 mg/kg (N = 10)	91.4* ($p < 0.05$)	142.2	81.5* ($p < 0.005$)	98.4
l-α-Acetylmethadol				
2 mg/kg (N = 8)	113.8	113.6	104.0	101.0
5 mg/kg (N = 8)	84.6* ($p < 0.005$)	133.5	80.0* ($p < 0.005$)	100.2
10 mg/kg (N = 8)	82.1* ($p < 0.005$)	110.1	63.0* ($p < 0.0005$)	97.2
Levorphanol				
2 mg/kg (N = 7)	93.6* ($p < 0.05$)	139.6	92.8	98.5
10 mg/kg (N = 7)	91.8* ($p < 0.05$)	104.5	79.0* ($p < 0.005$)	97.4
30 mg/kg (N = 7)	77.5* ($p < 0.005$)	92.4	67.3* ($p < 0.0005$)	97.8
60 mg/kg (N = 7)	69.8* ($p < 0.0005$)	83.7	64.4* ($p < 0.0005$)	97.8
Dextrorphan				
2 mg/kg (N = 7)	99.8	98.8	99.6	98.8
10 mg/kg (N = 7)	98.4	87.6	92.0	100.1
30 mg/kg (N = 7)	98.8	97.7	97.9	99.6
60 mg/kg (N = 7)	99.0	99.3	101.8	100.1

* Value significantly different from control.

† Mean base-line values of the control mice recorded over the 4 days preceding treatment are taken as 100%; ethanol consumption was 226.2 ml/kg; water 64.8 ml/kg; food 170.8 g/kg; and body weight 22.43 g.

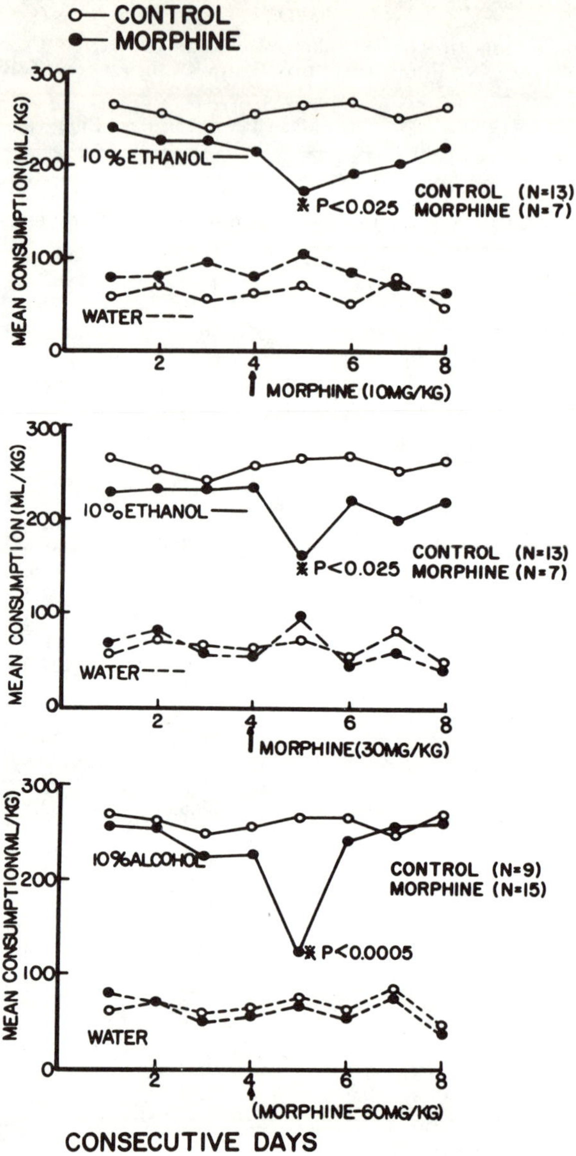

FIGURE 1. Acute effects of varying doses of morphine on ethanol selections in C57BL/6J mice.

TABLE 2

EFFECTS OF SINGLE INJECTION OF DIFFERENT DOSES OF NARCOTICS AND ANTAGONISTS ON CONSUMPTIONS OF ETHANOL, WATER, AND FOOD, AND BODY-WEIGHT CHANGES IN LONG-EVANS HOODED RATS

	Mean Percent of Base-Line Values†			
Treatment	Ethanol (5%) Consumption	Water Consumption	Food Consumption	Body Weight
Saline controls (N = 15)	103.5	98.6	125.9	100.6
Morphine				
10 mg/kg (N = 8)	76.1* ($p < 0.005$)	188.1	114.0	100.8
30 mg/kg (N = 8)	68.6* ($p < 0.005$)	288.5	91.1	102.0
Levorphanol				
30 mg/kg (N = 8)	47.9* ($p < 0.0005$)	201.4	70.2* ($p < 0.005$)	99.1
Dextrorphan				
30 mg/kg (N = 11)	111.5	103.5	103.8	101.6
Methadone				
15 mg/kg (N = 11)	75.1* ($p < 0.005$)	217.9	90.0	101.6
Naloxone				
0.1 mg/kg (N = 8)	95.6	77.5	94.5	100.6
1 mg/kg (N = 8)	101.2	107.9	91.9	100.0
5 mg/kg (N = 8)	105.4	100.0	116.7	99.4
Naltrexone				
0.1 mg/kg (N = 8)	110.0	122.7	98.8	99.7
1 mg/kg (N = 8)	95.8	191.7	94.5	101.2
5 mg/kg (N = 8)	98.1	61.5	102.9	99.4

* Significantly different from control.

† Mean base-line values of the control rats recorded over the 4 days preceding treatment are taken as 100%; ethanol consumption 102.7 ml/kg; water 48.0 ml/kg; food 90.7 g/kg; and body weight 188.8 g taken as 100%.

Chronic Studies

To demonstrate that the animals were made physically dependent on morphine following chronic injections or pellet implantation, abstinence signs (as outlined under "*Morphine Withdrawal*") were observed after treatment with either naloxone or naltrexone using doses of 0.1 mg/kg or 0.4 mg/kg s.c. The effects of morphine withdrawal on the selection of ethanol (5% v/v) and water were observed in adult Sprague-Dawley rats. Data obtained showed that body weight, food, and water but not ethanol consumption were significantly reduced on the first day after morphine withdrawal. However, during the next 4 days, the selection of ethanol increased significantly compared with the controls, whereas the other parameters observed returned to control levels during this period (FIGURE 2).

To study the effects of morphine withdrawal on ethanol preference in

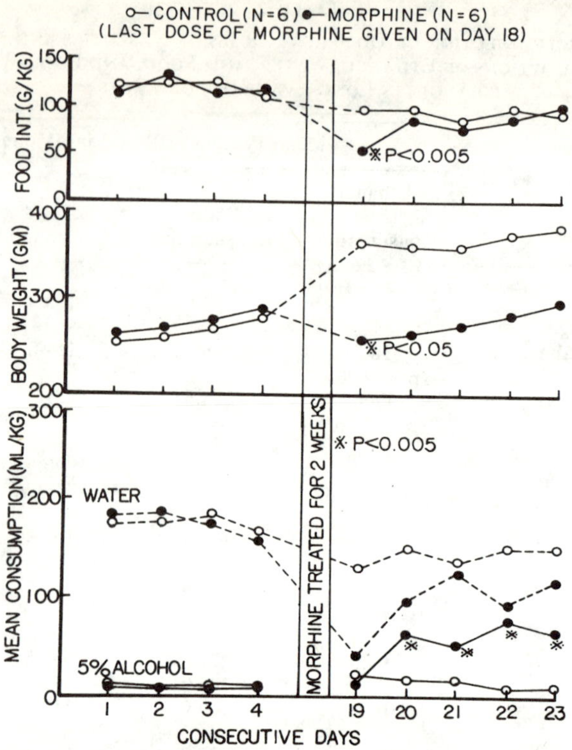

FIGURE 2. Effects of withdrawal from chronic morphine on food intake, body weight, water, and ethanol in adult rats.

neonatal rats, the preference aversion cutoff concentration and the volume of ethanol consumed were determined in neonates pretreated with morphine for 6 weeks. In a group of 18 treated rats (one of which died), 9 animals reached their preference-aversion cutoff concentration at 11% (v/v) ethanol, compared with only 1 in the controls. About one-fourth of the treated rats showed a preference-aversion cutoff concentration greater than 13% (v/v) ethanol, whereas all the control animals had a preference-aversion cutoff concentration at 13% or lower (FIGURE 3).

In two other groups of neonatal rats similarly treated with morphine for 6 weeks, the specificity of the withdrawal effects on ethanol consumption was studied. Following withdrawal from morphine, one group was allowed free choice between water and quinine solution ($4 \times 10^{-4}\%$), and the other group was given free choice between sucrose solution (3%) and a mixture of sucrose (3%) plus ethanol (5%). There was no significant difference between morphine-treated and control rats in the selection between water and quinine solution. Both groups showed preference for water. On the other hand, the morphine-treated rats showed a marked preference for ethanol-sucrose solution, whereas the controls showed a marked preference for sucrose solution (FIGURE 4).

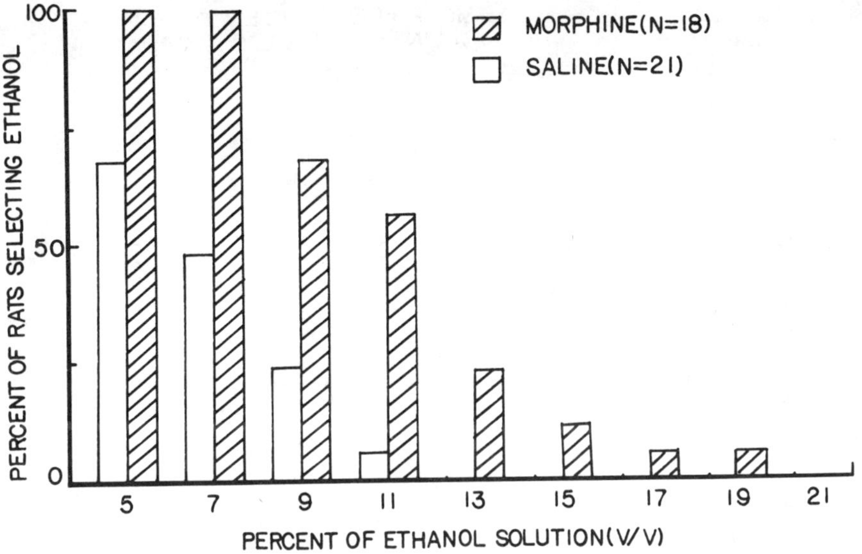

FIGURE 3. Effects of morphine withdrawal on the selection of ethanol at different concentrations.

Effect of Prior Chronic Treatment with Morphine or Methadone Followed by Chronic Forced Ethanol Ingestion on Ethanol Withdrawal Signs

Major ethanol withdrawal signs (as described under *"Ethanol Withdrawal"*) were observed in Sprague-Dawley rats that had been exposed to the ethanol forced-drinking schedule for periods varying from 1 to 5 months. The frequency and severity of these withdrawal signs appeared to be directly related to the period of exposure to ethanol. This was particularly true with the provoked withdrawal jumping, and thus the effects of morphine and methadone on ethanol withdrawal in rats were estimated using this parameter.

Following treatment with morphine for 2 weeks, a group of Sprague-Dawley rats were placed on an ethanol forced-drinking schedule for 60 days. The control animals injected with saline were similarly exposed to ethanol. At 1 and 2 months, provoked withdrawal jumping was observed 6 hours after ethanol withdrawal. Rats that had been previously exposed to morphine showed higher incidence of jumping as well as other withdrawal symptoms, such as tremor and hyperreflexia. About one-third of the morphine-pretreated animals showed withdrawal jumping, whereas none of the controls showed jumping. At 2 months of ethanol exposure, both the controls and treated animals showed similar frequency of withdrawal jumping.

In adult rats pretreated chronically with methadone for 1 month prior to ethanol exposure for 1 month, 20% showed withdrawal jumping, whereas none of the animals in the control groups showed jumping. The amount of ethanol consumed by rats pretreated with morphine was not higher under the forced-drinking schedule but appeared to be similar and at times less than that of the controls.

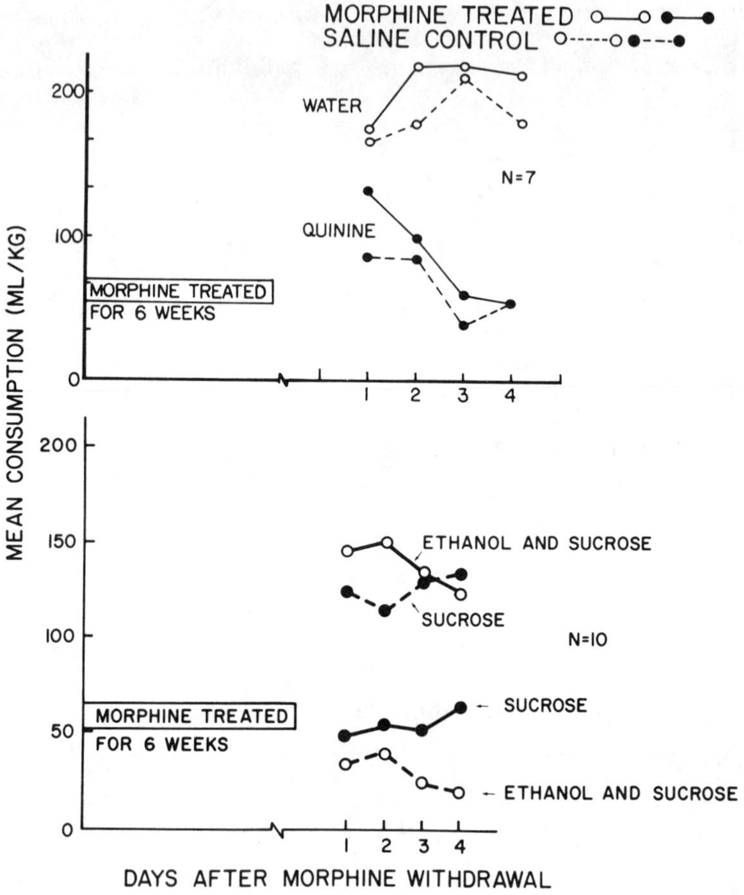

FIGURE 4. Effects of withdrawal from chronic morphine treatment on the selections of quinine (4×10^{-4}) versus water and sucrose (3%) versus ethanol (5%) and sucrose (3%).

In another experiment using neonates that had been pretreated with morphine for 6 weeks, withdrawal jumping was observed after 1, 2, and 3 months of ethanol forced-drinking, and the percentages of animals that showed jumping were 56, 73, and 70, respectively, compared with 0, 11, and 50 for the controls (FIGURE 5).

Effects of Acute and Chronic Narcotic Treatment on Ethanol Blood Levels

Measurements of blood ethanol levels showed that in rats treated with either morphine or methadone, the levels of ethanol were significantly different from those in the saline controls. At the higher doses, both morphine (10 and 20 mg) and methadone (5 and 10 mg/kg) suppressed the initial rise in blood

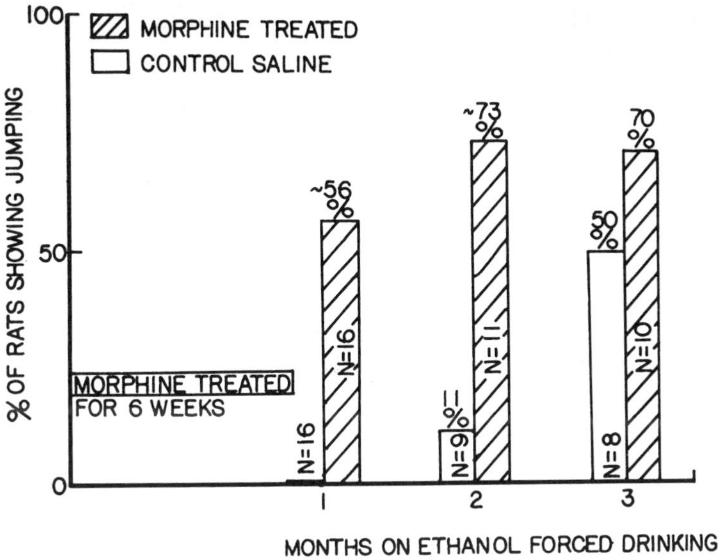

FIGURE 5. Comparison between control and prior chronic treatment with morphine followed by chronic alcohol ingestion on withdrawal symptoms in neonatal Sprague-Dawley rats.

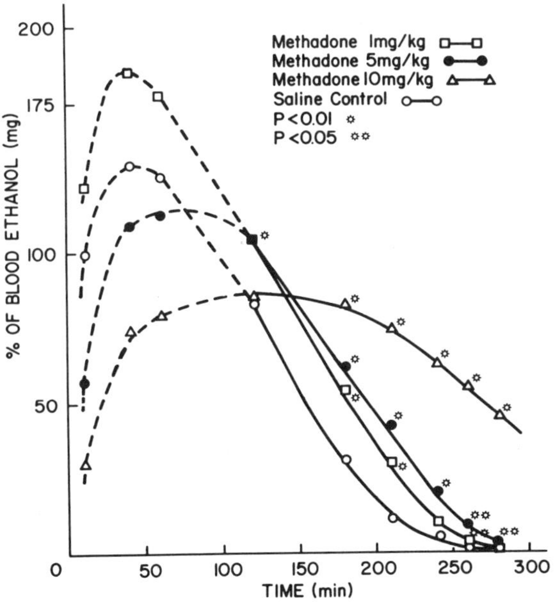

FIGURE 6. Effects of acute methadone on the blood level of ethanol after a loading dose (2g/kg i.p.) in Sprague-Dawley rats.

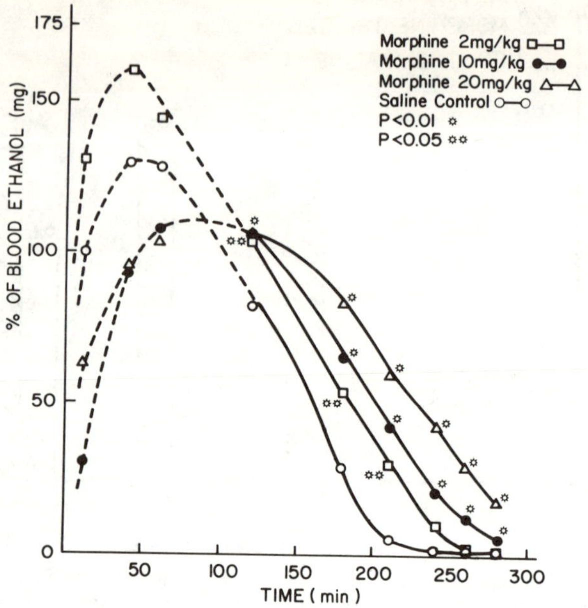

FIGURE 7. Effects of acute morphine on the blood level of ethanol after a loading dose (2g/kg i.p.) in Sprague-Dawley rats.

ethanol level, whereas the rate of decline was significantly prolonged (FIGURES 6, 7).

DISCUSSION

The results presented in this study indicated that narcotics modify ethanol consumption in both rats and mice during the acute, chronic, and withdrawal states.

In the acute experiments, single injections of morphine, methadone, LAAM, and levorphanol suppressed volitional consumption of ethanol. It is interesting to note that only the narcotics but not the antagonist naloxone, or the pharmacologically inactive stereoisomer of levorphanol, dextrorphan, suppressed ethanol consumption. These findings suggest that the effect of the narcotics on ethanol consumption is relatively specific. Both C57BL/6J mice and Long-Evans Hooded rats used in this study have the advantage that they voluntarily consume a much greater volume of 5% or 10% ethanol than the Sprague-Dawley rats. Yet, the effects of narcotics were similar in all three strains. These findings suggest that the effects of narcotics on ethanol consumption are independent of the ethanol-preference status of the animals.

In the chronic experiments, withdrawal from morphine increased the selection and consumption of ethanol in both adult and neonatal rats. The treated animals showed increases not only in the volume of ethanol consumed but also in the preference-aversion cutoff concentrations reached. The selection of ethanol appeared to be specific since the morphine-treated rats showed no preference for quinine solution but exhibited a high preference for the ethanol-sucrose mixture and not the sucrose solution, whereas the opposite was observed for the controls.

During a period of forced drinking of ethanol, the quantity of ethanol consumed by morphine-pretreated rats was not significantly greater than that consumed by the saline-treated controls. Yet the appearance of the abstinence signs was significantly more severe and developed earlier in the rats pretreated with either morphine or methadone. This would seem to indicate that pretreatment with narcotics causes an increase in the degree of physical dependence subsequently produced by ethanol. The similar findings in neonates were interesting in that exposure to narcotics during the postnatal period to 6 weeks of age also significantly increased the degree of physical dependence later produced by ethanol (using withdrawal jumping as an index). It has been our experience, as well as that of others, that the development of physical dependence on ethanol is significantly more rapid when rats were exposed to ethanol during the postnatal period.[8] However, the potentiation of physical dependence on ethanol by morphine or methadone has not been reported, although suggestions have been made that some degree of cross-tolerance may exist.[9] These phenomena warrant further studies on the mechanistic aspects of ethanol-narcotic interactions.

The findings that acute morphine and methadone at the higher concentrations both delayed the initial rise in blood ethanol and were followed by a prolongation of its disappearance may be attributed to interference with absorption and distribution of ethanol by the narcotics. It should be noted that in this study, ethanol was administered intraperitoneally, and any circulatory changes induced by the narcotics may alter absorption and distribution of ethanol in the gastrointestinal tract.

In addition to these pharmacokinetic changes, other mechanisms may play a role in the interactions between opiates and ethanol. Recently, several studies in the literature have suggested a relationship between narcotics and ethanol. For example, Ross *et al.*,[10] describing ethanol preference in the hamster, reported that morphine or levorphanol, but not dextrorphan, suppress ethanol consumption, and this is in good agreement with our findings. These investigators further suggested that naloxone blocks the ethanol-induced decrease in brain calcium as a possible common opiate-alcohol addictive mechanism. Blum *et al.*[11] furthered the earlier suggestions that acetaldehyde, the major metabolite of ethanol, condenses with catecholamines to produce a tetrahydroisoquinoline alkaloid, which may be responsible for the mechanism of ethanol dependence. These investigators showed that salsolinol and 6, 7-dihydroxy-tetrahydroisoquinoline intensify the ethanol withdrawal reactions. Amit and Levitan[12] proposed that the catecholaminergic activity may be critical in the development of self-administration of ethanol and morphine and that dopamine and norepinephrine may be differentially involved in the voluntary intake of these two compounds.

From the findings presented here and those reported recently in the literature, there appears to be good agreement on the interactions between narcotics and ethanol in animals. During withdrawal from opiates ethanol consumption is increased, and this may ease some of the withdrawal discomforts. Whether these findings also bear some relevance to the widespread use of ethanol by narcotic users remains to be determined.

References

1. Roizin, L. 1969. Interaction of methadone and ethanol. Presentation at meeting of Eastern section of American Psychiatric Association, New York.
2. Isbell, H., N. F. Fraser, A. Wikler, R. E. Belleville & A. J. Eisenman. 1955. An experimental study of the etiology of "rum-fit" and delirium tremens. *Q. J. Stud. Alcohol* **16:** 1.
3. Jackson, G. W. & A. Richman. 1973. Alcohol use among narcotic addicts. Alcohol World **1:** 25–28.
4. Venho, I., R. Eerola, E. V. Venho & O. Vartiainen. 1955. Sensitization to morphine by experimentally induced alcoholism in white mice. Ann. Med. Exp. Biol. Fenn. **33:** 249–252.
5. Eerola, R., I. Venho, O. Vartiainen & E. V. Venho. 1975. Acute alcoholic poisoning and morphine: An experimental study of the synergism of morphine and ethyl alcohol in mice. Ann. Med. Exp. Biol. Fenn. **33:** 253–26.
6. Forney, R. B., H. R. Hulpien & F. W. Hughes. 1962. The comparative enhancement of the depressant action of alcohol by eight representative ataractic and analgesic drugs. Experientia **18:** 468–470.
7. Sinclair, J. D., J. Adkins & S. Walker. 1973. Morphine-induced suppression of voluntary alcohol drinking in rats. Nature **246:** 425–527.
8. Cicero, T. J., S. R. Snider, V. J. Perez & L. W. Swanson. 1971. Physical dependence on and tolerance to alcohol in the rat. Physiol. Behav. **6:** 191–198.
9. Kissin, B. 1974. Interactions of ethyl alcohol and other drugs. *In* The Biology of Alcoholism. B. Kissin & H. Begleiter, Eds. Vol. **3:** 109–161. Plenum Press. New York, N.Y.
10. Ross, D., R. J. Hartmann & I. Geller. 1976. Ethanol preference in the hamster: effects of morphine sulfate and naltrexone, a long-acting morphine antagonist. Presented in Proceedings of Western Pharmacology Society Meeting. San Francisco, Calif.
11. Blum, K., J. D. Eubanks & J. E. Wallace. 1975. Proceedings 37th Annual Meeting Committee of Problems on Drug Dependence, Washington, D.C.
12. Amit, Z. & D. E. Levitan. 1975. Ethanol and morphine self-administration: A possible relationship based on differential involvement of catecholamines. *In* Proceedings of Satellite Symposium 6th International Congr. Pharmac. Helsinki, 1975. J. D. Sinclair & K. K. Kilanaa, Eds.: 85–100.
13. Bonnichsen, R. K. & H. Thoerell. 1951. An enzymatic method for the microdetermination of ethanol. Scand. J. Clin. Lab. Invest. **3:** 58–62.

POLYDRUG ABUSE AND THE MATURING NATIONAL DRUG ABUSE DATA BASE*

Robert L. DuPont

Director
National Institute on Drug Abuse
Rockville, Maryland 20852

Let me begin by describing the word "polydrug." I confess my involvement with the first official use of the word. It is a Federal political term, rather than a scientific term, which captures some important ideas. Despite its utility, it is difficult to relate to the word in a scholarly or scientific way. This word became big in the field about 2½ years ago. That was the time when the Federal Government's drug abuse response appeared to be preoccupied with the heroin problem. There was also a quite separate Federal concern with the alcohol problem, but there was a growing recognition that there were drug problems that were distinct from either the alcohol problem or the heroin problem. It was this concern with these other drug problems that led to the coining of the term "polydrug." A tremendous bureaucratic shoving and tugging went on within the Federal establishment at that time about how to react to this concept. Many budgeteers feared that we were talking about some overwhelming new drug problem that would break the Federal budget. Others worried that the new interest in the polydrug problem signaled the premature end of the Federal anti-heroin efforts. Some treatment experts doubted that we knew how to treat polydrug abuse.

I am happy to tell you that today, to a substantial extent, the polydrug hysteria has quieted down. It's clear that the Federal Government's interest in the drug problem extends to more than heroin. About 55 percent of the people who are in federally funded treatment programs have problems with heroin; the remaining 45 percent do not. This rough relationship has not changed over the last couple of years. So there is a clear Federal emphasis on other drug problems as well as on heroin. The polydrug concept helped give that concern with other drug problems a status with the Government, without reducing the primary concern with heroin problems. But it is curious to me that the word "polydrug" has now gotten mixed up in the public dialogue with the concept of "multiple drug use." As polydrug was used, at least in the Federal Government, it included problems with the use of any drug other than alcohol or heroin, even if these problems involved the use of only one drug. A person who was abusing marihuana, for example, in some curious way was considered a "polydrug abuser"—a very strange concept. But that is the way that word was used.

Now, having dispensed with the slippery word polydrug, I would like to tell you about the National Institute on Drug Abuse (NIDA). NIDA's top priority is on *knowledge development*. This commitment is something we have talked about a great deal within the staff, and I am happy to say it is a clear Institute priority. NIDA invests about $34 million a year in research projects

* After-dinner speech.

and an additional $12 million in demonstration projects. This total of $46 million is about 21 percent of NIDA's total budget. The remainder of NIDA's budget supports a variety of activities, but most supports community-based treatment.

Drug abuse is today a major knowledge opportunity area for people with many different interests. Drug abuse offers an opportunity to focus attention in generating major new understanding. In the basic research area, the work with the opiate receptor and the endogenous morphine-like substance is a fundamental new area of understanding with exciting potential therapeutic implications, but in addition, this research area promises new understanding of nerve and brain functioning. This is a basic area of knowledge breakthrough which has grown out of the drug abuse field. I am proud to say that virtually all the major investigators now working in this area are supported by NIDA.

In the clinical area of treatment efficacy, there is also a major potential for knowledge development with direct relevance for the whole rehabilitation-treatment area. In the past, there has been a paucity of clearly defined measurable goals. Being a psychiatrist, I am painfully aware of this deficiency in the psychiatric fields. Reluctance to get at the hard issues of evaluation has characterized broad areas of contemporary health and social programming. In the modern drug abuse treatment area, we have from the beginning, only a decade ago, been uniquely concerned with measurable outcomes and the definition of objectives. We have often fallen short of achieving the objectives we want, but at least we in the drug abuse treatment field have been committed to trying to achieve specified objectives. There has also been a commitment to measure results right from the beginning. That is a sign of strength.

In the epidemiologic area, the tremendous increase in drug use in the late 1960's is a major social change. The understanding of why that happened and what the consequences of that change were remain to me among the most fascinating aspects in the drug abuse field. I'm going to say more about that in a minute.

In the management area, and I know that this is not an area that many of you are interested in, the problem of managing scarce resources in order to achieve community-wide objectives is an area in which the drug abuse field is way ahead of any similar field. The emphasis that has been placed by the Federal Government on the management of resources, using the concept of "slot costs" and "matrix management"—not very attractive words perhaps to some of you scientists—helps achieve specific objectives within strict cost constraints.

In 1971 the drug abuse issue hit as a national concern leading to the creation of the White House Special Action Office for Drug Abuse Prevention. There has been talk about that as a political reaction as if some people in office then created the drug abuse issue. A little more reflective view of this would show that whoever had been President in 1971 would have reacted strongly to the drug abuse issue. The drug abuse issue simply had to be dealt with then because there was a significant change in American society which triggered a major public reaction. One of the first things to be worried about at that time was the nature and extent of the drug abuse problem—who was using, how much, with what consequences, and what were the trends in drug-using behavior. We are now beginning to reap the rich harvest from those initial investments of sizeable Federal funds in drug abuse research. I am going to review tonight a couple of the newer data bases which resulted from that investment because they have important potentials for all drug abuse research. This new data can help answer questions about what the most common types of drug problems are and who is using which drugs alone and in various combinations. These answers will help focus our concerns in the area of multiple drug use. In this regard, I would like to particularly pay my respects to Jerry Jaffe, the fellow who took the terrific political heat of that moment in 1971. To his credit, he began many of the programs that I am going to talk about tonight. It is interesting to me also, perhaps somewhat of a sign of the times, that the drug abuse issue has been moved from the Oval Office of the White House in 1971 to the Oval Room of the Hotel Roosevelt, where we are meeting tonight. This movement from a political area to a scientific area is important. I don't think we could have been here tonight without the political involvement. I am not one who thinks politics is insignificant or unimportant. In our field, the politics provided the public support for many of our current efforts. The maturing process of using this public support is well under way. One of these new data bases is the annual national surveys of drug use. The most recent reported survey was made in late 1974 and early 1975. Data collection is not yet complete on this year's survey. The 1974 survey followed up the Marihuana Commission data for 1971 and 1972. To select a few numbers from this rich data source, I will focus on the numbers of people who are current users of the most commonly used drugs. These are the numbers of Americans aged 12 and over who used each of these drugs at least once in the 30 days prior to the 1974 survey: alcohol—94 million; tobacco—67 million; marihuana—13 million; nonmedical use of psychotropic medications—2 million; hallucinogens—1 million; and cocaine—1 million. Somewhat lower numbers reported current use of heroin, inhalants, and other drugs. In terms of trends, the increase in marihuana use among young people was one of the most striking changes between 1972 and 1974. This means that 12 percent of the Nation's 12- to 17-year-olds were current marihuana users in late 1974. I find this an astoundingly high figure. There was no increase during those 2 years in the marihuana consumption of those over 25 years of age. Many of us thought there would be a sharp rise in marihuana use by oldsters—over 25—but that has not been the case. The big increase has been and continues to be among the young, the under-21 age group. Another random figure: Back in 1967 only 5 percent of college students in the United States reported they had ever used marihuana, but by 1975 that number stood at 55 percent. That figure gives some idea of the historic change in American drug use over the last decade. Currently, we have a major exposure of the population to substances about which we know not nearly enough. Both the exposure and the knowledge are growing. I cannot confidently say that the rate of growth of the latter is greater than the former. In addition to the annual national survey of all people 12 years of age and older, NIDA also supports an annual survey of the Nation's high school senior classes by Lloyd Johnston from the Survey Research Center at the University of Michigan. Lloyd will study a sample of 16,000 high school seniors each year for 5 years, beginning in 1975. He will follow each of these cohorts over a 5-year period. Thus, we can follow trends within and between cohorts over time. Let me share a few of Lloyd's interesting 1975 numbers with you. Twenty-eight percent of last year's graduating class reported marihuana use within the 30 days preceding the survey, and 6.2 percent reported daily marihuana use at the time of the survey. Thus, in a national sample, 6.2 percent reported daily marihuana use. This was 0.2 percent more than reported daily alcohol use in the same survey. This is the first time I have seen a national sample where marihuana consumption at the heavy end of the spectrum exceeded alcohol consumption. Current psychedelic drug use stood at 6 percent. Our common professional wisdom tells us that this particular drug problem went away several years ago. That wisdom is plainly wrong. The numbers continue to rise nationally for psychedelic use. Amphetamines were currently used by 9 percent, barbiturates—5 percent, tranquilizers (this is nonmedical use)—4 percent, cocaine—2 percent, and heroin—1 percent. Of the high school seniors surveyed, 2.3 percent reported they had used heroin at least once in their lifetimes. Again, this is a startlingly high figure.

Now I would like to call your attention to the tables and go over these quickly in the hopes of interesting you in these important new data sources. The first table is taken from a one-time study done by Louis Judd in San Diego. He looked at 131 treatment agencies serving substance abusers in six cities. He

TABLE 1

PERCENTAGE OF WEEKLY INTAKE OF EACH TYPE OF AGENCY BY TYPE OF DRUG USE

	All Agencies	Alcohol Agencies	Narcotics Agencies	Mixed Substance Agencies	CMH Agencies
Solely alcohol	51	87	0	37	20
Solely narcotics	16	0	52	22	9
Narcotics with alcohol	6	2	32	7	3
Narcotics with non-opiate drugs	8	0	32	7	7
Alcohol with non-opiate drugs	17	11	0	21	55
Solely non-opiate drugs	2	0	0	5	5

asked the question, *What specific drug problems do the clients you are helping have?* You see in TABLE 1 that only 2 percent of the drug abuse clients did not have a problem with either alcohol or heroin even though, of course, many had problems with more than one substance. This suggests that the Federal focus around alcohol on the one hand and heroin on the other is not inappropriate to the needs of many substance abusers.

TABLE 2 shows primary and secondary drug problems for our Federal Treatment System Admissions Report. This comes to a total of 15,000 admissions a month—a massive data collection system with unique data on each of these patients. This table shows the primary drug problem for which the client is being treated. This is shown across the top, whereas the secondary drug problem is shown along the left-hand side. If you look at the secondary drugs, you will see that heroin and alcohol have the lowest percentage of any secondary drug or the highest percentage of "none," 54 and 62 percent, respectively. Notice that barbiturates, amphetamines, and cocaine show that only 16 to 18 percent of the people who have problems with those drugs do not have a problem with some other drug. These CODAP data show a different pattern in terms of the existence of a secondary drug problem for various primary drug problems. If you will notice the row labeled "marihuana" and read across, you will see that in

TABLE 2

PRIMARY BY SECONDARY DRUG PROBLEM AT ADMISSION—ALL DRUGS (IN PERCENTAGES)

	Primary Drug												
Secondary Drug	Heroin	Illegal Metha-done	Other Opiates	Alcohol	Barbi-turates	Other Seda-tives	Am-phet-amines	Cocaine	Mari-huana	Hallu-cinogens	Inhal-ants	Over-the-Counter	Other
None	54	24	34	62	16	33	18	16	41	13	39	41	49
Heroin	N/A*	40	23	4	7	4	8	17	3	3	2	4	6
Illegal methadone	4	N/A	1	0	0	0	0	0	0	0	0	0	1
Other opiates	5	4	2	0	3	3	2	2	1	1	0	1	4
Alcohol	4	5	6	N/A	14	17	11	6	26	7	12	18	9
Barbiturates	6	11	11	5	N/A	10	15	9	7	12	3	5	5
Sedatives	1	4	7	4	10	N/A	4	2	2	3	1	7	5
Amphetamines	3	2	4	4	16	8	N/A	10	8	16	5	4	1
Cocaine	10	3	3	1	3	1	4	N/A	2	5	0	0	1
Marihuana	12	7	7	18	22	18	26	31	N/A	39	35	15	13
Hallucinogens	1	0	2	1	6	4	11	6	9	N/A	3	4	3
Inhalants	0	0	0	0	1	1	1	1	1	1	N/A	1	0
Over-the-counter	0	0	0	1	1	1	0	0	0	0	0	N/A	1
Other	0	0	0	0	1	0	0	0	0	0	0	0	2
Total percentage	100	100	100	100	100	100	100	100	100	100	100	100	100
Total N	30736	352	1102	3890	2318	1110	2138	531	7204	1205	641	82	241
Cramer's V = .19													
Excluded cases = 2163													

* N/A = Not Applicable.

the opiate area there are relatively small numbers in terms of secondary problems, whereas if you look at cocaine, hallucinogens, and inhalants, they are all over 30 percent for secondary problems associated with primary marihuana problems. This pattern of seeing cocaine, hallucinogens, and inhalants associated with marihuana problems is a very common one in several data sources. My major point, however, is not related to either primary or secondary drugs, but it is that this source, covering admissions each month to over 1,600 clinics located throughout the Nation, contains valuable data which can answer many basic questions about demographic characteristics and drug use patterns.

Next is TABLE 3, which comes from the DAWN system. DAWN is a program sponsored jointly by the Drug Enforcement Administration and NIDA.

TABLE 3

DRUGS MOST FREQUENTLY MENTIONED IN COMBINATION WITH AMPHETAMINES—DAWN SYSTEM*

Amphetamines and:	Number	Percentage
1. Hallucinogens	813	27.8
2. Narcotic analgesics	732	25.1
3. Barbiturate sedatives	664	22.8
4. Alcohol	599	20.5

* Based on 2917 mentions of amphetamines with up to two other drugs: 7/73–6/74.

DRUGS MOST FREQUENTLY MENTIONED IN COMBINATION WITH DIAZEPAM–DAWN SYSTEM*

Diazepam and:	Number	Percentage
1. Alcohol	2179	33.3
2. Narcotic analgesics	1231	18.8
3. Barbiturate sedatives	1006	15.3
4. Non-barbiturate sedatives	994	15.2

* Based on 6540 mentions of Diazepam with up to two other drugs: 6/73–7/74.

It covers 24 major metropolitan areas in the United States, plus samples from 200 representative communities, so that we have a national panel which is representative of the whole U. S. population. DAWN reports on a monthly basis in three areas: (1) emergency rooms, where there are about 15,000 emergency-room episodes reported each month, (2) medical examiners, who report about 800 overdose deaths a month, and (3) crisis centers, which report about 6,000 treatment episodes a month. This totals about 22,000 health-related events a month associated with drug use. In TABLE 3 you see which drugs were used most commonly in association with amphetamines and diazepam (Valium®). Again, these are only illustrative data that are available in mind-boggling richness from this new data source.

The CODAP reports are now published on a quarterly basis, and any of you could write to us and get them. I am interested in your criticisms, comments, and questions about these and other reports I have mentioned. The DAWN study comes out on a monthly basis. However, its current format makes it difficult to use. The National Survey of Drug Use and the Lloyd Johnston high school cohort studies are done annually and published in many places.

TABLE 4 comes from one of my favorite studies, the Jack O'Donnell study of drug use of young men. The basic population described in TABLE 4 is a national sample of males who were 20 to 30 years old in 1974. Thus, it describes the birth cohorts of 1944 to 1954. I have picked out one table to review with you. It relates to multiple drug use in this population. Note that the use of any substance is positively associated with the use of all the others. Notice that a "yes" answer in each column is associated with a higher rate of use of each other substance than is a "no" answer. The differences vary with different drugs, but that characteristic association runs throughout these data. The association has nothing to do with whether the index substance is a licit drug or an illicit drug. If you look in the row for marihuana and read across, you will notice that 59 percent who use tobacco also use marihuana, whereas only 27 percent who do not use tobacco use marihuana. Clearly, this is a strong correlation. Now compare that with the alcohol numbers. Of the people in this sample who use alcohol, 57 percent also use marihuana, whereas only 4 percent of those—admittedly a very small number—who do not use alcohol use marihuana. Now if you will look down the entire column for alcohol, you will see that if a person does not use alcohol, it is very unlikely he will use any of the other drugs. Notice all the zeroes and the ones running down that "no" alcohol column. It is clear that if a person does not use alcohol, he does not use these other drugs, although again the numbers are relatively small. Now if you will look over to the marihuana column, the figures are even more interesting—partly because there are many people in the sample who do not use marihuana. That is, in this sample, 1,128 report no marihuana use. The striking aspect of this column is that if people do not use marihuana, they simply do not use other illicit drugs. We are not talking about just a few Christian Scientists or Mormons—a big chunk of society is represented in that column. This is one of the sources of data which supports the concept that marihuana is the gateway into illicit drug use in America today. If a person does not go through that marihuana gate, he is not likely to use other illicit substances. O'Donnell in his study also shows that there is a chronological order of use. Thus, marihuana use does occur before the use of these other illicit drugs. For example, young men who report use of psychedelics used marihuana before they used psychedelics. Let's look at the marihuana numbers in a slightly different way. Read across the marihuana row. You will see that in terms of the other drugs, starting with the psychedelics, the marihuana "yes" numbers are: psychedelics—100 percent, stimulants—97 percent, sedatives—97 percent, heroin—99 percent, other opiates—91 percent, and cocaine—100 percent. This makes the same point once again in a compelling fashion. If you look down the heroin "yes" column, you see that the people who use heroin also use all the other drugs right down the line. The lowest number is 80 percent for sedatives. Thus, heroin users use all other drugs. In fact, O'Donnell shows (not in this table) that 60 percent of the people in this group who have ever used heroin have used all nine of the other categories as well, so that a heroin positive in a general sample signals a high probability of the use of all other illicit (and licit) drugs.

The most common double drug use pattern in the O'Donnell study is the combination of alcohol and tobacco. This pattern accounts for 33 percent of the entire population. If you include marihuana with alcohol and tobacco, you find that 22 percent of the population fall into that category. Four percent of

TABLE 4

PERCENTAGE OF USERS AND NONUSERS OF EACH DRUG WHO HAVE USED THE OTHER DRUGS*

	Tobacco		Alcohol		Marihuana		Psychedelics		Stimulants		Sedatives		Heroin		Opiates		Cocaine	
	Yes	No	Yes	No	Yes	No	Yes	No	Yes	No	Yes	No	Yes	No	Yes	No	Yes	No
Number	2211	299	2434	76	1382	1128	550	1960	581	1929	409	2101	148	2362	493	2017	352	2158
Tobacco	—	—	90	41	94	81	95	86	96	86	95	87	99	87	96	86	96	87
Alcohol	99	85	—	—	100	94	100	96	100	96	100	96	100	97	100	96	100	96
Marihuana	59	27	57	4	—	—	100	43	97	42	97	47	99	52	91	46	100	48
Psychedelics	24	9	23	0	40	†	—	—	71	7	80	11	92	18	72	10	89	11
Stimulants	25	7	24	0	41	1	75	9	—	—	82	12	86	19	71	21	86	13
Sedatives	18	6	17	1	29	1	60	4	58	4	—	—	80	12	60	6	72	7
Heroin	7	†	6	0	11	†	25	1	22	1	29	1	—	—	27	1	38	1
Opiates	21	7	20	0	33	4	65	7	60	7	73	9	91	15	—	—	79	10
Cocaine	15	5	14	0	25	†	57	2	52	3	62	5	90	9	56	4	—	—

* For stimulants, sedatives, and opiates, quasi-medical use was defined as no use.
† Less than half of one percent.

the total group of these young men report the use of all nine drugs at least once in their lives. Remarkably, only 2 percent of the sample report the use of none of the nine categories of drugs.

I will conclude with two final points related to the major issue of our conference here in New York. The question of specific drug interaction is one of tremendous importance. There is a lot of mythologizing about it, and I am sure that those of you who are devoted to a scientific approach to problems share my frustration with the oppressive talk about "garbage heads," as if there were somehow something magical or unspecifiable going on in the area of multiple drug use. This poorly focused talk unfortunately flourishes in the absence of solid fact. As a physician, it is depressing to read the equally fuzzy-headed package inserts about drug infractions which tend to be written by the drug companies' legal departments. These are generally not helpful to clinicians or patients in terms of thinking about specific drug interactions.

One small study that I was involved with in this area investigated the etiology of heroin overdoses. Mark Greene and I conducted the study in the District of Columbia, comparing people who died of overdoses of methadone and heroin with a group of heroin and methadone users who were murdered. We found that among the heroin positives in the two groups, there was an excess of alcohol in the group that died of overdoses. This suggested to us that there was an addictive or perhaps even a synergistic effect between alcohol and heroin, such that a dose of heroin which would not have been lethal became lethal because the person was also drinking. Interestingly, we did not find this among the methadone deaths. I do not know why. Lou Gottschalk has done a multicity study which went a step beyond what Mark and I did. He looked at the concentrations of substances in the tissues of the decedents and showed that the concentrations of various drugs, including heroin and methadone, for people who had alcohol in addition to the other substances were only half as great as for those who had the lethal outcome without alcohol.

Another area of great interest is the issue of the oral pharynx cancer and the increased risk associated with alcohol and tobacco use. Heavy use of each drug alone appears to increase the risk three times above the risk for nonusers. For simultaneous heavy use of alcohol and tobacco, the risk is 15 times as great as that of nonusers.

The most recent issue of the *Toronto Journal* has an article reporting that dogs injected with Penicillin G when smoking marihuana have gradual seizures. This does not occur if the dogs are given either penicillin or marihuana alone. What the significance of that is, I don't know, but both of those drugs are widely used.

Another area of great concern is the effect of the combination of marihuana and alcohol on driving. We are now sensitive to the problems of alcohol and driving, but I think we haven't begun to grasp the impact of these new high levels of youthful marihuana consumption. Marihuana use is correlated with alcohol use. The old idea that if people used marihuana they wouldn't use alcohol, or vice versa, is not borne out by any of our recent studies. The increasingly common simultaneous use of both drugs appears to be particularly devastating to driving performance.

I hope I have wetted your appetite for some new national data sources. There are still lots of problems with these data systems. But they are producing data right now, and I hope that it will be useful to you as you try to put multiple drug use into perspective. The next time you say, "I wish we knew what percentage of a certain group were using_____," or "What is the likelihood of two specific drugs being used in conjunction with each other within a population?" I hope you will think again about what I have said tonight. Maybe we do know what those numbers are. If you will get in touch with us at NIDA, we will try to get you the data.

The second point that I want to make sure that I made is that NIDA's top priority is *knowledge development.* This remains and will remain our top interest, not just in the research area, but across-the-board. We consider drug abuse not a field of a fad, but a field filled with opportunity. Drug abuse is one of the most exciting areas of contemporary research opportunity.

Thank you.

INTERACTIONS OF PSYCHOACTIVE DRUGS WITH NARCOTIC AGONISTS AND ANTAGONISTS*

Roger P. Maickel, Carol S. Lambert, and Joseph E. Zabik

Department of Pharmacology, Medical Sciences Program
Indiana University
Bloomington, Indiana 47401

Monique C. Braude

Division of Research, National Institute on Drug Abuse
Rockville, Maryland 20852

There is no question that the problems with drug usage generated by the widespread drug abuse phenomenon of the 1960's have led to a vast increase in the incidence of drug-drug interactions. Some of these interactions may have been beneficial to the subject, such as using barbiturates to come down from an amphetamine-induced high. Others were obviously harmful to the subject—even to the point of death—such as adding strychnine to a dosage of lysergic acid diethylamide. In addition to usage of various combinations and permutations of drugs on the "street," the drug abuse phenomenon increased the likelihood for unexpected drug combinations to occur in various therapeutic situations. For example, physicians found themselves in the unenviable situation of treating bad trips evoked by a hallucinogen with other psychoactive agents such as antipsychotic drugs. While such pharmacotherapy often produced the desired amelioration of the psychotomimetic state, it led, not infrequently to some other sort of adverse effect because of a drug-drug interaction.

A particular subcategory of the overall drug abuse problem is that dealing with the chronic user of opiate narcotic drugs such as heroin, morphine, or meperidine. The narcotic abuser represents a modestly unique individual with a variety of problems: pharmacological, such as physical dependence and tolerance; medical; and sociological.[1] Such an individual may readily turn to polydrug abuse in a sort of "mix and match" approach to self-medication, an approach further complicated by the lack of quality control (especially with regard to labeling and purity) of street drugs.[2]

Polydrug problems—and consequently, the potential adverse drug-drug interactions—for the abuser of narcotic drugs may arise in a number of ways.

1. On the street, the individual may, in addition to his or her use of heroin, concomitantly ingest alcohol, other opiates, or other drugs, in the quest for a longer, better, or different "high." The number of possible combinations is virtually unlimited; a new textbook of pharmacology could almost be generated from the anecdotal reports of interactions from such polydrug usage.[3]

2. When supplies of heroin become scarce, the dependent individual may turn to other agents as "substitutes" to alleviate the discomforts of withdrawal, or to achieve a maintenance state until heroin is once more available. In such a situation, "downers" such as alcohol, barbiturates, or other sedative drugs, or

* Supported in part by contract PHS HSM 42-73-226.

even amphetamines have been used, often with resulting adverse drug-drug interactions.[4]

3. Acceptance of an addict into a treatment program, often with substitution of an agonist (such as methadone or alpha-acetylmethadol) or with chronic administration of an antagonist (such as naloxone or naltrexone), may produce yet another opportunity for drug-drug interactions. This is especially true if psychotherapeutic agents such as anxiolytic, antidepressant, or antipsychotic agents are included in all overall therapeutic regimen.[5]

Despite this rather significant likelihood for drug-drug interactions to occur, carefully designed studies of such interactions, especially in terms of animal models for evaluating undesirable or toxic effects, are relatively few in number. As recently as 1975, the paucity of such studies could be seen in the fact that various reports to the Committee on Drug Dependence of the National Academy of Sciences contained virtually no information on drug-drug interactions. In fact, few, if any, drug combinations, other than classical narcotic agonist-narcotic antagonist interactions, had been examined at all.

Materials and Methods

Adult, male Swiss-Webster mice and Sprague-Dawley rats were obtained from Murphy Breeding Laboratories, Plainfield, Ind. Animals were maintained in a temperature-controlled animal room on a 14/10 light-dark lighting cycle for 7–10 days prior to use in any experimental studies. Food (Wayne Lab Blox) and tap water were available *ad lib*.

Standard experimental procedures, all previously used or developed in this laboratory, formed the basis for all experiments. Open field behavior was assessed by the method of Maickel and Johnson;[6] actophotometer activity (mice) by the method of Maickel *et al.*;[7] and actophotometer activity (rats) by the method of Light;[8] rotorod measurements by the method of Zabik *et al.*;[9] body temperature measurements by the method of Maickel[10]; and deprivation-induced fluid consumption by the method of Gerald and Maickel.[11]

Drugs were administered by subcutaneous injection as solutions in distilled water or as aqueous suspensions using 0.5% methylcellulose. Volumes of injection were held constant at 0.1 ml per 100 g body weight. Control animals were dosed with the appropriate vehicle.

Results

Against this rather sketchy (at best) background, it seemed reasonable to examine the problem using relatively simple test systems in the hope of gathering information useful to the therapeutic community in preventing toxic or fatal interactions. The first studies were designed to see if simple combinations of a fixed dose of a test drug with varying doses of a second agent could alter dose-response curves to yield information regarding antagonism or potentiation. Dose-lethality curves for single doses of a variety of narcotic agonists and antagonists were obtained in mice under standard conditions; these data are presented in Table 1. As can be seen, the 2 hour and 24 hour LD_{50} values

TABLE 1

LETHALITY OF NARCOTIC AGONISTS AND ANTAGONISTS IN MICE*

	2 Hour		24 Hour	
Compound	LD_{50}	95% C.L.	LD_{50}	95% C.L.
Cyclazocine	197	178–214	177	163–193
Levallorphan	204	198–210	200	183–219
Naloxone	260	254–267	261	237–288
Naltrexone	586	567–608	551	529–575
LAMM	595	542–640	111	91–130
Methadone	66	62–69	62	54–69
Morphine	870	727–1052	738	629–840

* Each LD_{50} value (mg/kg free base) was obtained from 8–10 groups of 20–25 adult, male Swiss-Webster mice (20–25 g), maintained in individual beakers at an environmental temperature of 22–25° C. Drugs were administered in aqueous solution by s.c. injection at log dose intervals. Data were processed by the Litchfield-Wilcoxon procedure.

were generally similar except for LAAM, which showed a marked decrease in LD_{50} (i.e., an increase in potency) at the 24 hour point. It is important to note also that to achieve tight confidence limits, such as those reported in TABLE 1, large numbers of animals (160–250 per compound) were required. Attempts to obtain closely reproducible estimations of LD_{50} values with fewer mice (3–5 doses, 5–10 mice per dose) met with failure, presumably owing, at least in part, to the generally steep slope of the dose-response curves.

Several studies were made of the effects of pretreatment of mice with a second drug on the lethality curve subsequently produced by methadone. The results are presented in TABLE 2. With naloxone as the pretreatment agent, the results indicated a classical antagonist-agonist relationship, with an increase in the LD_{50} value for methadone and no significant change in the slope of the dose-response curve. Pretreatment with chlordiazepoxide at a fixed dose of 40 mg/kg, s.c., had no significant effect on the LD_{50} value for methadone, although the slope of the lethality curve was significantly increased. Conversely, pretreatment with chlorpromazine at a fixed dose of 20 mg/kg, s.c., significantly

TABLE 2

EFFECTS OF PRETREATMENT WITH DRUGS ON METHADONE LETHALITY CURVES*

Pretreatment	LD_{50} (mg/kg)	Slope
Saline	64	92.3
Naloxone (60 mg/kg)	143†	89.7
Chlordiazepoxide (40 mg/kg)	59	127.7†
Chlorpromazine (20 mg/kg)	66	53.7†

* Each value was determined by pretreating mice with the stated dosage s.c. 1 hour prior to administration of methadone at various doses from 10–110 mg/kg, s.c. Each LD_{50} curve represents 80–140 mice.

† Values differing significantly from the corresponding control ($p < 0.05$).

decreased the slope of the lethality curve, also without significantly influencing the LD_{50}.

These studies were performed using a fixed pretreatment time of 1 hour. Pilot studies with varying pretreatment times and a variety of drugs indicate the complexity of the test system in terms of the confounding variable of differing rates of drug metabolism. For example, pretreatment with nalorphine, a potent narcotic antagonist, was effective only when pretreatment time was <1 hour before methadone administration, possibly reflecting the rapid metabolic degradation rate of that antagonist. In contrast, naltrexone was most effective when administered >1 hour before methadone, suggesting slow absorption and distribution or the possibility of an active metabolite.

TABLE 3

EFFECTS OF AGGREGATION ON LETHALITY IN MICE*

Compound	Dose	#/Beaker	% Dead (2 Hours)
Cyclazocine	130	1	12.5
		2	20.8
		4	55.6
Levallorphan	179	1	16.7
		2	25.0
		4	38.9
Naloxone	220	1	20.8
		2	50.0
		4	63.9
LAMM	350	1	12.5
		2	25.0
		4	55.6
Methadone	53	1	8.3
		2	37.5
		4	91.7
d-Amphetamine	100	1	45.8
		2	70.8
		4	94.4

* Doses are in mg/kg, s.c., for animals maintained at 22–25° C environmental temperature. Each value for % deaths is based on 20–36 animals; as animals died, they were replaced in the individual groups.

A chance observation, namely that some drugs tested seemed to be more toxic when animals were grouped in test cages, led to a detailed investigation of the effects of aggregation. Groups of one, two, or four mice were dosed with approximately an LD_{20}, then placed in beakers having 79 cm^2 of floor space. A dose of 100 mg/kg of *d*-amphetamine was tested under similar conditions for comparison. The data presented in TABLE 3 clearly demonstrate a significant degree of aggregation toxicity for both agonists and antagonists.

Since the increased lethality for *d*-amphetamine-induced aggregation toxicity has been reported to be reduced by lowering the environmental temperature,[12] a similar test was applied to the narcotic agonists and antagonists. The data presented in TABLE 4 clearly demonstrate that these compounds are quite different from *d*-amphetamine. For each of the narcotic agonists and antagonists

TABLE 4

MODIFICATION OF AGGREGATION LETHALITY BY ENVIRONMENTAL TEMPERATURE*

Compound	Dose	Deaths at 24° C	Deaths at 5° C
Cyclazocine	130	55.6	85.0
	110	8.3	58.3
Levallorphan	179	38.9	100.0
	150	8.3	91.7
Naloxone	215	56.2	87.5
	190	0.0	35.0
LAAM	350	55.6	100.0
	300	5.6	58.3
Methadone	40	63.3	91.7
	30	8.3	75.0
d-Amphetamine	100	94.4	5.0
		3.4	0.0

* Doses are in mg/kg., s.c. Experimental conditions were as described in TABLE 3.

treated, lowering the environmental temperature potentiated the lethality. This was in sharp contrast to *d*-amphetamine, where the lowered environmental temperature produced the expected protection from the lethal effects of the drug.

Since these drug effects may have been correlated with maintenance of body temperature in the animals, a series of studies were performed in which rectal temperature of isolated and aggregated mice was measured at environmental temperature of 24°C and 5°C. The data are presented in TABLE 5; as can be seen, all of the drugs tested produced a modest hypothermia in animals maintained at a 24° C environmental temperature, and a pronounced hypothermia when the animals were exposed to the lower environmental temperature of 5° C. Of particular interest is the fact that no differences were observed

TABLE 5

EFFECTS OF AGGREGATION ON DRUG EFFECTS ON BODY TEMPERATURE*

Drug	Dose (mg/kg)	N	#/Beaker	Body Temperature at 60 min at 24° C (° C + S.D.)	Body Temperature at 60 min at 5° C (° C + S.D.)
None	—	12	1	36.5 ± 1.7	34.5 ± 2.8
		16	4	37.5 ± 1.9	36.3 ± 1.9
Cyclazocine	130	12	1	29.6 ± 2.1	11.6 ± 4.1
		16	4	29.5 ± 3.7	15.0 ± 1.9
Levallorphan	179	12	1	28.5 ± 1.4	14.5 ± 1.9
		16	4	31.5 ± 1.9	18.3 ± 3.0
Naloxone	215	12	1	31.6 ± 1.1	17.3 ± 2.0
		16	4	34.5 ± 4.1	19.5 ± 3.3
Methadone	40	12	1	32.7 ± 1.8	13.8 ± 3.1
		16	4	33.0 ± 1.7	16.0 ± 1.9

* Drugs were administered by s.c. injection, and rectal temperatures were measured using a YSI Telethermometer with small animal probe.

with single or aggregated housing of the animals. Preliminary studies indicate that the hypothermic effects of methadone show the development of tolerance to repeated drug dosage, whereas those of naloxone do not.

While testing various drug regimens under repetitive dosage schedules, it became apparent that mice were not the most appropriate animals for chronic studies using the subcutaneous route of administration, so a shift was made to permit the use of rats and other test systems developed in this laboratory. Initial studies indicated that repetitive dosage with behaviorally active quantities of a variety of narcotic agonists and antagonists had no significant effect on liver microsomal oxygenase activity, as measured by aniline hydroxylase

TABLE 6

DRUG EFFECTS IN RATS TREATED CHRONICALLY WITH LAAM*

Chronic Drug	Acute Drug	Dose (mg/kg)	Open Field (Squares/30 min ± S.D.)	Actophotometer (Counts/30 min ± S.D.)	Rotorod (% Failures)
Water	Water	—	82 ± 17	1183 ± 192	2.8%
,,	Chlorpromazine	2.5	58 ± 14†	863 ± 184†	33.3%†
,,	Thiordiazine	4.0	56 ± 9†	812 ± 117†	41.7%†
,,	Desipramine	5.0	77 ± 11	1099 ± 206	11.1%
,,	Imipramine	5.0	81 ± 19	1102 ± 133	8.3%
,,	Chlordiazepoxide	10.0	59 ± 17†	976 ± 174†	52.8%†
,,	Diazepam	4.0	47 ± 11†	821 ± 119†	63.9%†
LAAM	Water	—	115 ± 28	1857 ± 306	4.0%
,,	Chlorpromazine	2.5	78 ± 17†	1132 ± 195†	58.3%†
,,	Thioridazine	4.0	74 ± 27†	1096 ± 244†	44.4%†
,,	Desipramine	5.0	105 ± 20	1931 ± 176	13.9%
,,	Imipramine	5.0	90 ± 11	1616 ± 206	69.4%†
,,	Chlordiazepoxide	10.0	201 ± 39†	2116 ± 222†	47.2%†
,,	Diazepam	4.0	39 ± 17†	799 ± 114†	38.9%†

* Chronic dosage with LAAM was 1 mg/kg, s.c., for days 1–10, 2 mg/kg for days 11–20 and 4 mg/kg for days 21–30. Animals were tested during the period 4–6 hours after the last dose of LAAM. Open-field measurements had N = 12; actophotometer had N = 9; rotorod measurements were 36 tests, 3 on each of 12 rats.

† Values significantly different from corresponding control ($p < 0.05$).

and *p*-nitroanisole demethylase activities *in vitro*. Consequently, it was felt that chronic administration of such dosages would not be confounded by the variable of liver microsomal oxygenase induction.

The first attempt to examine drug interactions in rats utilized a battery of simple behavioral test systems in which standard drugs are known to have reproducible effects. The open-field exploratory behavior of rats has been utilized as a measure of overall activity and as an evaluation of characteristic behavioral typing; the actophotometer has been used as a measure of exploratory motor activity in a novel situation; and the rotorod has been used as a measure of coordinated muscular activity. Rats were treated chronically with LAAM, then given single acute dosages of various psychoactive drugs. The results are summarized in TABLE 6. The only unexpected results were an increased open-field and actophotometer activity in chronic LAAM-treated rats given chlordiazepoxide and an increased rate of rotorod failures of chronic LAAM rats given imipramine. Detailed evaluation of the various subcategories of behavior in the open-field exploratory situation showed no dramatic patterns of change for any of the drug combinations tested.

Previous work by this laboratory has indicated that drug effects on deprivation-induced fluid consumption by rats are a sensitive measure of drug action.[11, 13–16] This is especially true for narcotic agonists and antagonists.[17] On chronic daily administration, the results obtained showed some tolerance with both methadone and LAAM, but none with naloxone (TABLE 7). Of particular interest is the fact that on cessation of chronic dosage of both LAAM and methadone, the animals showed a marked decrease in fluid consumption ("withdrawal"). In fact, after five additional days, the levels of fluid intake had still not returned to normal. In contrast, the chronically dosed naloxone animals

TABLE 7

EFFECTS OF CHRONIC DRUG DOSAGE ON FLUID CONSUMPTION*

Days of Treatment	Dosage	Methadone	LAAM	Naloxone
1	Water	17.9 ± 1.2	18.3 ± 1.0	17.5 ± 0.8
3	"	17.8 ± 1.6	17.9 ± 1.4	17.9 ± 1.1
4	Drug	20.3 ± 1.4	19.3 ± 1.0	12.4 ± 0.3
7	"	19.8 ± 1.7	20.9 ± 1.4	10.9 ± 0.9
10	"	19.1 ± 1.5	21.4 ± 0.4	9.6 ± 1.0
13	"	18.9 ± 1.0	19.9 ± 2.6	10.4 ± 1.1
17	"	18.3 ± 1.0	19.2 ± 1.0	10.6 ± 1.8
18	Water	12.5 ± 1.0	11.0 ± 1.7	14.5 ± 0.6
20	"	15.8 ± 0.8	14.9 ± 2.0	17.4 ± 0.8
23	"	15.8 ± 0.5	16.0 ± 1.7	17.8 ± 1.1

* Animals were dosed daily with methadone (4 mg/kg, s.c.), LAAM (2 mg/kg, s.c.), or naloxone (10 mg/kg, s.c.). Each value is the mean ± S.D. of values obtained from 8 animals.

TABLE 8

EFFECTS OF CHRONIC AGONIST DOSAGE ON FLUID CONSUMPTION ALTERATIONS*

Acute Test Drug	Dose (mg/kg, s.c.)	Chronic Dosage Agent: Vehicle	Methadone	LAAM
Naloxone	10	70.1 ± 4.0%	32.6 ± 6.3%†	27.8 ± 5.1%†
Chlorpromazine	2	42.7 ± 6.1%	42.0 ± 6.5%	47.1 ± 9.7%
Desipramine	10	51.7 ± 6.3%	82.2 ± 6.0%†	83.4 ± 4.0%†
Chlordiazepoxide	10	150.3 ± 10.1%	153.4 ± 5.4%	142.0 ± 8.1%
Methadone	4	117.6 ± 8.2%	—	103.0 ± 4.9%
LAAM	2	114.7 ± 10.3%	101.3 ± 7.4%	—

* Values reported are in percent of previous day fluid consumption for that animal. Each value is the mean ± S.D. of values obtained from 7–8 animals.

† Values different from corresponding chronic vehicle effects of the acute test drug ($p < 0.05$).

showed a return toward normal values on the first day after cessation of drug dosage, with a complete return to predrug baseline values on the next day. In an attempt to utilize this test system to examine drug-drug interactions, groups of rats were dosed chronically with LAAM or methadone for 21 days under the conditions described in TABLE 7. By this time, fluid consumption levels of the animals had returned to predrug baseline levels. On the 22nd day, the animals were dosed with both their regular daily dose of the narcotic agonist plus an additional dose of a second drug prior to the session of fluid consumption. The results obtained are presented in TABLE 8. Naloxone clearly had a greater decremental effect in the chronic LAAM and methadone rats than in rats dosed only with vehicle for 21 days; this presumably reflects agonist-antagonist interactions and is similar to the withdrawal effects shown in TABLE 7. The decremental effects of chlorpromazine and the stimulatory actions of chlordiazepoxide were not influenced by the treatment with the narcotic agonists. In contrast, the ability of desipramine to reduce deprivation-induced fluid consumption was markedly attenuated in the animals treated chronically with LAAM or methadone.

DISCUSSION

In this paper an attempt has been made to describe a variety of test systems examined as possible procedures for studying drug-drug interactions involving narcotic agonists and antagonists. Interactions can be shown in systems as simple and obvious as alteration of a dose-lethality curve; however, the simplicity of the test belies the complexity of subsequent interpretation. A shift to the right of a dose-lethality curve with no change in slope is typical of antagonist activity. But what is the meaning of an increase or decrease in slope with no significant change in LD_{50}? Further complications arise in the design of such experiments when factors such as drug metabolism rates, physiological disposition phenomena such as protein binding, and time design of dosages and lethality points are considered.

Toxicity studies of this type are additionally complicated by the fact that both narcotic agonists and antagonists show an increased toxicity under conditions when the animals are aggregated. This increased toxicity is, like that of *d*-amphetamine, directly proportional to the density of animals in a given space. However, in sharp contrast to amphetamine aggregation toxicity, which is reversed by lowering the environmental temperature, the increased sensitivity of aggregated mice to narcotic agonists and antagonists is further enhanced by lowering the environmental temperature. Indeed, narcotic agonists and antagonists are both hypothermic in cold-exposed mice, with a clear demonstration of tolerance development in animals treated with repeated dosages of methadone. Thus, attempts to utilize the hypothermic effects as an interactive measure are also subject to a variety of confounding variables.

Attempts to use a battery of simple, nonoperative behavioral test systems with rats as the experimental subjects were relatively unsuccessful in studying drug-drug interactions. While some deviations from expected results were observed, no clear-cut rationale could be assigned to the data. Since these simplistic measurements of open field behavior and exploratory activity were not amenable to use, more complex test procedures involving operant conditioning are obviously also fraught with difficulties and complexities, as other papers in this symposium clearly demonstrate.

Perhaps the simplest test procedure useful for the examination of narcotic agonists and antagonists, as well as for studying drug-drug interactions with such agents, is that of deprivation-induced fluid consumption. This test system has been studied extensively in this laboratory and shows responsivity to a wide variety of pharmacologic agents with excellent sensitivity and good reproducibility. For example, significant increases in volume consumed are seen at doses of morphine or methadone as low as 0.5 mg/kg, s.c. Narcotic agonists show a biphasic response, with stimulation of fluid consumption at lower doses and a decremental action at higher doses. In contrast, narcotic antagonists show only the decremental effect, again with excellent sensitivity; threshold doses for naloxone and naltrexone are 0.6 and 6.0 mg/kg, s.c., respectively.

This test system shows the development of tolerance to repeated dosages of LAAM or methadone, with evidence for cross-tolerance and clear-cut withdrawal actions. In contrast, repetitive dosage of naloxone shows no tolerance development; cessation of the drug elicits no evidence for withdrawal. Chronically dosed LAAM or methadone animals show clear-cut evidence for interactions with chlorpromazine and chlordiazepoxide. The latter finding seems of particular interest, since chlordiazepoxide is of itself dipsogenic. This test system seems to be the most useful one developed; further study and extension to other interactions is a future plan.

Acknowledgments

The assistance of a number of people in producing the data included in this paper must be gratefully acknowledged: David Bowman, Judith Chioli, Lorraine Ide, Shu-Shen Liao, Gerald Longa, Sandy Martin, Kimberly Porter, Robert Sexton, Rod Tipton and Deborah Wagner.

In addition, we wish to thank the following for supplying the drugs used in this study:

CIBA-Giegy: desipramine, imipramine
Eli Lilly & Co.: methadone
Endo Laboratories: naloxone, naltrexone
Hoffman-LaRoche: chlordiazepoxide, diazepam, levallorphan
Sandoz: thioridazine
Smith Kline & French: *d*-amphetamine, chlorpromazine
U.S. Public Health Service: L-alpha-acetylmethadol (LAAM)

References

1. National Commission on Marijuana and Drug Abuse (2nd Report). 1973. Drug Use in America: Problem in Perspective. U.S. Govt. Printing Office. Washington, D.C.
2. Bourne, P. G. 1974. Polydrug abuse—considerations in a national strategy. Amer. J. Drug Alcohol Abuse **1:** 141–158.
3. Simpson, D. D. & S. B. Sells. 1974. Patterns of multiple drug abuse: 1969–1971. Int. J. Addictions **9:** 301–314.

4. HOFMANN, F. G. 1975. A Handbook on Drug and Alcohol Abuse. Oxford Univ. Press. New York, N.Y.
5. BOURNE, P. G., Ed. 1974. Addiction. Academic Press. New York, N.Y.
6. MAICKEL, R. P. & S. A. JOHNSON. 1973. Effects of various anorexigenic agents on open field behavior of rats. Res. Commun. Chem. Pathol. Pharmacol. **6:** 733–739.
7. MAICKEL, R. P., R. M. LEVINE & C. M. QUIRCE. 1974. Differential effects of *d*- and *l*-amphetamine on spontaneous motor activity in mice. Res. Commun. Chem. Pathol. Pharmacol. **8:** 711–714.
8. LIGHT, K. E. 1975. Differential effects of amphetamine enantiomers. M.S. Thesis. Indiana Univ. Bloomington, Ind.
9. ZABIK, J. E., D. P. VAN DAM & R. P. MAICKEL. 1974. Pharmacological and toxicological studies with 1,4-butanediol. Res. Commun. Chem. Pathol. Pharmacol. **8:** 83–90.
10. MAICKEL, R. P. 1970. Interaction of drugs with autonomic nervous function and thermoregulation. Fed. Proc. **29:** 1973–1979.
11. GERALD, M. C. & R. P. MAICKEL. 1969. Evidence for peripheral cholinergic components in thirst-induced water consumption. Int. J. Neuropharmacol. **8:** 337–346.
12. COSTA, E. & S. GARATTINI, Eds. 1970. Amphetamines and Related Compounds. Raven Press. New York, N.Y.
13. MAICKEL, R. P. & G. J. MALONEY. 1972. Effects of barbital on deprivation-induced water consumption in rats. Physiol. Behavior **8:** 1175–1178.
14. MAICKEL, R. P. & R. W. WEBB. 1972. Taste phenomena and drug effects on thirst-induced fluid consumption by rats. Neuropharmacol. **11:** 283–280.
15. MAICKEL, R. P. & G. J. MALONEY. 1973. Effect of various depressant drugs on deprivation-induced water consumption. Neuropharmacol. **12:** 777–782.
16. MAICKEL, R. P. & G. J. MALONEY. 1974. Taste phenomena influences on stimulation of deprivation-induced fluid consumption by rats. Neuropharmacol. **13:** 763–768.
17. MAICKEL, R. P., M. C. BRAUDE & J. E. ZABIK. 1976. The effect of various narcotic agonists and antagonists on deprivation-induced fluid consumption. Neuropharmacol. In press.

EVALUATION OF NARCOTIC AND NARCOTIC ANTAGONIST INTERACTIONS IN PRIMATES*

K. F. Killam, Jr., M. J. Brocco, and C. A. Robinson

Department of Pharmacology
School of Medicine, University of California
Davis, California 95616

In many studies classic interactions between opiate agonists and antagonists have focused upon receptor characteristics as demonstrated by the precipitation of an abstinence syndrome or by blockade of the development of tolerance. In the former, the subject is made dependent upon the opiate by either serial parenteral administrations[1] or by using a depot form of the opiate with a subcutaneous implantation.[2] Once tolerance is developed the purported antagonist may be evaluated. The obverse of the latter from above are studies in which the antagonist is administered followed by effective doses of the opiate. Alterations of the pharmacological effects observed are interpreted as variations on receptor blockade phenomena.

The studies to be reported here are designed to investigate more clinically oriented problems. One strategy for the treatment of narcotic addiction is to make the subject dependent upon a relatively long acting opioid given under medical supervision.[3] Then cross tolerance prevents the subject from behavioral highs from the illicit use of opiates. A possible alternate strategy is to administer a long acting opiate antagonist, again under medical supervision. The presumed receptor blockade should also prevent behavioral highs from illicit opiates. Thus, the same therapeutic goals should be possible from agonists and antagonists.

It is also readily apparent, however, that drug users rarely restrict their drug usage to one or two substances. Thus, drug interactions across classes of substances may result in a variety of responses from reinforcement to frank toxicities.

In the studies to be reported here, rhesus monkeys maintained their dependence on morphine by self-infusion. The effects of methadone, L-alpha-acetylmethadol (LAAM), cyclazocine, naloxone, and naltrexone in these subjects were established. The multiple interactions were then evaluated comparing alterations of established patterns when either alcohol, *d*-amphetamine, diazepam, secobarbital or diphenylhydantoin were combined wth one of the above.

Methods

Adolescent *M. mulatta* of both sexes served as the subjects. The animals were divided into two groups. Group A (20 monkeys) was catheterized using

* Supported by Contract HSM-42-73-263 from NIDA. The authors are grateful for the valuable assistance of Ms. Susan Linkhart, Ms. Julia McNeal, Mr. Douglas Lytle, Mr. William Virgin, and Mr. James Springer. Special thanks are due for the counsel of Dr. G. A. Deneau. d-Amphetamine was supplied by Smith, Kline, and French Labs; diazepam by Roche; LAAM and naltrexone by NIDA; and cyclazocine by Winthrop Labs.

either the jugular or femoral veins and attached to reservoirs arranged for self-infusion. In these animals, alterations in morphine intake and gross behavioral changes were evaluated following methadone, L-alpha-acetylmethadol (LAAM), naloxone, naltrexone, and cyclazocine. Group B (24 monkeys) underwent a two-stage preparation. At stage one, the animals were anesthetized, and eight stainless steel screws with connecting wires were affixed to the skull. The lead wires were soldered to a modified size 16-9 pin Amphenol receptacle. The center pin was removed to allow the passage of a length of silastic tubing. The receptacle was affixed to the skull with screws and dental cement. The emerging catheter was led under the skin and sewn to the musculature in the mid-scapular region. The second stage consisted of the catherization of either the jugular or femoral veins and connection with the exteriorized segment of silastic tubing. An umbilicus made up of the catheter and eight cables within a case-hardened spring was connected to the Amphenol connector. The cables were led to an adjoining room and attached to a master switchboard. The catheter was attached to a reservoir arranged for self-infusion.

The cage behavior of the animal was observed, described, and scored by trained observers. The categories and scoring followed the rating scales developed at the University of Michigan.

Following recovery from surgery, the animals from both groups underwent a stabilization period. In addition to daily handling, the animals were hand fed for the most part. They were also weighed weekly in order to adjust the concentration of morphine in the individual reservoirs. The unit dose level for the infusions was either 1 or 2 mg/kg/infusion.

The dose range over which LAAM and methadone were studied was 1.0 to 4.0 mg/kg i.m. From preliminary studies this range spanned the range of pharmacological activity to respiratory arrest in non-addict monkeys. The dose ranges for the opiate antagonists were 32–320 mg/kg i.m. for cyclazocine, 10–100 mg/kg i.m. for naloxone, and 5–50 mg/kg i.m. naltrexone. These ranges were established as those that would elicit graded symptoms including a maximal withdrawal syndrome in morphine-dependent monkeys maintained by multiple injections. Dose ranges for *d*-amphetamine (0.25 to 1.0 mg/kg i.m.), for ethanol (1 to 5 ml/kg 70%–ethanol p.o. in fruit juice), for diazepam (0.1 to 1.0 mg/kg i.m.), and secobarbital (5.0 to 15.0 mg/kg i.m.) were established in drug-free monkeys as those producing the characteristic neuropsychopharmacological changes for those drugs. A dose range of 7.5 to 30.0 mg/kg i.m. for diphenylhydantoin was selected as that used for anticonvulsant activity.

The brain-wave activity of Group B animals was recorded in parallel on magnetic tape and paper with an indexing time code coupling the two media. The animal selection and the recording montage were made remotely without disturbing the animals. The multi-channeled taped data were analyzed on a Time Data 100 computer driven by a PDP-12. Autospectral densities were calculated every 4 seconds over specified time periods. These spectra were averaged and compared with control or other time epochs with a point-for-point comparison. The results were plotted using a Calcomp Digital Plotter driven by a LINC II computer.

Results

Over the first 3 months of study three monkeys took excessive amounts of morphine, which led to convulsions. The amount self-infused ranged from 150–

210 mg/kg in 2 hours. Following the convulsive period, the animals lapsed into post-ictal depression and then into successive bouts of seizures. Effective treatment was found to be the administration of both diazepam and naloxone. Neither of the two was effective alone. Following effective treatment, the animals exhibited normal cage behavior in 2–3 hours and restabilized on their pattern of morphine intake the following day. Neither previous baseline of morphine intake nor exposure to other substances predicted this behavior. Furthermore, these animals displayed the same behavior aperiodically. Inevitably, when the session occurred in the early morning hours, the animals could not be treated. A parallel study confirmed the efficacy of the combination of diazepam and naloxone in reversing the "overdose phenomenon." Other combinations of either anticonvulsants or antagonists were not studied.

TABLE 1 summarizes the influence of single and double drug interactions on the level of intake of morphine. The symbols represent normalization, animal by animal, of the percentage change from control intake. As can be seen, the daily intake of morphine was significantly increased following the administration of each of the three antagonists: naloxone, naltrexone, and cyclazocine. With naloxone and naltrexone, the dose level needed was that which induced overt signs of the withdrawal syndrome. Usually the increment in intake followed the period of vomitting induced by these drugs. Following multiple exposures to these drugs, the animals became "conditioned" and began to step up their drug intake when it was obvious that they were about to be injected. For the most part, this immediate increment was not sufficient to abort the initial bout(s) of vomitting but did shorten the duration of the effect of the antagonist.

TABLE 1

ALTERATIONS OF SELF-ADMINISTRATION OF MORPHINE BY *M. mulatta* IN THE PRESENCE OF OTHER DRUGS

	Secondary Drugs				
Tertiary Drug	LAAM	Methadone	Naltrexone	Naloxone	Cyclazocine
Control	I (3) NC (5) D (2)	I (4) NC (9) D (1)	II (4) I (2) NC (3)	II (2) I (5) NC (4)	I (6) NC (8) D (1)
Secobarbital	I (1) NC (3) D (2)	II (1) I (1) NC (3)	II (1) NC (3)	I (1) NC (4) D (1)	I (3) NC (3)
Amphetamine	II (1)* NC (2) D (1)	NC (2)	II (1) I (1) NC (1)	II (1) I (3) NC (1) D (1)	II (2) I (1) DD (1)* D (1)*
Diazepam	NC (2) D (1)	I (1) D (1)	II (1) NC (1)	II (2)	I (2) NC (1)
Ethanol	II (1)* NC (1)	I (1) NC (2)	I (1)	II (2)	NC (2)
Dilantin®	NC (1) D (2)	II (1) NC (1)	II (1) I (1)	II (3)	NC (1) D (1)

Numbers of animals indicated in parentheses.

Symbols: I = increase, D = decrease, NC = no change, DD, II = more than 2× difference from both prior and following days.

* Unexpected and potentially serious interactions; see text.

The mixed agonist-antagonist properties of cyclazocine presented less of a clear-cut pattern, but it was necessary to approach dose ranges in which a frank withdrawal syndrome was initiated. No obvious "conditioning" effect was observed with animals treated with multiple exposures of cyclazocine.

The effects of the agonists LAAM and methadone were biphasic. At the upper dose ranges, 2–4 mg/kg for the first 4 to 8 hours, there was a reduction in morphine intake. This was followed over the next 24 to 48 hours by an increase in morphine intake for a net increase over the period of drug action.

For the most part, the alterations in morphine intake were the same with multiple combinations as were seen with the agonist-antagonist interactions alone. Three combinations, however, produced isolated responses that were different and potentially hazardous. The first was the interaction observed following cyclazocine and amphetamine. Early in the study, historically, the combination produced an increase in morphine intake; late in the study the combination produced a decrease in morphine intake. At both times amphetamine potentiated the withdrawal syndrome elicited by cyclazocine for the particular level of morphine intake. The difference may be explained by a variation of the concept that a particular effect is related to basal or initial values. Early, when the mean daily intake of the animals was 30 mg/kg of morphine, the abstinence syndrome produced was motivating but not debilitating. Later, with a daily intake of 100 mg/kg of morphine, the abstinence syndrome produced was so disorganizing that the usual motivating stimuli to increase morphine intake were ineffective.

The second combination was LAAM (4 mg/kg) plus *d*-amphetamine (0.75 mg/kg). One animal with a baseline intake of 280 mg/kg of morphine had an intake of 426 mg/kg of morphine in the 4-hour period following the administration of the combination. Seizures and death followed this large increment in the body burden of morphine. Treatment with naloxone and diazepam was ineffective in controlling the seizures in this case.

The third combination was LAAM (4 mg/kg) plus ethanol (5 ml/kg of 70%). the animal given this treatment had a baseline intake of 120 mg/kg/day of morphine. Following the combination, the intake per time interval tripled until behavioral incapacitation interfered with coordinated responding. Subsequent intake patterns were characteristic of recovery periods.

The effects on general comportment paralleled the modifications of morphine intake for the combined studies. The usual behavioral depressions seen with ethanol, secobarbital, and diazepam were not seen when any of these drugs was combined with the antagonists. However, after the initial effects of the antagonists abated, a marked behavioral depression was seen in animals treated with secobarbital. A similar pattern appeared following the combination of ethanol, secobarbital, or diazepam with LAAM and methadone. Again, secobarbital was the only depressant exhibiting depressant activity.

The psychomotor stimulant effects were apparent only in the animals treated with LAAM and naltrexone plus amphetamine. In all other combinations, the agonist-antagonist effects were dominant.

EEG signs for the most part paralleled the behavioral changes. The detailed data will be presented elsewhere.

Discussion

It was of interest to find that despite the establishment of tolerance, i.e., a basal intake of 70 mg/kg/day or more, animals with free access to morphine may on occasion increase their intake to toxic levels. The manifestation of toxicity under such conditions was epileptiform convulsions progressing to status epilepticus. A combination of diazepam and naloxone was found to be an effective anticonvulsant treatment. There were no indicators, either EEG or behavioral, that would predict the sudden shift of behavior to excessive intake.

It is interesting that excessive morphine intake resulting from combined amphetamine and LAAM treatment and resulting seizures was not susceptible to control by naloxone and diazepam. No ready explanation is apparent.

The so-called pure antagonists, naloxone and naltrexone, both produced similar patterns of response in terms of altering morphine intake, induction of conditioning, and generalized behavior responses. Cyclazocine exhibited a qualitatively different pattern, with the antagonist effects predominating.

The agonist pattern with LAAM and methadone was similar: little or no effect on spontaneous behavior with a short-term suppression of morphine intake followed by a rebound with overshoot. The net increase in morphine intake did not appear to alter the basal behavior of the animals.

The most dramatic effects with the multiple combinations have been life threatening for the animals. Whether these are idiosyncratic or general responses cannot be determined in this limited study. However, the lack of sedative effects with ethanol and diazepam when given as combined therapy was striking. The ranges studied produced marked depression in otherwise drug-free animals. Diphenylhydantoin (Dilantin®) had no effect on the agonist-antagonist pattern.

The psychomotor stimulant effects of amphetamine were enhanced when combined with LAAM; following the initial autonomic fusillade after naltrexone, an enhanced stimulant activity was also seen.

The combination of secobarbital with the antagonist induced a "delayed" response of secobarbital. There was no alteration of the withdrawal syndrome, but subsequently a marked behavioral depression was seen.

Summary

Multiple and single drug interactions were studied in morphine-dependent monkeys whose dependency was maintained by self-infusion. Naloxone, naltrexone, and cyclazocine precipitated abstinence syndrome which the animals generally controlled with increased morphine intake. Methadone and L-alpha-acetylmethadol (LAAM) initially reduced, then increased, the morphine intake. Multiple interactions were studied using ethanol, seconal, diazepam, amphetamine, and diphenylhydantoin.

References

1. Villarreal, J. E. 1973. The effects of morphine agonists and antagonists on morphine-dependent rhesus monkeys. *In* Agonist and Antagonist Actions of Narcotic Analgesic Drugs. H. W. Kosterlitz, H. O. J. Collier & J. E. Villereal, Eds.: 73–93. University Park Press. Baltimore, Md.
2. Way, E. L., H. H. Loh & F. Shen. 1969. Simultaneous quantitative assessment of morphine tolerance and physical dependence. J. Pharmacol. Exp. Ther. **167:** 1–8.
3. Dole, V. P., M. E. Nyswander & M. J. Kreek. 1966. Narcotic blockade. Arch. Intern. Med. **118:** 304–309.

SUSCEPTIBILITY TO AMPHETAMINE-ELICITED DYSKINESIAS FOLLOWING CHRONIC METHADONE TREATMENT IN MONKEYS*

Kristin R. Carlson and Robert D. Eibergen†

Department of Pharmacology
University of Pittsburgh School of Medicine
Pittsburgh, Pennsylvania 15261

The interaction of drugs of abuse that are administered in close temporal contiguity is a well-recognized clinical problem, as witness the present conference. Considerably less attention has been directed toward the topic of delayed interactions, or altered sensitivity to a drug after chronic administration of another drug has ceased. Various psychoactive drugs are prescribed for long-term therapeutic use; obvious examples are neuroleptic agents in the treatment of schizophrenia, and methadone for maintaining former heroin addicts.[16] Since the ultimate goal of methadone maintenance treatment programs is detoxification from methadone and a narcotics-free existence, the potential *delayed* interaction of methadone with other drugs of abuse becomes of increasing clinical significance. In fact, patients do abuse other drugs following their participation in methadone maintenance programs; although the drugs of choice are alcohol and other sedatives, an appreciable percentage use amphetamines.[8, 9, 28, 43, 59] In this paper we present evidence that rhesus monkeys become highly sensitive to the effects of amphetamine as a direct consequence of prior methadone treatment.

Amphetamines elicit repetitive stereotyped movements in many species, including man. In the rhesus monkey,[20, 21] low doses of methamphetamine initially produce searching, jerking, picking at the skin, and hand examining. After several months of intoxication with doses attaining 10–20 mg/kg, monkeys eventually exhibit an intense form of stereotypy, oral dyskinesias. Consisting of repetitive tongue protrusions, jaw displacements, and other mouth movements, these behaviors are virtually identical with the symptoms of tardive dyskinesia in humans.

Tardive dyskinesia is an iatrogenic disease resulting from long-term neuroleptic therapy,[12–15, 17, 30, 31, 54, 61] and typically appears when treatment is terminated or drug dosage reduced.[7, 13–15] It is thought to result from chronic blockade of dopamine receptors in the striatum by neuroleptics,[3, 32, 33] a pharmacological denervation which induces a state of latent receptor supersensitivity. When the blockade is lifted, endogenous dopamine activates supersensitive receptors, resulting in the exaggerated oral behaviors.[32, 33] The role of the dopaminergic nigrostriatal system in the pathogenesis of this condition is supported by clinical reports that the symptoms can be alleviated by reinstituting dopaminergic blockade with a neuroleptic,[23, 26, 36, 58] and that administration of dopaminergic agonists not only exacerbates present symptoms but can pre-

* Supported by USPHS Grants MH20121 and DA00883 to Dr. Carlson.
† Present address: Dept. of Psychiatry, Duke University Medical Center, Durham, North Carolina 27710.

cipitate them in symptom-free patients.[22, 26, 36] In addition, autopsies on patients suffering from tardive dyskinesia have revealed lesions in the substantia nigra.[10]

In experimental animals, stereotyped behaviors including oral dyskinesias are also thought to depend on the dopaminergic nigrostriatal system. Dopamine agonists elicit stereotyped behaviors, as was mentioned earlier, and dopamine blockers such as neuroleptics eliminate them.[11, 24, 40, 46, 51, 57] Furthermore, dopaminergic supersensitivity develops during chronic neuroleptic administration; after discontinuation of these agents, lower doses of dopaminergic agonists are sufficient to elicit stereotyped behaviors.[34, 49, 51, 60]

There is considerable evidence that methadone blocks striatal dopamine receptors. Several studies have revealed biochemical changes in rat striatum indicative of receptor blockade.[1, 2, 37, 41, 46, 50] In addition, stereotyped behaviors elicited by dopaminergic agonists can be blocked by methadone.[50] Thus, it is reasonable to hypothesize that chronic treatment with methadone might induce

TABLE 1

DRUG HISTORY OF MONKEYS THAT HAD BEEN TREATED WITH P.O. METHADONE

Monkey	Methadone: Mean Dose Consumed (mg/kg)	Methadone: Duration (months)	Subsequent Drug-Free Period (months)
M1	2.2	10	2
M2	1.8	10	2
M3	0.9	22	6
M4	2.3	12	5
M5	2.6	10	2
M6	0.5	12	17
M7	2.2	10	2
M8	1.8	11	10

dopaminergic receptor supersensitivity and consequent susceptibility to the effects of dopaminergic agonists. We (Eibergen & Carlson, in press) have demonstrated such an effect in the guinea pig as a consequence of methadone or chlorpromazine administration. In the present paper we discuss analogous results obtained in rhesus monkeys.

ELICITATION OF ORAL DYSKINESIAS FOLLOWING CHRONIC ORAL METHADONE TREATMENT[18]

Eight adolescent male rhesus monkeys (*M. mulatta*) in the methadone (M) group had formerly drunk methadone hydrochloride (Dolophine®, 10 mg/ml, Lilly) mixed with 100 ml Tang® orange drink once daily.[6] TABLE 1 presents their drug histories and duration of subsequent drug-free period before the start of the present experiments. The doses of methadone consumed were well below those required to produce physical dependence; these monkeys had not responded to naloxone challenge nor to abrupt drug withdrawal. Eleven monkeys of comparable ages having had no experience with narcotics or amphetamines comprised the control (C) group.

In an observation cage (identical with the home cage except for a squeeze-back), intramuscular injections of freshly prepared methamphetamine hydrochloride in sterile saline (50 mg/ml as the salt) were administered. Each monkey received one injection per day on a schedule of four consecutive injection days followed by three rest days, mimicking human "spree" abuse.[20] Methamphetamine (MA) doses began at 1.0 or 2.0 mg/kg and were gradually increased, usually to 5.0–7.5 mg/kg.

The nature, frequency, and duration of each monkey's MA-elicited stereotyped behavior were recorded regularly for a minimum of 6 hr post-injection and periodically thereafter. Oral dyskinesias were considered present if one or more of the following behaviors persisted for at least 4 hr post-injection: tongue protrusion; widely open mouth with tongue rotation inside cheek; lateral jaw displacement; sucking of inside of the cheek; copious salivation, probably resulting from these movements; expulsion of air from mouth with a loud grunt. Lip-smacking and rapid teeth-chattering, which are characteristic of normal rhesus monkeys, were not considered dyskinesias.

As seen in TABLE 2, oral dyskinesias were elicited almost immediately in seven of the eight M monkeys by only 2.0 mg/kg MA. An example of the most common oral dyskinesia, tongue protrusion, is illustrated in FIGURE 1. The behaviors appeared 5–10 min after injection and occurred at rates of 25–60 events/min. These monkeys did not appear distressed or hyperactive; instead, they typically sat quietly in a corner of the cage while engaging in their oral dyskinesias. A dose-effect relationship was obtained with respect to the duration of the oral dyskinesias. After 2.0 mg/kg MA they persisted for 36 hr, whereas after 5.0 mg/kg they were apparent throughout the 72 hr rest period of the MA cycle.

Once they had been elicited, oral dyskinesias appeared in response to all subsequent MA injections in every M monkey. For example, M1 and M4 received MA on more than 30 occasions, and it never failed to elicit oral dyskinesias.

With two exceptions, no C monkey displayed oral dyskinesias in response to MA, even after prolonged administration of higher doses. In C8, MA elicited tongue protrusions early in the MA injection schedule. His oral dyskinesia differed from that of the M monkeys in that it lacked rhythmicity, occurred sporadically post-injection, and was not elicited on every injection day. After prolonged MA administration, another C monkey, C6, developed tongue protrusions which were identical with those of the M monkeys.

These results clearly indicate that monkeys with a history of oral methadone consumption are disposed to elicitation of oral dyskinesias. Doses of MA much lower than those necessary in control monkeys were immediately effective in eliciting oral dyskinesias in the former methadone monkeys. It is important to note that those monkeys had consumed amounts of methadone which were equivalent on a mg/kg basis to those used in methadone maintenance treatment programs, but which were functionally much lower since they did not induce physical dependence. Those doses were certainly sufficient, however, to sensitize the monkeys to MA administered as long as 17 months after methadone was terminated. We suggest, therefore, that the chronic receptor blockade imposed by methadone had led to striatal dopaminergic supersensitivity. Oral dyskinesias

TABLE 2

RESULTS OF METHAMPHETAMINE ADMINISTRATION

Monkey	Dys*	Day†	Methamphetamine Dose (mg/kg)	Principal Behaviors
M1	+	1	2.0	Tongue protrusion
M2	+	1	2.0	Tongue protrusion
M3	+	1	2.0	Jaw displacement
M4	+	1	2.0	Sucking and blowing out cheek
M5	+	4	2.0	Wide mouth opening
M6	+	4	2.0	Tongue protrusion
M7	+	59	6.0	Lip grooming, mild chewing; Tongue protrusion
M8	+	2	2.0	Tongue protrusion
C1	0	8	1.0 → 2.0	Mild chewing
C2	0	8	1.0 → 2.0	Body jerk
C3	0	31	2.0 → 5.0	Shuffling movements
C4	0	45	2.0 → 5.0	Body jerk
C5	0	40	2.0 → 5.0	Facial grimace‡, writhing
C6	+	47	5.0	Biting finger, vocalization; Tongue protrusion
C7	0	48	2.0 → 5.0	Body jerk
C8	+	2	1.0	Tongue protrusion
C9	0	8	1.0 → 2.0	Mild chewing
C10	0	8	1.0 → 2.0	No response
C11	0	8	1.0 → 2.0	Circling, mild chewing

* Oral dyskinesias: + indicates presence, 0 indicates absence.

† Day indicates the injection day using the dose specified on which dyskinesias were first observed, or the total number of injection days covering the dosage range specified for those monkeys not exhibiting dyskinesias.

‡ Although this behavior may be seen in human tardive dyskinesia, it was not considered a dyskinesia for this monkey inasmuch as the same behavior was observed prior to methamphetamine administration.

resulted from the stimulation of supersensitive receptors by the dopamine released by MA.

CONVERSION OF CONTROL MONKEYS TO ORAL DYSKINESIAS BY PARENTERAL METHADONE, CHLORPROMAZINE, OR HALOPERIDOL

Nine C monkeys had received increasing doses of MA on up to 48 occasions (see TABLE 2) and had failed to develop oral dyskinesias. We next asked whether these monkeys could be converted to oral dyskinesias by a period of methadone administration. In order to compare this condition with tardive dyskinesia following neuroleptic drug therapy, we administered to some of them chlorpromazine or haloperidol. If dopaminergic blockade is responsible for subsequent supersensitivity to MA, then one would expect that monkeys which had not displayed oral dyskinesias in response to MA previously would do so following chronic methadone or neuroleptic treatment.

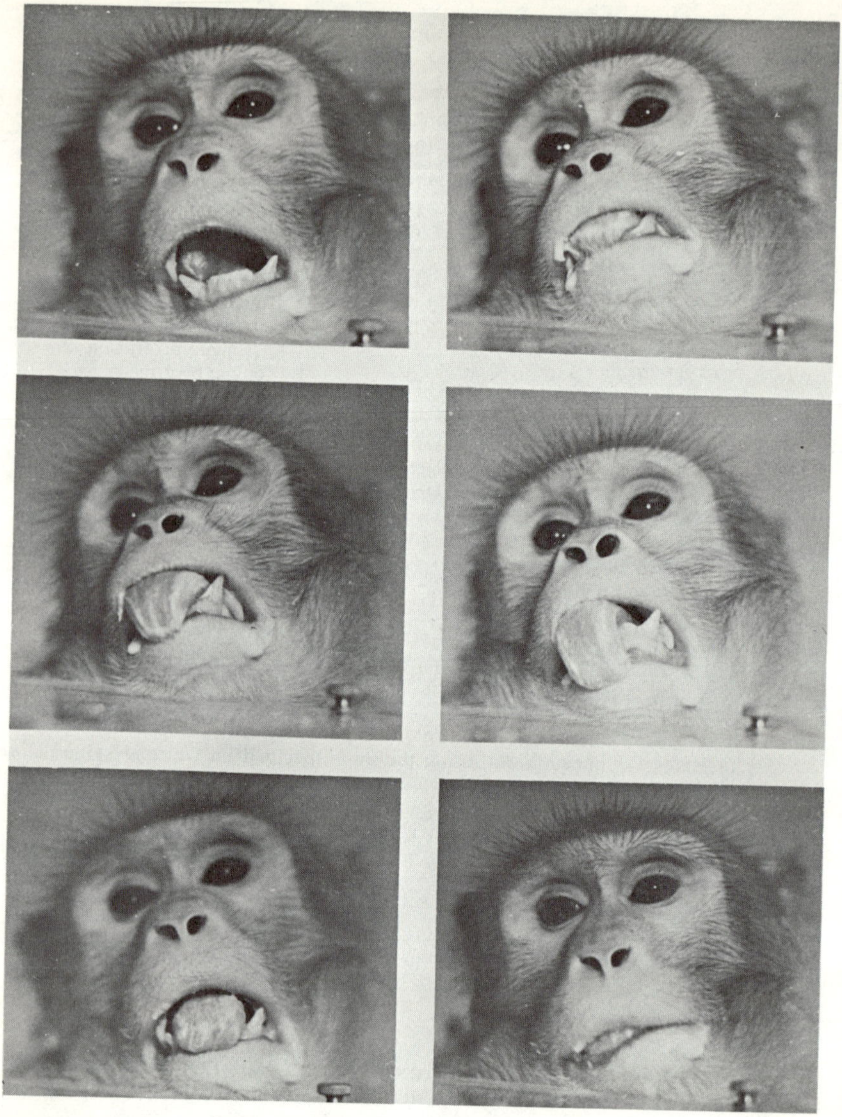

FIGURE 1. Sequence illustrating a typical tongue protrusion in Ml following administration of 4.0 mg/kg MA.

Thus, the following drugs were administered at 12-hr intervals: Methadone (MD), s.c. for 45 days; chlorpromazine (CPZ), i.m. Thorazine® (25 mg/ml, Smith Kline & French) for only 31 days due to profound anorexia; haloperidol (HPD), i.m. Haldol® (5.0 mg/ml, McNeil) for 45 days, the dosage was not increased because of persistent anorexia; saline (SAL), s.c. sterile physiological saline, in a volume equivalent to that given the MD monkeys, for 45 days.

On days 42 and 44 of this chronic drug regimen, monkeys were subjected to challenge with 0.10 and 0.15 mg/kg naloxone[5] (Narcan, 0.4 mg/ml, Endo). Only the two MD monkeys responded; their symptoms were indicative of a moderate level of physical dependence.[55, 56]

A 10-day drug-free period followed the chronic drug administration phase. On days 11–14, monkeys were injected i.m. each morning with 2.0 mg/kg MA, and examined for dyskinesias in the same fashion as in the previous experiment.

As can be seen in TABLE 3, both MD monkeys exhibited oral dyskinesias in response to MA. The case of C7 is particularly interesting, since he responded to this low dose on the first injection day, whereas he had not shown any oral dyskinesia over 48 days at doses up to 5.0 mg/kg prior to MD treatment. It is unlikely that his earlier experience with MA sensitized him, however, since the second MD monkey had received only eight previous injections of low doses and

TABLE 3

CONVERSION TO METHAMPHETAMINE-ELICITED ORAL DYSKINESIAS IN CONTROL MONKEYS BY CHRONIC DRUG TREATMENT

Chronic Drug (mg/kg/day)	Monkey	Response to Methamphetamine (2.0 mg/kg for 4 Days) Dyskinesia	Days	Principal Behaviors
Methadone 1.0 → 10.0	C2	+	3–4	Tongue protrusion
	C7	+	1–4	Tongue protrusion, jaw displacement
Chlorpromazine 2.0 → 10.0	C9	+	2–4	Jaw displacement
Haloperidol 0.2	C1	0	1–4	Vacant facial expression
	C4	0	1–4	Body jerk
Saline	C11	0	1–4	Circling

also was converted to oral dyskinesias. In addition, chronic CPZ administration was effective in converting C9 to MA-elicited oral dyskinesias, even though he underwent a shorter course of chronic drug treatment. These data show that even a relatively short period of MD or CPZ treatment can predispose monkeys to subsequent elicitation of oral dyskinesias by MA. Since both these drugs block dopamine receptors, our suggestion that chronic blockade results in the development of dopaminergic supersensitivity is supported.

However, the dopaminergic blocker HPD failed to convert two monkeys to oral dyskinesias, a result which superficially contradicts a dopaminergic supersensitivity theory but which was not unexpected. Other experiments have shown that long-term administration of CPZ to rhesus monkeys eventually results in the spontaneous appearance of oral dyskinesias,[42, 44] whereas HPD, even in much higher doses than we used, is ineffective in this regard.[44] In addition, HPD seems to be responsible for very few instances of tardive dyskinesia.[31] Thus, although dopaminergic blockade is necessary for the development of supersensitivity, it alone does not appear to be sufficient, suggesting the involvement of another neurotransmitter system.

ANTAGONISM OF METHAMPHETAMINE-ELICITED BEHAVIORS

Symptoms of tardive dyskinesia are often alleviated by reinstating dopaminergic blockade via a resumption of neuroleptic therapy,[23, 26, 36, 58] and in some cases by administering the cholinergic drug physostigmine.[7, 23, 26] Similarly, amphetamine-induced stereotyped behaviors in experimental animals are eliminated by both dopaminergic antagonists[11, 24, 40, 46, 51, 57] and cholinergic agents.[4, 35, 52] Thus, we wished to assess the role of these neurotransmitter systems in mediating oral dyskinesias and other stereotyped behaviors elicited by MA in our monkeys.

The effects of potential blocking drugs were tested in two ways; in some cases the drug was administered 60 min before MA, to see if it would block the appearance of stereotyped behaviors, and in other instances it was administered 45 min after MA, to determine whether it would antagonize on-going stereotyped behaviors. The effects of antagonists were compared with the effect of saline administered in other sessions before or after the same MA dose.

The following drugs were administered by i.m. injection: dopamine blockers were chlorpromazine, haloperidol, spiroperidol (0.2 mg/ml), and clozapine (2 mg/ml). The cholinergic drug was physostigmine salicylate (Antilirium, 1 mg/ml, O'Neil, Jones & Feldman). To assess possible chlorpromazine effects mediated via noradrenergic receptor blockade, the a-receptor blocking agent phentolamine mesylate (Regitine®, 5 mg/ml, Ciba) was used. Finally, to control for any non-specific depressant effects produced by the neuroleptics, sodium phenobarbital (Luminal®, 130 mg/ml, Winthrop) and diazepam (Valium®, 5 mg/ml, Roche) tests were conducted.

Monkeys were observed in the experimental cage, where the rate/min of stereotyped behaviors was determined during the 30 min preceding MA administration, for 90 min immediately following MA, and for 30 min beginning at 2, 4, and occasionally 6 hr after MA injection. The protocols and complete results of this study are presented in TABLE 4; typical examples of the effect of each drug are shown in FIGURES 2–5.

Both chlorpromazine and spiroperidol completely prevented the development of stereotyped behaviors when administered prior to MA, and rapidly antagonized ongoing stereotyped behaviors (FIGURE 2). The monkeys appeared mildly sedated by both drugs, but were definitely not incapacitated. Haloperidol, however, had no effect on oral dyskinesias (FIGURE 3). We attribute this result to the very low dose employed, since recent reports indicate that doses 10–20 times higher reduce amphetamine-elicited behaviors in primates.[25, 57]

As would be expected from other evidence indicating the lack of participation of adrenergic systems in stereotyped behaviors,[29, 47, 48, 53] the a-noradrenergic blocker phentolamine had no effect (FIGURE 3).

The results with the final dopaminergic antagonist, clozapine, were particularly interesting. It substantially reduced or eliminated oral dyskinesias (FIGURE 4), while having no effect on non-oral stereotyped grooming. The differential effectiveness of this drug is consistent with other evidence. It only weakly antagonizes stereotyped behaviors elicited by dopaminergic agonists in normal animals,[39, 58] but strongly suppresses stereotyped behaviors thought to be mediated by supersensitive receptors. For example, it alleviates symptoms of tardive dyskinesia,[58] and reduces the exaggerated responses to dopaminergic agonists produced by chronic neuroleptic administration in animals.[51]

The cholinergic agent physostigmine delayed the onset of oral dyskinesias

TABLE 4

DRUG ADMINISTRATION PROTOCOLS AND RESULTS OF ANTAGONISM STUDY

Blocking Drug and Dose (mg/kg)	Before or After Meth-amphetamine Dose (mg/kg)	Mon-key	Methamphetamine-Elicited Behavior	Effect of Blocking Drug on Behavior
Chlorpromazine				
0.5	After 3.5	M7	Searching behind	Completely eliminated
1.0	After 2.0	M8	Body jerk	Completely eliminated
1.0	After 2.0	M8	Body jerk	Completely eliminated (FIGURE 2)
1.0	Before 2.0	C4	Body jerk	Completely blocked (FIGURE 2)
Spiroperidol				
0.025	After 5.0	M1	Tongue protrusion	Completely eliminated
0.05	After 5.0	M7	Lip grooming	Completely eliminated
0.025	After 2.0	C7	Body jerk	Completely eliminated (FIGURE 2)
0.025	Before 5.0	M7	Lip grooming	Completely blocked (FIGURE 2)
0.1	Before 2.0	C7	Body jerk	Completely blocked
Haloperidol				
0.05	After 6.0	C6	Tongue protrusion	No effect (FIGURE 3)
Phentolamine				
0.5	Before 2.5	C4	Body jerk	No effect (FIGURE 3)
0.5	After 2.5	C7	Body jerk	No effect
Clozapine				
p.o. 0.1	Before 5.0	M2	Tongue protrusion	Cut number in half (FIGURE 4)
0.5	Before 6.0	M2	Tongue protrusion	Cut number in half
1.0	Before 5.0	M7	Lip grooming	Delayed onset 1 hr, no effect on number
i.m. 2.5	After 5.0	M4	Sucking cheek	Completely eliminated (FIGURE 4)
Physostigmine				
0.1	Before 6.0	M7	Jaw displacement	Delayed onset 4 hr (FIGURE 4)
0.1	After 6.0	C6	Tongue protrusion	No effect (FIGURE 4)
Phenobarbital				
30.0	Before 6.0	M7	Jaw displacement	No effect
10.0	Before 2.5	M8	Body jerk	No effect
10.0	After 2.5	C4	Body jerk	No effect (FIGURE 5)
20.0	After 5.0	C6	Tongue protrusion	No effect
Diazepam				
1.0	After 4.0	M4	Sucking cheek	No effect (FIGURE 5)

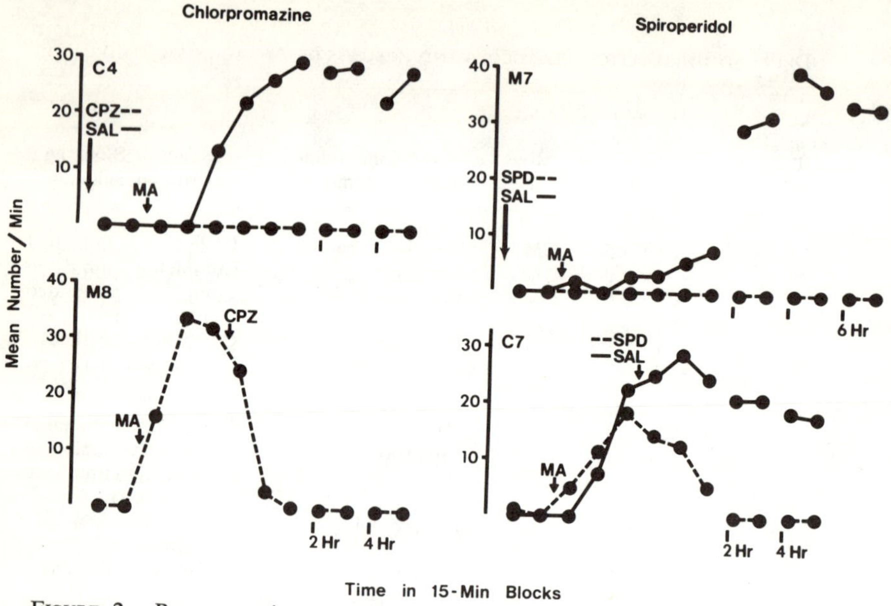

FIGURE 2. Representative examples of the effect on MA-elicited stereotyped behavior of chlorpromazine (CPZ) and spiroperidol (SPD). Each panel depicts the mean number/min of a monkey's characteristic behavior over time. The monkey is identified in the upper left corner of each panel. The solid line represents data from the session in which saline (SAL) was administered, and the dashed line data from the session in which the monkey received the potential blocking drug. Arrows indicate the times at which the blocking drug or SAL, and MA, were injected. Drug doses are specified in TABLE 4. (No SAL control session was run with M8.)

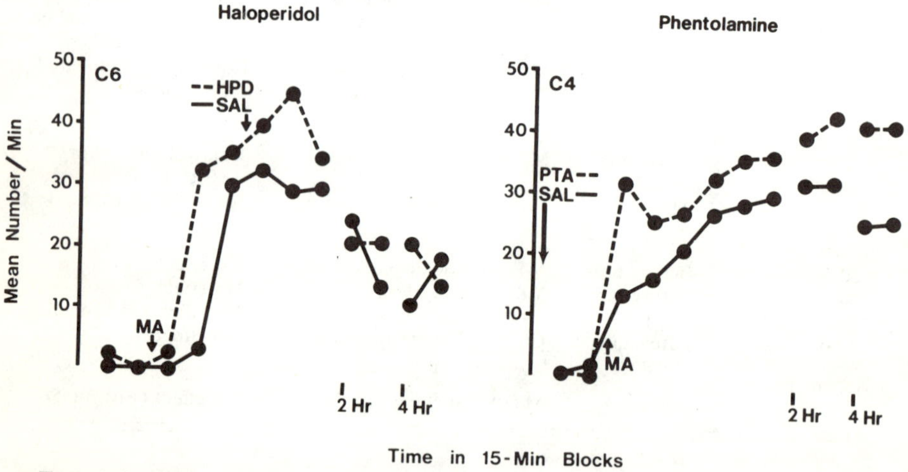

FIGURE 3. Representative examples of the effect on MA-elicited stereotyped behavior of haloperidol (HPD) and phentolamine (PTA). For further explanation of symbols, see legend to FIGURE 2.

in one monkey (FIGURE 4) but at the same dose had no effect on the oral dyskinesia of another. We are puzzled by these results, since we would have expected physostigmine to be consistently effective. A recent hypothesis of a malfunctioning dopaminergic-cholinergic balance in the striatum as responsible for tardive dyskinesia[26] has been supported by the effectiveness of physostig-

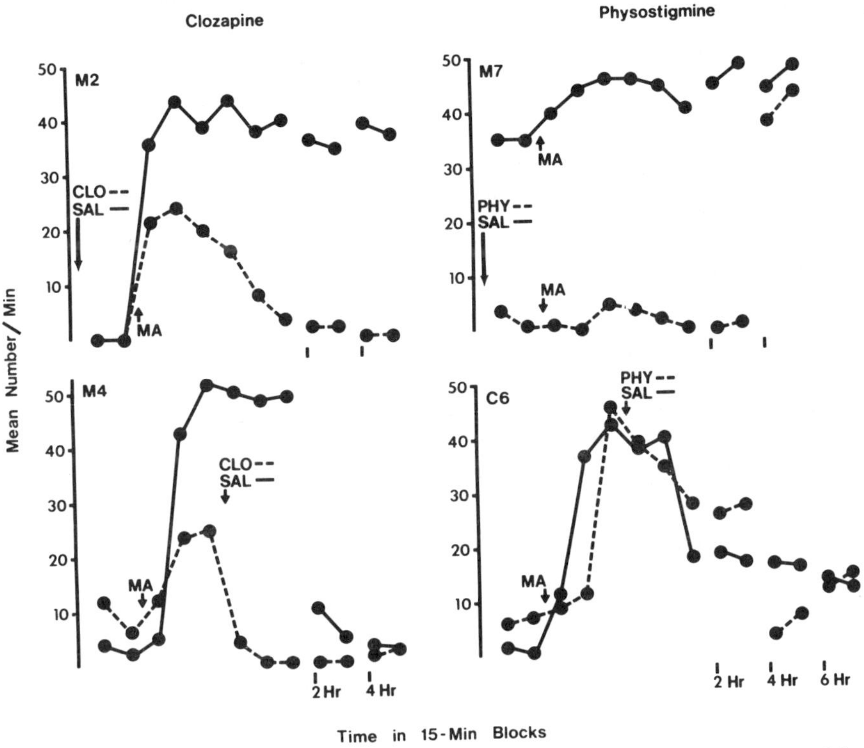

FIGURE 4. Representative examples of the effect on MA-elicited stereotyped behavior of clozapine (CLO) and physostigmine (PHY). For further explanation of symbols, see legend to FIGURE 2. Concerning the results with M7 (upper right panel), the initial high rate of stereotyped behavior in the SAL session, before MA was administered, represents a continuation of that behavior from MA administration on the previous day.

mine in alleviating the symptoms.[23, 26] Furthermore, cholinergic drugs antagonnize stereotyped behaviors in rodents, and anticholinergic agents potentiate them.[4, 35, 52] We are continuing to investigate the basis of these equivocable results.

Finally, neither phenobarbital nor diazepam had any effect on oral dyskinesias or other stereotyped behaviors (FIGURE 5), even though the monkeys were obviously sedated, and ataxic at the higher doses. Thus, one cannot attribute the effectiveness of the dopaminergic antagonists to non-specific depression of activity.

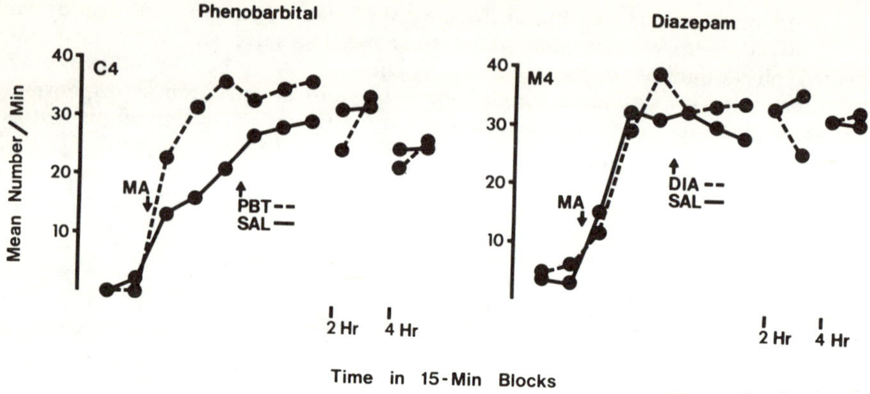

FIGURE 5. Representative examples of the effect on MA-elicited stereotyped behavior of phenobarbital (PBT) and diazepam (DIA). For further explanation of symbols, see legend to FIGURE 2.

DISCUSSION AND CLINICAL IMPLICATIONS

The present experiments have shown that prior experience with methadone greatly enhances the rhesus monkey's sensitivity to MA. This effect was obtained in monkeys that had had lengthy exposure to very low doses of methadone p.o., and persisted for as long as 17 months after this methadone treatment was terminated. Furthermore, parenteral treatment with dependence-producing doses of methadone for only 45 days was sufficient to induce supersensitivity to MA.

The stereotyped behaviors elicited by MA in these animals, oral dyskinesias, qualitatively resemble the symptoms of tardive dyskinesia in humans. In addition, parenteral treatment with chlorpromazine, which has been held responsible for cases of tardive dyskinesia,[49] also produced subsequent sensitivity to MA.

In tardive dyskinesia, however, the symptoms often appear "spontaneously" when neuroleptic therapy is halted or the dosage reduced, whereas it was necessary to elicit the monkeys' dyskinesias with MA. Thus, it appears that in the monkeys a state of "latent supersensitivity" was present, dependent on exogenous stimulation for expression.

The currently accepted theory concerning the development of tardive dyskinesia is that chronic neuroleptic administration creates a dopaminergic receptor blockade, rendering the receptors supersensitive to the dopamine reaching them when the blockade is lifted.[32, 33] We suggest that sensitivity to MA, subsequent to chronic methadone treatment, may be explained by the same mechanism. There is considerable biochemical evidence that methadone blocks dopamine receptors in the striatum,[1, 2, 37, 41, 46, 50] and several behavioral studies have shown enhanced responses to dopamine agonists immediately after termination of chronic narcotic administration.[19, 38, 45] In addition, it has been shown that rats formerly dependent on morphine are more sensitive to the dopamine agonist apomorphine for 30 days after withdrawal,[27] and we have demonstrated enhanced sensitivity to MA in the guinea pig for 3 weeks after chronic methadone or chlorpromazine treatment was terminated (Eibergen & Carlson, in press). Thus, we suggest that chronic blockade creates a long-lasting supersensitivity of nigrostriatal dopaminergic functions. The results of our last experiment support this explanation, since only dopaminergic antagonists were effective in blocking oral dyskinesias.

Finally, we raise a point of obvious clinical significance; the data indicate that methadone maintenance patients might be highly sensitive to amphetamines for an extended period of time after they terminate treatment. Although the use of amphetamines by these patients during and following treatment is well-documented,[8, 9, 28, 43, 59] we are unaware of any clinical reports of unusual motor effects consequent to amphetamine self-administration. We certainly hope that the lack of evidence indicates that humans are for some reason not subject to methadone-induced supersensitivity, even though they are to that induced by neuroleptics. We suspect, however, that this difference might derive from inadequate medical follow-up on methadone-maintenance patients, particularly program drop-outs, and from differences in the populations receiving methadone as opposed to neuroleptics. For example, tardive dyskinesia is thought to be most prevalent in elderly female patients;[13] the predominantly younger male population of methadone maintenance programs might be less susceptible to the development of supersensitivity.

Whatever the reason for the failure to date to observe symptoms of dopaminergic supersensitivity following methadone treatment in humans, on the basis of our research as well as other evidence in experimental animals we strongly suggest that further work should be undertaken to assess the degree to which such patients might be at risk to the elicitation of extrapyramidal dyskinesias.

Summary

Eight rhesus monkeys that had drunk subdependence-producing doses of methadone daily for 10–22 months, and had subsequently been drug-free for 2–17 months, were injected with low doses of methamphetamine (MA). They immediately exhibited oral dyskinesias resembling the symptoms of tardive dyskinesia in humans, a condition resulting from chronic blockade of striatal dopamine receptors by neuroleptics. Eleven control monkeys failed to develop dyskinesias during prolonged MA administration. Control monkeys then received parenteral methadone, chlorpromazine, haloperidol, or saline for 45 days. Upon subsequent retest with MA, the methadone and chlorpromazine monkeys immediately displayed oral dyskinesias. Dopaminergic antagonists blocked MA-elicited dyskinesias, whereas neither a noradrenergic blocker nor sedative doses of phenobarbital and diazepam had any effect on dyskinesias. We suggest that receptor supersensitivity is produced by chronic treatment with methadone or other dopamine receptor blockers. Following treatment, stimulation of hypersensitive striatal receptors by the dopamine released by MA results in oral dyskinesias. The clinical implications for methadone maintenance treatment program patients are discussed.

References

1. AHTEE, L. 1973. J. Pharm. Pharmacol. **25:** 649–651.
2. AHTEE, L. & I. KAARIAINEN. 1973. Eur. J. Pharmacol. **22:** 206–208.
3. ANDEN, N.-E., S. G. BUTCHER, H. CORRODI, K. FUXE & U. UNGERSTEDT. 1970. Eur. J. Pharmacol. **11:** 303–314.
4. ARNFRED, T. & A. RANDRUP. 1968. Acta Pharmacol. Toxicol. **26:** 384–394.
5. BROCCO, M., G. A. DENEAU & K. F. KILLAM. 1974. Proc. West. Pharmacol. Soc. **17:** 56–58.
6. CARLSON, K. R. & M. PAVSEK. 1974. Physiol. Psychol. **2:** 383–386.
7. CASEY, D. E. & D. DENNEY. 1975. Amer. J. Psychiatry **132:** 864–867.
8. CHAMBERS, C. D. & J. J. BERGEN. 1973. *In* Methadone: Experiences and Issues. C. D. Chambers & L. Brill, Eds.: 131–142. Behavioral Publications. New York, N.Y.
9. CHAMBERS, C. D., W. J. R. TAYLOR & P. V. WALTER. 1973. *In* Methadone: Experiences and Issues. C. D. Chambers & L. Brill, Eds.: 203–213. Behavioral Publications. New York, N.Y.
10. CHRISTENSEN, E., J. E. MOLLER & A. FAURBYE. 1970. Acta Psychiatr. Neurol. Scand. **46:** 14–23.
11. COSTAL, B., R. J. NAYLOR & J. E. OLLEY. 1972. Eur. J. Pharmacol. **18:** 95–106.
12. CRANE, G. E. 1968. Amer. J. Psychiatry **124:** 40–48.
13. CRANE, G. E. & E. R. NARANJO. 1971. Arch. Gen. Psychiatry **24:** 179–184.
14. CRANE, G. E. & G. PAULSON. 1967. Int. J. Neuropsychiatry **3:** 286–291.
15. CURRAN, J. P. 1973. Amer. J. Psychiatry **130:** 406–410.
16. DOLE, V. P. & M. E. NYSWANDER. 1965. JAMA **193:** 646–650.
17. DRUCKMAN, R., D. SEELINGER & B. THULIN. 1962. J. Nerv. Ment. Dis. **135:** 69–76.
18. EIBERGEN, R. D. & K. R. CARLSON. 1975. Science **190:** 588–590.
19. EIDELBERG, E. & R. ERSPAMER. 1975. J. Pharmacol. Exp. Ther. **192:** 50–57.
20. ELLINWOOD, E. H., JR. 1971. Biol. Psychiatry **3:** 25–32.
21. ELLINWOOD, E. H., JR. & O. DUARTE-ESCALANTE. 1970. *In* Current Concepts on Amphetamine Abuse. E. H. Ellinwood, Jr. & S. C. Cohen, Eds.: 59–68. U.S. Govt. Printing Office. Washington, D.C.
22. FANN, W. E., J. M. DAVIS & I. C. WILSON. 1973. Amer. J. Psychiatry **130:** 922–924.
23. FANN, W. E., C. R. LAKE, C. J. GERBER & G. M. MCKENZIE. 1974. Psychopharmacologia **37:** 101–107.
24. FOG, R. 1972. Acta Neurol. Scand. **48** (Suppl. 50)**:** 11–64.
25. GARVER, D. L., R. F. SCHLEMMER, JR., J. W. MAAS & J. M. DAVIS. 1975. Amer. J. Psychiatry **132:** 33–38.
26. GERLACH, J., N. REISBY & A. RANDRUP. 1974. Psychopharmacologia **34:** 21–35.
27. GIANUTSOS, G., M. D. HYNES, S. K. PURI, R. B. DRAWBAUGH & H. LAL. 1974. Psychopharmacologia **34:** 37–44.
28. GOLDSTEIN, A. & B. A. JUDSON. 1973. *In* Proc. 5th Nat. Conf. on Methadone Treatment: 21–44. Nat. Assoc. for Prevention of Addiction to Narcotics. New York, N.Y.
29. HERMAN, Z. S. 1967. Psychopharmacologia **11:** 136–142.
30. HUNTER, R., C. J. EARL & S. THORNICROFT. 1964. Proc. Royal Soc. Med. **57:** 24–28.
31. JACOBSON, G., R. J. BALDESSARINI & T. MANSCHRECK. 1974. Amer. J. Psychiatry **131:** 910–913.
32. KLAWANS, H. L., JR. 1973. Amer. J. Psychiatry **130:** 82–86.
33. KLAWANS, H. L., JR. 1973. *In* The Pharmacology of Extrapyramidal Move-

ment Disorders. Monographs in Neural Sciences. Vol. **2:** 64–70. S. Karger. Basel, Switzerland.
34. Klawans, H. L., Jr. & R. Rubovits. 1972. J. Neural Trans. **33:** 235–246.
35. Klawans, H. L., Jr., R. Rubovits, B. C. Patel & W. J. Weiner. 1972. J. Neurol. Sci. **17:** 303–308.
36. Kline, N. S. 1968. Amer. J. Psychiatry **124:** 48–54.
37. Kuschinsky, K. & O. Hornykiewicz. 1972. Eur. J. Pharmacol. **19:** 119–122.
38. Lal, H., J. O'Brien & S. K. Puri. 1971. Psychopharmacologia **22:** 217–223.
39. Matz, R., W. Rick, D. Oh, H. Thompson & S. Gershon. 1974. Curr. Ther. Res. **16:** 687–695.
40. McKenzie, G. M. & M. Sadof. 1974. J. Pharm. Pharmacol. **26:** 280–282.
41. Merali, Z., P. K. Ghosh, P. D. Hrdina, R. L. Singhal & G. M. Ling. 1974. Eur. J. Pharmacol. **26:** 375–378.
42. Messiha, F. S. 1974. Arch. Int. Pharmacodyn. Ther. **209:** 5–9.
43. Moffett, A. D., I. H. Soloway & M. X. Glick. 1973. *In* Methadone: Experiences and Issues. C. D. Chambers & L. Brill, Eds.: 215–227. Behavioral Publications. New York, N.Y.
44. Paulson, G. W. 1973. *In* Advances in Neurology. A. Barbeau *et al.*, Eds. Vol. **1:** 647–650. Raven Press. New York, N.Y.
45. Puri, S. K. & H. Lal. 1973. Psychopharmacologia **32:** 113–120.
46. Puri, S. K., C. Reddy & H. Lal. 1973. Res. Commun. Chem. Pathol. Pharmacol. **5:** 389–401.
47. Randrup, A. & I. Munkvad. 1964. Acta Pharmacol. Toxicol. **21:** 272–282.
48. Randrup, A., I. Munkvad & P. Udsen. 1963. Acta Pharmacol. Toxicol. **20:** 145–157.
49. Rubovits, R., B. C. Patel & H. L. Klawans, Jr. 1973. *In* Advances in Neurology. A. Barbeau *et al.*, Eds. Vol. **1:** 671–679. Raven Press. New York, N.Y.
50. Sasame, H. A., J. Perez-Cruet, G. DiChiara, A. Tagliamonte, P. Tagliamonte & G. L. Gessa. 1972. J. Neurochem. **19:** 1953–1957.
51. Sayers, A. C., H. R. Burki, W. Ruch & H. Asper. 1975. Psychopharmacologia **41:** 97–104.
52. Scheel-Kruger, J. 1970. Acta Pharmacol. Toxicol. **28:** 1–16.
53. Scheel-Kruger, J. & A. Randrup. 1967. Life Sci. **6:** 1389–1398.
54. Schmidt, W. R. & L. W. Jarcho. 1966. Arch. Neurol. **14:** 369–377.
55. Seevers, M. H. 1936. J. Pharmacol. Exp. Ther. **56:** 147–156.
56. Seevers, M. H. & G. A. Deneau. 1963. *In* Physiological Pharmacology. W. Root & F. Hoffman, Eds.: 565–640. Academic Press. New York, N.Y.
57. Shintomi, K. & M. Yamamura. 1975. Eur. J. Pharmacol. **31:** 273–280.
58. Simpson, G. M. & E. Varga. 1974. Curr. Ther. Res. **16:** 679–686.
59. Taintor, Z. & C. D'Amanda. 1973. *In* Proc. 5th Nat. Conf. on Methadone Treatment: 1002–1009. Nat. Assoc. for Prevention of Addiction to Narcotics. New York, N.Y.
60. Tarsy, D. & R. J. Baldessarini. 1974. Neuropharmacology **13:** 927–940.
61. Urhbrand, L. & A. Faurbye. 1960. Psychopharmacologia **1:** 408–418.

DRUG INTERACTIONS WITH METHADONE*

Mary Jeanne Kreek, Chai Leng Gutjahr, Jane W. Garfield,†
David V. Bowen, and Frank H. Field

The Rockefeller University
New York, New York 10021

† *The Department of Medicine*
New York University School of Medicine
and Chest Service, Bellevue Hospital
New York, New York 10016

Chronic methadone maintenance is now being used to treat over 85,000 heroin addicts in the United States alone. It is also being widely used throughout the world. It has been suggested anecdotally that various sedatives, tranquilizers, other depressants and stimulants including alcohol, diazepam, barbiturates, cocaine and amphetamines may have additive, potentiating, or antagonistic effects when taken by methadone maintenance patients. Few of these postulated drug interactions have been documented in human subjects on chronic methadone maintenance. None of these pharmacologic agents have been shown to alter methadone disposition in patients receiving methadone on a chronic basis, although certainly such drug interactions might be documented in the future.

Two different types of drug interactions, both resulting in the same clinical picture of acute narcotic withdrawal, have been observed in methadone-maintained subjects. Both of these drug interactions have been studied to determine whether or not the clinical observations of narcotic withdrawal could be related to any alterations in methadone disposition. Gas liquid chromatography techniques developed in this laboratory and chemical ionization mass spectrometry techniques developed in the collaborative laboratory were used in this study for the quantitative and qualitative analyses of methadone and its metabolites in plasma, urine, and feces.

Following oral administration and absorption, methadone is widely distributed in the body. Plasma levels are relatively low, even after a chronic daily maintenance dose of 50 to 100 mg.[1–3] Methadone is metabolized primarily in the liver by the hepatic microsomal drug-metabolizing enzymes. In the major pathway of biotransformation, methadone is first N-demethylated and then undergoes cyclization to form its major pyrrolidine metabolite (FIGURE 1).[4] This compound is excreted in urine in amounts approximately equal to those of unchanged methadone.[1, 3, 5] It is also the major excretory product in feces.[6, 7] The pyrrolidine metabolite may be metabolized by a second N-demethylation to form a pyrroline. Both the pyrrolidine and pyrroline may be hydroxylated.[4] Methadone may also be metabolized by several alternate minor pathways to form hydroxymethadone, a pyrrolidone, and various methadol metabolites (FIGURE 2).[4] Only this last group of metabolites are known to be pharmaco-

* Supported by grants from the National Institute of Drug Abuse (DA-01138); the National Institutes of Health, Division of Research Resources (RR-00862); the National Institutes of Health, General Clinical Research Center Grant (RR-00102); and the New York State Office of Drug Abuse Services (ODAS-84854). The opinions expressed within are not necessarily those of the Office. Dr. Kreek is a recipient of a Career Scientist Award of the Health Research Council of the City of New York.

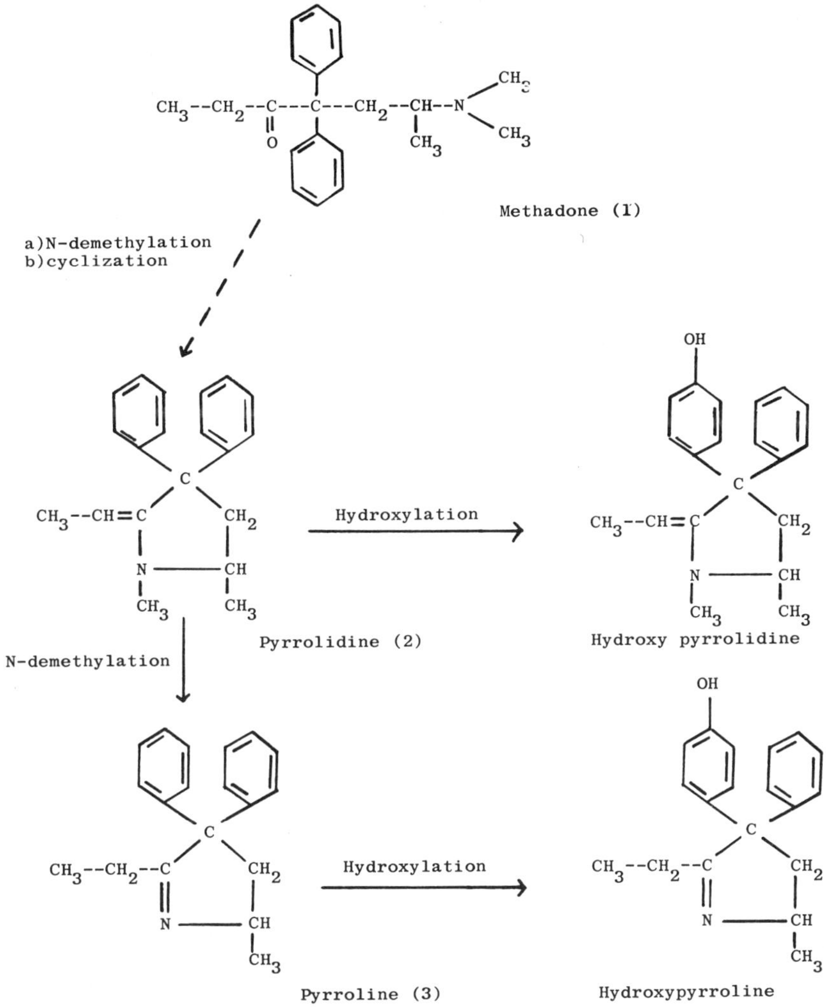

FIGURE 1. Major pathway of *dl*-methadone metabolism in man. After Sullivan & Due.[4] Compounds 1, 2 and 3 are major products excreted in human urine.

logically active. All of these metabolites have been identified in human urine by Dr. Hugh Sullivan and colleagues, and the identification of several has been confirmed by other investigators.[4]

Gas liquid chromatographic methods have been developed in this laboratory, as well as in others, for the quantitative analysis of methadone in plasma.[1-3] Using our method, in which radiolabeled methadone is added to determine recovery and docosane is added as an internal standard for gas chromatography, methadone can be measured down to 0.01 μg (or 10 ng) per ml. A gas liquid chromatographic method has also been developed to quantitate levels of both

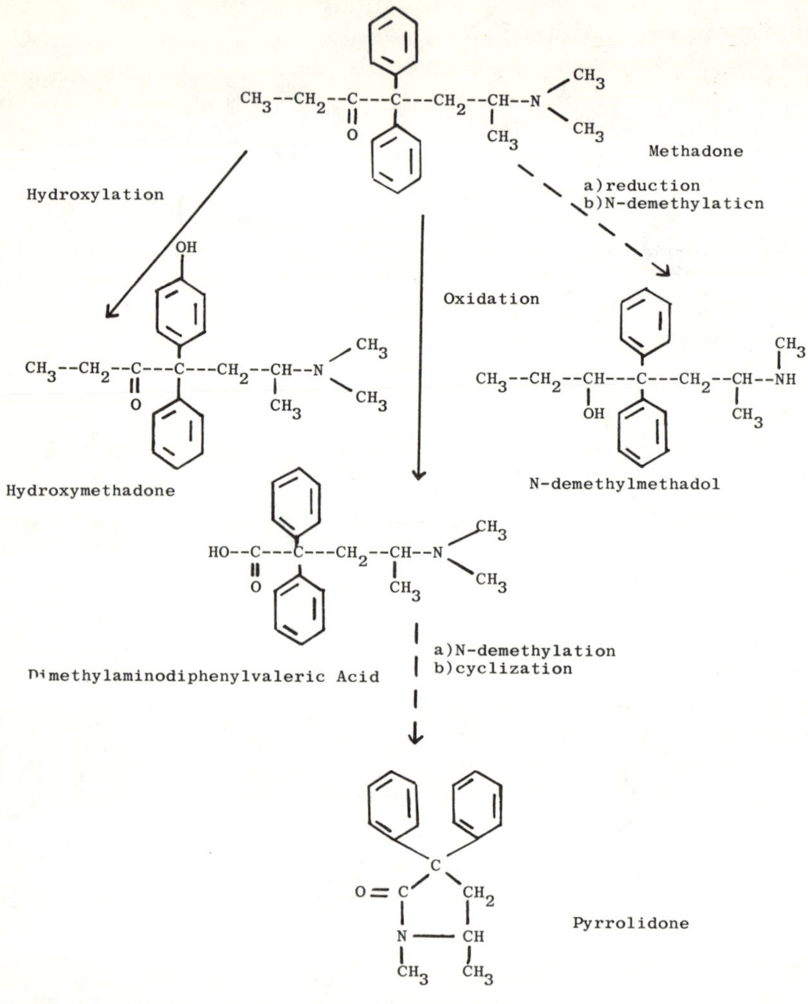

FIGURE 2. Minor pathways of *dl*-methadone metabolism in man. After Sullivan & Due.[4]

methadone and the major pyrrolidine metabolite in urine, again with sensitivities down to about 0.01 μg/ml. Recently, these methods have been modified in this laboratory to quantitate levels of methadone and to estimate levels of the major pyrrolidine metabolite in feces. All of these methods have been used in the drug-interaction studies to be reported.

Gas Liquid Chromatography Methods

Method for Quantitation of Methadone in Plasma

Blood to be used in measuring plasma levels of methadone is drawn into oxalated tubes, promptly centrifuged, separated, and either analyzed immediately or quick frozen and stored in a freezer. (Methadone will break down into various degradation products, especially the N-oxide, if it is left in solution at room temperature for extended time periods.)[8]

To 2 ml of plasma pipetted into a conical tube is added 10 μl of an aqueous solution of [^{3}H]methadone (*dl*, *d*-, or *l*-methadone with a specific activity of 92 mCi/mM, New England Nuclear) containing 1500–1800 cpm, to determine recovery of methadone through the extraction procedure. The plasma is vortexed and allowed to equilibrate for 1 hour at room temperature. Then 2 ml of 0.1 N ammonium hydroxide and 5 ml of ethyl acetate are added, shaken, and centrifuged. The upper phase (ethyl acetate) is transferred to a tapered conical tube and dried under nitrogen at room temperature. The residue is dissolved in 1 ml of ethyl acetate containing 0.12 μg docosane (as an internal standard for the final preparation steps and chromatography). A 500 μl aliquot is transferred to a second conical tube. Then 100 μl aliquots, in triplicate, of the remaining solution are transferred to counting vials for liquid scintillation counting, to calculate recovery through the extraction procedure. The 500 μl aliquot is dried under nitrogen at room temperature. It is then redissolved in carbon disulfide, 10 μl if low levels are expected or if magnitudes of levels are unknown, or 20 μl if moderate to high levels are anticipated. Then 1–2 μl (approximately equivalent to 0.05 to 0.2 ml of plasma) is injected onto the gas chromatography column (FIGURE 3). Standard calibration curves are constructed regularly and are linear within the range of 0.02–2.0 μg per ml (usual plasma concentration ranges observed in patients receiving 30–120 mg oral methadone daily in maintenance treatment).

Gas liquid chromatography is carried out using a Hewlett-Packard Research Chromatograph model 7620-A or 5700-A. A 6-foot stainless steel column with an internal diameter of 1/8 inch, packed with 10% methyl vinyl silicone gum rubber coating (UC–W–982) on 80–100 mesh High Performance Chromosorb W is used. The injection port temperature is 220° C, column temperature 210° C, and flame detector 225° C. Nitrogen carrier gas is adjusted to a flow of 30 ml/minute, and hydrogen and air are adjusted to give maximum sensitivity for flame detection.

Method for Quantitation of Methadone and Pyrrolidine Metabolite in Urine

Urine to be used in measuring levels of methadone and its metabolites is either analyzed immediately or quick frozen and stored in a freezer. (This is essential since the pyrrolidine is extremely labile and will undergo degradation to various products, especially the pyrrolidone metabolite, if left at room temperature for an extended time.[9] Methadone itself is also labile, and if left in solution at room temperature for over 24 hours, appreciable amounts of the N-oxide are formed.) The pH of all urines is determined before processing.

To 0.5 ml of urine pipetted into a conical tube is added 10 μl of an aqueous solution of [^{3}H]methadone (*dl*, *d*- or *l*-methadone with a specific activity of 92 mCi/mM, New England Nuclear) containing 1500–1800 cpm, to determine recovery of methadone through the extraction procedure. The urine is then vortexed and allowed to equilibrate at room temperature for 1 hour. Then 0.5 ml of concentrated ammonium hydroxide and 4 ml of ethyl acetate are added, shaken, and centrifuged. The upper phase (ethyl acetate) is transferred to a second conical tube. Two ml of 0.1 *N* ammonium hydroxide is added, shaken

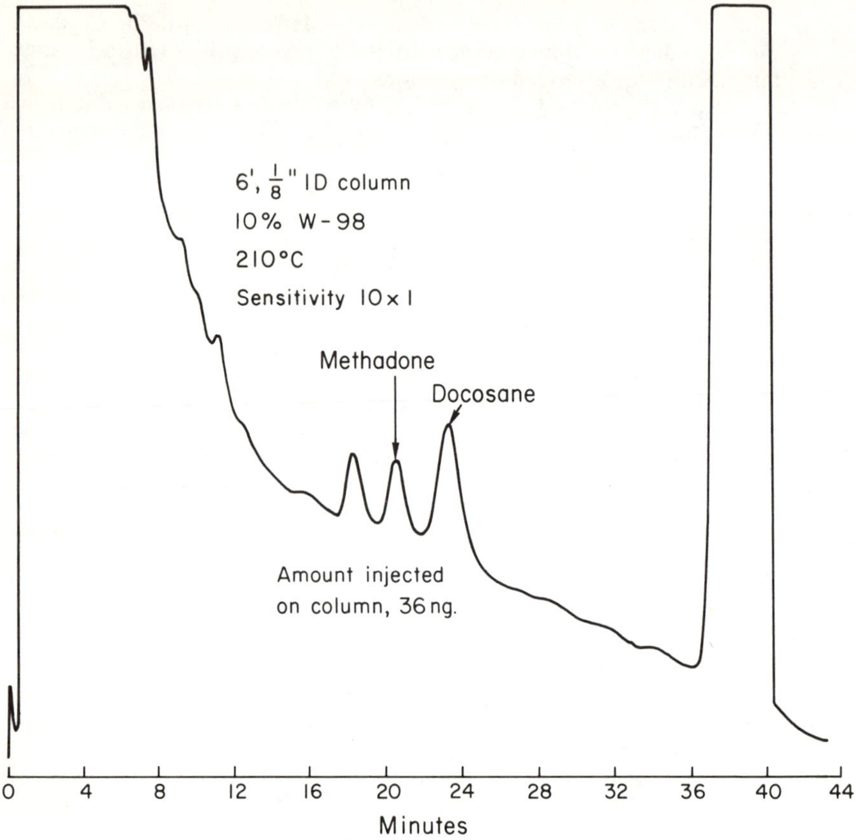

FIGURE 3. Gas liquid chromatogram of methadone in human plasma. Methadone extracted from plasma pH 9–10.

and centrifuged. The upper phase (ethyl acetate) is transferred to a tapered conical tube and dried under nitrogen at room temperature. The residue is dissolved in 1 ml of ethyl acetate containing 0.12 μg of docosane (as an internal standard for the final preparation steps and chromatography). A 500 μl aliquot is transferred to another conical tube. Then 100 μl aliquots, in triplicate, of the remaining solution are transferred to counting vials for liquid scintillation counting, to calculate recovery through the extraction procedure. The 500 μl aliquot is dried under nitrogen at room temperature. It is then redissolved in 20 μl carbon disulfide. Then 2 μl (equivalent to 0.025 ml urine) is injected on column (FIGURE 4). Separate calibration curves for both methadone and the pyrrolidine metabolite are constructed regularly and are linear in the concentration ranges of 1.0 to 50.0 μg per ml (range of concentrations observed in urines of most patients receiving 30–120 mg oral methadone daily in maintenance treatment).

Gas liquid chromatography conditions are the same as with determinations of methadone in plasma.

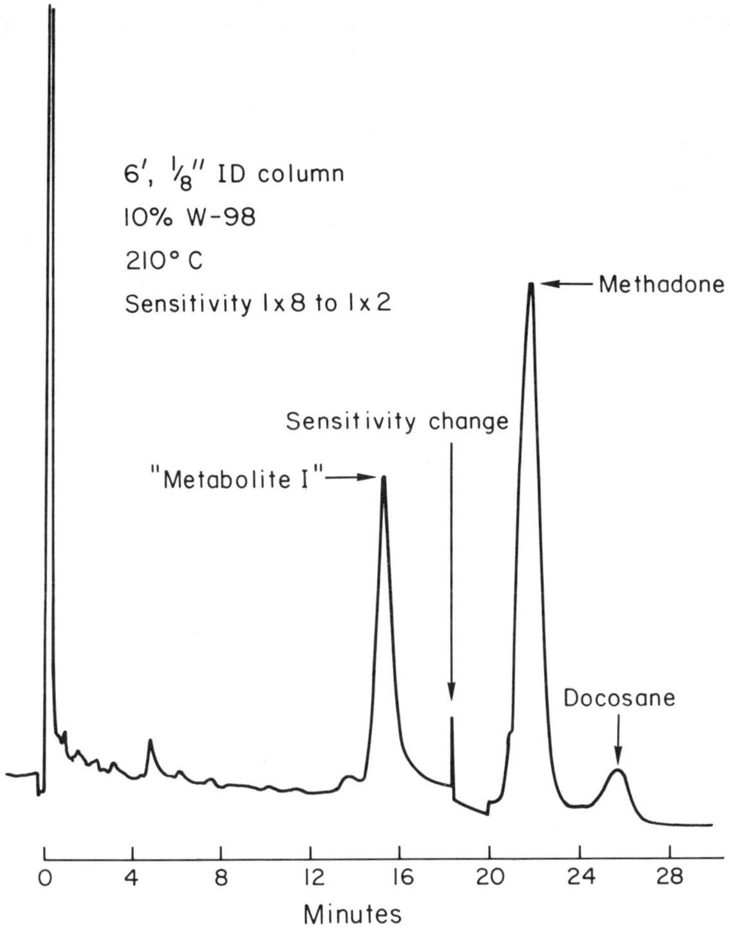

FIGURE 4. Gas liquid chromatogram of methadone and pyrrolidine metabolite of methadone in human urine. "Metabolite I" pyrrolidine extracted from urine pH 11–12.

Method for Quantitation of Methadone in Feces

Feces to be used in measuring levels of methadone are weighed and then either processed immediately or frozen and stored in a freezer until processing. Feces are processed by homogenization in distilled water of sufficient volume to make a slurry of moderate thickness which can be pipetted with accuracy (usually approximately 3 g water per 1 g feces). The final volume is measured and recorded. Aliquots of fecal homogenates may also be frozen for further subsequent qualitative and quantitative analyses.

To 1 ml of fecal homogenate is added 10 μl of an aqueous solution of [^{3}H] methadone (*dl*, *d*- or *l*-methadone with a specific activity of 92 mCi/mM, New England Nuclear) containing 1500–1800 cpm, to determine recovery of methadone through the extraction procedure. The homogenate is vortexed and allowed to equilibrate for 1 hour at room temperature. Then 4 ml of 0.5 *N* HCl is added and vortexed. This is placed in a refrigerator overnight. On the following day, the mixture is vortexed and then centrifuged. The aqueous phase is transferred to a 35 ml centrifuge tube. One ml of 3.5 *N* ammonium hydroxide and 10 ml of ethyl acetate are added, shaken, and centrifuged. The ethyl acetate phase is pipetted to a conical tube and partially dried under nitrogen until approximately 1 ml is left in the tube. Then 2 ml of 0.5 *N* HCl is added, vortexed, and centrifuged. The upper phase (ethyl acetate) is discarded. To the lower phase (aqueous) are added 1 ml of 3.5 *N* ammonium hydroxide and 5 ml of ethyl acetate. This is shaken and then centrifuged. The upper phase (ethyl acetate) is pipetted to another conical tube and dried under nitrogen at room temperature. The residue is dissolved in 1 ml of ethyl acetate containing 0.12 μg docosane (as an internal standard for the final preparation steps and chromatography). A 500 μl aliquot is transferred to a second conical tube. Then 100 μl aliquots, in triplicate, of the remaining solution are transferred to counting vials for liquid scintillation counting to calculate recovery through the extraction procedure. The 500 μl aliquot is dried under nitrogen at room temperature and redissolved in 10 μl carbon disulfide. Then 2 μl (equivalent to 0.1 ml of fecal homogenate) is injected onto the gas chromatography column. Standard calibration curves are constructed regularly and are linear with a range of 0.5 to 4.0 μg/ml (usual fecal homogenate concentration ranges observed in patients receiving 30–120 mg oral methadone daily in maintenance treatment).

Precision and Accuracy of Methods

Precision of each of these assays was determined by performing replicate analyses of several specimens over a wide concentration range. The precision, or reproducibility, of a measurement for each of the analytical procedures was: (1) methadone in plasma, $\pm$3.3% relative standard deviation (% S.D.) over a concentration range of 0.02 to 1.00 μg/ml; (2) methadone in urine, $\pm$2.6% S.D. over a concentration range of 1.0 to 20.0 μg/ml; (3) methadone in feces, $\pm$6.0% S.D. over a concentration range of 0.5 to 2.0 μg/ml of homogenate; and (4) pyrrolidine in urine, $\pm$6.6% S.D. over a concentration range of 1.0 to 20.0 μg/ml.

Accuracy of each method was determined by replicate analyses of blank plasma, urine, or fecal homogenate specimens to which known amounts of methadone or pyrrolidine were added. Recovery of added methadone to (1) plasma was 98 $\pm$ 3.4% S.D.; (2) urine, 101 $\pm$ 2.5% S.D.; and (3) fecal homogenates, 96 $\pm$ 5.0% S.D.; and recovery of added pyrrolidine to urine was 95 $\pm$ 6.5% S.D. Accuracy determinations were carried out over the concentration ranges used in construction of respective calibration curves.

Mass Spectrometry Methods

Very recently, an even more sensitive method for the measurement of methadone in biological fluids has been developed in collaboration with Drs. Peter Klein and David Hachey of the Argonne National Laboratory. For this method, a stable isotope of methadone, pentadeuteromethadone, has been synthesized.[10, 11] Pentadeuteromethadone is used as an internal standard in a reverse isotope dilution method, in which the ratios of known or unknown amounts of unlabeled methadone are measured using gas chromatography-chemical ionization mass spectrometry, with a stable isotope ratiometer-multiple ion detection system. These stable isotope techniques also are now being used for pharmacokinetic studies of methadone metabolism in man.[6] In our future drug-interaction studies, this more sensitive technology will be available for use as indicated.

Qualitative analyses of methadone and its metabolites have been carried out using both direct probe and gas chromatographic-chemical ionization mass spectrometry, with isobutane, modified with ethylenediamine as the reactant gas, a procedure developed by Drs. Field and Bowen to increase sensitivity in the detection of methadone and its metabolites.[12]

TABLE 1

QUALITATIVE ANALYSIS OF METHADONE AND ITS METABOLITES BY GAS CHROMATOGRAPHY-CHEMICAL IONIZATION MASS SPECTROMETRY*

Retention Time†	m/e‡	Compound
0.56	264	pyrroline§
0.70	280	OH-pyrroline
0.73	278	pyrrolidine§
0.82	294	OH-pyrrolidine
1.00	266	pyrrolidone§
1.00	310	methadone§
1.01	326	OH-methadone
1.13	312	methadol§

* Dupont mass spectrometer. Isobutane reactant gas modified with ethylenediamine.
† Relative to unchanged methadone; on 10% UC-W-982 GCL column-220° C.
‡ $(M + 1)^+$ ion.
§ Authentic standards available.

Gas chromatography-mass spectrometry is done using a DuPont 21-492 mass spectrometer modified for chemical ionization by these laboratories and interfaced to a Varian 1400 gas chromatograph. A 6-foot (× 2 mm) glass column packed with 10% UC-W-982, kept at 220° C, is used with a helium carrier gas flow of 20 ml/minute. Spectra are obtained under chemical ionization conditions with a resolution of about 1000. The reactant gas used is isobutane, usually modified with ethylenediamine. Direct insertion probe chemical ionization or electron impact mass spectrometry is used in the analysis of some specimens. Data are acquired and processed with a Vacuum Generator 2040 data system.

Compounds can be identified by their gas chromatography retention times coupled with the mass of their respective protonated molecules detected by chemical ionization mass spectrometry (TABLE 1). Using these techniques, six metabolites of methadone have been detected in human feces, including the pyrrolidine and its hydroxylated derivative, pyrroline and its hydroxylated derivative, hydroxymethadone, and the pyrrolidone.

Further analyses using these techniques are in progress to determine whether any qualitative or quantitative changes in fecal excretion of methadone and its metabolites occur in the setting of drug interactions.

Clinical Studies

The first observations and studies of an unanticipated drug interaction, resulting in symptoms of narcotic withdrawal in patients on chronic methadone maintenance treatment, were made during studies of bioavailability of methadone during treatment with various oral dosage forms.[3] Nine patients, including

Table 2

Patients Studied to Determine Plasma Levels of Methadone After Oral Methadone and Methadone:Naloxone*

Patient	Age (years)	Sex	Weight (kg)	Years Heroin Addiction	Years Methadone Treatment	Methadone Dose (mg)
1	36	M	84	18	2	100
2	27	M	67	10	2	100
3	31	M	83	15	2	100
4	50	M	69	23	4	100
5	36	M	81	3	5	100
6	43	M	70	19	5	100
7	30	F	78	8	5	100
8	41	F	65	21	3	100
9	45	F	66	22	1	100
Range	27–50	6M–3F	65–84	3–23	1–5	100

* From Kreek.[3] By permission of *New York State Journal of Medicine*.

six males and three females, all of whom had been on chronic methadone maintenance treatment for more than one year and had been reliable patients with no evidence on history or urine monitoring of polydrug abuse, were studied after obtaining informed consent (Table 2). These patients ranged in age from 27 to 50 years and had a past history of 3 to 23 years of heroin addiction. Although five patients had a history of hepatitis prior to starting methadone treatment, all were clinically well and had normal liver function tests before and during the studies. All were maintained on 100 mg of methadone each day. Each patient was studied after 2 weeks of daily treatment with 100 mg of methadone and after 2 weeks of treatment with a combined preparation of 100 mg methadone and 10 mg naloxone (Bristol Laboratories), a research preparation designed to prevent parenteral drug abuse. It was presumed that naloxone would not be absorbed if the medication were taken orally as instructed, but would prevent any narcotic effect if it were used parenterally. This combined preparation was not expected to cause any symptoms when administered orally. The two medication forms were each presented in synthetic orange juice on a single-blinded basis.

Of the nine patients studied, two developed severe symptoms of narcotic withdrawal when given the combined methadone-naloxone preparation. These two patients experienced an acute precipitation of withdrawal symptoms within 30 minutes after oral ingestion of this medication. The symptoms included anorexia, nausea, vomiting, abdominal cramps, diarrhea, diaphoresis, pilocarpal erection, irritability, tremulousness, and severe anxiety. The symptoms persisted for 2 to 3 hours and then subsided but returned with equal intensity after each subsequent dose of the combined preparation, necessitating discontinuation of this medication after three and nine doses, respectively. Three additional patients suffered milder withdrawal symptoms after each dose of the combined medication, but these patients found the symptoms tolerable for the limited 2-week period. The remaining four patients could not distinguish between the methadone-naloxone combination and methadone alone.

Plasma levels of methadone were determined at 24 hours (or time zero), 2, and 6 hours after each dose form. The mean plasma levels of methadone after

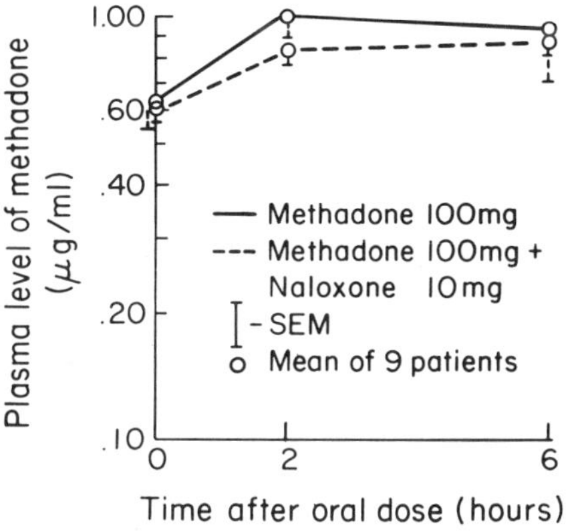

FIGURE 5. Methadone plasma disappearance curves on methadone: naloxone or methadone alone.

receiving methadone alone were typical of all similar studies in maintenance patients (FIGURE 5). At 24 hours after the last oral dose, there was a low but sustained plasma level of methadone, followed by a modest peak level 2 to 6 hours after the next oral dose. There were no significant differences in plasma levels of methadone during treatment with the combined methadone-naloxone preparation.

Single urine specimens were obtained from each patient at 24 hours after each dose form and were analyzed for methadone, the major pyrrolidine metabolite, and creatinine (FIGURE 6). There were no significant differences in the ratios of urinary concentrations of methadone to creatinine or of pyrrolidine to creatinine during treatment with methadone alone and during treatment with the methadone-naloxone combination.

Thus, a classical interaction of a narcotic agonist, methadone, and narcotic antagonist, naloxone, was observed. Narcotic withdrawal symptoms were precipitated by the small amount of naloxone which must have been absorbed from the combined oral preparation. However, no changes in plasma levels of methadone and no changes in the urinary excretion of methadone and its major pyrrolidine metabolite accompanied these clinical symptoms. As a result of these studies and other similar clinical observations, the combined methadone-naloxone preparation was modified to contain a much lower percentage of naloxone (methadone:naloxone ratio, 20:1; Bristol Laboratories).

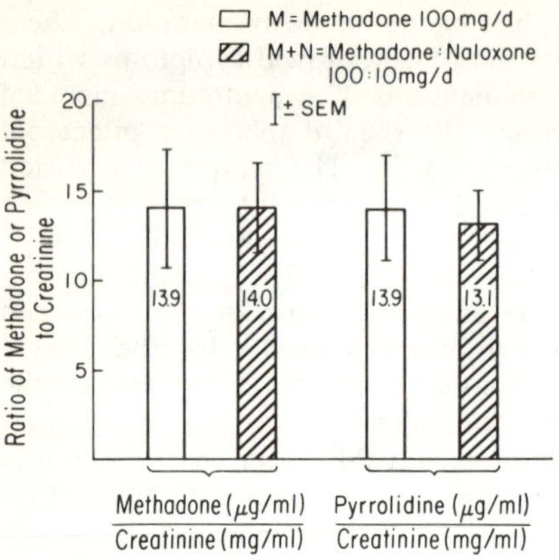

FIGURE 6. Urinary excretion of methadone and pyrrolidine metabolite during methadone or methadone:naloxone treatment. Urine specimens taken 24 hours after last oral dose of methadone in 9 patients. Mean values shown.

The second type of drug interaction observed and studied was that of the alterations of methadone metabolism and disposition by another drug, the antituberculosis agent rifampin.[13] This is the first time that this type of drug interaction with a narcotic used on a chronic basis has been observed in man. Symptoms of narcotic withdrawal were observed in patients receiving methadone for treatment of heroin addiction and rifampin as part of combined drug chemotherapy for tuberculosis. A study, carried out in collaboration with Dr. Jane Garfield of the Bellevue Chest Service and Department of Medicine at the New York University School of Medicine, was performed to determine whether rifampin altered plasma levels, metabolism, and excretion of methadone.

Eighty-six patients were treated for tuberculosis in the Bellevue Chest Methadone Maintenance Program.[13] Fifty-six received isoniazid with or without a second antituberculosis drug. Thirty patients with advanced tuberculosis were also treated with rifampin, in addition to isoniazid and/or other agents.[14-17] Nine of these patients treated with rifampin developed no symptoms. However, 21 of the 30 patients who received rifampin treatment developed mild, moderate, or severe symptoms of narcotic withdrawal. These 21 patients did not differ significantly from the 9 who did not develop symptoms or the remainder of the tuberculosis patients, with respect to age, ethnicity, or sex.

The interval between the beginning of combined rifampin-methadone treatment and onset of withdrawal symptoms was less than 2 weeks in most of these 21 symptomatic patients and was within 6 days in 6 of the 7 severely affected patients (TABLE 3). The withdrawal symptoms began each day 6 to 8 hours

TABLE 3

INTERVAL BETWEEN INSTITUTION OF COMBINED RIFAMPIN-METHADONE THERAPY AND WITHDRAWAL SYMPTOMS

21 Symptomatic Patients	1–6 Days	7–14 Days	15–30 Days	>30 Days
14 patients with mild symptoms	4	7	0	3
7 patients with severe symptoms	6	0	1	0

after the combined methadone and rifampin therapy was given and increased until 1 to 2 hours after methadone was given on the following day.

The mild symptoms observed in 14 patients included abdominal cramps, rhinorrhea, lacrimation, pilocarpal erection, yawning, irritability, and restlessness. Severe symptoms observed in 7 patients included nausea, vomiting, anorexia, chills, joint pains, insomnia, tremulousness, and severe anxiety. One patient treated these symptoms by self-administration of heroin. Others repeatedly asked for their methadone dose to be increased. Some patients suspected that rifampin might be causing their withdrawal symptoms and refused further treatment with the drug. Their symptoms promptly abated. Some patients with mild symptoms could be encouraged to tolerate these symptoms for the duration of a 20-week course of treatment with rifampin.

Six of the seven patients who had developed severe withdrawal symptoms during combined methadone-rifampin treatment were studied after obtaining informed consent (TABLE 4).[13] These patients were all males, ranging in age from 29 to 74 years. They had been heroin addicts for 6 to 30 years before entering methadone maintenance treatment. Three were studied first on and then off rifampin, and three were studied first off and then again on rifampin. Three patients had been receiving rifampin for at least 3 weeks when the first studies were carried out and then were off rifampin for 4 to 7 days before the studies were repeated. In addition to far-advanced pulmonary tuberculosis, one of these patients had adult onset diabetes requiring insulin treatment. Another patient was a chronic abuser of alcohol. A third patient had idiopathic seizures, unrelated to drug withdrawal, and was receiving phenobarbital during the rifampin treatment period, but not during the study period when off rifampin. The doses of methadone ranged from 30 to 60 mg per day and of rifampin from 600 to 900 mg per day. The remaining three patients were studied initially at least 3 weeks after rifampin treatment had been discontinued and then were restudied following resumption of rifampin treatment for at least 4 to 7 days. Each of these patients redeveloped narcotic withdrawal symptoms when rifampin treatment was reinstituted. One of these patients was also a chronic abuser of alcohol, and one had chronic persistent hepatitis. Each of these three patients was maintained on 90 mg of methadone daily, and each received 600 mg per day of rifampin.

Methadone is metabolized primarily in the liver. Over half of all patients in methadone maintenance treatment have clinical and/or biochemical evidence of chronic liver disease.[18, 19] Therefore, since rifampin has been reported to be hepatotoxic in some patients, liver function tests and serum proteins were followed off and on rifampin treatment. Although the exact frequency of rifampin-induced hepatitis is unknown, liver function test abnormalities, and in some cases, abnormal liver biopsies, have been reported in patients receiving this drug.[20, 21] Since most of the patients are concomitantly receiving other antituberculosis drugs, many of which are known to be potential hepatotoxins, these findings have frequently been difficult to interpret. Also many patients in whom deterioration of liver function has been noted during rifampin treatment have had documented chronic liver disease prior to starting rifampin treatment. In this study, both patients who were chronic abusers of alcohol (Nos. 2 and 4) and the patient with chronic persistent hepatitis (No. 5) had abnormal tests of hepatocellular function both before and during rifampin treatment (FIGURE 7A). These abnormalities did increase during rifampin treatment, but the patients did not develop clinical signs or symptoms. The three patients without

TABLE 4

PATIENTS STUDIED TO DETERMINE EFFECTS OF RIFAMPIN ON METHADONE METABOLISM*

Patient	Age (years)	Sex	Weight (kg)	Years Heroin Addiction	TBc. Diagnosis‡	Other Diagnosis	Other Drugs	Rifampin Dose (mg)	Methadone Dose (mg)
A. Patients studied first on and then off rifampin treatment†									
1	43	M	56	6	FAA	Severe diabetes (adult onset)	Isoniazid Ethambutol Insulin	600	60
2	53	M	51	20	FAA	Chronic alcohol abuse; past history hepatitis	Ethambutol	600	45
3	43	M	75	15	FAQ	Idiopathic seizures; past history hepatitis	Isoniazid (Phenobarbital while on rifampin only)	900	30
B. Patients studied first off and then on rifampin treatment†									
4	29	M	57	7	FAA	Chronic alcohol abuse; past history hepatitis	Isoniazid	600	90
5	74	M	55	30	FAA	Chronic persistent hepatitis	Isoniazid Ethambutol	600	90
6	64	M	50	20	FAA	—	Isoniazid Ethambutol	600	90
Range	29–74	6M	50–75	6–30					

* From Kreek *et al.*[13] By permission of *New England Journal of Medicine*.
† A. On rifampin at least 3 weeks; then off rifampin 4 to 7 days.
B. Off rifampin at least 3 weeks; then on rifampin 4 to 7 days.
‡ FAA, Far advanced active pulmonary tuberculosis.
FAQ, Far advanced quiescent pulmonary tuberculosis.

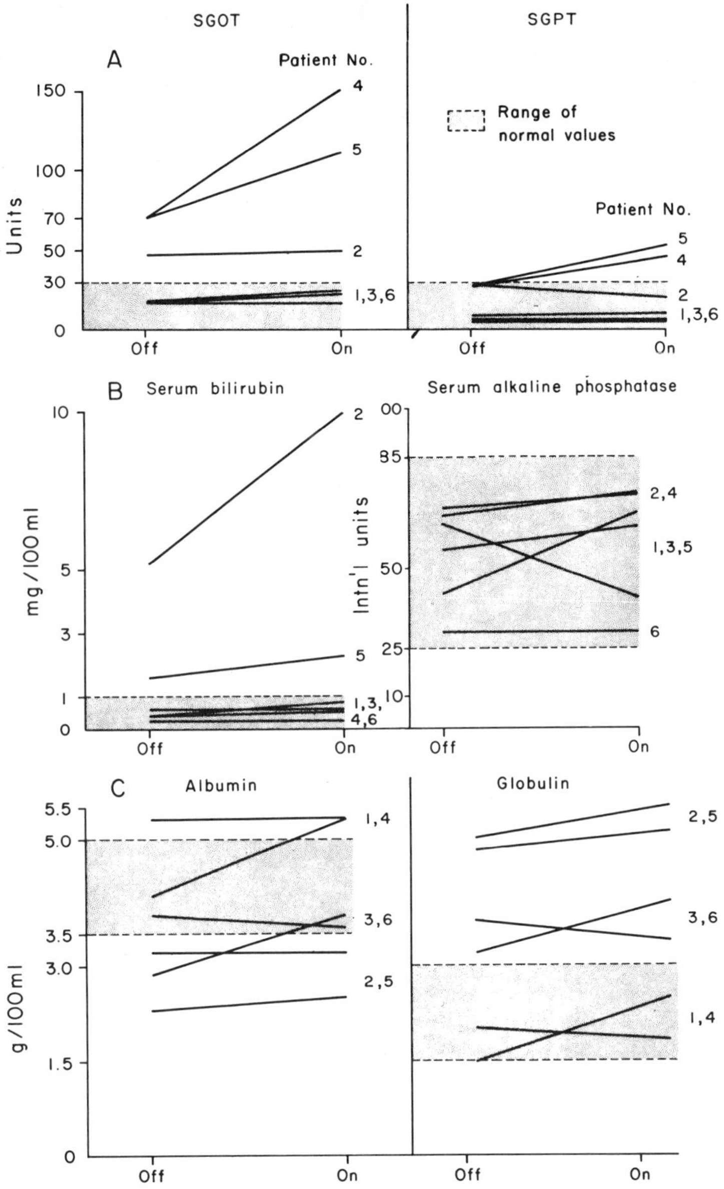

FIGURE 7. Liver function and serum protein tests off and on rifampin treatment.

previous evidence of liver disease did not develop abnormalities during rifampin treatment.

It has been shown that rifampin alters hepatic clearance of both bilirubin and bromsulphthalein, probably by competition for both hepatic uptake and biliary excretion. This effect may result in abnormal serum bilirubin levels and bromsulphthalein retention tests.[22-24]

In this study, only two patients with chronic liver disease had abnormal bilirubin levels before rifampin treatment, and in one, bilirubin levels markedly increased during treatment (FIGURE 7B). This patient was never rechallenged with rifampin. Alkaline phosphatase levels were normal in all patients studied. Before rifampin treatment, one patient had elevated albumin levels, two had normal levels, and three patients had reduced levels (FIGURE 7C). These levels

TABLE 5

PLASMA LEVELS OF METHADONE OFF AND ON RIFAMPIN TREATMENT

Patient	Dose (mg)	Rifampin Treatment	Hours After Oral Methadone Dose 0	3	6	24
1	60	off	<0.01	0.48	0.40	<0.01
		on	<0.01	0.18	0.22	<0.01
2	45	off	0.06	0.14	0.18	0.02
		on	<0.01	<0.01	0.09	<0.01
3	30	off	0.04	0.08	0.06	0.04
		on	<0.01	0.03	0.04	<0.01
4	90	off	<0.01	1.61	1.19	<0.01
		on	<0.01	0.75	0.46	<0.01
5	90	off	0.31	0.55	0.33	0.23
		on	0.10	0.18	0.14	0.11
6	90	off	0.47	—	0.75	0.39
		on	0.23	0.65	0.47	0.14

Significance: $p < 0.001$ differences between plasma levels off and on rifampin treatment.

did not change significantly during treatment. As in previous studies of heroin addicts and methadone maintenance patients, two-thirds of these patients had elevated globulin levels before rifampin treatment, and these levels also did not change during treatment.[18, 19]

Since 90% of plasma methadone is bound to serum proteins, including both albumin and globulin fractions, serum protein levels were followed both off and on rifampin treatment.[25]

Clinical histories and urine monitoring showed no evidence of polydrug abuse during these studies.[26] Plasma and fecal levels of methadone and urine levels of methadone and its major pyrrolidine metabolite were determined using gas liquid chromatography, and chemical ionization mass spectrometry was used to confirm, identify, and compare the pattern of methadone metabolites off and on rifampin treatment.

Plasma levels of methadone were determined at "time zero" or 24 hours after the last oral dose of methadone, and again at 3, 6, and 24 hours after the full daily oral dose of methadone (TABLE 5). Plasma levels of methadone during rifampin treatment were consistently lower (33–68%) at each comparable time point after oral methadone doses, except in the cases where the plasma levels of methadone were at the lower limit of detection (0.01 μg/ml), 24 hours after a dose of methadone when off, as well as when on, rifampin.[13] Plasma levels of methadone during rifampin treatment weie significantly reduced at the $p < 0.001$ level. Marked reduction in plasma levels of methadone during rifampin treatment was noted both in patients studied first on and then off rifampin (Nos. 1–3), and in patients studied first off and then on rifampin (Nos. 4–6).

Satisfactory 24-hour urine collections, both while off and on rifampin treatment, were completed in four of the six patients. Twenty-four hour urinary excretion of the major pyrrolidine metabolite increased in all four patients during rifampin treatment, with a mean 150% increase (FIGURE 8). Twenty-

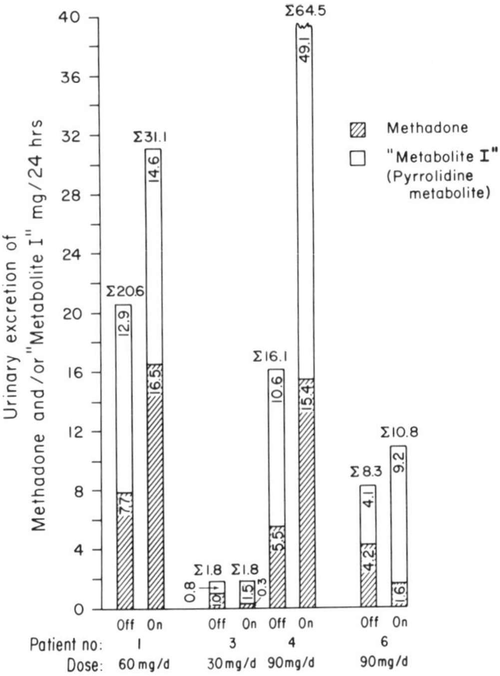

FIGURE 8. Urinary excretion of methadone and pyrrolidine metabolite off and on rifampin treatment.

four hour urinary excretion of unchanged methadone increased during rifampin treatment in two patients only. In these patients, as in other maintenance patients studied while receiving methadone alone, less than 50% of the daily oral dose of methadone was excreted as the sum of unchanged methadone and the major pyrrolidine metabolite when off rifampin treatment. In three patients the total excretion of methadone and metabolite was greater while on concomitant rifampin treatment, and in two (patient No. 1 receiving 60 mg/day and patient No. 4 receiving 90 mg/day) the total amount excreted exceeded 50% of the daily dose.

Satisfactory 24-hour fecal collections were completed in two patients both off and on rifampin treatment and in two additional patients while on rifampin only. Less than 1 mg of unchanged methadone was excreted in feces both while on, and while off, rifampin, suggesting that rifampin did not interfere with the intestinal absorption of methadone (TABLE 6). Fecal excretion of the

TABLE 6

FECAL EXCRETION OF METHADONE OFF AND ON RIFAMPIN TREATMENT*

Patient	Off Rifampin	On Rifampin
1	0.13	0.41
3	0.63	0.44
4	—	0.47
6	—	0.68

* Mg excreted in feces per 24 hours (gas chromatographic analysis).

major pyrrolidine metabolite was approximately 5 to 10 times greater than that of unchanged methadone while off rifampin and increased three- to five-fold while on rifampin treatment.

These data show three rifampin effects on methadone metabolism: (1) a lowering of plasma levels of methadone, coupled with (2) an increased urinary excretion, and (3) an increased fecal excretion of the major pyrrolidine metabolite. These findings could be interpreted as showing that rifampin was exerting its effect by its previously demonstrated ability to enhance hepatic microsomal drug-metabolizing enzyme activities.

Rifampin itself is cleared from the blood by the liver and is primarily excreted in bile as the unchanged compound and its major deacetylated metabolite. Using the rat bile fistula preparation, it has been shown that low doses of rifampin produce a choleresis and that higher doses produce true cholestasis.[27] Plasma levels of rifampin are higher in patients with liver disease than in normal subjects.[28-30] Alterations in the metabolism of rifampin in the setting of liver disease may accentuate its known effects on the liver. Rifampin has been shown to alter its own metabolism.[28, 31-33] Following repeated administration of rifampin in normal subjects, serum levels of rifampin are lower at 6 to 12 hours after oral administration of a dose than at the beginning of treatment. Increased biliary excretion of rifampin and its metabolites has been observed in this setting.[28] In patients with chronic liver disease, no such lowering of serum levels is observed, although a decrease in serum half-life after repeated administration has been observed in patients without and with liver disease.[28] Also, barbiturate-induced sleeping time has been shown to be reduced by chronic rifampin treatment in guinea pigs.[34] It has been postulated that these effects are due to an enhancement of microsomal drug-metabolizing enzyme activities by rifampin.

Rifampin has been shown to induce proliferation of the smooth endoplasmic reticulum in guinea pigs and, to a lesser extent, in human hepatocytes.[35] In studies using human liver biopsy material, it has been shown that rifampin treatment results in moderate, though not marked, enhancement of hepatic cytochrome P450 content, and of activities of the drug hydroxylating system.[36]

It has been suggested that some or all of the observed effects of rifampin on the clinical effectiveness of oral anticoagulants or contraceptive agents may be due to its effects on microsomal drug-metabolizing enzyme activity.[37–41] In the case of oral anticoagulants, rifampin has been shown to lower the plasma levels of the anticoagulants and to decrease their effects on prothrombin activity.[38, 39] In the case of the oral contraceptive drugs, effects on metabolism of the synthetic steroids have not been defined.[38, 39]

If enhancement of activity of microsomal drug-metabolizing enzymes were the sole mechanism by which rifampin lowers plasma methadone levels, one might expect to see a change in apparent plasma half-life of methadone, which is the slope when plasma levels are plotted semilogarithmically (FIGURE 9). In two patients studied (Nos. 3 and 6), in addition to the lowering of plasma levels of methadone during rifampin treatment, a more rapid plasma disappearance of methadone or shorter apparent half-life was also observed. However, one of these patients (No. 3) was receiving phenobarbital during rifampin treatment only, and phenobarbital could have altered the half-life. In three patients (Nos. 1, 2, and 4), although the plasma levels of methadone were lowered during rifampin treatment, plasma disappearance rates of methadone were not altered. Finally, in one patient (No. 5), again with lowered plasma levels of methadone on rifampin treatment, the apparent half-life was, in fact, prolonged during rifampin treatment.

TABLE 7

PLASMA HALF-LIFE OF METHADONE OFF AND ON RIFAMPIN TREATMENT*

Patient	Off Rifampin	On Rifampin
1	3.4	4.0
2	5.7	5.7
3	30.8	9.0
4	2.6	3.3
5	36.9	51.7
6	19.1	13.8

* Apparent terminal plasma half-life of methadone expressed in hours (determined from plasma levels at 6–24 hours after oral dose).

The data of the apparent plasma terminal half-lives of methadone based on the plasma levels of methadone at 6 and 24 hours show decreases in half-life in two patients, increases in one, and no changes in three during rifampin treatment (TABLE 7). These data suggest that the distribution of methadone may also be altered by rifampin treatment.

It has been shown by this laboratory that methadone is avidly extracted by the liver. Using an isolated perfused rabbit liver preparation, 85–90% of an injected bolus of methadone over a wide concentration range is extracted in one pass through the liver.[42] Since it has been shown that rifampin impairs the hepatic uptake of bilirubin and bromsulphthalein dye, its effect on hepatic extraction of methadone was studied. Preperfusion with rifampin did not alter the hepatic uptake of methadone.

Thus, it has been shown that rifampin significantly lowers plasma levels of methadone and that this effect is clinically paralleled by the appearance of

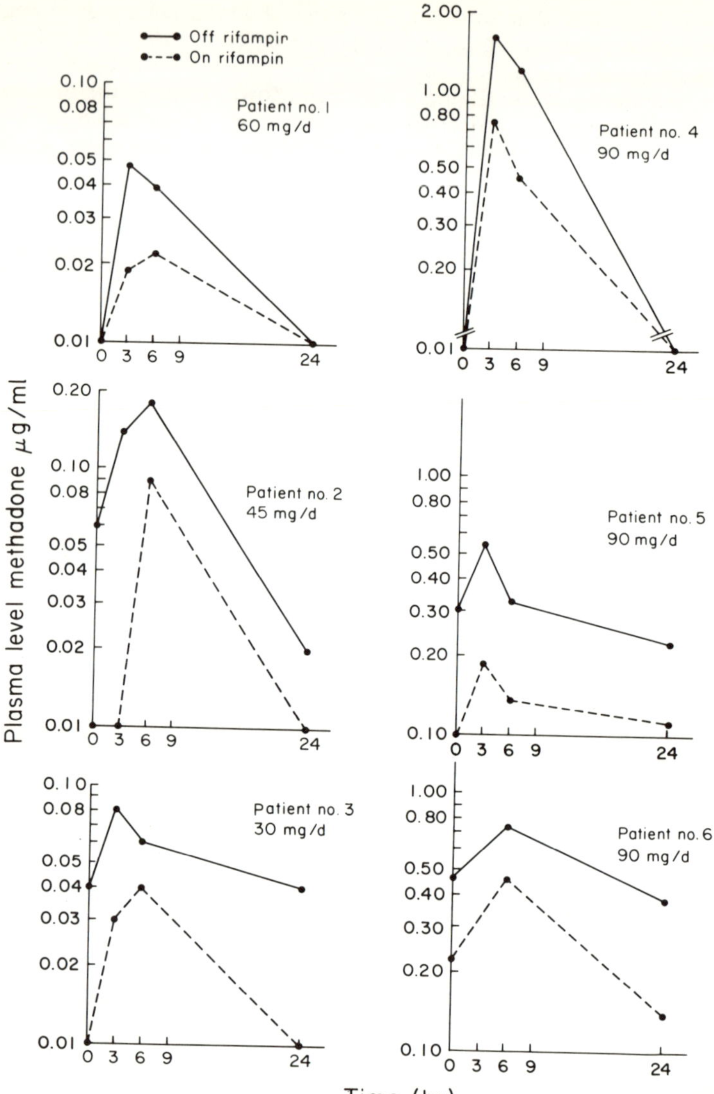

FIGURE 9. Methadone plasma disappearance curves off and on concomitant rifampin treatment. (From Kreek *et al.*[13] By permission of *The New England Journal of Medicine.*)

narcotic withdrawal symptoms in patients previously well maintained on that dose of methadone.[13] The mechanism by which rifampin lowers plasma levels of methadone is not fully understood. It may be due, in part, to enhanced microsomal drug-metabolizing enzyme activities. However, since during rifampin treatment there were inconsistent changes both in plasma disappearance rates, and in urinary and fecal excretion of methadone and its major metabolite, the consistent lowering of plasma levels of methadone may be due in part to some other alterations in drug disposition. Recent studies in animals have suggested that rifampin may interfere with the development of tolerance to morphine.[43] The clinical observations of narcotic abstinence symptoms in these studies might be related to some interaction of rifampin and methadone at the level of a central narcotic receptor. There is no evidence for this, however. Conversely, the observations made in animals may have been due to effects of rifampin on morphine metabolism similar to the effects of rifampin on methadone metabolism observed in these studies.

In summary, two types of drug interactions have been observed and studied in former heroin addicts maintained on the long-acting narcotic methadone. In both, the clinical symptoms resulting from the drug interaction were those of acute narcotic withdrawal. In the first, a classical narcotic agonist-antagonist interaction occurred between methadone and naloxone, with no concomitant changes in methadone disposition. In the second, significant changes in methadone disposition occurred during combined treatment with rifampin, which may have been partially or completely responsible for the observed concomitant clinical symptoms.

References

1. Sullivan, H. R. & D. A. Blake. 1972. Quantitative determination of methadone concentrations in human blood, plasma, and urine by gas chromatography. Res. Commun. Chem. Pathol. Pharmacol. **3:** 467-478.
2. Inturrisi, C. E. & K. Verebely. 1972. A gas-liquid chromatographic method for the quantitative determination of methadone in human plasma and urine. J. Chromatogr. **65:** 361–369.
3. Kreek, M. J. 1973. Plasma and urine levels of methadone. Comparison following four medication forms used in chronic maintenance treatment. N.Y. State J. Med. **73:** 2773–2777.
4. Sullivan, H. R. & S. L. Due. 1973. Urinary metabolites of *dl*-methadone in maintenance subjects. J. Med. Chem. **16:** 909–913.
5. Inturrisi, C. E. & K. Verebely. 1972. The levels of methadone in plasma in methadone maintenance. Clin. Pharmacol. Ther. **13:** 633–637.
6. Kreek, M. J. & D. L. Hachey. 1975. Use of pentadeuteromethadone in clinical studies of methadone disposition. Clin. Res. **23:** 571A.
7. Kreek, M. J. *et al.* 1976. Proceedings of the 3rd National Drug Abuse Conference (in preparation).
8. Sullivan, H. R., S. L. Due & R. E. McMahon. 1973. Methadone N-oxide in the urine of methadone maintenance subjects—an artifact? J. Pharm. Pharmacol. **25:** 1009–1010.
9. Kreek, M. J., C. L. Gutjahr, R. J. Korn, D. V. Bowen & F. H. Field. 1976. (unpublished observations).
10. Kreek, M. J., D. L. Hachey & P. D. Klein. 1975. Quantitative analysis of methadone in biological fluids using deuterium labeled internal standards. Second International Conference on Stable Isotopes: A-26.
11. Hachey, D. L. & M. J. Kreek (in preparation).
12. Bowen, D. V. & F. H. Field. 1974. Chemical ionization mass spectrometry. i-butane reactant gas modified by ethanolamine or ethylenediamene. Org. Mass Spectrom. **9:** 195–203.
13. Kreek, M. J., J. W. Garfield, C. L. Gutjahr & L. M. Giusti. 1976. Rifampin-induced methadone withdrawal. New Engl. J. Med. **294:** 1104–1106.

14. Garfield, J. 1974. Isoniazid-rifampin for initial treatment of pulmonary tuberculosis: Preliminary Report of the Public Health Service Cooperative Trial. Amer. Rev. Respir. Dis. **109:** 717.
15. Newman, R., B. C. Doster, F. J. Murray & S. F. Woolpert. 1974. Rifampin in initial treatment of pulmonary tuberculosis. A U.S. Public Health Service Tuberculosis Trial. Amer. Rev. Respir. Dis. **109:** 216–232.
16. Constans, P., A. Baron, R. Parrot & C. Coury. 1972. A study of 200 cases of active, recent pulmonary tuberculosis treated with rifampin-isoniazid. Chest **61:** 539–544.
17. Fox, W. & D. A. Mitchison. 1975. Short-course chemotherapy for pulmonary tuberculosis. Amer. Rev. Respir. Dis. **111:** 325–353.
18. Kreek, M. J., L. Dodes, S. Kane, J. Knobler & R. Martin. 1972. Long-term methadone maintenance therapy: effects on liver function. Ann. Int. Med. **77:** 598–602.
19. Kreek, M. J. 1973. Medical safety and side effects of methadone in tolerant individuals. JAMA **223:** 665–668.
20. Capelle, P., D. Dhumeaux, M. Mora, G. Feldmann & P. Berthelot. 1972. Effect of rifampicin on liver function in man. Gut **13:** 366–371.
21. Scheuer, P. J., J. A. Summerfield, S. Lal & S. Sherlock. 1974. Rifampicin hepatitis. A clinical and histological study. Lancet **1:** 421–425.
22. Acocella, G., F. B. Nicolis & L. T. Tenconi. 1965. The effect of an intravenous infusion of rifamycin SV on the excretion of bilirubin, bromsulphalein, and indocyanine green in man. Gastroenterology **49:** 521–525.
23. Acocella, G. & B. H. Billing. 1965. The effect of rifamycin SV on bile pigment excretion in rats. Gastroenterology **49:** 526–530.
24. Kenwright, S. & A. J. Levi. 1973. Impairment of hepatic uptake of rifamycin antibiotics by probenecid, and its therapeutic implications. Lancet **2:** 1401–1405.
25. Olsen, G. D. 1973. Methadone binding to human plasma proteins. Clin. Pharmacol. Ther. **14:** 338–343.
26. Dole, V. P., A. Crowther, J. Johnson *et al.* 1972. Detection of narcotic, sedative, and amphetamine drugs in urine. N.Y. State J. Med. **72:** 471–476.
27. Keberle, H., K. Schmid & H. G. Meyer-Brunot. 1968. The metabolic fate of Rimactane in the animal and in man. A Symposium on Rimactane. Pharmaceutical Division of CIBA Limited. Basle, Switzerland: 20–27.
28. Acocella, G., L. Bonollo, M. Garimoldi *et al.* 1972. Kinetics of rifampicin and isoniazid administered alone and in combination to normal subjects and patients with liver disease. Gut **13:** 47–53.
29. Curci, G., E. Claar, N. Bergamini *et al.* 1973. Studies on blood serum levels of rifampicin in patients with normal and impaired liver function. Chemother. **19:** 197–205.
30. Pozzi, E. & P. Menghini. 1974. Blood levels of rifampicin in liver diseases. Int. J. Clin. Pharmacol. **10:** 44–49.
31. Acocella, G., V. Pagani, M. Marchetti *et al.* 1971. Kinetic studies on rifampicin. 1. Serum concentration analysis in subjects treated with different oral doses over a period of two weeks. Chemother. **16:** 356–370.
32. Curci, G., N. Bergamini, F. D. Veneri *et al.* 1972. Half-life of rifampicin after repeated administration of different doses in humans. Chemother. **17:** 373–381.
33. Nitti, V., A. Ninni, G. Meola *et al.* 1973. Comparative investigations of the enzyme-inducing activity of rifampicin and barbiturates in man. Chemother. **19:** 206–210.
34. Curci, G., A. Ninni & V. Fabbrocini. 1970. Richerche sul legame farmacoproteico e sul metabolismo della Rifampicina. La Riforma Medica **84:** 197–202.
35. Jezequel, A. M., F. Orlandi & L. T. Tenconi. 1971. Changes of the smooth

endoplasmic reticulum induced by rifampicin in human and guinea-pig hepatocytes. Gut **12:** 984–987.
36. REMMER, H., B. SCHOENE & R. A. FLEISCHMANN. 1973. Induction of the unspecific microsomal hydroxylase in the human liver. Drug Metab. Dispos. **1:** 224–230.
37. MICHOT, F., M. BURGI & J. BUTTNER. 1970. Rimactane (rifampicin) and anticoagulant therapy. Schweiz. Med. Wochenschr. **100:** 583–584.
38. O'REILLY, R. A. 1974. Interaction of sodium warfarin and rifampin. Ann. Int. Med. **81:** 337–340.
39. ROMANKIEWICZ, J. A. & M. EHRMAN. 1975. Rifampin and warfarin: a drug interaction. Ann. Int. Med. **82:** 224–225.
40. REIMERS, D. & A. JEZEK. 1971. Rifampicin und andere Antituberkulotika bei gleichzeitiger oraler Kontrazeption. Prax. Pneumol. **25:** 255–262.
41. NOCKE-FINCK, L., H. BREUER & D. REIMERS. 1973. Wirkung von Rifampicin auf den Menstruationszyklus und die Ostrogenausscheidung bei Einnahme oraler Kontrazeptiva. Dtsch. Med. Wochenschr. **98:** 1521–1523.
42. KREEK, M. J., M. A. ROTHSCHILD, D. BOWEN *et al.* 1974. Hepatic extraction and metabolism of methadone and other narcotics by the perfused rabbit liver. Gastroenterology **67:** 805.
43. GISPEN, W. H., W. KRIVOY, D. DE WIED & E. ZIMMERMANN. 1975. Effect of rifampicin on development of tolerance to analgesic actions of morphine. Life Sci. **17:** 247–252.

COMMENT

DR. I. K. HO (*University of Mississippi, Jackson, Miss.*): Some interesting new data concerning interactions between methadone and barbiturates should be mentioned, as they may have chemical implications for methadone maintenance programs. For instance, Spaulding & Takemori[2] and Alvares & Kappas[1] observed that repeated administration of phenobarbital increased the V_{max} of N-demethylase activity of methadone and decreased the analgetic effect of methadone in rats.[1, 2] In mice implanted with pentobarbital pellets (75 mg) for 3 days, we observed a reduction of methadone toxicity and attenuation of methadone analgesia which correlated with an induction of hepatic microsomal N-demethylase activity.[3] As the recent studies by Verebely *et al.*[4] have shown that an increased biotransformation rate of methadone is partly responsible for the development of tolerance following chronic administration of methadone in man, the response to methadone of a narcotic user who is also a chronic barbiturate user may be modified. In other studies, we have also shown that continuous morphine treatment (pellet) potentiated pentobarbital narcosis and enhanced pentobarbital hypothermia.[5] In this case, the clinical implications are that the toxic effects of both drugs are additive and the duration of action of the barbiturates could be prolonged in addicts, thus leading to increased toxicity.

[1] A. P. Alvares & A. Kappas. 1972. J. Lab. Clin. Med. **79:** 439–451.
[2] T. C. Spaulding & A. E. Takemori. 1975. Fed. Proc. **34:** 814.
[3] I. K. Ho & W. O. Berndt. 1976. Life Sciences **18:** 1305–1314.
[4] K. Verebely, J. Volanka, S. Mulé & R. Resnick. 1975. Clin. Pharmacol. Ther. **18:** 180–190.
[5] I. K. Ho, I. Yamamoto, K. E. Becker, H. H. Loh & E. L. Way. 1976. Life Sciences **19:** 357–366.

MOLECULAR BIOLOGY OF PHENOBARBITAL ACTIONS AND INTERACTIONS

Steven J. Smith, Dai Kee Liu, Thomas B. Leonard, Barry W. Duceman, and Elliot S. Vesell

Department of Pharmacology
The Pennsylvania State University College of Medicine
Hershey, Pennsylvania 17033

Phenobarbital is a prototype compound for investigating the actions and interactions of depressant drugs at the molecular level. The effects of phenobarbital on the metabolism of macromolecules have been studied much more thoroughly in liver than in brain.[1-4] Regulatory mechanisms that could affect protein synthesis will be discussed in this paper, with emphasis being placed on potential interactions of phenobarbital with other drugs of abuse.

Phenobarbital can alter the pharmacokinetic parameters of other compounds through effects exerted on the processes of drug absorption, distribution, metabolism, excretion, or any combination of these. For most of these processes specific effects produced by phenobarbital at the molecular level remain to be defined. With regard to metabolism, the potent inducing effects of phenobarbital on liver drug-metabolizing enzymes located in smooth endoplasmic reticulum are abundantly documented.[1] By this mechanism, phenobarbital can increase the biotransformation of other drugs of abuse, decreasing their plasma half-lives and duration of activity.

Before discussing the actions of phenobarbital at the molecular level in hepatocytes and neurons, we shall review certain fundamental differences between the anatomy and physiology of brain and liver. Hepatocytes constitute approximately 90% of the liver mass. Although some differences exist among hepatocytes, they are for the most part a homogeneous cell type acting in concert to perform similar metabolic functions. Each hepatocyte contributes to liver function independently of other hepatocytes. In contrast, the brain contains not only heterogeneous cell types, but anatomically distinct subregions exhibiting discrete roles in brain function. Phenobarbital exerts its biological effects in specific subregions of the brain. In particular, phenobarbital is believed to act on the neocortex and reticular activating system (FIGURE 1),[5] whereas in liver, phenobarbital is believed to act equivalently on all hepatocytes.

Nerve cells communicate with each other through numerous synaptic connections, by which nerve cell bodies in one region of the brain can control other areas of the brain. Between sensory input and motor output, there is a complexity of synaptic integration that renders understanding of normal brain function exceedingly difficult. When exogenous drugs enter the brain via parenteral or oral routes, some answers emerge in terms of specific functions of certain brain areas, but in the final analysis there arise more questions than answers.

The structural features required for cell function are depicted in FIGURE 2. Events occurring in the nucleus control both the amount as well as the type of protein synthesized. Messenger RNA carries the code for protein synthesis. Messenger RNA precursors are transcribed from DNA in the nucleoplasm,

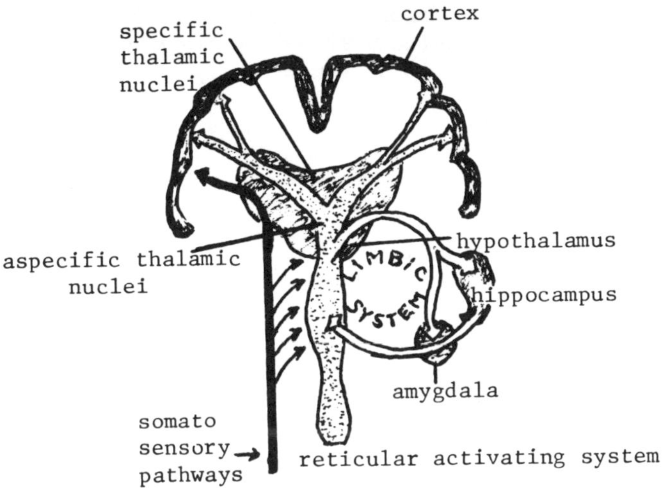

FIGURE 1. Brain areas affected by phenobarbital.

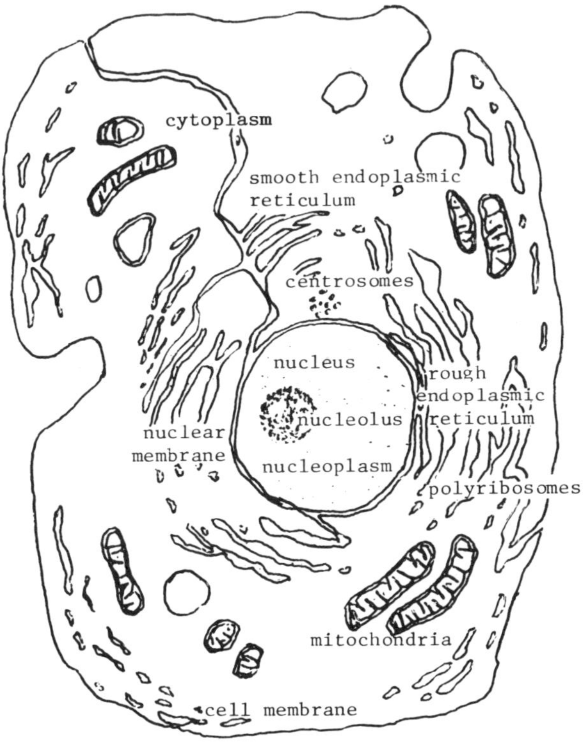

FIGURE 2. Diagrammatic representation of a cell.

whereas ribosomal RNA precursor is transcribed from DNA in the nucleolus. Both messenger RNA and ribosomal RNA are transported in the form of ribonucleoprotein particles from the nucleus to the cytoplasm, where they form the polyribosome complex and initiate protein synthesis (FIGURE 2).

Neurotransmitters acting at synapses play a primary role in normal brain function, as well as in the behavioral changes produced by some psychoactive agents.[6] However, the role of protein synthesis in maintaining normal brain function remains to be defined. Enzymes and other constituents of the nerve ending are synthesized in the perikarya. The nerve cell nucleus and its adjacent cytoplasm actively produce proteins, as indicated by several different lines of evidence including electron microscopy showing clusters of ribosomes in dendrites and in areas adjacent to the nucleus.[7] Rapid and slow axonal transport systems transfer essential enzymes and other materials to nerve endings.[8] The steps involved in synthesizing protein molecules in nerve cells may participate in the actions and interactions of certain drugs of abuse. Little research has been performed in this area. Since phenobarbital affects many of these processes

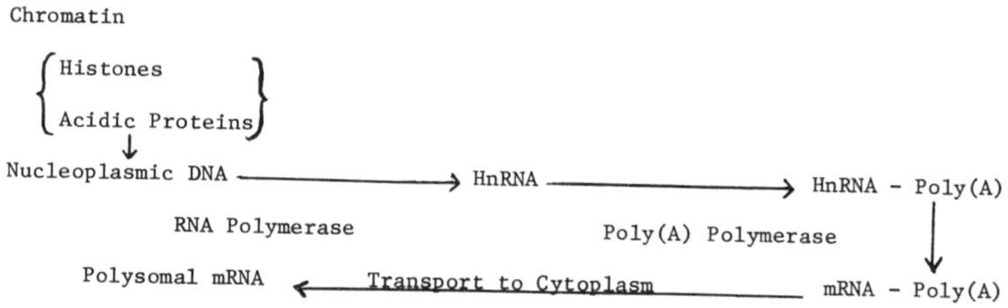

FIGURE 3. A model illustrating potential sites for action and interaction of drugs of abuse with respect to synthesis and transport of messenger RNA.

in the hepatocyte, it is a useful tool to explore mechanisms controlling protein synthesis.

FIGURE 3 is a schematic representation of the pathway for messenger RNA synthesis and processing. Because mature nerve cells and hepatocytes rarely divide, DNA turnover itself cannot constitute the primary site of action of psychoactive agents. However, drugs can interact with DNA or with proteins bound to DNA, thereby altering DNA function. Drug-induced changes in the structure of proteins attached to DNA, such as acidic proteins or histones, could unmask normally inactive DNA segments, thereby rendering them active with respect to RNA synthesis.[9] In rat liver, Bresnick and coworkers[10, 11] demonstrated that 2–6 hr after a single dose of phenobarbital acetylation of certain histones,[10] as well as phosphorylation of acidic nuclear proteins, is enhanced,[11] suggesting that RNA synthesis is increased.

FIGURE 3 reveals other possibilities. For example, DNA-dependent RNA polymerase may also be affected by these drugs. RNA polymerase II synthesizes messenger RNA. Some investigators claim that phenobarbital stimulates hepatic RNA polymerase II activity.[4]

In normal hepatocytes approximately 70 to 90% of messenger RNA precursor is destroyed within the nucleus and thus never reaches the cytoplasm[12] (FIGURE 3). Therefore, this material constitutes a reservoir of potentially usable messenger RNA. Messenger RNA coding for proteins different from those normally made could exist within this pool of "wasted" messenger RNA but never function under normal circumstances because it never reaches the cytoplasm. Several mechanisms could explain how phenobarbital and other agents of abuse might affect post-transcriptional processing of messenger RNA within the nucleus. Individual agents, as well as two or more agents in combination, could alter 1) protein addition, 2) methyl group addition, 3) poly(A) addition, and 4) the activity of specific nucleases. Nearly all cellular RNA is in the form of ribonucleoprotein particles. Newly transcribed RNA complexes with protein almost immediately. Drugs of abuse could alter the proteins added to newly synthesized RNA, thereby changing its conformation and subsequent processing. Recently, the presence of small numbers of methyl groups within messenger RNA molecules has been demonstrated.[13] Methyl groups appear at the 5′ end, as well as within the messenger RNA molecule. Protein synthesis *in vitro* does not occur in the absence of the 5′ methyl groups.[14] It has been suggested that the methyl groups within the messenger RNA molecule may serve as sites of

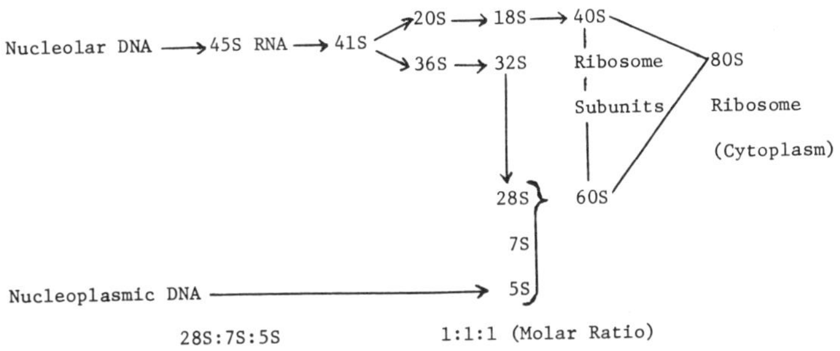

FIGURE 4. A model illustrating potential sites for action and interaction of drugs of abuse with respect to synthesis and maturation of ribosomal RNA.

specific cleavage of the large heterogeneous messenger RNA precursor molecules to the much smaller molecules of mature messenger RNA.[14] Although not all messenger RNA contains sequences of polyadenylate residues at the 3′ end, for most messenger RNA this could be a site of drug action. Specific endo- and exonucleases that physiologically cleave messenger RNA precursor have not been well defined.[15]

In a consideration of nuclear synthesis and processing of ribosomal RNA, processes similar to those described for messenger RNA could operate (FIGURE 4). However, the specific steps in cleavage of ribosomal RNA precursors are much better defined than those for messenger RNA.[16, 17] Each 45S RNA molecule produces a single molecule of 18S and 28S ribosomal RNA. Almost immediately after synthesis, 45S RNA is methylated at the 2′-O-ribose position. Approximately half of the 45S molecule is conserved during processing as mature 18S and 28S ribosomal RNA, but all methyl groups are retained. Degraded portions of 45S RNA are not methylated.

As mentioned previously with respect to messenger RNA precursor, potential sites for action and interaction of ribosomal RNA precursor with drugs of abuse are: 1) effects on nucleolar histones and/or acidic nucleolar proteins, 2) effects on RNA polymerase I, and 3) effects on post-transcriptional processing of ribosomal precursor RNA. Approximately 50 to 80% of newly formed 45S RNA, being degraded within the nucleus, never reaches the cytoplasm; and, as with messenger RNA, this source constitutes a pool of potentially usable ribosomal RNA precursor.

In answer to the question of where drugs of abuse could affect processing of ribosomal RNA precursor, the following sites should be considered: 1) protein addition, 2) methylation, and 3) the activity of specific nucleases. These sites of possible drug action are similar to those described previously for messenger RNA. Changes in stability of RNA newly formed from brain cells occur under certain circumstances. For example, newly synthesized RNA is much more stable in brains of mature than of immature mice.[18] Moreover, increased stability of newly formed RNA has been observed in brains of rats tolerant to morphine analgesia.[19]

Various sites exist in the cytoplasm for possible drug action at the molecular level (FIGURE 2). Direct effects on the efficiency of translation at the level of the polyribosome could occur in both liver and brain. Evidence exists that phenobarbital enhances protein synthesis in liver. Phenobarbital increases the uptake of labeled amino acids into rat liver proteins[20–22] and also decreases hepatic microsomal ribonuclease activity.[23, 24] Phenobarbital may increase the biological half-life of certain messenger RNA. Recent evidence suggests that phenobarbital decreases protein synthesis in the cerebral cortex.[25]

At the cell membrane, phenobarbital and other agents of abuse could act on the adenylate cyclase system.[26] In addition, those agents or their active metabolites may form drug receptor complexes similar to steroid hormones, thereby exerting effects within the cell.[27] Arias's studies on the binding of bilirubin and other drugs by ligandin could be generalized to apply to the transport of many drugs across cells.[28] Arias's group demonstrated that phenobarbital administration induces ligandin, thereby accelerating the transport of bilirubin across liver cells.

In liver, phenobarbital may produce some of its effects by direct action on the electron transport system that metabolizes some endogenous and many exogenous compounds. Phenobarbital may increase the synthesis of membrane components of the smooth endoplasmic reticulum where these reactions occur.[29] In addition to these sites of drug action, others may exist.

Data from our laboratory suggest that single doses of phenobarbital increase synthesis of ribosomal RNA but do not alter synthesis of ribosomal precursor RNA in rat liver.[30, 31] In the following experiments, adult male Sprague-Dawley rats received phenobarbital in a dose of 100 mg/kg intraperitoneally. Control rats were given an equal volume of 0.9% saline.

TABLE 1 shows that after a single dose of phenobarbital an increase of approximately 50% occurs in the incorporation of [^{3}H]orotic acid into ribosomal RNA.[30] Four daily doses of phenobarbital result in no increase in labeling of this RNA. Similar data were obtained when [^{3}H]adenine was used as the isotope. Other laboratories[32, 33] reported that within 16 hr after a single dose of phenobarbital, incorporation of various labeled RNA precursors into 28S and 18S ribosomal RNA is increased. These observations agree with the morphometric data of Staubli *et al.*,[29] who, using the electron microscope, estimated the number of bound ribosomes in phenobarbital rats. Sixteen hours after a single dose of phenobarbital, the number of bound ribosomes increased 60%. Even when phenobarbital administration was continued for five daily doses, these values returned toward normal.

TABLE 2 shows the effects of phenobarbital treatment on the labeling *in*

TABLE 1

EFFECT OF PHENOBARBITAL TREATMENT ON LABELING OF MICROSOMAL RNA WITH OROTIC ACID–5–^{3}H*

		28S RNA		18S RNA	
Time	Treatment	dpm/mg RNA	Ratio PB/C	dpm/mg RNA	Ratio PB/C
16 hr	Phenobarbital	8,272 (±350)	1.59†	6,394 (±330)	1.46†
	Control	5,202 (±360)		4,378 (±410)	
4 days	Phenobarbital	2,006 (±266)	0.82‡	1,738 (±202)	0.81‡
	Control	2,452 (±130)		2,154 (±124)	

* Rats were sacrificed 16 hr after a single dose or 4 daily doses of either phenobarbital (100 mg/kg) or 0.9% NaCl intraperitoneally. Each rat was injected intraperitoneally with [^{3}H]orotic acid 4 hr prior to decapitation. Microsomes were prepared; RNA was extracted by the sodium-dodecyl sulfate-phenol procedure. RNA was precipitated overnight in ethanol and dissolved in distilled H_2O. RNA was analyzed on 10 to 40% sucrose density gradients, and the 18S and 28S RNA peaks were collected from the gradient for determination of specific activity.[30] The results are the average of 3–5 experiments, and standard errors are indicated.

† Differences between controls and treatment are significant by the Student's t-test ($p < 0.05$).

‡ Differences between controls and treatment are not significant.

TABLE 2

EFFECTS OF PHENOBARBITAL ON THE LABELING OF RAT LIVER NUCLEAR 45S RNA*

		Ratio of Specific Activities Phenobarbital: Control	
Time	Pulse (min)	45S RNA (dpm/mg RNA)	Acid-Soluble Nucleotides (dpm/OD 260)
Orotic Acid [^{3}H]:			
4 days	10	0.67	1.00
4 days	60	0.66	1.02
3 days	10	0.94	—
16 hrs	15	0.98	1.02
Adenine (^{14}C):			
4 days	20	1.04	1.12
Guanine (^{14}C):			
4 days	20	1.15	1.15

* Rats were given a single dose or multiple doses of phenobarbital as described in TABLE 1. [5-^{3}H]Orotic acid, [8-^{14}C]guanine was injected at various times before death. The 45S RNA was precipitated from the sucrose gradients and dissolved in 1 ml of water; absorbance was determined at 260 nm, and radioactivity was measured by liquid scintillation counting.[30] The results are the average of 5 to 8 separate experiments.

TABLE 3

EFFECTS OF SINGLE AND MULTIPLE DOSES OF PHENOBARBITAL ON HEPATIC NUCLEOLAR RNA POLYMERASE ACTIVITY*

Treatment	Time	Picomoles UMP Incorporated/mg DNA ($Mn^{++}/(NH_4)_2SO_4$ + α-Amanitin)
Control		650 ± 31
Phenobarbital	16 hr	702 ± 20
Phenobarbital	4 days	660 ± 17

* Rats were treated with phenobarbital as described in TABLE 1. Control rats received a single daily injection of 0.9% NaCl for 2 days. Nuclei from 3 or 4 rats were isolated in sucrose-magnesium-spermine, and assays were performed as described previously.[30] Enzyme activity was linear, with increasing concentrations of nuclei from drug-treated rats and NaCl controls. Each assay was carried out in triplicate. The results are the averages of 3 separate experiments; standard errors are indicated. There were no significant differences between control and phenobarbital-treated animals by the Student's t-test.

vivo of nuclear 45S RNA. In rats sacrificed 16 hr after a single phenobarbital injection or 16 hr after four daily injections, no increase was observed in labeling of nuclear 45S RNA.[30] These same effects occur when various purines or pyrimidines are used as isotopic precursors of RNA. Because of the possibility that phenobarbital and other drugs alter the RNA precursor pool size, the results of *in vivo* labeling studies require confirmation by other techniques.

We measured the effects of phenobarbital treatment on synthesis of ribosomal RNA precursor. In rats sacrificed 16 hr after a single dose of phenobarbital or 16 hr after four daily doses of phenobarbital, no significant increase was observed in nucleolar RNA polymerase activity (TABLE 3).[31] Similar results are obtained in rats sacrificed 6 hr after a single dose of phenobarbital. Therefore, decreased degradation of newly formed 45S RNA, rather than increased synthesis, appears to explain the increased labeling of microsomal RNA. To test the hypothesis that 45S RNA is more stable in phenobarbital-treated than in control rats, we devised a nuclear incubation technique. In the following experiments, rats were sacrificed either 6 hr or 16 hr after a single dose or four daily doses of phenobarbital. Labeled nuclei from phenobarbital-treated or control animals were suspended in 0.25 M sucrose containing 5 mM $MgCl_2$ and divided into two equal parts. One part, incubated at 37° C in a water bath for 2 minutes, was then placed in an ice bath; the other part remained in the ice bath for 2 minutes. Nuclei were precipitated by centrifugation, and RNA extracted and analyzed on sucrose density gradients. FIGURE 5 shows sucrose density gradient patterns of RNA extracted from these nuclei. Analysis of control nuclear RNA extracted from nuclei heated at 37° C revealed loss of both optical density and label from the 45S RNA. The degraded RNA sedimented in the 18S to 28S region of the gradient. In contrast, 45S RNA of nuclei from phenobarbital-treated rats was only slightly degraded. These results suggest that phenobarbital pretreatment protected 45S RNA from degradation.[30]

We explored the possibility that newly synthesized 45S RNA of phenobarbital-treated rats exhibits more methylation than does 45S RNA from control rats. The incorporation of labeled *S*-adenosylmethionine into isolated nucleoli from phenobarbital-treated or saline-treated rats was measured. In rats sacri-

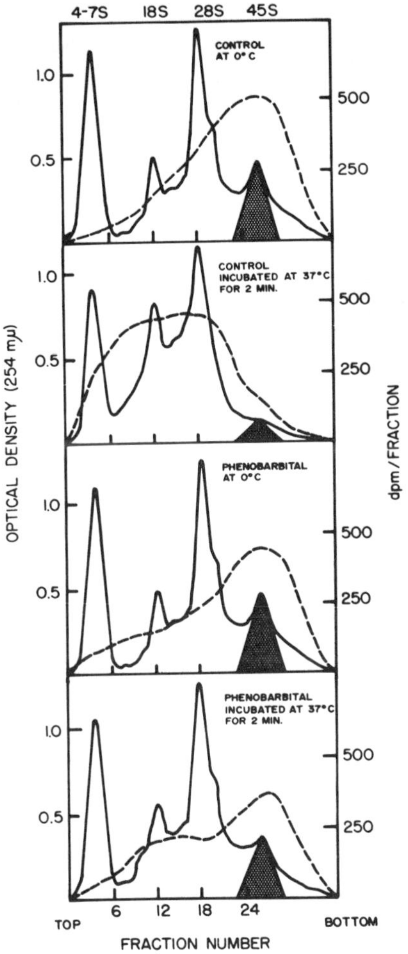

FIGURE 5. Effect of treatment with phenobarbital on stability of liver nuclear 45S RNA. Rats were sacrificed either 6 hr, 16 hr, or after 4 daily doses of phenobarbital or saline. Each rat received an intraperitoneal injection of 20 μCi of [5-^{3}H]orotic acid 10 min before death. Liver nuclei of NaCl- and drug-treated animals were suspended in 0.25 M sucrose containing 5 mM $MgCl_2$ and left in an ice bath or incubated at 37° C for 2 min as described in the text. RNA was extracted from the nuclei with hot sodium dodecyl sulfate-phenol and analyzed on 10–40% sucrose gradients. This figure is a composite showing that phenobarbital treatment for various times protects newly formed 45S RNA from intranuclear degradation.

ficed 6 hr or 16 hr after a single dose of phenobarbital, a significant increase occurred in nucleolar RNA methyltransferase activity (TABLE 4). Increased incorporation *in vitro* of labeled methyl group into isolated nucleoli of phenobarbital-treated rats should be reflected by an increase of similar magnitude in the amount of labeled dinucleotides/mg DNA. In two separate experiments, rats were sacrificed 16 hr after a single dose of phenobarbital or saline; nucleoli were isolated; and the assay for nucleolar RNA methyltransferase activity was performed as described in TABLE 4.

Since sugar methylation of a nucleotide confers to adjacent nucleotides resistance to alkali digestion, alkaline stable dinucleotides containing methyl groups are formed after incubation of ribosomal RNA overnight in 1 M sodium hydroxide. TABLE 5 shows that increased nucleolar RNA methyltransferase activity in phenobarbital-treated rats is reflected by similar elevations in labeled alkaline stable dinucleotides.

TABLE 4

EFFECT OF A SINGLE DOSE OF PHENOBARBITAL ON HEPATIC NUCLEOLAR RNA METHYLTRANSFERASE ACTIVITY*

Treatment	Time	SAM Incorporation Picomoles/mg DNA	Ratio of Phenobarbital to Control†
Control	6 hr	980 ± 28 (4)	
Phenobarbital		1263 ± 80 (4)	1.29
Control	16 hr	718 ± 51 (6)	
Phenobarbital		976 ± 34 (6)	1.36

* Rats were sacrificed 6 or 16 hr after receiving a single dose of phenobarbital as described in TABLE 1. Liver nucleoli were prepared by sonication. Nucleolar methyltransferase activity was assayed using a modification of the RNA polymerase assay developed by Jacob *et al.*[36] [^{3}H]*S*-adenosylmethionine (SAM) was used as the methyl donor. The incubation mixture contained a final volume of 0.5 ml. The reaction was carried out for 30 min at 30° C. The reaction was stopped by adding 100 mg of cold SAM and 1.5 ml of 0.4 N PCA containing 0.04 M $Na_4P_2O_7$. After sitting in an ice bath for 20 min, the acid-insoluble fraction was precipitated by centrifugation at 1000 × *g* for 10 min. RNA was extracted using the Munro and Fleck procedure.[35] The precipitate was washed twice with 0.2 N PCA, and 0.6 ml of 0.3 N KOH was added to it. After incubation in alkali for 90 min to hydrolyze RNA, DNA and protein were precipitated with PCA to a final concentration of 0.3 N. The tubes, placed in an ice-water bath for 20 min, were then centrifuged to sediment DNA, protein, and salt. The supernatant was analyzed for incorporation of [^{3}H]SAM into RNA. The number of experiments are shown in parentheses; standard errors are indicated.

† Differences between controls and treated at 6 and 16 hr are significant by the Student's t-test ($p < 0.01$).

TABLE 5

RECOVERY OF ALKALINE STABLE DINUCLEOTIDES FROM NUCLEOLAR RNA LABELED *in vitro* WITH [^{3}H]*S*-ADENOSYLMETHIONINE*

Group	Nucleolar RNA Methyltransferase Assay: pm SAM incorp/mg DNA	Nucleolar RNA Methyltransferase Assay: PB/CO	Recovery of Alkaline Stable Dinucleotides: cpm/mg DNA	Recovery of Alkaline Stable Dinucleotides: PB/CO
Control	659	1.00	14079	1.00
Phenobarbital	1046	1.59	22673	1.61

* Rats were sacrificed 16 hr after receiving a single dose of phenobarbital or saline. Nucleoli were prepared using the sonication technique.[30]. The assay was carried out as described in TABLE 4. After extraction of RNA methylated *in vitro* with hot sodium dodecylsulfate-phenol, and alkaline hydrolysis of the purified RNA, the nucleotides were eluted by DEAE-cellulose chromatography.[34] Each fraction was collected and analyzed for radioactivity. The results shown are the average of two separate experiments.

To determine whether phenobarbital administration *in vivo* altered hepatic nuclear ribonuclease activity, we measured in rat liver the effects of phenobarbital administration on total nuclear alkaline ribonuclease activity assayed *in vitro* (FIGURE 6).[30] Labeled 45S RNA served as a substrate for total alkaline ribonuclease activity. The results shown in FIGURE 6 represent nuclear ribonuclease activity in rats sacrificed after four single daily doses of phenobarbital.

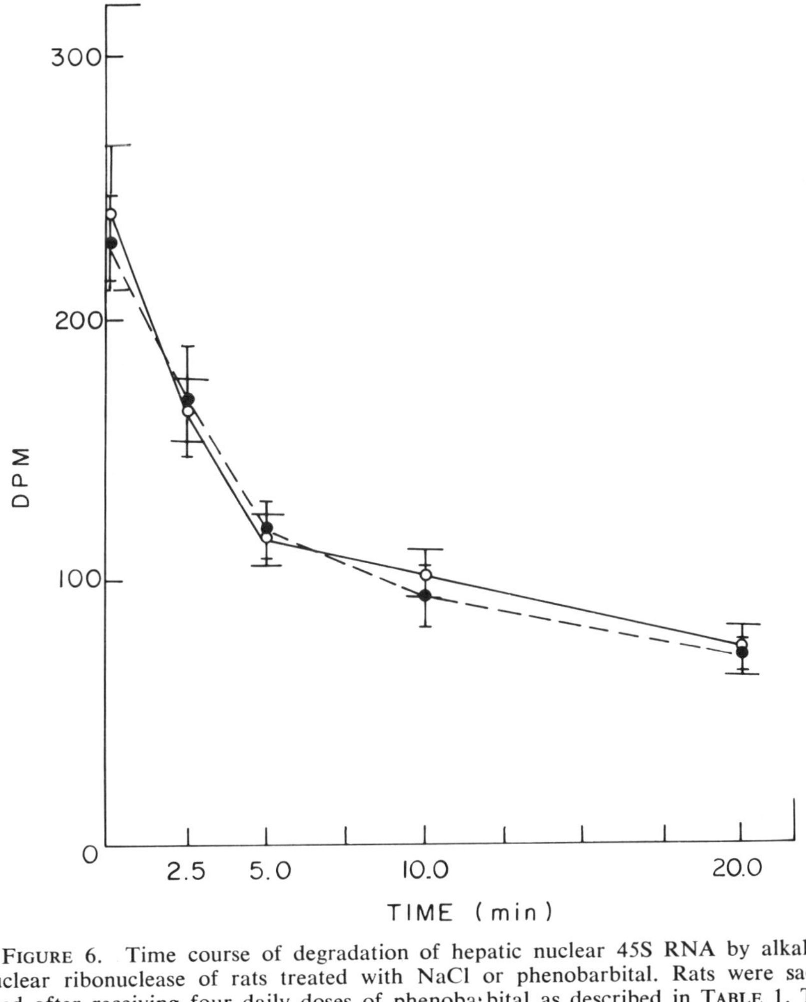

FIGURE 6. Time course of degradation of hepatic nuclear 45S RNA by alkaline nuclear ribonuclease of rats treated with NaCl or phenobarbital. Rats were sacrificed after receiving four daily doses of phenobarbital as described in TABLE 1. The assay for total alkaline ribonuclease was carried out as previously described.[30] The data are expressed as radioactivity remaining in the acid-insoluble fraction after incubation for the times indicated. The same results were obtained using nuclei of rats sacrificed 16 hr after receiving a single dose of phenobarbital. The results are the averages of five separate experiments. Standard errors are indicated. ●---●, phenobarbital; ○——○, NaCl controls.

Similar results were obtained in rats sacrificed 16 hr after a single dose of phenobarbital. Studies performed using nonlabeled ribosomal RNA as the substrate for nuclear ribonuclease yielded results similar to those shown here.[30] Although phenobarbital treatment had no effect on total nuclear alkaline ribonuclease activity (FIGURE 6), two qualifications should be made: 1) Deproteinated 45S RNA served as a substrate. In the *in vitro* nuclear incubation system, 45S RNA was present in the form of ribonucleoprotein. 2) Small amounts of specific nucleases may be physiologically active, but their activities could be masked by measurement of total nuclear ribonuclease activity.

In summary: 1) Phenobarbital decreases degradation of newly formed ribosomal precursor RNA from rat liver, thereby increasing the number of molecules of 45S RNA available for processing and transport to the cytoplasm. 2) Therefore, the stimulatory effects of this inducer on hepatic drug-metabolizing enzymes may be related in part to enhanced metabolic stability of newly formed ribosomal RNA. 3) The mechanism by which phenobarbital stabilizes newly formed molecules of 45S RNA may involve increased nucleolar RNA methyltransferase activity, which in turn increases the amount of methylated 45S RNA.

Recent studies in our laboratory revealed that in brain nuclei of rats sacrificed 2 hr after a single intraperitoneal injection of phenobarbital (100 mg/kg), RNA polymerase II, but not polymerase I, activity decreased by almost twofold. Whether diminished synthesis of messenger RNA in brains of phenobarbital-treated rats is a primary or secondary effect remains to be defined. We are currently investigating effects of phenobarbital and other drugs of abuse on RNA metabolism in brain cells. In neurons the relationship between altered RNA metabolism and the psychopharmacological actions of these drugs is under study.

REFERENCES

1. VALERINO, D. M., E. S. VESELL, K. C. AURORI & A. O. JOHNSON. 1974. Drug Metab. Disp. **2:** 448–457.
2. REMMER, H. 1972. Eur. J. Clin. Pharmacol. **5:** 116–136.
3. TRAGL, K. H. & R. CHIARI. 1974. Acta Hepato-Gastroenterol. **21:** 433–437.
4. GELBOIN, H. V. 1971. *In* Fundamentals of Drug Metabolism and Drug Disposition. B. N. LaDue, H. G. Mandel & E. L. Way, Eds.: 279–306. Williams & Wilkins Co. Baltimore, Md.
5. SHULMAN, A. 1970. Med. J. Aust. **1:** 1199–1204.
6. GAITO, J., Ed. 1972. Macromolecules and Behavior. Appleton-Century-Crofts. New York, N.Y.
7. TALWAR, G. P. & Z. IQBAL. 1972. *In* Macromolecules and Behavior. J. Gaito, Ed. Appleton-Century-Crofts. New York, N.Y.
8. SJÖSTRAND, I. & M. FRIZELL. 1974. *In* Dynamics of Degeneration and Growth in Neurons. K. Fuxe, L. Olson & Y. Zotterman, Eds. Pergamon Press. Oxford and New York.
9. KLEINSMITH, L. J. 1972. Biol. Sci. **22:** 343–348.
10. PROCACCINI, R. L. & E. BRESNICK. 1975. Chem. Biol. Interact. **11:** 523–533.
11. BLANKENSHIP, J. & E. BRESNICK. 1974. Biochim. Biophys. Acta **340:** 218–227.
12. JELINEK, W., M. ADESNIK, M. SOLDITT, D. SHEINESS, R. WALL, G. MOLLOY, L. PHILIPSON & J. E. DARNELL. 1973. J. Mol. Biol. **75:** 515–532.
13. PERRY, R. & D. KELLEY. 1974. Cell **1:** 37–42.

14. DESROSIERS, R. C., K. H. FRIDERICI & F. M. ROTTMAN. 1975. Biochemistry **14:** 4367–4374.
15. KWAN, C. N., S. GOTOH & D. SCHLESSINGER. 1974. Biochim. Biophys. Acta **349:** 428–441.
16. MADEN, B. E. H., M. SALIM & D. F. SUMMERS. 1972. Nature [New Biol.] **237:** 5–9.
17. DARNELL, J. E. 1968. Bacteriol. Rev. **32:** 262–290.
18. BANKS, S. P. & T. C. JOHNSON. 1972. Brain Res. **41:** 155–169.
19. CASTLES, T. R., S. CAMPBELL, R. GOUGE & C. C. LEE. 1972. J. Pharmacol. Exp. Ther. **181:** 399–406.
20. VENKATESAN, N. & W. J. STEELE. 1975. Chem. Biol. Interact. **11:** 41–54.
21. GELBOIN, H. V. & L. SOKOLOFF. 1961. Science **134:** 611–612.
22. KATO, R., W. R. JONDORF, L. A. LOEB, T. BEN & H. V. GELBOIN. 1966. Mol. Pharmacol. **2:** 171–186.
23. MYCEK, M. J. 1971. Biochem. Pharmacol. **20:** 325–337.
24. LECHNER, M. C. & C. R. POUSADA. 1971. Biochem. Pharmacol. **20:** 3021–3028.
25. JONES, G. L. & D. M. WOODBURY. 1976. Biochem. Pharmacol. **25:** 53–61.
26. PASTAN, I. & R. L. PERLMAN. 1971. Nature [New Biol.] **229:** 5–7.
27. BULLER, R. E. & B. W. O'MALLEY. 1976. Biochem. Pharmacol. **25:** 1–12.
28. REYES, H., A. J. LEVI, R. LEVINE, Z. GATMAITAN & I. M. ARIAS. 1971. Ann. N.Y. Acad. Sci. **179:** 520–528.
29. STAUBLI, W., R. HESS & E. R. WEIBEL. 1969. J. Cell Biol. **42:** 92–113.
30. SMITH, S. J., R. N. HILL, R. A. GLEESON & E. S. VESELL. 1972. Mol. Pharmacol. **8:** 691–700.
31. SMITH, S. J., S. T. JACOB, D. K. LIU, B. DUCEMAN & E. S. VESELL. 1974. Mol. Pharmacol. **10:** 248–256.
32. COHEN, A. M. & R. W. RUDDON. 1970. Mol. Pharmacol. **6:** 540–547.
33. MCCAULEY, R. & D. COURI. 1971. Biochim. Biophys. Acta **238:** 233–244.
34. VAUGHAN, JR., M. H., R. SOEIRO, J. R. WARNER & J. E. DARNELL, JR. 1967. Proc. Natl. Acad. Sci. U.S.A. **58:** 1527–1534.
35. MUNRO, H. N. & FLECK, A. 1966. Methods Biochem. Anal. **14:** 113–176.
36. JACOB, S. T., E. M. SAJDEL & H. N. MUNRO. 1966. Eur. J. Biochem. **7:** 449–453.

INTERACTIONS OF DRUGS OF ABUSE WITH ALCOHOL

Cedric M. Smith

Research Institute on Alcoholism
New York State Department of Mental Hygiene and
Department of Pharmacology and Therapeutics
State University of New York
Buffalo, New York 14203

The reasons for interest in alcohol-drug interactions stem from three different, distinct areas of concern. First, the frequency and degree with which alcohol is used by members of our society means that most, if not all, other drugs will be used with appreciable frequency before or after alcohol. In fact, many alcoholic beverages are classed as foodstuffs rather than as drugs. The concerns, then, are clinical and epidemiological in terms of altered actions, changed intensity of effect of either the drug or alcohol, and the frequency and import of such combinations. Of course, prime among these are the possibilities for increased toxicity.

The second concern is the potential for increased understanding of the nature of either the drug or alcohol's action based on studies of interactive effects of two or more agents.

The third concern deals with possible influence of effects or experiences with one agent with respect to the probability of use of a second. For example, does heavy caffeine ingestion during the day predispose one to the use of alcohol in the evening? Does experience with alcohol intoxication in any way predispose an individual to explore or adopt other means of intoxication? Reference is made to extensive previous reviews on alcohol-drug interactions.[1–6, 58]

There is little I can add with respect to the clinical import, other than the generalizations that are relatively common knowledge among laymen as well as professionals. In general, among the various psychoactive drugs, including the so-called drugs of abuse, on acute administration all produce the combination of effects of the two agents, both with reference to qualitative effects of the drugs and their quantitative effects. Thus, from a clinical point, they are all "additive," and their combination results in the combined effects of both.

Moreover, I am aware of no instances of striking antagonism—such as that seen between naloxone and morphine. Of recent interest are reports of antagonism between chlordiazepoxide and alcohol.[8–13] Conversely, marked potentiation of an active drug by a relatively inactive one is rarely observed either, except for the toxicity of certain combinations of amphetamine and alcohol.[14, 15] Over rather broad ranges, drugs that depress a given function tend to be synergic and, within the narrow physiological limits, depressants may antagonize certain stimulant effects, for example, the induction of sleep by a barbiturate in an individual who has received amphetamine or the mutual antagonism between low doses of pentobarbital and caffeine.[16] None of the agents, however, reveal any neural or biochemical processes not observable in the undrugged individual. To date, there are no known specific or competitive antagonists of ethanol (or of the inhalational or barbiturate anesthetics as well).

With respect to interactions with either the drug or the alcohol being present for some time prior to the other agent, a variety of clinical concerns can be identified. (These factors are so complex in their impact that an analysis of the usual clinical situation is nearly impossible; thus, practically speaking, interactions are not predictable.) Among these are:

1. *Additive,* qualitatively and quantitatively on simultaneous administration.

2. *Acute acquired, functional tolerance* among most, if not all, sedative hypnotics and ethanol. The time course of onset of acute tolerance is 3 hours or more (i.e., within the usual acute administration situation), and its magnitude is dose-related and such that up to some 2 to 4 hours the previously effective dose will be required to produce a given effect.[17-21] (See FIGURE 1 and 2.) The acute tolerance varies in degree with the dose, the agent, the time

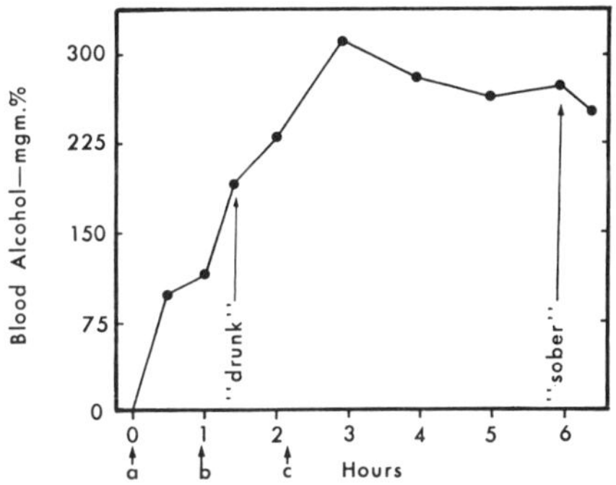

FIGURE 1. Graph showing blood-alcohol concentration consequent to drinking at "a" (1.0 g per kg), "b" (0.25 g per kg), and "c" (0.25 g per kg). Arrows indicate the point at which the patient revealed the signs and symptoms of alcoholic intoxication, and the point at which the patient subsequently became sober. (From Mirsky *et al.*[57] By permission of *Quarterly Journal of Studies on Alcohol.*)

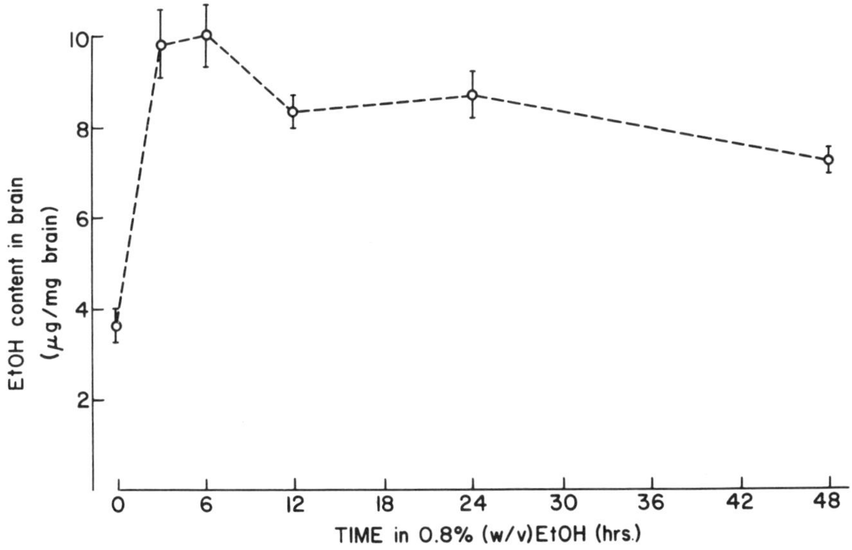

FIGURE 2. Time course tolerance development in groups of fish exposed to ethyl alcohol (ETOH) in aquarium water. Ordinate is mean of the ethanol concentration in brain required for loss of righting reflex (brackets depict standard error). Note maximal tolerance with the 3 to 6 hour exposure to ethanol. (From Greizerstein & Smith.[20] By permission of *Journal of Pharmacology and Experimental Therapeutics.*)

of testing, and, very importantly, with the system and function used to measure the drug effect.

3. I postulate that following a single acute dose of ethanol or barbiturates there follows what might be called an acute hypersensitivity to sedative drug during the "common" hangover period. However, the very large physiological alterations characteristic of severe hangovers make assessment of drug effects during that period difficult. Obviously, the nervous system is altered; then how can one actually denote a given action, such as relief of tremor, or altered motor function, as analogous to that seen prior to the intoxication and subsequent hangover?

This postulated "*acute withdrawal syndrome*" has been suggested in some animal studies. It has not been clearly described in man except in terms of the sustained alterations in sleep patterns observed after single doses of hypnotics or benzodiazepines[22, 23] or possibly with ethanol in epileptic patients.[24]

4. With *chronic administration* there are various possibilities for functional and dispositional tolerance, cross-tolerance, and sensitization. Included among these are metabolic alterations in terms of ethanol metabolism, its induction, alterations in barbiturate and other drug metabolism, plus the complex alterations in metabolism consequent to acute or chronic liver disease. This extensive literature and the recent important findings of groups coordinated by Israel and by Lieber will not be reviewed here.[25] In addition, other extraneuronal interactions may be important with alcohol; for example, its oral administration alters absorption of many agents, including barbiturates and diazepam.[26, 27] Distribution of a second drug would also be expected to be altered, because of vasodilation and diuresis if for no other reason.[28] Among the sedative/hypnotics and ethanol there is also marked chronic acquired, functional tolerance and cross-tolerance. Upon withdrawal, a *withdrawal syndrome* occurs. Its intensity depends on prior dose, frequency, and duration, and it may be fully reversed by administration of any of the sedative hypnotics; during withdrawal there is decreased apparent sensitivity to such drugs.[29]

Stimulants such as amphetamine would tend to partially antagonize the somnolence and sedation of the depressants, as well as aggravate the withdrawal syndrome, although this latter has been little studied. Although no antagonism or synergy was found between ethanol and amphetamine by measuring lethal effects in mice,[30] Rech[14] has found extensive and complex interactions between these two agents. (See also Garattini[15].)

Appreciable confusion exists regarding the possible influence of sedatives/hypnotics on the withdrawal syndrome to opiates and vice versa. Although this has not been extensively studied in either man or experimental animals, some of the results obtained are relatively plausible and predictable and can be summarized by saying that the agents continue to have their characteristic effects such that the hyperactivity and anxiety, for example, in mild withdrawal from opiates, is partially alleviated by sedatives or alcohol.[12] The reverse, i.e., the treatment of alcohol or barbiturate withdrawal with an opiate, has been less studied.

A specific combination of interest is marihuana and alcohol. The subject is complex since the acute interaction of modest doses appears to be a mixture of the two syndromes, such that there is both qualitative and quantitative combined additive effects. As a generalization, when subjects receiving both are queried regarding the experience, relative to effects of either agent alone, they report that it is "different, bigger, and better." Chronic experimental studies demonstrate complex interactions relative to dispositional and metabolic aspects of both the active tetrahydrocannabinols and ethanol; cross-tolerance also occurs.[25, 31–36]

Much is made of the differences between potentiation and addition, and the distinction is important when it can be drawn from precise dose-effect determinations such as those of Gessner and Cabana[37] or Gebhart *et al.*[38] It is important, however, to observe precisely what the dose-effect curves with ethanol and such agents actually detect and measure. In man such "dose-effect" relationships usually entail little more than assessment of two doses, and the effect is a complex mixture of actions on various neuronal systems. Frequently these are demonstrably different neural systems, such as those involved in sleep versus those involved in motor coordination. Thus, what is being detected with various doses is not only an increase in action on a given cell but the appearance of actions on other cells. In addition, many studies confound time course of action with intensity, and very few control for possible alterations in distribution.

What has been referred to above as "additive" might, on close examination with isobolographic techniques, exhibit more than quantitative addition, and thus may be "potentiated" interactions; however, the point being made is that such potentiation, to my knowledge, is not marked with any of the combinations of drugs of abuse of concern. Such combinations may well be hazardous to life, and this, as well as the unpredictability of large single or combination doses, are facts that the public needs to be continually aware of.

Perhaps more significant, but less well recognized, are the interactions among drugs, alcohol, the individual, and toxic agents that take place over a longer time span than is being considered in this symposium. Certainly, senile dementia and the chronic brain syndromes commonly associated with alcohol need much further study.[39]

From the clinical management point of view, it becomes academic to nitpick over the terminology of the quantitative aspects. All of the studies stress the finding that the drugs act as combinations (as just one of many examples, the study of Morland *et al.*[40] on combinations of diazepam and ethanol). Only rarely can these syndromes be described as antagonistic such as that reported between chlordiazepoxide and alcohol with respect to behavioral endpoints and possible utility in anesthesia.[8–11, 41, 42]

A variety of brief reports have appeared on interactions between ethanol and various drugs,[2] but how these can be assessed is difficult to state. For example, Smith[43] reports that alcoholics are remarkably resistant to the effects of 200 to 400 mg of LSD administered orally.

Wiberg *et al.*[44] appropriately emphasize that the unidimensional categorization of the terms "additive" or "synergistic" does not help clarify understanding of the effects of combinations of drugs.

Results with the subjective rating scales employed by the Lexington group raise the question of perhaps the converse of antagonism—i.e., there are overlaps between the various drugs barbiturates and amphetamines in terms of feeling better or relief of worry. Is there, perhaps, a common thread of actions that are positively reinforcing and these are what underlie certain patterns of self-administration?

Not only are the amphetamines and barbiturates or benzodiazepines (and probably alcohol) not direct antagonists, the subjective effects of the two taken simultaneously are detectably different from either alone or even what might have been predicted.[45]

The second of the primary concerns is the opportunity to deduce the possible sites or mechanism of action of the various agents by examining the quantitative interrelationships of effects of various concentrations of two or more agents. As part of his extensive studies on peripheral nerve and red cell permeability Seeman[46, 47] found that three different classes of blocking agents were simply additive in their actions over wide concentration ranges—the anesthetics including ethanol, the amine local anesthetic, such as procaine, and tetrodotoxin. Each agent appeared to act by altering action potential generation and passive sodium permeability.

The fact that ethanol, anesthetics, including barbiturates, and even hypoxia[48, 49] are usually approximately additive in their effects on a given isolated neural or behavioral system in many varied investigations leads to one or more of the following conclusions: (1) Each agent or chemical class of an agent has a different site(s) of action—on the same or on a different neuron; and/or (2) Even if there may be common receptor sites, the concentration of receptor sites probably is far in excess of the relative concentration of the agents, such that there is no detectable competition between agents or evidence for saturation of sites; and/or (3) The number of receptor sites that must be occupied for the given or a maximal drug action is far less than the total number available. (The maximum may well be limited by the appearance of other effects, e.g., the assessment of drug-induced depression of spinal reflexes that becomes confounded by cardio-respiratory failure.)

These possible inferences are analogous to a variety of treatments of theories of biochemical kinetics.

Note that it is *not* concluded that alcohol or any of its synergists or antagonists act "non-specifically." Alcohols and general anesthetics neither produce an identical syndrome nor do they act on all excitable cells with the same intensity or action. Nevertheless, there are no specific, competitive antagonists of alcohol or the sedative/hypnotic agents, even of some of the barbiturates which exhibit a degree of stereo-specific binding characteristics.[50]

The relevant action of alcohol, related drugs, or antagonists is the alteration in a specific synaptic system. To date none of such synaptic systems have been examined for the nature of the interactions between synergists and antagonists of ethanol, with perhaps the exception of the neuromuscular junction. The specification of site and mechanism of action is clearly being established at this site.[51] The neuromuscular junction is not a particular applicable model of central synaptic systems, but the extensive studies point to the methodology and approaches that may prove fruitful.[52–54]

[With respect to mechanism of action of alcohol and anesthetics, much is made of correlations between the passive distribution of the agents in lipid or water phases and potency or translocation kinetics. I would continue to emphasize, however, that although such factors are of critical and necessary importance, they are not sufficient to explain anesthetic, sedative, or anti-anxiety action any more than the demonstration of stereo-specific blocking or binding constitutes isolation of the receptor.]

A variety of curious or incidental interactions among these drugs have been reported. Among the more intriguing are the reports of Ross[55] on calcium levels in cerebral tissue. Both alcohol and morphine, separately, evoke a marked decrease in brain calcium; this effect is blocked or reversed by naloxone. Furthermore, this depletion exhibits tolerance and cross-tolerance between ethanol and morphine! Whether the calcium depletion is related to the central nervous system depression or is secondary to other phenomena remains to be determined. Reference is made to the extensive interactions between ethanol, morphine, and naloxone detailed in this symposium by Ho.[12]

I refer the reader to other participants in this symposium who have reviewed specific interactions of drug of abuse with alcohol, amphetamines and cocaine, cannabis, narcotics.

The third concern can only be touched on because of the paucity of concrete information. Alcoholic beverages and sedative/hypnotics are used and abused by many people, they say, to produce relaxation, sleep, or relief of anxiety, worry, and insomnia. In some individuals such internal manic or anxiety states may indeed be induced by another drug—e.g., caffeine or cocaine, amphetamines; the see-saw of stimulant and depressant drug use are frequently described clinical situations. Whether or not the alternate drug use is causally or strongly related is not known and is a prime area for future study. The degree to which the use of one drug may predispose to the use of another remains to be determined. Relevant animal models are just beginning to be defined.[56]

References

1. Kissin, B. 1974. Interactions of ethyl alcohol and other drugs. *In* The Biology of Alcoholism. B. Kissin & H. Begleiter, Eds. Vol. **3:** 109–161. Plenum Press. New York, N.Y.
2. Polacsek, E., T. Barnes, N. Turner, R. Hall & C. Weise. 1972. Interaction of Alcohol and Other Drugs: An Annotated Bibliography. 2nd edit. (revised). Addiction Research Foundation. Toronto, Ontario, Canada.
3. Forney, R. B. & F. W. Hughes. 1970. Interaction between alcohol and psychopharmacological drugs. *In* International Encyclopedia of Pharmacology and Therapeutics. J. Tremolieres, Ed. Vol. II. Pergamon Press. New York, N.Y.
4. Maling, H. M. 1970. Toxicology of single doses of ethyl alcohol. *In* International Encyclopedia of Pharmacology and Therapeutics. J. Tremolieres, Ed. Vol. II: 277–299. Pergamon Press. New York, N.Y.
5. Forney, R. B. 1972. The interactions of alcohol and other drugs including psychotomimetics. Drug information Journal. January/June: 59–63.
6. Milner, G. 1970. Interaction between barbiturates, alcohol and some psychotropic drugs. Med. J. Aust. **1:** 1204–1207.
7. Gruber, C. M., Jr. 1955. A theoretical consideration of additive and potentiated effects between drugs with a practical example using alcohol and barbiturates. Arch. Int. Pharmacodyn. Ther. **102:** 17–32.
8. Hoffer, A. 1962. Lack of potentiation by chlordiazepoxide (Librium) of depression or excitation due to alcohol. Can. Med. Assoc. J. **87:** 920–921.
9. Dundee, J. W. & M. Isaac. 1970. Interaction between intravenous alcohol and some sedatives and tranquillizers. Brit. J. Pharmacol. **39:** 199–200.
10. Dundee, J. W. & M. Isaac. 1970. Interaction of alcohol with sedatives and tranquillizers (a study of blood levels at loss of consciousness following rapid infusion). Med. Sci. Law **10:** 220–224.
11. Dundee, J. W. & M. Isaac. 1971. Interaction between intravenous alcohol and some sedatives and tranquillizers. Med. Sci. Law **11:** 49–50.
12. Ho, A. K. S., R. C. A. Chen & J. M. Morrison. 1976. Potential interactions between narcotics and narcotic antagonists with ethanol during acute, chronic and withdrawal states. This volume.

13. KILLAM, K. F., M. J. BROCCO & C. A. ROBINSON. 1976. Evaluation of narcotic and narcotic antagonist interactions in primates. This volume.
14. RECH, R. H., M. K. VOMACHKA, D. RICKERT & M. C. BRAUDE. 1976. Interactions between amphetamine and alcohol and their effect on rodent behavior. This volume.
15. GARATTINI, S., A. JORI & R. SAMANIN. 1976. Interactions of various drugs with amphetamine. This volume.
16. FORREST, W. H., JR., J. W. BELLVILLE & B. W. BROWN, JR. 1972. The interaction of caffeine with pentobarbital as a nighttime hypnotic. Anesthesiology **36:** 37–41.
17. KALANT, H., A. E. LEBLANC & R. J. GIBBINS. 1971. Tolerance to, and dependence on, some non-opiate psychotropic drugs. Pharmacol. Rev. **23:** 135–191.
18. HUG, C. C. 1972. Characteristics and theories related to acute and chronic tolerance development. *In* Chemical and Biological Aspects of Drug Dependence: 307–345. CRC Press. Cleveland, Ohio.
19. MAYNERT, E. W. & G. I. KLINGMAN. 1960. Acute tolerance to intravenous anesthetics in dogs. J. Pharmacol. Exp. Ther. **128:** 192–200.
20. GREIZERSTEIN, H. B. & C. M. SMITH. 1973. Development and loss of tolerance to ethanol in goldfish. J. Pharmacol. Exp. Ther. **187:** 391–399.
21. LEBLANC, A. E., H. KALANT & R. J. GIBBINS. 1975. Acute tolerance to ethanol in the rat. Psychopharmacologia **41:** 43–46.
22. OSWALD, I. 1968. Drugs and sleep. Pharmacol. Rev. **20:** 273–303.
23. DAVID, J., R. S. GREWAL & G. P. WAGLE. 1974. Persistent electroencephalographic changes in rhesus monkeys after single doses of pentobarbital, nitrazepam and imipramine. Psychopharmacologia **35:** 61–75.
24. MATTSON, R. H., J. K. STURMAN, M. L. GRONOWSKI & H. GOIEO. 1975. Effect of alcohol intake in non-alcoholic epileptics. Neurology **25:** 361.
25. KHANNA, J. M., H. KALANT, Y. YUVONNE, S. CHUNG & A. J. SIEMENS. 1976. Effect of chronic ethanol treatment on metabolism of drugs *in vitro* and *in vivo*. Biochem. Pharmacol. **25:** 329–335.
26. SELLMAN, R., J. KANTO, E. RAIJOLA & A. PEKKARINEN. 1975. Human and animal study on elimination from plasma and metabolism of diazepam after chronic alcohol intake. Acta Pharmacol. Toxicol. **36:** 33–38.
27. SELLMAN, R., A. PEKKARINEN, L. KANGAS & RAIJOLA. 1975. Reduced concentrations of plasma diazepam in chronic alcoholic patients following an oral administration of diazepam. Acta Pharmacol. Toxicol. **36:** 25–32.
28. COLDWELL, B. B., G. S. WIBERG & H. L. TRENHOLM. 1970. Some effects of ethanol on the toxicity and distribution of barbiturates in rats. Can. J. Physiol. Pharmacol. **48:** 254–264.
29. PATEL, G. J. & H. LAL. 1973. Reduction in brain gamma-aminobutyric acid and in barbital narcosis during ethanol withdrawal. J. Pharmacol. Exp. Ther. **186:** 625–629.
30. IVERSON, F., B. B. COLDWELL, R. H. DOWNIE & L. W. WHITEHOUSE. 1975. Effect of ethanol on toxicity and metabolism of amphetamine in the mouse. Experientia **31:** 679–680.
31. FORNEY, R. B., R. MARTZ, L. LEMBERGER & B. RODDA. 1976. The combined effect of marihuana and dextroamphetamine. This volume.
32. DEWEY, W. L. 1976. Interactions of active constituents of marihuana with other drugs in the neuron. This volume.
33. HOLLISTER, L. E. 1976. Interactions of Δ^9-tetrahydrocannabinol with other drugs. This volume.
34. LEMBERGER, L., B. DALTON, R. MARTZ, B. RODDA & R. FORNEY. 1976. Clinical studies on the interaction of psychopharmacologic agents with marihuana. This volume.
35. MANNO, J. E., G. F. KIPLINGER, N. SCHOLZ & R. B. FORNEY. 1971. The in-

fluence of alcohol and marihuana on motor and mental performance. Clin. Pharmacol. Ther. **12:** 202–211.

36. Siemens, A. J., H. Kalant & J. C. deNie. 1975. Metabolic interactions between Δ^9-tetrahydrocannabinol and other cannabinoids in rats. *In* The Pharmacology of Marihuana. M. C. Braude & S. Szara, Eds.: 77–92. Raven Press. New York, N.Y.
37. Gessner, P. K. & B. E. Cabana. 1970. A study of the interaction of the hypnotic effects and of the toxic effects of chloral hydrate and ethanol. J. Pharmacol. Exp. Ther. **174:** 247–259.
38. Gebhart, G. F., G. L. Plaa & C. I. Mitchell. 1969. The effects of ethanol alone and in combination with phenobarbital, chlorpromazine, or chlordiazepoxide. Toxicol. Appl. Pharmacol. **15:** 405–414.
39. Rankin, J. G., Ed. 1975. Alcohol, Drugs and Brain Damage. Addiction Research Foundation. Toronto, Ontario, Canada.
40. Morland, J., J. Setekleiv, J. F. W. Haffner, C. E. Stromsaether, A. Danielson & G. H. Wethe. 1974. Combined effects of diazepam and ethanol on mental and psychomotor functions. Acta Pharmacol. Toxicol. **34:** 5–15.
41. Goldberg, L. 1966. Interaction between alcohol and tranquilizing agents. *In* Proceedings of the Fourth International Conference on Alcohol and Traffic Safety. R. N. Harger, Ed.: 235–244. Indiana University Press. Bloomington, Indiana.
42. Hughes, F. W., R. B. Forney & A. B. Richards. 1965. Comparative effect in human subjects of chlordiazepoxide, diazepam, and placebo on mental and physical performance. Clin. Pharmacol. Ther. **6:** 139–145.
43. Smith, C. M. 1958. A new adjunct to the treatment of alcoholism: the hallucinogenic drugs. Q. J. Stud. Alcohol **19:** 406–417.
44. Wiberg, G. S., B. B. Coldwell & H. L. Trenholm. 1970. Toxicity of ethanol barbiturate mixtures. J. Pharm. Pharmacol. **22:** 465.
45. Rushton, R., H. Steinberg & M. Tomkiewicz. 1973. Effects of chlordiazepoxide alone and in combination with amphetamine on animal and human behavior. *In* The Benzodiazepines. S. Garattini, E. Mussini & L. O. Randall, Eds.: 355–366. Raven Press, New York, N.Y.
46. Seeman, P. 1972. The membrane actions of anesthetics and tranquilizers. Pharmacol. Rev. **24:** 583–655.
47. Seeman, P. 1975. The membrane expansion theory of anesthesia. *In* Progress in Anesthesiology. B. R. Fink, Ed. Vol. **1:** 243–252. Raven Press. New York, N.Y.
48. Stewart, R. D. 1975. The effects of carbon monoxide on humans. Ann. Rev. Pharmacol. **15:** 409–423.
49. Roseler, P. 1961. Observations and investigations on the interaction of alcohol and carbon monoxide. Dissertation, Faculty of Medicine of the Free University of Berlin, West Germany.
50. Downes, D. A., J. H. Woods & M. E. Llewellyn. 1975. The behavioural pharmacology of addiction: some conceptual and methodological foci. *In* Biological and Behavioural Approaches to Drug Dependence. S. L. Lambert, Ed. House of Lind. Ontario, Canada.
51. Colquhon, D. 1975. Mechanisms of drug action at the voluntary muscle endplate. Ann. Rev. Pharmacol. **15:** 307–325.
52. Gage, P. W., R. N. McBurney & D. VanHelden. 1974. Endplate currents are shortened by octanol: possible role of membrane lipid. Life Sci. **14:** 2277–2283.
53. Gage, P. W., R. N. McBurney & G. T. Schneider. 1975. Effects of some aliphatic alcohols on the conductance change caused by a quantum of acetylcholine at the toad end-plate. J. Physiol. **244:** 409–429.

54. KENNEDY, R. D. & A. GALINDO. 1974. Comparative site of action of various anesthetics at the mammalian myoneural junction. Fed. Proc. **33:** 579.
55. ROSS, D. H. 1976. Selective action of alcohols on cerebral calcium levels. Ann. N.Y. Acad. Sci. **273:** 280–294.
56. MELLO, N. K. 1973. A review of methods to induce alcohol addiction in animals. Pharm. Biochem. Behav. **1:** 89–101.
57. MIRSKY, I. A., P. PIKER, M. ROSENBAUM & H. LEDERER. 1941. "Adaptation" of the central nervous system to varying concentrations of alcohol in the blood. Q. J. Stud. Alcohol **2:** 35–45.
58. WALLGREN, H. & H. BARRY. 1970. Drug actions in relation to alcohol effects. *In* Actions of Alcohol **2:** 621–714. Elsevier Pub. Co. Amsterdam–London–New York.

STIMULANTS: INTERACTION WITH CLINICALLY RELEVANT DRUGS*

Everett H. Ellinwood, Jr., Robert D. Eibergen, and M. Marlyne Kilbey

Department of Psychiatry
Behavioral Neuropharmacology Section
Duke University Medical Center
Durham, North Carolina 27706

INTRODUCTION

Several common patterns of drug abuse involve stimulant use along with other drugs; these patterns present a variety of potential interactions. In this report we will attempt to outline the important temporal relationship in these various abuse patterns and to consider the available laboratory data in terms of these temporal relationships. Potentially hazardous combinations of abused drugs will be considered, as well as interaction effects that may hinder treatment of the stimulant abuser. Persistent effects of chronic stimulant intoxication and the potential for a residual interaction will be emphasized.

MAIN PATTERNS OF DRUG COMBINATIONS WITH STIMULANTS

A pattern of oral stimulant use, prevalent in middle-class businessmen, professionals, and housewives, involves the use of amphetamines to awaken in the morning and stimulate mood and activity during the day, and alcohol or sedative use at night to calm the "jitters" and to induce sleep. Not infrequently the individual acquires a dual pattern of dependence.[1] Variations on this pattern are, of course, well known, such as the truck driver who uses amphetamines to sustain alertness over a 24–48 hour period and then uses sedatives or alcohol to come down. The other major pattern of use is one in which the "street" user injects intravenous doses of amphetamine or other stimulants at short intervals and in immense quantities over a period of 4–6 days, during which time he does not sleep. Gradually the user becomes more tense, irritable, and exhausted and finally "crashes," usually after ingestion of large doses of alcohol and/or sedatives.[2] The sedative drug or alcohol may be taken under entirely different states: 1) the individual may be intoxicated with stimulants, 2) withdrawing from the stimulant and exhausted from hyperactivity and sleep loss, 3) combinations of both conditions.

In addition to these two major patterns of stimulant/sedative abuse, the effects of other stimulants combined with sedatives should be considered. In one double blind study, 15 mg of amphetamine plus 300 mg of cyclobarbitone produced significantly greater euphoria, elation, and excitation than either of the two drugs taken singly.[3] The combination of sedative and stimulant is re-

* This research was supported by NIDA Grants #DA 00057 and #DA 01665.

ported to reduce the haziness and jitteriness and autonomic effects of amphetamine alone, in addition to the "synergistic" effect on euphoria.[4] A variety of combinations of amphetamine and sedative drugs have appeared on the market, capitalizing on the combined effect.

In addition, street users have discovered the properties of the combined drugs.[5] Thus, a considerable number of street users, as well as individuals using medically prescribed drugs, have come to prefer the concurrent combined effect of sedatives and stimulants, which may result in a pattern of dual dependency. Finally, amphetamines are also used in order to increase one's capacity for drinking huge quantities of alcohol without "passing out."[6] Interviews of court cases by one of the authors (E.H.E.) indicate that such individuals can become quite inebriated, yet are still physically active; in an aggressive or unstable individual, or in an adverse environment, violence is not uncommon. There are no systematic data illustrating this latter point, and in fact there are data indicating that at lower doses, amphetamine can antagonize alcohol-induced cognitive impairments. In humans, amphetamine reduced the amount of alcohol-induced impairment of a number of intellectual tasks, such as coding and mental addition.[7]

Abuse of narcotic/stimulant combinations has a long history, beginning with combined injection of heroin and cocaine, a so-called "speed-ball." Amphetamine is also used this way. Both stimulants are touted to increase the initial rush of the herion injection. Amphetamines have also been used extensively by narcotic addicts to sustain the activity level needed to "hustle" the necessary funds for their habits. Additionally, methadone clinics periodically report a high rate of stimulant use among clients.

The uncertainties of the street marketplace make any number of contaminant-drug combinations a real possibility. Not infrequently, anticholinergic drugs, amphetamine, as well as tryptaminergic hallucinogens, are found in various combinations. In reality, almost any combination is possible, depending on the supply of drugs and the financial need of the seller. Incidence studies have been helpful primarily in demonstrating that combinations of stimulants with other drug use occur not infrequently. The actual figures demonstrate an extreme variability dependent on local drug supply and subcultural patterns (see TABLE 1). Perhaps the most nonvariable finding is that of Eckerman *et al.*[8] that everyone who abuses cocaine also uses other drugs.

Temporal Relationship Between Drugs

In perusing the drug combinations abused, one factor is outstanding: Multiple dose and temporal relationships are involved. TABLE 2 depicts the spectrum of temporal relationships. This outline also helps to organize the laboratory data that relate to each of the temporal patterns. TABLES 3 and 4 list pertinent laboratory data on stimulant/other drug interactions. The classical paradigm for study of drug interactions involves the concurrent administration of two or more drugs. When patterns of drug abuse are considered, however, the need arises for an extension of this definition. Chronic drug abuse may result in an altered physiology that endures beyond the cessation of drug administration, and subsequent administration of other drugs may thus result in an altered response. We have used the term "residual-drug interaction" to indicate that the

TABLE 1

INCIDENCE OF POLYDRUG ABUSE INVOLVING STIMULANTS (AMPHETAMINE, COCAINE, PHENMETRAZINE)

Drug	Location	Method of Establishing Use	% Positive	Year	References
heroin	N.Y. City	history	33.6	'71	106
heroin	Washington, D.C.	urinalysis	48.0	'73	107
heroin	N.Y. City	history	24.0	'75	108
methadone	N.Y. City	hospital records	5.0	'71	109
methadone	Philadelphia	history	69.2	'72	110
alcohol	Two communities, eastern Mass.	history	20.0	'73	111
alcohol & heroin	N.Y. City	history	8.0	'75	108
barbiturates, heroin, & alcohol	N.Y. City	history	4.0	'75	108
barbiturates	N.Y.City	history	1.0	'75	108

TABLE 2

TEMPORAL PATTERNS OF INTERACTION EFFECTS

I. Concurrent administration of stimulant and non-stimulant drugs
   A. Acute interaction
   B. Chronic interaction
II. Sequential administration of stimulant and non-stimulant drugs: residual effects
   A. Residual non-stimulant effect on subsequent stimulant administration
   B. Residual stimulant effect on subsequent non-stimulant administration
   C. Residual stimulant effect on subsequent stimulant administration

effects of a second drug are changed owing to the residual effects of earlier, chronic administration of a first drug. Similar altered responses following multiple administrations of a single drug typically are labeled tolerance, reverse tolerance, or supersensitivity. In the sequential administration paradigm of TABLE 4, all the drugs listed require chronic administration to obtain the full effect. The major classes of drugs of abuse are presented in these examples. We have included chronic stimulant potentiation of subsequent stimulant effects as a residual interaction; more typically, this interaction would be considered a case of reverse tolerance. Keeping in mind these temporal relationships, we would like to review laboratory data that relate to combinations that are of clinical concern.

POTENT OR HAZARDOUS ABUSE COMBINATIONS

Stimulant use combined with alcohol, sedatives, or minor tranquilizers is, in our estimation, potentially the most dangerous combination. When a chronic amphetamine abuser who has become paranoid, fearful, and even panic-stricken subsequently drinks or takes sedatives to "come down," he is taking a chance on losing the last remnants of judgement inhibiting his aggressive acting out of

TABLE 3

EXAMPLES OF CONCURRENT INTERACTIONS

Observed Interactions	Mechanisms Proposed in Literature
1) Alcohol increases blood level of amphetamine[11–14]	Inhibition of amphetamine hydroxylation
2) Barbiturates/benzodiazepines enhance amphetamine hypermotility[22–26]	Unknown
3) Benzodiazepines enhance amphetamine stereotypy[20, 21]	Possible elevation of striatal dopamine
4) Tricyclics increase brain level of amphetamine[46–48]	Tricyclic inhibition of amphetamine hydroxylation
5) Tricyclics increase brain level of cocaine[49]	Possible increased cerebrovascular permeability
6) MAOI enhanced peripheral toxic effects of amphetamine[34]	Decreased degradation of sympatho-mimetic amines
7) Chlorpromazine prolongs amphetamine hypermotility[43–45]	Elevated brain levels of amphetamine
8) Amphetamine/cocaine potentiation of narcotic analgesia[53–56]	Possible catecholaminergic effects
9) Methylphenidate potentiation of tricyclic, hexobarbital, diphenylhydatoin action[28]	Inhibition of microsomal metabolism
10) Narcotics inhibit amphetamine stereotypies[57–60]	Dopamine receptor blockade
11) Alkaline urine elevates amphetamine levels[33, 34]	Decreased excretion of unchanged amphetamine
12) Disulfiram potentiates amphetamine stereotypy, motor abnormalities, and seizures[83, 84]	Disruption of norepinephrine synthesis; increased "toxic" effect of disulfiram

TABLE 4

STIMULANTS: EXAMPLES OF SEQUENTIAL ADMINISTRATION INTERACTIONS

Observed Residual Interactions Following Last Dose of Prior Chronic Treatment	Time Residual Interaction Observed	Mechanisms Proposed in Literature
1) Phenobarbital produces a delayed cocaine lethality[30]	24 hrs	Induced abnormal metabolism to toxic *N*-oxide metabolite
2) Norepinephrine increases response to hexobarbital[29]	4 days	Reduction of microsomal enzymatic metabolism
3) Neuroleptics enhance stimulant stereotypy[75–77]	7–28 days	Hypersensitivity of dopamine receptor
4) Narcotics enhance stimulant		
a) stereotypy/aggression[60, 62–66]	3–28 days	Hypersensitivity of dopamine receptor
b) dyskinesias[67, 68]	10–17 mos	
5) Thyroid state influences stimulant response[36–39]	24 hrs	Altered sensitivity of catecholamine receptor
6) Stimulant administration potentiates subsequent stimulant response[89–92]	5–54 days	Increased sensitivity of dopamine receptor/possible neurophysiological reorganization

distorted thoughts. Chronic sleep loss may augment this process. Individuals have been known to become quite violent and indeed to commit homicide during these periods.[9, 10] Other drugs that would contribute to loss of judgement include tryptaminergic hallucinogenic drugs or drugs having anticholinergic properties.

Experimental studies have shown that ethanol prolongs amphetamine-induced stereotypies and startle response in the rat.[11] This potentiation of amphetamine-induced behaviors in the rat may in part be due to the influence of ethanol on the metabolism of amphetamine. Ethanol has been shown to inhibit hydroxylation, the major metabolic pathway of amphetamine in the rat, so that the concentration of unchanged amphetamine in urine is increased, whereas the concentration of metabolites of amphetamine is decreased.[12–14] An *in vitro* study has also demonstrated that the parahydroxylation of amphetamine by rat liver microsomes is inhibited by ethanol.[11] These studies indicate that ethanol potentiates the behavioral actions of amphetamine by inhibiting its metabolic breakdown. The relevance of these studies to humans is still under question, as will be discussed later.

In the rabbit and mouse, amphetamine antagonizes ethanol-induced narcosis[15, 16] and antagonizes ethanol-induced depression of Y-maze activity in the rat.[17] Results of EEG studies demonstrate that amphetamine blocks ethanol-induced cortical depression in the rabbit.[18] Amphetamine probably does not antagonize alcohol-induced depression by lowering blood levels of alcohol, since in the two studies above in which blood levels were measured, the concentration in amphetamine and control pretreated subjects was not significantly different.[7, 18] There are no reports in the literature examining the possibility that beer or wine that contains quantities of tyramine may interact with the reported action of amphetamine to potentiate tyramine pressor effects.[19]

Pretreatment with a number of benzodiazepine derivatives has been demonstrated to prolong methamphetamine-induced stereotyped behavior in rats.[20] This effect may be mediated through dopamine metabolism, since Taylor and Laverty[21] found that benzodiazepines significantly increase the concentration of striatal [^{3}H]dopamine. Also, combined amphetamine and chlordiazepoxide treatment elevated exploratory activity of mice and rats on a hole board or in a Y-maze, whereas neither drug given separately did so.[22, 23] A similar potentiation of behavior has been demonstrated for mixtures of amphetamine and amylobarbitone.[24–26] In these studies, an amphetamine-amylobarbitone mixture increased exploration of a Y-maze by rats. However, this increased exploration was prevented when subjects were given prior nondrugged experience with the maze.[27]

Amphetamine has a moderate inhibitory effect on liver microsomal enzyme metabolism of hexobarbital; methylphenidate is a more potent inhibitor[28] and has been demonstrated clinically to increase serum levels of phenobarbital and diphenylhydantoin. At least part of this effect may be mediated by potentiation of norepinephrine, since norepinephrine, administered chronically, has a potent (same order of effect as SKF 25) inhibitory effect on microsomal drug metabolism that lasts for at least 4 days.[29]

An interesting delayed cocaine toxicity has been demonstrated recently following phenobarbital treatment.[30] Pretreatment with phenobarbital for 4 days has been shown to produce a differential effect on cocaine-induced mortality in mice. Cocaine was administered 24 hours following 4 days of pretreatment with phenobarbital or saline. Phenobarbital pretreatment protected mice against the immediate cocaine toxicity but produced a delayed toxicity attributed to organ damage. Fifty-five percent of saline-pretreated mice died within 3 hours after receiving cocaine, but the remaining animals all survived during the subsequent 3-day period. Only 14 percent of the phenobarbital subjects died during the initial 3 hours following cocaine administration; however, 62 percent of those surviving the acute effects of cocaine died within the next 3 days.[30] The authors present the possibility that phenobarbital stimulation of microsomal enzymes enhances the activity of mixed function oxidase, thereby increasing the *N*-dealkylation of cocaine. They speculate further that an *N*-oxide intermediate could result in the focal liver damage noted, thus inducing a delayed toxicity. Whatever the mechanism, the results indicate a delayed toxicity of potential importance to combined barbiturate/cocaine abuse.

One simple interaction by which a variety of compounds could potentiate amphetamine involves urinary pH. Several researchers[31–33] have demonstrated that a considerable proportion of amphetamine is excreted unchanged in the urine and that an acid pH markedly increases the excretion rate. The administration of an alkalinizing agent such as sodium bicarbonate reduces the urinary excretion[33] and is stated to prolong the amphetamine psychosis.[34] There are anecdotal accounts of amphetamine abusers taking sodium bicarbonate to enhance the effect of amphetamine. Acetazolamide and thiazide diuretics are also urinary alkalinizers.[35]

Historically, one major source of initiates to amphetamine abuse comes from the incredible number of persons for whom prescriptions were written for diet purposes.[1] In certain of the more questionable diet regimens, thyroid medication is added to the amphetamine prescription. These diet combinations have been known as "rainbow pills" because often they are given in addition to sedatives, diuretics (see effect on urinary pH), vitamins, etc. in a brightly colored array of pills. Patients report that the combination of thyroid and amphetamine creates a much greater sense of well-being. One of the authors (E.H.E.) has interviewed two patients who developed behavioral pathology on only moderately high doses of amphetamine, taken concurrently with thyroid medication. There are no direct human studies in this area; however, there is a variety of experimental evidence supporting the hypothesis that thyroid state can influence the sensitivity to catecholamines and consequently to stimulant drugs.

In thyroxine-pretreated rats, intracerebral norepinephrine elicits greater locomotor behavior than in control animals,[36] and apomorphine, a dopamine-receptor stimulator, elicits stereotyped behavior in thyroxine-pretreated guinea pigs at doses that had little effect in untreated animals.[37] Amphetamine induced enhanced locomotor activity (in the morning but not afternoon) in rats pretreated with thyroid-releasing hormones,[38] while in hypothyroid mice, amphetamine elicited less motor activity.[39] Finally, chronic thyroxine pretreatment markedly potentiates barbiturate action.[40, 41] Thus, the effects of both amphetamine and barbiturates found in "rainbow" combinations could be potentiated by the concurrent thyroid medication.

Interaction with Treatment Efforts

A potential problem involving drug interactions may arise in the care of amphetamine addicts. Chlorpromazine is an effective drug in the treatment of acute amphetamine overdose or poisoning.[42, 10] However, in treating the amphetamine psychosis where tolerance has developed to the peripheral toxic effects, it is probably wiser to use a drug such as haloperidol, which does not increase the half-life of amphetamine as does chlorpromazine.[43, 45] Sulser and Dingell[44] have found that chlorpromazine prolongs hypermotility induced by amphetamine in the rat and elevates the amphetamine levels. Another potential therapeutic interaction problem involves the post-amphetamine depression. Following chronic amphetamine withdrawal, there is mild-to-moderate depression, with marked fatigue, lassitude, and psychasthenia, that may wax and wane for 6 to 8 months. The recommended treatment for this condition is tricyclic antidepressants,[10] but with careful warning to the patient that the surreptitious addition of amphetamine to the tricyclic regimen may produce a potentiation of amphetamine effects. Valzelli *et al.*,[46] Sulser *et al.*,[47] Dolfini *et al.*,[48] as well as others, have found that in rats tricyclic antidepressants prolong amphetamine psychomotor activation associated with an increased level of amphetamine induced by blocking amphetamine hydroxylation. Similarly, a number of tricyclic antidepressants also have been shown to increase brain levels of cocaine.[49] These authors speculated that administration of antidepressants altered the blood-brain barrier to cocaine but provided no direct evidence other than showing increased levels of cocaine at 20 minutes. Electrical convulsive treatment had a similar effect.[49] As with mice, which do not hydroxylate amphetamines,[48] the relevance of the tricyclic effects to metabolism in man is questionable. Amphetamine in man is mainly excreted unchanged in the urine (about 60–70% at usual pH) or as deaminated metabolites. Thus, one would not expect the tricyclic drugs to have any major effect on amphetamine metabolism.[34] In pilot studies in only a few subjects, Davis *et al.*[34] found no effect of tricyclic antidepressants on metabolism of amphetamine in man. However, until this relationship is confirmed, it would be wise to continue to warn patients against the combined use, especially since both drugs enhance adrenergic effects. In addition, monoamine oxidase (MAO) inhibitors should not be used for post-amphetamine depression where there is a chance of reversion to amphetamine use, because of the potentially fatal sympathetic crisis. It is well established that MAO inhibitors block degradation of sympathomimetic amines,[34] and fatal reactions of amphetamine in combination with an MAO inhibitor have occurred.[50]

Sedatives (especially the barbiturates), narcotics and cocaine, depress the respiratory center.[51] Thus, there is a potential cocaine additive effect with these agents that may lead to a fatal brain-stem respiratory center depression. The incidence of respiratory depression might be potentiated with a bolus of drug, for example, a speedball injection. Sedative and alcohol withdrawal seizures, or a lowered threshold for seizures, could certaintly interact with the epileptogenic properties of cocaine and high doses of amphetamine. In this regard, overdose of amphetamine and/or cocaine leading to status epilepticus tyically would be treated with high doses of one of the benzodiazepines, most likely Valium.®[10] Although Valium® is quite effective in treating status epilepticus, the successful treatment of seizures may be followed by a potentiation of less life-threatening dopaminergic effects, since there is evidence from animal studies that the benzodiazepines potentiate these effects.[20, 21]

The concurrent combination of narcotic and stimulant drugs for i.v. injection apparently affords the narcotic addict a more intensely pleasurable rush. More pertinent to treatment concerns, a high incidence of cocaine and amphetamine use is often found among methadone maintenance patients.[52] In the laboratory, amphetamine has been shown to potentiate morphine analgesia in the rat.[53-55] Nott[56] demonstrated that concurrent administration of either cocaine or amphetamine with low doses of morphine markedly enhanced analgesia in mice. Conversely, a number of studies indicate that concurrent narcotics administration reduces or eliminates the stereotypies elicited by amphetamine or apomorphine,[57-60] and it has been suggested that this antagonistic action is mediated by dopamine receptor blockade by the narcotic. However, McKenzie and Sadof[61] have reported intensification of amphetamine stereotypies with high doses of morphine.

Laboratory experiments demonstrate that prior chronic narcotic treatment has a residual effect of enhancing subsequent behavioral response to stimulants. For example, doses of amphetamine, L-dopa, or apomorphine (all drugs with dopamine effects), at doses that produced no response in control rats, elicited severe fighting in animals formerly morphine-dependent.[62-64] This enhanced stimulant-induced aggressive response occurred as long as 30 days following the terminal morphine injection.[64] Further, L-dopa produced greater locomotor activity in mice pretreated with morphine than in control animals,[65] and amphetamine elicited enhanced stereotypies in morphine-dependent rats.[66] Recent studies have shown also that methadone pretreatment can potentiate a dyskinetic response to stimulants for as long as 17 months.[67, 68]

Methadone pretreatment also enhances the response to methamphetamine in the guinea pig. When tested up to 3 weeks following termination of chronic administration of methadone, methamphetamine elicited greater stereotyped behavior and open field activity.[60] Several authors have suggested that the enhanced behavioral responses to stimulants in subjects with a history of narcotic administration are mediated by supersensitive dopaminergic receptors. The supersensitivity is thought to be induced by the previous chronic narcotic blockage of these receptors.[64-66, 68] There is considerable evidence that the stimulant-elicited behaviors, i.e., aggression, locomotor activity, stereotyped behavior, oral dyskinesias, and open field activity, which are enhanced following narcotic administration are mediated via CNS dopaminergic systems.[62, 69-72] This position derives from a large body of evidence indicating that when dopaminergic transmission is disrupted by surgical or pharmacological means, the dopamine receptors become hypersensitive to endogenously released dopamine agonists. For example, following administration of neuroleptic drugs that block dopamine receptors,[73, 74] dopamine agonists produce enhanced stereotyped behaviors.[75-77] Since narcotic drugs are also thought to block dopamine receptors,[78, 59] it is possible that the enhanced response to dopamine agonists following chronic narcotic administration represents an increased sensitivity at the dopamine receptor. Neurochemical evidence supports the hypothesis of a narcotic-induced supersensitivity of dopamine receptors. Apomorphine, a dopamine agonist, at appropriate doses decreases dopamine turnover in rat brain, presumably via a feedback message to presynaptic terminals, indicating that the postsynaptic receptors are receiving excessive stimulation.[9, 80] Apomorphine, at doses that had no effect on control rats, produced significant decreases in dopamine turnover in rats formerly morphine-dependent at 3 and 30 days following termination of morphine administration, indicating a hypersensitivity of the postsynaptic receptors.[81] Kuschinsky[103] also found enhanced apomorphine-induced decreases in dopamine turnover in morphine-dependent rats, although apomorphine did not induce enhanced stereotypies. Since in this experiment morphine was administered for only 7 days, however, and stereotypies were measured only at 16 to 20 hours after the last morphine injection, the results are difficult to interpret. In summary, it seems probable that chronic narcotic administration can produce a residual hypersensitivity to stimulant drugs.

The use of disulfiram to decrease alcohol abuse in methadone maintenance patients has been considered and tested.[82] Given the rate of stimulant use by methadone patients, this practice should be examined. Disulfiram prolongs amphetamine-induced stereotyped behavior in rats,[83] and the drug combination induces severe dystonias, dysjunctive behaviors, and seizures in cats.[84-86] One of us (E.H.E.) has seen a patient with a severe cataleptic reaction to an overdose of disulfiram and amphetamine. Thus, disulfiram for patients who are potential stimulant abusers should be considered very cautiously.

Importance of Stimulant-Stimulant Interactions

The narcotic-induced supersensitivity of the dopamine receptor may contribute to the residual effects of chronic stimulant intoxication. These residual effects include a lowered threshold for stimulant-induced dyskinesias, as well as bizarre and psychotic behaviors. We have included chronic stimulant intoxication resulting in a subsequent lowered threshold for stimulant effects among the residual drug interaction examples. Following long-term chronic stimulant intoxication, subsequent doses of stimulants frequently induce a qualitatively different behavior than that seen originally. These end-stage behaviors include constricted stereotypies, hyperreactive behaviors, postural abnormalities, and dyskinesis, and have been noted in monkeys, cats, rats, and guinea pigs.[87-89] Even with shorter periods of chronic stimulant intoxication (10 to 14 days), one finds that there is an augmentation of stimulant-induced locomotor activity[90] and stereotypy[88, 89, 91, 92] to the same unit dose. These effects are persistent. Klawans and Margolin[89] have demonstrated a shorter onset and increased intensity of stereotyped behavior in guinea pigs administered amphetamine over a 3-week period and increased sensitivity to amphetamine and apomorphine at 3, 7, and 10 days following pretreatment. Kilbey and Ellinwood[91] and Stripling and Ellinwood[92] have demonstrated that during chronic administration of either amphetamine or cocaine, the latency of onset decreases and intensity of the maximum stereotypy increases over days, and that following 14 days of treatment increased responsivity is noted over a period of several weeks (Figure 1). There is also a significant cocaine-induced augmentation of electrical activity in the amygdala and a lowered behavioral-seizure threshold that persists following cessation of the chronic cocaine treatment (Stripling and Ellinwood),[92] possibly indicating a neurophysiological reorganization (Ellinwood *et al.*).[104] The importance of these findings may relate not only to the induction of movement disorders, which are found in chronic amphetamine addicts,[93, 94] but also to the lowered threshold for psychotic behavior in abstinent amphetamine addicts reported to follow only moderately high doses of amphetamine.[95, 96, 1] It has been noted in animal studies that apomorphine, a direct dopamine-receptor activator, also has a lowered threshold for induction of stereotypies following chronic stimulant intoxication;[89, 91] this suggests that the dopamine receptors are supersensitive. Similarly, dyskinesias found in high-dose L-dopa-treated parkinsonian patients are attributed to increased receptor

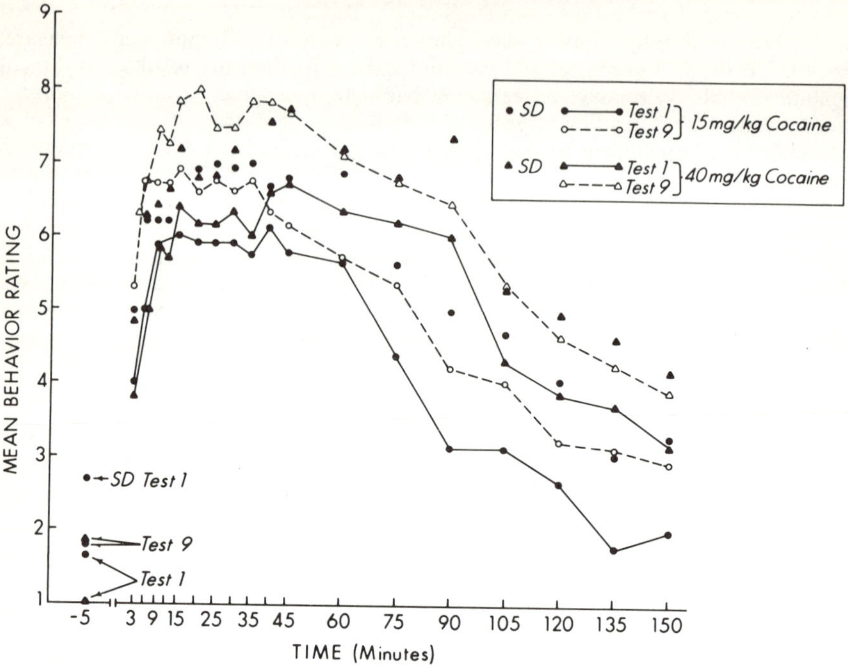

FIGURE 1. Mean and standard deviation of behavior ratings following initial administration of cocaine (test 1) and 54 days following cessation of 14 daily administrations (test 9).

sensitivity (Chase *et al.*[105]). That chronic stimulation of dopamine receptors and chronic dopamine-receptor blockade both lead to receptor supersensitivity would appear to be paradoxical. Several explanations are possible. One series of findings involves a chronic residual catecholamine depletion. Amphetamine is known to stimulate circuits that are already active;[97] thus, a local circuit overactivity may lead to hypermetabolic exhaustion of certain catecholamine neurons, resulting in neuronal catecholamine depletion and/or chromatolysis, as we have previously demonstrated in cats undergoing chronic amphetamine intoxication.[98, 99] Neuronal chromatolysis was found in areas with marked neuronal catecholamine depletion when examined histochemically. Gunne and Lewander[100] in 1967 originally reported that chronic administration of amphetamine for 6 days reduced brain norepinephrine to 75% and dopamine to 50% of control levels in rats. More recently, Seiden *et al.*[101] have demonstrated that there is a striking depletion of dopamine in the caudate nucleus (70% reduction) and a marked depletion of norepinephrine in the midbrain and frontal cortex that persisted for 3 to 6 months after cessation of chronic methamphetamine administration in monkeys. Thus, there is evidence for either persistent catecholamine depletion or neuronal death, establishing the setting for a functional deficit and/or a postsynaptic supersensitivity, at least in animals chronically intoxicated with high doses of stimulants. Since the augmented stereotype response begins to develop after 3 to 4 days of repeated amphetamine intoxication, other explanations are also possible. The immediate effect of amphetamine stimulation results in high levels of dopamine following injection. This would, in turn, lead to a feedback inhibition of catecholamine synthesis. Thus, the post-amphetamine period each day might be characterized by a functional deficit of catecholamine synthesis. Whether such cyclic excess/deficiency exists and, moreover, is sufficient to establish receptor supersensitivity has not been experimentally tested yet. Whatever the mechanism involved, there is a series of studies indicating that postsynaptic supersensitivity is established with repeated moderately high doses of stimulants. The supersensitivity phenomena may be an important factor in the stimulant psychosis and in the induction of dyskinesias in chronic amphetamine users.[102] Whether the concurrent or sequential interaction of drugs that block the dopamine receptor, such as narcotics, potentiates this postsynaptic supersensitivity in the chronic stimulant-intoxication state remains unanswered.

References

1. Ellinwood, E. H. 1973. The amphetamine and stimulant drugs. *In* Drug Use in America: Problem in Perspective. Second report of the National Commission on Marihuana and Drug Abuse: 140–157. U.S. Govt. Printing Office. Washington, D.C.
2. Kramer, J. C., C. Fischman & D. C. Littlefield. 1967. Amphetamine abuse—pattern and effect of high doses taken intravenously. JAMA **201:** 305–309.
3. Legge, D. & H. Steinberg. 1962. Actions of a mixture of amphetamine and barbiturate in man. Brit. J. Pharmacol. **18:** 495–500.
4. Grinspoon, L. & P. Hedblon. 1975. The Speed Culture: 47. Harvard Univ. Press. Cambridge, Mass.
5. Fiddle, S. 1968. The case of "peak user" John. *In* Amphetamine Abuse. J. R. Russo, Ed.: 123–124. Charles C. Thomas, Publisher. Springfield, Ill.
6. Kipperman, A. & E. W. Fine. 1974. The combined abuse of alcohol and amphetamines. Amer. J. Psychiat. **131:** 1277–1280.
7. Wilson, L., J. D. Taylor, C. W. Nash & D. F. Cameron. 1966. The combined effects of ethanol and amphetamine sulfate on performance of human subjects. Can. Med. Ass. J. **94:** 478–484.
8. Eckerman, W. C., J. D. Bates, J. U. Rachel & W. K. Poole. 1971. Drug usage and arrest charges. Prepared for the Bureau of Narcotics and Dangerous Drugs. Contract No. J-70-35.
9. Ellinwood, E. H. 1971. Assault and homicide associated with amphetamine abuse. Amer. J. Psychiat. **127**(9)**:** 1170–1175.
10. Ellinwood, E. H. 1975. Treatment of reactions to amphetamine-type stimulants. *In* Current Psychiatric Therapies. J. Masserman, Ed. Vol. **15:** 163–170. Grune & Stratton. New York, N.Y.
11. Todzy, I. & W. Becker. 1974. Alteration of the effects and the metabolism of *d*-amphetamine by ethanol. Naunyn-Schmiedebergs Arch. Pharmakol. **282**(& Suppl.).
12. Creaven, P. J. & T. Barbee. 1969. The effect of ethanol on the metabolism of amphetamine by the rat. J. Pharm. Pharmacol. **21:** 859–860.
13. Creaven, P. J., T. Barbee & M. K. Roack. 1970. The interaction of ethanol and amphetamine metabolism. J. Pharm. Pharmacol. **22:** 828–831.
14. Iversen, F., B. B. Coldwell, R. H. Downie & L. W. Whitehouse. 1975. Effect of ethanol on toxicity and metabolism of amphetamine in the mouse. Experientia **31:** 679–680.

15. Reifenstein, E. C. 1941. Amphetamine sulfate-ethyl alcohol antagonism in the rabbit. J. Lab. Clin. Med. **27:** 131–139.
16. Abdallah, A. H. & D. M. Roby. 1975. Antagonism of depressant activity of ethanol by DH-524; a comparative study with bemegride, doxapram, and *d*-amphetamine. Proc. Soc. Exp. Biol. Med. **148:** 819–822.
17. Leonard, B. E. & B. D. Wiseman. 1970. The effect of ethanol and amphetamine mixtures on the activity of rats in a Y-maze. J. Pharm. Pharmacol. **22:** 967–968.
18. Greenberg, R. E. 1967. Prevention of alcohol-induced cortical depression with stimulants and tertiary amines. Q. J. Stud. Alcohol **28:** 1–10.
19. Elbe, J. N. & A. D. Rudzik. 1969. Tyramine and amphetamine. Lancet **1:** 877.
20. Babbini, M. N. Montanaro, P. Strocchi & M. Gaiardi. 1971. Enhancement of amphetamine-induced stereotyped behavior by benzodiazepines. Eur. J. Pharmacol. **13:** 330–340.
21. Taylor, K. M. & R. Laverty. 1969. The effect of chlordiazepoxide, diazepam and nitrazepam on catecholamine metabolism in regions of the rat brain. Eur. J. Pharmacol. **8:** 296.
22. Cox, C., P. E. Harrison, H. Steinberg & M. Tomkiewicz. 1971. Lithium attenuates drug-induced hyperactivity in rats. Nature **232:** 336–337.
23. Poitou, P., R. Boulu & C. Bohuon. 1975. Effect of lithium and other drugs on the amphetamine chlordiazepoxide hyperactivity in mice. Experientia **31:** 99–101.
24. Rushton, R. & H. Steinberg. 1963. Mutual potentiation of amphetamine and amylobarbitone measured by activity in rats. Brit. J. Pharmacol. **21:** 295–305.
25. Weijnen, J. A. W. M. 1969. Effects of amphetamine-amylobarbitone mixtures on ambulation of rats in the Y-maze. Eur. J. Pharmacol. **5:** 180–184.
26. Kumar, R. 1971. Extinction of fear. I: effects of amylobarbitone and dexamphetamine given separately and in combination on fear and exploratory behaviour in rats. Psychopharmacologia **19:** 163–187.
27. Rushton, R., H. Steinberg & C. Tinson. 1963. Effects of a single experience on subsequent reactions to drugs. Brit. J. Pharmacol. **20:** 99–105.
28. Lal, H., S. K. Puri & G. C. Fuller. 1970. Inhibition of hexobarbital metabolism by dextroamphetamine. Psychopharmacologia **16:** 395–398.
29. Dixon, R. L., L. A. Rogers & J. R. Fouts. 1964. The effects of norepinephrine treatment on drug metabolism. Biochem. Pharmacol. **13:** 623–631.
30. Evans, M. A., C. Dwivedi & R. D. Harbison. 1976. Enhancement of cocaine-induced lethality by phenobarbital. *In* Cocaine and Other Stimulants. E. H. Ellinwood & M. M. Kilbey, Eds. Plenum Press. New York, N.Y. In press.
31. Asatoor, A., B. R. Galman, J. R. Johnson & M. D. Milne. 1965. The excretion of dextro-amphetamine and its derivatives. Brit. J. Pharm. **24:** 293–300.
32. Rowlan, M. & A. H. Beckett. 1966. The amphetamine: clinical and pharmokinetic implications of recent studies, assay procedures and urinary excretion in man. Arzneim. Forsch. **16:** 1369–1372.
33. Davis, J. N., W. E. Sand, J. Griffith & L. Lemberger. 1971. Pharmacological aspects of the treatment of amphetamine abuse: the effects of urinary pH. *In* Advances in Neuropsychopharmacology. O. Zinar, Z. Bolza & P. B. Bradley, Eds. North Holland Publishing Co. Amsterdam, Netherlands.
34. Davis, J. N., H. J. Sekerke & D. S. Janowsky. 1973. Drug interaction involving the drugs of abuse. *In* Drug Use in America: Problem in Perspective. Second report of the National Commission on Marihuana and Drug Abuse: 181–208. U.S. Govt. Printing Office. Washington, D.C.

35. HANSTEN, P. 1971. Drug Interaction. Lea & Febiger Co. Philadelphia, Pa.
36. EMLEN, W., D. S. SEGAL & A. J. MANDELL. 1972. Thyroid state: effects on pre- and postsynaptic central noradrenergic mechanisms. Science **175:** 79–82.
37. KLAWANS, H. L., C. GOETZ & W. J. WEINER. 1973. Dopamine receptor site sensitivity in hyperthyroid guinea pigs: a possible model of hyperthyroid chorea. J. Neural Trans. **34:** 187–193.
38. BREESE, G. R., B. R. COOPER, A. J. PRANGE, J. M. COTT & M. A. LIPTON. 1974. Interactions of thyrotropin-releasing hormone with centrally acting drugs. *In* The Thyroid Axis, Drugs, and Behavior. A. J. Prange, Ed.: 115–127. Raven Press. New York, N.Y.
39. MANTEGAZZA, P., K. M. NAIMZADA & M. RIVA. 1968. Activity of amphetamine in hypothyroid rats. Eur. J. Pharmacol. **5:** 10–16.
40. ELLINWOOD, E. H. & A. J. PRANGE. 1964. Effect of epinephrine pretreatment on pentobarbital sleeping time of mice with altered thyroid states. Nature **201:** 305–306.
41. ELLINWOOD, E. H. 1966. Paradoxical effect of dichlorioproterenol on pentobarbital sleep time in hyperthyroid mice. Nature **209:** 1250–1251.
42. ESPELIN, D. E. & A. K. DONE. 1968. Amphetamine poisoning: effectiveness of chlorpromazine. New Engl. J. Med. **278:** 1361–1365.
43. LEMBERGER, L., E. WITT, J. DAVIS & I. TOKIN. 1970. The effects of haloperidol, chlorpromazine on amphetamine metabolism and amphetamine stereotyped behavior in the rat. J. Pharmacol. Exp. Ther. **174:** 428–433.
44. SULSER, F. & J. DINGELL. 1969. Potentiation and blockage of the central action of amphetamine by chlorpromazine. Can. J. Physiol. Pharm. **47:** 7–13.
45. BORELLA, L. E. 1969. Effect of chlorpromazine on urinary excretion of amphetamine in rats. Pharmacologist **11:** 292.
46. VALZELLI, L. L., S. CONSOLO & C. MORPURGO. 1967. Influence of imipramine like drugs on metabolism of amphetamines. *In* Antidepressant Drugs. S. Garattini, Ed. Excerpta Medica Press. Amsterdam, Netherlands.
47. SULSER, S., OWENS, M. L. & J. V. DINGELL. 1966. Mechanism of amphetamine potentiation by desipramine. Life Sci. **5:** 2005–2010.
48. DOLFINI, E., M. TANSELLA, L. VALZELLI &. S. GARATTINI. 1969. Further studies on the interaction between desipramine and amphetamine. Eur. J. Pharmacol. **5:** 185–190.
49. ANGEL, C. & A. J. ROBERTS. 1966. Effect of electroshock and antidepressant drugs on cerebrovascular permeability to cocaine in the rat. J. Nerv. Men. Dis. **142:** 376–380.
50. LEWIS, E. 1965. Hyperpyrexia with antidepressant drugs. Brit. Med. J. **1:** 1671–1672.
51. RITCHIE, J. M. & P. J. CHEN. 1975. Local anesthetics. *In* The Pharmacological Basis of Therapeutics. L. S. Goodman & A. Gilman, Eds.: 379–403. Macmillan Co. New York, N.Y.
52. CHAMBERS, C. D. & J. J. BERGEN. 1973. Self-administered methadone supplementation. *In* Methadone: Experiences and Issues. C. D. Chambers & L. Brill, Eds.: 131–142. Behavioral Publications. New York, N.Y.
53. EVANS, W. O. 1962. The synergism of autonomic drugs on opiate or opioid analgesia, a discussion of its potential utility. Military Med. **127:** 1000–1003.
54. EVANS, W. O. & D. P. BERGNER. 1964. A comparison of the analgesic potencies of morphine, tentazocine, and a mixture of methamphetamine and tentazocine in the rat. J. New Drugs. **4:** 82–85.
55. EVANS, W. O. 1967. The effect of stimulant drugs on opiate induced analgesia. Arch. Biol. Med. Exp. **4:** 144–149.
56. NOTT, M. W. 1968. Potentiation of morphine analgesia by cocaine in mice. Eur. J. Pharmacol. **5:** 93–99.
57. FOG, R. 1970. Behavioral effects in rats of morphine and amphetamine and of a combination of the two drugs. Psychopharmacologia **16:** 305–312.

58. PURI, S. K., C. REDDY & H. LAL. 1973. Blockade of central dopaminergic receptors by morphine: Effect of haloperidol, apomorphine or benztropine. Res. Commun. Chem. Path. Pharmacol. **5:** 389–401.
59. SASAME, H. A., J. PEREZ-CRUET, G. DICHIARA, A. TAGLIAMONTE, P. TAGLIAMONTE & G. L. GRESSA. 1972. Evidence that methadone blocks dopamine receptors in the brain. J. Neurochem. **19:** 1953–1957.
60. EIBERGEN, R. D. & K. R. CARLSON. 1976. Behavioral evidence for dopaminergic supersensitivity following chronic treatment with methadone or chlorpromazine in the guinea pig. Psychopharmacologia. In press.
61. MCKENZIE, G. M. & M. SADOF. 1974. Effects of morphine and chlorpromazine on apomorphine-induced stereotyped behavior. J. Pharm. Pharmacol. **26:** 280–282.
62. LAL, H., J. O'BRIEN & S. K. PURI. 1971. Morphine withdrawal aggression: Sensitization by amphetamines. Psychopharmacologia **22:** 217–223.
63. PURI, S. K. & H. LAL. 1973. Effect of dopaminergic stimulation or blockade on morphine-withdrawal aggression. Psychopharmacologia **32:** 113–120.
64. GIANUTSOS, G., M. D. HYNES, S. K. PURI, R. B. DRAWBAUGH & H. LAL. 1974. Effect of apomorphine and nigrostriatal lesions on aggression and striatal dopamine turnover during morphine withdrawal: evidence for dopaminergic supersensitivity in protracted abstinence. Psychopharmacologia **34:** 37–44.
65. EIDELBERG, E. & R. ERSPAMER. 1975. Dopaminergic mechanisms of opiate actions in brain. J. Pharmacol. Exp. Ther. **192:** 50–57.
66. VASQUEZ, B. J., D. H. OVERSTREET & R. W. RUSSEL. 1974. Psychological evidence for increase in receptor sensitivity following chronic morphine treatment. Psychopharmacologia **38:** 287–302.
67. CARLSON, K. R. & R. D. EIBERGEN. Susceptibility to amphetamine-elicited dyskinesias following chronic methadone treatment in monkeys. This volume.
68. EIBERGEN, R. D. & K. R. CARLSON. 1975. Dyskinesias elicited by methamphetamine: susceptibility of former methadone-consuming monkeys. Science **190:** 588–590.
69. SNYDER, S. H., S. P. BANERJEE, H. I. YAMAMURA & D. GREENBERG. 1974. Drugs, neurotransmitters, and schizophrenia. Science **184:** 1243–1253.
70. UNGERSTEDT, U. 1974. Brain dopamine neurons and behavior. *In* The Neurosciences, third study program. F. O. Schmitt & F. G. Worden, Eds. MIT Press. Cambridge, Mass.
71. SCHEEL-KRUGER, J. & A. RANDRUP. 1967. Stereotyped hyperactive behavior produced by dopamine in the absence of noradrenaline. Life Sci. **6:** 1389–1398.
72. KLAWANS, H. L. 1973. The pharmacology of tardive dyskinesia. Amer. J. Psychiat. **130:** 82–86.
73. CARLSSON, A. & M. LINDQVIST. 1963. Effect of chlorpromazine of haloperidol on formation of 3-methoxytyramine and noradrenaline in mouse brain. Acta Pharmacol. Toxicol. **20:** 140–144.
74. CORRODI, H., K. FUXE & T. HOKFELT. 1967. The effect of neuroleptics on the activity of central catecholamine neurons. Life Sci. **6:** 767–774.
75. KLAWANS, H. L. & R. RUBOVITZ. 1972. An experimental model of tardive dyskinesia. J. Neural Trans. **33:** 235–246.
76. TARSY, D. & R. J. BALDESSARINI. 1974. Behavioral supersensitivity to apomorphine following chronic treatment with drugs which interfere with synaptic transmission of catecholamines. Neuropharmacology **13:** 927–940.
77. SAYERS, A. C., H. R. BURKI, W. RUCH & H. ASPER. 1975. Neuroleptic-induced supersensitivity of striatal dopamine receptors in the rat as a model of tardive dyskinesias. Effects of clozapine, haloperidol, loxapine, and chlorpromazine. Psychopharmacologia **41:** 97–104.

78. AHTEE, L. & I. KAARIANINEN. 1973. The effect of narcotic analgesics on the homovanilic acid content of rat nucleus caudatus. Eur. J. Pharmacol. **22:** 206–208.
79. ANDEN, N-E., A. RUBENSON, K. FUXE & T. HOKFELT. 1967. Evidence for dopamine receptor stimulation by apomorphine. J. Pharm. Pharmacol. **191:** 627–629.
80. ROOS, B. 1969. Decreases in homovanilic acid as evidence for dopamine receptor stimulation by apomorphine in the neostriatum of the rat. J. Pharmacol. **21:** 263–264.
81. PURI, S. K. 1974. Interaction of naloxone, haloperidol, apomorphine, and benzotropine with morphine on catelepsy and striatal dopamine turnover. Ph.D. Thesis. Univ. Rhode Island. Kingston, R.I.
82. PASCARELLI, E. F. 1973. Disulfiram (antabuse) in the treatment of methadone maintenance alcoholics. *In* Proceedings of the 5th National Conference on Methadone Treatment, Washington, D.C.: 316–323.
83. ELLINWOOD, E. H. & M. M. KILBEY. 1975. Species differences in response to amphetamine. *In* Psychopharmacogenetics. B. E. Eleftheriou, Ed.: 323–375. Plenum Press. New York, N.Y.
84. ELLINWOOD, E. H., JR. & A. SUDILOVSKY. 1973. Chronic amphetamine intoxication: Behavioral model of psychoses. *In* Psychopathology and Psychopharmacology. J. Cole *et al.,* Eds.: 51–70. Johns Hopkins Univ. Press. Baltimore, Md.
85. ELLINWOOD, E. H., A. SUDILOVSKY & R. S. GRABOWY. 1973. Olfactory forebrain seizures induced by methamphetamine and disulfiram. Biol. Psychiat. **7:** 89–99.
86. ELLINWOOD, E. H. 1974. Behavioral and EEG changes in the amphetamine model of psychosis. *In* Neuropsychopharmacology of Monoamines and their Regulatory Enzymes 12. E. Usdin, Ed.: 281–297. Raven Press. New York, N.Y.
87. ELLINWOOD, E. H. 1971. Effect of chronic methamphetamine intoxication in rhesus monkey. Biol. Psychiat. **3:** 25–32.
88. ELLINWOOD, E. H. & M. M. KILBEY. 1975. Amphetamine stereotypy: the influence of environmental factors and prepotent behavioral patterns on its topography and development. Biol. Psychiat. **10:** 3–16.
89. KLAWANS, H. L. & D. I. MARGOLIN. 1975. Amphetamine-induced dopaminergic hypersensitivity in guinea pigs. Arch. Gen. Psychiat. **32:** 725–732.
90. SEGAL, D. S. & A. J. MANDELL. 1974. Long-term administration of *d*-amphetamine: progressive augmentation of motor activity and stereotypy. Pharmacol. Biochem. Behav. **2:** 249–255.
91. KILBEY, M. M. & E. H. ELLINWOOD. 1976. Chronic administration of stimulant drugs: response modification. *In* Cocaine and Other Stimulants. E. H. Ellinwood & M. M. Kilbey, Eds. Plenum Press. New York, N.Y. In press.
92. STRIPLING, J. S. & E. H. ELLINWOOD. 1976. Sensitization to cocaine following chronic administration in rats. *In* Cocaine and Other Stimulants. E. H. Ellinwood & M. M. Kilbey, Eds. Plenum Press. New York, N.Y. In press.
93. ELLINWOOD, E. H. 1967. Amphetamine psychosis. I: description of the individuals and process. J. Nerv. Ment. Dis. **144:** 273–283.
94. RYLANDER, G. 1972. Psychosis and the punding in choreiform syndromes in addition to central stimulant drugs. Psychiatr. Neurol. Neurochir. **75:** 203–313.
95. KRAMER, J. C. 1969. Introduction to amphetamine abuse. J. Psychedelic Drugs **2:** 1.
96. BELL, D. S. 1973. The experimental reproduction of amphetamine psychosis. Arch. Gen. Psychiat. **29:** 35.

97. MOORE, K., G. ZELDES & C. C. CHIUEH. 1976. Release of neurotransmitters from brain *in vivo* by amphetamine, methylphenidate and cocaine. *In* Cocaine and Other Stimulants. E. H. Ellinwood & M. M. Kilbey, Eds. Plenum Press. New York, N.Y. In press.

98. ESCALANTE, O. D. & E. H. ELLINWOOD. 1970. Central nervous system cytopathological changes in cat with chronic methedrine intoxication. Brain Res. **21:** 555.

99. ESCALANTE, O. D. & E. H. ELLINWOOD. 1972. Effects of chronic amphetamine intoxication on adrenergic and cholinergic structures in the central nervous system: histochemical observation in cats and monkeys. *In* Current Concepts on Amphetamine Abuse. E. H. Ellinwood & S. Cohen, Eds.: 97–106. U.S. Govt. Printing Office. Washington, D.C.

100. GUNNE, L. & T. LEWANDER. 1967. Long term effects of some dependence-producing drugs on the brain monoamines. *In* Molecular Basis of Some Aspects of Mental Activity. O. Wahaas, Ed.: 75–81. Academic Press. New York, N.Y.

101. SEIDEN, L. S., M. W. FISCHMAN & C. R. SCHUSTER. 1976. Changes in brain catecholamines induced by long-term methamphetamine administration in rhesus monkeys. *In* Cocaine and Other Stimulants. E. H. Ellinwood & M. M. Kilbey, Eds. Plenum Press. New York, N.Y. In press.

102. ELLINWOOD, E. H., STRIPLING, J. S. & M. M. KILBEY. 1976. Chronic changes with amphetamine intoxication: underlying processes. *In* Neuro-regulators and Hypotheses of Psychiatric Disorders. E. Usdin & J. Barchas, Eds. Oxford Univ. Press. London, England. In press.

103. KUSCHINSKY, K. 1975. Does chronic morphine treatment induce a supersensitivity of dopamine receptors in the rat? Psychopharmacologia **42:** 225–229.

104. ELLINWOOD, E. H., M. M. KILBEY, S. CASTELLANI & C. KHOURY. 1976. Amygdala hyperspindling and seizures induced by cocaine. *In* Cocaine and Other Stimulants. E. H. Ellinwood & M. M. Kilbey, Eds. Plenum Press. New York, N.Y. In press.

105. CHASE, T. N., E. M. HOLDEN & J. A. BRODY. 1973. Levodopa-induced dyskinesias. Arch. Neurol. **29:** 328–330.

106. LANGROD, J. 1971. Secondary drug use among heroin users. Report to the Commission on Problems of Drug Dependence. Vol. **2:** 1012–1045. U.S. Govt. Printing Office. Washington, D.C.

107. GREENE, M., N. TURNER & R. DU PONT. 1974. Amphetamines in the District of Columbia. Int. J. Addictions **9:** 653–662.

108. RICHMAN, A. 1975. Narcotics addicts, multiple drug abuse and psychological distress. Report to the Committee on Problems of Drug Dependence. Vol. **5:** 1115–1123. U.S. Govt. Printing Office. Washington, D.C.

109. GEARING, F. R. 1971. Evaluation of methadone maintenance treatment program. *In* Methadone Maintenance. Marcel Dekker. New York, N.Y.

110. CHAMBERS, C. D. & W. J. R. TAYLOR. 1972. Patterns of "cheating" among methadone patients. *In* Drug Abuse, Current Concepts and Research. W. Keup, Ed.: 328–336. C. C. Thomas. Springfield, Ill.

111. WECHSLER, H. & D. THUM. 1973. Teen-age drinking, drug use and social correlates. Q. J. Stud. Alcohol **34:** 1220–1227.

INTERACTIONS OF VARIOUS DRUGS WITH AMPHETAMINE

S. Garattini, A. Jori, and R. Samanin

Instituto di Ricerche Farmacologiche "Mario Negri"
Milan 20157, Italy

Introduction

A meaningful analysis of drug interactions with amphetamine is impossible without a preliminary, although brief, discussion of some basic aspects of amphetamine pharmacology. Since the literature on amphetamine is enormous, no attempt will be made in this review to be exhaustive; preference will be given to those aspects of drug interactions which have been the contribution of these laboratories.

Kinetics and Metabolism of (+)Amphetamine

Amphetamine exists as a racemate and as the respective (—) and (+) optic isomers. For the purpose of this review only the (+) form will be considered because this is the isomer provided with the therapeutic activity and showing the potential of drug abuse. (+)Amphetamine is rapidly absorbed by oral route[1] and distributed in various organs.[2] The drug easily enters the red blood cells[3] and blood-brain barrier,[4, 5] being distributed in various brain areas without special localizations.[5, 6] (+)Amphetamine is excreted by renal route, the rate of such excretion being pH dependent; in fact, at acidic urinary pH, (+)amphetamine is excreted in higher amounts than at basic pH.[4, 7] Depending on the animal species, several metabolite pathways exist.[8]

Essentially, (+)amphetamine can be oxidatively deaminated with the formation of benzoic acid,[8] which is then conjugated with glycine and excreted as hippuric acid.[9] Another route of metabolism is represented by hydroxylation in the para position,[10] followed by glucuronide conjugation.[9] This hydroxylation is, for instance, more prominent in rats than in mice.[11] p-OH-amphetamine, when formed, can be hydroxylated in the beta position yielding p-OH-norephedrine,[12] a false metabolite which accumulates in adrenergic terminals by displacing catecholamines.[13] (+)Amphetamine can also be hydroxylated in the adrenergic nerve terminals, both peripherally and centrally, in the beta-position to form norephedrine by means of dopamine-beta-hydroxylase.[12] The distribution of (+)amphetamine and its metabolites in two brain areas is shown in Table 1, and the metabolic pattern of (+)amphetamine is summarized in Figure 1.

Some Pharmacological and Biochemical Effects of (+)Amphetamine

The discussion will be limited to some basic pharmacological effects of (+)amphetamine, which include increase of body temperature and locomotor

TABLE 1

CONCENTRATIONS OF AMPHETAMINE, P-HYDROXYAMPHETAMINE AND P-HYDROXYNOREPHEDRINE IN TWO AREAS OF THE RAT BRAIN AFTER AMPHETAMINE*

Brain Areas	Interval Between Treatment and Death	Amphetamine	p-OH-Amphetamine ng g^{-1} ± S.E.	p-OH-Norephedrine
Striatum	1	11615 ± 874	92 ± 6	<25
	2	6006 ± 242	79 ± 6	38 ± 1.5
	5	1099 ± 86	46 ± 5	57 ± 3
	8	266 ± 30	31 ± 1	44 ± 5
	12	100 ± 11	<25	31 ± 1
Brainstem	1	14763 ± 778	105 ± 18	32 ± 3
	2	5826 ± 822	62 ± 5	81 ± 7
	5	852 ± 87	37 ± 6	168 ± 15
	8	248 ± 20	<25	87 ± 9
	12	75 ± 8	—	53 ± 1

* (+)Amphetamine sulfate was given intraperitoneally at the dose of 15 mg kg^{-1}. Each figure is the average of 4 determinations.

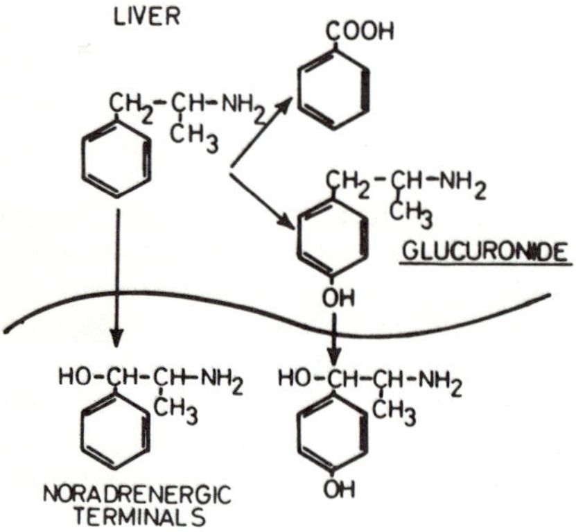

FIGURE 1. Scheme of the main metabolic pathways of (+)amphetamine.

activity, decrease of food intake, and stereotypy, because these are the parameters on which most of the studies on drug interactions are based. The degree of the parmacological actions of (+)amphetamine cannot be discussed here because it depends on many factors, including animal species and the precise experimental conditions under which a given effect of (+)amphetamine is tested and evaluated. It is sufficient in this respect to recall that (+)amphetamine exerts quite a different effect in relation to the number of mice present in the cage (grouping effect).[14] It is also interesting to note that within the same animal species, i.e. rats, the reported effects of (+)amphetamine require different doses in order to become evident. Usually, low doses of the drug (1–2.5 mg/kg i.p.) produce a marked increase of locomotor activity and a depression of food intake (anorexia), whereas the doses necessary to induce hyperthermia and stereotyped behavior range from 5 to 10 mg/kg i.p. (TABLE 2). A remarkable amount of data exist as far as biochemical effects are con-

TABLE 2

VARIOUS PHARMACOLOGICAL EFFECTS OF (+)AMPHETAMINE IN RATS

Experimental Groups	Food Intake* (g/rat ± S.E.)	Body Temperature† (° C ± S.E.)	Motor Activity‡ (counts ± S.E.)	Stereotypy§ (proportion of positive animals)
Controls	8.0 ± 0.4	37.5 ± 0.4	21 ± 4	0/10
(+)Amphetamine	1.7 ± 0.4¶	39.9 ± 0.2¶	203 ± 36¶	9/10¶

Groups of at least 6 animals were used in each experiment.

* Measured for 2 hours after injection of (+)amphetamine sulfate (2.5 mg/kg i.p.).

† Measured 60 min after intraperitoneal injection of 10 mg/kg of (+)amphetamine sulfate.

‡ 10 min recording by an actometer (Basile, Italy) 30 min after the injection of (+)amphetamine sulfate (1.5 mg/kg i.p.).

§ Continuous licking, biting or gnawing at 90 min after (+)amphetamine sulfate (10 mg/kg i.p.).

¶ $p < 0.01$ with respect to controls.

TABLE 3

EFFECT OF (+)AMPHETAMINE ON BRAIN MONOAMINES AND THEIR METABOLITES

Monoamine in Brain (B) or Striatum (S)		Monoamine Content (μg/g + S.E.)	
		Controls (saline)	(+)Amphetamine Sulfate (15 mg/kg i.p.)
5HT	(B)	0.43 ± 0.01	0.40 ± 0.01
5HIAA	(B)	0.34 ± 0.01	0.34 ± 0.03
NA	(B)	0.40 ± 0.01	0.21 ± 0.02*
MOPEG-SO_4	(B)	0.58 ± 0.02	0.58 ± 0.02
DA	(S)	8.2 ± 0.5	7.5 ± 0.3
HVA	(S)	0.21 ± 0.06	0.42 ± 0.01*
Ach	(S)	3.9 ± 0.1	5.1 ± 0.5*
Choline	(S)	9.8 ± 0.3	9.4 ± 0.2

Each figure represents the mean of 6 animals.

* $p < 0.01$ in respect to controls.

cerned in the area of brain chemical neurotransmitters. As shown in TABLE 3, (+)amphetamine produces, at high doses, selective effects because it significantly reduces the steady-state levels of brain noradrenaline (NA) without affecting the levels of brain dopamine (DA) or serotonin (5HT). The major metabolites of NA, 3-methoxy-4-hydroxy-phenyl glycol sulfate (MOPEG-SO_4), and of 5HT, 5-hydroxyindoleacetic acid (5HIAA), are not affected by (+)amphetamine, whereas the final DA metabolite, homovanillic acid (HVA), shows a marked increase in the striatum. Several studies indicate that (+)amphetamine acts mainly by releasing catecholamines from presynaptic terminals and by inhibiting their uptake.[15, 16] As a consequence of the increased release, the O-methyl metabolite of NA, normetanephrine, is increased.[17] The lack of increase of MOPEG-SO_4 (TABLE 2) may be related to an inhibition of NA uptake[15] and to a reversible inhibition of monoamineoxidase,[16] an important enzyme for the intraneuronal metabolism of NA and normetanephrine. As a consequence of the release of NA, (+)amphetamine at relatively high doses increases the turnover of brain NA.[15] In addition, it appears that amphetamine shows a direct stimulatory effect (partial agonist) on postsynaptic NA receptors.[18, 19] As far as the effect of (+)amphetamine on DA, it has been shown that amphetamine exerts several effects, such as increased release,[15,16] inhibition of uptake,[15] together with the already mentioned inhibition of monoamineoxidase.[16] An increase of DA turnover has been observed in the striatum as a consequence of (+)amphetamine administration.[15] (+)Amphetamine does not appear to stimulate DA receptors directly because it is inactive *in vitro* on the DA-dependent adenylcyclase,[20, 21] which is considered a reliable *in vitro* model of a DA receptor in the striatum.[22] In the striatum (TABLE 3), but not in the whole brain,[23] (+)amphetamine produces a significant increase of acetylcholine (Ach) without changes in choline levels.[23] This increase of Ach is with all probability secondary to the stimulation of DA receptors,[24] as indicated by the fact that drugs stimulating directly or indirectly the dopaminergic system increase striatal Ach levels,[25] whereas drugs, such as neuroleptics, that block the DA receptors exert the opposite effect.[26] The increase of striatal Ach depends on a reduced release, as indicated by the fact that (+)amphetamine decreases the Ach turnover in the striatum.[27] However, (+)amphetamine may be a releaser of Ach in other brain areas, such as the cerebral cortex.[28]

Some authors have reported that high doses of (+)amphetamine increase the turnover of brain 5HT,[29] but this effect appears to be secondary to the hyperthermic effect of (+)amphetamine.[29] Moreover, the possibility exists that high doses of amphetamine may produce some changes in the serotonergic system through their effects on brain catecholamines, since it has been shown that a functional connection exists between these systems in the brain.[30]

DISSOCIATION OF (+)AMPHETAMINE EFFECTS

An important aspect in the pharmacological effects of (+)amphetamine is represented by the fact that the various activities of this drug can be dissociated in some instances, suggesting the involvement of different mechanisms.

It has been shown, for instance, that various strains of mice do not respond with the same intensity to (+)amphetamine.[31-34] The C3H strain is different from several albino strains (Swiss, CD_1, NMRI) because it is almost insensitive to the stimulant and to the hyperthermic effect of (+)amphetamine,[35] whereas in all the strains the same drug is effective in increasing the level of plasma FFA and in decreasing the amount of food intake[36] (TABLE 4). The mechanism for this dissociation of effects apparently does not lie in differences of drug distribution and metabolism in the various strains, since the concentrations of brain amphetamine[37] and p-OH-norephedrine[37] are comparable in C3H and CD_1 mouse strains. It was instead observed that C3H mice show a lower turnover rate of striatum DA in respect to albino mice,[35] a finding which may explain the fact that (+)amphetamine elicits a higher increase of HVA in the striatum of CD_1 than of C3H mice.[35]

Furthermore, a depletion or brain NA occurs in a higher degree in the albino than in the C3H strain.[35]

TABLE 4

DIFFERENT SENSITIVITY TO VARIOUS EFFECTS OF (+)AMPHETAMINE IN TWO STRAINS OF MICE

Effect of (+)Amphetamine	Mouse Strain C$_3$H	Mouse Strain NMRI
Hyperthermia (Δ° C)	−0.7 ± 0.1*	+2.5 ± 0.1
NE decrease (ng/g)	−60 ± 15*	−150 ± 20
HVA increase (ng/g)	−14 ± 20*	+224 ± 15
Food intake (g/2 hr/6 mice)	1 ± 1	2 ± 1
Plasma FFA increase (meq/l)	+715 ± 35	+727 ± 39

* $p < 0.01$ versus the NMRI strain; for details see Reference 36.

Another possible mechanism by which some of the activities of amphetamine are dissociated is shown in rats submitted to discrete electrolytical brain lesions. Animals lesioned in the ventral noradrenergic bundles[38] respond to (+)amphetamine with the usual stereotyped movements and an increase of locomotor activity, whereas the anorectic effect is markedly reduced in these animals (TABLE 5). These findings indicate that in studying interaction of drugs with amphetamine it is important to consider that an interaction in respect to a given pharmacological or biochemical effect of amphetamine does not necessarily apply to all the effects of this drug.

TRICYCLIC ANTIDEPRESSANT DRUGS

Potentiation of locomotor hyperactivity or hyperthermia of (+)amphetamine by tricyclic antidepressant drugs (TAD) has been suggested as a test to

TABLE 5

VARIOUS PHARMACOLOGICAL EFFECTS OF (+)AMPHETAMINE IN RATS LESIONED IN THE VENTRAL NORADRENERGIC BUNDLE (VNB)

Experimental Groups	Food Intake* (g/rat ± S.E.)	Motor Activity† (counts ± S.E.)	Stereotypy‡ (proportion of positive animals)
Sham operated			
saline	10.8 ± 1.2	40 ± 6	—
(+)amphetamine	2.7 ± 0.4	183 ± 15	8/10
VNB lesioned			
saline	11.3 ± 1.6	52 ± 4	—
(+)amphetamine	6.2 ± 1.0§	207 ± 20	7/10

* Measured for 2 hours after the injection of (+)amphetamine sulfate (2.5 mg/kg i.p.).
† 10 min recording 30 min after (+)amphetamine sulfate (1.5 mg/kg i.p.).
‡ Continuous licking, biting, or gnawing 120 min after (+)amphetamine sulfate (10 mg/kg i.p.).
§ $p < 0.01$ when compared with sham operated (Duncan's test).

differentiate this class of psychotropic drugs[39] from that of neuroleptics, the latter characterized, as discussed below, by the capacity to block several actions of (+)amphetamine. The hypothesis to explain the interaction between TAD and (+)amphetamine was based on the fact that TAD, by blocking the uptake of NA at nerve terminals,[40, 41] would have been able to increase at the receptor sites the concentrations of NA released by (+)amphetamine. This attractive hypothesis is no longer tenable, however, because TAD interacts with (+)amphetamine by increasing the concentration of (+)amphetamine in the brain.[42] A series of studies has been conducted in this respect on the interaction between desipramine and (+)amphetamine. Thus, it was shown that the prolongation

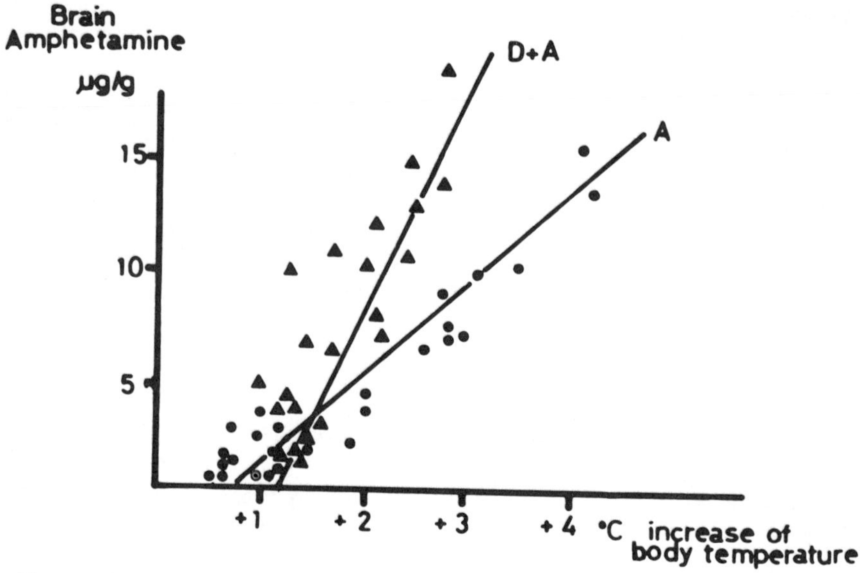

FIGURE 2. Correlation between hyperthermia and levels of brain amphetamine in rats treated with amphetamine alone (A) or with a combination of desipramine and amphetamine (D + A).

of the hyperthermia by (+)amphetamine is temporally related to an increased brain level of (+)amphetamine in rats.[42] This increase is due to the fact that desipramine blocks the hydroxylation of (+)amphetamine[43, 44] by liver microsomal enzymes,[10] reducing, therefore, the major metabolism pathway in rats. Since the hyperthermia is directly related to brain (+)amphetamine concentrations, it appears that when equal concentrations of (+)amphetamine in brain are considered, the animals pretreated with desipramine are actually less responsive than the controls[45] (FIGURE 2). Desipramine also prevents the formation of p-OH-norephedrine, because this metabolite depends upon the availability of p-OH-amphetamine.[10, 12] That the potentiating effect of desipramine is almost entirely related to an inhibition of amphetamine hydroxylation is indirectly confirmed by the fact that desipramine does not potentiate (+)amphetamine, and it does not increase brain amphetamine concentration in mice,[46] an animal species in which amphetamine is only poorly hydroxylated.[11] Furthermore, iprindole, a tricyclic antidepressant drug which does not inhibit the NA uptake in brain,[47] can also increase brain amphetamine concentration and potentiate psychomotor stimulation induced by amphetamine.[48] The interaction between TAD and (+)amphetamine in rats can be minimized when (+)amphetamine is given by oral route, because TAD blocks gastrointestinal motility and decreases the oral absorption of several drugs in relation to their anticholinergic activity.[49] There is, therefore, at the same time less amphetamine being absorbed but also less drug being metabolized in the presence of a pretreatment with TAD.

Neuroleptics

In contrast to antidepressant drugs, neuroleptics such as phenothiazines, butyrophenones and related drugs antagonize various effects of amphetamine.[50, 51] Depending upon the dose and the type of drug used, certain neuroleptics may preferentially inhibit the stereotyped movements and have little or no effect on other activities, such as anorexia or locomotor activity.[52, 53] A clear example is shown in Table 6, where the same dose of pimozide or penfluridol strongly antagonizes stereotypy, with little or no effect on anorexia. Even an increase of amphetamine-induced locomotor activity has been reported by a low dose of perphenazine, which inhibited the stereotyped movements.[52] Inhibition of stereotypy induced by (+)amphetamine appears to be a common effect of all neuroleptics, with the exception only of reserpine.[51] The anti-stereotypy effect shown by neuroleptics does not appear to be due to their interference with the metabolism or distribution of amphetamine, since drugs such as haloperidol or chlorpromazine have no effect or even decrease the disappearance of amphetamine in the rat brain.[54] Moreover, various pharmacological and biochemical findings suggest that this interaction is likely to occur at

Table 6

Effect of Pimozide or Penfluridol on the Stereotypy and Anorexia Induced by (+)Amphetamine in Rats*

Experimental Group	Food Intake (g/rat/2 hr ± S.E.)	Stereotypy† (proportion of positive animals)
Controls	6.7 ± 0.3	0/8
Pimozide	6.9 ± 0.6	0/6
Penfluridol	7.8 ± 0.6	0/6
(+)amphetamine	1.3 ± 0.3	7/8
Pimozide + (+)amphetamine	2.3 ± 0.5	0/8
Penfluridol + (+)amphetamine	4.0 ± 0.2‡	0/8

* Pimozide (0.2 mg/kg i.p.) and penfluridol (2.5 mg/kg i.p.) were administered 4 and 18 hours, respectively, before amphetamine. (+)Amphetamine sulfate was injected intraperitoneally at doses of 2.5 and 10 mg/kg for food intake and stereotypy, respectively.

† Animals showing continuous licking, biting, or gnawing 120 min after amphetamine were taken as positive.

‡ $p < 0.01$ when compared with amphetamine-treated animals (Dunnet's test).

the level of DA receptors in the striatum. In fact, as previously mentioned, (+)amphetamine is commonly believed to produce the stereotyped movements by releasing DA from the presynaptic terminals in the striatum,[55] whereas neuroleptics are known to be potent blockers to DA receptors in the brain.[56] Particularly suggestive of the specificity of this interaction are the data showing a fairly good agreement between the relative blockade of neuroleptics on amphetamine stereotypy and the inhibition of DA-stimulated cyclic AMP production in rat striatum.[57] Also, the inhibition of (+)amphetamine stereotypy by fenfluramine has been interpreted as the result of the dopaminergic blockade exerted by the latter drug.[90]

The lack of antiamphetamine effect by reserpine is explained on the basis of the fact that this drug has no blocking activity on central catecholamine receptors, which appear to be even in a state of hypersensitivity in the animals treated with reserpine.[59] Together with the fact that reserpine increases the turnover rate of catecholamines in the brain,[60] this can explain why some effects of amphetamine have been found to even be potentiated in animals treated with reserpine.[61, 62]

Other Drugs Acting on Catecholamines

Various drugs believed to exert a specific effect on brain catecholamines have been studied for their ability to modify the activity of amphetamine in various experimental conditions. It has been found, for instance, that alpha-methyl-para-tyrosine, a potent inhibitor of tyrosine hydroxylase, antagonizes various effects of amphetamine[63, 64] without changing amphetamine concentrations in the brain,[64] indicating that catecholamine can mediate its effects. Various attempts have been made to separate the relative role of brain dopamine and noradrenaline in amphetamine action. On the basis of comparisons between the potencies of (+) and (—)amphetamine in producing biochemical and behavioral effects, it has been suggested that NA is selectively involved in the increase of locomotor activity induced by amphetamine.[65] However, data have been presented that are not consistent with this hypothesis,[66, 67] and an increase of motor activity in rats has been found recently with a dose of amphetamine that increases the turnover of brain DA but not that of NA.[68] Although diethyldithiocarbamate or disulfiram have been reported to reduce the effect of amphetamine on motor activity without affecting the stereotyped movements,[69, 70] recent experiments using more specific inhibitors of dopamine-beta-hydroxylase, such as U-14,624 or FLA-63, have not confirmed these findings.[71–73] Alpha and beta blockers such as phentolamine, phenoxybenzamine, and propanolol have been also studied for their interaction with various effects of amphetamine, but no consistent results have been obtained.[74–78] The complexity of the various levels at which these drugs act and the uncertainty about their real effectiveness in blocking central noradrenergic receptors make interpretation of experiments with these drugs particularly difficult. The use of 6-hydroxydopamine (6-OHDA), a compound that produces a selective degeneration of catecholamine containing neurons when injected intracerebrally,[79] appears to offer better possibilities to separate the role of dopamine and noradrenaline in the action of amphetamine. We have found (Table 7) that in rats pretreated with desipramine, an intrastriatal injection of 6-OHDA, that

TABLE 7

EFFECT OF AN INTRASTRIATAL INJECTION OF 6-HYDROXYDOPAMINE (6-OHDA) ON VARIOUS PHARMACOLOGICAL EFFECTS* OF (+) AMPHETAMINE

Experimental Group	Food Intake (g/rat/2 hr ± S.E.)	Stereotypy† (proportion of positive animals)	Locomotor Activity‡ (counts/10 min ± S.E.)
Vehicle			
Saline	8.0 ± 0.4	0/6	—
(+)Amphetamine	2.4 ± 0.3§	10/10	203 ± 26
6-OHDA			
Saline	8.8 ± 0.7	0/6	—
(+)Amphetamine	3.9 ± 0.4	0/10¶	110 ± 20¶

* 6-OHDA (20 μg × 2) was administered bilaterally in the striatum, and the experiments were performed 10 days after. (+)Amphetamine sulfate was administered intraperitoneally at doses of 1.5, 2.5, and 10 mg/kg for locomotor activity, food intake, and stereotypy, respectively.

† = animals showing continuous licking, biting or gnawing 120 min after amphetamine were considered positive.

‡ = recorded by an actometer (Basile, Italy) 30 min after the injection of (+)amphetamine sulfate.

§ $p < 0.01$ when compared with saline.

¶ $p < 0.01$ when compared with the vehicle group receiving (+)amphetamine.

completely protects the noradrenergic neurons from the action of 6-OHDA,[80] strongly antagonizes the stereotypy and the increase of locomotion induced by amphetamine without significantly altering the anorectic effect. The anorexia by (+)amphetamine is instead inhibited when both DA and NA terminals are destroyed by the combination of pargyline and 6-OHDA.[81] The preferential role of brain dopamine in stereotypy and locomotor activity appears to be suggested by various recent experiments of interaction in which various compounds were injected intracerebrally in either noradrenergic or dopaminergic brain areas.[82-84] The use of 6-OHDA has revealed that (+)amphetamine accumulates in catecholaminergic terminals. In fact, the destruction of these terminals reduces the levels of (+)amphetamine in given brain areas, particularly at later times after (+)amphetamine administration.[85] Furthermore, the destruction of noradrenergic terminals leads to a decreased accumulation of p-OH-norephedrine, the metabolite of (+)amphetamine which, in order to form, requires DA-beta-hydroxylase.[85]

As far as the anorectic activity is concerned, although our data suggest a preferential role for brain NA, the possibility cannot be excluded that DA also contributes to this effect, particularly in view of the antagonism toward amphetamine anorexia that various authors have found with some neuroleptics believed to possess a rather specific effect in blocking DA receptors in the brain.[77, 86, 87] Therefore, the exact role of brain NA and DA in the anorectic action of amphetamine needs to be further explored. Various drugs acting on the serotonergic system have been studied in their ability to interact with amphetamine. With a few exceptions, neither 5-HT depletors such as p-chlorophenyl-alanine nor 5-HT antagonists such as methysergide or methergoline have been found to change significantly the stereotypy or anorexia induced by amphetamine.[88-91]

Recently, various authors have found a significant potentiation of amphetamine-induced locomotor activity in rats in which brain 5-HT levels were depleted either by p-chlorophenyl-alanine or by 5,6-HT,[92, 93] a compound which produces a preferential degeneration of 5-HT neurons when injected intracerebrally.[94] However, these data have been interpreted as indicative of an inhibitory role of brain 5-HT or some catecholaminergic mechanisms specifically related to behavioral arousal, rather than to a direct effect of these drugs on amphetamine or to a role of 5-HT in amphetamine action.[93]

Autointeraction

This term is used to describe the fact that repeated treatments with (+)amphetamine make animals insensitive to a subsequent administration of the same drug. This tolerance situation has been described for the hyperthermic, the anorectic, and the stimulant effect of (+)amphetamine.[13, 95, 96] It was established that tolerance is not related to an increased metabolism of amphetamine because the brain levels of (+)amphetamine of normal and tolerant rats are comparable.[97] Also, the increase of striatum HVA induced by (+)amphetamine is abolished if the rats are pretreated with several administrations of (+)amphetamine or of p-OH-amphetamine.[97] Pretreatment with (—)amphetamine, which also increases HVA levels,[98] does not make the rats tolerant to (+)amphetamine as far as the increase of striatum HVA is concerned. On the other hand, rats made tolerant to (+)amphetamine can still respond to an increase of striatum HVA induced by other agents, such as fenfluramine.[97] The intimate mechanism for explaining the tolerance is not known, although the hypothesis has been advanced that tolerance may depend on the accumulation of the metabolite of (+)amphetamine, p-OH-norephedrine, which by displacing NA is stored as a false transmitter at nerve terminals.[13] This explanation may be valid for the effect of (+)amphetamine mediated by a release of NA, but on this basis it is difficult to explain the tolerance toward the increase of HVA because p-OH-norephedrine cannot be synthesized in dopaminergic terminals owing to the lack of the necessary enzyme, dopamine-beta-hydroxylase.

Drugs Acting on the Thyroid Function

Animals that are made hyperthyroid by repeated administration of triiodothyronine become more susceptible to the toxic and hyperthermic effects of (+)amphetamine.[99] Also, the previously mentioned C3H mice become sensitive to the hyperthermic effects of (+)amphetamine if they are pretreated with thyroid hormones.[100] This effect does not involve any change in the concentrations of brain (+)amphetamine.[99] Conversely, rats submitted to thyroidectomy or made hypothyroid after the administration of propylthiouracil become insensitive to the hyperthermic effect of (+)amphetamine, despite the fact that the concentrations of brain amphetamine are higher than in euthyroid rats,[99] probably owing to an inhibition of amphetamine metabolism.

The interaction of thyroid function with amphetamine activity can be explained on the basis of the known permissive effect exerted by thyroid hormones on catecholamine activities.[101]

Aspecific Interactions

Although these interactions have already been alluded to in several parts of this review, it seems appropriate to summarize here aspecific effects that may be present in different classes of drugs. For instance, all the compounds showing an inhibition of gastric emptying and intestinal motility should be expected to interact with (+)amphetamine by reducing the intestinal absorption of this drug given orally and also decreasing, therefore, the pharmacological effects.

All the compounds that decrease or enhance the aromatic hydroxylation through liver microsomal enzymes should be expected to potentiate or to inhibit pharmacological effects of (+)amphetamine, but only in those animal species where hydroxylation of (+)amphetamine represents an important metabolic pathway. In man, where the hydroxylation of (+)ampthetamine is subjected to individual variability,[8] it is likely that an interaction with this metabolic step will also show a high degree of variability. Finally, drugs that change urinary pH are likely to interact with (+)amphetamine excretion, since the acidifying agents are able to decrease the effect of amphetamine, while the opposite holds true for the alkalinizing drugs.

Conclusion

This brief review gives some examples of the possible interactions that a number of drugs may exert on (+)amphetamine. These interactions may occur at different levels, including the distribution and the metabolism of (+)amphetamine as well as the sites on which (+)amphetamine affects catecholamine functions. Due to the multiplicity of action of (+)amphetamine, it is impossible to draw general conclusions. Each interaction should therefore be studied on the many pharmacological and biochemical parameters that are relevant for (+)amphetamine activity. Since it is not yet completely clear which effects of amphetamine are the result of the release of DA and/or NA, the interaction of drugs with (+)amphetamine is also difficult to interpret. It should be stressed in this respect that the studies on drug interactions have thrown considerable light on the mechanism of action of (+)amphetamine. This in turn may be of enormous importance because (+)amphetamine is utilized as a model of acute psychosis and as a tool to detect new neuroleptic agents.

References

1. Beckett, A. H., R. N. Boyes & E. J. Triggs. 1968. Kinetics of buccal absorption of amphetamines. J. Pharm. Pharmacol. **20:** 92–97.
2. Maickel, R. P., R. H. Cox, Jr., F. P. Miller, D. S. Segal & R. W. Russell.

1969. Correlation of brain levels of drugs with behavioral effects. J. Pharmacol. Exp. Ther. **165:** 216–224.
3. MORSELLI, P. L., G. F. PLACIDI, C. MAGGINI, R. GOMENI, M. GUAZZELLI, G. DE LISIO, S. STANDEN & G. TOGNONI. 1976. An integrated approach for the evaluation of psychotropic drug in man. Psychopharmacologia. In press.
4. VAN ROSSUM, J. M. 1970. Mode of action of psychomotor stimulant drugs. Int. Rev. Neurobiol. **12:** 307–383.
5. PLACIDI, G. F., D. T. MASUOKA & R. W. EARLE. 1972. Distribution of [14C] amphetamine in mouse brain: an autoradiographic study. Brain Res. **38:** 399–405.
6. JORI, A. & S. CACCIA. 1974. Distribution of amphetamine and its hydroxylated metabolites in various areas of the rat brain. J. Pharm. Pharmacol. **26:** 746–748.
7. BECKETT, A. H. & M. ROWLAND. 1965. Urinary excretion kinetics of amphetamine in man. J. Pharm. Pharmacol. **17:** 628–639.
8. SMITH, R. L. & L. G. DRING. 1970. Patterns of metabolism of β-phenylisopropylamines in man and other species. *In* Amphetamines and Related Compounds. E. Costa & S. Garattini, Eds.: 121–139. Raven Press. New York, N.Y.
9. ELLISON, T., L. GUTZAIT & E. J. VAN LOON. 1966. The comparative metabolism of d-amphetamine-C^{14} in the rat, dog and monkey. J. Pharmacol. Exp. Ther. **152:** 383–387.
10. AXELROD, J. 1954. Studies on sympathomimetic amines. II. The biotransformation and physiological disposition of d-amphetamine d-p-hydroxyamphetamine and d-methamphetamine. J. Pharmacol. Exp. Ther. **110:** 315–326.
11. DRING, L. G., R. L. SMITH & R. T. WILLIAMS. 1966. The fate of amphetamine in man and other mammals. J. Pharm. Pharmacol. **18:** 402–404.
12. GOLDSTEIN, M. & B. ANAGNOSTE. 1965. The conversion "in vivo" of d-amphetamine to (+)-p-hydroxynorephedrine. Biochim. Biophys. Acta **107:** 166–168.
13. BRODIE, B. B., A. K. CHO & G. L. GESSA. 1970. Possible role of p-hydroxynorephedrine in the depletion to norepinephrine induced by d-amphetamine and in tolerance to this drug. *In* Amphetamines and Related Compounds. E. Costa & S. Garattini, Eds.: 217–230. Raven Press. New York, N.Y.
14. CHANCE, M. R. A. 1946. Aggregation as a factor influencing the toxicity of sympathomimetic amines in mice. J. Pharmacol. Exp. Ther. **87:** 214–224.
15. GLOWINSKI, J. 1970. Effects of amphetamine on various aspects of catecholamine metabolism in the central nervous system of the rat. *In* Amphetamines and Related Compounds. E. Costa & S. Garattini, Eds.: 301–316. Raven Press. New York, N.Y.
16. GLOWINSKI, J., J. AXELROD & L. L. IVERSEN. 1966. Regional studies of catecholamines in the rat brain. IV. J. Pharmacol. Exp. Ther. **153:** 30–41.
17. GLOWINSKI, J. & J. AXELROD. 1965. Effect of drugs on the uptake, release, and metabolism of H^3-norepinephrine in the rat brain. J. Pharmacol. Exp. Ther. **149:** 43–49.
18. SMITH, C. B. 1965. Effects of d-amphetamine upon brain amine content and locomotor activity in mice. *J. Pharmacol. Exp. Ther.* **147:** 96–102.
19. VAN ROSSUM, J. M., J. B. VAN DER SCHOOT, & J. A. TH. M. HURKMANS. 1962. Mechanism of action of cocaine and amphetamine in the brain. Experientia **18:** 229–231.
20. KRUEGER, B. K., J. FORN & P. GREENGARD. 1975. Dopamine-sensitive adenylate cyclase and protein phosphorylation in the rat caudate nucleus. *In* Pre- and Post-Synaptic Receptors. E. Usdin & W. E. Bunney Jr., Eds.: 123–147. Marcel Dekker. New York, N.Y.

21. IVERSEN, L. L., A. S. HORN & R. J. MILLER. 1975. Structure-activity relationships for agonist, and antagonist drugs, at pre- and post-synaptic dopamine receptor sites in rat brain. *In* Pre- and Post-Synaptic Receptors. E. Usdin & W. E. Bunney Jr., Eds.: 207–243. Marcel Dekker. New York, N.Y.
22. KEBABIAN, J. W., G. L. PETZOLD & P. GREENGARD. 1972. Dopamine-sensitive adenylate cyclase in caudate nucleus of rat brain, and its similarity to the dopamine receptor. Proc. Natl. Acad. Sci. **69:** 2145–2149.
23. CONSOLO, S., H. LADINSKY, G. PERI & S. GARATTINI. 1972. Effect of central stimulants and depressants on mouse brain acetyl-choline and choline levels. Eur. J. Pharmacol. **18:** 251–255.
24. LADINSKY, H., S. CONSOLO, S. BIANCHI, S. SAMANIN & D. GHEZZI. 1975. Cholinergic-dopaminergic interaction in the striatum: the effect of 6-hydroxydopamine or pimozine treatment on the increased striatal acetylcholine levels induced by apomorphine, piribedil and d-amphetamine. Brain Res. **84:** 221–226.
25. CONSOLO, S., H. LADINSKY & S. GARATTINI. 1974. Effect of several dopaminergic drugs and trihexyphenidyl on cholinergic parameters in the rat striatum. J. Pharm. Pharmacol. **26:** 275–277.
26. CONSOLO, S., H. LADINSKY & S. BIANCHI. 1975. Decrease in rat striatal acetylcholine levels by some direct- and indirect-acting dopaminergic antagonists. Eur. J. Pharmacol. **33:** 345–351.
27. TRABUCCHI, M., D. L. CHENEY, G. RACAGNI & E. COSTA. 1975. *In vivo* inhibition of striatal acetylcholine turnover by L-DOPA, apomorphine and (+)-amphetamine. Brain Res. **85:** 130–134.
28. PEPEU, G. 1975. The release of acetylcholine from the brain: an approach to the study of the central cholinergic mechanisms. *In* Progress in Neurobiology. G. A. Kerkut & J. W. Phillis, Eds. Vol. **2**(3): 257–288. Pergamon Press. Oxford, England.
29. REID, W. D. 1970. Turnover rate of brain 5-hydroxytryptamine increased by d-amphetamine. Brit. J. Pharmacol. **40:** 483–491.
30. SAMANIN, R. & S. GARATTINI. 1975. The serotonergic system in the brain and its possible functional connections with other aminergic systems. Life Sci. **17:** 1201–1210.
31. BROWN, A. M. 1965. Pharmacogenetics of the mouse. Lab. Animal Care **15:** 111–118.
32. BROWN, A. M. & T. JULIAN. 1968. The body temperature response of two inbred strains of mice to handling, saline and amphetamine. Int. J. Neuropharmacol. **7:** 531–541.
33. DOLFINI, E., S. GARATTINI & L. VALZELLI. 1969. Activity of (+)-amphetamine at different environmental temperatures in three strains of mice. J. Pharm. Pharmacol. **21:** 871–872.
34. DOLFINI, E., S. GARATTINI & L. VALZELLI. 1969. Different sensitivity to amphetamine of three strains of mice. Eur. J. Pharmacol. **7:** 220–223.
35. CACCIA, S., G. CECCHETTI, S. GARATTINI & A. JORI. 1973. Interaction of (+)-amphetamine with cerebral dopaminergic neurones in two strains of mice, that show different temperature responses to this drug. Brit. J. Pharmacol. **49:** 400–406.
36. JORI, A. & S. GARATTINI. 1973. Catecholamine metabolism and amphetamine effects on sensitive and insensitive mice. *In* Frontiers in Catecholamine Research. E. Usdin & S. H. Snyder, Eds.: 939–941. Pergamon Press. New York, N.Y.
37. JORI, A. & S. CACCIA. 1975. Further studies on brain concentrations of amphetamine and its metabolites in strains of mice showing different sensitivity to pharmacological effects of amphetamine. J. Pharm. Pharmacol. **27:** 886–888.

38. UNGERSTEDT, U. 1971. Stereotaxic mapping of monoamine pathways in the rat brain. Acta Physiol. Scand. **82**(suppl. 367): 1–48.
39. MORPURGO, C. & W. THEOBALD. 1965. Influence of imipramine-like compounds and chlorpromazine on the reserpine-hypothermia in mice and the amphetamine-hyperthermia in rats. Med. Pharmacol. Exp. **12:** 226–232.
40. CARLSSON, A., K. FUXE, B. HAMBERGER & M. LINDQVIST. 1966. Biochemical and histochemical studies on the effects of imipramine-like drugs and (+)-amphetamine on central and peripheral catecholamine neurons. Acta Physiol. Scand. **67:** 481–497.
41. CARLSSON, A., H. CORRODI, K. FUXE & T. HÖKFELT. 1969. Effects of some antidepressant drugs on the depletion of intraneuronal brain catecholamine stores caused by 4, α-dimethyl-meta-tyramine. Eur. J. Pharmacol. **5:** 367–373.
42. VALZELLI, L., S. CONSOLO & C. MORPURGO. 1967. Influence of imipramine-like drugs on the metabolism of amphetamine. *In* Antidepressant Drugs. S. Garattini & M. N. G. Dukes, Eds.: 61–69. Excerpta Medica. Amsterdam, Netherlands.
43. DINGELL, J. V. & A. D. BASS. 1969. Inhibition of the hepatic metabolism of amphetamine by desipramine. Biochem. Pharmacol. **18:** 1535–1538.
44. CONSOLO, S., E. DOLFINI, S. GARATTINI & L. VALZELLI. 1967. Desipramine and amphetamine metabolism. J. Pharm. Pharmacol. **19:** 253–256.
45. GARATTINI, S. 1969. Importance of a knowledge of drug metabolism for the assessment of drug interactions. *In* Importance of Fundamental Principles in Drug Evaluation. D. H. Tedeschi & R. E. Tedeschi, Eds.: 129–139. Raven Press. New York, N.Y.
46. DOLFINI, E., M. TANSELLA, L. VALZELLI & S. GARATTINI. 1969. Further studies on the interaction between desipramine and amphetamine. Eur. J. Pharmacol. **5:** 185–190.
47. GLUCKMAN, M. I. & T. BAUM. 1969. The pharmacology of Iprindole, a new antidepressant. Psychopharmacologia **15:** 169–185.
48. MILLER, K. W., J. J. FREEMAN, J. V. DINGELL & F. SULSER. 1970. On the mechanism of amphetamine potentiation by Iprindole. Experientia **26:** 863–864.
49. CONSOLO, S. & S. GARATTINI. 1969. Effect of desipramine on intestinal absorption of phenylbutazone and other drugs. Eur. J. Pharmacol. **6:** 322–326.
50. BRADLEY, P. B. & A. J. HANCE. 1957. The effect of chlorpromazine and methopromazine on the electrical activity of the brain in the cat. Electroencephalog. Clin. Neurophysiol. **9:** 191–215.
51. JANSSEN, P. A. J., C. J. E. NIEMEGEERS, K. H. L. SCHELLEKENS & F. M. LENAERTS. 1967. Is it possible to predict the clinical effects of neuroleptic drugs (major tranquillizers) from animal data? Arzneim.-Forsch. **17:** 841–854.
52. RANDRUP, A. & I. MUNKVAD. 1965. Special antagonism of amphetamine-induced abnormal behaviour. Psychopharmacologia **7:** 416–422.
53. FOG, R. 1972. On stereotypy and catalepsy: Studies on the effect of amphetamines and neuroleptics in rats. Acta Neurol. Scand. **48** (suppl. 50).
54. LEMBERGER, L., E. D. WITT, J. M. DAVIS & I. J. KOPIN. 1970. The effects of haloperidol and chlorpromazine on amphetamine metabolism and amphetamine stereotype behavior in the rat. J. Pharmacol. Exp. Ther. **174:** 428–433.
55. SCHEEL-KRÜGER, J. & A. RANDRUP. 1967. Stereotype hyperactive behaviour produced by dopamine in the absence of noradrenaline. Life Sci. **6:** 1389–1398.
56. ANDÉN, N.-E., S. G. BUTCHER, H. CORRODI, K. FUXE & U. UNGERSTEDT. 1970. Receptor activity and turnover of dopamine and noradrenaline after neuroleptics. Eur. J. Pharmacol. **11:** 303–314.

57. MILLER, R. J., A. S. HORN & L. L. IVERSEN. 1974. The action of neuroleptic drugs on dopamine-stimulated adenosine cyclic 3′,5′-monophosphate production in rat neostriatum and limbic forebrain. Mol. Pharmacol. **10:** 759–766.
58. JORI, A., G. CECCHETTI, D. GHEZZI & R. SAMANIN. 1974. Biochemical and behavioral antagonism between fenfluramine and apomorphine in rats. Eur. J. Pharmacol. **26:** 179–183.
59. DAHLSTRÖM, A., K. FUXE, B. HAMBERGER & T. HÖKFELT. 1967. Uptake and storage of catecholamines in rabbit brain after chronic reserpine treatment. J. Pharm. Pharmacol. **19:** 345–349.
60. NEFF, N. H. & E. COSTA. 1968. Application of steady-state kinetics to the study of catecholamine turnover after monoamine oxidase inhibition or reserpine administration. J. Pharmacol. Exp. Ther. **160:** 40–47.
61. STOLK, J. M. & R. H. RECH. 1967. Enhanced stimulant effects of d-amphetamine on the spontaneous locomotor activity of rats treated with reserpine. J. Pharmacol. Exp. Ther. **158:** 140–149.
62. STOLK, J. M. & R. H. RECH. 1968. Enhanced stimulant effects of d-amphetamine in rats treated chronically with reserpine. J. Pharmacol. Exp. Ther. **163:** 75–83.
63. WEISSMAN, A., B. K. KOE & S. S. TENEN. 1966. Antiamphetamine effects following inhibition of tyrosine hydroxylase. J. Pharmacol. Exp. Ther. **151:** 339–352.
64. VALZELLI, L., E. DOLFINI, M. TANSELLA & S. GARATTINI. 1968. Activity of centrally acting drugs on amphetamine metabolism. J. Pharm. Pharmacol. **20:** 595–599.
65. TAYLOR, K. M. & S. H. SNYDER. 1971. Differential effects of d- and l-amphetamine on behaviour and on catecholamine disposition in dopamine and norepinephrine containing neurons of rat brain. Brain Res. **28:** 295–309.
66. SCHEEL-KRÜGER, J. 1972. Behavioural and biochemical comparison of amphetamine derivatives, cocaine, benztropine and tricyclic anti-depressant drugs. Eur. J. Pharmacol. **18:** 63–73.
67. THORNBURG, J. E. & K. E. MOORE. 1973. Dopamine and norepinephrine uptake by rat brain synaptosomes: Relative inhibitory potencies of l- and d-amphetamine and amantadine. Res. Commun. Chem. Pathol. Pharmacol. **5:** 81–89.
68. COSTA, E., A. GROPPETTI & M. K. NAIMZADA. 1972. Effects of amphetamine on the turnover rate of brain catecholamines and motor activity. Brit. J. Pharmacol. **44:** 742–751.
69. RANDRUP, A. & J. SCHEEL-KRÜGER. 1966. Diethyldithiocarbamate and amphetamine stereotype behaviour. J. Pharm. Pharmacol. **18:** 752.
70. PFEIFER, A. K., E. GALAMBOS & L. GYÖRGY. 1966. Some central nervous properties of diethyldithiocarbamate. J. Pharm. Pharmacol. **18:** 254.
71. JOHNSON, G. A., S. J. BOUKMA & E. G. KIM. 1970. In vivo inhibition of dopamine β-hydroxylase by 1-phenyl-3-(2-thiazolyl)-2-thiourea (U-14,624). J. Pharmacol. Exp. Ther. **171:** 80–87.
72. SVENSSON, T. H. 1970. The effect of inhibition of catecholamine synthesis on dexamphetamine induced central stimulation. Eur. J. Pharmacol. **12:** 161–166.
73. THORNBURG, J. E. & K. E. MOORE. 1973. The relative importance of dopaminergic and noradrenergic neuronal systems for the stimulation of locomotor activity, induced by amphetamine and other drugs. Neuropharmacology **12:** 853–866.
74. MANTEGAZZA, P., E. E. MÜLLER, M. K. NAIMZADA & M. RIVA. 1970. Studies on the lack of correlation between hyperthermia, hyperactivity and anoressia induced by amphetamine. *In* Amphetamines and Related Compounds. E. Costa & S. Garattini, Eds.: 559–575. Raven Press. New York, N.Y.

75. LEIBOWITZ, S. F. 1975. Amphetamine: possible site and mode of action for producing anorexia in the rat. Brain Res. **84:** 160–167.
76. FREY, H.-H. & R. SCHULZ. 1973. On the central mediation of anorexigenic drug effects. Biochem. Pharmacol. **22:** 3041–3049.
77. GARATTINI, S. & R. SAMANIN. 1976. Anorectic drugs and brain neurotransmitters. Presented at Dahlem Workshop on Appetite and Food Intake, Berlin, Dec. 8–12, 1975. In press.
78. SIMON, P., R. CHERMAT, M. TH. FOSSET & J. R. BOISSIER. 1972. Inhibiteurs β-adrénergiques et stéréotypies provoquées par l'amphetamine ou l'apomorphine chez la rat. Psychopharmacologia **23:** 357–364.
79. URETSKY, N. J. & L. L. IVERSEN. 1970. Effects of 6-hydroxydopamine on catecholamine containing neurones in the rat brain. *J. Neurochem.* **17:** 269–278.
80. BREESE, G. R. & T. D. TRAYLOR. 1971. Depletion of brain noradrenaline and dopamine by 6-hydroxydopamine. Brit. J. Pharmacol. **42:** 88–99.
81. SAMANIN, R., S. BERNASCONI & S. GARATTINI. 1975. The effect of selective lesioning of brain catecholamine-containing neurons on the activity of various anorectics in the rat. Eur. J. Pharmacol. **34:** 373–375.
82. CREESE, I. & S. D. IVERSEN. 1973. Blockage of amphetamine induced motor stimulation and stereotypy in the adult rat following neonatal treatment with 6-hydroxydopamine. Brain Res. **55:** 369–382.
83. FIBIGER, H. C., H. P. FIBIGER & A. P. ZIS. 1973. Attenuation of amphetamine-induced motor stimulation and stereotypy by 6-hydroxydopamine in the rat. Brit. J. Pharmacol. **47:** 683–692.
84. IVERSEN, S. D. & P. H. KELLY. 1975. The use of 6-hydroxydopamine (60 HDA) techniques for studying the pathways involved in drug-induced motor behaviours. *In* Chemical Tools in Catecholamine Research. G. Jonsson, T. Malmfors & Ch. Sachs, Eds. Vol. **1:** 327–333. North-Holland. Amsterdam, Netherlands.
85. GARATTINI, S., A. JORI, L. MANARA & R. SAMANIN. 1975. 6-Hydroxydopamine, a tool to study distribution of drugs in the catecholaminergic system. *In* Chemical Tools in Catecholamine Research. G. Jonsson, T. Malmfors & Ch. Sachs, Eds. Vol **1:** 303–309. North Holland. Amsterdam, Netherlands.
86. CLINESCHMIDT, B. V., J. C. MCGUFFIN & A. B. WERNER. 1974. Role of monoamines in the anorexigenic actions of fenfluramine, amphetamine and p-chloromethamphetamine. Eur. J. Pharmacol. **27:** 313–323.
87. FREY, H.-H. & SCHULZ, R. 1973. On the central mediation of anorexigenic drug effects. Biochem. Pharmacol. **22:** 3041–3049.
88. RANDRUP, A. & I. MUNKVAD. 1964. On the relation of tryptaminic and serotonergic mechanisms to amphetamine induced abnormal behaviour. Acta Pharmacol. Toxicol. **21:** 272–282.
89. GARATTINI, S., A. BIZZI, G. DE GAETANO, A. JORI & R. SAMANIN. 1975. Recent advances in the pharmacology of anorectic agents. *In* Recent Advances in Obesity Research. A. Howard, Ed. Vol. **1:** 354–367. Newman Publ. London, England.
90. GARATTINI, S., A. BONACCORSI, A. JORI & R. SAMANIN. 1974. Appetite suppressant drugs: Past, present and future. *In* Obesity: Causes, Consequences and Treatment. L. Lasagna, Ed.: 70–80. Medcom Press. New York, N.Y.
91. JESPERSEN, S. & J. SCHEEL-KRÜGER. 1973. Evidence for a difference in mechanism of action between fenfluramine- and amphetamine-induced anorexia. J. Pharm. Pharmacol. **25:** 49–54.
92. BREESE, G. R., B. R. COOPER & R. A. MUELLER. 1974. Evidence for involvement of 5-hydroxytryptamine in the actions of amphetamine. Brit. J. Pharmacol. **52:** 307–314.
93. MABRY, P. D. & B. A. CAMPBELL. 1973. Serotonergic inhibition of catecholamine-induced behavioral arousal. Brain Res. **49:** 381–391.

94. BAUMGARTEN, H. G., A. BJÖRKLUND, L. LACHENMAYER, A. NOBIN & U. STENEVI. 1971. Long-lasting selective depletion of brain serotonin by 5,6-dihydroxytryptamine. Acta Physiol. Scand. **84**(Suppl. 373): 1–15.
95. HARRISON, J. W. E., C. M. AMBRUS & J. L. AMBRUS. 1952. Tolerance of rats toward amphetamine and methamphetamine. J. Amer. Pharm. Assoc. **41:** 539–544.
96. KOSMAN, M. E. & K. R. UNNA. 1968. Effects of chronic administration of the amphetamines and other stimulants on behavior. Clin. Pharmacol. Ther. **9:** 240–254.
97. JORI, A. & D. BERNARDI. 1972. Further studies on the increase of striatal homovanillic acid induced by amphetamine and fenfluramine. Eur. J. Pharmacol. **19:** 276–280.
98. JORI, A., E. DOLFINI, G. TOGNONI & S. GARATTINI. 1973. Differential effects of amphetamine, fenfluramine and norfenfluramine stereoisomers on the increase of striatum homovanillic acid in rats. J. Pharm. Pharmacol. **25:** 315–318.
99. DOLFINI, E. & M. KOBAYASHI. 1967. Studies with amphetamine in hyper- and hypothyroid rats. Eur. J. Pharmacol. **2:** 65–66.
100. DOLFINI, E., A. RAMIREZ DEL ANGEL, S. GARATTINI & L. VALZELLI. 1970. Brain catecholamine release by dexamphetamine in three strains of mice. Eur. J. Pharmacol. **9:** 333–336.
101. HARRISON, T. S. 1964. Adrenal medullary and thyroid relationships. Physiol. Rev. **44:** 161–185.

INTERACTIONS BETWEEN AMPHETAMINE AND ALCOHOL AND THEIR EFFECT ON RODENT BEHAVIOR*

R. H. Rech, M. K. Vomachka, and D. Rickert

Department of Pharmacology
Michigan State University
East Lansing, Michigan 48824

M. C. Braude

Division of Research
National Institute on Drug Abuse
Rockville, Maryland 20852

Introduction

Central nervous system (CNS) stimulants of the amphetamine type have generally been understood to antagonize the central depressant actions of alcohol, barbiturates, and other agents in the broad category of the CNS depressants. Indeed, stimulant drugs such as *d*-amphetamine have had trial as analeptics in the treatment of overdose with CNS depressants.[1] On the other hand, it seems clear that certain of the effects of *d*-amphetamine are not appreciably reduced by the concomitant administration of a CNS depressant. Thus, the rationale for combining *d*-amphetamine and amobarbital (Dexamyl) in the treatment of obesity is to reduce the insomnia and restlessness of the stimulant without appreciably interfering with the anorexic effect of amphetamine.[2] However, relatively few experimental studies have been attempted to document the interactions between these stimulants and depressants.[3–8] These previous efforts have used a variety of biological responses to characterize the interactions of only one or two combinations and have usually examined effects over a narrow dose range.

The purpose of this study was to evaluate the interactions of sympathomimetic stimulants with several examples of the CNS depressants. The biological response that was chosen for comparison of these interactions was rotarod performance. This test has the advantages of simplicity and efficiency, and yet it appears to be a reasonable measure of alertness and motor coordination in rodents.[9–12]

Methods

Female rats of the Sprague-Dawley strain (Spartan Farms, Haslett, Mich.) weighing from 225 to 280 g were used for this study. Animals were housed in animal rooms with controlled diurnal lighting and temperature except for days

* This study was supported by Contract ADM-45-74-146 from the National Institute on Drug Abuse.

of training and testing. The mice were female Swiss-Webster (Spartan Farms) weighing about 25 g. Food (Purina Rat Chow) and water were available *ad lib.*, except when oral administration of ethanol was scheduled; in this latter case the subjects were fasted overnight.

Rotarod

The rats or mice were trained to walk a rotating cylinder (rotarod) for a period of 3 minutes.[9, 12] The cylinder, 5 inches in diameter and 6 inches in width, was rotated at about 8 revolutions per minute. Rats usually walked the cylinder for the 3-minute period after two or three training trials. They were then treated with 0.9% saline or drugs and tested at various times thereafter. The measure taken was the number of seconds that each subject maintained its balance on the cylinder, up to a maximum of 180 sec.

Chemical Assays

Gas chromatographic techniques were employed to quantify levels of ethanol and *d*-amphetamine in brain tissue and serum. Rats were sacrificed by decapitation at 5, 15, 30, 90, and 180 minutes following treatment with ethanol, *d*-amphetamine, or a combination of the two. Blood was collected in tubes over ice and allowed to clot. Whole brains were removed rapidly, and a 33% homogenate was prepared in ice-cold distilled water.

Ethanol was measured in serum and supernatants of brain homogenates after centrifugation. Twenty μl aliquots of serum or brain homogenate supernatant fluid were added to 20 μl of a methanol solution (1 mg/ml). One μl aliquots of the resultant mixtures were introduced into a gas chromatograph (Shimadzu, 4BMPFE) equipped with a flame-ionization detector and a 2.5 m Porapak Q column. Injection post and detector temperatures were held at 300° C; the column temperature was 160° C. Ethanol was quantified by the peak height ratio method using methanol as the internal standard. Standard curves were prepared and run daily. They were linear between 0.05 and 2.5 mg ethanol per ml of serum or supernatant. Recovery of ethanol added to serum or brain homogenates from untreated rats was 100 $\pm$ 2%. Acetaldehyde levels in brain and serum were also assayed. The method was accurate to a level of 0.01 mg/ml.

d-Amphetamine was assayed according to modifications of published methods.[13–15] Ten μg of methamphetamine was added to 2 ml of serum or brain homogenate as the internal standard. Protein was precipitated by the addition of 2 ml 1.2*N* perchloric acid, the solution was made alkaline with 5*N* NaOH, and the amphetamines were extracted into methylene chloride. This was followed by black-extraction of the amphetamines into 1*N* HCl, after which the organic layer was removed and the aqueous layer again made basic with NaOH. Methylene chloride, 100 μl, was added, and the layers were mixed and then separated by centrifugation. Three μl aliquots of the methylene chloride layer were introduced into the gas chromatograph. The column was 2.5 m in length and packed with 10% apiezon—2% KOH. Injection port and flame ionization detector were maintained at 300°C; the column was held at 150° C. *d*-Amphetamine was quantified by the peak height ratio method using methamphetamine as the internal standard. Standard curves for *d*-amphetamine, prepared and run daily, were linear from 0.5 to 10 μl/ml of serum or brain homogenate extract. Comparison of unextracted standard curves with those extracted from water, serum, or brain extracts showed that, whereas absolute recoveries varied depending upon the matrix from which the amphetamines were extracted, the relative recoveries of *d*-amphetamine and methamphetamine did not. The method was thus validated for both serum and brain extracts.

Drugs and Statistics

With a few exceptions, all drugs were administered by i.p. injection as an aqueous solution (0.9% saline). In one series of rats, alcohol (ethanol) was administered orally via gastric intubation as a 30% (w/v) solution. Alcohol for injection was prepared as a 10% solution for rats and as a 40% solution for mice. Powdered diazepam or methaqualone was suspended in 1% methylcellulose for the injectable preparation. Rotarod data were analyzed statistically using Mann-Whitney U test. Chemical assay data were compared by linear regression analysis.

RESULTS

To initiate the study of drug interactions on behavior, we first established a dose-response pattern for disruption of rotarod performance of rats by alcohol. Alcohol was administered i.p. in varying doses from 0.5 to 3.0 g/kg to groups of trained rats, and their performance was monitored at various times thereafter. The effects are illustrated in FIGURE 1. The dose of 0.5 g/kg did not provoke a significant disruption of this behavior. A prominent but very transient disruption of rotarod performance was noted following the 1.0 and 1.5 g/kg doses. However, increasing the dose slightly, to 2.0 g/kg, greatly prolonged the behavioral disruption, and recovery required more than 2 hours. Larger doses prolonged the rotarod impairment even more, although all subjects recovered within the 4-hour period of testing, and none of the rats exhibited lasting effects of this treatment.

The effects of *d*-amphetamine alone were determined for any impairment of rotarod performance to serve as control data for the study of interactions. The stimulant was injected i.p. into rats in doses ranging from 2 to 8 mg/kg. None of these doses induced a deficit in rotarod behavior, as can be seen by the results depicted in FIGURE 2. Although there is a trend for the drug treatment to disrupt this behavior, most evident at the 8 mg/kg dose, the subjects did not differ significantly from saline controls. At no time over the 4-hour test period did any of these subjects exhibit a prominent incapacity to walk the rotating drum.

A dose of 1.5 g/kg of alcohol was chosen as the dose to interact with the dose range of *d*-amphetamine. The consequences of this combined treatment on rotarod performance are illustrated in FIGURE 3. The effect of alcohol alone at this dose is indicated in each panel by the dashed line. Alcohol combined with 2 mg/kg *d*-amphetamine (upper left panel) resulted in a definite prolongation of the behavior disruption. Scores after the combination were

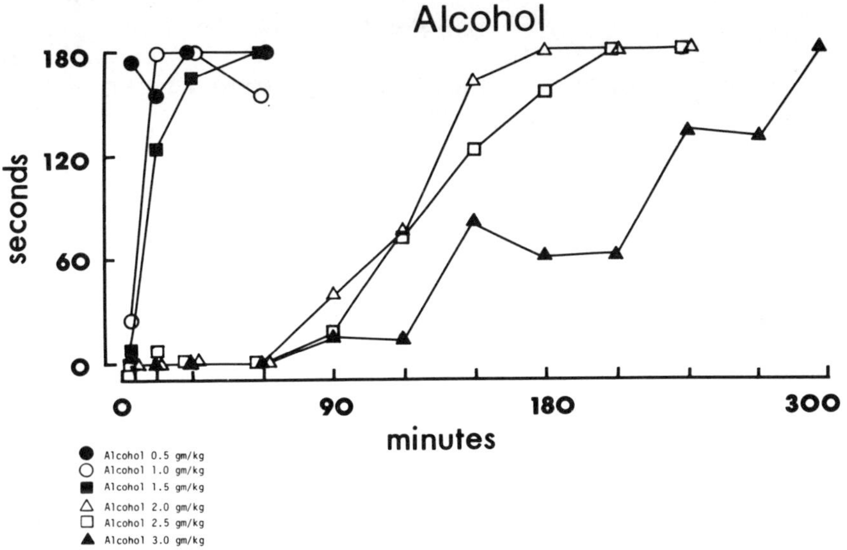

FIGURE 1. Dose-response-duration patterns for alcohol disruption of rotarod performance in rats. The vertical scale indicates number of seconds the subjects maintained balance on the rotarod, up to a maximum of 180 seconds, in this and FIGURES 2–11. The horizontal scale indicates time of the test following the drug treatment. Alcohol was injected i.p. as a 10% solution. Each point represents the mean score derived from six subjects. Rotarod scores of less than 120 seconds generally represent significant impairments.

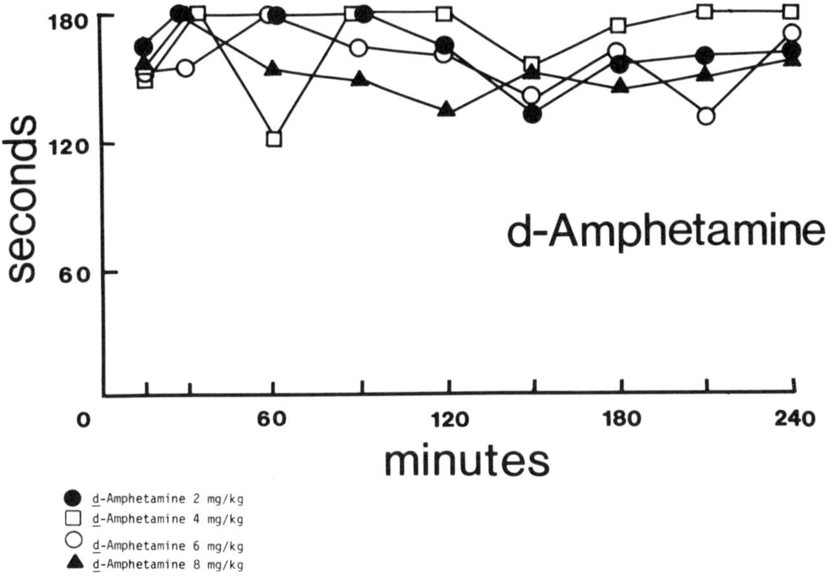

FIGURE 2. Lack of effects of various doses of *d*-amphetamine on the rotarod performance of rats. The trend for disrupted behavior was not significant at any single point for any dose. However, pooled data for the 8 mg/kg dose over the 60 to 240-minute time period showed a significant impairment. Each point represents the mean score from six subjects, in this and FIGURES 3–12.

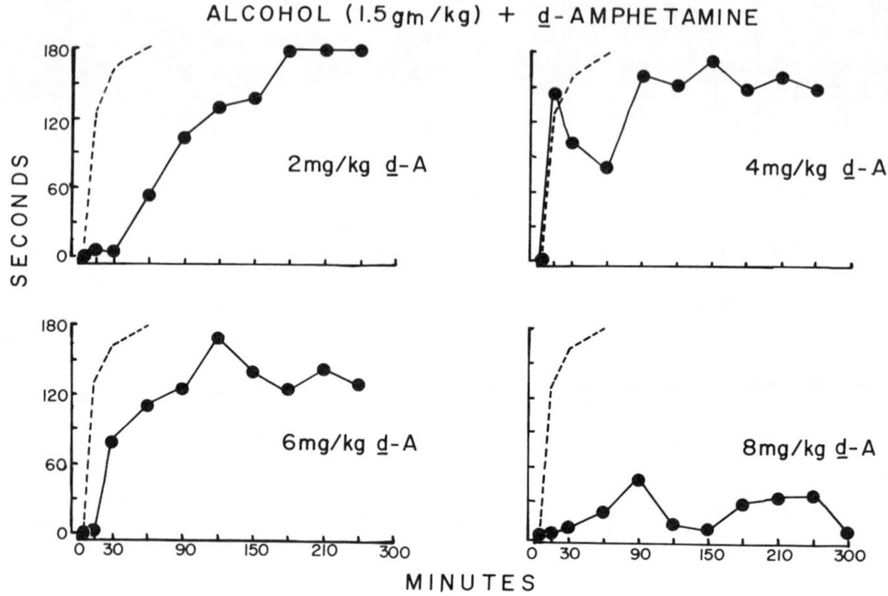

FIGURE 3. Dose-response-duration patterns for alcohol disruption of rotarod performance of rats when administered in combination with a dose range of *d*-amphetamine. The extent of disruption due to i.p. injection of 1.5 g/kg ethanol alone is indicated in each panel as the dashed line.

significantly decreased for at least 1 hour, as compared to the 5-min. disruption due to alcohol alone. The combination of alcohol with 4 mg/kg *d*-amphetamine (upper right panel) or 6 mg/kg of the stimulant (lower left panel) caused less of a prolongation of the alcohol impairment than did the 2 mg/kg *d*-amphetamine dose. When the alcohol was combined with 8 mg/kg of the stimulant, a very prolonged disruption of this behavior was observed, outlasting the 5-hour period of rotarod testing. In addition, most of these subjects became comatose, and about two-thirds died within a 24-hour period.

Since the combination of alcohol and *d*-amphetamine yielded these unexpected results, we decided to examine interactions between alcohol and cocaine. Cocaine is a stimulant which produces central effects closely related to *d*-amphetamine, at least over its lower dose range.[1] The effects of this combination on the rotarod behavior of rats are depicted in FIGURE 4. This stimulant combined with alcohol in a dose range of 10 to 25 mg/kg did significantly prolong the alcohol disruption, thus resembling the alcohol-low dose *d*-amphetamine combination. On the other hand, the largest dose of cocaine used in combination with alcohol (25 mg/kg, lower right panel) did not result in the very prolonged disruption, coma, or lethality seen with the alcohol and 8 mg/kg *d*-amphetamine combination. This dose range of cocaine (10–25 mg/kg) did not significantly impair rotarod performance when administered alone (not illustrated). A larger dose of cocaine in combination with alcohol was not tested since these larger doses induced tremors and preconvulsive spasms when administered alone.

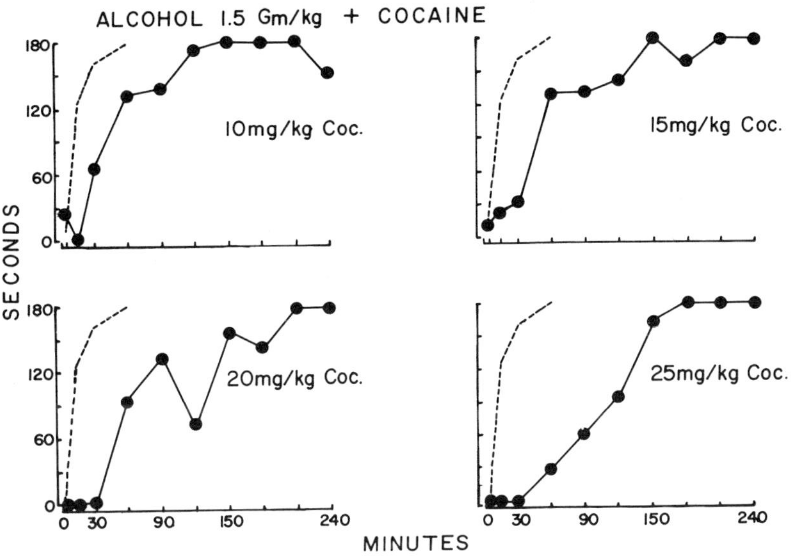

FIGURE 4. Dose-response-duration patterns for alcohol disruption of rotarod performance of rats when administered in combination with a dose range of cocaine. The extent of disruption due to i.p. ethanol alone is indicated in each panel as the dashed line.

The influence of a combination of alcohol and methylphenidate on rotarod behavior of rats was also explored (results not illustrated). In a dose range of 10 to 40 mg/kg, methylphenidate prolonged the impairment induced by alcohol with a pattern similar to that described for the alcohol-cocaine combination. None of these subjects showed the prolonged depression or lethality associated with the alcohol and 8 mg/kg *d*-amphetamine combination.

In further exploring the nature of these drug interactions, we combined pentobarbital and *d*-amphetamine for their effects on the rotarod behavior of rats. Pentobarbital alone, 12 mg/kg, impaired performance for about 2 hours, as shown in FIGURE 5 by the dashed lines. The combination of this depressant with 2 mg/kg *d*-amphetamine prolonged the behavioral disruption in a manner similar to that noted with the alcohol-*d*-amphetamine combination. The combinations with 4 (upper right panel) or 6 mg/kg (lower left panel) *d*-amphetamine did not prolong the disruption beyond that due to pentobarbital alone. With the combination of pentobarbital and 8 mg/kg *d*-amphetamine (lower right panel), the impairment of rotarod performance was again prolonged. Nevertheless, this prolongation did not extend beyond 5 hours, as was the case with the alcohol and 8 mg/kg *d*-amphetamine combination, nor were there signs of late coma or deaths as seen with the latter combination.

FIGURE 6 plots the interactions between diazepam and *d*-amphetamine on the rotarod scores of rats. In this case, the depressant combined with 2 mg/kg of the stimulant prolonged the duration of impairment after diazepam alone, while the combination with 4, 6, or 8 mg/kg *d*-amphetamine did not interact

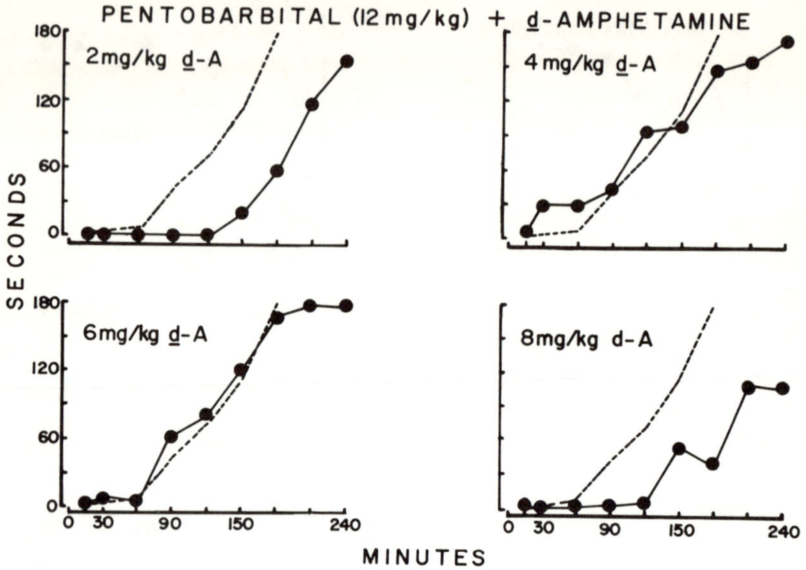

FIGURE 5. Dose-response-duration patterns for pentobarbital disruption of rotarod performance of rats when administered in combination with a dose range of *d*-amphetamine. The extent of disruption due to i.p. pentobarbital alone is indicated in each panel as the dashed line.

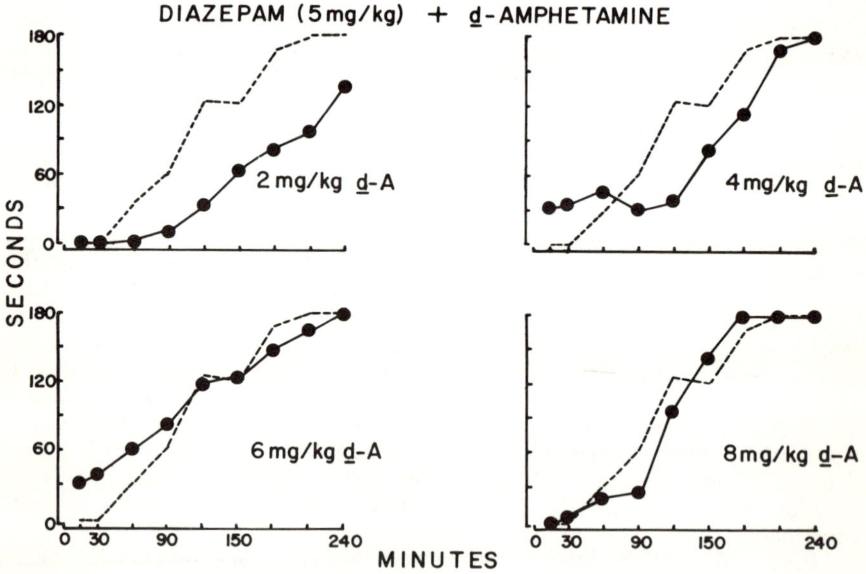

FIGURE 6. Dose-response-duration patterns for diazepam disruption of rotarod performance of rats when administered in combination with a dose range of *d*-amphetamine. The extent of disruption due to i.p. diazepam alone is indicated in each panel as the dashed line.

in this manner. In fact, the combination of diazepam with 4 (upper right panel) or 6 mg/kg (lower left panel) indicated significant antagonism of the depressant effects by the stimulant at a few of the earlier determinations.

The last example of a CNS depressant chosen to study for interactions with *d*-amphetamine was methaqualone. The effects of methaqualone-*d*-amphetamine combinations on the rotarod behavior of rats are shown in FIGURE 7. Here the presence of the stimulant (2 or 6 mg/kg) did not prolong the disruption seen with 15 mg/kg of methaqualone alone. In fact, at the 6 mg/kg dose *d*-amphetamine appeared to antagonize the depressant at the earlier determinations (lower panel). Methaqualone, then, differs from the other three CNS

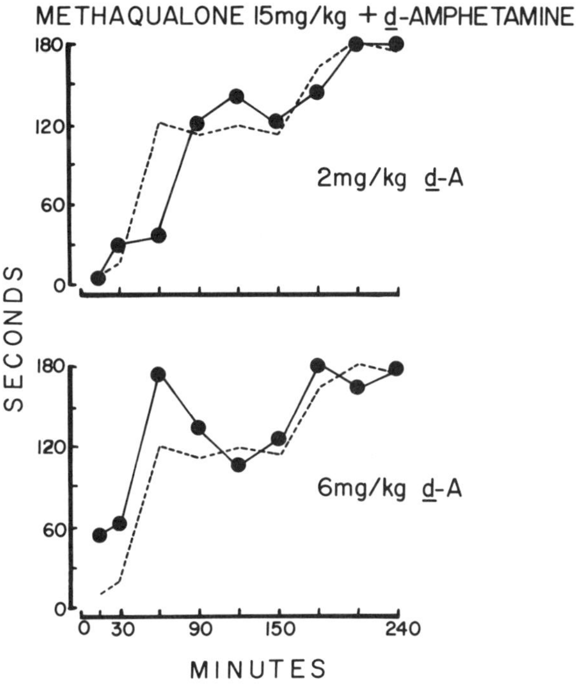

FIGURE 7. Dose-response-duration patterns for methaqualone disruption of rotarod performance of rats when administered in combination with several doses of *d*-amphetamine. The extent of disruption due to i.p. methaqualone injected in the absence of *d*-amphetamine is indicated in each panel as the dashed line.

depressants in that the 2 mg/kg dose of *d*-amphetamine does not prolong the impairment of rotarod described after methaqualone alone.

The interaction between alcohol and *d*-amphetamine in rats described above could have been a peculiarity of this one species. Therefore, we tested the interactions between these two agents in mice, once again utilizing subjects trained to walk the rotarod. Two g/kg of alcohol administered i.p. to mice provoked a transient disruption of this behavior, as described by the dashed line in each panel of FIGURE 8. Alcohol combined with 1 mg/kg *d*-amphetamine caused a prolongation of the rotarod disruption, but 2 and 4 mg/kg *d*-amphetamine in combination with the depressant yielded the same duration curve as alcohol alone. When this dose of alcohol was combined with 8 mg/kg *d*-amphetamine, the disruption was prolonged once more. On the other hand, the variability of this interaction was much greater than in rats,

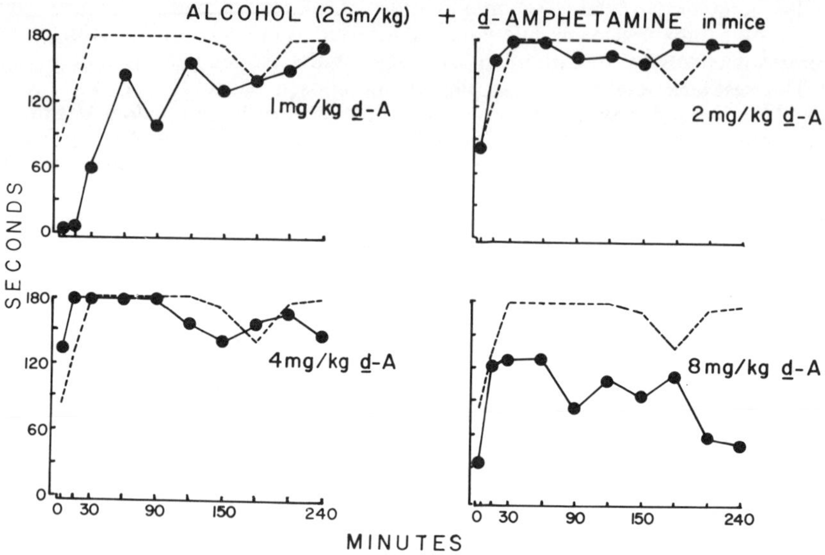

FIGURE 8. Dose-response duration patterns for alcohol disruption of rotarod performance of mice when administered in combination with a dose range of *d*-amphetamine. The extent of disruption due to i.p. alcohol alone is indicated in each panel by the dashed line.

when several additional groups of mice were studied. Furthermore, the lethality of this combination was quite unpredictable, one group of mice suffering 50% mortality, while no deaths were observed in two other groups identically treated. Thus, the pattern of interactions was somewhat different from that observed in the rat.

Another concern was that the paradoxical interactions between alcohol and *d*-amphetamine might somehow relate to an artifact developing from the near-simultaneous injection of the two drugs into the peritoneum. For this reason we administered alcohol orally in other rats trained to walk the rotarod. FIGURE 9 illustrates the duration of rotarod impairment in rats treated with oral alcohol alone, 2 g/kg, the plot marked by the filled squares. In subjects treated with oral alcohol plus 8 mg/kg *d*-amphetamine, injected i.p., there was a prominent potentiation and prolongation of the behavioral disruption, as obvious from the plot marked by the filled circles in FIGURE 9. In accordance with previous findings, most of these latter subjects lapsed into coma, and about two-thirds died.

The interactions between alcohol and *d*-amphetamine as described above were shown to vary with doses of the stimulant. In the next series of experiments involving rats, we administered a fixed dose of *d*-amphetamine (4 mg/kg) but varied the dose of alcohol, injected i.p., from 1 to 3 g/kg. The effects of these combinations on rotarod performance are depicted in FIGURE 10. The combination of the stimulant with 1 g/kg (upper left panel) or 2 g/kg alcohol (lower left panel) did not appreciably influence the duration of impairment. On the contrary, the combinations with 1.5 g/kg (upper right panel) or 3 g/kg (lower right panel) of alcohol caused a significant prolonga-

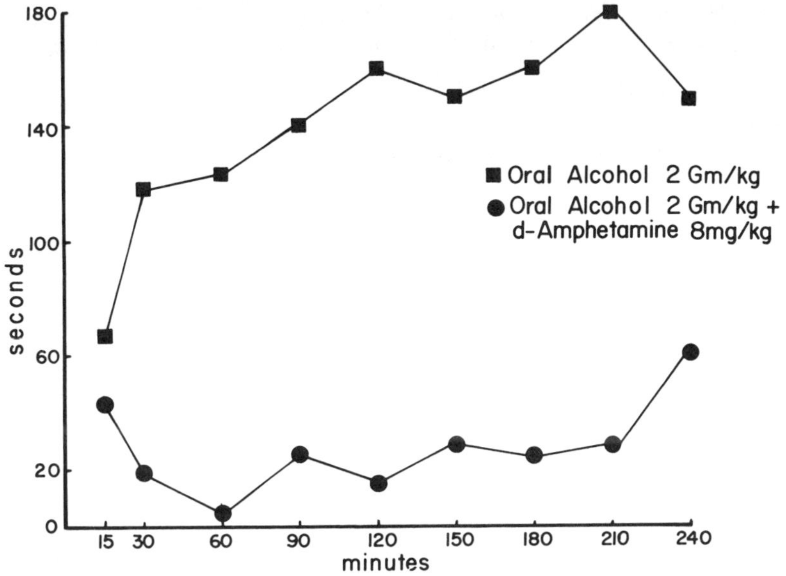

FIGURE 9. Patterns of impairment of rotarod performance of rats treated with oral alcohol alone or in combination with *d*-amphetamine.

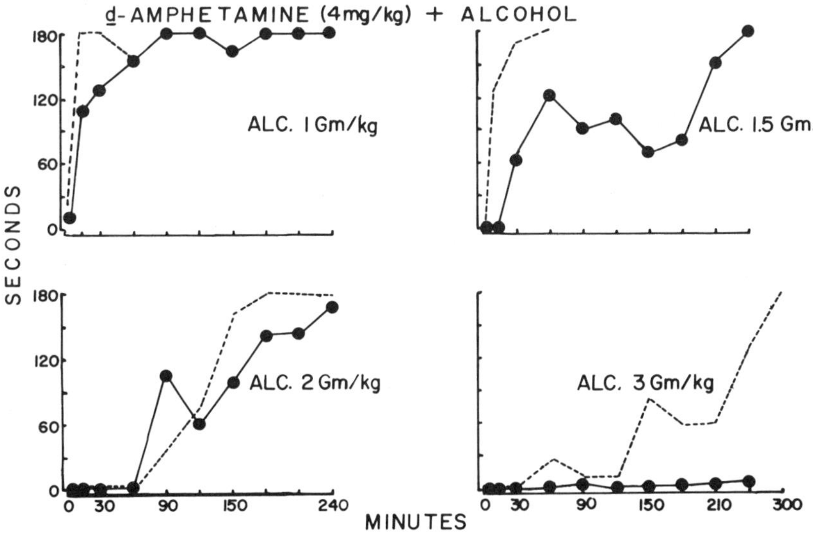

FIGURE 10. Dose-response-duration patterns for alcohol disruption of rotarod performance of rats when administered in combination with a fixed dose of *d*-amphetamine. The extent of disruption due to the i.p. injection of each indicated dose level of ethanol in the absence of *d*-amphetamine is plotted by the dashed line in each panel.

tion of the behavioral disruption. Thus, it is clear that the interaction between alcohol and *d*-amphetamine varies as a function of dosage levels of both drugs. Nevertheless, the group treated with *d*-amphetamine, 4 mg/kg, and alcohol, 3 g/kg, although impaired in rotarod capabilities for a period beyond 5 hours, did not demonstrate the very prolonged coma and lethality as described above for rats treated with alcohol and 8 mg/kg *d*-amphetamine. That is, none of the rats contributing to the data of FIGURE 10 had lasting complications from the drug treatments.

The last series of behavioral experiments examined the combination of a subthreshold dose of alcohol and a dose range of *d*-amphetamine. Alcohol,

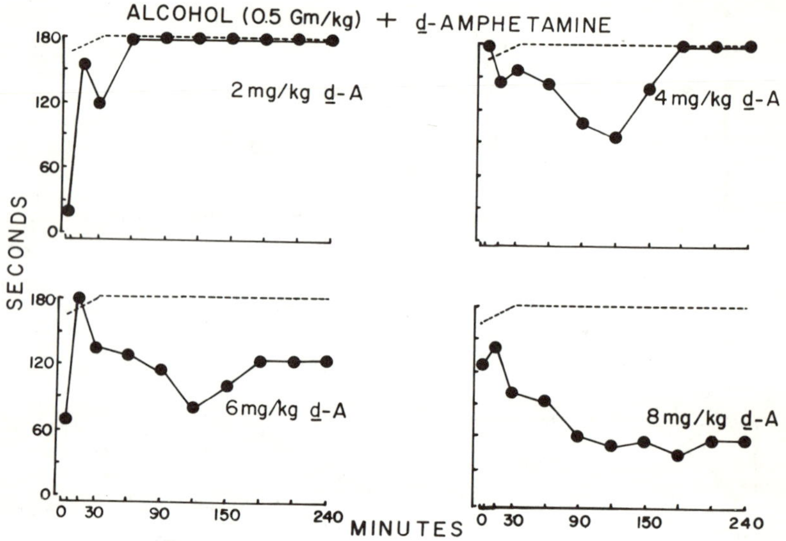

FIGURE 11. Dose-response-duration patterns for alcohol effects on rotarod performance of rats, when administered in a subthreshold dose, in combination with a dose range of *d*-amphetamine. The lack of effect of i.p. alcohol, 0.5 g/kg injected alone, is indicated in each panel as the dashed line.

0.5 g/kg i.p., did not significantly influence the rotarod performance of rats, as depicted in FIGURE 11 as the dashed line in each panel. Combining this dose of alcohol with 2 mg/kg *d*-amphetamine caused a prominent but transient impairment of behavior (upper left panel) occurring only at the 5-minute determination. The combination with 4 mg/kg, on the other hand, did not initially disrupt performance, but caused a later decrease in scores (upper right panel). Alcohol plus 6 mg/kg of the stimulant appeared to incorporate these two effects, an initial impairment and a later delayed one being seen (lower left panel). The combination with 8 mg/kg *d*-amphetamine (lower right panel) showed an exaggeration of this delayed impairment. This latter group also exhibited a prolonged comatose state, and about two-thirds died. Therefore, the severe depression and death suffered as a consequence of being treated with the combination appears best related to a high dose of *d*-amphetamine administered in the presence of any reasonable dose level of alcohol.

To gain further insight into the nature of these interactions, we analyzed serum and brain levels of alcohol and *d*-amphetamine in rats administered each drug alone and in subjects receiving the combination of 1.5 g/kg alcohol (i.p.) and 8 mg/kg *d*-amphetamine. The curves for decay of blood and brain concentrations of the drugs at various times after administration are plotted in FIGURE 12. It is clear that the elimination of alcohol from the body is not delayed as a consequence of the presence of *d*-amphetamine. The rate of decay of *d*-amphetamine in brain and serum extracts does, however, seem to be slowed appreciably by administering the stimulant in combination with alcohol (two lower panels, FIGURE 12). In brain, *d*-amphetamine levels attained a higher peak 15 minutes after administering the amine in combination with alcohol, and levels were higher at 90 and 180 minutes after administration of the combination as compared with the injection of *d*-amphetamine alone. The picture in serum is similar, although treatment wth the combination did not result in as great a difference in *d*-amphetamine levels. Higher initial levels of *d*-amphetamine in serum were found after the combination at the 5 and 90 minute determinations, whereas the levels of the stimulant reached about the same concentrations with or without the presence of alcohol by the 180 minute determination. No measurable levels of acetaldehyde were apparent in either brain or serum samples, regardless of the treatment administered, at the level of sensitivity of the method.

DISCUSSION

The results of this study clearly demonstrate prominent interactions, in terms of behavioral effects and drug levels attained in the body, between stimulant drugs of the sympathomimetic class and drugs of the CNS depressant category. The behavioral test employed is presumed to measure components of altertness and skeletal muscle coordination. The stimulant agents appear to enhance rather than antagonize the disruptive influences of the CNS depressant drugs, at least at certain dose combinations. The most complex interaction was observed with alcohol and *d*-amphetamine. A low dose of the stimulant prolonged the impairment of rotarod when combined with alcohol, while somewhat larger doses of *d*-amphetamine yielded a lesser interaction. At the highest dose of *d*-amphetamine (8 mg/kg), a second type of interaction with alcohol was described, a prolonged disruption of rotarod performance occurring in association with severe CNS depression and lethality. The dose of *d*-amphetamine appeared to be more critical to this latter interaction than was the dose of alcohol.

It must be emphasized that the severe depression and lethality observed in rats after administering a large dose of *d*-amphetamine along with alcohol was also a function of the behavioral testing procedure. Rats that were administered the drug combination but not tested periodically on the rotarod did not show the same intensity or duration of overt CNS depression, and the lethality was much lower in this group. Thus, this interaction may relate to the provocation of a stress reaction that disturbs homeostasis mechanisms for peripheral and/or CNS vital functions. Support for this hypothesis may be derived from the analyses of blood and brain levels of the drugs. The onset of coma and the lethality often occurred in these subjects 4 hours or more

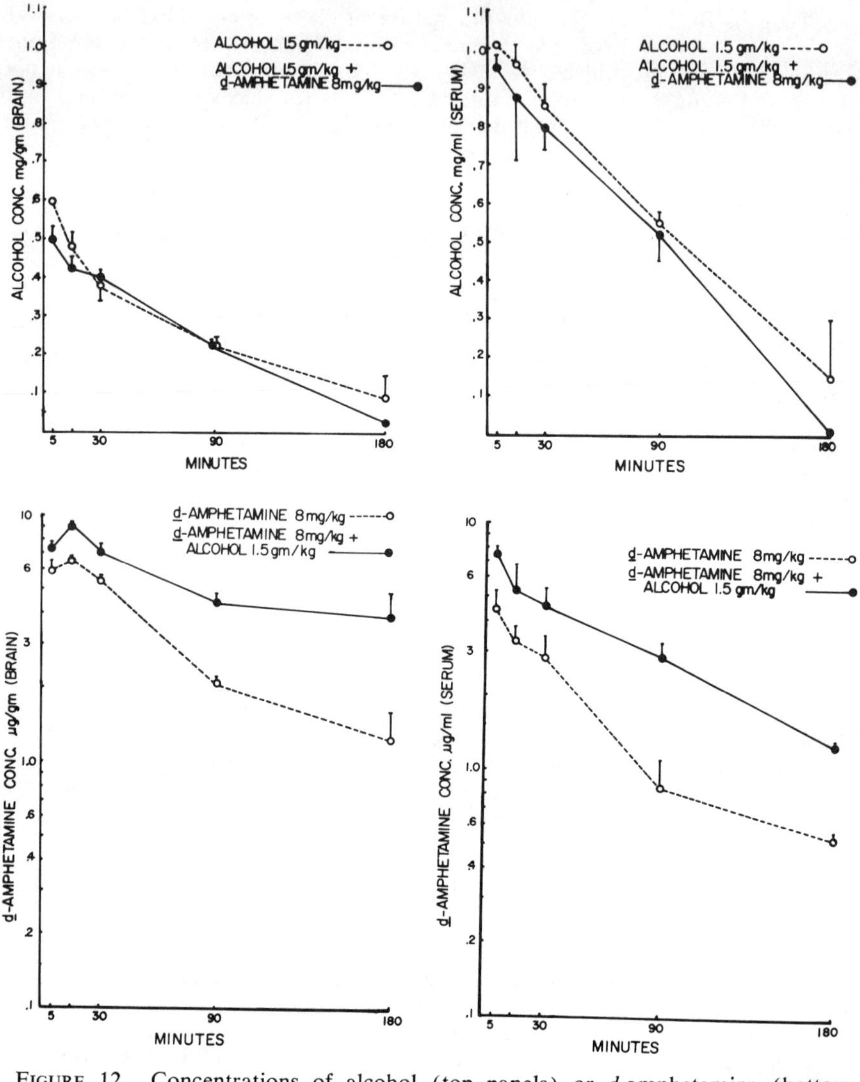

FIGURE 12. Concentrations of alcohol (top panels) or *d*-amphetamine (bottom panels) in brain extracts (left-hand panels) or serum (right-hand panels) derived from rats treated with either drug alone or with the combination. Each point represents the mean, and the vertical projection on it ± the standard error, of a group of six rats. The assay procedures utilized are described in detail under "Methods." The horizontal axis indicates the time in minutes following drug injection when the subjects were sacrificed.

after administration, when drug concentrations of alcohol in the body would have been at insignificant levels. The possible involvement of both central and peripheral mechanisms in these interactions should not be lost sight of, since the drug concentrations of *d*-amphetamine in brain and serum persisted at higher levels when this agent was combined with alcohol. Jonsson and Lewander[6] have previously described a persistence of *d*-amphetamine blood and brain levels when the agent was coadministered with alcohol. In view of the differences we noted in lethality between rats and mice, it would be useful to repeat these chemical assays in mice treated with alcohol plus the large dose of *d*-amphetamine.

The combinations of pentobarbital and diazepam with *d*-amphetamine also showed interactions on the behavioral test. These were confined, however, to the type observed with the alcohol plus a low dose of *d*-amphetamine. No comatose state or lethality was found with any dose combination of *d*-amphetamine plus pentobarbital or diazepam. The interaction of methaqualone with *d*-amphetamine appeared to be of an antagonistic nature rather than an enhancement of the rotarod impairment. The combination of other examples of adrenergic-type stimulants, cocaine and methylphenidate, with alcohol also demonstrated an enhanced behavioral impairment. Once again, this was of the alcohol-low dose of *d*-amphetamine type, being a prolongation of rotarod disruption over the earlier times of testing and without the later onset of coma or death, even at the highest dose of the stimulant used.

There are experimental data in the literature supporting the idea that *d*-amphetamine prolongs the depressant effects of alcohol, at least for the low-dose *d*-amphetamine type of interaction.[16, 17] The clinical relevance of these interactions is, however, obscure at present. The literature contains mainly anecdotal accounts of severe reactions in people who have combined amphetamines and alcohol.[18, 19] The authors have also been informed of several deaths in the Chicago area during the latter part of 1974 that were associated with the combined intake of an amphetamine and alcohol (D. Yacavone, personal communication). The ultimate importance of these drug interactions in terms of mechanisms of action of the agents and deleterious or toxic manifestations in humans must be determined by future research.

Acknowledgments

The authors gratefully acknowledge the technical assistance of Laurie Soderberg, Cindy Knight, and Glenna Frazer in the performance of these studies.

References

1. Goodman, L. S. & A. Gilman, Eds. 1975. The Pharmacological Basis of Therapeutics. 5th edit. MacMillan Co. New York, N.Y.
2. Shapiro, R. & K. Michaile. 1956. The use of sustained-release D-amphetamine-amobarbital preparation in the treatment of obesity. Intern. Rec. Med. **169:** 638.
3. Rushton, R. & H. Steinberg. 1967. Drug combinations and their analysis

by means of exploratory activity in rats. *In* Neuro-Psychopharmacology. H. Brill, Ed.: 464–470. Excerpta Medica Foundation. Amsterdam, The Netherlands.
4. PRABHU, V. G. 1972. Amphetamine aggregation effect in mice under conditions of altered microsomal enzymes. Arch. Int. Pharmacodyn. **195:** 81–86.
5. HATCH, R. C. 1973. Experiments on antagonism of barbiturate anesthesia with adrenergic, serotonergic and cholinergic stimulants given alone and in combination. Amer. J. Vet. Res. **34:** 1321–1331.
6. JONSSON, J. & T. LEWANDER. 1973. Effects of diethyldithiocarbamate and ethanol on the *in vivo* metabolism and pharmacokinetics of amphetamine in the rat. J. Pharm. Pharmacol. **25:** 589–591.
7. ABDALLAH, A. H., H. D. WHITE & A. S. KULKARNI. 1974. Interaction of D-amphetamine with central nervous system depressants on food intake and spontaneous motor activity of mice. Eur. J. Pharmacol. **26:** 119–121.
8. BRANCH, M. N. 1974. Behavior as a stimulus: joint effects of D-amphetamine and pentobarbital. J. Pharmacol. Exp. Ther. **189:** 33–41.
9. RECH, R. H., H. K. BORYS & K. E. MOORE. 1966. Alterations in behavior and brain catecholamine levels in rats treated with α-methyltyrosine. J. Pharmacol. Exp. Ther. **153:** 412–419.
10. MOORE, K. E. & R. H. RECH. 1967. Antagonism by monoamine oxidase inhibitors of α-methyltyrosine-induced catecholamine depletion and behavioral depression. J. Pharmacol. Exp. Ther. **156:** 70–75.
11. PIRCH, J. H., R. H. RECH & K. E. MOORE. 1967. Depression and recovery of the electrocorticogram, behavior and brain amines in rats treated with reserpine. Neuropharmacol. **6:** 375–385.
12. RECH, R. H., L. A. CARR & K. E. MOORE. 1968. Behavioral effects of α-methyltyrosine after prior depletion of brain catecholamines. J. Pharmacol. Exp. Ther. **160:** 326–335.
13. RAMSEY, J. & D. B. CAMPBELL. 1971. An ultra rapid method for the extraction of drugs from biological fluids. J. Chromatogr. **63:** 303–308.
14. JAIN, N. C., T. C. SNEATH & R. D. BUDD. 1974. Rapid gas-chromatographic determination of amphetamine and methamphetamine in urine. Clin. Chem. **20**(11): 1460–1462.
15. O'Brien, J. E., W. ZAZULAB, V. ABBEY & O. HINSVARKS. 1972. Determination of amphetamine and phentermine in biological fluids. J. Chromatogr. Sci. **10:** 336–341.
16. BREESE, G. R., J. M. COTT, B. R. COOPER, A. J. PRANGE, JR. & M. A. LIPTON. 1974. Antagonism of ethanol narcosis by thyrotropin releasing hormone. Life Sci. **14:** 1053–1063.
17. IVERSON, F., B. B. COLDWELL, R. H. DOWNIE & L. W. WHITEHOUSE. 1975. Effect of ethanol on toxicity and metabolism of amphetamine in the mouse. Experientia **31:** 679–680.
18. COLEMAN, J. H. &. W. E. EVANS. 1975. Drug interactions with alcohol. Med. Times **103**(6): 145–150, 155.
19. ANDERSON, L. B. & P. WHYTE. 1975. The Amphetamine Follies. Comic book published by the National Council on Drug Abuse. Chicago, Ill.

COCAINE, AMPHETAMINE, AND LITHIUM INTERACTIONS: NEUROBIOLOGICAL CORRELATES*

Arnold J. Mandell and Suzanne Knapp

Department of Psychiatry
University of California at San Diego
La Jolla, California 92093

Theoretical Framework

Since the mid-1960's the major model used to predict and explain psychotropic drug effects on central biogenic amine synapses has involved what we have come to call first-order effects: primary drug-induced changes in presynaptic reuptake, release, access to the receptor, and associated changes in the metabolism of the specificed biogenic amine. FIGURE 1 depicts such a model, which requires the presence of the drug and predicts short latency to action on the brain mechanism(s) involved, as well as rapid reversibility of the effects when the drug disappears. Thus, the three drugs we will speak about here (amphetamine, cocaine, and lithium) work as follows when the explanation is based on first-order mechanisms in the serotonergic system: Amphetamine releases and blocks reuptake of serotonin.[1, 2] Cocaine may release, and appears to block, the reuptake of serotonin, although the data have been questioned recently.[3] Lithium appears to retard the release of serotonin, although its effect on transmitter release has been studied more extensively in the catecholamine system.[4]

Recent developments have cast doubt on the sufficiency of such a first-order model, however. The most telling evidence from the clinic demands that when one tries to explain the actions of such psychotherapeutic drugs as the antipsychotics, the antidepressants, and lithium, he must explain a latency to full effect of days to weeks, in spite of the achievement of "therapeutic" blood levels within hours or a few days. In addition, neurobiological effects triggered in animals by these drugs may outlast the disappearance of the drugs by hours, days, or weeks. For example, we have recently shown that a single administration of fenfluramine to rats induces a sequence of apparently compensatory changes in elements of the serotonergic biosynthetic system in the brain that lasts almost two weeks, although significant levels of the drug are gone from the brain after only a few days.[5]

Our group, and others, have been studying mechanisms which, because of their tendency to be affected some time after a drug is administered, we call *second-order* mechanisms. FIGURE 2, a diagram of these adaptive mechanisms, shows 1) a mechanism to transport substrate into the nerve endings, which we have shown in the serotonergic system to be a high-affinity tryptophan-uptake system that is drug-sensitive;[6, 7] 2) the activity state of the transmitter synthesizing apparatus in intact nerve endings, which we have shown to change independently of the measure of soluble rate-limiting biosynthetic enzyme activity in lysed synaptosomes, and which might involve such influences

* This work is supported by United States Public Health Grant DA-00265-04.

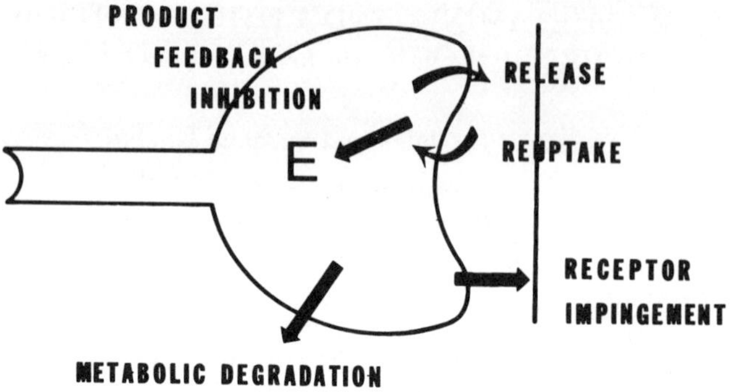

FIGURE 1. First-order drug-sensitive mechanisms.

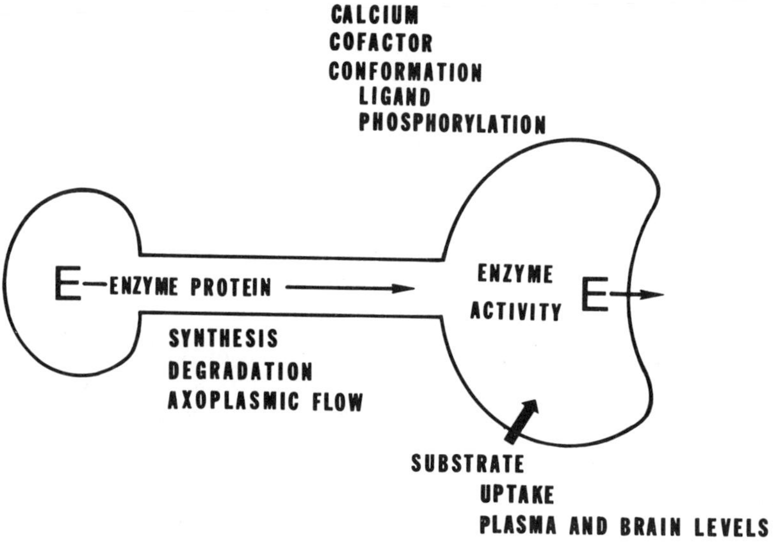

FIGURE 2. Second-order drug-sensitive mechanisms for the regulation of neurotransmitter biosynthesis in biogenic amine nerve endings.

as activation by calcium,[8] allosteric modulation by such ligands as heparin[9] or phosphatidyl-L-serine,[10] occlusive binding of the enzyme by nerve-ending membrane fractions,[11] changes in conformation (and thereby activity) by reversible phosphorylation,[12] and alterations in nerve-ending pterin cofactor levels induceable by psychotropic drugs, a potential influence elicited recently by Wilson Bullard in our laboratories; and 3) the amount or activity of soluble rate-limiting enzyme in the cell bodies and nerve endings, and the axonal transport time for changes appearing in the cell bodies to reach the nerve endings.[13, 14] Confirmation of this last parameter has been begun by Joh *et al.*[15] in work in which they use antibody determination of enzyme protein.

Relative to synaptic function, changes in these second-order mechanisms generally move in directions opposite to first-order effects. Thus, whereas reserpine releases and reduces stored biogenic amine (first-order mechanisms), it leads to both an increase in the activity state of the nerve-ending transmitter-synthesizing apparatus and an increase in soluble enzyme (second-order mechanisms).[13, 14] Whereas tricyclics block reuptake of biogenic amine neurotransmitter (first order), they lead to reductions in the relevant soluble enzyme levels in cell body and nerve-ending regions of the brain.[11] Similar contrasting effects on first and second-order mechanisms have been reported for the antipsychotics; the drugs block dopamine receptors but increase its synthesis.[16, 17]

The present report focuses on the effects of amphetamine, cocaine, and lithium on second-order mechanisms in the rat-brain serotonergic biosynthetic system and on two types of antagonism that appear among second-order effects when lithium is given as pretreatment before challenge by amphetamine or cocaine respectively. Although to our knowledge no adequate study of the effect of lithium pretreatment on cocaine-induced behavioral changes in animals has been reported, there have been several studies demonstrating that lithium can antagonize the effects of amphetamine on such diverse behavioral parameters as hyperactivity, stereotypy, and intracranial self-stimulation.[18–20] The problems raised by having to attribute the lithium-induced neurobiological antagonism of amphetamine and/or cocaine to either first or second-order mechanisms will be discussed, as will the potential clinical relevance of lithium-induced alterations in neurobiological substrate, with special reference to the systems' reactivity to stimulant drugs.

Effects of Amphetamine on Second-Order Serotonergic Mechanisms

As can be seen in Figure 3, 2 hours after the administration of D-amphetamine there is, in an appropriate dose-response manner, a decrease in the capacity of rat-brain striate synaptosomes to convert radioactive tryptophan to serotonin.[13] Figure 4 illustrates the reversibility of this phenomenon; the biosynthetic capacity of the striate serotonergic nerve endings returns to 80 percent of control in about 4 hours and is at control levels 24 hours after drug administration.

Dissecting this amphetamine-induced reduction in synaptosomal biosynthetic capacity for serotonin, we find it apparently made up of two components. As illustrated in the top graph in Figure 5, there is an initial decrease in the capacity of the striate synaptosomes to synthesize serotonin *before* there is a decrease evident in the soluble tryptophan hydroxylase activity there (second graph). According to very recent work by Wilson Bullard, this initial decrease may be associated with a decrease in endogenous pterin cofactor, which he examined by means of an assay coupling dyhydropteridine reductase and tyrosine hyroxylase in which cofactor was limiting. Thus, the first change among second-order mechanisms (visible 15 and 30 minutes after drug administration) is a reduction in the activity state of striate serotonergic nerve endings. The second change among second-order mechanisms, 30 minutes later (1 hour after drug administration) is a decrease in soluble tryptophan hydroxylase beginning in the lateral midbrain raphe cell bodies (drawn in the third graph). Whether these second-order decreases in enzyme activity and nerve-ending biosynthetic capacity compensate for the

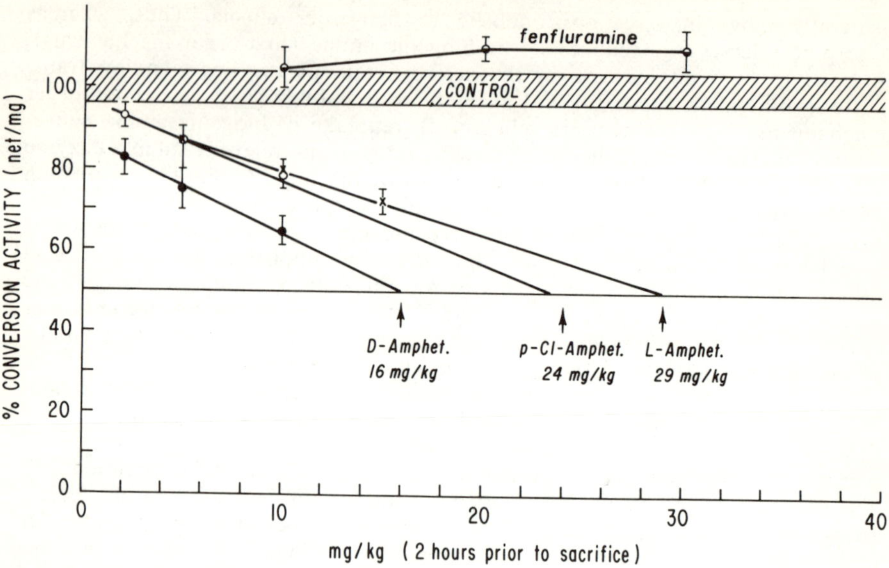

FIGURE 3. The effects of the acute administration of various doses of amphetamines on striate synaptosomal conversion of tryptophan to serotonin. The weights of D- and L-amphetamine were those of their sulfate salts; of fenfluramine and *p*-chloroamphetamine, their hydrochloride salts. Theoretical extrapolation to the point of 50 percent inhibition is shown by the broken lines. Control conversion specific activity = 130 ± 4 pmol/mg/45 min. Each point is the mean of at least eight determinations.

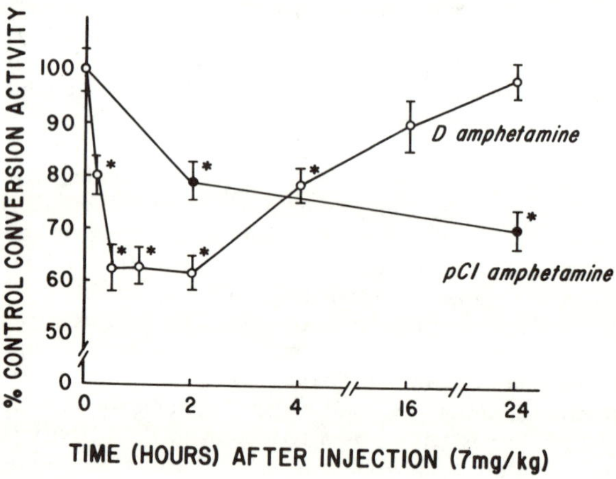

FIGURE 4. The temporal relationship between the effects of D-amphetamine and *p*-chloroamphetamine on rat striate synaptosomal tryptophan to serotonin conversion activity. Drugs were administered as their sulfate and hydrochloride salts respectively, and animals were sacrificed at the times indicated. $^*p < 0.05$.

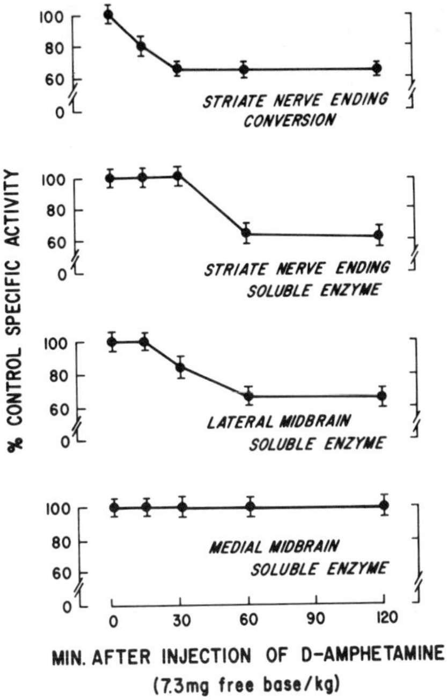

FIGURE 5. The effects of D-amphetamine on serotonergic biosynthetic mechanisms. Drug was administered to rats at specified times before sacrifice. Control specific activities (represented at 0 min) were 150 ± 4 pmol/mg/45 min for conversion; 100 ± 4 pmol/mg/45 min for nerve-ending soluble enzyme; 206 ± 8 pmol/mg/45 min for lateral midbrain soluble enzyme, and 987 ± 40 pmol/mg/45 min for medial midbrain soluble enzyme. The decrease in conversion activity was significant at 15 minutes ($p < 0.05$) and thereafter ($p < 0.001$). Nerve-ending soluble enzyme activity was significantly decreased at 60 minutes ($p < 0.02$). Lateral midbrain soluble enzyme activity was decreased at 30 minutes ($p < 0.05$) and thereafter ($p < 0.02$). Medial midbrain enzyme activity apparently was not affected.

amphetamine-induced potentiation of synaptic transmission by the first-order mechanisms of facilitated release and blockade of reuptake, or are induced by some other drug action, remains to be resolved.

Effects of Cocaine on Second-Order Serotonergic Mechanisms

In 1972 our group reported that cocaine reduced the synaptosomal conversion of tryptophan to serotonin by blocking the high-affinity uptake of tryptophan ($K_m = 10\ \mu M$).[21] FIGURE 6 is a representation of the results of that study—read "particulate" as "synaptosomal." FIGURE 7 shows that, concomitant with an apparent blockade in the uptake of the substrate tryptophan, when animals are sacrificed 1 hour after the administration of cocaine, there is a reduction of synaptosomal conversion of tryptophan to serotonin. This is shown in the first pair of bars in FIGURE 7. The second pair shows the compensatory *increase* in tryptophan hydroxylase activity in the nerve ending within an hour. The final pair indicates that cocaine administered *in vivo* does not affect the uptake of radioactive serotonin. Thus, cocaine appears to affect two second-order mechanisms in the serotonergic biosynthetic system: It reduces the high-affinity uptake of tryptophan into synaptosomes and reduces the capacity of those nerve-ending preparations to convert radioactive tryptophan to serotonin. Concomitantly there is an increase in soluble tryptophan hydroxylase in the nerve ending. Two aspects of this cocaine-induced increase in enzyme should be noted: 1) The cocaine-induced increase in tryptophan hydroxylase in serotonergic cell body regions is best seen in the lateral

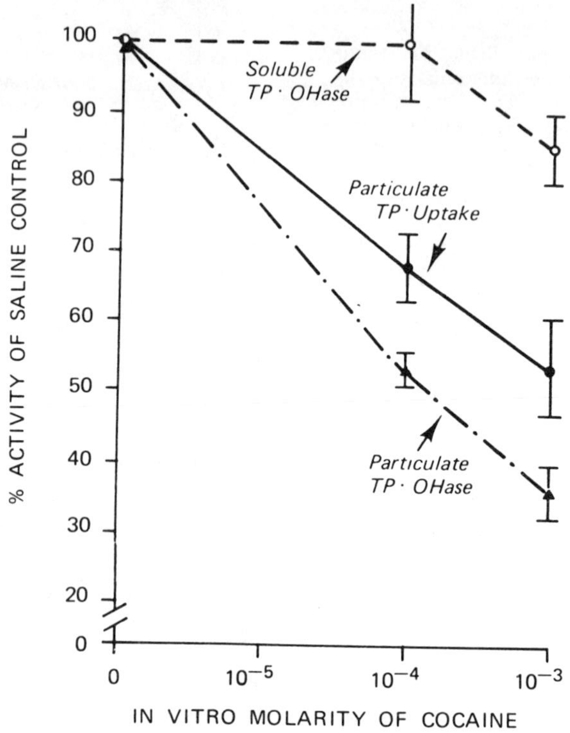

FIGURE 6. The effects of three concentrations of cocaine hydrochloride on the uptake and conversion of tryptophan to serotonin by particulate (synaptosomal) preparations and on soluble tryptophan hydroxylase activity. Note that cocaine does not inhibit soluble enzyme significantly, but does reduce substrate uptake and conversion. Each point represents the mean ± S.E.M. from six experiments.

midbrain raphe nuclei (B9, according to the nomenclature of Dahlstrom and Fuxe[22]), as was the case with the amphetamine-induced decrease. 2) Whereas the amphetamine effect on synaptosomal conversion was reversed to 80 percent of control in 4 hours and completely absent in 24 hours, the cocaine-induced effect on soluble tryptophan hydroxylase returned to control level within 2 hours. This is interesting in view of the very short behavioral effect of cocaine compared to that of amphetamine in animals and in humans.

EFFECTS OF LITHIUM CHLORIDE ON SECOND-ORDER SEROTONERGIC MECHANISMS

Our work on the mechanisms of action of lithium on the serotonergic biosynthetic system in brain[6, 7] suggests an interacting sequence of events among the second-order mechanisms. Lithium first stimulates the high-affinity uptake of radioactive tryptophan into synaptosomes. This augmented uptake of substrate remains during the course of treatment and is represented in FIGURE 8 as an increase in V_{max} estimated from a Lineweaver-Burk double

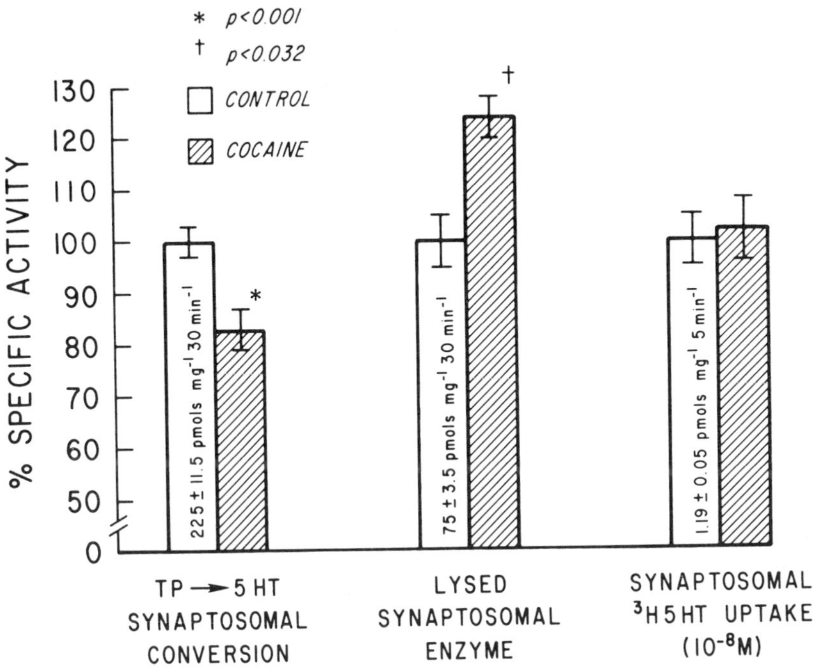

FIGURE 7. The effects of cocaine hydrochloride (100 mg/kg) administered to rats 1 hour before sacrifice on three synaptosomal serotonergic mechanisms, graphed as mean percentages ± S.E.M. of their respective control specific activities, shown in the white bars. Substrate concentration was 10 μM for the assays; 0.08 μM for the uptake determination.

reciprocal plot. As a concomitant of this increase in substrate uptake there is an increase in synaptosomal conversion of tryptophan to serotonin in preparations made from nerve endings, and with time there is a gradual compensatory decrease in midbrain cell body tryptophan hydroxylase activity (FIGURE 9). This increase in intraneuronal enzyme is seen finally in the nerve-ending region as a decrease to control values for the synaptosomal capacity to convert tryptophan to serotonin in spite of the maintenance of stimulated uptake of substrate. By 21 days a new steady state is achieved, in which striate synaptosomal biosynthetic capacity, returned to "normal," is made up of reduced intraneuronal tryptophan hydroxylase activity (in both cell bodies and nerve endings) combined with the maintained increase in the high-affinity tryptophan uptake system (FIGURE 10).

INFLUENCE OF LITHIUM PRETREATMENT ON THE EFFECTS OF AMPHETAMINE OR COCAINE CHALLENGE ON SECOND-ORDER SEROTONERGIC MECHANISMS—TWO FORMS OF PHARMACOLOGICAL ANTAGONISM

In terms of second-order events, it appears that repeated administration of lithium chloride moves the serotonergic mechanisms slowly in the same

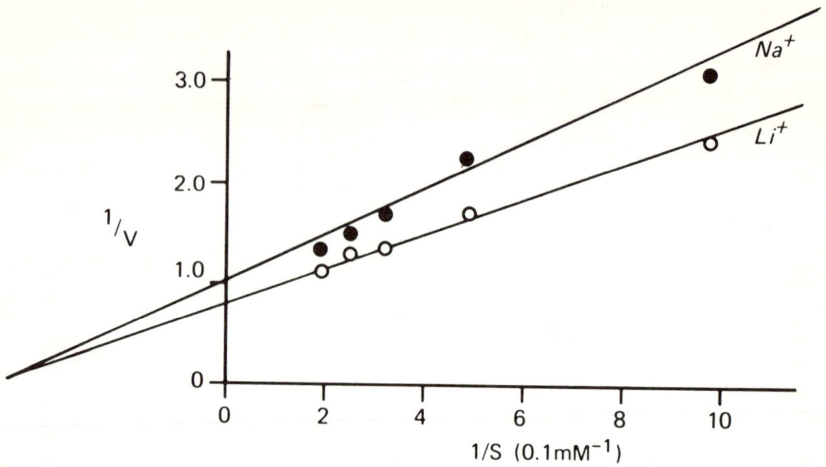

FIGURE 8. The effect of short-term (3 days) repeated injections of lithium chloride (10 meq/kg) on the uptake of L-[3-^{14}C]-tryptophan into rat striate synaptosomes. Controls received equimolar amounts of sodium chloride. Synaptosomal pellets from 12,000 × *g* centrifugation were used for the kinetic studies. Substrate concentrations ranged from 15 to 53 μM. Velocity is plotted as nanomoles of labeled substrate retained per milligram per 4 minutes. V_{max} and $K_m \pm$ S.E. were estimated according to the method of Wilkinson. Control $V_{max} = 10 \pm 2$ nmol/mg/4 min; $K_m = 2 \pm 0.5 \times 10^{-5}$ M. Lithium-treated $V_{max} = 13 \pm 2$ nmol/mg/4 min; $K_m = 2 \pm 0.1 \times 10^{-5}$ M.

direction that a single administration of amphetamine does quickly (decreased intraneuronal tryptophan hydroxylase activity) and slowly in the direction opposite to that in which a single administration of cocaine moves it quickly. (Lithium chloride produces an increase in tryptophan uptake and a decrease in intraneuronal tryptophan hydroxylase activity.) TABLE 1 summarizes the changes seen in both striate synaptosomal conversion of tryptophan to serotonin and intraneuronal (cell body in this case) soluble tryptophan hydroxylase activity when rats were challenged with D-amphetamine (5 mg/kg) after pretreatment with lithium chloride (5 meq/kg/day) for varying lengths of time.

TABLE 1

DECREASING RESPONSES TO AMPHETAMINE WITH LONG-TERM LITHIUM TREATMENT

	Percent Change in Amphetamine Effect*	
Days of Lithium Treatment	Synaptosomal Conversion TRP to 5-HT	Raphe Soluble TRP Hydroxylase Activity
3	−32	+22
6	−18	+10
9	−11	− 3
16	− 9	+ 4

$$* \frac{(\text{NaCl} \cdot \text{Amphetamine}) - (\text{LiCl} \cdot \text{Amphetamine})}{(\text{NaCl} \cdot \text{Amphetamine})} \times 100$$

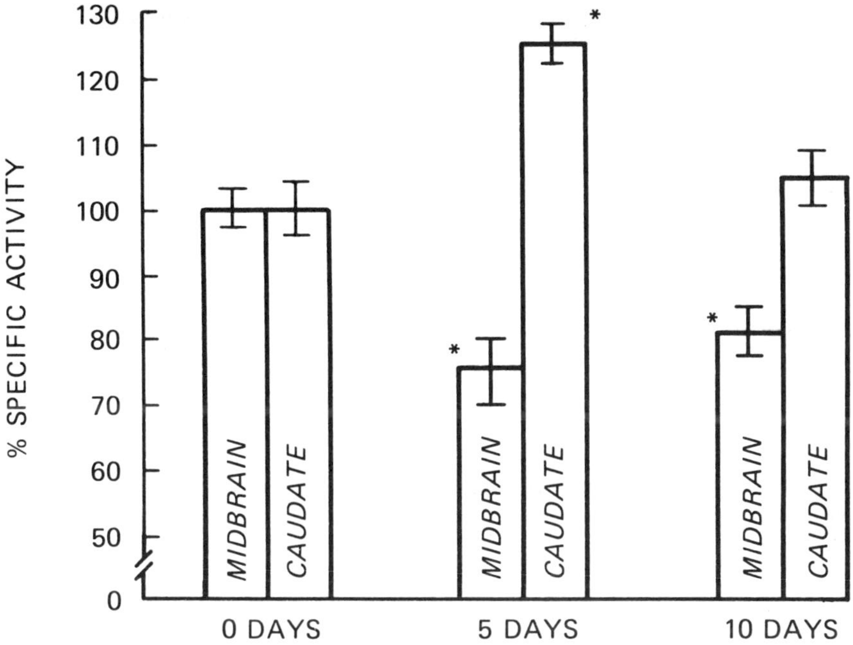

FIGURE 9. The effects of daily lithium chloride treatment on rat midbrain tryptophan hydroxylase activity and on rat caudate synaptosomal conversion of tryptophan to serotonin. Controls, treated with sodium chloride, are represented at 0 days; control midbrain enzyme activity was 100 pmol/mg/hr; caudate conversion, 130 pmol/mg/hr. Both parameters changed significantly* ($p < 0.005$). Within 10 days the conversion of substrate to transmitter in caudate nerve endings had returned to control levels, while the decrease in midbrain tryptophan hydroxylase persisted.

Note that with longer periods of lithium pretreatment there was, in both parameters, a progressive decrease in the differences between the group treated with lithium chloride and challenged with amphetamine and the group treated with sodium chloride and challenged with amphetamine.

We have viewed this lithium-induced progressive decrease in the amphetamine-induced change in various ways. We have considered the idea of lithium-induced cross-tolerance, in which the lithium-induced change in soluble enzyme would move slowly toward its biological limit, leaving less "room" for change to be induced by the amphetamine challenge. Invoking a first-order mechanism, one could argue that a lithium-induced decrease in enzyme may simply mirror the state and experience of a concomitantly desensitized receptor. If the reduction in soluble enzyme were a compensatory change related to an increase in receptor activation, one could think of the amphetamine-induced reduction in tryptophan hydroxylase and the nerve-ending activity state as compensating for amphetamine-facilitated release of serotonin, as shown in FIGURE 11. Pretreatment with lithium might be represented (as in FIGURE 12) as increasing receptor bombardment by serotonin through stimulation of uptake and conversion, culminating in a lithium-initiated decrease in enzyme. Thus, an acute amphetamine challenge after lithium pretreatment

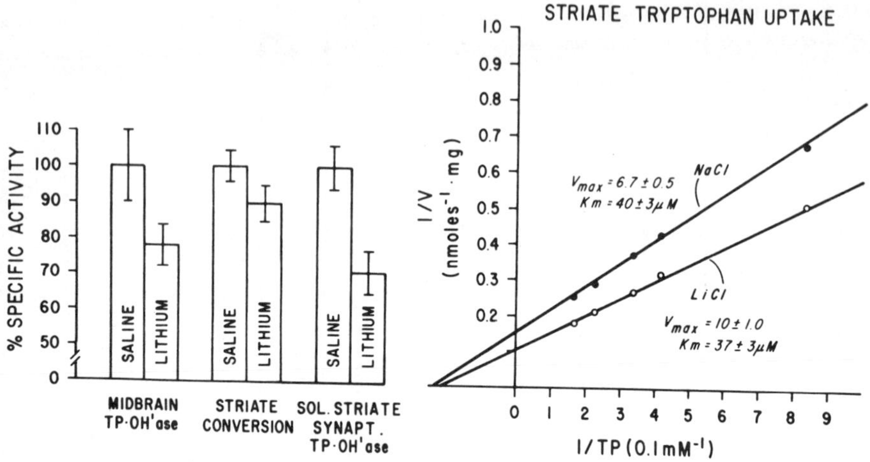

FIGURE 10. The effects of 21 daily lithium chloride injections (5 meq/kg) on four measures relevant to serotonin synthesis. Control velocities: midbrain soluble enzyme = 475 ± 20 pmol/mg protein/45 min ($p < 0.05$); striate synaptosomal conversion = 200 ± 10 pmol/mg/45 min; striate solubilized enzyme = 160 ± 5 pmol/mg/45 min ($p < 0.001$). High affinity uptake (12 μM to 53 μM substrate) is plotted as nmol L-[3-^{14}C]-tryptophan retained/mg/4 min, and V_{max} and K_m ± S.E. are estimated according to the method of Wilkinson.

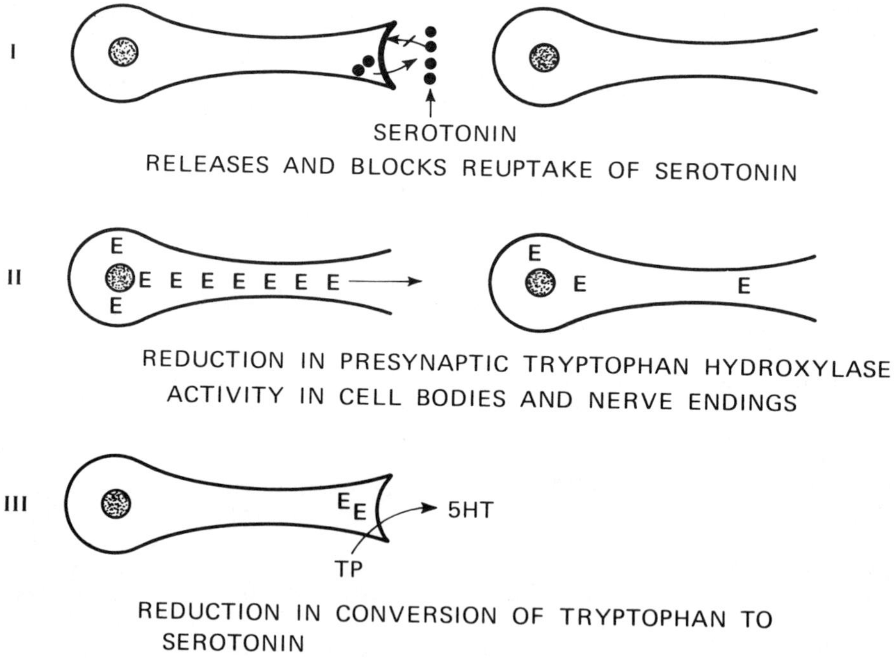

FIGURE 11. A model for serotonergic adaptation to the acute administration of D-amphetamine.

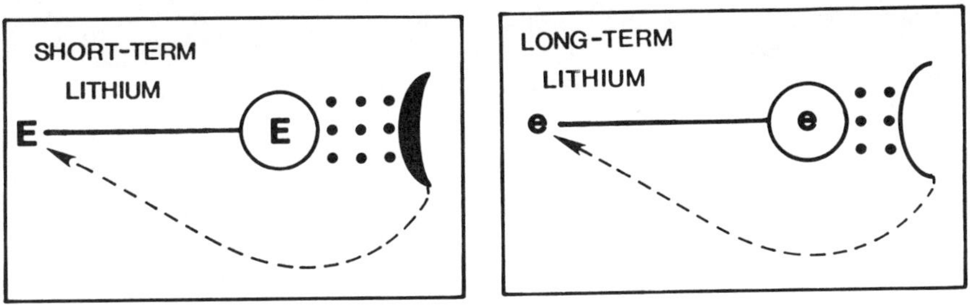

FIGURE 12. Hypothetical post-synaptic mechanisms in the action of lithium.

might fail to invoke changes in the serotonergic systems because such changes have already occurred gradually—perhaps receptor desensitization as well as enzyme decrease. This proposed lithium-amphetamine antagonism is reminiscent of the cross-tolerance mechanisms used to explain the loss or reduction of opiate effects in patients being maintained on methadone. We have also described this interaction as resulting in a drug-induced restriction in the possible range of response to another drug—when the first drug "uses up" the latent adaptive potential in a given neurobiological mechanism.

The lithium-cocaine antagonism in second-order mechanisms appears, at least on the surface, to be more straightforward. Treatment with lithium chloride or sodium chloride (10 meq/kg/day) was begun 3 days before cocaine administration, and the animals were sacrificed 2 hours after an injection of cocaine (100 mg/kg). The rats were sacrificed, then, 24 hours after the last lithium or sodium chloride injection. TABLE 2 indicates the individual effects of cocaine and lithium on four parameters related to serotonin biosynthesis, as well as the effects of the interaction of the drugs. Note that cocaine alone reduced the high affinity uptake of radioactive tryptophan, lithium alone stimulated the uptake system, and their interaction led to values in the vicinity of 100 percent of con-

TABLE 2

EFFECTS OF LITHIUM AND COCAINE ALONE AND TOGETHER

	Percent Control Specific Activity ± S.E.M.*		
	Lithium	Cocaine	Lithium + Cocaine
Striate uptake of ^{14}C-tryptophan	119 ± 7.5	89 ± 5.0	105 ± 7.2
Striate conversion of ^{14}C-tryptophan to serotonin	120 ± 3.9†	85 ± 2.2†	103 ± 4.5
Lateral midbrain tryptophan hydroxylase	79 ± 3.5‡	130 ± 3.5‡	90 ± 5.6
Striate synaptosomal tryptophan hydroxylase	81 ± 3.2‡	121 ± 4.3‡	103 ± 3.4

* Control specific activities: Uptake = 1150 ± 60 pmol/mg/5 min; conversion = 180 ± 7 pmol/mg/30 min; lateral midbrain enzyme = 200 ± 5 pmol/mg/30 min; striate synaptosomal enzyme = 111 ± 4.5 pmol/mg/30 min.

† $p < 0.05$.

‡ $p < 0.028$.

trol. Similar changes were seen in the capacity of striate synaptosomes to convert radioactive tryptophan to serotonin: cocaine reduced it, lithium increased it, and their interaction resulted in approximately control values. Cocaine, while reducing the uptake of tryptophan and its conversion to serotonin, led to an increase in tryptophan hydroxylase activity in the midbrain and the striate cortex. Lithium, while increasing the uptake and conversion of tryptophan to serotonin, produced a decrease in tryptophan hydroxylase activity in both the midbrain and the striate cortex. When lithium and cocaine treatments were combined as described above, the values for soluble enzyme activity approached control. Thus, it appears that for all four parameters involved with serotonin biosynthesis examined in this study, the cocaine-induced changes are antagonized by those induced by lithium. In this case, lithium pretreatment appears to restrict the ranges of response of the second-order mechanisms to the cocaine challenge *not* by using them up (as was the case with the amphetamine challenge) but by creating neurobiological counterforces that reduce or dampen the second drug's effects.

Discussion

One could argue that these drug-drug interactions among second-order mechanisms are simply reflections of the drug-drug interactions of the first order. Such a case would be more easily built for the catecholamine system, in which lithium has been shown to retard the neural activation-linked release of catecholamines,[4] and amphetamine[23] and cocaine[24, 25] have been shown to promote the release of catecholamines. For the serotonin system, such a first-order antagonistic interaction is less defensible. Grahame-Smith and Green[26] and others[27, 28] have produced both biochemical and behavioral evidence suggesting that treatment with lithium chloride increases serotonin biosynthesis and turnover in rat brain. Using, then, a first-order mechanism alone to explain the actions of amphetamine on the lithium-treated serotonergic system without invoking receptor and/or enzymatic adaptation, one might predict a potentiation of the amphetamine effect from a lithium-induced increase in synthesis and the amphetamine-induced facilitation of release. As noted above, both biochemical and behavioral evidence suggest antagonism. Moreover, an argument for cocaine-facilitated release of serotonin from nerve endings is rather weak, whereas the evidence for a cocaine-induced decrease in serotonin synthesis *in vivo* is good.[29] In addition, both cocaine and lithium effects on the uptake of substrate and conversion can be demonstrated *in vitro*,[6, 7] which suggests that explaining the cocaine-lithium antagonism in the intact brain by a functional link to first-order mechanisms, with resulting feedback-regulated modulation, is not necessary. Thus, the antagonistic interactions between lithium chloride and amphetamine and cocaine among second-order mechanisms seem to be the functionally important ones.

FIGURE 13 is a diagram of the first and second-order interactions described in this paper. The rationale for minimizing the purely first-order interactions in the serotonin system has been discussed. The amphetamine-lithium interaction has been described as the gradual induction by lithium of increased receptor bombardment by neurotransmitter and a compensatory decrease in presynaptic enzyme—both changes induced by amphetamine challenge with reduced effect

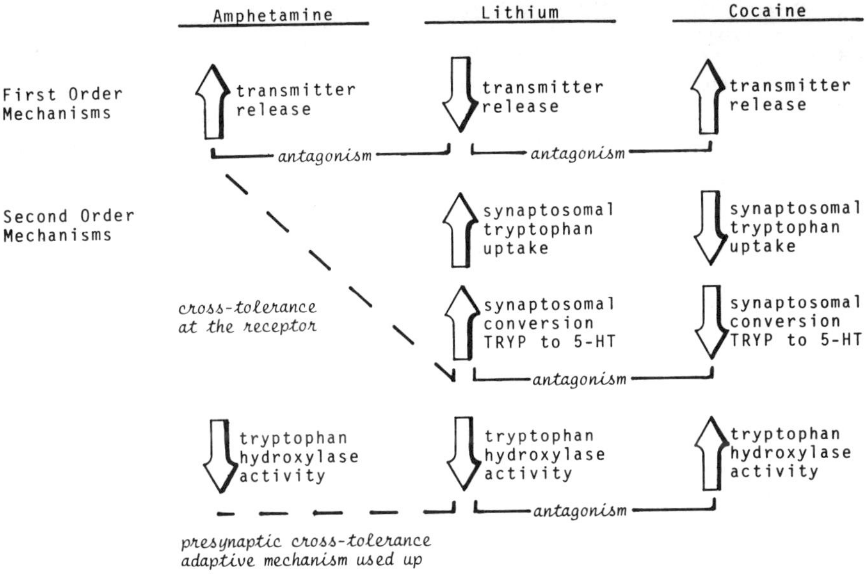

FIGURE 13. A model for first and second-order interactions between lithium and amphetamine or cocaine in the serotonergic biosynthetic system of brain.

after lithium pretreatment. The lithium-cocaine interaction is represented as a sequence of three changes induced in opposite directions. In the case of amphetamine after lithium pretreatment, one would predict an antagonism of the acute behavioral response. In the case of cocaine, one might predict a more significant antagonism in mechanisms of the second order—perhaps altering the delayed post-cocaine subjective and behavioral responses. Perhaps lithium in this case does not alter, so to speak, the splash of a rock tossed into water, but dampens or eliminates the secondary wave-circles of neurobiological change.

ACKNOWLEDGMENTS

Our thanks are offered to Arnetta McPherson and Nancy Anson for excellent technical assistance.

REFERENCES

1. AZZARO, A. J. & C. O. RUTLEDGE. 1973. Selectivity of release of norepinephrine, dopamine, and 5-hydroxytryptamine by amphetamine in various regions of rat brain. Biochem. Pharmacol. **22:** 2801–2813.
2. WONG, D. T., J. S. HORNG & R. W. FULLER. 1973. Kinetics of serotonin accumulation into synaptosomes of rat brain—effects of amphetamine and chloroamphetamines. Biochem. Pharmacol. **22:** 311–312.

3. Ross, S. B. & A. L. Renyi. 1969. Inhibition of the uptake of tritiated 5-hydroxytryptamine in brain tissue. Eur. J. Pharmacol. **7:** 270–277.
4. Katz, R., T. N. Chase & I. J. Kopin. 1968. Evoked release of norepinephrine and serotonin from brain slices: inhibition by lithium. Science **162:** 466–467.
5. Knapp, S. & Mandell, A. J. 1976. Coincidence of blockade of synaptosomal 5-hydroxytryptamine uptake and decrease in tryptophan hydroxylase activity: effects of fenfluramine. J. Pharmacol. Exp. Ther. **198:** 123–132.
6. Knapp, S. & A. J. Mandell. 1973. Short and long-term lithium administration: effects on the brain's serotonergic biosynthetic systems. Science **180:** 645–647.
7. Knapp, S. & A. J. Mandell. 1975. Effects of lithium chloride on parameters of biosynthetic capacity for 5-hydroxytryptamine in rat brain. J. Pharmacol. Exp. Ther. **193:** 812–823.
8. Knapp, S., A. J. Mandell & W. P. Bullard. 1975. Calcium activation of brain tryptophan hydroxylase. Life Sci. **16:** 1583–1594.
9. Kuczenski, R. T. & A. J. Mandell. 1972. Allosteric activation of hypothalamic tyrosine hydroxylase by ions and sulfated mucopolysaccharides. J. Neurochem. **19:** 131–137.
10. Lloyd, T. & S. Kaufman. 1974. The stimulation of partially purified bovine caudate tyrosine hydroxylase by phosphatidyl-L-serine. Biochem. Biophys. Res. Commun. **59:** 1262–1269.
11. Mandell, A. J., S. Knapp, R. T. Kuczenski & D. S. Segal. 1972. Methamphetamine-induced alteration in the physical state of rat caudate tyrosine hydroxylase. Biochem. Pharmacol. **21:** 2737–2750.
12. Guidotti, A., A. Kurosawa, D. M. Chuang & E. Costa. 1975. Protein kinase activation as an early event in the trans-synaptic induction of tyrosine-3-monooxygenase in adrenal medulla. Proc. Nat. Acad. Sci. USA **72**(3): 1152–1156.
13. Knapp, S., A. J. Mandell & M. A. Geyer. 1974. Effects of amphetamines on regional tryptophan hydroxylase activity and synaptosomal conversion of tryptophan to 5-hydroxytryptamine in rat brain. J. Pharmacol. Exp. Ther. **189:** 676–689.
14. Segal, D. S., R. T. Kuczenski & A. J. Mandell. 1974. Theoretical implications of drug-induced adaptive regulation for a biogenic amine hypothesis of effective disorder. Biol. Psychiat. **9**(2): 147–159.
15. Joh, T. H., C. Geghman & D. J. Reis. 1973. Immunochemical demonstration of increased tyrosine hydroxylase protein in sympathetic ganglia and adrenal medulla elicited by reserpine. Proc. Nat. Acad. Sci. USA **70:** 2767–2771.
16. Carlson, A., M. Lindqvist & T. Magnusson. 1960. On the biochemistry and possible functions of dopamine and noradrenaline in brain. *In* Ciba Symposium on Adrenergic Mechanisms. J. R. Vane, G. E. W. Wolstenholme & M. O'Connor, Eds.: 432–439. J. & A. Churchill, Ltd. London, England.
17. Carlsson, A. 1974. Antipsychotic drugs and catecholamine synapses. J. Psychiat. Res. **11:** 57–64.
18. Furukawa, T. 1975. Modification by lithium of behavioral responses to methamphetamine and tetrabenazine. Psychopharmacologia **42:** 243–248.
19. Segal, D. S., M. Callaghan & A. J. Mandell. 1975. Alterations in behaviour and catecholamine biosynthesis induced by lithium. Nature **254:** 58–59.
20. Cassens, G. P. & A. W. Mills. 1973. Lithium and amphetamine: opposite effects on threshold of intracranial reinforcement. Psychopharmacologia **30:** 283–290.
21. Knapp, S. & A. J. Mandell. 1972. Narcotic drugs: effects on the serotonin biosynthetic systems of the brain. Science **177:** 1209–1211.
22. Dahlstrom, A. & K. Fuxe. 1964. Evidence for the existence of monoamine-

containing neurons in the central nervous system. Acta Physiol. Scand. **62** (suppl. 232): 1–55.
23. Besson, M. I., A. Charamy, P. Feltz & J. Glowinski. 1969. Release of newly synthesized dopamine from dopamine-containing terminals in the striatum of the rat. Proc. Nat. Acad. Sci. U.S.A. **62:** 741–748.
24. Farnebo, L-O. & B. Hamberger. 1971. Drug-induced changes in the release of ^{3}H-monoamines from field stimulated rat brain slices. Acta Physiol. Scand. (suppl. 371): 35–44.
25. Starke, K. & H. Montel. 1973. Alpha-receptor-mediated modulation of transmitter release from central noradrenergic neurones. Naunyn-Schmiedeberg's Arch. Pharmakolog. **279:** 53–60.
26. Grahame-Smith, D. G. & A. R. Green. 1974. The role of brain 5-hydroxytryptamine in the hyperactivity produced in rats by lithium and monoamine oxidase inhibition. Brit. J. Pharmacol. **52:** 19–26.
27. Perez-Cruet, J., A. Tagliamonte, P. Tagliamonte & G. L. Gessa. 1971. Stimulation of serotonin synthesis by lithium. J. Pharmacol. Exp. Ther. **178:** 325–330.
28. Poitou, P., F. Guerinot & C. Buhuon. 1974. Effect of lithium on central metabolism of 5-hydroxytryptamine. Psychopharmacologia **38:** 75–80.
29. Friedman, E., S. Gershon & J. Rotrosen. 1975. Effects of acute cocaine treatment on the turnover of 5-hydroxytryptamine in the rat brain. Brit. J. Pharmacol. **54:** 61–64.

INTERACTIONS OF HALLUCINOGENS AT THE CLINICAL LEVEL

Richard Jed Wyatt, Eleanor H. Cannon, David M. Stoff, and J. Christian Gillin

Laboratory of Clinical Psychopharmacology
Division of Special Mental Health Research, IRP, NIMH
Saint Elizabeths Hospital
Washington, D.C. 20032

Introduction

Although our knowledge of hallucinogens is expanding rapidly, hallucinogenic agents have been used by man to produce mystical experiences for thousands of years. The plants and their extracts from which many of the natural drugs are derived are used both separately and in combinations. When used in combination, there is reason to believe that they might potentiate one another.[1] How the use of these drugs was discovered, how their appropriate dosages and proper combination were derived, is a fascinating area of investigation. Even if we do not now understand how "Dawn Age Psychopharmacologists" came to their conclusions, we know that they did.

Today modern-day alchemists are interested in drugs which augment the hallucinogens to produce the "golden drug experience." We are also interested in treating bad trips, producing models of psychosis, as well as being just curious about how things work.

Here we explore some of what is known about interactions of hallucinogens with drugs which might be used in treating "bad trips." We also examine the interactions of hallucinogens with themselves (tolerance and cross tolerance).

Hallucinogens and Drugs Which Interact With Them Clinically

LSD

LSD has been the hallucinogen most extensively studied in almost every regard—its interactions with other drugs included. Clinical studies (Table 1) have focused primarily on LSD interactions with the neuroleptics on the theory that if these drugs are effective in attenuating major psychiatric symptoms they may also affect the same symptoms when they are produced by a hallucinogen. Probably the most widely used compound for treatment of "bad" LSD trips is chlorpromazine (CPZ) (Figure 1). CPZ has been administered as a pretreatment to, simultaneous with, or following a dose of LSD. Pretreatment experiments have used CPZ doses ranging from 0.35 to 9 mg/kg given 30 minutes to several days prior to LSD ingestion. CPZ has proven to be an incomplete antagonist of LSD. At low doses (0.35 mg/kg), given shortly before LSD, CPZ increased the LSD threshold dose needed to produce pupil dilatation.[2] Pretreatment with higher doses (0.70 mg/kg), for longer periods of

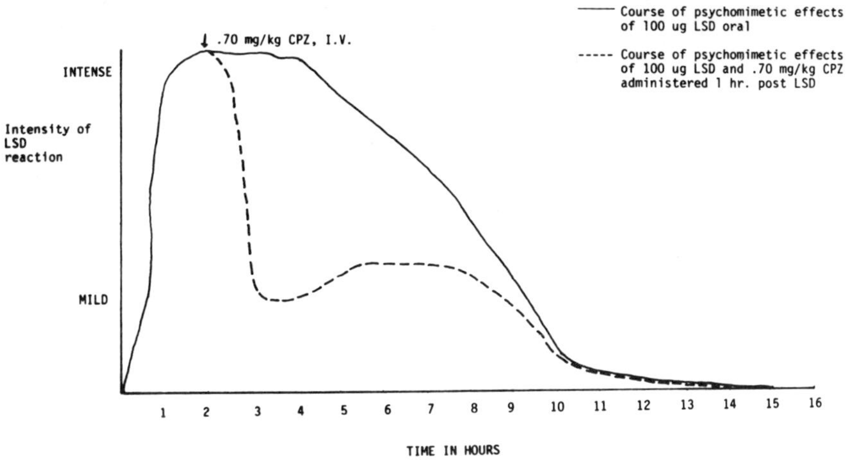

FIGURE 1. Course of psychotomimetic effects of LSD alone and with chlorpromazine administered at the peak of the LSD reaction. (From Hoch.[5] By permission of Grune & Stratton, Inc.)

time, tended to reduce LSD-induced psychomotor activity,[3] reduced anxiety and improved mood, delayed the onset of the "trip," and reduced its duration.[4]

When CPZ was given simultaneously with LSD to humans in small doses (below 0.40 mg/kg), it produced no change in the LSD effect.[2] At higher doses (0.70 mg/kg), disappearance of symptoms such as nausea, vomiting and dizziness, reduction in motor activity, anxiety, and unpleasant affect feelings of unreality have been reported.[5] CPZ did not appreciably alter the production of hallucinations or delusions, but the unpleasant feelings associated with these symptoms were reduced or eliminated.[4] In some instances, exacerbation of adverse effects of LSD have been reported when CPZ was administered at 0.70 mg/kg simultaneously with LSD.[3, 6]

Animal studies (TABLE 2) using various measures such as rage reaction in cats,[7] conditioned behaviors,[8] or observation of changes in normal behaviors[9, 10] indicate that CPZ pretreatment partially or completely antagonizes the effects of LSD. It is interesting to note, however, that in animal studies there also have been reports of potentiation of LSD effects by CPZ (FIGURE 2). Halasz *et al.* studied the effects of various doses of CPZ together with LSD on conditioned learning performance in monkeys and cats.[8] In cats, at 200 μg/kg, CPZ protected against behavior impairment produced by LSD. CPZ alone at 300 μg/kg doses did not disrupt learned behavior, but when 300 μg/kg of CPZ was given together with LSD, potentiation of impairment beyond that produced by the LSD alone was observed. Halasz hypothesized that the additive effect may reflect competition for receptors between LSD and CPZ; that CPZ itself is a weak psychotogen which, at low doses, takes up receptor sites and protects against the activity of the stronger psychotogen, but at greater doses, adds to the effect instead. CPZ has also been reported to aggravate the hallucinogenic effects of 2,5-dimethoxy-4-methylamphetamine (DOM [STP]).[11]

Studies of interactions of LSD with other anti-psychotic substances have included reserpine, adrenergic and serotonergic blockers, monoamine oxidase

TABLE 1
EFFECTS OF LSD WITH OTHER DRUGS IN MAN

Author	Drug*	Dose and Schedule	Subjects	Results
Giberti & Gregoretti[4] (1955)	CPZ	3–9 mg/kg daily for "a few days" prior to LSD	Psychoneurotic patients	Reduced anxiety, improved mood. LSD experience was subjectively better. Onset of "trip" was delayed. Duration shortened. Did not affect perceptual changes, memory distortion, or orientation.
	Reserpine	0.06–0.32 mg/kg daily for for "a few days" prior to LSD	Psychoneurotic patients	Reduced psychomotor and behavioral effects, reduced nausea and anorexia, delayed onset, duration shortened.
Himwich[33] (1955)	LSD	"Huge doses" prior to small dose, exact dosage not stated	Human and/or monkey	Reversed initial effects. Sleep pattern restored. Evoked EEG arousal. In monkey, appeared to be tranquilizing rather than hallucinogenic.
Fabing[34] (1955)	Frenquel	After LSD, time and dose unstated	Volunteer normals	"Cured" LSD psychotic-like episode and prevented effects of subsequently administered LSD.
Hoffer[35] (1955)	Nicotinic acid	0.30 mg/kg at peak of LSD "trip"	Normals	Within 2–5 min "almost all" LSD phenomena disappeared. Some slight perceptual changes left.
Abramson[3] (1955)	CPZ	0.70 mg/kg 2 hr before 0.70 mg/kg 2 hr after	Non-psychotic	Psychomotor activity decreases.
		0.70 mg/kg simultaneous		Potentiation may occur.
Hoch[5] (1955)	Sodium amytal	3–6 mg/kg i.v. (after LSD trip began)	Unstated	Sodium amytal and peruitin both tend to shorten duration of drug effect. Autonomic and psychotic symptoms not completely removed but reduced in intensity.
	Peruitin	0.3–0.55 mg/kg i.v. (after LSD trip began)	Unstated	
	CPZ	0.70 mg/kg i.v. at height of psychotic reaction	Unstated	Rapid and complete disappearance of autonomic symptoms such as vomiting, nausea, and dizziness, later reduction in motor activity and verbal productivity. Anxiety reduced. Hallucinations and delusions may remain.

Murphree[2] (1962)	CPZ	0.35 mg/kg 30 min prior	Normals	Elevation of threshold dose (threshold measured was significant change in pupil dilation). Not a complete antagonist.
	CPZ	0.35 mg/kg simultaneous or after	Normals	No effect.
	Phenoxy-benzamine	0.14 mg/kg 30 min prior	Normals	Elevation of threshold dose for significant changes in pupil dilation.
Freedman[14] (1963)	Reserpine	0.14 mg/kg 2 days prior to LSD	Schizophrenic females	Potentiated LSD effect. Prolonged toxic reactions (tremor, akathesia), increased duration of effects, "trip" significantly "less pleasant."
Hollister[13] (1964)	CPZ	In advance of LSD, dose and times unstated	Unstated	
	Phenoxy-benzamine	In advance of LSD, dose and time unstated	Unstated	Effective antagonist, if given at height of syndrome in sufficient doses.
	Reserpine	In advance of LSD, dose and time unstated	Unstated	Fails to block LSD reaction. May enhance it.
Matussek & Halbach[36] (1964)	Ergotamine	0.03–0.03 mg/kg 3–5 days before LSD, then 0.03 mg/kg together with LSD and 0.03 mg/kg 4 hr later	Normals	Excitement, euphoria, and depression prolonged.
Resnick, Krus & Raskin[37] (1964)	Isocarboxide	0.42 mg/kg daily for 3–5 weeks	Normals	Attenuated subjective effects.
	Reserpine	0.70 mg/kg daily for 2 weeks	Normals	Potentiated LSD effects.

* CPZ, Chlorpromazine. LSD, Lysergic acid diethylamide.

TABLE 2
EFFECTS OF LSD WITH OTHER DRUGS IN ANIMALS

Author	Drug*	Dose and Schedule	Subjects	Results
Himwich[33] (1955)	Frenquel	18 mg/kg after LSD	Rabbit	LSD produced an alerting response in EEG. Frenquel reversed this effect and restored the sleep pattern.
Elder & Dille[7] (1962)	CPZ	5 mg/kg daily for 3 days and 1 dose 30 min before LSD	Cat	Observed "rage reaction." CPZ blocked all aspects of the rage reaction except hissing and mydriasis, but the latter was reduced in intensity.
	Reserpine	0.5 mg/kg daily for 6 days	Cat	Duration of reaction shortened. Animals were catatonic post-LSD.
	Phenoxybenzamine	15 mg/kg 30–60 min before	Cat	LSD reaction was markedly reduced in intensity or abolished. Tracking, hissing, and startle remained, but very little aggression.
Freedman[14] (1963)	Reserpine	2 mg/kg 3–4 days before	Rat	Showed prolonged reaction to a subthreshold dose of LSD (40 mg/kg). Stated that reserpine had already been metabolized.
Appel & Freedman[9] (1964)	Reserpine	1.4 mg/kg over 4 days	Rat	These three drugs potentiated behavioral effects. LSD induced impairment in bar-pressing performance.
	Tetrabenzine	4 mg/kg 5 hr before	Rat	
	Tranylcypromine	1.5 mg/kg 6 hr before	Rat	
	CPZ	30 mg 1 hr before	Rat	Attenuated LSD-induced disruption of bar-pressing performance.
Weckowicz[38] (1967)	5-hdroxytryptophan	Unstated	Rat	Prevented LSD's confusing effect on the rat's trained behavior. Prevented dragging abdomen along the floor.

Dixon[10] (1968)	Phenoxybenzamine	7.5, 15, and 30 mg/kg	Rat	Inhibited aberrant behavior (motor excitation, stereotypy, compulsive biting and chewing).
	Propranolol	7.5, 15, and 30 mg/kg prior	Rat	Same as above.
	AMPT	120 mg/kg 20 hr prior	Rat	Inhibited LSD effect, almost no aberrant behavior.
	Disulfiram	300 mg/kg 5 hr prior	Rat	Reduced LSD effect.
	Reserpine	1.5, 3, and 6 mg/kg 20 hr prior	Rat	Potentiated effect.
	Desmethylimipramine	7.5, 15, 30 mg/kg prior	Rat	Potentiated effect.
	PCPA	3 × 100 mg/kg daily or 24, 48, or 72 hr before	Rat	No effect.
	CPZ	1, 3, or 10 mg/kg prior	Rat	Inhibited aberrant behavior at all doses.
Sugrue[16] (1969)	Reserpine	5 mg/kg 18 hr prior	Rat	No effect on intensity of LSD-produced excitation, except to shorten its duration.
	AMPT	50 mg/kg 4 hr prior	Rat	Slightly decreased initial response to LSD and attenuated the duration of excitation.
Halasz *et al*[8] (1969)	CPZ	0.15 mg/kg 30 min prior	Monkey	Protects against LSD-induced disruption of conditioned lever pressing for food.
		1 mg/kg 30 min prior	Monkey	Potentiation of LSD-induced disruption of conditioned lever pressing for food.
		200 μg/kg	Cat	Protects against LSD-induced disruption of discrimination task performance.
		300 μg/kg	Cat	Potentiates LSD-induced disruption of discrimination task performance.
Martin & Eades[17] (1970)	CPZ	5 mg/kg 30 min prior	Dog	Antagonized LSD-induced facilitation of flexor reflex.
	Cyproheptadine	0.2 mg/kg 30 min prior	Dog	
	Phenoxybenzamine	4 mg/kg	Dog	No effect.
Smythies *et al.*[2] (1970)	THPC	15 mg/kg 45 min prior	Rat	Blocked the disrupting effects of LSD (avoidance conditioning paradigm).

* CPZ, chlorpromazine, AMPT, alpha-methyl-para-tyrosine. PCPA, para-chlorophenylalanine. THPC, 1, methyl-1,2,5,6-tetrahydropyridine-3-(N,N-diethylcarboxamide).

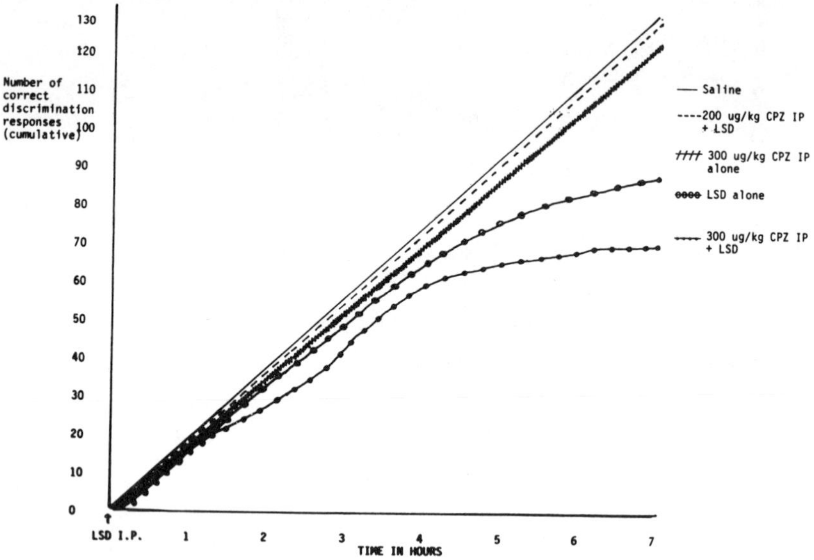

FIGURE 2. Effect of different doses of chlorpromazine pretreatment on LSD-induced impairment of discrimination performance in cats. (From Halasz *et al.*[8] By permission of *Science*.)

inhibitors, and a variety of compounds such as vitamin B_3, sodium succinate, and huge doses of LSD itself (TABLE 1). Most reports of the interactions of LSD and reserpine indicate that reserpine pretreatment in both normal and psychiatric subjects enhances the subjective effects of LSD.[12–14] An exception to this general finding is the study by Giberti and Gregoretti, who observed a reduction in LSD effects, particularly psychomotor effects, nausea, and anorexia.[4] The onset of LSD effect was also reported to be delayed and the duration shorter. Reserpine administered 24–48 hr before LSD prolonged disturbed consciousness, mydriasis, and the occurrence of numerous extrapyramidal symptoms.[15]

In animals, daily pretreatment with reserpine (0.5 mg/kg for 6 days) prior to LSD shortened the duration of the LSD reaction in cats, but after the normal LSD reaction wore off, the animals became catatonic and remained so for several hours.[7] In rats, reserpine pretreatment potentiated behavioral effects,[9, 10] or, when given in a single dose 3–4 days before LSD, prolonged the response to a sub-threshold dose of LSD.[14] Sugrue found that 5 mg/kg reserpine 18 hr prior to LSD had no effect on the intensity of LSD-produced excitation but did shorten the duration of the excitation.[16]

Phenoxybenzamine (an adrenergic blocker) in man increased the threshold dose of LSD[2] for pupil dilatation. In animals, phenoxybenzamine, 15 mg/kg given 30 to 60 min prior to LSD, markedly reduced LSD effects in one study[7] and was ineffective when given at a lower dosage.[17]

The literature on interactions of LSD with various other substances is a pot-pourri of ancedotes and inconsistent or scant information; it will not be discussed here. The LSD tables (TABLES 1 and 2) contain brief summaries of some of these reports.

N,N-Dimethyltryptamine (*DMT*)

Little data are available in the clinical literature regarding the interactions of DMT with other drugs (TABLE 3). In animals, CPZ may prolong disruption of bar pressing produced by DMT,[18] but it was ineffective in blocking DMT-induced excitation of hippocampal cells.[19] An interesting biphasic effect of neuroleptics on DMT is now being investigated by Moore *et al.*[20] As in the case of CPZ and LSD, the nature of the interaction between DMT and certain neuroleptics (CPZ, haloperidol, thiothixine, molindone, methiothepin, and octoclothepin) is dose-dependent. Low (1 mg/kg) doses of all these neuroleptics except molindone potentiated DMT's effect on evoked potentials in the visual system of the cat. Higher doses (10 mg/kg) antagonized the effects of DMT.

In our laboratory, Stoff *et al.*[39] found that chronic pretreatment with CPZ attenuates DMT disruption of avoidance behavior, but acute CPZ is ineffective. To our knowledge, this is the only study on chronic neuroleptic pretreatment before DMT and may provide a model for the clinical response of schizophrenics to CPZ, where the drug is initially sedating and gradually takes on antipsychotic effects with continued administration.

Studies in the literature dealing with the interactions of DMT and other compounds are not numerous. Sai-Halasz investigated the monoamine oxidase inhibitors in combination with DMT.[21] He pretreated normal human subjects with iproniazid at 100 mg for 4 days and observed the effects of DMT following this pretreatment. Iproniazid reduced the effects of DMT. At a low dose of DMT, subjects pretreated with iproniazid experienced no hallucinations or disturbances in time and space orientations, although nearly all stated that they did not feel "normal" but rather had a definite "odd" feeling. At a higher dose of DMT, the subjects experienced the typical effects of DMT, but in a much milder form, and then proceeded to pass into the state experienced by the low-dose group, that of absence of "psychotic symptoms" but an "odd" sensation. On the other hand, when Sai-Halasz pretreated subjects with methylsergide, a serotonin receptor blocker, he observed intensification of DMT symptoms.[22] Sai-Halasz concluded that DMT and serotonin have antagonistic effects.

Mescaline

A study of interactions of mescaline (TABLE 4) with phenothiazines was done by Shah *et al.*[23] in mice. Pretreatment with CPZ effectively prevented mescaline effects. It was also noted that CPZ appeared to elevate tissue concentrations of mescaline in the brain and other organs. Administration of 2.5 mg/kg CPZ or 10 mg/kg thioridazine 45 min post-mescaline resulted in a partial block of gross mescaline-induced behavior (i.e., mescaline-induced scratching and locomotor activity were reduced, and the animals no longer "seemed frightened"). At higher doses, 5 mg/kg CPZ and 30 mg/kg thioridazine, all the mescaline effects were blocked. Increasing the CPZ post-treatment to 15 mg/kg resulted in catatonia. Post-mescaline treatment with thioridazine blocked mescaline effects without producing a catalepsy until the dose was pushed up to 45 mg/kg.

In man, pretreatment with phenothiazines has been reported to attenuate

TABLE 3

EFFECTS OF DMT WITH OTHER DRUGS IN MAN AND ANIMALS

Author	Drug	Dose and Schedule	Subjects	Results
Sai-Halasz[21] (1963)	Iproniazid	1.42 mg/kg for 4 days	Normals	0.35–0.55 mg/kg DMT dose: no hallucinations or disturbances in time and space orientation. Subjects just felt "odd." 0.65–0.88 mg/kg DMT: 1st phase was usual DMT effect but milder. Subjects then went into a 2nd phase which resembled the reaction above for the low DMT dose.
Sai-Halasz[22] (1962)	Methysergide	0.07 mg/kg 30–40 min before	Normals	DMT symptoms markedly intensified. Experimental psychosis accentuated.
Moore *et al.* (unpublished data)	CPZ*	1–10 mg/kg 15 min prior	Cat	Observed effect of DMT on evoked potentials in visual system. Low doses of neuroleptics potentiated DMT effect. High doses antagonized DMT effect. Methiothepin and octoclothepin were the most potent antagonists. Molindone was essentially ineffective.
	Haldol	1–10 mg/kg 15 min prior	Cat	
	Thiothixene	1–10 mg/kg 15 min prior	Cat	
	Molindone	1–10 mg/kg 15 min prior	Cat	
	Methiothepin	0.032–1 mg/kg 15 min prior	Cat	
	Octoclothepin	1–10 mg/kg 15 min prior	Cat	
Smythies *et al.*[111] (1972)	DBA (N,N-diethylbutyramide)	20 mg/kg 30 min before	Rat	Reduced DMT disruption of avoidance conditioning.
Kovacic & Domino[18]	CPZ	Unknown (unpublished data, anecdotal)	Rat	Prolonged disruption of bar pressing produced by DMT.
Moore *et al.*[20] (1974)	Methiothepin	1 mg/kg	Rabbit	Antagonized DMT-induced hypothermia, mydriasis and EEG activation.
	CPZ	1 mg/kg	Rabbit	
Moore *et al.*[20] (1974)	Methiothepin	1 mg/kg	Cat	Antagonized DMT effects (depression of visual evoked potential).
	CPZ	1 mg/kg	Cat	Potentiated effect of DMT.
	Haldol	1 mg/kg	Cat	
De France *et al.*[19] (1975)	CPZ	1–2.5 mg/kg i.v.	Cat	Ineffective in blocking DMT-induced excitation of cells in hippocampus.
Stoff *et al.*[39,79] (1976)	CPZ	0.5 mg/kg 30 min prior	Rat	No effect on DMT disruption of shuttlebox avoidance.
	Haloperidol	0.05 mg/kg 30 min prior	Rat	Attenuation of DMT disruption
	CPZ	0.5 mg/kg 30 min prior/28 days	Rat	Dose-response attenuation of DMT disruption (time-related).

* CPZ, chlorpromazine.

TABLE 4

EFFECTS OF MESCALINE WITH OTHER DRUGS IN MAN AND ANIMALS

Author	Drug*	Dose and Schedule	Subjects	Results
Cholden[25] (1955)	CPZ	0.70 mg/kg given twice after onset of mescaline trip	Unstated	After 2nd dose, mescaline effect was blocked.
Himwich[33] (1955)	Frenquel	18 mg/kg after mescaline	Rabbit	Mescaline evokes an EEG alerting reaction. Frenquel eliminated alerting response and established features of sleep.
Hollister[24] (1968)	Phenothiazine	Unstated	Unstated	Reduced behavioral effects of mescaline.
	Diethazine	Unstated	Unstated	Potentiated behavioral effects of mescaline.
Martin & Eades[17] (1970)	CPZ	5 mg/kg	Dog	Antagonized mescaline-induced facilitation of flexor reflex.
	Cyproheptadine	0.2 mg/kg 30 min prior	Dog	Antagonized mescaline-induced facilitation of flexor reflex.
	Phenoxybenzamine	4 mg/kg 30 min prior	Dog	No effect.
Dittrich[26] (1971)	2,4,5-MPEA	100–200 mg/kg 45 min prior	Normal	2,4,5-MPEA intensified effects of mescaline as measured by increases in time to do a task and decreased ability to concentrate.
Smythies *et al.*[111] (1972)	THPC	15 mg/kg 45 min prior	Rat	Potentiated behavior disruption effect of mescaline as measured by avoidance conditioning.
Shah *et al.* (1975)	CPZ	15 mg/kg 45 min after	Mice	CPZ and haloperidol effectively reversed mescaline effects in mice. Also found elevated tissue mescaline levels in the brain and other organs.
	Haloperidol	10 mg/kg 45 min after	Mice	
Shah *et al.*[23] (1975)	CPZ	2.5, 5, 15 mg/kg 45 min or 120 min post	Mice	Partial or complete block of gross mescaline-induced behavior (increased scratching and locomotor activity) at higher CPZ and thioridazine doses. Got catatonic-like effect and hypothermia. Tissue levels of mescaline were increased after CPZ. Mice no longer seemed frightened at 2.5 mg/kg CPZ. At 5 mg/kg CPZ, all mescaline effects were blocked. 15 mg/kg CPZ produced catatonia. Thioridazine blocked effects without catalepsy until dose of 45 mg/kg.
	Thioridazine	10, 30, 45 mg/kg post mescaline		

* 2,4,5-MPEA, 2,4,5-trimethoxyphenylethyamine. CPZ, chlorpromazine. THPC, 1-methyl-1,2,5,6-tetrahydroxypridine-3-(N,N-diethylcarboxamide).

the effects of mescaline.[24] Post-treatment, two doses of 0.70 mg/kg each, with CPZ also reduced the effects of mescaline.[25]

Reported interactions of mescaline with other substances are scarce. One study by Dittrich involved pretreating a single subject with 2,4,5-trimethoxyphenylethylamine (2,4,5-MPEA), a substance identical with mescaline in structure except for the placement of one methoxy group.[26] Administered alone, 2,4,5-MPEA was not psychotomimetic in man. Pretreatment at doses of 100 to 200 mg/kg 45 min prior to 100 mg/kg mescaline resulted in an intensification of the mescaline effects, as measured by an increase in time required to accomplish a task and decreased ability to concentrate. Duration of effects was also increased. This study conflicts with a rat study in which 2,4,5-MPEA pretreatment reportedly antagonized mescaline response.[27]

5-Methoxy-DMT (5-MeO-DMT)

Interactions of various substances with 5-MeO-DMT generally indicate that CPZ pretreatment inhibits 5-MeO-DMT-induced tremor in rats,[28] rage induced in cats,[29] and hyperactivity in rats.[30, 31] Antagonism of 5-MeO-DMT is also produced by pretreatment with reserpine,[29, 30] 5-HTP, disulfiram, and L-DOPA.[30] Hyperactivity produced by 5-MeO-DMT in tranylcypromine-pretreated rats was inhibited by alpha-methyl-para-tyrosine.[32]

Potentiation of 5-MeO-DMT action has been shown to occur with SK-525-A, pargyline,[28] para-chlorophenylalanine and dihydroxyphenylserine,[30] and tranylcypromine.[31]

Of other substances known to be hallucinogenic, such as psilocin and psilocybin, some animal studies are available which discuss drug interactions. A few of these are summarized in Table 5.

Tolerance and Cross Tolerance

Operationally speaking, tolerance may be defined in terms of an acquired change within the same individual as a result of repeated exposure to the drug,

Table 5

Effects of Psilocin and Psilocybin With Other Drugs in Animals

Author	Drug*	Dose and Schedule	Subjects	Results
Martin & Eades[17] (1970)	CPZ	5 mg/kg 30 min prior	Dog	Antagonized psilocin-induced facilitation of flexor reflex.
	Cyproheptadine	0.2 mg/kg 30 min prior	Dog	No effect.
Sugrue[16] (1969)	Reserpine	5 mg/kg 18 hr prior	Rat	No effect on intensity of psylocybin-induced excitation, but duration of effect was reduced.
	AMPT	50 mg/kg 4 hr prior	Rat	

* CPZ, chlorpromazine. AMPT, α-methyl-para-tyrosine.

so that an increased amount of drug is required to produce the designated degree of effect that was produced by the same dose of drug on the first exposure. This definition of tolerance carries no implications with respect to mechanisms.

The data of TABLES 6 and 7 strongly suggest that tolerance develops to the autonomic and psychological effects of LSD, mescaline, DOM, and psilocybin in humans.[40–46] In the only human study with DMT tolerance probably did not develop.[42] All the studies demonstrated tolerance to "good trip" effects (e.g., perceptual distortions) occurring under relatively supportive environmental conditions in the laboratory in normal-health volunteers who were informed about the kind of drug ingested. Tolerance may not develop to stress-related effects of these drugs in unsuspecting individuals. This may explain the report by the CIA of bad trips (e.g., paranoid ideation) in unaware individuals,[109] the finding that thought disturbances increased with more prolonged drug intake,[110] and the few animal studies[80–83] where tolerance did not develop to stress-related excitatory effects of LSD or mescaline. Pretreatment with BOL-148, a non-hallucinogenic congener of LSD[48] having serotonin antagonist properties like LSD,[49] does not protect against the effects of LSD.[50–54] There is two-way (cross tolerance from drug A to drug B and from drug B to drug A) partial cross tolerance among LSD, mescaline, and psilocybin. The most complete cross tolerance is to mescaline in LSD-tolerant humans.[50, 55–58] There is one study suggesting that one-way cross tolerance from LSD to DMT[60] does not occur.

Further studies are required to determine the potential for DMT to induce tolerance and the degree of cross tolerance to mescaline or psilocybin in LSD-tolerant humans. There are no studies reported on cross tolerance between any of the methoxylated amphetamines (e.g., DOM) and the other hallucinogens. An interesting approach may be to determine whether or not cross tolerance among hallucinogens depends upon their chemical structure. For example, the hallucinogens with catechol nuclei (mescaline, DOM) and those with indole nuclei (DMT, psilocybin) may share similar effects, but there may not be cross tolerance between a catechol and indole-related hallucinogen. LSD is a good test compound in this regard since it has an indole ring but also sympathomimetic properties.

The reports cited in TABLE 6 show that tolerance develops to disruptive effects of LSD, mescaline, psilocybin, and nutmeg constituents on a variety of operant behaviors;[60–68] these effects are cross tolerant among all four drugs.[69–75] Furthermore, tolerance may not develop for DMT[76–79] and for excitatory effects of LSD or mescaline.[80–83]

The interesting finding that there was no cross tolerance to mescaline given intraperitoneally after the development of tolerance to the ventricular administration of mescaline on operant behavior (and vice versa)[67] suggests that there may be separate mechanisms for the effects and formation of tolerance, depending upon whether the route of administration is central or peripheral.

Cross-Discriminated Responding

In general, the reports on cross-discriminated responding (TABLE 8) are consistent with the cross tolerance (TABLE 7) studies. The basic paradigm employed is one in which rats are trained to make differential responses under the drug and non-drug control conditions where the drug serves as a discriminative cue. The differential response is reinforced by reward for the correct choice

TABLE 6A
STUDIES OF TOLERANCE IN HUMANS AND ANIMALS

Author	Subject	Index	Drug Regimen*	Tolerance
Isbell *et al.*[40] (1955)	Psychiatric patients	Mental effects via questionnaire	LSD 50–180 μ/7 days	Yes
Cholden *et al.*[41] (1955)	Chronic schizophrenics	Clinical reactions in terms of intensification or reversal of symptoms	LSD 100 μg/2–3 days	Yes
Isbell *et al.*[42] (1956)	Ex-morphine addicts	Abramson[3] questionnaire. Clinical grade (e.g., anxiety, perceptual distortion, hallucinations)	LSD 10–30 μg twice daily/3 days	Yes
Abramson *et al.*[43] (1956)	Normal humans	Positive questionnaire responses about intensity of perceptual and physiological state (e.g., I am trembling, palpitations) and verbal report about psychic changes (e.g., hallucinations, mood)	LSD 5–100 μg/3–6 days	Yes
Hoffer[44] (1964)	Normal humans	Psychological effects	LSD 100–200 μg/2 days	Yes
Hollister *et al.*[45] (1969)	Psychiatric patients	Clinical syndrome, physiological measures, psychometric tests	DOM 1–12 mg, 1–3 times day/9 days	Yes
Angrist *et al.*[46] (1974)	Normal humans	True items of Addiction Research Center Inventory, Perceptual Experience Inventory, subjective estimates of intensity of drug experience	DOM 6 mg/3 days	Yes
Kaplan *et al.*[47] (1976)	Normal humans	Ratings of "subjective high," blood concentrations, pupillary diameter	DMT 0.7 mg/kg twice daily/5 days	Probably none
Gogerty & Dille[91] (1956)	Rabbits	Pyretogenesia	LSD 50 μg/4–5 days	Yes
Freedman *et al.*[69] (1958)	Rat	Disruption of rope climbing for food	LSD 130–260 mg/kg at 24-hr intervals/4 days	Yes
			LSD 130 mg/kg at 48-hr intervals/14 days	Yes (partial)
			LSD 130 mg/kg at 72-hr intervals/14 days	No
Mahler & Hummoller[60] (1958)	Rat	Disruption of pole climbing for food	Mescaline 10 mg/kg/10 days	Yes
			LSD	Yes
Jarvik & Chorover[61] (1958)	Monkey	Disruption of memory and delayed alternation task maintained by liquid reward	LSD 0.01 μg/kg/several consecutive days	Yes

Jarvik & Chorover[62] (1960)	Monkey	Disruption of memory and delayed alternation task maintained by liquid reward	LSD 0.005–0.2 mg/kg/2 days	Partial
Gillett[92] (1960)	Rat	Inhibition of sexual behavior in terms of reduction of number of copulations preceding ejaculation	LSD 130 μg/kg 3 times at 96-hr intervals	No
Hamilton[80] (1960)	Rat	Facilitation of well-learned nonsignalled escape response	LSD 0.13–0.50 mg/kg/7 days	No
Adey *et al.*[63] (1962)	Cat	Disruption of discriminated delayed motor response maintained by food	LSD 100–200 μg/kg 2 times at intervals of	Yes
Koella *et al.*[93] (1964)	Goat	Increased motor activity in open field	LSD 7.5–15 μg/kg/4 days	Cyclical
Freedman *et al.*[64] (1964)	Rat	Disruption of rope climbing for food	LSD 130 μg/kg/14 days at 48-hr intervals Mescaline 10 mg/kg/10 days	Variable
Freedman *et al.*[64] (1964)	Rat	Disruption of fixed-ratio or variable-interval bar pressing maintained by food	LSD 130 μg/7–8 days	Yes
Jonas & Downer[94] (1964)	Monkey	Gross behavioral changes (e.g., tame, loss of placing and hopping reactions, visual perception disappeared)	LSD 1 mg/kg/4 days	No
Smythies *et al.*[95] (1966)	Rat	Disruption of performance in shuttlebox avoidance	Mescaline 25 mg/kg/7 days	Yes
Becker *et al.*[65] (1967)	Pigeon	Disruption of fixed-ratio visual discrimination for food	LSD 20–80 μg/kg 27 times over 10 months	Yes
Carlini *et al.*[66] (1967)	Rat	Disruption of rope climbing for food	Mescaline 40 mg/kg/9 days	Yes
Banerjee[81] (1971)	Rat	Excitement, increased alertness, hyperkinesia, jumps, myoclonic jerks	LSD 0.05 mg/kg/6–7 days	No
Tilson & Sparber[67] (1971)	Rat	Disruption of fixed-ratio bar pressing maintained by food	Mescaline 10 mg/kg/3–5 days	Yes
Bailey & Pradhan[96] (1972)	Rat	Depression of hypothalamic self-stimulation responding	Mescaline 25 mg/kg/11 days	Yes
Bignami[97] (1972)	Rat	Facilitation of ongoing performance in shuttlebox avoidance	LSD 0.05–0.20 mg/kg/4 days	No
Wallach *et al.*[98] (1972)	Cat	Gross behavioral abnormalities including arousal and aggressivity	DOM 8 mg/kg/2 days	Yes
Cole & Pieper[76] (1973)	Monkey	Disruption of fixed-ratio bar pressing for food.	DMT 10.8 μmoles/kg 36–38 days	No

TABLE 6A (*cont'd.*)

Author	Subject	Index	Drug Regimen*	Tolerance
Bridger *et al.*[82] (1973)	Rat	Facilitation of acquisition on shuttlebox avoidance	Mascaline 12.5 mg/kg/5 days	No
Kulkarni[99] (1973)	Mice	Scratching response	Mescaline 25–50 mg/kg/2 days DOM 5–2 mg/kg/2 days	Yes Yes
Bridger *et al.*[82] (1973)	Rat	Disruption of continued performance in shuttlebox avoidance	Mescaline 100 mg/kg/5 days	Yes
Gillin *et al.*[77] (1973)	Cat	Decrease in spontaneous locomotor activity. Abnormalities of posture and coordination	DMT 3 mg/kg twice daily/7–15 days or every 2 hr for 24 hr	No
Stoff *et al.*[83] (1973)	Rat	Facilitation of acquisition on shuttlebox avoidance	LSD 0.50 mg/kg/5 days	No
Kovacic & Domino[78] (1974)	Rat	Disruption of fixed-ratio bar pressing for liquid reward	DMT 3.2 or 10 mg/kg every 2 hr/21 days	Variable
Dykstra & Appel[68] (1974)	Rat	Changes in response bias on fixed ratio temporal and frequency discrimination	LSD 0.08 mg/kg 3 times at 1-hr intervals	Yes
Stoff *et al.*[79] (1976)	Rat	Disruption of ongoing performance in shuttlebox avoidance	DMT 4 mg/kg twice daily for 14 days	No

* DOM, 2,5-dimethoxy-4-methylamphetamine; DMT, N,N-dimethyltryptamine.

TABLE 6B

NUMBER OF EXPERIMENTS SHOWING TOLERANCE

	LSD	Mescaline	DOM*	DMT†	Psilocybin
Humans	13/13	2/2	2/2	0/1	1/1
Animals	17/23	12/13	2/2	1/4	1/1

* DOM, 2,5-Dimethoxy-4-methylamphetamine.
† DMT, *N,N*-Dimethyltryptamine.

under the particular condition and by non-reward or punishment for the alternative, incorrect choice. After the differential response becomes well established, the animals are given tests with novel drug conditions. Choice of the drug or control response in these tests measures whether the novel test conditions are perceived by the animal as similar to the familiar drug (i.e., generalization) or control condition (i.e., no generalization). The data suggest that there is generalization of responding among hallucinogens (e.g., between LSD and mescaline [and vice versa],[84, 85] from LSD to psilocybin,[85] from mescaline to DOM or DOET)[86] but not among hallucinogens and non-hallucinogens (e.g., from mescaline to DMPEA,[87] TMPEA,[88] amphetamine or cocaine,[86] between LSD and morphine [and vice versa],[89] from *d*-amphetamine to DOM, DOET, nicotine, mescaline, LSD).[90] There are no reports on whether DMT has the ability to serve as a discriminative cue. Two drugs that demonstrate generalization of responding with each other may show similar behavioral effects and/or mechanisms (like drugs that are cross tolerant with each other).

DISCUSSION

When assessing interactions between drugs, in particular, the effects of various pretreatments on the action of hallucinogens, it is important to take into account the effects produced by the pretreatment drug alone. The effects of phenothiazines, in particular chlorpromazine (CPZ), the most frequently mentioned drug in the interactions discussed here, vary depending upon the dose. In general, in those studies which mention the effects of CPZ (and not many do), high doses produce impairment in conditioned learning, moderate depression of activity, and some decrease in appetite. Observed attenuation of hallucinogenic drug effects may, in some instances, be partly due to a sedating action of CPZ, (e.g., in reduction of motoric excitation or subjective anxiety), but it is probably not possible to ascribe all protective effects to sedation, especially in instances that involve selective blockage of stereotypy or aberrant behavior such as gnawing.

Reserpine given by itself has been shown to have fairly definite behavioral effects, among them moderate to severe depression of activity and appetite as well as ataxia. Interaction studies involving reserpine, when they mention the effect of reserpine itself, usually do not begin administration of hallucinogens until the behavior of interest has returned to normal levels or stabilized.

Reserpine appears to potentiate most effects of hallucinogens. It is unclear whether the potentiation is produced by reserpine altering the metabolism of

Table 7A

Studies of Cross Tolerance in Humans and Animals

Author	Subject	Index	Drug Regimen*	Tolerance	Cross Tolerance
Balestrieri & Fontanari (1954)	Psychiatric and neurological patients	Scale of autonomic and kinesthetic effects, motor, emotional, related to consciousness, psychosensorial	LSD 200 μg/4–7 days Mescaline 500 mg	Yes	Yes
			Mescaline 500 mg/7–10 days LSD 200 μg	Yes	Partial
			BOL-148 2.5 μg/4–8 days LSD 200 μg	—	Partial
Cholden *et al.*[41] (1955)	Chronic schizophrenics	Clinical reactions	LSD/3 days BOL-148	Yes	Yes
			LSD/3 days Mescaline Doses not reported	Yes	No
Abramson *et al.*[43] (1956)	Normal humans	Abramson[3] (1955) questionnaire	BOL-148 100 mg twice daily/2 days LSD 25 μg	Yes	Partial
Ginzel & Mayer-Gross[51] (1956)	Normal humans	Psychological symptoms (e.g., euphoria, depersonalization, sensory symptoms)	BOL-148 2–3 mg/1–2 days LSD 50–75 μg	—	Yes
Balestrieri[56] (1957)	Psychiatric and neurological	Autonomic and kinesthetic effects, motor, emotional, related to consciousness, psychosensorial	LSD 200–250 μg/3–5 days Mescaline (dose not reported)	Yes	Yes
Abramson *et al.*[52] (1958)	Normal humans	Abramson[3] (1955) questionnaire	MLD-41 100–350 μg/5–6 days LSD 100 μg	—	Yes
			BOL-148 1000 μg/5–6 days LSD 50 μg	—	Partial
Balestrieri[55] (1959)	Psychiatric and neurological patients	Autonomic and kinesthetic effects, motor, emotional, related to consciousness, psychosensorial	LSD 200 μg/kg/4–8 days JB-336 10 mg	—	No
			LSD 200 μg/5–8 days Psilocybin 6 mg	—	No
			UML-491 2–4 mg/5–6 days LSD 200 μg	—	Yes

Turner *et al.*[53] (1959)	Chronic schizophrenics	Descriptions of agitation, anxiety, defensive hostility, hallucinations	BOL-148 30 mg/28–35 days	—	
			LSD 150–200 μg		Yes
Isbell *et al.*[54] (1959)	Former opiate addicts	Temperature, pulse rate, blood pressure, pupillary change, knee jerk threshold, positive response, questionnaire, clinical Grole	BOL-148 3 mg/5 days	—	
			LSD 1 μg/kg		Yes
Isbell *et al.*[57] (1961)	Former opiate addicts	Same as Isbell *et al.*[54] (1959)	LSD 1.5 μg/kg/12 days	Yes (except knee jerk)	
			Psilocybin 210 μg/kg		Yes (except pulse rate, blood pressure, knee jerk)
			Psilocybin 210 μg/kg/12 days	Yes (except temperature, pulse rate, blood pressure, knee jerk)	
			LSD 1.5 μg/kg		Yes (except temperature, blood pressure, knee jerk)
Wolbach *et al.*[58] (1962)	Former opiate addicts	Same as Isbell *et al.*[54] (1959)	LSD 1.5 μg/kg/14 days	(Yes except pulse rate and temperature)	
			Mescaline 5.0 mg/kg		Yes (except temperature)
			Mescaline 5.0 mg/kg/14 days	Yes (except pulse rate and temperature)	
			LSD 1.5 mg/kg		Yes (except temperature, pulse rate, knee jerk)

TABLE 7A (*continued*)

Author	Subject	Index	Drug Regimen*	Tolerance	Cross Tolerance
Rosenberg *et al.*[59] (1964)	Former opiate addicts	Same as Isbell *et al.*[54] (1959)	LSD 1.5 μg/kg/13 days DMT 1.0 mg/kg	Yes	No
			LSD 3.0 μg/kg twice daily/36 days DMT 0.5 mg/kg	Yes	No (Physiological measures) Yes (Questionnaire, clinical grade)
Isbell *et al.*[100] (1967)	Former opiate addicts	Same as Isbell *et al.*[54] (1959)	LSD 1.5 μg/kg THC 250 mg/kg (No data reported on number of injections)	Yes	No
Isbell & Jasinski[101] (1969)	Former opiate addicts	Same as Isbell *et al.*[54] (1959)	LSD 0.5–1.5 μg/kg/11 days THC 250 mg/kg	Yes	No
Freedman & Aghajanian[70] (1959)	Rat	Disruption of pole-climbing for food	LSD 130–260 g/kg/3–4 days Mescaline 10 μg/kg	Yes	Yes
			Mescaline 10 mg/kg/10 days LSD 130–260 μg/kg	Yes	No
Appel & Freedman[71] (1968)	Rat	Disruption of FR bar pressing for food	LSD 0.195 mg/kg/7–8 days Psilocybin 1.5 mg/kg	Yes	Yes
			LSD 0.195 mg/kg/7–8 days Mescaline 10 mg/kg	Yes	Yes
			Mescaline 10 mg/kg/7–8 days LSD 0.13 mg/kg	Yes	Yes
			Psilocybin 1.5 mg/kg/7–8 days LSD 0.13 mg/kg	Yes	Yes (Partial)
			BOL 1.3 mg/kg/7–8 days LSD 0.13 mg/kg	Yes	Yes (Partial)
			LSD 0.195 mg/kg/7–8 days BOL 1.3 mg/kg	Yes	Yes (Partial)
			BOL 1.3 mg/kg/7–8 days Psilocybin 1.5 mg/kg	Yes	Yes (Partial)
			LSD 0.195 mg/kg/7–8 days Amphetamine 1–2 mg/kg	Yes	No

Silva *et al.*[72] (1968)	Rat	Rope climbing for food	Mescaline 40 mg/kg/9 days	Yes	
			THC 10 mg/kg		No
			THC 10 mg/kg/22 days	Yes	
			Mescaline 40 mg/kg		No
			Cannabis extract 1 mg/18 days	Yes	
			Mescaline 40 mg/kg		No
		Disruption of VI bar pressing for water	LSD 130 g/kg/3 days	Yes	
			THC 10 mg/kg		No
			THC 10 mg/kg/10–28 days	Yes	
			LSD 200 μg/kg		No
Knoll & Vizi[102] (1970)	Rat	Disruption of one-way avoidance and escape behavior on modified jumping test	V-III 10 mg/kg/21 days	Yes	
			LSD 0.5–2.0 mg/kg		Yes
	Rabbit	Hyperthermia	V-III 10–100 mg/kg/3–40 days	Yes	
			LSD 50 mg/kg		Yes
Tilson & Sparber[67] (1971)	Rat	Disruption on FR bar press for food	Mescaline 10 mg/kg (i.p.)/3–5 days	Yes	
			Mescaline 100–240 mg (intraventricular)		No
			Mescaline 100–240 mg (intraventricular)/3 days	Yes	
			Mescaline 10 mg/kg (i.p.)		No
Winter[73] (1971)	Rat	Disruption of FR bar press for milk	LSD 0.2 μmoles/kg/3 days	Yes	
			Mescaline 40 μmoles/kg/2 days	Yes	
			LSD 0.2 μmoles/kg		Yes
Martin & Eades[103] (1972)	Chronic spinal dog	Increased heart rate, respiratory rate, pupillary diameter, facilitate flexor reflex, evoke stepping response	LSD 15 μg/kg/twice daily/1–2 weeks	Yes	
			Tryptamine 0.5 mg/kg		Yes
de Mello *et al.*[74] (1973)	Rat	Disruption of rope climbing for food	Myristicin 40 mg/kg/30–34 days	Yes	
			THC 7.5 mg/kg		No
			Elemicin 20 mg/kg		Yes
			Mescaline 20 mg/kg		No

TABLE 7A (*continued*)

Author	Subject	Index	Drug Regimen*	Tolerance	Cross Tolerance
de Mello *et al.*[74] (1973) (*continued*)	Rat	Disruption of rope climbing for food	Elemicin 20 mg/kg 30–34 days	Yes	
			THC 7.5 mg/kg		No
			Myristicin 40 mg/kg		No
			Mescaline 20 mg/kg		No
			THC 7.5 mg/kg/30–34 days	Yes	
			Myristicin 40 mg/kg		No
			Elemicin 20 mg/kg		No
		Disruption of FI bar pressing for food	Myristicin 20 mg/kg/15 days	Yes	
			THC 7.5 mg/kg		No
			Elemicin 10 mg/kg		Yes
			Mescaline 20 mg/kg		No
			Elemicin 10 mg/kg/15 days	Yes	
			THC 7.5 mg/kg		No
			Myristicin 20 mg/kg		Yes (Partial)
			Mescaline 20 mg/kg		No
			(myristicin and elemicin are major constituents of nutmeg)		
Tilson & Sparber[75] (1973)	Rat	Disruption of FI lever press for food	Mescaline 3 mg/kg/3 days	Yes	
			Amphetamine 0.15 mg/kg		Yes
			Amphetamine 0.15 mg/kg/4–8 days	Yes	
			Mescaline 3 mg/kg		No
			LSD 0.045 mg/kg/3–4 days	Yes	
			Mescaline 3 mg/kg		No
			Mescaline 3 mg/kg/4–7 days	Yes	
			LSD 0.045 mg/kg		Yes (Partial)
			LSD 0.015 mg/kg/4–6 days	Yes	
			Amphetamine 0.15 mg/kg		No
			Amphetamine 0.15 mg/kg/6–9 days	Yes	
			LSD 0.015 mg/kg		No

* BOL-148, 2 bromo-d-lysergic acid diethylamide; MLD-41, 1-methyl-d-lysergic acid diethylamide; JB-336, N-methyl-3-piperidyl benzilate; UML-491, L-methyl-d-lysergic acid butanolamide; THC, delta-trans-tetrahydrocannabinol; V-III, para-bromo-methamphetamine; FR, fixed ratio; FI, fixed interval.

TABLE 7B

NUMBER OF EXPERIMENTS SHOWING CROSS TOLERANCE

	LSD to Mescaline	Mescaline to LSD	LSD to DMT	LSD to Psilocybin
Humans	3/4	2/2	0/1	1/2
Animals	3/3	3/4	—	1/1
	Psilocybin to LSD	BOL* to LSD	BOL to Psilocybin	LSD to BOL
Humans	1/1	0/6	—	1/1
Animals	1/1	1/1	1/1	1/1
	LSD to Tryptamine	LSD to Amphetamine	Amphetamine to LSD	Mescaline to Amphetamine
Humans	1/1	—	—	—
Animals	1/1	0/1	0/1	1/1

* BOL, 2-bromo-d-lysergic acid diethylamide.

the hallucinogens or whether it represents additive effects. A study by Freedman may be relevant. He reported that a single dose of reserpine, 3–4 days prior to LSD administration, resulted in a prolonged response to a subthreshold dose (40 μg/kg) of LSD. He stated that the time elapsed between pretreatment and LSD was enough for reserpine to have been metabolized.[14]

Adrenergic blockers, such as the neuroleptics, propranolol, and phenoxybenzamine, generally act as incomplete antagonists of LSD, mescaline, psilocybin, and DMT. In the case of LSD and DMT, some neuroleptics, especially CPZ, may act as agonists or antagonists, depending upon the dose and time of administration.

Clinically, the drugs of choice for treatment of effects of hallucinogens have most often been the phenothiazine antipsychotics, especially CPZ. Treatment with at least 50 mg i.m. CPZ or its equivalent is the usual dose which is probably necessary for a beneficial effect. While CPZ at this dose may be beneficial, it does not completely reverse the response to hallucinogens, and caution should be used in its administration so that potentiation does not occur. Potentiation of LSD symptoms by CPZ seems to occur when CPZ is introduced simultaneously with or very close to time of LSD administration. When given as a pretreatment, 2 hours or more before LSD, or if given at the peak of the LSD experience, adverse effects appear to be avoided (FIGURE 3).

A final note of clinical advice should be added in regard to interactions of hallucinogens and anaesthetics. It has been suggested that LSD and similar substances "may potentiate the narcotic analgesics and sympathomimetic drugs and delay metabolism of ester-type local anaesthetics."[108]

Probably the best way of preventing a LSD reaction is pretreatment with LSD itself. The same thing holds for mescaline, DOM, and psilocybin. It does not appear to hold for DMT. There appears to be considerable cross tolerance to these drugs as well.

The studies of cross tolerance and discriminative stimulus properties of the hallucinogens may allow us to understand what physiological change they pro-

TABLE 8A
STUDIES OF CROSS-DISCRIMINATED RESPONDING

Author	Subject	Index	Drug Regimen*	Generalization
Hirschorn & Winter[84] (1971)	Rat	VI lever press for food	Mescaline 40 μmoles/kg	
			LSD 0.06 μmoles/kg	Yes
Schechter & Rosecrans[85] (1972)	Rat	Discrimination in T-maze maintained by positive/negative reinforcement	LSD 0.1 μmoles/kg	
			Psilocybin 9.0 μmoles/kg	Yes
			Mescaline 90–120 μmoles/kg	Yes
			Amphetamine 14.8–29.6 μmoles/kg	No
Schechter & Rosecrans[104] (1973)	Rat	Shock escape in 3-chambered compartment	*d*-Amphetamine 4.0 mg/kg	
			l-Amphetamine 8.0 mg/kg	Yes
			Nicotine 0.2 mg/kg	No
			Mescaline 7.4–29.7 mg/kg	No
			LSD 0.048 mg/kg	No
			Fenfluramine 4–8 mg/kg	No
Winter[88] (1973)	Rat	VI positive/negative lever press	Mescaline 10 mg/kg	
			TMPEA 10 mg/kg	No
Frey & Winter[87]	Rat	Positive/negative operant response	Mescaline	
			DMPEA	No
			(Doses not reported)	No
Browne *et al.*[105] (1974)	Rat	Lever press DRL for food	Mescaline 25 mg/kg	
			Mescaline (intraventricular) 10–75 mg	Yes
			NMM (intraventricular) 25–200 mg	No
			DMM 50 mg/kg	Yes
			DMM (intraventricular) 200–300 mg	Transient
Hirschorn & Rosecrans[89] (1974)	Rat	VI lever press for milk	LSD 0.15 μmoles/kg	
			Morphine 10 mg/kg	No
			Morphine 10 mg/kg	
			LSD 0.15 μmoles/kg	No

Huang & Ho[90] (1974)	Rat	Lever press DRL for food	*d*-Amphetamine 0.8 mg/kg	
			l-Amphetamine 1.6 mg/kg	Yes
			Ephedrine 8.0 mg/kg	Yes
			Norephedrine 8.0 mg/kg	Yes
			4-Methoxyamphetamine 2.0 mg/kg	Yes
			Methylphenidate 2.5 mg/kg	Yes
			(Lower doses of these 5 drugs do not produce generalization)	
			Methamphetamine 0.8–1.6 mg/kg	Yes
			Cocaine 7.5 mg/kg	Yes
			Mescaline 12.5–25 mg/kg	No
			DOM 0.25–1.0 mg/kg	No
			DOET 0.25–0.5 mg/kg	No
			3-Methoxyamphetamine 2.0–4.0 mg/kg	No
			4-Methylamphetamine 1.0–2.0 mg/kg	No
			2,5-Dimethoxyamphetamine 1.0–4.0 mg/kg	No
			4-Hydroxyamphetamine 1.0–2.0 mg/kg	No
			Tryamine 1.0–4.0 mg/kg	No
Winter[106] (1974)	Rat	VI positive/negative lever press	Mescaline 10 mg/kg	
			DMPEA 10–30 mg/kg	No
Tilson *et al.*[107] (1975)	Rat	RI bar press for food	Amphetamine 1.0 mg/kg	
			DOM 0.5–0.75 mg/kg	Yes
			DOM 1.5–2.2 mg/kg	No
			DOM 0.75 mg/kg	
			Amphetamine 0.5–0.75 mg/kg	Yes
			Amphetamine 1.5–2.2 mg/kg	No
Winter[86] (1975)	Rat	FR positive/negative lever press	Mescaline 10 mg/kg	
			DOM 0.3 mg/kg	Yes
			DOET 0.3 mg/kg	Yes
			Amphetamine 1.0 mg/kg	No
			Cocaine 30 mg/kg	No

* TMPEA, 2,3,4-trimethoxyphenylethylamine; DMPEA, 3,4-dimethoxyphenylethylamine; NMM, *N*-methylmescaline; DMM, *N,N*-dimethylmescaline; DOM, 2,5-dimethoxy-4-methylamphetamine; DOET, 2,5-dimethoxy-4-methylamphetamine; DOET, 2,5-dimethoxy-4-ethylamphetamine; VI, variable interval; RI, random interval; FR, fixed ratio; DRL, differential reinforcement for low rate of responding.

TABLE 8B

DRUGS WITH DISCRIMINATIVE STIMULUS PROPERTIES AND GENERALIZATION TO OTHER DRUGS

	Generalization To:								
	Mescaline	LSD	TMPEA	DMPEA	DOM	DOET	Psilocybin	*d*-Amphet-amine	Morphine
Discriminative Stimulus									
LSD	1/1						1/1	0/1	0/1
Mescaline		1/1	0/1	0/2	1/1	1/1		0/1	
Morphine		0/1							
d-Amphetamine	0/2	0/1			1/2	0/1			
DOM								0/1	

TMPEA, 2,3,4-trimethoxyphenylethylamine; DMPEA, 3,4-dimethoxyphenylethylamine; DOM, 2,5-dimethoxy-4-methlamphetamine; DOET, 2,5-dimethoxy-4-ethylamphetamine.

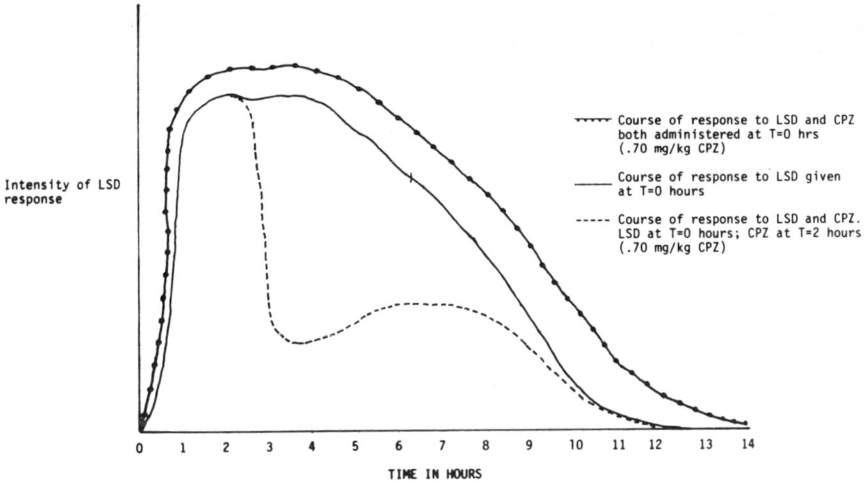

FIGURE 3. Course of psychotomimetic effects of LSD alone and with chlorpromazine administered simultaneously (hypothetical) or at the peak of the LSD reaction.

duce in common as well as animal perceptions of hallucinogens. This should help us understand structure-activity relationships and eventually how the hallucinogens work on a biochemical level.

REFERENCES

1. EFRON, D. H., B. HOLMSTEDT & W. S. KLINE. 1967. *In* Ethnopharmacologic Search for Psychoactive Drugs. Superintendent of Documents, U.S. Government Printing Office. Washington, D.C.
2. MURPHREE, H. G. 1962. Quantitative studies in humans on the antagonism of lysergic acid diethylamide by chlorpromazine and phenoxybenzamine. Clin. Pharmacol. Ther. **3:** 314–320.
3. ABRAMSON, H. A. 1955. Some observations on normal volunteers and patients. *In* Lysergic Acid Diethylamide and Mescaline in Experimental Psychiatry. L. Cholden, Ed.: 51–54. Grune & Stratton. New York, N.Y.
4. GIBERTI, F. & L. GREGORETTI. 1955. Prime esperienze di antagonismo psicofarmacologico. Sistema Nervoso **4:** 301–309.
5. HOCH, P. H. 1955. Studies in routes of administration and counteracting drugs. *In* Lysergic Acid Diethylamide and Mescaline in Experimental Psychiatry. L. Cholden, Ed.: Grune & Stratton, Inc. New York, N.Y.
6. SILVERMAN, J. 1971. Research with psychedelics: some biopsychological concepts and possible clinical applications. Arch. Gen. Psychiat. **23:** 498–510.
7. ELDER, J. T. & J. M. DILLE. 1962. An experimental study of the participation of the sympathetic nervous system in the lysergic acid diethylamide (LSD) reaction in cats. J. Pharmacol. Exp. Ther. **136:** 162–168.
8. HALASZ, M. G., J. FORMANEK & A. S. MARRAZZI. 1969. Hallucinogen-tranquilizer interaction: its nature. Science **164:** 569–571.
9. APPEL, J. B. & D. X. FREEMAN. 1964. Chemically-induced alterations in the behavioral effects of LSD-25. Biochem. Pharmacol. **13:** 861–869.

10. DIXON, A. K. 1968. Evidence of catecholamine mediation in the "aberrant" behavior induced by lysergic acid diethylamide (LSD) in the rat. Experientia **24**(7): 743–747.
11. FDA Science Desk Release. 1967. (67–90).
12. RESNICK, O., D. M. KRUS & M. RASKIN. 1965. Accentuation of the psychological effects of LSD-25 in normal subjects treated with reserpine. Life Sci. **4:** 1433–1437.
13. HOLLISTER, L. E. 1964. Chemical Psychoses. Ann. Rev. Med. **13:** 203–213.
14. FREEDMAN, D. X. 1963. Psychotomimetic drugs and brain biogenic amines. Amer. J. Psychiat. **119:** 843–850.
15. GIARMAN, N. J. & D. X. FREEDMAN. Biochemical aspects of the actions of psychotomimetic drugs. Pharmacol. Rev. **17**(1): 1–25.
16. SUGRUE, M. F. 1969. A study of the role of noradrenaline in behavioral changes produced in the rat by psychotomimetic drugs. Brit. J. Pharmacol. **35:** 243–252.
17. MARTIN, W. R. & C. G. EADES. 1970. The action of tryptamine on the dog spinal cord and its relationship to the agonistic actions of LSD-like psychotogen. Psychopharmacologia **17:** 242–257.
18. KOVACIC, B. & E. F. DOMINO. 1975. Personal Communication.
19. DEFRANCE, J. F., R. A. MCCREA & H. YOSHIHARA. 1975. Effects of certain indoleamines in the hippocampal-septal circuit. Exp. Neurol. **48**(2): 352–377.
20. MOORE, R. H., S. K. DEMETRIOU & E. DOMINO. 1975. Effects of iproniazid, chlorpromazine and methiothepin on DMT-induced changes in body temperature, pupillary dilation, blood pressure and EEG in the rabbit. Arch. Int. Pharmacodyn. **213:** 64–72.
21. SAI-HALASZ, A. 1963. The effect of MAO inhibition on the experimental psychosis induced by dimethyltryptamine. Psychopharmacologia **4:** 385–388.
22. SAI-HALASZ, A. 1962. The effect of antiserotonin on the experimental psychosis induced by dimethyltryptamine. Experientia **18:** 137–138.
23. SHAH, N. S., J. R. JACOBS, J. T. JONES & M. P. HEDDEN. 1975. Interaction of mescaline with phenothiazines: effect on behavior, body temperature and tissue levels of hallucinogen in mice Biol. Psychiat. **10**(5): 561–573.
24. HOLLISTER, L. E. 1968. Chemical Psychoses: LSD and Related Drugs. Charles C Thomas. Springfield, Ill.
25. CHOLDEN, L. 1956. Lysergic Acid Diethylamide and Mescaline in Experimental Psychiatry. Grune & Stratton, Inc. New York, N.Y.
26. DITTRICH, A. 1971. Alteration of behavioral changes induced by 3,4,5-trimethoxyphenylethylamine (mescaline) by pretreatment with 2,4,5-trimethoxyphenylethylamine. Psychopharmacologia **21:** 229–237.
27. SMYTHIES, J. R., J. S. JOHNSTON & R. S. BRADLEY. 1967. Alteration by pretreatment with iproniazid and inactive mescaline analogue of a behavior change by mescaline. Nature **216:** 196–197.
28. AHLBOORG, V., B. HOLMSTEDT & S. E. LINDGREN. 1968. Fate and metabolism of some hallucinogenic indolealkylamines. Adv. Pharmacol. **68:** 213–228.
29. BENINGTON, F., R. D. MORIN & L. C. CLARK. 1965. 5-methoxy-N,N-dimethyltryptamine, a possible endogenous psychotoxin. Adv. J. Med. Sci. **2:** 397–403.
30. GESSNER, P. K. 1970. Pharmacological studies of 5-methoxy-N,N-dimethyltryptamine, LSD and other hallucinogens. *In* Psychotomimetic Drugs. D. H. Efron, Ed.: 105–122. Raven Press. New York, N.Y.
31. GRAHAME-SMITH, D. G. 1971. Inhibitory effect of chlorpromazine on the syndrome of hyperactivity produced by *l*-tryptophan or 5-methoxy-N,N-dimethyltryptamine in rats treated with a monoamine oxidase inhibitor. Brit. J. Pharmacol. **43:** 856–864.

32. Green, A. R. & D. G. Grahame-Smith. 1974. The role of brain dopamine in the hyperactivity syndrome produced by increased 5-hydroxytryptamine synthesis in rats. Neuropharmacology **13:** 949–959.
33. Himwich, H. E. 1955. The effect of Frenquel on EEG changes produced by LSD-25 and mescaline. *In* Lysergic Acid Diethylamide and Mescaline in Experimental Psychiatry. L. Cholden, Ed.: 19–26. Grune & Stratton, Inc. New York, N.Y.
34. Fabing, H. D. 1955. New blocking agent against the development of LSD-psychosis. Science **121:** 208.
35. Hoffer, A. 1955. Studies in niacin and LSD. *In* Lysergic Acid Diethylamide and Mescaline in Experimental Psychiatry. L. Cholden, Ed.: 44–45. Grune & Stratton, Inc. New York, N.Y.
36. Matussek, N. & A. Halbach. 1964. Uber den Einpluss von Ergstamin und die LSD-psychose beim Menschen. Psychopharmacologia **5:** 158–160.
37. Resnick, O., D. M. Krus & M. Raskin. 1964. LSD-25 action in normal subjects treated with a monoamine oxidase inhibitor. Life Sci. **3:** 1207–1214.
38. Weckowicz, T. E. 1967. Animal studies of hallucinogenic drugs. *In* The Hallucinogens. A. Hoffer & H. Osmond, Eds. Academic Press. New York, N.Y.
39. Stoff, D. M., E. A. Moja, J. C. Gillin & R. J. Wyatt. 1976. Chronic but not acute chlorpromazine attenuates disruptive effects of N,N:Dimethyltryptamine on shuttlebox avoidance in rats. Paper presented at 6th Annual Meeting of Society For Neurosciences, Toronto, Canada.
40. Isbell, H., H. F. Fraser, A. Wilkler & R. E. Belleville. 1955. Tolerance to diethylamide of lysergic acid (LSD-25). Fed. Proc. **14:** 354.
41. Cholden, L. S., A. Kurland & C. Savage. 1955. Clinical reactions and tolerance to LSD in chronic schizophrenia. J. Nerv. Ment. Dis. **122:** 211–221.
42. Isbell, H., R. E. Belleville, H. F. Fraser, A. Wikler & C. R. Logan. 1956. Studies on lysergic acid diethylamide (LSD-25). Effects in former morphine addicts and development of tolerance during chronic intoxication. Arch. Neurol. Psychiat. **76:** 468.
43. Abramson, H. A., M. E. Jarvik, M. H. Gorin & M. W. Hirsch. 1956. Lysergic acid diethylamide: XVII Tolerance development and its relationship to a theory of psychosis. J. Psychol. **41:** 81–105.
44. Hoffer, A. 1964. D-Lysergic acid diethylamide (LSD): A review of its present status. Clin. Pharmacol. Ther. **6:** 183–255.
45. Hollister, L. E., M. F. Macnicol, H. K. Gillespie. 1969. An hallucinogenic amphetamine analog (DOM) in man. Psychopharmacologia **14:** 62–73.
46. Angrist, B., J. Rotrosen & S. Gershon. 1974. Assessment of tolerance to the hallucinogenic effects of DOM. Psychopharmacologia **36:** 203–207.
47. Kaplan, J., R. Stillman, J. C. Gillin, R. W. Walker, L. Mandel & R. J. Wyatt. 1976. Absence of tolerance to DMT in normal experienced subjects. Arch. Gen. Psychiat. Submitted.
48. Rothlin, E. 1957. Lysergic acid diethylamide and related substances. Ann. N.Y. Acad. Sci. **66:** 668–676.
49. Cerletti, A. & E. Rothlin. 1955. Role of 5-hydroxytryptamine in mental diseases and its antagonism to lysergic acid derivatives. Nature **176:** 785-786.
50. Balestrieri, A. & D. Fontanari. 1959. Acquired and cross-tolerance to mescaline, LSD-25, and BOL-148. Arch. Gen. Psychiat. **1:** 279–282.
51. Ginzel, K. H. & W. Mayer-Gross:. 1956. Prevention of psychological effects of d-lysergic acid diethylamide (LSD-25) by its 2-Brom derivative (BOL-148). Nature **178:** 210.
52. Abramson, H. A., B. Sklarofsky, M. O. Baron & N. Fremont-Smith.

1958. Lysergic acid diethylamide (LSD-25) antagonists. II. Development of tolerance in man to LSD-25 by prior administration of MLD-41 (1-methyl-d-lysergic acid diethylamide). Arch. Neurol. Psychiat. **79:** 201–207.
53. Turner, W. J., M. Almudevar & S. Merlis. 1959. Chemotherapeutic trials in psychosis. III. Addendum 2-Brom-d-lysergic acid diethylamide (BOL-148) Amer. J. Psychiat. **116:** 261–262.
54. Isbell, H., E. J. Miner & C. R. Logan. 1959. Cross tolerance between d-2 Brom-lysergic acid diethylamide (BOL-148) and d-diethylamide of lysergic acid (LSD-25). Psychopharmacologia **1:** 109–116.
55. Balestrieri, A. 1959. Studies in cross tolerance with LSD-25, UML-491 and JB-336. Psychopharmacologia **1:** 257–259.
56. Balestrieri, A. 1957. Crossed tolerance between LSD-25 and mescaline. *In* Psychotropic Drugs. S. Garattini & V. Ghetti, Eds.: 581. Elsevier Publishing Co., Inc. New York, N.Y.
57. Isbell, H., A. B. Wolbach, A. Wikler & E. J. Miner. 1961. Cross tolerance between LSD and Psilocybin. Psychopharmacologia **2:** 147–159.
58. Wolbach, A. B., Jr., H. Isbell & E. J. Miner. 1962. Cross tolerance between mescaline and LSD-25 with a comparison of the mescaline and LSD reactions. Psychopharmacologia **3:** 1–14.
59. Rosenberg, D. E., H. Isbell, E. J. Miner & C. R. Logan. 1964. The effect of N,N-dimethyltryptamine in human subjects tolerant to lysergic acid diethylamide. Psychopharmacologia **5:** 2, 7–227.
60. Mahler, D. J. & F. L. Hummoller. 1959. Effect of lysergic acid diethylamide and bufotenin on performance of trained rats. Proc. Soc. Exp. Biol. **102:** 697–701.
61. Jarvik, M. E. & S. Chorover. 1958. Effects of lysergic acid diethylamide upon certain aspects of memory (delayed alternation) in monkeys. Fed. Proc. **17:** 381.
62. Jarvik, M. E. & S. Chorover. 1960. Impairment by lysergic acid diethylamide of accuracy in performance of a delayed alteration test in monkeys. Psychopharmacologia **1:** 221–230.
63. Adey, W. R., F. R. Bell & B. J. Dennis. 1962. Effects of LSD-25, psilocybin and psilocin on temporal lobe EEG patterns and learned behavior in the cat. Neurology **12:** 591–602.
64. Freedman, D. X., J. B. Appel, F. R. Hartman & M. E. Mollner. 1964. Tolerance to behavioral effects of LSD in the rat J. Pharmacol. Exp. Ther. **143:** 309–313.
65. Becker, D. I., J. B. Appel & D. X. Freedman. 1967. Some effects of LSD on visual discrimination in pigeons. Psychopharmacologia **11:** 354–364.
66. Carlini, E. A., M. Teressa, A. Silva, L. C. Cesare & R. M. Endo. 1967. Effects of chronic administration of β-(3,4-dimethoxyphenyl)-ethylamine and β-(3,4,5-trimethoxyphenyl)-ethylamine on the climbing rope performance of rats. Med. Pharmacol. Exp. **17:** 534–540.
67. Tilson, H. A. & S. B. Sparber. 1971. Differences in tolerance to mescaline produced by peripheral and direct central administration. Psychopharmacologia **19:** 313–323.
68. Dykstra, L. A. & J. B. Appel. 1974. Effects of LSD on auditory perception: a signal detection analysis. Psychopharmacologia **34:** 289–307.
69. Freedman, D. X., G. K. Aghajanian, E. M. Ornitz & B. S. Rosner. 1958. Patterns of tolerance to lysergic acid diethylamide and mescaline in rats. Science **127:** 1173–1174.
70. Freedman, D. X. & G. K. Aghajanian. 1959. Time parameters in acute tolerance, cross-tolerance, and antagonism to psychotogens. Fed. Proc. **18:** 390.
71. Appel, J. B. & D. X. Freedman. 1968. Tolerance and cross-tolerance among psychotomimetic drugs. Psychopharmacologia **13:** 267–274.

72. SILVA, M. T. A., E. A. CARLINI, U. CLAUSSEN & F. KORTE. 1968. Lack of cross-tolerance in rats among (-) Δ^9-trans-tetrahydrocannabinol (Δ^9-THC). Cannabis extract, mescaline, and lysergic acid diethylamide (LSD-25). Psychopharmacologia **13:** 332–340.
73. WINTER, J. C. 1971. Tolerance to behavioral effect of lysergic acid diethylamide and cross-tolerance to mescaline in the rat: absence of a metabolic component. J. Pharmacol. Exp. Ther. **178:** 625–630.
74. DE MELLO, A. C., E. A. CARLINI, K. DRESSLER, J. P. GREEN, S. KANG & S. MARGOLIS. 1973. Behavioral observations on compounds found in nutmeg. Psychopharmacologia **31:** 349–363.
75. TILSON, H. A. & S. B. SPARBER. 1973. Similarities and differences between mescaline, lysergic acid diethylamide-25 (LSD) and d-amphetamine on various components of fixed interval responding in the rat. J. Pharmacol. Exp. Ther. **184:** 376–384.
76. COLE, J. M. & W. A. PIEPER. 1973. The effect of N,N-dimethyltryptomine on operant behavior in squirrel monkeys. Psychopharmacologia **29:** 107–112.
77. GILLIN, J. C., E. CANNON, R. MAGYAR, M. SCHWARTZ & R. J. WYATT. 1973. Failure of N,N-dimethyltryptamine to evoke tolerance in cats. Biol. Psychiat. **7:** 213–220.
78. KOVACIC, B. & E. F. DOMINO. 1976. Tolerance and limited cross-tolerance to the effects of N,N-Dimethyltryptamine (DMT) and lysergic acid diethylamide (LSD) on food-rewarded bar pressing in the rat. J. Pharmacol. Exp. Ther. **197:** 495–504.
79. STOFF, D. M., E. A. MOJA, J. C. GILLIN & R. J. WYATT. 1976. Disruption of conditioned avoidance behavior by N,N-Dimethyltryptamine (DMT) and stereotypy by β-phenylethylamine (PEA): Animal models of attentional defects in schizophrenia. J. Psychiat. Res. In press.
80. HAMILTON, C. L. 1960. Effects of LSD-25 and amphetamine on the running response in the rat. Arch. Gen. Psychiat. **2:** 104–109.
81. BANERJEE, U. 1971. Acquisition of the conditioned avoidance response in rats under the influence of addicting drugs. Psychopharmacologia **22:** 133–143.
82. BRIDGER, W. H., I. J. MANDEL & D. M. STOFF. 1973. Mescaline: No tolerance to excitatory effects. Biol. Psychiat. **7:** 129–138.
83. STOFF, D. M., I. J. MANDEL, D. A. GORELICK & W. H. BRIDGER. 1974. Acute and chronic effects of LSD and 3,4-dimethoxyphenylethylamine on shuttle-box escape/avoidance in rats. Psychopharmacologia **36:** 301–312.
84. HIRSCHORN, I. D. & J. C. WINTER. 1971. Mescaline and lysergic acid diethylamide (LSD) as discriminative stimuli. Psychopharmacologia **22:** 64–71.
85. SCHECHTER, M. D. & J. A. ROSECRANS. 1972. Lysergic acid diethylamide (LSD) as a disriminative cue: drugs with similar stimulus properties. Psychopharmacologia **26:** 313–316.
86. WINTER, J. C. 1975. The effects of 2,5-dimethoxy-4-methylamphetamine (DOM), 2,5-dimethoxy-4-ethylamphetamine (DOET), d-amphetamine, and cocaine in rats trained with mescaline as a discriminative stimulus. Psychopharmacologia **44:** 29–32.
87. FREY, L. G. & J. C. WINTER. 1973. Stimulus properties of mescaline and 3,4-dimethoxyphenylethylamine (DMPEA). Pharmacologist **15:** 236.
88. WINTER, J. C. 1973. A comparison of the stimulus properties of mescaline and 2,3,4-trimethoxyphenylethylamine. J. Pharmacol. Exp. Ther. **185:** 101.
89. HIRSCHORN, I. D. & J. A. ROSECRANS. 1974. A comparison of the stimulus effects of morphine and lysergic acid diethylamide (LSD). Pharmacol. Biochem. Behav. **2:** 361–366.
90. HUANG, J. T. & B. T. HO. 1974. Discriminative stimulus properties of d-amphetamine and related compounds in rats. Pharmacol. Biochem. Behav. **2:** 669–673.

91. GOGERTY, J. H. & J. M. DILLE. 1956. Tolerance to the pyretogenic effects of lysergic acid diethylamide. J. Pharmacol. Exp. Ther. **116:** 450.
92. GILLETT, E. 1960. Effects of chlorpromazine and d-lysergic acid diethylamide on sex behavior of male rats. Proc. Soc. Exp. Biol. **103:** 392–394.
93. KOELLA, W. P., R. F. BEAULIEU & J. R. BERGEN. 1964. Stereotyped behavior and cyclic changes in responses produced by LSD in goats. Int. J. Neuropharmacol. **3:** 397–403.
94. JONAS, S. & J. DOWNER. 1964. Gross behavioral changes in monkeys following administration of LSD-25 and development of tolerance to LSD-25. Psychopharmacologia **6:** 303–306.
95. SMYTHIES, J. R., E. A. SYKES & C. P. LORD. 1966. Structure-activity relationship studies on mescaline: II. Tolerance and cross-tolerance between mescaline and its analogues in the rat. Psychopharmacologia **9:** 434–446.
96. BAILEY, P. T. & S. N. PRADHAN. 1972. Effects of Δ^9-tetrahydrocannabinol and mescaline on self-stimulation. Neuropharmacol. **11:** 831–838.
97. BIGNAMI, G. 1972. Facilitation of avoidance asquisition by LSD-25: possible effects on drive modultaing systems. Psychopharmacologia **25:** 146–151.
98. WALLACH, M. G., E. FRIEDMAN & S. GERSHON. 1972. 2,5-dimethoxy-4-methylamphetamine (DOM). A neuropharmacological examination. J. Pharmacol. Exp. Ther. **182:** 145–154.
99. KULKARNI, A. S. 1973. Scratching response induced in mice by mescaline and related amphetamine derivatives. Biol. Psychiatry **6:** 177–180.
100. ISBELL, H., C. W. GORODETSKY, D. JASINSKI, U. CLAUSSEN, F. V. SPULAK & F. KORTE. 1967. Effects of delta-trans-tetrahydrocannabinol in man. Psychopharmacologia **11:** 187–188.
101. ISBELL, H. & D. R. JASINSKI. 1969. A comparison of LSD-25 with (-)-Δ^9-trans-tetrahydrocannabinol (THC) and attempted cross-tolerance between LSD and THC. Psychopharmacologia **14:** 115–123.
102. KNOLL, J. & E. S. VIZI. 1970. Cross-tolerance between para-bromo-methamphetamine (V-111) and LSD-25. Pharmacology **4:** 278–286.
103. MARTIN, W. R. & O. G. EADES. 1972. Cross-tolerance to tryptamine in the LSD tolerant dog. Psychopharmacologia **27:** 93–98.
104. SCHECHTER, M. D. & J. A. ROSECRANS. 1973. d-amphetamine as a discriminative cue: drugs with similar stimulus properties. Eur. J. Pharmacol. **21:** 212–216.
105. BROWNE, R. G., R. T. HARRIS & B. T. HO. 1974. Stimulus properties of mescaline and N-methylated derivatives: difference in peripheral and direct central administration. Psychopharmacologia **39:** 43–56.
106. WINTER, J. C. 1974. The effects of 3,4-dimethoxyphenylethylamine in rats trained with mescaline as a discriminative stimulus. J. Pharmacol. Exp. Ther. **189:** 741–747.
107. TILSON, H. A., T. G. BAKER & J. A. GYLYS. 1975. A comparison of the discriminative stimulus properties of R-2,5-dimethoxy-4-methylamphetamine and S-amphetamine. Psychopharmacologia **44:** 225–228.
108. ELLIOTT, H. W. 1975. Effects of street drugs on anesthesia. Int. J. Clin. Pharmacol. **12:** 134–140.
109. Commission on CIA Activities Within the United States. 1975. U.S. Government Printing Office: Washington, D.C., 225–228.
110. TUCKER, Q. J., D. QUINLAN & M. HARROW. 1972. Chronic hallucinogenic use and thought disturbance. Arch. Gen. Psychiat. **27:** 443–447.
111. SMYTHIES, J. R., J. M. BEATON, F. BENNINGTON & R. D. MORIN. 1972. The design of some new compounds to block psychotomimetic drugs. Eur. J. Pharmacol. **17:** 270–272.

INTERACTION OF HALLUCINOGENS WITH OTHER DRUGS

Stephen Szara

Biomedical Branch
National Institute on Drug Abuse
Rockville, Maryland 20852

There are essentially two major rationales for studying drug interaction of hallucinogens with other drugs: the psychotomimetic model and the drug abuse model.

The investigator using the psychotomimetic model assumes that hallucinogens are drugs that produce a reasonable model of psychosis, presumably similar to an endogenous psychosis, such as schizophrenia. Interaction of hallucinogenic drugs with other drugs is frequently used in this model with the hope that (1) the mechanism by which an exogenous drug is able to produce psychotic-like symptoms can be elucidated; (2) clues may be obtained as to the nature and identity of a hypothetical endogenous "schizotoxin" responsible for the etiology of schizophrenia; and (3) interaction with therapeutic drugs may give some clues and guide us to obtain a more effective therapeutic agent for the endogenous psychoses.

The more recent clinical studies along these lines have been described by Dr. Wyatt[1] and expanded to include the interaction with chlorpromazine (CPZ), not only in the context of endogenous psychosis, but also in reference to treatments of "bad trips." The earlier literature, including my contributions to the psychotomimetic model, has been reviewed in a book published some five years ago.[2] This model need not be further elaborated on here.

The second major rationale for studying hallucinogenic drug interaction stems from the facts of life: Hallucinogens are frequently obtained illegally and used or abused, sometimes in conjunction with other drugs, so that there is a concern that potentially dangerous drug interaction may represent a serious public health hazard. I refer to this as the "Drug Abuse Model" and will elaborate on it a little to show the need for more valid information in this area.

A "MEDLARS" search by our library, using "Hallucinogens" and "Drug Interaction" as key words, turned up 125 citations for the 3-year period 1972–75 inclusive. Most papers dealt with interaction with cannabis, which is, apparently, classified as a hallucinogen by the National Library of Medicine. Only 34 citations were found to deal with the more generally accepted hallucinogens, such as LSD, mescaline, DMT, psilocybin, or the amphetamine-type hallucinogen STP or DOM. Of these 34, again a majority (24) appeared to investigate drug interaction in terms of the psychotomimetic model, and only 10 seemed to be motivated by the "Drug Abuse Model." Of these 10, two papers were clinical case reports and eight could be considered as bona fide scientific reports of experimental data on drug interaction involving hallucinogens. For a 3-year period, this is a relatively meager result in an effort to obtain valid, scientific data on a phenomenon that may have considerable public health consequences.

Let me quote from the statistics that are available and may be indicative of the size and perhaps the seriousness of the problem. According to the 1974 nationwide survey (conducted by Ira Cisin), LSD and other hallucinogens have been tried by a small percentage (4.6–4.8%) of the total population, and the percentage of regular users is even smaller, around 1% of youth (ages 12–17) and less than ½% of adults (18 and over).[3, 4] Nevertheless, LSD and other hallucinogens can cause a number of side effects including panic reactions and can occasionally trigger longer lasting psychotic or depressive episodes. The potential severity of this problem may be reflected by the fact that for a 12-month period (September 1974–August 1975) LSD continued to rank fourth as a drug mentioned by persons treated at crisis centers (over 70 located in major cities in the United States), as reported by the Drug Abuse Warning Network[5] (1st, diazepam; 2nd, heroin; 3rd, marihuana).

LSD sold on the street is usually made in illegal laboratories and almost always contains contaminants from the manufacturing process. Sometimes it is not even LSD but other drugs. Most frequently, phencyclidine or PCP is passed off as LSD.[8]

In a street-drug identification program conducted by two members of the Department of Pathology, University of Southern California School of Medicine, well over half of some 572 samples collected were not at all what they were represented to be. The most consistent misrepresentations included 192 samples sold as mescaline, of which only three were mescaline alone and one a mixture. The usual drugs sold as mescaline were lysergic acid diethylamide (LSD), phencyclidine (PCP), or a combination of the two. Of 53 samples sold as psilocybin, only one was legitimate; most of the others were LSD, PCP, or LSD-PCP. The percentage of serious problems with PCP was particularly high, with convulsions, paranoia, and psychosis being reported.[8]

Furthermore, it is well known that drugs are not always used alone but in combination with alcohol or some other drug, as polydrug use is now becoming the rule rather than the exception.[11]

Some of the statistics again are revealing. The statistical data, collected by the CODAP System[6] from federally funded drug abuse treatment units during a 3-month period of January–March 1975, lists 1,463 admissions that involved hallucinogens as primary drugs of problem. Of this total, only 12% stated the use of hallucinogen alone, without any secondary drug (lowest similar percentage among the 12 other categories of abused drugs!). Most frequent secondary drugs were marihuana (39%), amphetamines (16%), and barbiturates (10%).

A recent report on multiple drug abuse in the United States Army suggests that hallucinogens are also frequently used in that population in combination with marihuana and stimulants, as well as depressants.[7]

Although these statistical reports do not specify whether the combination is used simultaneously or sequentially, the case reports suggest that serious complications often involved the simultaneous use of hallucinogens with other drugs.[8–10] Also, the statistical data and the case reports quoted do not establish unequivocally the etiological role of hallucinogens interacting with other drugs. Nevertheless, these reports cannot be simply dismissed or ignored but rather should be regarded as an invitation, or even a demand, for a more systematic, scientific exploration of the field.

I think that these reports have a clear message: there are good reasons to be concerned with potential hazards associated with hallucinogenic drug use and its interaction with other, commonly used or abused drugs.

References

1. Wyatt, R. J. *et al.* Interactions of hallucinogens at the clinical level. This volume.
2. Weil-Malherbe, H. & S. Szara. 1971. The Biochemistry of Functional and Experimental Psychoses. C. C. Thomas. Springfield, Ill.
3. Glen, W. A. & L. G. Richards. 1974. Recent Surveys of Nonmedical Drug Use: A Compendium of Abstracts. NIDA Publication.
4. White Paper on Drug Abuse: A Report to the President from the Domestic Council Drug Abuse Task Force. Sept. 1975. U.S. Govt. Printing Office. Washington, D.C.
5. DAWN Statistical Summary. August 1975 (Report of Contract #DEA-75-22).
6. NIDA Statistical Series. Quarterly Reports. Series 1, Suppl. 2, No. 3 (NIDA Report of Contract No. 271-75-5137) Jan. 1976.
7. Cook, R. E., R. S. Hostetter & D. A. Ramsey. 1975. Patterns of illicit drug use in the Army. Amer. J. Psychiatry **132**(10): 1013–1017.
8. 1972. Impurities tied to "bad trips" in drug abusers. Med. Trib. Med. News **13**(43): 3–4.
9. Klaut, Robert R. 1973. Homicide and LSD. JAMA **224**(2): 246.
10. Liskow, Barry. 1972. LSD and prolonged psychotic reactions. Amer. J. Psychiatry **128**(9): 144.
11. DuPont, Robert. Polydrug abuse. This volume.